THE
SELECTED
LETTERS
OF
CHARLES
SUMNER

THE
SELECTED
LETTERS
OF
Charles
Sumner

EDITED BY
Beverly Wilson Palmer

Volume Two

Northeastern University Press
Boston

Northeastern University Press

Copyright © 1990 by Beverly Wilson Palmer

Some of the annotated letters have appeared in *Ohio History* (Summer–
Autumn 1984; Winter–Spring 1990) and are used with permission.

Publication of this volume was assisted by a grant from the National
Historic Publications and Records Commission.

Library of Congress Cataloging-in-Publication Data
Sumner, Charles, 1811–1874.
   The selected letters of Charles Sumner / edited by Beverly Wilson
Palmer.
      p.   cm.
   Includes bibliographical references.
   ISBN 1-55553-078-8 (alk. paper)
      1. Sumner, Charles, 1811–1874—Correspondence. 2. Legislators—
United States—Correspondence. 3. Abolitionists—United States—
Correspondence. 4. Slavery—United States—Anti-slavery movements.
5. United States—Politics and government—1849–1877. I. Palmer,
Beverly Wilson, 1936–   .   II. Title.
E415.9.S9A4   1990
973.7′092—dc   90-6925
                        CIP

1002081114 T

Designed by Virginia Evans

Composed in Garamond #3 by Graphic Composition, Inc., Athens,
Georgia. Printed and bound by Edwards Brothers, Inc., Ann Arbor,
Michigan. The paper is Glatfelter Offset, and acid-free sheet.

MANUFACTURED IN THE UNITED STATES OF AMERICA
96 95 94 93 92 91 90 5 4 3 2 1

CONTENTS

ILLUSTRATIONS

V

THE
LINCOLN
YEARS
AND
THE
CIVIL
WAR

November 1859 – April 1865

ABOUT THE eruption of the Civil War, Sumner wrote Longfellow, elliptically, "my system would have made it unnecessary" (17 April 1861). Yet Sumner gave little indication of any plan to avoid war. As a lifelong pacifist, he dreaded a civil conflict. "Much as I desire the extinction of Slavery, I do not wish to see it go down in blood," he wrote the duchess of Argyll, 14 December 1860. Still, as he watched the secession crisis deepen, Sumner advocated both firm adherence to constitutional principles against disunion and resistance to Southern demands. He wrote Cordelia Walter Richards on 16 April 1861 that perhaps if the government had "been more prompt," the South might have given in and returned to the Union. Sumner was probably wrong, however, in believing that Northern hesitation had caused the South to become even more defiant.

Once the states in the lower South had voted to secede from the United States, Sumner opposed any compromise. "I do not tremble at any thing from our opponents, whoever they may be, but from our friends," he wrote John Andrew, 10 February 1861. Reflecting (to Richard Cobden, 4 September 1863) on the outbreak, Sumner wrote that he had not originally "counselled a war for Emancipation." He professed to have "accepted the conditions imposed by the other side," but added, significantly, "I would not surrender to Slavery." Despite his profession of cooperation, Sumner did not entertain any "conditions" from either Southerners or Northern moderates. From the beginning of the crisis Sumner regarded the rebellion as "slavery in arms"; slavery was the Confederacy's "cornerstone." Southern insistence on the right to secede ironically gratified Sumner because he saw how it would strengthen Northern resolve and prevent compromise. "The inordinate demands of the South are now the *safeguard* of Northern principles," Sumner wrote Edward L. Pierce, 5 February 1861. Emancipation thus became a real possibility.

During the war Sumner carried on his own legislative battle for emancipation. He rejoiced over every proclamation, military edict, and congressional act giving the federal government power not only to prosecute the war but also to free slaves and treat them like whites. Sumner saw Thomas A. Scott's order of 14 October 1861 to employ slaves fleeing from Confederate lines as the beginning of a tortuous but steady path toward the ultimate repeal of the Fugitive Slave Law (to Harriet Martineau, 29 October 1861). He argued that black troops should receive the same pay as whites and before the war's end was insisting on black suffrage in returning states.

Like other officials who regarded the war solely as a means to abolish slavery, Sumner feared that early Northern victories might lead to restoration of the Union with slavery intact. He wrote Wendell Phillips that Bull Run was both the "worst" (in terms of "calamity & shame") and the "best event in our history . . . as it made the extinction of slavery inevitable" (3 August 1861). Instead of exulting over Gettysburg and Vicksburg, on 21 July 1863 Sumner wrote John Bright that a "collapse" of the Confederacy at this time would be a "calamity." Questions of restoration of the Union should not be considered before all blacks were freed. *"Time is essential,"* wrote Sumner. "So great a revolution cannot come to a close at once."

Exalted principles could give way to personal jealousy, and Sumner engaged in a running feud with Seward over control of foreign policy during the Civil War. In 1860, Sumner seemed agreeable to Seward's presidential candidacy, but when Seward became Lincoln's secretary of state and Sumner the chair of the Senate Foreign Relations Committee, the two men held rival positions in Washington. Sumner began to complain confidentially about the secretary of state's policies, which he saw as exacerbating relations with Great Britain and France. Seward was simply "infatuated" and far too optimistic, Sumner wrote John Jay on 27 March 1861; Seward promoted a *"policy of insincerity"* (to Richard Henry Dana, Jr., 14 April 1861). Although Sumner blamed Seward for the war hysteria surrounding the *Trent* affair, ultimately the two agreed that war with Britain would be disastrous for the Union. Thereafter, as British minister Lord Lyons observed, Seward became more moderate. Sumner then turned to domestic differences with Seward and sought to expose the secretary's ambivalence on abolition (see to Sydney H. Gay, 26 July 1862). By October Sumner was criticizing abroad Seward's "contrivances" (to John Bright, 28 October 1862). After Lincoln supported Seward in the cabinet crisis of December 1862, Sumner declined open opposition (see to James W. White, 1 March 1863) but never missed an opportunity to snipe privately at his rival (see to Bright, 16 March 1863).

As Seward adopted a less truculent attitude toward Britain, Sumner's animosity increased. Considering his later emphasis on the Queen's 1861 Proclamation of Neutrality, Sumner at first reacted mildly (to the duchess of Argyll, 4 June 1861) because at that time he hoped for Britain's condemnation of the Confederacy. In addition, in the spring of 1863 Sumner worked to prevent U.S. issuance of letters of marque, an act he knew could provoke hostile relations. However, a combination of the British-built Confederate cruisers' rampage, Britain's failure to see that the morally correct Union deserved Her Majesty's wholehearted support, and Sumner's desire to establish his role as chief foreign policy expert brought about his speech "Our Foreign Relations" in September 1863 (see to Francis Lieber, 15 September 1863, and to Horace Greeley, 21 September 1863). Sumner wrote the duke of Argyll, "the people here naturally look to me for an explanation of their Foreign Relations" (10 November 1863).

Thereafter, despite Britain's refusal to release additional Confederate cruisers, Sumner repeatedly railed to his sympathetic British correspondents about the damage, moral and physical, that British neutrality inflicted on the North. Sumner prided himself on his mastery of international law, but admitted to the duke of Argyll that, like a shield, the law could be "read differently on the two opposite sides, & with equal honesty in the two." Sumner then proceeded to read the law on the Union side of the shield, contending that Britain had violated international law in conceding belligerent rights to the Confederacy (tantamount to recognition, in Sumner's eyes). He called British construction of the Confederate cruisers a "hostile act" (to the duke of Argyll, 10 May 1863) and consistently blamed Britain for the war's continuing.

Sumner's letters reveal that toward France, the other major European power, he pursued a more diplomatic and less chauvinistic policy. Seeking to avoid war with France, Sumner sought to suppress public condemnation of Napoleon III's intervention in Mexico. Sumner kept hostile resolutions in his committee (see to Francis Lieber, 4 May 1864, 20 January 1865). At the same time he wrote Nathaniel Niles that he did not wish to encourage "any concession to this new-fangled imperialism" (2 April 1864).

Sumner was at first wary of Lincoln. Although he initially employed careful language about the president in letters abroad, Sumner bemoaned the president's lack of foreign policy and administrative expertise and, more importantly, Lincoln's deliberate moves to free the slaves. "A wise, courageous & humane statesman, with proper forecast might from the begining have directed this whole war to the suppression of Slavery, & have ended it by this time," Sumner wrote Bright, 18 November 1862. Lincoln's homely style disarmed the courtly Sumner, but he gradually came to admire the president's prose. Recognizing Lincoln's authority, Sumner steadily pressured Lincoln for immediate emancipation and complete conquest of the South; Lincoln rarely responded. In 1864, Sumner, along with other Republicans, blamed Lincoln for Northern defeats and stalemates and cautiously, privately encouraged Republican consideration of another candidate, if Lincoln withdrew (to John Andrew, 24 August 1864). Sumner wrote Bright that Lincoln "does not know how to help or is not moved to help," and complained about Lincoln's lack of "instinct or inspiration" (27 September 1864). On Reconstruction, Sumner found Lincoln, as before, "slow in accepting truths" (to Bright, 13 March 1865), the truth for Sumner being refusal to admit rebel states until freedmen were granted suffrage. Sumner's last words on the living president showed his mixture of admiration and exasperation. He wrote Chase 12 April 1865, "The more I have seen of the Presdt. the more his character in certain respects has risen, & we must all admit that he has said some things better than any body else could have said them. But I fear his policy now." That Sumner and Lincoln operated in wholly different ways needs no elaboration here. Summing up Lincoln's shortcomings to his fellow senator Lot Morrill (15 June 1865), Sumner wrote that, for signing the Emancipation Proclamation and making "speeches that nobody else could have made," Americans must respect Lincoln and, besides, "Fame takes him by the hand." Of the three presidents under whom Sumner served, only with Lincoln did he have a working relationship, a phenomenon that reveals more about Lincoln's ability than about Sumner's.

To Samuel Gridley Howe

Boston 23 Nov. '59

My very dear Howe,

I feel a void in being here without seeing you, & still hope that this will not endure too long.[1] My voyage was long & dreary, & I suffered much from sea-sickness. I leave my maledictions with the sea; I spit in it—, that is strong for me! My head still tosses, & this brick house is going up & down like a ship.

Of the great event, I know little more than I have caught in conversation.[2] To-day I shall try to read up on it.

Without delay I went the first forenoon to S. Boston, & then to yr office but without the good fortune of finding yr wife. I try the office again to-day. From her I hope to learn about yr plans. Of course, in my profound ignorance, I cannot judge the step you have taken. But for my own sake I wish you were here.

I have seen T. P. Chandler,[3] but not [*John*] Andrew.

You tell me to see [*Edward*] Jarvis. I shall send for him. I wish you could see me now & my bounding step, & yet I am not without solicitude as to the effect of continuous work. Paris & Boston Drs. say— "caution." Very well; but I long to be fully in the harness, & to drag my part of the load. I long also *liberare animam meam.*[4]

Good bye! God bless you!

Ever & ever Yrs,   Charles Sumner

ALS   MH-H   (64/072, PCS)

1. CS returned to Boston from Liverpool on 21 November 1859.
2. On 16 October, John Brown and his band raided Harper's Ferry. Howe, Gerrit Smith, T. W. Higginson, Theodore Parker, Franklin B. Sanborn (1831–1917; Concord journalist), and George L. Stearns (1809–67; Boston manufacturer) helped finance Brown's raid. During his trial, Brown refused to name any of his backers, but Virginia authorities discovered among Brown's papers letters from Howe, Sanborn, and Smith. On 14 November, after he had fled to Canada, Howe had a notice published in local papers stating that he had no knowledge of the raid (Stephen B. Oates, *To Purge this Land With Blood: A Biography of John Brown* [1984], 312–14; Harold Schwartz, *Samuel Gridley Howe* [1956], 221–23; 234–40; *New York Times*, 16 November 1859:8).
3. Theophilus P. Chandler (1807–86), Boston attorney.
4. "To free my soul."

To Samuel Gridley Howe

Washington 9th Dec. '59

Dear Howe,

At last I found Judge Blair at his own house.[1]

It is as I supposed. He knows nothing more than the rest of us, but suspects the enemy of a design to cause mischief by seizing a Northern man under the witness statute.[2] But he has no *facts*; nor does he know any body through whom he can ascertain the real purposes of the Virginians. In short you & Andrew can judge the point as well as he. I mention this so as to relieve you from any pressure on account of his supposed opinions.

You will note Mason's resolution still pending in the Senate, which will pass as soon as the speaking ceases.[3] Under this witnesses can be brought from any part of the country, & I doubt not you would be summoned at once. Of course, I know nothing of the circumstances, but I presume you can have no objection to tell yr story before that Committee.[4]

Hanscomb[5] is now in the employ of the N.Y. *Herald*. I have not found any body through whom I can learn the Virginia purposes, nor do I think it important to seek them.

I think you must judge by the well-known facts, & by yr own knowledge of what you might [*rest of MS missing*]

AL   MH-H   (64/076, PCS)

1. Howe had tried to get the Washington lawyer Montgomery Blair (1813–83) to defend Brown (Harold Schwartz, *Samuel Gridley Howe* [1956], 235).

2. CS wrote both Howe and John Andrew, Howe's attorney, regularly in December 1859 and January 1860, offering advice as to Howe's conduct regarding his connection with John Brown's raid (see reels 64 and 73, PCS). On 9 December 1859, he wrote Andrew, "More than ever I am convinced, that it was a mistake in him to leave Boston, & that, as he is now there, the sooner he shews himself openly the better, with the statement that he has returned at the close of his vacation for his accustomed duties" (73/548).

3. At the opening session of the 36th Congress, 5 December, James Murray Mason had introduced a resolution that a committee be appointed to determine whether the Harper's Ferry raid was undertaken by any organization with subversive intentions against a state and whether any citizens not present at the raid were also implicated (*Globe*, 36th Cong., 1st sess., 1).

4. CS wrote Andrew (10 December, 73/550), "I assume that there was no legal offence committed. That is enough."

5. Howe, having returned from Canada to Boston, asked if CS could hire, at Howe's expense, a Washington correspondent named Hanscom to find out all he could about "the movement in Virginia touching witnesses" (6 December [misdated 1857], 72/654). Hanscom had evidently been dismissed from the New York *Evening Post* as Washington correspondent sometime before February 1859 (*Letters of William Cullen Bryant*, ed. William Cullen Bryant II and Thomas G. Voss, 4 [1984]: 96). CS informed Howe 12 December that CS had been told it was not "safe" to communicate with Hanscom (64/078).

To John Greenleaf Whittier

Washington 12th Dec. '59

My very dear Whittier,

Often in my seclusion & suffering I have thought of you & felt stronger. Although I read little from home I did not miss the generous word which you put forth.[1]

My situation was peculiar, & I was much perplexed as to the course I should pursue. Had I foreseen how my disability was to run on I should at once have resigned. But, like other invalids, I looked to every to-morrow for health.

But at last I am well again, with only the natural solicitude as to the effect of work & the constant pressure of affairs on a system which is not yet hardened & annealed. My physicians enjoined for the present caution & a gradual resumption of my old activities.

Should I speak on recent occurrences it would be in the spirit of yr article, which I admire & adopt.[2]

God bless you! Cheer me now & then by a word!

Ever affectionately Yrs,   Charles Sumner

ALS   MSaE   (73/554, PCS)

1. On 11 September 1858 Whittier had written a letter to the Boston *Atlas and Daily Bee* criticizing those who called for CS's resignation from the Senate. Praising CS as senator, Whittier asked Massachusetts citizens to let CS make his own decision (*Letters of John Greenleaf Whittier*, ed. John B. Packard [1975], 2:378–79).

2. Whittier enclosed an article on the Harper's Ferry raid he had written for the Amesbury *Villager* (17 November 1859) with his letter to CS of 8 December (18/241, PCS). In the article, "Lesson of the Day," Whittier reiterated his belief in nonresistance, but stated that continued Southern aggression was likely to provoke violence (*Letters of John Greenleaf Whittier*, 2:439). In his letter to CS Whittier said Northerners should distinguish between "the natural sympathy with the *man*" and support for John Brown's "most dangerous & unjustifiable *act*."

To Samuel Gridley Howe

Senate Chamber 12½ o'clk—
{15 December 1859}

Dear Howe,

The Committee is just appointed, & is *very strong & not unfair.*

Mason of Va		
Jeff. Davis of Miss.	}	Slavery
Fitch of Ind		
Collamer	}	Anti-Sl.
Doolittle[1]		

The two last are excellent for our side, inasmuch as they have ability & judicial xperience.

The Committee is called together for Sat morng at 11 o'clk, when, of course, its course will be determined. As there will be an adjournment for the holidays next week, it does not seem to me probable that witnesses will be summoned till after New Year's Day.

Private —Doolittle, with whom I have just conversed, thinks with me, that no body, who is not an accomplice in the recent affair, need have any anxiety—that, indeed, this is the *only question!* He thinks that every such witness should come without hesitation. If harm comes to him, so much the worse for Slavery!—

Hale, who sits beside me, says the same.

Therefore, I beseech you banish the M.B. letter from your mind.[2]

I hope to be in Boston next week when we can discuss these things. But my first, 2nd & 3d request are to consider the M.B. letter as never written!

God bless you!

Ever & ever yrs,   C. S.

ALS   MH-H   (64/082, PCS)

1. Members of the Harper's Ferry Investigating Committee not previously identified are Graham N. Fitch (1809–92; U.S. senator [Dem., Ind.], 1857–61), Jacob Collamer (1792–1865; U.S. senator [Rep., Vt.], 1855–65), and James R. Doolittle (1815–97; U.S. senator [Rep., Wis.], 1857–69).

2. Howe wrote CS from Boston 13 December 1859 that he was going "openly about my business." But he wondered if a witness who was "an ultra abolitionist" was safe in Washington (73/556, PCS). Montgomery Blair had written Andrew that Southern "mischief makers" might contrive to have a Northerner arrested (Washington, 7 December, Andrew Papers, Massachusetts Historical Society). However, CS repeatedly urged both Andrew and Howe to ignore Blair's advice; Blair was "naturally nervous & cautious," wrote CS to Howe (8 December, 64/074).

To the Duchess of Argyll

Washington 20th Dec. '59

My dear Duchess,

These tardy words are the first which I send to England, & I hardly know where to begin in my story.

My voyage was long & disagreeable. Out of its 16 days I was sea-sick 12; so that I was most happy to touch the firm earth. I found conversation & the press much occupied by the recent inroad into Virginia, of which only a hint had reached England before I embarked. Every where the enterprize has been condemned, while it has seemed almost mad, but the singular courage & character shewn by its author have awakened very general admiration. People find in his conversation & letters since his imprisonment & in his death much of the Covenanter, the Puritan & even the early Xtian martyr.[1]

Of course his act must be deplored, & yet it was the pedestal which has shewn to the world a most remarkable character, whose courageous example is destined to influence powerfully our dreadful question.

I wish that I could talk with you on this theme. For a practical statesman, believing Slavery a wrong, the subject is not without its difficulties. Not, indeed, that I hestitate to judge the *act*; but how can I refuse my admiration to many things in the *man?* The subject has been discussed in the Senate, on a motion for a Committee of Inquiry, but I took no part. My absence from the country when it all occurred inclined me to follow the suggestion of my physician.

The lower House still continues without its Speaker, & nobody can tell when it will be organized.[2] This is caused by the near equality of the opposing political forces. The Republicans, representing the Anti-Slavery sentiment, have almost a majority—*not quite*; opposed to them are the Democrats, & what are called Americans, Pro-Slavery. If the two latter could agree they might choose a Speaker. It will end in the choice of the Republican, whose success, it is supposed, will foreshadow that of his party next year in the Presidential contest.

The Presdt's Message is kept back until the House is organized.

The San Juan difficulty seems for the present settled. Good!—I did not doubt this result when I saw that General Scott had been sent there.[3]

Meanwhile difficulties seem still imminent in Europe. When will the Italian question be settled? I trust that England, in the approaching Congress,[4] will throw her [buckler?] over the weak & oppressed.

Since my return I have read Mr Gladstone's volumes on Homer,[5] which, in my long sojourn on the continent, had escaped me. Perhaps my great interest in him personally added to the interest of the work, but it seemed to me on every ground a most remarkable contribution to literary history. Several of the chapters are charming. Mure[6]—Grote—Gladstone—are three Englishmen, who have done much for Greek literature—a good triumvirate.

You have noticed the death of Washington Irving.[7] He died just as life was beginning to be a burthen, & has been mourned by the public almost as a personal loss.

I found Mr Palfrey much absorbed in the 2nd vol. of his History, but very anxious to hear about you & glad to know that you had not forgotten him. Dana, in his circumnavigation of the globe, must be now in

China—& soon in India.[8] Not far from the Sandwich Islands his ship took fire, & all must have perished but for the timely meeting with another vessel, which took off the passengers & crew.

How often I think of Europe—of friends there—of England & her beautiful civilization! I imagine you now at Trentham, with yr mother (God bless her!), & surrounded by yr children including the boys from Eton. Good bye! Best regards to the Duke, for whom I have some locust seeds.

Ever Yours,   Charles Sumner

Is it true that yr neighbor is about to publish 2 more vols.?[9]

ALS CSmH (73/564, PCS)

1. John Brown was hanged for treason against the state of Virginia on 2 December 1859.
2. On the thirteenth ballot, 19 December, John Sherman (1823–1900; U.S. congressman [Rep., Ohio], 1855–61; U.S. senator, 1861–77) was still four votes short of the necessary majority (*Globe*, 36th Cong., 1st sess., 189).
3. Reviving questions about the U.S.–Canadian northwest boundary, the British insisted that the island of San Juan belonged to Her Majesty's government. Buchanan stood firm, and wrote the British Foreign Office that he was sending Winfield Scott to assert U.S. claims to the island (Lewis Einstein, "Lewis Cass," in *American Secretaries of State*, ed. Samuel Flagg Bemis, 6 [1928]: 314–16).
4. A congress of European powers to discuss the unification of Italy was announced for 5 January 1860 (*New York Times*, 19 December 1859:2).
5. *Studies on Homer and the Homeric Age*, 3 vols. (1858).
6. William Mure (1799–1860), British historian.
7. On 28 November.
8. Dana was then en route to China (*Journal of Richard Henry Dana, Jr.*, ed. Robert F. Lucid [1968], 3:891).
9. Thomas Macaulay lived near the Argylls in Kensington and had been working on volume 5 of the *History of England* (*The Letters of Macaulay*, ed. Thomas Pinney 6 [1981], 10).

To Hamilton Fish

Washington, 13th Jan. 60.

My dear Fish:

I recd. a visit last evng. from yr successor.[1] Our conversation was long & intimate on the nomination. He thinks Seward will have it, & will be elected.

Of course, I naturally inquired as to the prospects in Pennsylvania. To which he said—"Penn will go for the nominee of the Convention—

& for the cause." He seemed confirmed in this view by his recent visit to Wilmot.[2]

[*Solomon*] Foot says that the constant abuse of Seward will make him the candidate. You know that he did not incline this way originally, but he seemed to think that circumstances had changed.

Judge Read,[3] whom I saw as I passed through Phila, was sure that he could not carry Penn. or N.J. This also was the opinion of an intelligent gentleman with whom I conversed in the cars on my way here.

Seward is cheerful &, I think, looks to the nomination—alluding more than once—in conversation with me to the prospect of representing the party. He says—what is fame? & then tells the story of a person in the cars, (while he was on his way to Auburn, & guns were firing & speeches making), asking his neighbor—"Who is this Govr. Seward? Is he of N.Y."!—

Good bye!

Ever yours,   Charles Sumner.

ALS ICbs (73/592, PCS)

1. Preston King was elected senator in 1857 when Fish retired.
2. David Wilmot, now a Pennsylvania judge, had been active in the state Republican party since its formation.
3. John Meredith Read (1797–1874), judge of the Supreme Court of Pennsylvania, 1858–73.

To the Duchess of Argyll

Washington 17th Jan. '60

My dear Duchess,

I have this morning learned of the death of Macaulay.[1] Though not surprized I am oppressed by this event. I am unhappy. I last saw him at yr house the last day I was in London, & I felt painfully his invalid condition. There seemed to be no physical health in him.

His fame in America is prodigious; I think, perhaps, the most widely diffused & solid of any living Englishman. His style, has had more imitators here than that of any other person.

It is sad to think that his great work is left a *torso*. Pray in what precise state is it, & who will edit it? I presume Mr Flower Ellis,[2] who seemed to be the bosom friend. To those who were in the habit of seeing him familiarly & enjoying his wonderful conversation his death will cause an incalculable void. What talk ever matched his in learned full-ness, force & variety?

I am so subdued by this loss & feel it so sharply, that I do not like to speak of other things. But I cannot write to you without a souvenir of all yr kindness. I wish that I could go to you now & tell you every thing.

I have sent to yr Duke a box of the locust-seed which he desired. I fear that the tree will not be as profitable as he seemed to anticipate. It suffers very much from a worm called the borer. In the same parcel he will find a copy of Emerson on the Trees of Massachusetts,[3] where is a full account of the locust-tree. Let me also call his attention to an ingenious criticism—somewhere about the 10th page—on a passage in Hallam criticising Spenser. I also send to you for yr eldest son, with my best regards, & constant interest, a copy of the late Boston edition of Plutarch's Lives[4]—the best I think that exists. You will perceive that it was edited by Mr Clough who is now in England. At the time the work was commenced he resided in Boston.

The "dead-lock" in our House of Reps. still continues, nor can any body tell when it will end. It is a part of the revolutionary state of affairs caused by Slavery. Truly the influence of this institution is worse than I had supposed.

I thought that I knew something of Slavery. But it looks in all its influences more *barbarous* than I had supposed. The men & society where it exists are degraded beyond all imagination. The threats of disunion are now louder than ever.

Yesterday I saw the President, who seemed well, & particularly glad to hear of Lord Clarendon, who he said—was not an Englishman in character—"Why" said he, "he talks laughs & smokes—*like an Ameri-can*"! He thought Miss Lane[5] was liked in England much better than himself.

Seward has returned from his extensive rambles full of health & spirit. Meanwhile the enemy has been busy in denouncing & pursuing him, & the threat is open that, should he be elected President, the Slave States, will break up the Union. All things shew that we are approach-ing a crisis—perhaps the beginning of the end. But why that odious article in the *Times* on our Slave Question?[6]

God bless you & yours

Ever sincerely Yrs,   Charles Sumner

In reading Dibdin's Memoirs[7] I have often been reminded of Camden Hill, where he lived so long & loved books.

ALS   CSmH   (73/608, PCS)

1. Macaulay died 28 December 1859.
2. Thomas Flower Ellis (1796–1861), law reporter and editor.
3. George Barrell Emerson, *A Report on the Trees and Shrubs Growing Naturally in the Forests of Massachusetts* (1846).
4. John Douglas Sutherland, marquess of Lorne, later ninth duke of Argyll (1845–1914); *Plutarch's Lives: The Translation called Dryden's, Corrected from the Greek and Revised* (1859).
5. Harriet Lane Johnston (1833–1903), Buchanan's niece.
6. In an editorial on the American reaction to John Brown's raid, 28 December 1859:6, the London *Times* criticized all abolitionists and described an increasing pro-Southern sentiment in the U.S. The editorial concluded, "the enforced equality of European and African tends, not to the elevation of the black, but the degradation of the white man."
7. Thomas Frognall Dibdin (1776–1847), bibliographer and author of *Reminiscences of a Literary Life* (1836).

To Samuel Gridley Howe

Senate Chamber 26th Jan. '60

Dear Howe,

The Committee, I learn, have considered the case of witnesses coming here, who might be exposed to indignity or trouble, & they will regard such witnesses for the time as under the protection of the Senate. How much this is worth you can judge.[1]

But I regard this intimation, which had been volunteered to me, as one of the signs of safety for witnesses coming here.

Mr Mason, to whom through Mr Doolittle, I communicated the letter you dictated to me, said—"tell Dr Howe to come on as soon as practicable without further summons—that is as soon as is consistent with his health & official business—& to let the Committee know the day before he comes, that they may be in session to go on with his examination without delay."

Mr Jackson has given his testimony,[2] which he is to read over tomorrow & depart with his $2 per diem & his mileage at 10 cents a mile each way. I doubt if they have got their money's worth!

Pray keep me informed of yr movements.[3]

I shall write you a note on Horace Mann.[4] Earlier I have not written, because I have only now touched my money, by the payment of the last draft.

God bless you!

Ever Yrs,   C. S.

ALS   MH-H   (64/096, PCS)

1. Howe wrote CS from Boston 21 January 1860 that he was awaiting his summons from the Harper's Ferry Investigating Committee. He said he would appear because he had made "one or two mistakes in this matter which the Committee are investigating & which I wish to retrace." Otherwise he would have defied the summons, which he regarded as an "outrageous stretch of power" on the part of the Senate committee (73/617, PCS).

2. In his testimony James Jackson of Boston said he had sent money to Francis J. Meriam of Boston, a participant in the Harper's Ferry raid, but denied knowing anything of Meriam's purpose (U.S. Senate, Harper's Ferry Investigating Committee, *Resolution and Inquiry into Late Invasion and Seizure of Public Property at Harper's Ferry*, Senate Report no. 278, 1860, serial set 1040, 129–32).

3. Howe wrote CS 26 January that he would leave for Washington the following Wednesday. He regretted following others' advice earlier; "the thought of any evasion was always repugnant to my feelings" (73/629).

4. Howe was trying to raise money for a statue of Horace Mann ([January 1860], 73/651).

To John Andrew

Senate Chamber Tuesday—
[7 *February* 1860]

My dear Andrew,

I have already sent you a telegram.[1]

The Committee has adjourned to Thursday, but will probably sit Friday,—especially if it is known before hand that you will be here that day.

The desire is to accommodate you. Come then when yr case is over. To arrive Monday might be inconvenient to you on account of Sunday. Monday or Tuesday will be agreeable, if you will by telegraph, let the day be known here which you select, that the Committee may be in session.

If the question with the Committee were made, it were better begun at home, by a refusal to obey the summons & a judgt. of our court on *hab. corp*. That failing, then the contest might be renewed here. All this provided one wished to raise this question. You I suppose will content yourself with a protest.[2]

Howe has recounted his experiences to you, Mare's nest![3]—

Ever Yrs,   Charles Sumner

ALS   MHi   (73/663, PCS)

1. Andrew had been summoned to testify before the Harper's Ferry Investigating Committee and wrote CS from Boston 4 February 1860 that he would do his best to

comply, even though he had legal business and doubted the committee's authority (James M. Mason to Andrew, 2 February, Andrew Papers, Massachusetts Historical Society; 18/511, PCS). CS telegraphed Andrew 7 February (73/662) telling him to, come to Washington Friday or Tuesday.

2. In his testimony on 9 February, primarily on his role in obtaining legal counsel for John Brown, Andrew stated he thought Brown's raid was unlawful but so was the Brooks attack on CS, which had been, "if not justified, at least winked at throughout the South" (U.S. Senate, Harper's Ferry Investigating Committee, *Resolution and Inquiry into Late Invasion and Seizure of Public Property at Harper's Ferry*, Senate Report no. 278, 1860, serial set 1040, 193).

3. Howe testified 3 February denying any knowledge of John Brown's plan to attack Harper's Ferry; he told the committee that he thought his financial contributions were to be used solely for "the defense of freedom in Kansas" and he had supported Brown as he would any cause for freedom (ibid., 159, 166–67).

To Nassau Senior

Washington 22nd Feb. '60

My dear Senior,

At last there is a certain degree of repose in our affairs. The excitement created by John Brown, which I found raging on my return, has subsided & a Speaker has been elected.[1] Both parties are preparing for the nomination of their respective candidates at the approaching Presidential struggle. The Democrats will nominate in April; the Republicans, or Anti-Slavery in June. Who will be the candidates nobody can tell.

On our side Seward continues the strongest, &, I think, counts upon the nomination. There is less certainty on the democratic side. Some are confident that Douglas will be the candidate; others regard him out of the question. I hope so; for he is an unprincipled & vulgar able man.

The pro-slavery men have moderated their tune much during the last few weeks. Of course, the Anti-Slavery moves on, amidst these excitements & temporary hindrances.

And you in old Europe have yr excitements. Surely you have sent us lately great news—the Cobden Treaty & the Pope's letter.[2] Cobden is the great volunteer without a musket in his hand! I hope my dear England is now convinced that there is to be no invasion. This I always said. As for Italy, it is better off than we anticipated it could be. At last, it seems to have a chance.

I cannot doubt that Savoy is to go to France; I think Nice also. Italy begins at Mentone. And since Sardinia is now commencing as a great Italian State, it may properly content itself with Italian boundaries. To this arrangement it seems to me natural forces tend, without much need to diplomacy.

I imagine you about to pass over to Paris, where I wish I were to meet you. But how goes the Education Commission?[3] And what is yr plan for the summer? Pray keep me informed.

Our new Minister to France, Mr Falkener,[4] is a Virginian, of considerable wealth, I am told, who early in life, surrendered to good inspirations & expressed himself against Slavery with positive power. Since then he has crawled back, & his power seems to have deserted him. He is now bitterly for Slavery—or he could not have been nominated by Mr Buchanan. Good bye!

Ever Yours, Charles Sumner

Pray give these cravats to yr servant. Seward speaks often of you & particularly Mrs Senior[5] & of certain canvass-backs which he has not yet been able to send.

ALS CSmH (73/699A, PCS)

1. On 1 February 1860 the House finally elected as speaker William Pennington (1796–1862), U.S. congressman (Whig/Rep., N.J.), 1859–61 (*Globe*, 36th Cong., 1st sess., 650).

2. Negotiated by Cobden in 1859–60, the Cobden Treaty, a commercial treaty between England and France, provided for reciprocal tariffs between the two countries. It also stipulated that neither country could impose any trade restrictions on the other that it did not also impose on other countries. By the "Pope's Letter," CS may refer to a pamphlet, *le Pape et le Congrès*, published anonymously in December 1859 by La Guéronnière, an advisor to Napoleon III. It proposed the reduction of papal authority in Italy and implied that Sardinia would exert greater authority in central Italy (Harry Hearder, *Italy in the Age of the Risorgimento, 1790–1870* [1983], 228). The letters Pius IX issued in early 1860 maintained his determination to hold onto Rome (*New York Times*, 6 February 1860:1; 13 February 1860:4; 25 February 1860:2).

3. Senior had been appointed to the Royal Commission on Education in 1857.

4. Charles James Faulkner (1806–84), U.S. congressman (Dem., Va.), 1851–59, served as U.S. minister from 1859–61.

5. Mary C. Mair Senior.

To the Duchess of Argyll

Washington 2nd March '60

My dear Duchess,

I seem daily to miss Macaulay,—as I think that he is gone, so that I shall never again listen to his marvellous talk, nor read other works from his wonderful pen. But I am happy that he reposes in the Abbey. That is his just place.

Pray, why has not Burke been removed from Beaconsfield to this same Abbey? He belongs there; nay, I might almost say, he is wanting there. I think the representatives of Lord Rockingham[1] might very properly charge themselves with this posthumous & most tardy act of justice to a name, which is surely among the first even in our well-filled English list.

Of course, I follow with attention European movements, & am not a little pleased to find that my ideas with regard to the assurance of pacific relations between England & France seem confirmed. Sympathizing with England & rejoicing in her glory, I was too intimate with France, &, perhaps also with the well-founded peace sentiment of England itself, not to feel that the excitement stimulated by Lord Lyndhurst's speech[2] was without adequate cause. And I am glad that it has now subsided. *À la bonne heure!*[3] I hope much from that Commercial Treaty.

Italy, too, seems full of promise. I live in the hope that the Imperial programme will be fulfilled, even to driving the Austrians out of Venice.

Meanwhile we are drawing towards our Presidential contest. For the last month there has been a comparative lull. Nobody can tell who will the democratic candidate. I incline now more than ever to think that Seward will be ours. He evidently counts upon it. You are aware that the election does not take place before Novbr; but the Democrats will nominate their candidate in April; the Republicans theirs in May.

Mr Seward only two days ago made an elaborate speech in the Senate on the Slavery Question, intended as a final declaration of his sentiments.[4] He says it is the last speech he shall ever make, for, that he never will return to the Senate again. This speech, as an intellectual effort, is most eminent, & is also marked by caution in statement, insight, & elegance. His object was to plead the good cause, & at the same time, to avoid disturbing the prejudices of those who differed from him & especially not to furnish any phrases or sentences which might be used by unprincipled partizans against him. In this respect he seems to have succeeded. But there is at least one passage which I regretted & his wife agrees with me.

Of this speech half a million copies will be printed & circulated at once in a pamphlet, besides the countless reprints in the newspapers.

I trust that yr two boys are still strong in health & study.[5] I think of them often in their scholastic retreat, & only hope that they may know their advantages & be true to them.

As I hear nothing of yr Mother, I trust that she is better—completely well as she merits to be from her goodness.

Who will be yr neighbor at Holly Lodge? And what is the promise of vols from Macaulay not yet published?[6]

Good bye! And believe me,

Ever most sincerely Yours,　Charles Sumner

ALS　CSmH　(74/001, PCS)

1. Charles Watson-Wentworth, second marquess of Rockingham (1730–82), British prime minister, 1782.

2. On 5 July 1859 Lyndhurst spoke in the House of Lords on "The National Defences." He argued for increased defense expenditures, especially against expanding French power (*Hansard's Parliamentary Debates*, 3rd series, 154:616–27).

3. "Very good!"

4. In his Senate speech 29 February 1860, Seward argued for the admission of Kansas as a free state, dwelling on the moral and political evils slavery produced. He declared that the Republican party, representing the best interests of the entire United States, did not favor disunion (*Globe*, 36th Cong., 1st sess., 910–14).

5. The duchess's sons, John Douglas and Archibald (1843–1913), were then at Eton.

6. The duchess answered that she had no information about future Macaulay publications (London, 22 March, 19/039, PCS).

To John Andrew

Washington Sunday—
[*18 March 1860*]

My dear Andrew,

Put not yr trust in politicians—or in lawyers. As a general rule, out of neither can you find leaders.[1]

The lawyer can oppose anything with ingenious ability, & can defend with equal ability a position which he is told to occupy. But do not look to him, where original principles are in question.

Why have not the papers said something for Hyatt? At least, why don't they print my speech? It is brief &, I believe, opens the whole case.[2]

I have visited him in prison several times. What a hole! He is calm & serene, & thinks that it will be seen at last that he was right. I fear not. The case has already passed into the limbo of things lost on earth.

God save us all from politicians—& lawyers!—

Good bye!

Ever Yours,　Charles Sumner

ALS   MHi   (74/015, PCS)

1. On 12 March 1860 James M. Mason, chairman of the Harper's Ferry Investigating Committee, introduced a resolution that Thaddeus Hyatt (1816–1901), an inventor and abolitionist, be imprisoned for refusing to testify before Mason's committee. CS spoke against this resolution, saying first that such an investigation was not properly Senate business, and second that a Senate resolution alone could not force a witness to testify. Mason's resolution passed, 44–10 (*Globe*, 36th Cong., 1st sess., 1100–1109). Andrew wrote CS on 14 March applauding CS's stand "against a merely arbitrary power" (Boston, 18/718, PCS).

2. Andrew informed CS 21 March that the *Boston Daily Advertiser* would print CS's speech, and that Andrew would seek other possibilities as well (19/030).

To Franklin B. Sanborn

Senate Chamber—6th April 60

My dear Sir,

I am grateful for the opposition you have already made to the enforcement of a tyrannical edict, &, I trust, that what has been done is simply an earnest of what will be done should the occasion rise.[1]

Inch by inch the ground must be fought.[2] Should the attempt be made again, then plant yourself before the court on the ground that in the pending matter the Senate has transcended its powers, & press for its decision.

But you will be let alone now.

It has been discovered here that the Sergt at arms is not entitled to command the *posse comitatus*. This is important, for it leaves you in the custody and protection of yr neighbors.[3]

Ever faithfully Yours,   Charles Sumner

Frank B. Sanborn Esq.

ALS   WvCDH   (74/032, PCS)

1. On 3 April 1860 Sanborn had resisted arrest in Concord from a representative of the sergeant at arms from the Senate. He was discharged by Judge Lemuel Shaw (1781–1861), who said the Senate's power to arrest could not be delegated to another (*Globe*, 36th Cong., 1st sess., 10 April 1860, 1626). Sanborn had written CS on 21 March, after refusing a summons to appear before the Harper's Ferry Investigating Committee, that he was "resolved" not to leave Massachusetts under such a questionable authority (Concord, 19/031, PCS).

2. On 10 and 13 April CS defended Sanborn in the Senate, asking that Sanborn's petition protesting his "kidnaping" be referred to the Judiciary Committee. Despite Mason's objections, the petition was referred on 17 April to that committee (*Globe*, 36th Cong., 1st sess., 1626, 1698–99, 1745).

3. Thanking CS for his speeches, Sanborn stated in his letter of 17 April that he would "try to resist to the End" (19/181).

To Samuel Gridley Howe

Washington 25th April '60

My dear Howe,

Nobody writes to me now, & I feel solitary enough here. Yr last letter was for the moment cheering.[1] But I feel more keenly than ever the Barbarism which I see about me, & which shews itself in speech, & sentiment. I feel also the little faith of our own men in the true principles of our cause.

The Judiciary com. to whom Sanborn's case is referred can not report for some time. I doubt if any further step will be proposed. At all events there will be ample notice by public action in the Senate, so that he may till then be at rest.[2]

I visit Hyatt constantly in his Jail. He continues unshaken, & refuses to harken to any proposition, either for the submission of his case to a tribunal here, or for discharging himself from his alleged contempt.

His case was sacrificed to the politicians & lawyers—two classes, invaluable when enlisted on our side, but not to be trusted as leaders where principles of Human Freedom are in question.

Pray don't forget to verify my account with the Barings, & then return it to me. As George [*Sumner*] is now at home this can be done completely. If you can save out of it an item which save me from being in debt I shall be too happy.

How is the subscription for Mann's statue? & who is to be the sculptor?[3]

Good bye! God bless you.

Yours ever—not very happy—   Charles Sumner

ALS MH-H (64/117, PCS)

1. Howe wrote CS 15 April 1860 from Boston congratulating CS for his attack on Senator Mason regarding the Sanborn petition (74/039, PCS).

2. Sanborn was never forced to testify.

3. Howe replied, 6 May, that no sculptor for Mann's statue had been decided upon and that, anyway, adequate funds had not yet been raised (74/065).

To William H. Seward

Washington 20th May '60

My dear Seward,

My personal feelings have been so much disturbed by the result at Chicago, that I cannot yet appreciate it as a public act.[1] But I long to see you again & I hope that we may all welcome you soon.

But to you what is the Presidency? A new & highest post of duty & influence. True. But this is not needed to yr fame, nor to the discharge of the debt which we all owe to our country. Yr labors & yr speeches will be yr praise always, when Presidents are forgotten.[2]

Good bye! God bless you!

Ever affectionately Yours,   Charles Sumner

ALS   NRU   (74/077, PCS)

1. Although Seward had led on the first two ballots at the Republican convention in Chicago, on 16 May 1860 the Republicans nominated Abraham Lincoln.

2. Seward replied from Auburn, 23 May (19/302, PCS), "I should have been worthy of *them* [*friends and supporters*] and they worthy of me had it been otherwise. The road is new to all of us."

To the Duchess of Argyll

Washington 22nd May '60

My dear Duchess,

I did not write at once on the receipt of yr most welcome letter of 22nd March because I was anxious to write something definite with regard to the approaching Presidential contest, & the way was not then open.

You may remember that, while in England, I always expressed a doubt whether Seward could be nominated. Perhaps my position enabled me to appreciate better than the public generally something of the impediments. It is hard for a person, who is in the Senate, exposed to bitter opposition & also to jealousies & rivalries, to rally for himself the whole party, & perhaps the very brilliancy of his position is against him. He is too much known, & the neutral men, whose votes are wanted, cannot sustain him. Thus far in our history no man in the Senate has been chosen President.

We have recently seen an illustration of these ideas. Seward was the favorite of earnest Anti-Slavery men, but men representing the great middle states, declared that their voters were not far enough advanced in the Anti-Slavery cause to sustain him. After an active contest he has been defeated in the Convention. I had not expected it, for during the last few weeks I thought there were signs that this conservative interest would yield to the pressure for his nomination. I was mistaken.

This will be a bitter disappointment to Seward, who is now at his home in New York. During all this winter he has regarded himself as the candidate, &, I think, has allowed his mind to be much occupied by the thought.

Mr Lincoln, who has been selected as the candidate, is a good honest Anti-Slavery man, who was never in the Senate, & has served two years only in the other House. He was brought forward, in order to make sure of carrying certain states at the North-West—Illinois & Indiana— & also Penn., which with Seward would have been doubtful. Those who know him speak of him as a person of positive ability, & of real goodness. But I think it is admitted that he has very little acquaintance with Govt., & is [uninformed?] on Foreign affairs. We think he will be the next President.

Meanwhile the Democratic party is split on the question of Slavery.[1] Should this continue, it will make our victory more certain.

I need not say to you that I find much to disappoint me in the tone of persons & things. I long to see my country beautiful, just & good, & I am unhappy at the short-comings which I see. But enough of this.

England—France & Italy—I continue to watch with my accustomed interest. Of all these England seems the only one that has true tran-quillity. The Emperor seems strong still, but who knows for how long? Italy does wonders, & there is now hope even for Naples. All this must gladden you.[2]

Mr Gladstone's fame seems constantly ascending. When I first met him at Clifton, at a time when he was out of office & much abused, I predicted what has taken place, though I hardly thought it would come so soon.

Be sure that I have sympathized in the sorrow of yr family. I remem-ber Lady Dover well, but I especially remember the way in which her brother spoke of her when he was in America.[3] As he left New York he told me that it was that dear sister who would be at Bristol to welcome him home.

The Commercial Treaty with France promises well. It will make war more & more difficult. All my anticipations have been fulfilled with regard to Savoy & Nice. I always thought they would go to France.

How are yr two Etonians? & how is yr mother? I hear nothing latterly of her health. Pray give her my constant & most grateful regards. I look for Dana soon in Europe on his tour of the globe.

Good bye!

Ever Yours & the Duke's,   Charles Sumner

ALS CSmH (74/080, PCS)

1. The Democratic national convention, meeting at Charleston, South Carolina, 23 April–3 May 1860, ended with delegates from eight Southern states leaving to nominate their own candidate, who would promote a proslavery territorial policy.

2. Napoleon III and Victor Emmanuel of Sardinia signed a treaty 12 and 14 March, giving Savoy and Nice to France and allowing Sardinia to annex the former duchies of Emilia and Tuscany. On 15 May Garibaldi, with a small army of Sardinians and other northern Italian republicans, defeated the royal Neopolitan army in Sicily (Harry Hearder, *Italy in the Age of the Risorgimento, 1790–1870* [1983], 229–31).

3. In her letter of 22 March (London, 19/039, PCS) Elizabeth Argyll had informed CS of the death of her aunt Georgina Howard (b. 1805), widow of George James Agar-Ellis, first Baron Dover. Lady Dover's brother was CS's friend Morpeth, the seventh earl of Carlisle.

To Abraham Lincoln

Senate Chamber 8th June '60

My dear Sir,

I venture to send you a copy of a speech made by me recently in the Senate, where I have endeavored to expose the true character of the assumptions now made by Slave-masters.[1] It is my earnest hope that what I said may help our great cause, by vivifying its principles, & by inspiring good men every where to join in their support.

Be assured, my dear Sir, of the joy with which I look forward to the opportunity of mingling with yr fellow-citizens in welcome to you here at the National Capitol next 4th March.[2]

Believe me, my dear Sir, with much respect,

Yours sincerely,   Charles Sumner

The Honble. Abraham Lincoln

ALS DLC (74/109, PCS)

1. CS delivered "The Barbarism of Slavery" 4 June 1860 (*Globe*, 36th Cong., 1st sess., 2590–2603).

2. Lincoln replied from Springfield 14 June thanking CS for his note and the speech. He had not read the speech, "but I anticipate much both of pleasure and instruction from it" (74/119, PCS).

To Lewis Tappan

Senate Chamber 25th June '60

My dear Sir,

In referring to "old-fashioned Abolitionists" I meant those of 1830 to 40, true & earnest men, who warred on Slavery, but did not find any power in the Constitution to enter the States.[1]

In reply to yr other suggestion, allow me to remark;[2] my theme was the *Barbarism* of Slavery. This, I said, appeared first in its *Law*, &, then, I shewed the *barbarous* elements of this *law*, & the *barbarous origin* of this law. Under the latter head I proceeded to shew that the law was not derived (1) from the common law (2) from the Roman law (3) from the Mahommedan law, nor (4) from the Spanish law—all possessing a certain character of civilization; but that it came, in the slave-ships, from the barbarous chiefs of Africa.

You do not suggest that the law was derived from either of the sources which I reject, but you criticise my theory by asserting that in Africa, the child is not born a slave. Even if this were so, I doubt if my theory would fail. It might require a simple modification to this extent; that is, the Law of Slavery was derived from Africa but that we had grafted upon it the slavery of children.

But I hope you will pardon me for suggesting that you are in error in yr fact. I know well the reports of Livingston & others, shewing in the interior of Africa a considerable degree of civilization & the absence of Slavery. But all testimony shews that in Guinea & on the slave-coast, the *slave-law* is maintained, especially by the African kidnappers, with every American detail of Barbarism. Even [some way?] in the interior we hear of "*home-born* slaves." I take this phrase from Bowen's book, which happens to be on my desk. (p. 320)[3]

Do not consider me obstinate, if I still insist that Slavery is Barbarous—that one evidence is its law—& especially its barbarous origin. Pray do not—you an Abolitionist—help grace it with civilization.[4]

Ever sincerely Yours,   Charles Sumner

ALS LAMA (74/133, PCS)

1. Tappan wrote CS first on 16 June 1860 from New York, praising his speech "The Barbarism of Slavery," but noting that an "old fashioned abolitionist" might

take offense. Tappan clarified his terminology in a subsequent letter of 19 June, after CS in an unrecovered letter apparently disputed the phrasing: Tappan wrote he meant "abolitionists of the age now closing," and intended no criticism of the speech, for he liked the speech the more he examined it (19/716, 20/035, PCS).

2. Tappan wrote on 19 June that he thought CS erred in attributing to Africa the cause of the "barbarous American Slave Code. . . . American missionaries in Africa say that the children are born free." After examining in his speech the four laws that CS said did *not* produce slavery, he went on to say, "No, sir; not from any land of civilization is this Barbarism derived. It comes from Africa; ancient nurse of monsters; from Guinea, Dahomey and Congo. There is its origin and fountain" (*Globe*, 36th Cong., 1st sess., 2592).

3. Thomas J. Bowen, *Central Africa: Adventures and Missionary Labors in Several Countries in the Interior of Africa, 1849–56* (1857).

4. Tappan replied 26 June (20/149), agreeing with CS about the barbarous origin of slavery. Tappan went on, however, to state: "Without venturing to 'criticise' your admirable speech I meant barely to suggest that you had attributed to Africa what belongs to this country—the ne plus ultra of barbarism." CS's answer to Tappan, 27 June (74/141), essentially repeated the points of CS's speech and his 25 June letter. CS's letters to friends at this time indicate his concern with Republican reaction; for example, he wrote Howe, 15 June (64/135), "I see clearly; there is an effort to disown me in the Republican party, & to *read me out*." To Jay CS lamented, "the heartlessness of politicians is past belief. Not one word of sympathy or welcome has be uttered by them towards me on resuming my old functions" (27 June, 74/137).

To Theodore Tilton
Private

Boston 21st. July '60

My dear Sir,

There was a reason why I repeated myself—so far as I did—which you do not present. I did not suppose that there were 3 persons who heard me, that knew anything I had ever said before, &, as my object was to press my idea home, I naturally adopted the language in which it most naturally presented itself. And in this I believe I imitate every speaker in the habit of frequent political addresses. Of course, I had no affectation of classical models. I was in earnest, & wished to do my work at the moment as strongly as I could.[1]

Perhaps, I used old language. No matter. Perhaps, I used old ideas. But in describing Slavery, can one be always new? Indeed, how can I do better than in addressing a new audience, unfolding *anew* the five-fold selfishness of Slavery. If I understand yr criticism, you would have me give up *that* description of Slavery, & find a new one. But can I find anything, which drives the subject home more?

In the paralelle which you present, you fail to print all of the description in the Senate speech—leaving it to be inferred that the resemblance was greater than it was in reality. In that respect, it seemed to me *almost* unfair, although I think unintentionally.

But I have become latterly so accustomed to paving-stones from friends, that I shall soon be able to bear them almost as well as the open attacks of enemies. One announces my speech as "ill-timed"; another as in "bad temper"; & now another—something else; thus furnishing weapons to the enemy. Perhaps, no person has ever recd. so many attacks, with so little of real assistance in his defence. Others, who have become equally obnoxious, have had earnest presses to beat back the enemy. I have none; not one that does not give the enemy something to hurl at me. Perhaps, I deserve it. At all events, I have labored for the Truth, & I accept the consequences.

Don't believe me over-sensitive. Nobody is less so. I bear without a word of complaint all hostile criticisms; but when friends at a moment of general attack, swell the onset & even give to the enemy new weapons, I may be pardoned for a simple most friendly protest.

But I hope you will not think me insensible to the good you say. And yet, so trivial a circumstance, as that on a hot night I indiscretely wore trousers without suspenders seemed hardly worthy of friendly criticism. And are you sure that in that very speech, there are not more illustrations from art & science—certainly from modern literature—than from medieval times, if not also from antiquity too? I know not.[2]

I have always had much sympathy with the *Indep.*—from the beginning;—as I had also with the *Tribune* & with the *Post*. I do not think that I expect too much from either. And yet, perhaps, I err. It is hard to be a judge in one's own case. And all these papers may be right in the *coups de pavé*,[3] which they have given me.

Pray pardon this note. I write what comes to me & commit it to yr indulgence. Honoring you always for yr stedfast support of Truth, believe me, my dear Sir,

Sincerely Yours,   Charles Sumner

ALS NBu (74/163, PCS)

1. Theodore Tilton (1835–1907), editor of the New York *Independent*, had written a generally favorable editorial, "Charles Sumner as Orator" (19 July 1860:3), on CS's 11 July Cooper Institute speech. In it, Tilton also criticized CS's deliberate repetition of some themes, such as the fivefold enormity of slavery, used in both "The Barbarism of Slavery" and the 11 July speech, "The Republican Party: Its Origin, Necessity, and Permanence." Tilton termed CS's adoption of this Greek practice "akin to affectation."

2. Besides contrasting the spontaneous and more effective oratory of Wendell Phillips and Henry Ward Beecher with CS's "recitation," Tilton also noted CS's distracting gestures: "he occasionally hitches his pantaloons, plays with his watch-chain." Tilton wrote that CS's speeches could be improved with more references from "nature, science, and art" and fewer "to classic and medieval history."

3. "Paving-stone blows."

To the Duchess of Argyll

Boston 31st July '60

My dear Duchess,

The session of Congress is over, & I am here & hereabouts for the summer & autumn. Looking over a late English paper, I was startled to read of measles in yr family, &, then, I was gladdened by yr letter, which told of the convalescence of all & made me happy on various accounts.[1]

It was the first letter I had recd from an English friend since the attack of the *Times*.[2] I had 2 or 3 from indignant strangers; but not a syllable from a friend. I thought that perhaps they had all been discomfited by that article & felt uneasy about writing.

The article was false as could be. I recognized at once its American origin with English pro-slavery additions. The first *animus* came from New York, & it was in all respects a misrepresentation of my speech, & of the circumstances under which it was made. The question directly before the Senate was—shall Slavery be extended into the Territory of Kansas—a region as large as England? Throughout the winter the partizans of Slavery had most audaciously insisted upon an untenable interpretation of the Constitution sanctioning this extension, &, in the debate, had openly vaunted Slavery as a "blessing alike to master & slave"—"ennobling to the master" & constituting the "highest type of civilization." Nobody in the Senate had met these assumptions. The real Anti-Slavery heart of the country longed for somebody to meet them. I undertook to do it.

From this simple statement, you will see that my speech was almost a necessity in the discussion. Feeling at last a consciousness of strength, I felt it my duty to make it. Of course, it should be done thoroughly,—avoiding all personality & so far as possible, all allusion to the present moment & absolutely all allusion to my own experience, but fearlessly exposing & characterizing Slavery as it had showed itself in our history. As I came to speak of some of these incidents, which testify so strongly to its barbarizing influence, I naturally used strong language, for only in this way can they be adequately depicted.[3] But in the main I allowed the facts to speak for themselves, &, so careful was I with regard to them, that though exposed to the most vindictive assaults, they have never been successfully impeached.

But beyond a direct reply to the assumptions of slave-master, I had still another purpose, which was to vindicate Freedom of debate struck down in my person; & this I wished to do, not by words & mere declarations, but by a speech, which, as a practical exercise of this right, should be a precedent & an example. My determination was to let it appear that nothing had occurred to deter me from the freeest exercise of this right.

The people from Kansas, in Washington at the time, were very desirous that I should speak, & afterwards expressed their gratitude. I had reason to believe that some of the *mere politicians*,—who had no interest in the Anti-Slavery cause except so far as it might serve personal ends— were concerned lest I might in some way disturb their plans; but not one ventured to make a suggestion to me on the subject, or give me so much as a hint. The speech found a prompt response from all the real Anti-Slavery men throughout the country. For a month I received more than a hundred letters daily,[4] some of them full of feeling & gratitude, & all expressing interest in my position. Meanwhile some of the politicians became frightened, lest the speech might be used in some of the doubtful states to deter weak-minded men, from voting for Lincoln. But I think this fear has now passed away. Still I would not convey to you the idea that I have the approbation completely of this class of men. On the contrary, they think too much of *mere political* success, carrying with it the offices of the country, to sympathize with a strenuous uncompromising support of principles.

But I beg to assure you, that now,—after all the criticism & objections—I would not have had it otherwise. Were I put back to the day when I made the speech, I would make it again. If I could make it better, I should be glad to do it. But it was what I thought best in form for our people. I know well that it is not in the tone of a Parliamentary speech, at least in the present day. But there are two reasons at least, why that tone seems to me,—who know it so well & admire it in its place—inappropriate for our purposes. *First*, the question in issue touches feelings more profound than any Parltry question, & finds its prototype more in discussions like those of Burke on the French Revolution. And, *secondly*, our speeches are not made strictly in debate, where there is a direct off-hand reply to the speaker who has just sat down, but they are addressed, somewhat as harangues to the whole country, & are intended for circulation as tracts. On this account it is important that they should have more of the completeness & elaboration of an article, with, however, the form of a speech. Whatever may be the value of these two points of difference, they have their effect on my mind.

The papers which have just arrived from California[5] announce that the speech has been published at length there & is to be extensively circulated as a pamphlet in the hope of "converting democrats."—Pray pardon these details. I feel humbled at giving them; but yr kind inquiry, & the assurance of yr interest in me, have drawn them out.

Notwithstanding hard work, my health is excellent. On my way home from Washington, I spoke at New York to an audience of 3000 persons for two hours, & was perfectly well afterwards, so that I feel at last *completely restored*. The latter speech was received with much enthusiasm. I shall send it to you in a few days, when it is in a pamphlet, & hope you will be able to look into it. You will find it in some respects a vindication of the other.

Meanwhile there is every reason to believe that Lincoln will be elected. The South concede it in advance, & already menace disunion. Of course, nobody can precisely foretell the complications that may ensue; but I look with confidence to the result. On these things I will write again very soon. Pray tell me something of yr Mother & remember me affectnly to all yr family.

Ever sincerely Yrs,   Charles Sumner

P.S. I enclose slips from 2 or 3 Republican papers, which will help answer yr inquiry.[6]

ALS CSmH (74/183, PCS)

1. Kensington, 9 July 1860, 20/251, PCS.
2. In an editorial, the London *Times* (18 June 1860:8) called CS's "Barbarism of Slavery" speech a "peevish effort of rhetoric" and suggested he be "muzzled" by his friends. CS, said the *Times*, was an example of the politician who "is an enemy to the cause in which he pours forth his acrimonious eloquence." The duchess reassured CS in her reply of 18 August from Kensington that the *Times* wrote "so wrongly & so arrogantly, & ignorantly that few care what they say" (20/457).
3. In his speech CS cited several examples of slave masters' cruelty to their slaves: "overshadowed constantly by the portentous Barbarism about him, the Slave-master naturally adopts the bludgeon, the revolver, and the bowie-knife" (*Globe*, 36th Cong., 1st sess., 2597).
4. The Sumner correspondence contains about 450 letters total in the month after his speech.
5. The San Francisco paper, *Alta California*, published an abstract on 28 June 1860:1.
6. No enclosures have been recovered regarding the duchess's question in her 9 July letter as to whether Lincoln's stand on slavery was more moderate than Seward's.

To Milton Sutliff

Boston 8th Aug. '60

My dear Sir,

It was only recently, while on an excursion from home, that I was able to read yr masterly judgment on the Fugitive Slave Bill.[1] Nothing from the bench for years has given me equal pleasure.

Sympathy, admiration & gratitude filled me as I proceeded in yr exhaustive discussion of this important topic. It astonishes me that yr learned colleagues did not allow yr opinion to be that of the Court. But whatever may its be character I know well that it contains the law which the Court sooner or later must declare.

That the Fug. Bill is absurdly & infamously unconstitutional seems to me as clear as an axiom, & I am sure it will be so regarded just so soon as the atmosphere of Slavery has been banished from our courts, so that the true principles of Freedom will be clearly discerned.

The true difficulty lies in the possible conflict between two jurisdictions. And here we must look to the moderation of reasonable men to avoid as much as possible pressing a case which may raise such a question. Do you remember the last sentence of the chapter on Gratuitous Loans by Judge Story in his work on Bailments?[2]—"if a loss or injury unintentionally occurs, an indemnity is either promptly offered or promptly waived." Something of this spirit must be established between the two jurisdictions generally, with the special understanding that a State is truly "sovereign" in fact as in name, when it undertakes to protect the liberty of any one within its borders.

In delivering yr opinion on this subject you have erected a monument to yourself in the judicial history of the country.

What greater mistake can a judge make than to attempt by artificial reasoning to do away the moral law & the principles of universal liberty? The passion or prejudice of the hour may sustain him; but the sober judgment of history must condemn him, & this unfortunately must be the position of yr colleagues.

Pardon, my dear Sir, the freedom with which I write, & believe me, with much regard,

Sincerely Yours,   Charles Sumner

The Honble Milton Sutliff

ALS   OCLWHi   (74/204, PCS)

1. Milton Sutliff (1806–78; Ohio Supreme Court Justice, 1860–70) had sent CS a copy of his "Dissenting Opinion of Hon. Milton Sutliff, One of the Judges. Ex parte Simeon Bushnell. Ex parte Charles Langston. On Habeas Corpus" (1859) with his letter of 30 June 1860 from Warren, Ohio (20/201, PCS). Although he believed his opinion on the Fugitive Slave Law contained some "imperfections," Sutliff wrote that he thought CS could "pick up here & there along the little brook smooth stones for your potent sling on some future occasion."
2. *Commentaries on the Law of Bailments* (1832).

To Hannibal Hamlin

Boston 23d Aug. '60

My dear Hamlin,

A thousand pardons! I ought to have written at once; but from yr letter, I inferred that if I could not go, an answer would not be expected.[1] I wish I could go.

I am to speak at our State Convention, which is next week,[2] & immediately afterwards must enter upon other engagements.

I hear that your canvass is conducted with much spirit, but with the best promise. Good! I see nothing in our way elsewhere. The enemy is desperate; but in closing up, it will lose many who will not fuse.

Good bye!

Ever Yours,   Charles Sumner

ALS   MeU   (74/219, PCS)

1. Hamlin, Republican vice presidential candidate, wrote from Hampden, Maine, 14 August 1860 (20/434, PCS), asking CS to come to Maine and "help us and the cause" by speaking at a mass meeting 31 August. He told CS the Republicans were doing "well" in Maine, but he was concerned about the "super human exertion" on the part of the "Slave Democracy."
2. CS enthusiastically endorsed the Republican ticket in his speech, "Presidential Candidates and the Issues," at the Republican state convention in Worcester, 29 August.

To the Duchess of Argyll

Boston 3d Sept. '60

My dear Duchess,

You are kind & good. Believe me—I feel truly the friendship with which you cheer me.[1] I imagine you now in Scotland—perhaps at Dunrobin—perhaps at Inverary; but wherever you may be, happy I hope & surrounded by family & children all well.

How is Mr Gladstone now? Of course, his ability shines always. But I fear that he is again exciting great bitterness. When I first met him, he was then much attacked & was out of power. I predicted his rehabilitation, & I foresaw his union with the Liberals. But for his Oxford education, he would have been from the beginning a Whig & *something more*; & I am inclined to think he is now getting free from his Oxford impediments. Surely all must respect his abilities, & his scholarship & reverence his purity of character.

I was glad to hear through you from Tennyson.[2] I trust that his charming wife is well. Would that I could pass another day with them. His fame among us is greater than ever. All who really love poetry feel that his is of unapproachable beauty.

That chance word from Ld Brougham at the Statistical Congress has produced considerable commotion here.[3] In some respects it was a blunder—but a happy one. It has shot far & wide the truth of the common humanity of the negro.

We follow with painful anxiety Garibaldi in Sicily & now in Naples. It seems as if Liberty was to assert her rights in Italy. I long to hear of the flight of Bambino—& then of the Pope.[4] If this could be followed by the flight of Louis Nap. himself, the peace of Europe might settle down upon a natural basis. Just so long as he holds his throne I am anxious. Besides I know that the best minds of France are all held in check.

You must be gratified by the reception of the Prince of Wales in Canada.[5] And thus far the interest in his visit seems hardly less in the United States. I doubt not that he will be welcomed cordially & completely. I fear, indeed, that it will be over-done. But this he will kindly pardon.

Meanwhile our Presidential canvass goes on.[6] The election is at the beginning of Nov. Till then newspapers & speakers will be constantly occupied. I do not doubt the result. Lincoln will be chosen. Then, however, will commence a new class of perils & anxieties. The threats of a dissolution of the Union have no force. But it remains to be seen how competent the new Presdt. will be to organize the govt. of a great country. Idealist as I am, I shall prepare myself in advance for many disappointments.—I have sent you in the papers another speech which I have recently made.

The course of the London *Times* seems almost Satanic on Slavery. It might do [us?] much good; but it has encouraged the slave-masters & slave-traders to believe that there is a real change of opinion in England, & from this they take hope. Its attack on me was originally implied from New York.[7]

Mr Palfrey was happy to know of yr inquiry. He has just finished the 2nd vol. of his most elaborate History of New England. I think yr Duke will read it with true interest, & will find himself aided even in English history. I am proud of this book.—Dana is, perhaps, at this moment in England on his way home from the East.[8]—Longfellow is at home with no present purpose of going abroad.—Good bye! Best regards to the Duke—

                  & Ever Yours,   Charles Sumner

ALS   CSmH   (74/221, PCS)

1. The duchess had written CS from Kensington 18 August 1860 (20/457, PCS), again praising CS's "Barbarism of Slavery" speech: "it must be truth—awful truth, that is spoken," she declared, even if such statements were to jeopardize the Republicans' chance for the presidency.

2. The duchess wrote that Tennyson had asked her to convey to CS his "warm approval" of CS's speech.

3. At the recent opening of the International Statistical Congress, Brougham had noted to the American minister, George M. Dallas, that one of the Canadian delegates was black (London *Times*, 21 July 1860:9).

4. After several bloody battles, Garibaldi's forces occupied all of the island of Sicily and looked toward conquering the Kingdom of Naples on the mainland, also ruled by Francis II ("Bambino") (1836–94).

5. The Prince of Wales, the future Edward VII, visited Canada and the U.S. from 24 July to 20 October.

6. Besides the Republicans, three other parties had nominated presidential candidates: the northern Democrats, Stephen A. Douglas; the southern Democrats, John C. Breckinridge of Kentucky; and the Constitutional Unionists, John Bell.

7. In an editorial 7 July 1860:9, the London *Times* declared the U.S. was unnecessarily agitated against Great Britain on the slave-trade issue; U.S. senators, Northerners and Southerners alike, said the *Times*, generally misunderstood British antislavery policy because of "national vanity and national rivalry." Another editorial stated that the slave trade should be left to die out on its own since the U.S. would rather breed its own slaves (1 August 1860:8). See also CS to the duchess of Argyll, 31 July 1860.

8. Dana was in fact in Switzerland en route to England (*Journal of Richard Henry Dana, Jr.*, ed. Robert R. Lucid [1968], 3:1124).

To John Evelyn Denison

                             Boston—U.S. of America—
                             23d Oct. '60—

Dear Mr Speaker,

Our discussions on the rules at the last session of Congress ended, like many other discussions, in very little. Should any thing be done at the approaching session, which commences the first Monday of Dec., I shall have pleasure in apprizing you of it.[1]

You are doubtless aware that the Hour Rule & the Previous Question prevail in the Lower House, but not in the Senate. I know no source of information on the differences between the American & the English systems better than Cushing's work on Parliamentary Law.[2]

Perhaps, this letter will reach you even before the arrival of the squadron with the Prince. You will be glad to know that he left in good health & unwearied by all the processions & hospitalities to which he was subjected. During his last day I was with the party & parted with him on the pier, as he was stepping into the barge.[3] You will have heard something of the uprising of the people to welcome him. But I doubt if any description can give you an adequate idea of its extent & earnestness. At every station on the rail-way, there was an immense crowd headed by the local authorities, while our national flags were blended together. I remarked to Dr Ackland that "it seemed as if a young heir long absent was returning to take possession."—"It is more than that," said he affected almost to tears. For the Duke of Newcastle, who has had so grave a responsibility in the whole visit, it is a great triumph. I took the liberty of remarking to him that he was carrying home an unwritten Treaty of Alliance & Amity between two great nations.

The suite of the Prince seemed well-chosen.[4] Nobody could be abler than the Duke, more clever than Ld Lyons, more courtly than Ld St Germain, or more polite & amiable than Genl. Bruce. I wish they could have seen the country in the simple way of common travellers. The only walk the Prince has had—except on the prairies, which he enjoyed much—was in the evening at Philadelphia. It happened to be on the day of the election for Governor, which has substantially decided the Presidential election, so that he saw something of the movement caused by the *demos*.[5]

It was very kind in you to write me, & I pray you to present my compliments to Lady Charlotte,[6] & believe me, dear Mr Speaker,

Ever sincerely Yours,   Charles Sumner

ALS GBNÜ (74/275, PCS)

1. John Evelyn Denison, later viscount Ossington (1800–73; Speaker of the House of Commons, 1857–72), had written CS from London 22 August 1860 (20/471, PCS) inquiring about any new procedural rules that had been passed in the U.S. Congress. He especially wanted to know the effect of "coercive & repressive Rules, such as the one Hour Rule."

2. Luther S. Cushing, *Elements of the Law and Practice of Legislative Assemblies in the United States* (1856).

3. The prince sailed from Portland, Maine, on 20 October (Henry J. Morgan, *The Tour of H.R.H. The Prince of Wales Through British America and the United States* [1860], 206–7). CS attended all the Boston and Cambridge celebrations for the Prince of Wales (Prc, 3:620).

4. Accompanying the prince on his tour were Henry W. Acland (1815–1900), Oxford professor of medicine; Henry Pelham Fiennes, fifth duke of Newcastle (1811–64), secretary of state for the colonies; Richard Bickerton Pemell, second baron and first earl of Lyons (1817–87), British minister to the U.S., 1858–65; Edward Granville Eliot, third earl of St. Germans (1798–1877), lord steward of the household; and Major General Robert Bruce, governor to the Prince of Wales (Morgan, 21).

5. The Pennsylvania gubernatorial election took place 9 October, with the Republicans winning by 32,000 votes. The *New York Times* described the Republican celebration that evening as the returns came in (10 October 1860:1).

6. Lady Charlotte Cavendish Bentinck Ossington.

To William H. Seward

Boston 7th Nov. '60

My dear Seward,

Yr last words at New York were simple, grave, impressive.[1] They fitly closed yr most remarkable series of speeches.

Here we can hardly rejoice in our great State & national triumph when we think that we [have?] lost Burlingame.[2] Through Mr Appleton Boston gives a *hand-shake* to the Pro-Slavery men of the South; & his table will become one of their council-boards. This is hard to bear.

We suspect the grossest frauds, but covered up too ingeniously. God bless you!

Ever Yrs,   Charles Sumner

ALS   NRU   (74/282, PCS)

1. On 2 November 1860 Seward spoke in New York City, promising that a Republican victory would contain slavery in the South and energize the nation's economy (Glyndon van Deusen, *William Henry Seward* [1967], 235).

2. Lincoln was elected president 6 November with 1,866,352 votes, followed by Douglas with 1,375,157 votes. Anson Burlingame was defeated by William Appleton (1786–1862; U.S. congressman [Whig, Mass.], 1851–55, 1861).

To Henry W. Longfellow

Sen. Chamber—Monday
[*3 December 1860*]

Dear Longfellow,

S.C. will go out; then Alab & Missip;[1] The great question is, can Georgia be saved? Some say yes; others say no. Then, if all these go,

where will the contagion stop? *Quien sabe?* But there must be no yielding on our part. Thank God! our friends are firm.

We are on the eve of great events. Good bye!

Ever Yrs,   Charles Sumner

ALS   MH-H   (74/306, PCS)

  1. On 10 November 1860 South Carolina had called for a state convention to meet
17 December and vote on secession. Similar conventions were scheduled for Mississippi and Alabama in January. Longfellow replied 12 December from Cambridge,
"When South Carolina has gone out of the Union, I shall believe she is going" (74/
318, PCS).

To the Duchess of Argyll

Washington
14th [and 18th] Dec. 60

My dear Duchess,

The Presidential election has been followed by the menaced storm.
It is clear that the South is more in earnest than ever before. The
election of Lincoln is felt as the signal of subordination & repression
while they stay in the Union. It is seen that ultra slavery-men can never
expect high office, & that the slave-trade cannot be re-opened. Therefore, the Govt. must be broken up.

The first step is taken by South Carolina, which before you receive
this letter, will have taken all formal steps for secession (that is the mild
phrase for treason!). She will be followed, in all probability, by the
"Cotton States," being the ultra slave states on the Gulf of Mexico.[1] All
this will be done before the 4th March, when the new Administration
comes into power. It could not take place, if Mr Buchanan were not
playing into their hands. His irresolution, timidity & positive sympathy have encouraged them in their treason.

The first question for the new Administration will be—shall force
be applied to hold back these communities? This would be civil war,
with, as I think, a servile insurrection, ending in Emancipation—
perhaps, as in St Domingo. Indeed, in any alternative this is imminent.
On this account, I approach the question with the greatest caution.[2]
Much as I desire the extinction of Slavery, I do not wish to see it go
down in blood. And yet the existing hallucination of the slave-masters
is such that I doubt if this calamity can be avoided. They seem to rush
upon their destiny.

If the secession can be restrained to the "Cotton States," I shall be willing to let them go. But can it be stopped there? That will be the difficult work of statesmanship to accomplish. They are confident that they shall carry off all the Slave States, & even some of the Middle States.

Thus far they have counted upon the sympathy of France & even of England. Recent articles in the English papers[3] are beginning to open their eyes; but still they declare that Cotton is King every where, & that these powers must admit its sceptre. If this plant could be cultivated elsewhere successfully, their confidence would abate. Napoleon, finding himself shut out from the West Indies, made sugar from the beet-root. Perhaps, under the pressure of coming events, we may find a substitute for cotton.

18th Dec. Four days have passed. The slave states seem as mad as ever. They even hope to enlist Virginia & Maryland before the 4th March so as to prevent the inauguration of the new President at the National Capital. The imbecility of Mr Buchanan is more apparent every day. A vigorous will on his part would have arrested this movement.

The North is to be touched through the pocket, & already the cry of merchants there is producing a certain degree of influence. They insist upon concession to the South, &, in the large cities, organize mobs to suppress all discussion of Slavery. I look forward to a winter of much anxiety &, possibly, of painful incidents. I doubt not also that there will be weakness in some of our friends, although thus far they hold their ground well. Perfect firmness with all possible moderation of manner is the rule which I hope to see followed.

One by one the President is losing his Cabinet. One has left him, in order to organize treason at home. Another, Genl. Cass—the oldest & most respectable—has just resigned, because he could not concur with the President in leaving the small garrison at Charleston, amidst the disunionists, without reinforcement.[4] His Administration will end in shame.

The course of the press in Europe is now of vast importance. It may at once make the slave-holders feel the *moral blockade* in which they will be placed.

All that we hear of the new President—who lives 800 miles from Washington—is favorable. He is calm & decided. But before his term commences dismemberment will have begun, & he will be obliged to meet this or the alternative of civil war.

For myself I know no better rule than to stand firmly by the great principles of justice & to meet the consequences.

Good bye! I think often of good kind dear English friends & of their strengthening sympathy. I trust that yr mother is again well. With kindest regards to all yr family.

Ever sincerely Yours,   Charles Sumner

ALS CSmH (74/320, PCS)

1. By this date state conventions to consider secession had been proposed in Alabama, Mississippi, Florida, Louisiana, and Georgia.

2. In her reply of 26 January 1861 (21/366, PCS) the duchess wrote that she remembered CS's look of horror in the summer of 1859 when she said that the North and South must eventually separate, that the North could not remain permanently connected with slaveholding states.

3. For example, the London *Times* editorial (26 November 1860:6) stated that, despite Southern secession threats, "the United States will continue to combine in one Federation two communities, with widely different politics and systems of social life, but forming essentially and unalterably one and the same people." And the Washington correspondent for the *New York Times* (14 December 1860:2) stated that the British press indicated that Great Britain was not willing to offer protection to seceding states.

4. Howell Cobb resigned as secretary of the Treasury 10 December; Cass resigned 14 December over federal reinforcement of Fort Moultrie in Charleston.

To John Andrew

Washington 8th Jan. '61

My dear Andrew,

Yr message is clear, strong & right. I feel happy that Mass. at last has found her voice.[1]

I deplore every backward step, whether here or in Boston.

The cotton States are doomed. Even the compromisers, who have been here from New York, admit that nothing can be done to arrest them. They are trying on the tobacco states; I think in vain. *They will all go.*[2]

Therlow Weed came to see me Sunday evng with Seward. He admitted that he was "alone,"—found that he was "not welcome here"— & that the Republicans had made up their mind to have no compromises. Good! I always like Mr Weed when I see him; but he is a *politician* —not a *statesman*. I think we are in too deep water for him. True; we are now away from shore, & can only steer by the sun & stars—God-given guides.

The President's change of policy disorganizes the traitors, who curse him as a "black Republican."[3] Genl. Scott says the President's change occurred on the "2nd Jan";—"yes, sir, since the 2nd Jan. the Presdt has done well."

If possible, we must avoid civil war; indeed, to avert this dread calamity, I will give up, if necessary, territory & state; but I will not give up our principles.

But the slave masters hurry to their doom.

Good bye! God bless you!

Ever Yours,   Charles Sumner

The sense of insecurity here seems to have passed away. Had not something been done, I do not doubt that the capital could have been taken—like the other posts in Southern territory.

Virginia will go, & will carry with her Maryland & Ky.

There is intestine unrevealed trouble in Tennessee which I do not yet comprehend.[4]

ALS   MHi   (74/364, PCS)

1. Andrew had been elected governor of Massachusetts 6 November 1860. In his inauguration address, 5 January 1861, Andrew strenuously defended Massachusetts' personal liberty laws, which prohibited state courts, jails, and militia from carrying out the Fugitive Slave Act. Boston leaders such as Lemuel Shaw and Benjamin R. Curtis had recently organized a movement to repeal these laws. Denouncing the secessionists, Andrew also affirmed that Massachusetts strongly supported the Union (Henry Greenleaf Pearson, *The Life of John Andrew* [1904], 1:71, 138–41; Prc, 4:20).

2. Andrew wrote CS 4 January (21/229, PCS) that he hoped CS's "prophecies of sorrow" (apparently stated in CS's letter to Andrew of 1 January, unrecovered) would not come true. At this date, no more states had seceded, but state conventions to consider secession were scheduled for 9, 10, and 11 January in Mississippi, Florida, and Alabama respectively.

3. On 31 December 1860 Buchanan informed commissioners from South Carolina, whom he had refused to recognize officially, that he would not remove federal troops from Fort Sumter, where they had been moved from Fort Moultrie. General-in-Chief Winfield Scott had repeatedly recommended to Buchanan that Fort Sumter remain fortified.

4. CS may have been referring to a special meeting of the Tennessee legislature held on 7 January 1861.

To Dorothea Dix

Senate Chamber 14th Jan. '61

Dear Miss Dix,

I was most happy in the opportunity you gave me of sending docts. to you.

Madness rules the hour—among our Southern friends. The Cotton States have taken the plunge & will not be saved. I think the contagion will spread through all the States South of M[ason] & D[ixon]'s line.

Mr Seward's speech was entirely unsatisfactory to the South. Toombs called it "a cheat." [1] Many republicans regretted that he should deem it his duty to make *offers* or *concessions* of any kind. It seems to me that the North has but one duty; quietly, calmly, but firmly to stand by its principles. The crisis will soon pass.

Every thing will be saved if the North is firm & tranquil. [2]

Ever Sincerely Yours,   Charles Sumner

ALS   MCR   (74/372, PCS)

1. Seward's speech, delivered in the Senate 12 January 1861, proposed five means by which the Union could be preserved. He offered such concessions to the South as a constitutional amendment denying Congress the power to interfere with slavery in any state and proposed a popular convention to consider amendments to "the organic national law" (*Globe*, 36th Cong., 2nd sess., 341–44). Robert Toombs (1810–85; U.S. senator [Dem, Ga.], 1853–61) resigned as senator on 4 February.

2. In her reply from Harrisburg, Pennsylvania, Dix urged senators, even though the South insulted and betrayed the Union, to maintain "prudence and forbearance" (16 January, 21/314, PCS).

To John Jay

Senate Chamber
17th Jan. '61

My dear Jay,

Pardon my silence, & do not measure by it my interest in all that you kindly write.

Genl. Scott says the capital is now safe:—His military character is staked upon its preservation. [1] He can hold it for 24 hours against all comers, & within that time can have 50,000 men from the North. Of course all assistance here must come through the Govt. A movement of volunteers without such a call would be a "first-move," which would directly provoke hostilities.

I deplore S[eward]'s speech. He read it to me 4 days before its delivery & I protested with all the earnestness of my soul & all the strength of language I could command against his propositions—*against any propositions*. [2] I fear that it will demoralize the Northern sentiments.

Yr father—Horace Mann—& Theodore Parker—are now wanting.
God bless you!

Ever Yours,   Charles Sumner

ALS NNCB (74/380, PCS)

1. Jay wrote 12 January 1861 from Katonah, New York, that newspapers warned
that militia in the District of Columbia were organizing; he feared that Washington,
D.C., would be "suddenly seized by the rebels" (21/277, PCS).

2. Jay replied 24 January, agreeing with CS that the North should not compromise. He advised CS that if he spoke in the Senate he should remain calm and "say
as little as need be on the slavery question" (21/356).

To John Andrew

Senate Chamber
18th Jan. '61

My dear Andrew,

I think that our friends are coming to the conclusion, that we can
offer no terms of Concession, or Compromise, in order to please the
border states.[1] The question must be met on the constitution *as it is* &
the *facts as they are*, or we shall hereafter hold our Govt. subject to this
asserted right of secession. Should we yield now—& any offer is concession—every Presidential election will be conducted with the menace of
secession by the defeated party.

There is a disposition also to *stand firm* together.
Private   Ten Eyck of N. J.[2] said at one of our conferences that he should
be glad to support the propositions brought forward by Seward. The
latter at once said that what he had said was only for a speech—*he had
no idea of bringing them forward*—that they would split the Republ.
party—that there were not *three* men on our side in the Senate who
would support them.—Do you remember the story of John Wilks?[3]—
"What!" said he "do you take me for a Wilksite—no such thing!"

Ever Yrs   C. S.

ALS MHi (74/385, PCS)

1. On 14 January 1861 in the House, the recently appointed Committee of
Thirty-three postponed debate on its compromise proposal, as well as on resolutions

regarding the role of the federal government toward seceding states (*Globe*, 36th Cong., 2nd sess., 362, 364–65, 378). In the Senate, a similar Committee of Thirteen on 16 January debated but did not adopt John J. Crittenden's compromise proposal, which revived the former Missouri Compromise line (36° 30′) as the separation between free and slave states and restricted congressional power to legislate on slavery. However, an amendment supporting the Constitution and "directing energies" to "the maintenance of the existing Union and Constitution" passed, 25–23 (ibid., 402–9).

2. John C. Ten Eyck (1814–79), U.S. senator (Rep., N.J.), 1859–65.

3. John Wilkes, the British civil libertarian, was associated in the popular mind with civil disorder.

To Salmon P. Chase

Senate Chamber, 19th Jan. '61

My dear Chase,

I have not written to you because until now I saw no occasion to trouble you with my hopes or fears. I looked forward to you as a colleague in the Senate & a pillar there of our cause, & I was unwilling to say a word to incline you to any change.[1] Indeed, I have been fixed in the opinion that you ought to be in the Senate—that there yr great powers could be most felt, & yr usefulness most eminent. If these times were not so unnatural, I think that I could not be shaken in this idea.

But our new Administration, under the peculiar circumstances which now surround us, will be called to deal directly with great questions of principle. It will be for a while in the place of Congress, & it may have the duty cast upon it to save a great cause even at the expense of the Republic. Such a responsibility can be adequately met only by firmness, courage & inflexible principle.

More than any thing else, I fear "surrender." Beyond my opposition to Slavery in every form—whether it shews itself in direct or indirect propositions—I am against any offer now, even of a peppercorn.[2] Let us know if we have a Govt. These troubles cannot now be [composed?] by any concession on our part without admitting secession as a constitutional right, & giving to recent proceedings the force of precedent, so that hereafter every Presidential election will be conducted under the menace of "disunion" by a single discontented state.

No; we must stand firm.

Therefore I trust that you will accept the post of Secretary of the Treasury.[3] I write this at my own [notion?], & with an anxious desire to help those principles for which we have so long labored together.

I deplore S's speech. He read it to me 4 days before he made it, & I supplicated him with all the ardor of my soul, to change its tone &

especially to abandon every proposition of concession,—ending his speech with the declaration that Mr Lincoln would be inaugurated 4th March President of the United States, & with a rally to sustain him. He did not hearken to me.

Govr. [*Kinsley S.*] Bingham, who is by my side, says that yr acceptance is "our only salvation."

We are on the eve of great events, & I doubt if any devices can do more than dishonor us.

You will judge the question wisely—I doubt not. God bless you! & yr daughter also

Ever Yours,   Charles Sumner

ALS   DLC   (74/387, PCS)

1. The Ohio legislature had recently elected Chase to the U.S. Senate.

2. On 19 January 1861 the Virginia assembly passed a resolution inviting delegates to a peace convention, 4 February, which would examine ways to prevent dissolution of the Union. Emphasizing his agreement with CS, Chase wrote, "The surrender will not save the Union; firmness, moderation, decision will,—if anything will" (Columbus, 26 January, 21/368, PCS).

3. A formal offer had apparently not yet been extended to Chase, for he responded to CS's entreaty by saying, "Nothing but an imperative sense of duty would convince me at this time under existing circumstances to accept the post of Secy. of the Treasy," and he doubted whether the "decision between duty and inclination will be imposed on me" (21/368). Chase accepted the appointment of secretary of the Treasury on 6 March (Chase to Lincoln, 6 March, Lincoln Papers, DLC).

To Charles G. Loring

Washington 26th Jan. '61

My dear Sir,

I have too long postponed my acknowledgments of yr kindness in sending me yr Reading on the Personal Liberty Laws of Mass.[1] I am well aware that my judgment can be of little value to you; but I take the liberty of saying that no abler article of a professional character has ever been published in Mass.

But you will pardon the frankness which is a part of my nature if I add that my admiration of its professional ability made me feel most painfully the willingness it shewed to surrender cherished safe-guards of Human Rights.[2] Again & again, as I read, I exclaimed; "Oh—that he had written this article in the summer on the sea-shore, & not at this season & on the pavements of Boston! Then would his soul have been filled with the spirit of Freedom, & he would have seen that no

safeguard of God-given Rights, endangered by cruel legislation elsewhere, should be abandoned under any pretext or apology." Thus I said
to myself as I read, & I have never thought of yr remarkable effort
without repeating the wish.

It seems to me that Govr. Andrew has spoken like a jurist & a
Governor of Mass. when in his message, he declared; "There can be no
doubt that the first & most sacred duty of Govt. is to protect the lives
& liberties of subjects." In the presence of this duty, I find no stringency
of legislation "vindictive;" but conservative, just & honorable.

But I do not yield to you in homage to the Constitution.[3] I accept it
as my guide. But within its requirements, I will spare no effort, &
shrink from no obloquy, in order to surround my fellow-citizens—
especially the humble & outraged—with protection or to ward off
peril. And especially at this moment, when fundamental principles are
denied, & the treason of Judas is repeated, & the cowardice of Peter
too, it is important that our beloved Massachusetts should stand an
example of adamant.

I see clearly our future, & my earnest prayer is that the State, where
I was born, & which I now humbly represent, may not join in the
surrender of those principles which constitute her glory.

Beyond all question, the most eminent service of yr professional life
was when you *volunteered* to defend a fugitive slave.[4] This will be remembered gratefully hereafter, & spoken of with pride by yr grand-
children. In the same spirit, I wish you would now *volunteer* to save for
our Cwlth an act of legislation, which proposes to do for all what you
so nobly did for one. God bless you! & believe me, my dear Sir

Sincerely yours,   Charles Sumner

ALS   MH-H   (74/423, PCS)

1. The articles, "Reading on the Personal Liberty Laws of Massachusetts," by
Charles G. Loring (1794–1868), Boston lawyer, were published in the *Boston Daily
Advertiser*, 31 December 1860:2 and 3 January 1861:4.

2. Given the threatened dissolution of the United States, it seemed "reasonable
and expedient," wrote Loring, to clarify what rights the Constitution bestowed on
individuals. In his "Reading" Loring argued that no state law could countermand the
constitutional rights of a master to reclaim his slave (*Boston Daily Advertiser*, 31
December 1860:2).

3. Loring stated that some provisions in Massachusetts laws were "unquestionably
unconstitutional as the law and judicial decisions now stand" and should be repealed
or revised (ibid.). He urged that such state laws be brought into conformity "without
condition or delay" with the U.S. Constitution or "Constitutional principles" (*Boston
Daily Advertiser*, 3 January 1861:4).

4. Loring had defended the fugitive slave Thomas Sims in April 1851. In his reply of 30 January 1861 Loring wrote that he did not believe the "modification" he suggested harmed free men in Massachusetts, especially since these present laws "annoy or irritate" the South. Patriotism demanded some "amendment," he believed, and "deeper questions" were now paramount (Boston, 21/427, PCS).

To John Andrew
Confidential

Senate Chamber
28th Jan. '61

My dear Andrew,

I did not unite with the delegation yesterday in recommending Commissioners, & I think they signed without much reflection, certainly without any general conference. [1]

My disposition is on any matter, which [does?] not involve principle, to keep the delegation *a Unit*, & I certainly would not stand in the way of this. Two considerations have been pressed, which are entitled to consideration, *first*, that, in the absence of Commissioners duly appointed, certain "Union-savers" from Mass. accidentally here would work into the Convention & undertake to represent Mass;[2] & *secondly*, that it is important that Mass should not be kept insulated. Both of these things you can judge, & I shall defer to yr judgment.

Preston King concurred with me as to the true policy of our States; but he did not think it worth while to interfere positively by writing to Albany.

Should you conclude to move in that direction, let two things be guarded; *first*, the principles, by letting it be known that Mass. can take no step towards any acceptance of the Resolutions, which are made the implied basis of the proposed Convention, & *secondly*, the men, by designating only the firmest, in whom there is no possibility of concession or compromise—like Judge Allen, Judge [*Ebenezer Rockwood*] Hoar, Dana, Erastus Hopkins, Howe, Longfellow, Boutwell: but you know the men better than I do.[3]

Last evng the Attorney General was with me for a long time till after midnight.[4] I know from him what I cannot communicate. Suffice it to say, *he does not think it probable, hardly possible* that we shall be here on the 4th March. The Presdt. has been trimming again; & a scene has taken place which will be historic, but which I know in sacred confidence. Genl. Scott is very anxious. *It is feared that the Departments will be seized & occupied as forts*. What then can be done by the General's dragoons & flying artillery?

Ever Yours,   Charles Sumner

ALS   MHi   (74/433, PCS)

1. Charles Francis Adams had circulated a petition among Massachusetts' congressional representatives urging Andrew to appoint a commission to the peace conference organized by the state of Virginia. CS refused to sign it (DD, 1:379).

2. Bostonians such as Amos A. Lawrence (1814–86) and Edward Everett (vice presidential candidate on the Constitutional Union ticket in 1860) were then in Washington to present a petition supporting the Crittenden compromise (Henry G. Pearson, *The Life of John A. Andrew* [1904], 1:155).

3. Andrew replied on 30 January that Massachusetts should place "good men" on the delegation rather than risk being "misrepresented by volunteers, or to be wholly outside," and thus "misinformed" of the conference proceedings (21/418, PCS).

4. Edwin M. Stanton (1814–69; counsel for the U.S. government) had been named attorney general 20 December 1860 when Jeremiah Black of Pennsylvania had taken over as secretary of state.

To Francis W. Bird

Senate Chamber—
28th Jan. '61

My dear Bird,

I read every word—although yr letter was one of 30 brought me at the same time.

I see the future clearly—all bright for Freedom, if the North will only keep its tranquility & firmness. If Mass. begins a retreat, I know not where it will stop. There is nothing of Freedom [at?] the North which will not be endangered. God guard her from any backward step!

I have written to Peirce an off-hand letter giving my sentiments on the madness which would now repeal the safeguards of Freedom.[1] I trust that, if there is any body at the State House who cares for my opinion, & who inclines to this madness, he will at least hesitate well & not act hastily.

Freedom is about to have her greatest peril;—to be followed by results of unspeakable importance. Men will press compromise; but I am happy to believe *in vain*. *The question is to be settled now.*

Virginia will secede carrying with her all the rest,—except, perhaps, Maryland which will be retained by the national capital.[2] There are some who think this cannot be done; but that the revolution which carries Maryland will seize the capital. Perhaps.

February will be an eventful month.

I have not spoken because I could say nothing which would not be perverted by the compromisers as an attempt to widen the breach.[3] Meanwhile I insist upon an inflexible "No," to every proposition. "No"—"No"—"No"; let the North cry out to every compromise & to every retreat; Then will be days of glory.

Ever yours, Charles Sumner

I have written twice to Charles G. Loring on the Pers. Lib. Laws.[4]

ALS MH-H (74/437, PCS)

1. On 29 January 1861 CS wrote Henry L. Pierce (1825–96), then a member of the Massachusetts legislature and later U.S. congressman (Rep., Mass., 1873–77), urging him to oppose steadfastly those "who seek to overthrow our Massachusetts safeguards of personal liberty" (74/444, PCS).

2. At this date Georgia and Louisiana had joined the other four Cotton States in forming the Confederacy.

3. CS gave no major speeches during the second session of the 36th Congress.

4. See CS to Loring, 26 January. CS also wrote Loring 30 January (21/427).

To Richard Henry Dana, Jr.

Senate Chamber—
1st Feb. '61

My dear Dana,

Yr letter & especially its P.S. interested me much.[1] *You are now where I have been from the beginning.* Mr [*Francis E.?*] Parker will tell you that when he was here I saw this Crisis in larger proportions than others, although I was not then so sure as now of the completeness with which it would envelope all the Slave States. The Conspiracy was not then exposed.

Many have mistaken the character of this movement—deeming it merely *political* & governed by the laws of such movements, to be met by reason, by concession, & by compromise; whereas it is a *revolution*, beginning in *conspiracy*, & governed by the laws of revolution, subject to all the impulses of passion, & discarding reason. Therefore, all propositions of adjustment, unless they assume the form of absolute "surrender," are absolutely vain & of no effect,—except to distract & demoralize the Northern sentiment. Of this be assured. It is my duty to study this question, & believe me I have done it most conscientiously.

The repeal of our Pers. Lib. Law in Mass. can have no effect, except to give the signal for greater surrenders in other states. Most earnestly do I hope that our beloved Cwlth will give no "uncertain sound." On this account, even if I thought our Law open to question, I would not touch it now.[2]

Its alleged "unconstitutionality" may be safely left to the courts; nor can I sympathize with the idea that its provisions are "vindictive." The maxims of the common law, & the example of Westminister Hall teach us to "seize hold of a twine-thread for the sake of Liberty"—indeed, to strain every thing to this end. You remember Ld Mansfield's[3] instructions to bring in a verdict that the thing stolen was worth only 5 shillings, because if its true value was declared the penalty would be death. In this spirit I think it proper to meet Congressional legislation, which is cruel & offensive, & I think unconstitutional.

A few days longer,—& events will supercede all compromises or questions of concession. *Virginia will secede* & carry with her—perhaps all the rest. If we can hold the national capital, it will be because events are more "forbearing" than men.

I pray for *firmness* at the North—especially in Mass.

God bless you!

Ever yours,   Charles Sumner

ALS   MHi   (74/457, PCS)

1. Dana wrote from Cambridge 26 January 1861 that the seceded states' position rendered any U.S. compromise impossible, for such action would only make secession appear constitutional; "we must not yield." His P.S. on 29 January criticized Buchanan's message of support for the peace convention (21/370, 372, PCS).

2. Dana, coauthor with CS of the personal liberty laws in 1855, was amenable, he wrote, to some changes in those laws, changes he had always sought: "If anything is found to violate the Constitution, I should repeal it. If anything is equivocal, make it clear." Dana believed some changes would not necessarily mean capitulation to the secessionists.

3. James Mansfield (1733–1821), lord chief justice of the Court of Common Pleas.

To John Andrew

Washington 3d Feb. '61

My dear Andrew,

I saw the Presdt. yesterday. He was astonished to learn that the resolutions had not been acknowledged, & said that they should be done.[1]

Afterwards I said to him; "Mr Presdt, what else can we do in Mass.

for the good of the country."—A pause. "Much, Mr S.—no State more."—"What?" said I.—"Adopt the Crittenden proposition?" said he. "Is that necessary" said I.—"Yes!" said he; to which I replied; "Massachusetts has not yet spoken directly on those propositions, but I feel authorized to say—at least I give it as my opinion—that such are the unalterable Convictions of her people, that they would see their state sink below the sea & become a sandbank before they would adopt those propositions, acknowledging ppty in man & disfranchising a portion of her population"—I think I was right.

In God's name stand firm! *Don't cave, Andrew!*[2]

God bless you!   C. S.

Save Mass from any "surrender"—*the least*

ALS   MHi   (74/463, PCS)

1. In his letter of 30 January 1861 (21/416, PCS), Andrew asked CS to ask President Buchanan why the Massachusetts resolutions offering financial aid to the U.S. government had not been acknowledged.
2. Andrew replied 6 February (21/483) that most of his appointed delegation were "rocks"; he asked CS to keep "good men" like John Murray Forbes and Richard P. Waters from the influence of "Philistines."

To William H. Claflin[1]

Senate Chamber—4th Feb. '61

My dear Claflin,

[*John B.*] Alley tells me that my despatch was misunderstood.[2] I am sorry. Of course, I can have no sympathy with any conference *called on the basis proposed*. Mass. has a great position, which I wish her to guard. Any participation in that conference, as it seems to me, must be a *first step* towards "surrender." I am against any such first step—as I am against any "surrender."

I doubt not that Govr. Andrew would send men true to Massachusetts principles; but for what purpose? Why? The very call excludes all, who are not ready to surrender.

Perhaps I am too sensitive; but I do feel keenly whenever I think our cause is endangered or the honor of Mass. is not kept above suspicion.[3]

It is this same feeling which makes me hope that you will not listen to any suggestion against our Personal Liberty Laws. If they are "unconstitutional," let us wait till they are so decided.[4] But until then let those safeguards be preserved as a part of our glory. Be assured that any act of humiliation by Mass. will be a signal for greater surrenders elsewhere—*all without doing any good.* God bless you! Let us all be firm!

Ever sincerely Yours,   Charles Sumner

ALS   OFH   (74/467, PCS)

    1. William H. Claflin (1818–1905), then a Massachusetts state senator.

    2. Apparently a reference to CS's protest against the Massachusetts delegation to the peace convention. See CS to Andrew, 28 January 1861.

    3. Replying on 7 February (Boston, 21/501, PCS), Claflin agreed with CS that a peace conference was unwise but stated that Massachusetts should go along with other northern states.

    4. Claflin had written CS on 4 January, stating that since Massachusetts Senate moderates "demand that our laws be made constitutional," Claflin believed the issue should be submitted to the state supreme court (21/232). In his reply of 7 February, Claflin assured CS that, although the personal liberty laws might be amended, they would not be repealed. He warned CS, however, that there existed a "desperate effort under, the surface, to drive you from the Senate next winter."

To Edward L. Pierce

Senate Chamber 5th Feb. '61

My dear Peirce,

If I have not written you do not believe that I have not often thought of you.

I was glad to see that you had appeared at the State House agnst the repeal of our Pers. Lib. Laws.[1] My constant prayer is for firmness. I believe in the people, & have faith that they will not fail *even if leaders do.*

But we are now in great danger. The tocsin must be rung. All influences for the right will be needed.

And yet I do not abandon the confidence I have uniformly expressed. But we shall be *saved by events in spite of men.* The inordinate demands of the South are now the *safeguard* of Northern principles. Shame that we should owe our safety to others than ourselves!

These things make me anxious & unhappy. Let me hear from you. Tell me of persons & things.

The news to-day from Va. *postpones* the result, without altering it.[2] At least this is the look it has to-day. The Unionists are for the Union, *with a condition*; & the condition is "a constitutional guarantee of Slavery." The revolutionary movt. in Maryland, endangering the nat. capital, is also postponed. *We are safe now* till after 4th March at least.[3]

Ever Yrs,   Charles Sumner

ALS   MH-H   (64/163, PCS)

1. Testifying before the committee investigating possible repeal of these laws, Pierce stated that they were *not* a violation of the U.S. Constitution (Prc, 4:21).

2. In an election 4 February 1861 just 32 seats, of a possible 152, were won by secessionists for the Virginia state convention, which would consider secession on 18 February (David M. Potter, *The Impending Crisis* [1976], 507–8).

3. Pierce replied from Boston 10 February (21/524, PCS) that compromising sentiments were stronger now in Massachusetts since Charles Francis Adams and Seward supported the peace convention, but that he and many others were strongly opposed to such measures.

To John Greenleaf Whittier

Senate Chamber
5th Feb. '61

My dear Whittier,

I deplored S's speech—1st & 2nd.[1] The first he read to me, & I supplicated him not to make it. The true-hearted here have been filled with grief & mortification.

People are anxious to save our forts—to save our Nat. capital; but I am more anxious far *to save our principles*, which leaders now propose to abandon—as Mr Buchanan proposed to abandon Fort Sumpter! The public pride arrested the latter; I hope that the conscience may arrest the former.

My old saying is revived in my mind. *Backbone.* This especially is needed here.[2]

If saved it will be by events & not by men. The inordinate demands of the Slave States will make it next to impossible to appease them. Even compromisers cannot go so far. If they asked less, we should be lost.

Pray keep Mass. firm & strong. She must not touch a word of her Personal Libty Laws. The lightest act of surrender by her would be a signal for the abasement of the Free States.[3] God bless you!

Ever yours,   Charles Sumner

ALS MiMp (74/475, PCS)

1. Seward had spoken again on 31 January 1861 on the "State of the Union." He endorsed the upcoming peace convention and stated that only if the differences were utterly irreconcilable should the Union resort to force (*Globe*, 36th Cong., 2nd sess., 657–60).

2. Whittier wrote CS 6 February that he, too, failed to see how the free states could agree to any concessions the peace convention might propose (Amesbury, Massachusetts, 21/497, PCS).

3. Whittier had already assured CS in his letter of 26 January not to worry about Massachusetts' personal liberty laws: "the great body of our people can no more hunt slaves than commit cannibalism" (21/387).

To Richard Henry Dana, Jr.

Senate Chamber—6th Feb. '61

My dear Dana,

The election in Va. seems to me a beneficent result to arrest a conflict. Had Va. voted for immediate unconditional secession, the revolutionary movt. now organized in Maryland would have been precipitated, & this capital put in jeopardy. This is now postponed, & with delay will come those influences of reason & common sense on which I now rely to save us from civil war.

But the Unionists of Va. are only for the Union *on condition that they can have the Crittenden proposition*. This cannot have a constitutional majority in Congress; &, then, comes the conclusion already announced in the Va. resolutions.

Mr [*William Cabell*] Rives, who is regarded among you as a Union-man is described to me by one who meets him habitually at breakfast as "bitter"—against Mr Johnson for his Union speech[1] & especially for saying that "secession is treason; also against Mr Everett for saying, "the Union must be preserved." This he says has a double maning. He does not doubt that Va. will secede.

Ever & ever Yrs,   Charles Sumner

Let Mass. be tranquil & firm.

ALS MHi (74/482, PCS)

1. Tennessee senator Andrew Johnson gave two Senate speeches, 5 and 6 February 1861, denouncing secession and supporting the Union (*Globe*, 36th Cong., 2nd sess., 744–47, 766–72).

To John Andrew
Confidential

Senate Chamber
8th Feb. '61

My dear Andrew,

Last evng I was gladdened by the first installment of the Commissioners. The rest I expect this morng.

Be assured I shall do all that I can for their comfort & information. I am glad to know that there is not a single weak joint in them. One, I am told, had hastily committed himself to the New Mexico proposition;[1] but he has disengaged himself & will act with the rest. That is the most dangerous because the most deceptive of all the pending propositions. As an abandonment of principle it seems to me hardly less offensive than the Crittenden proposition. Of course, it is against our old Buffalo platform & the Chicago platform justly interpreted; & it proceeds on a most fallacious & demoralizing suggestion, belittling our cause, that the presence of 24 slaves is a small affair. *To sanction the enslaving of a single human being* is an act which can not be called small— unless the whole moral law which it overturns or ignores is small.

This proposition, if pres[sed] to a vote, will split our party—as no other party ever has been split. *Seward will not vote for it.* He will use it as a lure; *but not vote for it.* I deplore its introduction, & think of it constantly with tears. My constant hope is that events in their rapid march, may save us from any legislative action upon it, so that it may be dismissed to oblivion.

Pray, what is this Govt. worth, if held on such a condition, with the recognition of the right of secession? This alone is answer to it—even if it were not repugnant to the moral sense. This is the first time I have ever made an allusion in writing to this proposition. The innumerable letters which I have recd. on the subject have all been left unnoticed. I have trusted that my known character would save me from suspicion of any sympathy with it. But the surrender of one public man brings all others into distrust.[2]

I pray *constantly for courage at home.* Let Mass. be true & firm; & keep our friends from divisions.

The news from Va. continues to reveal the same tendency—secession unless constitutional guarantees are secured for Slavery. Unless some change occurs, contrary to all legislative & other declarations Va. must go out.

I hope that our Legislature will not pause in offering its guarantee to the bonds of the Nation. Govt.[3] It ought to be done at once.

Did I ever tell you how much I enjoyed & admired yr *old musket speech?*[4] It was well-conceived & beautifully done. I am glad that Theodore P's name is enrolled in the capitol.

Ever yours,

I find yr commissioners noble, true, good columnar characters fit to support Massachusetts. That's enough.

God bless you!   C.S.

ALS   MHi   (74/486, PCS)

1. Since late December Congress had been considering a move to admit New Mexico as a slave state, largely to appease the border states. This proposal was backed by Adams and other moderates. Both the 1848 Free Soil party platform and the 1860 Republican party platform had opposed the existence of slavery in the U.S. territories.

2. CS refers to Charles Francis Adams, who strongly differed with CS over whether the Union or antislavery principles were paramount. For an analysis of this breakup, see DD, 1:377–80.

3. Andrew had strongly urged on the Massachusetts legislature a guarantee of $2 million in U.S. government bonds (30 January 1861, 21/418, PCS) as support for the Union. He wrote CS on 3 February that the Senate had endorsed the guarantee, but he wondered what benefit such an act carried if the capital were captured (21/461).

4. On 26 January Andrew had delivered a speech presenting two Revolutionary War muskets that Theodore Parker had willed to the state of Massachusetts (Henry G. Pearson, *The Life of John A. Andrew* [1904], 1:152–53).

To John Andrew

Washington 10th Feb. '61

Dear Andrew,

It is much to be regretted that our State has hesitated so long in giving its endorsement to the U.S. bonds. Let us give the Govt. the means of procuring money at once, & put its credit on its legs.

There is tranquility now. The Peace Conf. has not reached any point. It is evident that Va. & the other border States will have to decide the question—which to choose—the Union or Slavery? If they remain it must be in subjection to the Constitution & the Anti-Slavery policy of our Fathers.

Confidential

In our councils & conferences, the only question that gives trouble is the New Mexico proposition—*a fatal dismal mistake*—already the root of infinite discontent & bitterness, & destined, if pressed, to split the Republican party with a split such as no other party has had.

Why offer it? Nothing is gained by it. But every thing is lost—our principles—the cause for which we have contended; while we leave unsettled the *first of all questions*, "Have we a Govt"? What is this Govt. worth, if we are merely "tenants at will," to be turned out by any mad State?—

Preston King has said nothing to any of his colleagues on S[*eward*]'s course; but he went at once to see him alone, threw his arms about his neck & burst into tears. S. says he can make no more speeches. To C. F. A.[*dams*], who quoted Ld Bacon, King said that he liked better this remark of Ld B. "When a good man begins to fall where will he stop?"—There was a smile, when he said—if Ld B. didn't say this, he ought to have said it.

I do not tremble at any thing from our opponents, whoever they may be, but from our friends.

The N.Y. Commissioners, in a majority, are stiff & strong.[1]

Every word of concession thus far has done infinite mischief. (1) by encouraging the slave-holders & (2) by dividing & demoralizing our own friends & filling them with doubts & distrust.[2]

God bless you!

Ever Yrs,   C. S.

ALS MHi (74/494, PCS)

1. Eleven delegates representing both Republicans and Democrats in New York had been instructed by the New York state legislature to attend the peace conference, but not necessarily to accept Virginia's proposals (Robert G. Gunderson, *Old Gentlemen's Convention: The Washington Peace Conference of 1861* [1961], 37).

2. CS spoke briefly against "concession" on 12 February 1861, when he argued that Massachusetts petitioners supporting the Crittenden compromise were "ignorant" and misled by Crittenden's proposals (*Globe*, 36th Cong., 2nd sess., 862–63, 865).

To John Andrew

Washington 10th March '61

Dear Andrew,

I have written to Howe & asked him to confer with you on the Boston Post-office. Let me have yr frank opinion.

How wld. Otis Clapp's nomination do?[1]

The Mass. delegation has *abdicated* all just influence over nominations *out of State* & all *present* influences over nominations *within the State.* This seems to me a great mistake. They ought to have remained a few days & insisted upon the position that belongs to our State.[2]

I can do nothing in settling our Mass. cases,—except the Boston P.O. which *it seems*, depends upon me alone, according to the usage of the Depart. & I hesitate with regard to other matters. At this moment all foreign appointments are *in chaos.* I am much behind the scenes.[3] My desire is that, at this critical moment, we may win & not lose the confidence of foreign govts; but this can be done only by the best possible representatives abroad.

Albert Browne has conversed with me on several matters. He will tell you that I have no suggestion or hint with regard to myself; but that I shall continue in position to act hereafter, as I have always tried to do, according to the requirements of duty. It will be for friends to help me determine [where?] at this moment that can be best performed. But I shall neither say or do any thing on the matter to which he called my attention.[4]

It is probable that Tuck will have the Navy Office.[5] This will be a Presidential edict. What, then, for T. P. C.[*handler*]?

I am in a maze with the multitude of details.

Good bye!

Ever Yours,   Charles Sumner

ALS MHi (74/546, PCS)

1. The position of postmaster of Boston was eagerly sought after. According to Donald, Lincoln asked CS to fill the post (DD, 1:385), and the appointment accounted for many a letter from Boston on the subject. For example, Andrew wrote CS that the appointment must go to the "strongest, surest and boldest Republican in Massachusetts. . . . We *must* be *bold.* We must *use* power, when we have it." Andrew thought Clapp, a loyal Republican, "about the fittest man in many respects." Andrew also considered Theophilus P. Chandler a good candidate (Boston, 11 March 1861, 22/030, PCS).

2. Congress had adjourned 28 March.

3. CS's appointment as chairman of the Senate Foreign Relations Committee was announced on 8 March (*Globe,* 37th Cong., special sess., 1446).

4. Albert Browne (1805–85), a Boston businessman, was then private secretary to Andrew. Andrew, Longfellow, and others had urged that CS be appointed minister to England (see, e.g., Longfellow to Fessenden, 2 February, HWL, 4:219–20, and DD, 1:381–82).

5. Amos Tuck became a naval officer for the port of Boston.

To Henry W. Longfellow

Washington 16th March '61

Dear Longfellow,

I think that all yr letters have been recd. They have been always most pleasant to me.[1]

I am tired, sick & unhappy. My rooms are full from early morning till midnight, with debaters about "office," & the larger part go away discontented, & sometimes, I doubt not, hostile. Could you see what I do of Govt. you would be happier than ever in yr books & elegant seclusion.

The Presdt. makes the great mistake of trying to deal with all possible cases, & this fritters away his valuable time.

Believe me—I have done all that I could for Monti. Only yesterday I pressed his case again. His papers of course, I filed at once with a letter asking his appointment. But to-day I hear of two impediments. Mr [*Samuel*] Downer of Boston has called upon me to urge the retention of the present incumbent—Mr Barstow of N.H.[2]—appointed in '56— who is not a politician—who is a Republican—& who was a teacher of English there, when he was appointed at the request of the American merchants there. You will see how much of an impediment this is. Add—that Mr Barstow is married—with a large family, & has no other means of support; so it is said.

Next comes another impediment, which you will find in a letter enclosed. I have written to Mr [Spring?], that, if a change takes place, I shall try to secure the post for Sig. Monti. Can I do more?

There is uncertainty, dislocation, chaos in every thing here. But I hope that after a short time there will be something more of a Kosmos. Who knows?

Genl. Scott insists that the flag must fall at Fort Sumter—& this is a military necessity.

God bless you!

Ever Thine,   C. S.

ALS MH-H (74/567, PCS)

1. Longfellow had written CS several times in early March in hopes of securing for Luigi Monti (1830–1914), professor of Italian at Harvard, the consulship at Palermo. In his letter of 13 March 1861 Longfellow asked CS to let him know if his letters had arrived (Cambridge, 74/554, PCS).

2. Henry H. Barstow (1823–75). Longfellow replied that Barstow "cannot be

much of a Republican, for he was appointed by Pres. Pierce and continued by Pres. Buchanan" (20 March, 74/582).

To William H. Seward

Senate Chamber 18th March '61

My dear Sir,

I deem it my duty to urge with all possible earnestness the nomination of Mr Motley as Minister Resident at the Hague.

This will be especially grateful to Massachusetts, & I think it ought to be grateful to all who take a pride in the character of their country.

I write this in the sincere hope that the Govt. will not miss the opportunity of associating itself with a name already adopted into European history, which will be for us at the present moment a powerful ally.

My colleague Mr Wilson joins in this request. But we *both insist that Mr Burlingame shall not be neglected. In our desires he stands first*.[1]

Faithfully Yours,   Charles Sumner

The Honble. Wm. H. Seward

———————————

ALS   NRU   (74/571, PCS)

1. CS's recommendation for the historian John Lothrop Motley (1814–77) was one of many CS proffered to Seward soon after Seward became secretary of state (see letters of 14 March 1861, 74/559 et seq., PCS). Burlingame was confirmed as minister to Austria on 23 March, but when the Austrian government would not receive him, he became minister to China (*Executive Proceedings*, 11:328, 445).

To the Duchess of Argyll

Washington—19th March '61

My dear Duchess,

Only yesterday I read in the papers that the Duke of Sutherland was dead.[1] It pained me to think that he was gone, & that his family were in affliction. Amidst most pressing duties, I steal a moment to send you the assurance of my true sympathy. Pray let your Mother know how much I grieve with her.

I can never forget his elegant graceful manners, & his hospitable welcome to me at Dunrobin[.] I owe you a letter already; but I hope that you will let me know very soon something of your Mother, & how she bears this bereavement.

I wish that I had something pleasant to write with regard to our affairs. There is a lull for the moment; but the future is uncertain. Thus far in a most remarkable way events have been so tempered & restrained, as to avoid bloodshed. Can this be always? I hope so; but I am not certain.

Our new Administration comes to power at a moment of unprecedented difficulty. But beyond this, it has an awkwardness, which is partly attributable to its inexperience. I trust, however, that it will shew itself able to deal with events as they occur.

Mr Adams, a political & personal friend, whose grandfather was our first Minister to England in 1784, & whose father was our Minister in 1815, has been nominated to the English Mission. I have hoped to secure the Hague for Mr Motley; but I fear that I shall be disappointed.[2] The scramble for office is enormous & sickening.

My own duties as the head of the Committee on For. Relations in the Senate, are onerous; but I am plagued by "office-seekers." This you cannot understand. Good bye! God bless you!

Ever yours,   Charles Sumner

ALS CSmH (74/575, PCS)

1. The duchess's father, George Granville Leveson-Gower, second duke of Sutherland (1786–1861).

2. CS notified Charles Francis Adams on 20 March 1861 by telegram that he had been confirmed as minister to Great Britain (74/581, PCS). The duchess replied from Inverary 20 April, "Some hopes were given that you might have come here—but I thought you were more likely to think you were doing your duty best, at Home—where the work must be very hard;—and the anxiety great" (22/395). Motley was confirmed as minister to Austria on 22 January 1862 (*Executive Proceedings*, 12:96).

To John Jay

Senate Chamber 27th March '61

My dear Jay,

I despair.[1]

So far as our for. relat. go, L.[*incoln*] is ignorant; S.[*eward*] is infatuated.

The Paris Mission is a nullity. Better have none.

At Brussells is a person who was not a Republ. & with him a Secy of Legation from Minnesota, an incompetent, who had been S's fugleman at Chicago.[2]

Secties of Legat. at London & Paris—*unpresentable*![3]

But I forbear.

Every thing tends, as I have foreseen to a break-up of the Union. Things were never worse than now. But S.[*eward*] is infatuated. He says in 60 days all will be well!

Good bye! God bless you!

I have always had at heart that our country should be represented by you abroad. But other ideas prevail. Before leaving I shall press you especially.[4]

Ever yrs,   C. S.

ALS NNCB (74/596, PCS)

1. Jay wrote CS congratulating him on his chairmanship and laying out some foreign policy proposals. He added that he hoped that "no foreign refugees are to represent us in Europe. . . . [W]e need the kind regards of the Continental Government now more than ever" (18 March 1861 [and misdated 26 March 1861], 22/165, 260, PCS).

2. Henry S. Sanford (1823–91), who had been secretary of legation in Paris, 1849–54, served as minister to Belgium, 1861–69. His secretary of legation there was Aaron Goodrich (1807–87). Sanford was confirmed on CS's motion 20 March; CS voted for Goodrich's confirmation on 27 March (*Executive Proceedings*, 11:318, 351).

3. In London Charles Lush Wilson (1818–78), editor of the *Chicago Daily Journal*, was first secretary of legation; in Paris the secretary was William S. Pennington (b. 1818), son of the Speaker of the House. They were confirmed 25 and 26 March (ibid., 337, 350).

4. On 10 August CS wrote Jay a lengthy explanation as to why Motley, not Jay, had received the appointment as minister to Austria (Washington, 75/122).

To Richard Henry Dana, Jr.

Washington—29th March—'61

My dear Dana,

Will you not see that Mr Palfrey's case is fairly stated in the papers? It seems to me that his noble act with regard to his slaves ought to be told distinctly.[1] This alone would commend him.

Do not forget his speech in Congress on Postal matters.[2] Of this give extracts.

Dwell on his business talent; his success as Secy of the Cwlth; his industry; his order; his knowledge; his conscientiousness; his ability in details; & all those things which will make him the best Postmaster Boston has ever had. Let these be known.

I think it would also be proper to recall his early & important services for the Republican cause, &, *perhaps, foreshadow the advantage to our party which will come from his active identification with it at this moment.* The Republican party in Mass. & in Boston will look again to his talents, & fidelity, which will be to us all a source of strength.

I think that the question of the [site?] of the Post-office may be properly alluded to. Where shall it be? State St? Summer St? or some other place? In deciding this, we need the most careful judgment & the most perfect integrity.

But the topics are familiar to you.

A few positive articles in season will fix public opinion; & I believe I do not ask too much in expressing a hope that they may be written. The Adamses, each & all, will lend their admirable pens; so will Dr Howe.

In taking the responsibility which I have done of setting aside the numerous & most elaborate testimonials of other candidates, I have done what I thought was right & I rely upon the good sense of our people at home to sustain me.

You will pardon the trouble I give you.[3]

Ever Yours,   Charles Sumner

ALS   MHi   (74/602, PCS)

1. CS recommended Palfrey as postmaster of Boston on 23 March 1861, and he was appointed 29 March (CS to Howe, 29 March, 64/169, PCS). In 1844 Palfrey freed slaves that he had inherited (Frank O. Gatell, *John Gorham Palfrey and the New England Conscience* [1963], 112–16).

2. Apparently Palfrey delivered his speech on the postage bill on 21 February 1848 (CS to Palfrey, 6 June 1870, 83/457). The House, however, adjourned early that day because of John Quincy Adams's collapse, and the *Globe* does not record it.

3. Dana replied that he had written a favorable notice on Palfrey for the Boston *Traveller*, which would run as an editorial. He told CS not to worry about criticism of the appointment, for there was "a good deal of secret satisfaction" in Boston that the office had gone to someone other than a party hack (Boston, 4 April, 22/326).

To Henry W. Longfellow

Washington—7th April '61

My dear Longfellow,

I never forget Monti. Several times I have thought the appointment would be made without delay.

But action on consulships is now postponed—I trust only for a short time. I shall not leave here without a valedictory request.

I have seen so much behind the scenes latterly, that public life has lost all its illusions.

The Presdt. undertakes what no mortal can do, & defies the first principle of Polit. Econ. which is the *division of labor*. He ought to be meditating the condition of the country & his great public duties, instead of listening to the tales of office-seekers. I am humbled, chagrined, disappointed, & of course unhappy.

I wish that I could fly away to some other planet.

Good bye! God bless you. Be happy with wife & children & books & yr genius.

Ever & ever Yrs,   Charles Sumner

ALS MH-H (74/623, PCS)

To Richard Henry Dana, Jr.
Private

Washington—14th April '61

My dear Dana,

In conversing with the Presdt on our Mass. cases, I said, that—"as to Mr Dana he was already nominated by general Public Opinion, & all that remains now is to register it."[1] I then passed to the next case.

Of course, you will accept. But at all events, we have had the honor of enrolling yr name in our republican list, & I am proud of it.

Events are hastening. We are now reaping the fruits of *Sewardism* throughout the winter—demoralizing our energies & planting distrust every where but no where more than in the Slave States themselves.[2] I have deplored that *policy of insincerity*, & my chief hope now is that it will be renounced. I love truth, & believe that it must be the foundation of public as of private conduct. Already the same dismal *policy* has crept into our foreign relations, so that there is not a foreign minister here who does not distrust our Secy. This is bad at a moment when we need the confidence & good will of other Powers.—My labors latterly have been most trying, & I long to get away. Good bye!

Ever Yours,   Charles Sumner

P.S. I opened this letter to say, on the authority of the Secy of War,[3] that "Seward is now the fiercest of the lot."—

ALS MHi (74/640, PCS)

1. Dana had been appointed U.S. district attorney for Massachusetts on 12 April 1861 (see official appointment in Dana Papers, Massachusetts Historical Society); he served until 1866.

2. Seward opposed sending provisions to Fort Sumter, in hopes of avoiding civil war. He also recommended to Lincoln that, to reunite the country against foreign threats, the U.S. take the offensive against any interference from foreign nations in the western hemisphere.

3. Simon Cameron (1799–1889), U.S. secretary of war, 1861–62; U.S. minister to Russia, 1862; U.S. senator (Rep., Pa.), 1867–77.

To William Pitt Fessenden

Washington. 16th April '61

My dear Fessenden,

Here I am still, wishing to leave, & determined that I will not remain. But I have been able to say the *last word* for Mr Dorrance, who was to-day recommended to the Presdt by the Secy of the Treasury.[1]

At last the war has come.[2] The day of insincerity & duplicity is now passed, & *all* the cabinet is united in energetic action. It will be needed, for the Slave States will be united.

The Presdt speaks simply & plainly of the state of the country, & I think understands it. As I see more of him I like him better.

Meanwhile at the State Depart. the web is spinning—spinning—in infinite despatches—to what end God knows! Already the diplomatists here are afraid.

Good bye!

Ever yours,   Charles Sumner

ALS   MnHi   (74/650, PCS)

1. Fessenden had written CS asking his help in securing the appointment of Oliver Dorrance of Boston as a general appraiser ([N.P., March? 1861], 22/305, PCS).

2. Lincoln ordered that supplies should be sent to Fort Sumter on 6 April; when Major Robert Anderson (1805–71), the commander of the fort, refused to surrender to the Confederates, they fired on the fort on 12 April, and Anderson surrendered on 13 April.

To Cordelia Walter Richards

Washington 16th April '61

My dear Madam,

Allow me to offer you my thanks for yr very instructive letter from Richmond.[1] I have long foreseen the tendency of events, although I have never ceased to hope that the Southern States might take counsel of patriotism & civilization. In this hope I fear that we shall be disappointed.

You must have been struck by the long forbearance of the National Govt. Perhaps had it been more prompt, treason at this moment would be less demonstrative.

Be assured, you have rightly interpreted my sentiments when you encourage me in the cultivation of a spirit of conciliation. This spirit, of course, is widely different from that spirit which would sacrifice principles.

The Nat. Govt. must now maintain the Constitution as administered by George Washington. The responsibility & peril of the assault upon this precious inheritance will rest, of course, with the Southern States & upon none so much as Virginia.[2]

Believe me, dear Madam,

very faithfully yours,   Charles Sumner

ALS MHi (74/660, PCS)

1. Cordelia Walter Richards, who wrote that, like CS, she was a Bostonian and a Republican, had come to Richmond in March 1861 to care for an ailing daughter. In her letter of 3 April (22/340, PCS) she described the high level of secession excitement in Richmond, excitement she attributed to Lincoln's vacillating and uncertain policy. She asked CS to inform Lincoln "of the dangerous positions of affairs in this city—if he have a policy *conciliatory to the South* in any way—urge him, I pray you, to a less tedious manner of unfolding it." To save the Union, some concessions were now necessary, she wrote; "let your voice be heard in the privy councils at Washington, and *do* consider what a woman has written."

2. On 17 April the Virginia state convention voted to secede.

To Henry W. Longfellow

Washington 17th April '61

My dear Longfellow,

Twice since I last wrote, I have mentioned "Palermo" at the Depart. of State, & each State have been assured that at the proper moment, when these cases are considered, there could not be question with regard to Signor Monti.

For Mr Fiske at Elsinore I have already spoken.[1] He too must wait; but without the same hope.

I am very weary—working 15 hours a day in drudgery of which you know nothing—listening to the pleadings, & strifes of office-seekers. I long to leave. Tomorrow I will. Of course, my lectures are all abandoned. How could I lecture now with my country in civil war? And yet I must avoid Boston for the present, & the press of office-seekers there.

I have much to talk over with you. Often this winter I have said that we were on the eve of great events. Are we not?—

Alas! that I, loving Peace, vowed to Peace, should be called to take such great responsibility in a direful ghastly civil war! My system would have made it unnecessary. Good bye! God bless you!

Ever yrs,   C. S.

ALS   MH-H   (74/662, PCS)

1. Longfellow wrote CS from Cambridge 15 April 1861 (74/643, PCS) recommending Daniel W. Fiske (1831–1904), a Scandinavian language scholar, for the consulship at Elsinore.

To Joshua R. Giddings

Boston 28th April '61

My dear Consul General,

On my return to Boston, after a long detention in Washington, I found yr favor of 2nd April.

I have not examined the Abrdgt. of Debates, but am not surprized at what you say.[1] You will remember it was made in great haste, & I suppose it may be said with truth, that Col. Benton, with all his great merits, had no real sympathy with the Anti-Slavery cause—certainly in those early struggles where you & Mr Adams bore a conspicuous part.

But surely you are right in making yr protest against the injustice done. To render this effective, there should be a proper statement drawn up by yourself, the living witness of the truth, which the publishers ought to print & bind with the vols. in question.

From yr distant retreat I doubt not that you watch the great events of to-day with intense interest. Only a short time ago, it seemed as if there must be a separation; but this generous & mighty uprising of the North seems to menace defeat to the rebels & the extinction of Slavery in blood.[2] How does it look to you?

I hope that you are enjoying yr new position; but I can not reconcile myself to your not being at Washington.[3] Goodbye!

Ever sincerely Yours,   Charles Sumner

The Hnble. J. R. Giddings

ALS OHi (74/677, PCS)

1. Giddings had written CS from Jefferson, Ohio, seeking advice regarding false information in D. Appleton and Company's *Abridgment of Congressional Debates*. Giddings was exercised over the many examples of "gross injustice" that Thomas Hart Benton and others had tendered toward the antislavery leaders in the 1840s, and thought a protest to the publisher should be made (22/328, PCS).

2. On 15 April 1861 Lincoln issued a call for volunteers to put down the insurrection in the South, and all Northern states responded enthusiastically. CS left Washington for Boston 18 April, shortly before the capital was threatened by secessionists.

3. Giddings replied 30 April from his new post as consul general in Montreal. He wrote that he wished he were in Washington and that he was hopeful about a Northern victory: "The first gun fired at fort Sumter rang out the death knell of slavery" (22/429).

To John Andrew

Washington 24th May '61

Dear Andrew,

Capt. Stone is a person who enjoys fully the confidence of Genl. Scott & the War Depart. I understand him to have peculiar merit. He will be made a Colonel.[1]

You have already recd. my telegram saying that an Army Surgeon must, at his examination be under 30. This is not applicable to the volunteers.

I enclose a memorandum from the War Depart. which shews the officers, including assistant surgeons of regiments, which are appointed by the Govr.

I have seen Mr Dalton, & offered my services to aid him.[2]

The troops here under Col. L.[3] are impatient of inaction, but otherwise very well. Their drill is super-excellent.

The pressure upon the Admtion is great for active aggressive measures. You will hear of collision soon at Harper's Ferry & Fortress Munroe.[4]

Our foreign relations have got in a bad way—through the grossest mismanagement of Seward, who seems to understand foreign nations as little he understood our crisis.

Good bye!

Ever yours,   Charles Sumner

ALS MHi (75/019, PCS)

1. Charles P. Stone (1824–87) was then commander of the Massachusetts 16th and 20th Divisions. Andrew at this time was busily engaged in organizing Massa-

chusetts regiments to serve in the Civil War (see Henry G. Pearson, *The Life of John A. Andrew* [1904], vol. 1, chapter 5).

2. Andrew sent Charles H. Dalton to Washington to supervise Massachusetts volunteers in the army (ibid., 222).

3. Probably Andrew's aide, Henry Lee, Jr. (1817–98).

4. Harper's Ferry had been taken over by Virginia militia on 19 April 1861; the Federals held the U.S. garrison at Fort Monroe, Virginia.

To the Duchess of Argyll

Boston 4th June '61

My dear Duchess,

Since I last wrote I have had yr kind letter, which has been too long neglected; but meanwhile every thing with us has taken a more decisive character. I left Washington only a day before the bridges were destroyed & communication with it for a few days cut off. On the road & in New York I was a witness to the magnificent uprising of the country. After a short time in Boston I hurried back to Washington, especially to look after our foreign relations, & have again returned home.

The rebels relied upon two things. (1) First, division & discord at the North. This winter a brother-in-law of Jefferson Davis[1] said to me—"You [count?] without yr host, when the fighting begins it will all be North of the Susquehanna." He was miserably mistaken. North of the Susquehanna all are united as one man. (2) The next reliance was upon recognition by France & England. On this they counted absolutely. I have predicted that here they will be disappointed again. This I have said to the President. Indeed, I have become answerable for the good conduct of these two great nations—an immense responsibility, except, that I feel clearly that there is but one course which they can adopt. I have not for a moment doubted that their course will be such as to take from the rebels their last prop.

The President is honest & well-disposed. There has been a sinister influence; but I believe that it is now checked. At all events I did my best to this end. Let me say frankly, that we should all have been cheered, if there had been a word from Ld John [*Russell*] shewing sympathy with a constitutional Govt. struggling with a wicked rebellion founded upon a principle long ago repudiated by the people of England.[2]

I appreciate completely the embarassments of England; but I believe sincerely that her prosperity is linked with that of our Northern States. It is for her good as well as ours that this wretched rebellion be crushed out as it surely will be; & nothing can protract the crisis more than sympathy with the rebels. If left to ourselves we can deal with them;

but hope is a great ally, & I wish to have such a voice proceed from Europe as will cut this off absolutely.

Nothing could be more painful to me than this conflict, except that I feel that it was inevitable, & that its result will be the extinction of Slavery. Our Secy of War, who is no enthusiast, admitted to me only a week ago, that it would "wipe out Slavery." This is the expectation of all the more earnest & thoughtful.—Genl. Scott thinks he can finish the war in one year.—I did not write you by the Adamses; but should you see them, let me commend them kindly.[3]

God bless you!

Ever Yours & the Duke's   Charles Sumner

Francis Lawley[4] was good enough to call upon me. We talked England, & Mr Gladstone, & I enjoyed his conversation much.

ALS   CSmH   (75/039, PCS)

1. Most likely Becket Hempe Howell (1840–82), who spent much of his youth with the Davises, and in 1860 was a second lieutenant in the U.S. Marines (*Papers of Jefferson Davis*, vol. 5, ed. Lynda L. Crist [1985], 42).
2. On 13 May 1861 Queen Victoria, on the advice of her foreign secretary, Lord Russell, issued a proclamation recognizing both the U.S. and the Confederacy as belligerents, and affirming Britain's strict neutrality.
3. Charles Francis Adams and Abigail Brooks Adams, along with Henry Adams, acting as his father's secretary, arrived in London 13 May.
4. Francis Lawley (1825–1901), British Civil War correspondent, London *Times*, 1862–65.

To William H. Seward

Boston 12th June '61

My dear Secretary,

Mr Motley has just arrived, fresh from long-continued intimacy & recent conversations with Lord Palmerston & Lord John Russell,—in the course of which our affairs have been much discussed.

He is a true American, who knows well how to be thoroughly loyal to his own country & to inspire the confidence of foreign statesmen. As such, the precise report which he gives of recent conversations, is especially interesting. It has made me happy in the assurance that all will go right in England with regard to us.[1]

Mr Motley will visit Washington at the beginning of the week,[2] & I now announce his visit in order to bespeak for him during the short time he may be there an opportunity of laying his views before those who are most interested in our foreign relations.[3]

Faithfully Yours,   Charles Sumner

The Hnble Wm. H. Seward—

ALS NRU (75/046, PCS)

1. On 21 May 1861 Seward had instructed Charles Francis Adams to impose certain conditions on Great Britain, including agreement to the U.S. blockade of Southern ports. Adams was also instructed to "desist from all intercourse" with British officials as long as they continued to meet with Confederate emissaries. Seward threatened war if the British did not accede to these conditions (U.S. Senate, *List of Papers Relating to Foreign Affairs*, Senate Ex. Doc. no. 1, 1861, serial set 1117, 87–90). Writing Lord Russell on 21 May, Lyons stated that CS should be informed "of the real perils to which Mr. Seward and the Cabinet are exposing the country"; Lyons thought that CS could help avoid war with Great Britain (Thomas W. L. Newton, *Lord Lyons* [1913], 1:41).

2. In his letter later that month from Boston Motley wrote about his visit. He was not worried about the quality of Seward's dispatches to Great Britain, because those that he saw showed tact and good sense, and "a marked sense of the injustice which we have suffered" from that country. Motley wrote CS that he believed Britain "sees her error" in so quickly recognizing the Confederacy as a belligerent (29 June, 22/648, PCS).

3. Five days later CS wrote John Jay that "our foreign relations are conducted in a bad spirit, from which I have dissented; but I am sanguine that they cannot be disturbed" (Boston, 17 June, 75/055).

To Francis Lieber
Private

Washington 23d June '61

My dear Lieber,

I hoped that you would read the official list of appointments, containing the name of yr son. Give him my benediction.[1]

I have no dread of Congress.[2] The session will be very brief—a week or 10 days—both houses in secret session—every thing prepared in advance—(1) an Army Bill (2) Navy Bill (3) Loan Bill & War Taxes on the Free List, with, perhaps, an income tax. (4) Bill for treason & to arrest supplies for traitors (5) bill of embargo & non-intercourse for the whole Southern coast, in lieu of the blockade, which is a great mistake. Such at least is my programme, which I have submitted to the Presdt,

& his cabinet, & I hope it will be carried out without a single speech or one word of Buncombe—so that our short session may be a mighty act. Have you any thing to suggest?

Good bye!

Ever yours,   Charles Sumner

P.S. Our foreign relations especially concern me. The statement in the message [here?] *will be*—"All's well"—

ALS   MH-H   (64/175, PCS)

1. After eight years of estrangement, Lieber and CS had resumed their friendship. Breaking the silence on 24 May 1861, Lieber wrote from New York requesting CS's help in securing a lieutenant's commission for his son Norman Lieber (1837–1923). CS informed Lieber 30 May that he had recommended Norman to Secretary of War Cameron. He closed his cordial letter, "Count upon me if I can serve you & believe me, your old friend, Charles Sumner" (75/021, 64/173, PCS). Lieber replied on 22 June that he had just seen Norman's name on the list of appointments (75/059).

2. "Are you not dreading the approaching Congress?" asked Lieber on 22 June. He had heard rumors of a "Compromise bomb" from the Democrats. The first session of the 37th Congress ran longer than CS predicted, from 4 July to 6 August.

To Richard Henry Dana, Jr.

Washington 30th June '61

My dear Dana,

If you have any notes or hints with regard to legislation, pray send them *at once*.

By stat. of 1807 the Presdt. is authorized to employ "the navy" to suppress insurrection. Does this authorization carry with it, blockade, & all its incidents, prize courts & all?[1]

Prize is essentially *jure belli*;[2] but we are putting down an insurrection.

Immediately on my arrival I laid my views on the blockade before the Presdt. He read me his message,[3] which is characteristic. Some things I objected to frankly.

The statement on our For. Relations is that "All's Well"—in a single sentence. The Secretary of State has changed immensely during the last month, & is now mild & gentle.

Good bye!

Ever Yrs,   Charles Sumner

I have read *all* the foreign correspondence since 4th March!—

ALS MHi (75/070, PCS)

1. Approved 3 March 1807, the act stated that the president could call up "such part of the land or naval force of the United States, as shall be judged necessary" (*Annals of Congress*, 9th Cong., 2nd sess., appendix, 1286). Replying 3 July 1861 from Boston, Dana sent a draft (unrecovered) which, he said, "explains itself." Dana sought to recommend "judicial processes for seizing, detaining & forfeiting" to be used at the discretion of the government (22/675, PCS).

2. "The rights of war."

3. According to Donald, CS opposed Seward's plan to blockade Southern ports because he considered such policy tantamount to recognition of the Confederacy (DD, 2:19). Lincoln's presidential message of 4 July (*Globe*, 37th Cong., 1st sess., appendix, 1–4) stated that measures such as suspension of *habeas corpus* were necessary "for public safety" and to carry on the war. Lincoln stated that his proclamation to close ports in "the insurrectionary districts by proceedings in the nature of a blockade" was considered "strictly legal."

To Richard Henry Dana, Jr.

Senate Chamber 18th July '61

Dear Dana,

You have my heart's thanks for the letter you wrote me from Cambridge. Nothing but the press of business in Senate & Committee prevented me from going to Longfellow at once.[1] I long to be with him; & I wish very much that I had been at the last meeting with the dead. This has been to me a great affliction.

You have seen the bill authorizing the Presdt. to close the ports & put the rebel states under interdict.[2] I have not time now for its history.

Last Tuesday there was a very grave question in the cabinet, arising under that Bill, & a difference. In the evng the Presdt. stated the difficulties to me, asking my counsel. But I cannot touch this now.—I have drawn a Bill to meet the case; but find opposition from an important quarter, because I propose to shield Mr Seward; which, by the way I have done already several times.

Ever yours, Charles Sumner

ALS MHi (75/089, PCS)

1. On 10 July 1861 Fanny Longfellow died of burns suffered when her dress caught fire from sealing wax. Dana had written CS on 11 July from Cambridge (22/706, PCS) with details regarding the "fearful disaster & loss at Cambridge." CS's letter to Longfellow of 11 July (75/083, PCS) is printed in Prc, 4:37.

2. The bill on collection of duties also stipulated that ships belonging to rebel states would be seized and that the president was authorized to declare commerce between the U.S. and seceded states unlawful. It was considered and passed by the Senate 12 July (*Globe*, 37th Cong., 1st sess., 83–84).

To Wendell Phillips

Senate Chamber—3d Aug. '61—

My dear Phillips,

I doubt not you read events—as I do; but, perhaps, I have some lights which you have not.[1]

Be tranquil. Never did I feel so sure of the result. The battle & defeat have done much for the slave; & since then I have spoken to the Presdt & *a majority of the Cabinet* on the new power to be invoked. I assure you there are men who do not hesitate.

I told the Presdt that our defeat[2] was the worst event & the best event in our history; the worst, as it was the greatest present calamity & shame,—the best, as it made the extinction of Slavery inevitable.

Be hopeful. I am. Never so much so.

Good bye!

Ever yours,   Charles Sumner

Sumner to Wendell Phillips, 3 August 1861. By permission of The Houghton Library, Harvard University.

ALS   MH-H   (75/112, PCS)

1. On 1 August Phillips spoke at a celebration in Abington, Massachusetts, on West Indies emancipation. Phillips stated that "the old Union of '87 is gone beyond recovery" and it was only a "dream" that the North could subdue the South militarily. He criticized the absence of a definite policy, both military and foreign, in the U.S. government and called on the North to unite to emancipate the slaves, and to be less lenient toward potential secessionists in the government (*New York Times*, 6 August 1861:2).

2. Phillips called the defeat of Federal troops at Bull Run on 21 July "wholesale butchery, public murder," a defeat caused primarily by the North, because battle plans were leaked by spies in Washington to Confederate forces (ibid.).

To Wendell Phillips
private

Washington 8th Aug. '61

My dear Phillips,

Yr last speech is an inspiration. I think you discern the future—as it will be.

In many respects I am disappointed. Indeed, I am heavy-hearted. The Govt. is not what it ought to be. My friend Gurowski[1] is enraged because I will not openly denounce it. I find it better to try to lead it.

Cameron has promised me to issue an order from the War office, declaring every slave coming within our lines free.

There are other movements & declarations in the same sense.

Therefore, though much dejected at what I see & know, I feel sure of the Future.

People who ask for Peace should be told that peace is impossible while Slavery exists. Abolition is the Condition precedent.

Good bye!

Ever Yrs,   Charles Sumner

I was glad to recommend young May.[2] He will be appointed.

ALS   MH-H   (75/117, PCS)

1. Adam Gurowski (1805–66), expatriate Polish count and translator at the State Department, 1861–62.

2. Phillips had asked CS to help Edward May, son of Samuel May, Jr., secure a position as assistant paymaster on a U.S. ship (28 July 1861, 23/044, PCS).

To John Jay

Met. Hotel Saturday
[*New York, 11 August 1861*][1]

My dear Jay,

I am about to start for Boston—having just arrived from Washington.

I wish you would visit Washington at once to press upon the Presdt. the duty of Emancipation, *in order to save the country*. No time is to be lost.

Somebody should see the Presdt every day, & exhibit to him this supreme duty. I have discussed it with him much, & do not despair, but I am pained inexpressibly at the delay. Meanwhile all may be lost.

I hope that you will go *at once*, &, pray induce others to go.[2] The country must be saved.

This moment is full of peril—in every direction, at home & abroad.

Ever yours,   Charles Sumner

ALS   NNCB   (75/129, PCS)

1. Although CS has written "Saturday," he must mean Sunday, the day on which 11 August fell in 1861. He wrote John Andrew on that date from Washington that he was leaving immediately for Boston (75/127, PCS).
2. Jay visited Washington in late August, when he discussed the abolition of the slave trade with Seward. Jay advised CS to be patient; other causes should not detract from "vigorous prosecution of the war" (N.P., c. 2 September 1861, copy, 75/182).

To William H. Russell[1]

Boston 16th Sept. '61

Dear Mr Russell,

On my return to Boston I found yr two notes—each with a copy of the printed letter.[2]

As to the letter;—the same things might be said in yr regular correspondence & return to plague yr critics in due course of packet.

The publication as a separate letter would be earlier; but I doubt if it would be so extensively read.

I do not know Dr Ray intimately,[3] but have personal & political relations with him, & have always respected him as an honorable editor exerting an important influence through a widely circulated Journal. On this account I hesitate to mix my name in a controversy not only concerning him, but with him.

LINCOLN—"*I'm sorry to have to drop you, Sambo, but this concern won't carry us both!*"

From Frank Leslie's Illustrated Newspaper, *12 October 1861. "I wish you would . . .
press upon the Presdt. the duty of Emancipation, in order to save the country" (to John Jay,
11 August 1861). Courtesy, Special Collections, Honnold Library, Claremont, California.*

Beyond the personal question there is now unhappily something of a
national question, & it seems to me only proper husbandry for me to
avoid giving to malignant persons an opportunity of starting a cry that
I have taken sides against my country, which, however false, might at
this sensitive moment be prejudicial.

A letter addressed to me in print might seem to imply a judgment
by me on the points of observation opinion & sentiment involved;—
possibly even partizanship on my part.

Should these suggestions seem to you of any consequence, & I rely
upon yr candor to appreciate them, the name might be struck out &
the letter printed as addressed to a friend, or it might, with slight
changes, be addressed directly to one of our newspapers.

Let me add that I have been astonished at the minuteness of criticism directed against yr account of the panic, which I regarded very much as a battle-piece by Wouvermans[4] with his perpetual white horse.

If I can judge from what I hear people are much less sensitive with regard to your errors of fact than with regard to the tone in which you write. They feel that this is not friendly—that it is *de haut en bas*[5]—that you write down upon us; & this, you can imagine, is not pleasant. It becomes more conspicuous from its contrast with the real cordiality of one or two recent French writers:—who have struck cords which I wish had been struck by an Englishman. I hear from different quarters that the War will soon be ended. I do not see it so. And if Slavery is left to itself, I think you are right in the horoscope you cast.

But help us to a breath of generous strengthening sympathy from Old England, which will cheer the good cause & teach every body that there can be no terms of any kind with a swarm of traitors trying to build a State on Human Slavery.

Bon jour!

                           & ever sincerely Yours,   Charles Sumner

What is the look in Washington? Will there be a battle soon? & how will it go?

ALS MH-H (64/180, PCS)

1. William H. Russell (1820–1907), British journalist, was then American correspondent for the London *Times*. He met CS in Washington in July and in his diary described CS as "useful at allaying irritation" on the part of the Union toward Great Britain (*My Diary North and South* [1863], 377–79). His account, dated 22 July 1861, of the Federal defeat at Bull Run (London *Times*, 6 August 1861:7) emphasized the Northerners' panic and confusion as they retreated from battle.

2. Russell wrote CS twice on 10 September from Washington (23/198 and 200, PCS), enclosing for CS's response a letter he had prepared. Although the printed copy is unrecovered, Russell apparently had addressed the letter to CS and asked him his opinion of it as a "refutation of the charges against me." In his diary, Russell noted both personal and newspaper attacks on him for his unsympathetic picture of the Northern armies (516, 532). Russell stated in his letter that he was unwilling to "drag you into my quarrel" without CS's permission, but believed that the use of CS's name was "the chief moment of the letter."

3. Charles H. Ray (1821–70), editor, Chicago *Daily Tribune*. The *Tribune* had criticized Russell's account of the Battle of Bull Run (Rupert Furneaux, *The First War Correspondent: William Howard Russell* [1944], 137–38).

4. Philip Wouvermans (1619–68), Dutch painter known for his cavalry scenes.

5. "Haughty."

To Francis Lieber

Boston 17th Sept. '61

My dear Lieber,

To me the Presdt's letter is full—too full of meaning. It means that Slavery shall only be touched by Act of Congress & *not through Martial Law*. This weakens all our armies.[1]

The London Times is right. We cannot conquer the rebels as the War is now conducted. There will be a vain masquerade of battles,—a flux of blood & treasure & nothing done![2]

Never has there been a moment of history when so much was all compressed into a little time & brought directly under a single mind. Our Presdt is now dictator, Imperator—what you will; but how vain to have the power of a God if not to use it God-like.

I am sad; for I know that we are to spend energy & resource of all kinds & accomplish nothing;—until there is a change of policy.

Ever yours,   Charles Sumner

ALS   MH-H   (64/182, PCS)

1. On 30 August 1861 General John C. Frémont, in charge of western operations in St. Louis, had issued a proclamation stating that Missouri was under martial law and slaves of rebels there were freed. Lincoln's reply to Frémont, a copy of which he released to the newspapers, stated that the president objected to the clause in Frémont's proclamation "on confiscation of property and liberation of slaves." That clause, wrote Lincoln, did not conform to Congress's action of 6 August and therefore Lincoln ordered the clause to be modified so as to "conform to, and not to transcend, the provisions" of the congressional act (11 September, CWL, 4:517–18). The 6 August congressional act stipulated that a slaveholder's slaves could be freed only if they had been forced to serve in armies fighting the U.S. (*Globe*, 37th Cong., 1st sess., appendix, 42).

2. In its editorial of 4 September 1861:6, the London *Times*, citing Southern victories and Northern unpreparedness, stated, "Enough has now been learnt to show that the subjugation of the South is next to impossible, and its submission in the highest degree improbable."

To John Jay

Boston 4th Oct. '61

My dear Jay,

Unless the Secy of State has changed he will not hearken to suggestions.[1] He is too strong in egotism.

Prince Napoleon the evng before sailing expressed the strongest sentiments for our cause,[2] but thought we had erred in not obtaining an influence through the Paris & London press. Of course, we have. Months ago, I pleaded that the Secret Service fund should go in this way.

I wish I *knew* the real character & position of Fremont.[3]

I shall send you my little speech in a pamphlet corrected.[4] The whole convention or 9/10th cheered it most enthusiastically.

Ever yours,   Charles Sumner

ALS   NNCB   (75/186, PCS)

1. Jay wrote from Katonah, New York, 26 September 1861 (23/247, PCS) that he had written Seward suggesting that U.S. diplomats in Europe be made fully aware of the "pro-slavery aims of the Rebellion & the comparative resources of the North & South." He feared Northern representatives abroad were out of touch.

2. Joseph Charles Paul Napoleon Bonaparte (1822–91), a French soldier and cousin of Napoleon III, had recently visited the U.S.

3. Jay wrote that he was "somewhat anxious" about Frémont, but even more over Lincoln's conduct. "The pro-slavery press at the North is making great capital out of Mr. Lincolns letter to Fremont."

4. "Emancipation Our Best Weapon," given at the Republican State Convention, Worcester, 1 October.

To Wendell Phillips

Boston 13th Oct. '61

My dear Phillips,

Of course I am not responsible for a weak statement in the *Transcript* of what my speech of Friday is to be. But you have done me only *simple* justice.[1]

It is not in my nature to retreat.

My special object will be to shew Slavery as the *causa causas* of the War—all this with a view of directing the attention directly & exclusively upon that as our real Enemy.

I think I shall supply a link in the argt.

They do not charge me often with *feebleness* in stating my ideas.

I thought I knew the malignants well; but they are worse than I supposed. A good paper would have silenced them & driven them down to shame. But we have no paper. Not a Boston paper dares to speak in defence of a Mass. Senator.

Good bye!

Ever yours,   Charles Sumner

ALS   MH-H   (75/201, PCS)

1. Phillips wrote CS on 12 October 1861 (23/384, PCS) about an "unhappy phrase" in the *Boston Evening Transcript* (10 October 1861:2) about CS's forthcoming speech, "The Rebellion. Its Origin and Mainspring," to be delivered on 18 October at Tremont Temple. The *Transcript* stated that CS's address "will attract general attention from its thoroughness as well as moderation of the theme which he has chosen, viz., 'The Rebellion.'" Phillips urged CS not to give "an inch to the yelping curs at your heels."

To Harriet Martineau
private

Boston 29th Oct. '61

Dear Mrs Martineau,

The enclosed notes will explain to you the situation of our effort for Anderson's family.[1] Of course, with yr faithful hold of our affairs, you must be familiar with the cares & difficulties by which Fremont has been surrounded,—absorbing the attention of himself & all his officers. I shall not forget the case, &, when I reach Washington will take some other means to follow it up if I do not hear from it before. I am glad to know that Lord Shaftesbury[2] is interested in it. I wish that he had a truer sympathy for the North.

It is constantly said in England that this is not a war against Slavery. This is a mistake. It is a war to prevent the foundation of a slave-holding Confederacy, in which Slavery is to be soul & corner-stone, & which will insist upon the extension & perpetuation of Slavery. Surely in crushing such an attempt we are fighting for Freedom—& Civilization too. But you need no word from me on this point.[3]

I deplore the course of the English press & of many persons there, who mis-represent this contest; & for two reasons. First, they have caused a distrust & bitterness, which will influence for a long time the relations between our two countries—all of which is most painful to me & inconsistent with my policy & passion. And, secondly, English sympathy has actually fomented this Rebellion. Without the hopes they have derived from England, they would have been disheartened. It is not pleasant to think that we have been compelled to our present exertions, involving so many victims, in part by English encouragement to the Rebellion.

Meanwhile the tragedy moves on. I have never from the beginning doubted the result. Slavery must die. Had Fremont's Proclamation been maintained, & extended to other states, it would be equivalent to a decree of Emancipation. The letter of the Secy of War,[4] which you will receive by this packet, *does almost as much*, when it directs that all who come to the camp shall be received & put to *service* —not limiting it to work on trenches. I have for sometime expected this order. When I made my speech the other day I knew that it was coming. *The Secy of War & Secy of the Navy*[5] *are both determined to make the war bear on Slavery.* This is not known to the public; but I know it from their own lips. The Presdt. is honest & slow.—Pray continue to help in removing misunderstandings & keeping the peace between our countries.

Ever Yours,   Charles Sumner

I am sorry to learn that you still suffer; but I admire all the more the abilities you give to work.

ALS   GBUBi   (75/225, PCS)

1. No enclosures have been recovered. Martineau wrote CS from Ambleside asking his assistance in freeing and bringing to Great Britain the family of John Anderson, a fugitive slave from Missouri who had escaped to Canada and eventually made his way to Great Britain (2 August 1861, 23/069, PCS).

2. Martineau had enclosed a note (unrecovered) from Anthony Ashley Cooper, seventh earl of Shaftesbury (1801–85), stating, she said, his regard for CS and his support of Anderson's case.

3. Martineau replied on 14 November 1861 (23/556, PCS) that ninety-nine out of one hundred British sources "insist, loudly & persistently, that the war is not for the abolition of slavery; & that it is fully intended *not* to abolish it."

4. On 14 October Cameron's acting secretary of war, Thomas A. Scott, instructed Brigadier General Thomas W. Sherman, in charge of the Union land invasion at Port Royal, South Carolina, to employ any blacks who fled from the Confederate armies (*War of the Rebellion*, series 1, 6:176–77).

5. Gideon Welles (1802–78), secretary of the navy, 1861–69.

To Martin F. Tupper

Boston 11th Nov. '61

Dear Mr Tupper,

Amidst most engrossing cares I seize a moment to thank you for those generous poems, in which you touch the true keynote of our greater struggle, & also for yr personal kindness to me.[1]

There is but one way in which Peace can be restored here; & that is by the removal of Slavery. This is the cause & origin of the Rebellion; & nothing else. The Morrill Tariff has had nothing to do with it.[2]

All things now tend to an attack on Slavery. A majority of the cabinet is for this course. When this is openly done, then I count upon the unequivocal sympathy of the English people,—which has hesitated too long.

I am astonished that good generous Englishmen should have become so mystified with regard to our contest, which has always been Anti-Slavery, even if it did not propose the extinction of Slavery. Had they been less sympathetic with the slave-drivers, the contest would have been shorter.

I remember well the eminent Bishop from whose Palace you wrote,[3] & I envy you the opportunity of his hospitality.

I write now in Boston but when you receive this I shall be in Washington.

Ever sincerely yours,   Charles Sumner

ALS IU (75/241, PCS)

1. Martin F. Tupper (1810–89), a British writer and antislavery activist, had recently sent CS some verses he had written and told CS he had had CS's recent Worcester speech reprinted in several British newspapers (21 September and 23 October 1861, 23/236, 449, PCS).

2. Some people, especially British subjects, argued that the Morrill and other tariffs had forced the South to secede because of high import duties the U.S. had imposed on British manufactured goods.

3. Tupper's most recent letter came from Farnham Castle, residence of Charles Richard Sumner (1790–1874), bishop of Winchester.

To the Duchess of Argyll

Boston 18th Nov. '61

My dear Duchess,

I have just read the Duke's speech.[1] If that were the tone of the British press or of British speakers, I should be comforted. But every packet brings us voices much less wise & peaceful. The *Times* acts like a demon, & others follow it more or less. I regret also Lord Russell's little speech at Newcastle, where he made a fanciful distinction between "power" & "empire."[2] Even assuming that the war is not waged directly against Slavery, nothing is clearer than that its origin is in the determination at least to limit Slavery—that it is waged against the extension & perpetration of Slavery—against a slave-holding Propaganda. Of course, every word of sympathy for the South or coldness to the North encourages the Rebellion.

It is vain for the *Times* to say—separate. This is simply absurd & impossible. There can be no separation. Where shall it be? What line? Shall patriots in the slave states be sacrificed? What terms? How with the outlying territory? How with Slavery? And fugitive slaves? Even if these questions were all settled in a solemn treaty, what assurance have we that the Treaty would not be broken within six months? Slave-masters are naturally false & piratical. I know them well. *The only chance of Peace is in the suppression of the Rebellion.* How Englishmen can do anything which by any accident can encouage such a Rebellion, whose animating principle is Human Slavery—I cannot understand. They should next join Satan. I do not regard this as a common political Rebellion; but it is an odious & impious outbreak.

Don't think me ill-natured. You know my love for England & also something of my personal responsibilities here. Every thing that creates any ill-feeling between our two countries touches me sharply. But enough of this. Pray keep the peace. And now comes the arrest of the rebel commissioners on an English packet.[3] I hope there will be no trouble here. We have followed English precedent. In 1810 Lucien Bonaparte was taken by an English cruiser from a U.S. merchantman, the Hercules, & carried, I think to London.[4]

I greatly err—or English fortunes are linked with the re-establishment of our National Govt. Then will your manufacturers have cotton, & also a market for their goods—but not before.

You kindly inquire after Longfellow. His hands which were severely burned are now nearly well. He is tranquil, but unable to apply his mind to composition or study. He talks of the South of France, but he will not leave before spring.

What is Tennyson writing? Though I have little time I shall surely read at once whatever he writes.—I hope yr mother is still improving. Remember me most kindly to her.—I took the liberty of shewing yr note, which spoke particularly of her, to Mr Dana, & here is a little note which he wrote me afterwards.—Mr Palfrey is well & speaks constantly of you.

> Ever sincerely Yours & the Duke's   Charles Sumner

The landing of the Expedition in S. Carolina among slaves will give the latter an opportunity. The instructions to the General [*Thomas W. Sherman*] from the Depart. were in harmony with my speech. Thanks again to the Duke for his beautiful, sensible & adroit speech.

ALS   CSmH   (75/257, PCS)

1. In an address to his tenants at Inverary on 25 October 1861, the duke of Argyll stated that although Great Britain should remain officially neutral in the Civil War, he did not believe the North should allow the South to secede. He looked forward to a resolution of the conflict that would "promote the causes of human freedom" (London *Times*, 29 October 1861:9).

2. Lord John Russell stated on 14 October that the Civil War was not fought over

slavery but by "the one side for empire and the other for power" (*New York Times*, 30 October 1861:1).

3. On 8 November U.S. Captain Charles Wilkes stopped the British mail packet the *Trent* and removed the Confederate emissaries James M. Mason and John Slidell (1793–1871), who were bound for London and Paris respectively.

4. Lucien Bonaparte (1775–1840), brother of Napoleon I. In a letter of 17 November, CS called Seward's attention to this precedent as well as the British seizure of Henry Laurens from a Dutch ship during the Revolutionary War (Miscellaneous Letters, General Records of the Department of State, National Archives).

To Wendell Phillips

Washington 8th Dec '61

My dear Phillips,

You have already recd. an invitation from the Lecture Comttee. here.[1] Don't fail to accept. You will be received with all possible welcome, & I desire the honor of taking you on the floor of the Senate.

Private

The great end approaches. It cannot be postponed. The President assured me that in a month or six weeks we should all be together.

Therefore, we have before us, as I announced in Boston, the grave question of the reconstruction of Southern Society. Pray give me the benefit of yr counsels; & set others at work.

Send to me *any practical propositions touching Slavery*, & I will use them. The way is now clear. Washington is now as free to you & Garrison as Boston.

But I pray you quicken our friends to put their views in some practical form. My time is so devoured by my duties, that I have scarcely a moment for the pen, much less for technical work. Help me.

Ever yours,   Charles Sumner

ALS   MH-H   (75/277, PCS)

1. Enclosed with this letter is a flyer announcing the Washington Lecture Association's schedule for winter 1861–62, with Phillips listed as one of the featured speakers.

To John Bright

Washington 23d Dec. '61

Dear Mr Bright,

I wish that I could see the future in our relations with England.[1] Does England mean war? The impression here is that she does; & two

CAPTURE OF SECESSION VARMINTS.

BULL—"What are you about, sir! Picking pockets, eh!"
JONATHAN—"Don't get wrathy, now! You shouldn't be carryin' skunks about with you, John!"

(And Jonathan necks the varmints accordingly).

From Frank Leslie's Illustrated Newspaper, *7 December 1861. "Does England mean war? The impression here is that she does" (to John Bright, 23 December 1861). Courtesy, Special Collections, Honnold Library, Claremont, California.*

foreign ministers have given to-day the opinion that she does. If this be so then must I despair. It is said that if the Trent question is adjusted even on English terms another pretext will soon be found. Can this be so?

All this is to me inexpressibly painful; for I am almost a Quaker on principle. Besides my sympathies have always been thoroughly English, so much so as to expose me to frequent criticism. Thus on every account, I protest against such a contest; but I fear that it is coming. I cannot write this without emotion.

You have done all that you can I do not doubt, & so has Cobden. On my part I have tried. Yr letter & also Cobden's I shewed at once to the President,[2] who is much moved & astonished by the English intelli-

gence. He is essentially honest, & pacific in his disposition, with a
natural slowness. Yesterday he said to me "There will be no war unless
England is *bent* upon having one." Ld Lyons has left his instructions,
which are not yet answered.[3] But it is not known what will follow in
the event of the answer not being categorical. Will Ld Lyons then
withdraw & war begin—perhaps Copenhagen[4] be enacted anew? I fear,
while there has been no want of courtesy, there has been a want of
candor & frankness on the part of the English Govt. If this act were any
thing but an accident, there might be an apology for the frenzy which
seems to prevail.

The President himself will apply his own mind carefully to every
word of the answer, so that it will be essentially his; & he hopes for
peace. But if the English Govt chooses to take advantage of our present
misfortunes & to attack us in our weakness, it will be for the future
historian to judge the act. Of course such conduct will leave behind an
ineradicable undying sting. I speak simply of the fact, which must for
a long time be in the way of harmony between our two countries. Do
you remember the visit of the Prince of Wales? Think of the reciprocal
sympathy then abounding to be changed, I fear into hate. I cannot bear
the thought. What I can do to prevent this will be done sincerely &
earnestly.—We are all inexpressibly grateful for yr good noble words.[5]
There is no suggestion of Compromise. It is impossible.

Ever Yrs   Charles Sumner

I enclose a note from Seward suggested by yr present letter.[6]

ALS   GBL   (75/331, PCS)
Enc: W. H. Seward to Bright and CS, 11 October 1861

1. Until this letter, CS made few specific comments on the *Trent* affair either
publicly or privately.

2. In letters from London, Manchester, and Rochdale, Bright expressed his hope
that the U.S. government would take a moderate course and, if the administration
could not bring itself to release Mason and Slidell, would submit the issue to an
international tribunal (29 November, 30 November, 5 December, 7 December 1861,
23/624, 639, 678, 715, PCS).

3. Lord Russell instructed Lord Lyons on 30 November to inform the U.S. that
Great Britain considered Wilkes's capture of Mason and Slidell from the *Trent* an
"aggression" that was "not in compliance with any authority from his government."
Great Britain therefore asked that the men be returned to Great Britain and that the
U.S. offer an apology for the incident (*British Documents*, part 1, series C, 5:348–49).

4. The British bombarded Copenhagen in 1807 and captured the Danish fort.

5. In a speech to Rochdale townspeople 4 December, Bright lamented the Union's
poor treatment from both British authorities and the press. He further declared that
Great Britain should trust the Lincoln administration to review the *Trent* case carefully and should hope for a peaceful international settlement of it (London *Times*, 6
December 1861:5–6).

6. Seward's letter to CS and Bright thanked CS for sharing a recent letter from Bright and asked CS to inform Bright of the secretary of state's appreciation of Bright's support of the "preservation of the American Union" (copy, 23/376). In his letter of 7 December from Rochdale, Bright wrote, "You must put the matter in such a shape as to save your honor, & to put our Govt. in the wrong if they refuse your proposition." Bright continued, "At all hazards you must not let this matter grow to a war with England—even if you are right and we are wrong, war will be fatal to your idea of restoring the union, & we know not what may survive its evil influences" (23/715).

To Francis Lieber
private & confidential

Washington 24th Dec. '61

My dear Lieber,

The *special* cause of the English feeling is aggravated by the idea on their part that Seward wishes war,[1] &, they say—"very well—then we will not wait." All that has passed diplomatically since 4th March has inspired in Europe a profound distrust of our Secretary; then incidents, which have been reported, have caused something like animosity. Then the constant fire of letters. Then the circular to Northern Governors, co-incident in date with the supposed order to seize the emissaries. Then the unfortunate letter to Lord Lyons.[2] All these have left a deep impression in England. If the Govt & the people could be thoroughly satisfied of the *real good will* of this Administration, a great impediment to Peace would be removed. But amidst present frenzies how can this be done?

My letters from eminent public men all speak of the Secy with utter distrust.

The articles in the *Herald*, proposing to give up the emissaries; but to remember the incident & call England to account hereafter, will be in the way of Peace.[3] If England sees that war is inevitable, sooner or later, she will accept it *now*. The only chance of Peace is that the settlement shall be complete & without mental reservations which shall hereafter be forged into thunder-bolts.

Of course, I say these things daily to the Presdt, who is essentially pacific, & who declares that "there will be no war unless England is *bent* upon war."

Such a Congress as you suggest is impracticable.[4] The Congress of Paris went as far as possible—at that time. We must wait until the exigency is greater or Civilization more advanced. Of course, I should like to propose such a Congress; but not unless it can be presented in a practical form. Think of it, & tell me (1) what propositions you would submit. & (2) how would you enlist the other nations.

War with England involves—(1) instant acknowldgt of rebel States by England followed by France (2) breaking of present blockade with capture of our fleet—Dupont & all.[5] (3) the blockade of our coasts from Cheseapeake to Eastport. (4) the sponging of our ships from the ocean. (5) the *establishment* of the independence of rebel states (6) opening of these states by free trade to English manufacturers which would be introduced by contraband into our states, making the whole North American continent a manufacturing dependency of England.—All this I have put to the Presdt.

I agree with you on the Proclamations; but Phelps's was a set-off to Sherman's & Halleck's.[6]

It would not do *at this moment* to seem to follow the lead of the rebels on the seats of cabinet ministers.[7]

I have proposed to the Presdt. Arbitration (1) by a sovereign or (2) by learned publicists. And I like Prussia for this purpose. But in her present mood England will not arbitrate; & it has been suggested also that no nation can submit to arbitration a question with regard to its own subjects. But let us make a precedent.—Seward is tranquil & confident. But *me judice*,[8] no man can penetrate the future. Passion is too strong, & we are too little informed of the *real purposes* of England.

Ever Yrs   Charles Sumner

ALS   MH-H   (64/190, PCS)

1. On 27 November 1861 Richard Cobden wrote CS of the "impression" in Great Britain that "Mr. Seward wished to quarrel with this country" (23/606, PCS). Similarly, Bright wrote CS on 29 November (23/624) that he hoped the "feeling" in the British cabinet that Seward was "not so friendly" was unfounded.

2. In a circular of 14 October Seward asked Northern governors of states along the Canadian border to fortify their frontiers (Norman Ferris, *The* Trent *Affair* [1977], 95). Seward wrote Lord Lyons 14 October justifying the arrest of two British subjects and explaining that in such a time of crisis President Lincoln was duly exercising his right to suspend *habeas corpus*. He concluded that Great Britain "would hardly expect that the President will accept their explanations of the Constitution of the United States" (*British Documents*, part 1, series C, 5:322–24).

3. The *New York Herald* (21 December 1861:4) proposed that the U.S. give up Mason and Slidell and get on "with the suppression of the Southern rebellion," and repeated the advice on 24 December.

4. In his letter from New York of 19 December (75/321), Lieber proposed an international congress of European powers, Brazil, and the U.S. "*to settle, if not a code, at any rate a catachism for belligerents and neutrals.*"

5. Samuel F. Du Pont (1803–65), U.S. naval officer.

6. Lieber wrote CS that he thought all proclamations from Union generals should be issued from the secretary of war and adhere to a general policy. He thought Brigadier General John Wolcott Phelps (1813–85) "must be out of his mind" in issuing his 4 December proclamation from Ship Island, Mississippi, stating that slaves had equal right to free labor as did their owners and that all slave states admitted since

the U.S. Constitution was adopted were obliged to abolish slavery (*New York Herald*, 17 December 1861:1). For Sherman's orders, see CS to Martineau, 29 October 1861. Major Henry W. Halleck (1815–72), in command of the Department of the Missouri, had on 12 December issued an order that fined secessionists in Missouri $10,000 or the equivalent in provisions to pay for Confederate army damages (*New York Herald*, 19 December 1861:1).

7. Lieber, noting that his former pupils in South Carolina had adopted a measure for the Confederate constitution that he had long advocated, asked CS to see that cabinet ministers "have seats in Congress."

8. "In my opinion."

To William H. Seward

[*Washington*]
[*c. 24 December 1861*]

I have letters from Cobden & Bright—at length—marked *private & confidential*, which I am not to allow to go out of my hands, in which they suggest grounds on which they & their friends can stand in England.[1] I wish to read them to you & the President. When?—

I am believe me   Charles Sumner

ALS   DLC   (75/333, PCS)

1. By this date, CS had probably received Cobden's letters of 29 November, 5 and 6 December 1861 (23/626, 682, 697, PCS), as well as Bright's (noted in CS to Bright 23 December) informing CS as to the course of the British government in the *Trent* affair. Cobden argued that while the U.S. seizure of Mason and Slidell might be "right in point of law" it was "*wrong in point of policy*" (29 November). In his letter of 5 December, Cobden advised that the present British government was "the most friendly to your government which could be found in England, for, although Palmerston is fond of hot water, he boasts that he never got us into a serious war." He informed CS, "You will see that we [*Bright and Cobden*] stand in the breach as usual to stem the tide of passion." On 6 December, Cobden urged the U.S. to release Mason and Slidell and "propose that private property at sea should be exempt from capture by armed government ships."

To Francis Lieber
private

Washington Xtmas
[*25 December 1861*]

Dear Lieber,

Yr suggestion with regard to improvt in Maritime Law is so much in harmony with my own constant aspirations, that I am unwilling to dismiss it.[1] Pray, put it in practical form, or at least develop it more at length. I see impediments at this moment to a movement in Congress on this subject. But my anxious desire is to associate with our decision about M[*ason*] & S.[*lidell*] some triumph of our traditional policy with regard to Maritime Rights. Of course, this must come from the Administration, & I have to-day urged it.

The *immediate pending* question will be settled. My present solicitude is lest the deep-seated distrust of our Secy of State may break out anew—especially as the blockade begins to pinch.

L. N. is thoroughly false[2]—& is full as dangerous as England, even without the provocation which England has.

Ever yrs,   Charles Sumner

ALS MH-H (64/195, PCS)

1. Lieber wrote that his proposed congress of U.S. and European powers "would be a blessing" if they could prepare "some final document" (New York, 19 December 1861, 75/321, PCS).

2. CS evidently did not believe Napoleon III's professions of neutrality in the *Trent* affair and his apparent support of the U.S. stand (*New York Times*, 23 December 1861:4).

To John Bright

Washington
27th Dec. '61

My dear Mr Bright,

I write one word to say that the case of the Trent *is settled.*[1] I used yr letters & Cobden's—reading them to the Presdt & his cabinet in council on this question *Xtmas day.*

Now, let the settlement be accepted sincerely; &, in the name of Peace, let England banish all desire for other pretexts. God bless you

Ever Yrs,   Charles Sumner

ALS GBL (75/342, PCS)

1. On 26 December 1861 Seward wrote British minister Lord Lyons that since Wilkes's capture of Mason and Slidell had not been authorized by the U.S., the two commissioners would be released (letter published in *New York Times*, 29 December 1861:1, 8).

To Richard Cobden
private & confidential

Washington—
31st Dec. '61

My dear Cobden,

I cannot thank you enough for yr constant & most instructive letters down to the 12th Dec. Not a word has been lost. I have read them all to the Presdt, & the most important I read to the Presdt, & his whole cabinet, assembled Xmas day to consider the Trent Case. At the same time I read John Bright's letters. All were full of gratitude to two such good friends, who true to the best interests of their own country, so truly watched for us also.

Will the settlement of the Trent case be accepted in England as definitive, *I fear not*. The war fever is too intense, &, I fear there is a foregone determination in the public mind to have war with the U.S. Can this be so? *This must be stopped*. We are in earnest for peace. I can speak for the Presdt & his cabinet. If there have been incidents or expressions, giving a different impression, they must be forgotten. Last evng at a dinner by the Secy of War, where were Seward, Chase & two or three Senators, while we were seated at table, the Presdt entered, & took a seat at the table. I have never seen or known such an incident before; for our Presidents have some of the reserves of sovereigns. The conversation was much of it on the Trent case. Speaking of the course of England, Seward said he had no memory for injuries, & that, in surrendering M & S, he did it in good faith, *laying up nothing for future account or recollection*. I mention this conversation, & the surrounding circumstances that you may know the *inner sentiments* of our Cabinet & especially of the man who is most suspected by Englishmen. Seward may be careless or hasty; *he is not vindictive*. The Presdt is naturally & instinctively for peace—besides being slow to conclusion. He covets kindly relations with all the world & especially with England. I say this confidently; for I have seen him almost daily, & most intimately ever since the Trent question has been under discussion. Pardon me for pressing this upon you. *It is necessary that yr Govt should be cured of its distrust*. Unless this is done, you will continue yr preparations, & we shall be kept with yr great British sword hanging over us.

Meanwhile our efforts against the Rebellion will be pressed. For a moment they have been checked by the question with you. As long as that continued unsettled all our Expeditions were held back. Now they will start. It is believed that we shall occupy New Orleans by the 1st Feb., & also other important places. There must be soon a decisive battle in Kentucky where the Govt has an army of 100,000 men under an able General.[1] If England & France had not led the Rebels to expect foreign sympathy & support, our work would be easily accomplished. Meanwhile the Slavery Question will be associated more & more with the War. *The Presdt now meditates an early Message to Congress* proposing to buy the slaves in the still loyal states of Mo.—Ky.—Md.—& Del. & then proclaim Emancipation with our advancing armies.[2] These loyal states, which are still debated by the Rebellion, would then be fixed to the Union, & we should deal exclusively with the Cotton States. You see the magnitude of the questions which now occupy us. It is hard that with complications such as history has scarcely ever recorded, our position should be embarassed by foreign nations.

There are 660,000 men in arms under the pay of the Nat. Govt—& *not a single conscript*. But you conceive the terrible responsibilities of this enormous force. To sustain it will task the finances of our country. Already our banks have suspended specie payments—under the anticipated return from England of American securities.[3] It is deplorable that so much of bad influence should come to us from England.

We must strive to extract as much as possible for Maritime Rights out of the unfortunate Trent affair. I shall do what I can. The attention which the subject has received will prepare the way for *reform*. I note well yr suggestions about our Blockade.[4]

You know I am for Peace *quand même*—& especially with England. I believe that all the circumstances & considerations—in extenuation of the British outbreak—have been stated by me to the Presdt, as strongly as they could have been stated by Ld Palmerston. *I know them, intimately & completely*, & I desired that the Presdt should know them. *They explain but do not justify British conduct*. You, of course, will bear with me in saying this.

On reaching Washington for the opening of Congress, I learned from the Presdt. & from Mr Seward, that neither had committed himself on the Trent affair, & that it was absolutely an unauthorized act. Seward told me that he was reserving himself in order to see what view England would take. It would have been better to act on the case at once & to make the surrender in conformity with our best precedents; but next to that was the course pursued. Nothing was said in the message,—nor in conversation. Lord Lyons was not seen from the day of the first news until he called with his Letter from Ld Russell. The question was not touched in the cabinet. It was also kept out of the Senate, that there might be no constraint upon the absolute freedom that was desired in meeting it. I may add, that I had cultivated with regard to myself the same caution. The letter of my brother George,[5] which the Times announced as "inspired" by me, was written in my absence from Boston, & I first saw it in a newspaper which I read in the train. These circumstances will let you see how little there was of [study?] or effort against England. Meanwhile the British fever has gone on, & I doubt not our answer will find yr Navy & Army panting to be unleashed against us, & disappointed at the result.

Telling the Presdt. a few days ago, that it was now important to drive out from the British Govt. their distrust of his Administration & to plant confidence instead, he said at once with perfect simplicity—"I never see Lord Lyons. If it were proper I should like to talk with him that he might hear from my lips how much I desire Peace. If we could talk together he would believe me."

I send you by this packet all the despatches on Maritime Rights which have been published. That of Mr Cass to which you refer was addressed also to Mr [George M.] Dallas, who was directed to read it to Ld John R[ussell]. Presdt Pierce's statement was founded on unpublished despatches.[6] I once obtained a call for these by the Senate; but Mr Cass shewed them to me, & I was satisfied at the time that they contained too much familiar talk with ministers to bear publication. But I will look at them again.—Goodbye!

Ever gratefully & truly yours,   Charles Sumner

I write to John Bright also. If you see him, let him read this also.

There is another question at this moment pending before my Committee—the Presdt & cabinet declining to act. It is—what we shall do on the Mexican side.

That fleet of Eng. France & Spain in the Gulf of Mexico means no good to us.[7]

ALS   GBWSR   (75/365, PCS)

1. Brigadier General Don Carlos Buell was stationed in eastern Kentucky with 110,000 men (*New York Times*, 21 December 1861:4).

2. On 6 March 1862 Lincoln sent Congress a message encouraging gradual emancipation of slaves by giving financial aid to individual states to accomplish this purpose (*Globe*, 37th Cong., 2nd sess., 1112).

3. U.S. banks expected that the British would sell off their American securities and drain more gold from the U.S. economy.

4. Cobden advised that the U.S. abandon its blockade along the Confederate coast, arguing that not only was it ineffective, but that also, since the subjugation of the South would not be a "*speedy*" achievement, the North needed Europe's favorable opinion (6 and 12 December 1861, 23/697 and 24/022, PCS).

5. In a letter published in the *Boston Evening Transcript* (19 November 1861:2) George Sumner wrote that Wilkes's seizure of the *Trent* "was in strict accordance with the principles of international law."

6. In his letters of 27 November and 5 December (23/606, 682) Cobden asked CS to obtain a copy of Cass's dispatch (27 June 1859) to the American minister John Y.

Mason, which Lord Russell had referred to in Parliament on 18 February 1861. This dispatch stated that private property on belligerent vessels should be respected at sea and that blockades could be applied only in specific and limited situations. CS referred to this dispatch in his speech on the *Trent* (*Globe*, 37th Cong., 2nd sess., 243). Cobden also asked CS for the history behind Pierce's "message" (presumably the presidential message of 4 December 1854) that Russia and France agreed to the immunity of private property at sea.

7. When a newly established government in Mexico had declared that all foreign debt payments would be suspended for two years, France, Britain, and Spain formed a joint expedition to Mexico to force payment of these debts. The *New York Times* (28 December 1861:1) noted that the State Department was taking no stand on the joint expedition and that the chairman of the Senate Foreign Relations Committee also opposed any U.S. response.

To John Andrew

Washington
10th Jan. '61 [*1862*]

My dear Andrew,

I am authorized by the War Depart. to say, that, if you will send on yr programme with reference to Genl. Butler, it shall be carried out, & the Department given up.[1] Please let me know yr desires & they shall be presented & pressed.

Morse[2] is kept at Annapolis because he cannot be trusted in any real service.

General Stone is impertinent![3]—But he treats you very respectfully, according to his fashion.

Ever yours,   Charles Sumner

ALS   MHi   (75/396, PCS)

1. Major General Benjamin F. Butler (1818–93) and Massachusetts governor Andrew had been feuding since September 1861 over who was to control Massachusetts regiments, and Andrew now refused to sign commissions of officers nominated by Butler, who had set up his own Department of New England (Henry G. Pearson, *The Life of John A. Andrew* [1904], 1:286–304). Andrew wrote CS and Henry Wilson, 21 December 1861 (*War of the Rebellion*, series 3, 1:864–65), that Butler's behavior "seems to have been designed and adopted simply to afford means to persons of bad character to make money unscrupulously." CS responded on 7 January [1862] that he agreed Andrew had had "much to bear" because of Butler's independence and politicking (75/384, PCS).

2. Possibly Augustus Morse of Massachusetts, confirmed as a captain in the Subsistence Department in the volunteer force (*Executive Proceedings*, 5 August 1861, 11:554). Andrew complained that Morse should be replaced with a "better man" at Annapolis (Boston, 7 January, 24/264).

3. Brigadier General Charles Stone had recently written CS protesting CS's Senate attack on Stone for surrendering fugitive slaves (Stone to CS, Poolesville, Maryland, 23 December 1861, 24/142; *Globe*, 37th Cong., 2nd sess., 18 December, 130).

Stone was about to be arraigned for allegedly aiding the Confederates in the Battle of Ball's Bluff, 21 October 1861.

To Theodore Dwight Woolsey

Senate Chamber 12th Dec. '61
[*12 January* 1862][1]

My dear Sir,

I am grateful for yr instructive letter.[2] All my studies for this late debate were hasty, & I followed Hautefeuille in his recent statement with regard to "Despatches," which seemed to be in harmony with our treaties.[3] I was led to give special stress to the testimony of our treaties, because they were formed subsequent to Lord Stowell's decisions[4] on this identical question, which were well-known to all our negotiators.

And yet I confess that there are considerations in favor of yr more cautious conclusion. Were I to speak now I should express myself with more reserve.

But, beyond dealing with the late case, you will see that I had another object. I longed to do something for the completest emancipation of the sea. In adopting, therefore, the most liberal interpretation of neutral rights I simply spoke in the direction of my desires.[5] The report in the New York papers was imperfect, & I venture to ask you to look over the speech in the pamphlet edition. You will find a topic introduced which, I think, is not in the New York report. Believe me, my dear Sir,

Sincerely Yours,   Charles Sumner

ALS CtY (75/287, PCS)

1. CS assigned not only the wrong year but also the wrong month to three letters in January 1862.
2. Theodore Woolsey (1801–89; president of Yale College, 1846–71) wrote CS 11 January 1862 regarding CS's Senate speech, "The *Trent* Case and Maritime Rights," given 9 January. Defending the U.S. release of Mason and Slidell, CS stated, "Surely, that criminals, though dyed in guilt, should go free, is better than that the law of nations should be violated" (*Globe*, 37th Cong., 2nd sess., 241). While generally supporting CS's speech, Woolsey wrote that he wished CS had been more specific as to how to treat enemy dispatches found aboard a neutral vessel (New Haven, 24/357, PCS).
3. Terming Laurent-Basile Hautefeuille (1805–75) a "watchdog of neutrality," Woolsey cited the French legal scholar who wrote that dispatches were not contraband on a neutral ship. Hautefeuille's study of the *Trent* affair appeared in the *New York Times*, 4 January 1862:2–3.

4. William Scott, Baron Stowell (1745–1836), British maritime lawyer. CS had cited Stowell as an authority "recognizing dispatches as contraband" but stated that according to American principle the *Trent* "was not liable on account of dispatches on board" (*Globe*, 37th Cong., 2nd sess., 244).

5. In his speech CS stated that U.S. policy, based on the treaties formerly negotiated with foreign powers, had two rules regarding contraband: "First, that no article shall be contraband unless it be expressly enumerated and specified as such by name. Secondly, that when such articles, so enumerated and specified, shall be found by the belligerent on board a neutral ship, the neutral shall be permitted to deliver them to the belligerent whenever, by reason of their bulk in quantity, such delivery may be possible, and then the neutral shall, without further molestation, proceed with all remaining innocent cargo to his destination, being any port, neutral or hostile, which at the time is not actually blockaded" (ibid., 245).

To Richard Cobden

Senate Chamber 13th Dec. '61
[*13 January 1862*]

My dear Cobden,

The report of my speech on Maritime Rights in the New York papers, which, probably, was the first recd. in England, is incomplete. That of the *Globe* is precisely as I made it. But there will be a pamphlet tomorrow *revised* by myself. I mention these things, as I know yr interest in the question.

Should there be any disposition to reprint it, will you see that it is from the pamphlet.

I have called for our correspondence, yet unpublished on Maritime Rights.[1] It will be communicated, so far as is practicable. There is much loose talk of Ministers in Russia, Spain & elsewhere which cannot be communicated.

Our people are tranquil, &, I think, that my speech has satisfied the country as to the surrender. I hope also that it may not cause any counter-feeling in England. My whole system is Peace. This is my Alpha & Omega. And to make war difficult, if not impossible, I wish to enlarge Maritime Rights. It seems to me that much may be done now

Our new Secy of War is a personal *friend* of mine[2]—who is determined on a vigorous military policy & a positive policy on Slavery.

Ever Yrs,   Charles Sumner

ALS   GBWSR   (75/289, PCS)

1. On 6 January 1862 (*Globe*, 37th Cong., 2nd sess., 186).
2. Edwin M. Stanton was confirmed as secretary of war on 15 January 1862.

To Francis Lieber

Washington
19th Dec. '61 [*19 January 1862*]

Dear Lieber,

I have this moment recd. yr valued letter. I wish I could see you to *talk over* these events.

By letters mainly received since our decision I am satisfied that a proposition of Arbitration, couched in moderate language, would have prevented war.[1] But our relations with G.B. would have been held in suspense meanwhile, &, of course, all our military expeditions Southward *paralyzed*. This was the fact during the week of consideration. I think you will admit that it was decisive.

But is England held to any thing?[2] Perhaps not. And yet, when Ld Russell avers that the Trent was on "a lawful & innocent voyage," & when she notoriously was carrying rebel emissaries & despatches, is there not ground at least for inference? Besides, by declaring openly at this moment, that G.B. is bound to certain conclusions you will contribute to fix her in this position. At least so I thought & spoke.

Now what shall be done to fasten her? Another Congress might accomplish this.[3] But do you bear in mind that, while we have sought by direct propositions, to amend the law of Nations, we have always kept out of Congresses? The traditional policy of Washington against "entangling alliances" may have influenced us in this course.

But Mr Cobden will commence the discussion in England, & I look soon for propositions, from the Chambers of Commerce in that country.

If you will think of the question, whether we can consistently with our traditional policy, propose a Congress; & then reduce to forum the whole proposition, I shall be most grateful. But I dare not ask you to do it.

In calling for unpublished correspondence on Maritime Rights, I acted, after consultation at the Depart. of State. Seward declares his willingness, to act in that direction.

Mr Stanton, the new Secy of War is my *personal* friend, in confidential relations with me, & goes as far I do in directing the war against Slavery.—It belonged to me in Exec. session to vindicate Mr Cameron's nomination.[4] I think I did it.

Ever Yours,   Charles Sumner

ALS MH-H (64/186, PCS)

1. In his letter of 17 January 1862 Lieber asked if arbitration might not have been a better solution to the *Trent* affair (75/414, PCS).

2. Lieber expressed concern in his letter that for "practical international law . . . no point seems to have been positively settled." He thought the U.S. should try to get European powers, especially Great Britain, to see that the "principle by which we gave up Mason and Slidell [*is*] as broadly and as irrevocably acknowledged even by England herself, as possible."

3. Lieber suggested that the U.S. organize an international congress of "deputed publicists" to settle maritime rights.

4. Cameron was confirmed by a vote of 28–14 as minister to Russia on 17 January (*Executive Proceedings*, 12:87).

To Lord Lyons

F St Sat. Evng—
[*1 February 1862*]

Dear Lord Lyons,

I shall be glad to take advantage of yr kind invitation.

Permit me to say, that the prudence & delicacy with which yr course has been marked under circumstances of peculiar difficulty, deserve honor, & I am glad that they have been so promptly recognized. I congratulate you most sincerely upon the distinguished token you have received.[1]

The parcel which you have kindly sent me has a souvenir also from Mr Gladstone,[2] which I value much.

Ever Yours Sincerely, Charles Sumner

ALS GBWSR (75/434, PCS)

1. Lyons had recently been made a grand commander of the Order of the Bath.
2. Apparently a book, not identified (CS to Gladstone, 21 April 1863).

To Orestes A. Brownson

Washington 2nd Feb. '62

My dear Sir,

Yr son's nomination is now before the Senate. He will be confirmed.[1] *Soyez tranquille.*

The new Secy of War *is with us.*[2] I know him personally & well. I hope for great things for him. With a military education he might organize victory; now he will inspire it.

I think the President will rise.[3] Unless hostile influences should prevail, you will be satisfied with him. *Inter nos*. He has counselled with Chase & myself on a proposition of greater magnitude than was ever yet submitted to a deliberative assembly. I say to him constantly—Courage! Courage!

Yesterday I told the Presdt. that though I am against capital punishment, I am yet for hanging that slave-trader condemned in New York.[4] It must be done (1) to deter slave-traders, (2) to give notice to the world of a change of policy & (3) to shew that the Govt. can hang a man.

Ever sincerely Yours, Charles Sumner

ALS InND (75/437, PCS)

1. Brownson wrote CS on 30 January 1862 from Elizabeth, New Jersey, concerned about the nomination of his son, Edward, as an officer on Frémont's staff (24/564; Edward P. Brownson to CS, 8 April, 25/320, PCS).

2. Brownson asked, "Is the new Secretary of War with us, indifferent on the point, or strongly opposed to us?"

3. Brownson also asked if the president would "rise nearer to the level of his position & of the circumstances of the nation."

4. Nathaniel Gordon was condemned for "piracy and voluntarily serving on board a slaver" and hanged 21 February (*New York Times*, 21 February 1862:5 and 22 February 1862:8).

To John Bright
Private

Washington 3d Feb. '62

Dear Mr Bright,

I have yr instructive favor of the 11th, & note carefully its suggestions.[1] I took the liberty of reading it to the Presdt.

If I wrote anxiously on the 23d, it was because at that date the question had not been touched in the Cabinet.[2] It was not taken up there before Xmas day.

Those who ought to know are confident, that we shall soon be in the possession of Savannah, & that *before spring*, we shall have Mobile & New Orleans.[3] I think a more positive policy on Slavery will be declared also. Indeed, spring ought to find us in such a situation, that any recognition by European powers will be simply discreditable to them, without serious embarassment to us.

Shall we not obtain new securities for Maritime Rights & Universal Peace out of present discussions? It is pleasant to see England the Champion.[4]

Ever sincerely yours,   Charles Sumner

ALS   GBL   (75/442, PCS)

1. Bright wrote from Rochdale 11 January 1862 that he thought it possible that Parliament would urge the Palmerston government to recognize the South. If recognition seemed likely, Bright wrote, "your true policy, if it be a possible policy, is to declare all slaves free—& if this declaration preceded the recognition of the independence of the South, then England would be put in the position not of continuing merely, but of actually *restoring* the condition of slavery" (24/343, PCS).

2. Bright noted "such evidences of anxiety" in CS's letter of 23 December 1861 that he was surprised at the news that arrived on 8 January about the settlement of the *Trent* affair.

3. While calling Cobden's suggestions that the U.S. abandon its blockade "impracticable perhaps," Bright still considered the interruption of commerce with Great Britain "a great peril." He hoped that the U.S. could take New Orleans and Mobile and "at once raise the blockade—receive imports & permit exports, & the customs' receipts would go into your coffers. The cotton pressure here is considerable, & may become very formidable."

4. Bright answered CS 27 February from Rochdale stating, "I hope we *shall* get something out of the Trent business in favor of a wiser international maritime code. The subject comes on in the House of Commons on the 11th March" (25/062).

To Francis W. Bird

Senate Chamber
19th Feb. '62

My dear Bird,

The victories will help us abroad, but hurt *the* cause at home.[1] Already Seward speaks of authentic information from Va. that the Rebellion will be over there in 4 weeks.

Jefferson Davis will *not* proclaim Emancipation.[2]

I fear that the Presdt's good purposes will be suspended. The illness of his child[3] has prevented me from seeing him

Ever yours   C. S.

No Mass. paper publishes my speeches, or hardly notices them. The *Journal* had slips of my speech on Bright—on Legal Tender[4] &c—

ALS   MH-H   (75/467, PCS)

1. On 6 and 16 February 1862 Fort Henry and Fort Donelson in Tennessee had been captured by Union armies, and in North Carolina the Confederates lost Roanoke Island on 8 February.

2. CS's reference is unclear. He may be referring to Davis's forthcoming inaugural address on 22 February in light of the Northern victories.

3. Willie Lincoln died of typhoid 20 February.

4. CS delivered brief speeches, "Expulsion of Jesse D. Bright of Indiana," on 21 January and 4 February 1862, and "Treasury Notes A Legal Tender," on 13 February 1862 (*Globe*, 37th Cong., 2nd sess., 412–15, 628–29, 797–800). In its regular coverage of Congress, the *Boston Daily Journal* noted CS's speeches supporting Bright's expulsion (22 January 1862:4 and 5 February 1862:4). Excerpts from CS's speech favoring the issuance of treasury notes appeared in the *Journal* 19 February 1862:4; the *Journal* stated that lack of space prohibited printing the entire speech.

To William H. Seward

Senate Chamber 20th Feb. '62

My dear Seward,

I find that in printing the resolution *one clause* was left out accidentally.[1] I send you a corrected copy. —

There is opposition to our resolution.

Ever Yrs,   Charles Sumner

I have just consented to its postponement till next Tuesday.[2]

ALS   NRU   (75/475, PCS)

1. CS presented the Senate Foreign Relations Committee's recommendations on U.S. relations with Mexico on 19 February 1862. The committee advised that the U.S. conclude a treaty with Mexico in which the U.S. would pay the interest on Mexico's debt to Great Britain, France, and Spain as temporary satisfaction for their claims. In exchange, the European countries would then withdraw from Mexico (*Executive Proceedings*, 12:121–26). The clause stipulating the European powers' withdrawal had been omitted.

2. Ibid., 131. On 25 February the Senate voted 29–9, with CS opposed to the motion, not to negotiate any treaty with Mexico in which the U.S. would assume a part of Mexico's debt (ibid., 134).

To John Andrew
Private & Confidential

Washington 2nd March '62

My dear Andrew,

The Presdt told me yesterday that an incident had occurred, which excited him very much, so that he expressed himself angrily. It was this.

Genl. McLellan[2] announced to him an expedition, which was to cross the river in force & to occupy Winchester in Va.[1] The first crossing was to be by a pontoon, which was to be thrown over the river, *where the canal-boats were to be taken from the neighboring canal*, & turned into a bridge, which would be necessary for the large number of forces required.

The expedition failed, as on crossing the river it was discovered that the canal-boats could not be got into the river. *The Presdt. thought that Genl. M. should have ascertained this in advance, before he promised success.*

Since his return Genl. M. has not seen the Presdt, who has made up his mind to talk plainly to him. The subject was considered in cabinet Friday.

I hope Mass. will keep in advance on the Slavery Question. This war is nothing unless it finishes Slavery, & our State must lead.

God bless you.

Ever yours, Charles Sumner

ALS MHi (75/496, PCS)

1. The attempted expedition from Harper's Ferry had been planned for late February.
2. Major General George B. McClellan (1826–85) was then in command of the Army of the Potomac.

To Edward Atkinson

Senate Chamber.
5th March '62

My dear Sir,

The Territorial Committees—of Senate & House have each adopted a Bill, founded on my resolutions, for the establishment of Territorial Govts. in the rebel territory. I do not hear of any explosions. Yr friend knows very little of what is passing here or of the grander movement throughout the country.[1]

The rebel territory must be governed but the state govts. have ceased. How, then, shall it be governed? By Govts. organized by Congress,—call them provisional, territorial, or what you will.

There is a movement, in *which the Presdt. takes a deep interest* & on which he has repeatedly consulted Mr Chase & myself, by which the Border States will be brought completely into our ideas.[2]

You are in earnest; & I say to you—Courage! & do not be alarmed by idle threats from persons who know nothing of the real state of things.

Ever sincerely Yours,   Charles Sumner

ALS   MHi   (75/500, PCS)

1. Edward Atkinson (1827–1905), Boston textile manufacturer and economist, had written CS that an unidentified, "wellposted" friend had expressed concern over CS's resolutions on emancipation and reconstruction, which CS had proposed in the Senate 11 February 1862 (*Globe*, 37th Cong., 2nd sess., 736–37). The nine resolutions laid out the powers seceding states had lost and specified that these states reverted to the status of territories controlled by Congress. Atkinson said his friend feared that if CS's "treasonable bill" passed Congress, all border-state representatives would resign from that body (Boston, [c. 1 March], 25/087, PCS). By 5 March no bills from either the Senate or House territorial committees had been considered by either assembly. On 12 March James Mitchell Ashley (1824–96; U.S. congressman [Rep., Ohio], 1859–69), chair of the Committee on Territories, reported a bill to establish a provisional government over territory of seceded states; it was immediately tabled (*Globe*, 37th Cong., 2nd sess., 1193).

2. On Lincoln's gradual emancipation proposal of 6 March, see CS to Cobden, 31 December 1861, and DD, 2:51–52.

To Francis W. Bird

Senate Chamber 12th March '62

Dear Bird,

Can any legislation be proposed to carry out the clause of the Constitution securing to citizens their rights in other states? Pray think of this.

Also, send me any other proposition, needed to *clean out* our Govt. I am determined that the session shall not pass without a trial to make it clean in all respects.

The article of war forbidding military men to surrender fugitive slaves is a triumph.[1] It is the best act of the session. Had it existed originally it would have been next door to military Emancipation.

The proposition of the Presdt. is an epoch, & I hope it will commence the end.

Ever yours,   Charles Sumner

ALS   MH-H   (75/516, PCS)

1. The president approved the additional article of war on 13 March 1862 (*Globe*, 37th Cong., 2nd sess., appendix, 340). CS proposed it on 18 December 1861; it was approved by the House 25 February 1862, and by the Senate 10 March (ibid., 130, 959, 1143). The article forbade the U.S. armed forces from returning fugitive slaves to "any such persons to whom such service or labor is claimed to be due."

To Parke Godwin
private

Washington—23d March [*1862*]
Sunday morng.

My dear Godwin,

You say in yr letter that "the actual state functionaries are annihilated by their own acts."[1] The *Nat. Intelligencer* in criticising me says the States are *de facto* dead; but not *de jure*.[2] Others say that the State govts. are dead. Pray, what is the difference between us, then? Don't let us be lost in a discussion, only worthy of schoolmen, on the metaphysical entity of a State. I call myself practical, & I wish to deal with *facts*.

Now the great unquestionable *Fact* which dominates this whole discussion is that the old constitutional State organizations have ceased to exist in the territory claimed by Secession. The Govts pretending to exercise jurisdiction there are unconstitutional & we cannot recognize them.

But the *territory* cannot be destroyed or eloigned; nor can the Constitution of the U.S. be displaced.

Whatever, then, may be the fortunes of the old State Govts. the territory remains & the Constitution of the U.S. remains.

Now, you will not differ from me at this point; but *you may differ as to the legal & constitutional consequences from this condition*. I rejoice to believe that Slavery itself has lost its *slender legality* in this suicide. But you may disown this consequence. I don't think you can disown the statement of position.

The question then arises; in this suicide of the State organization, who shall exercise jurisdiction over this region or territory? Some say, the military. Very well. If this is thought best. To a certain extent, it must be so. But who shall set the old machinery in motion again? The military. If so, you will depart from constitutional usage, which discards the military if possible. To me it seems clear, that the *ultimate depository* of this lapsed jurisdiction is Congress, who may exercise it according to a just discretion. (1) It may simply instruct the military power. (2) It may organize a Provisional Govt over the whole or parts of States or (3) It may follow the original precedents with regard to the Orleans Territory.[3] To do this, in either of these forms, it is especially empowered, as is set forth in the last of my resolutions,[4] in its obligation "to guaranty a republican form of govt to the States." Nothing, of course, is said, of the forms of this guaranty. Shall it be by the military power or by Congress?—By either, according to the exigency. But, in an exigency like the present, I do not see how the great responsibility can be effectually met *without the intervention of Congress*; but this is the exercise of jurisdiction, which is all that is claimed by my resolutions.[5]

The resolutions do not even speak of "territories." In their title they speak of the territory once occupied &c. They leave open the whole question what the organization shall be; but insist, that, in the present exigency, the duty is cast upon Congress to undertake this organization. Surely you do not dissent from this view.

And yet yr writer speaks of me precisely as the pro-slavery Hunker-semi-secessionists.[6] If I deserve such censure, let it come. Few in the country have studied the present condition of things more constantly or carefully than I have, &, I am sure, that my first desire is the welfare of the country. Of course, yr article is used against me, as it is already used against Ashley in his District & against Wade in Ohio. But you & I cannot differ in purpose.

Perhaps I have erred; but I do not think yr writer has ever read my resolutions carefully & candidly enough to understand them, & I am sure the *Evng Post* has never printed them, so that others could read them. But enough & too much. I am exposed to criticism & abuse; but I do not feel them much unless from the house of friends.

Ever yours,   Charles Sumner

The *Evng Post* has come in since writing this letter. I abjure the whole metaphysical question; & I protest against your statement that "Mr S. contemplates doubtful themes of state existence or anti-constitutional means."[7] This seems strange when in the same article you concede that Congress "must establish a Provisional Power—its authority is ample & the duty to use it imperative." —*Ecce Sumner's resolutions*.

ALS NN (75/527, PCS)

1. Examining CS's resolutions on emancipation and reconstruction in detail, the New York *Evening Post* (13 March 1862:1) concluded that they exhibited "fallacies of constitutional doctrine." CS's resolutions, stated the *Post*, argued that secession destroys both "national and local existence, which is a double suicide." Parke Godwin (1816–1904), then an editor of the *Post*, wrote CS on 21 March 1862 that the bases for CS's Senate resolutions on emancipation and reconstruction were "fallacious"; Godwin believed that such resolutions would "complicate the difficulties of reconstruction by introducing new questions." He thought that CS's second resolution outlawing functionaries of treasonable governments was "clear enough," but such representatives "do not make the State which is defined and created by the [organic?] law" (New York, 25/235, PCS).

2. In an article, "Political Metaphysics" (19 March 1862:3), the Washington *Daily National Intelligencer* called for a clearer discrimination between a state (which could be "terminated" only by "joint consent of Congress and the state legislature") and a state government whose "functionaries" could be "considered civilly dead."

3. The state of Louisiana was originally called the Orleans Territory.

4. CS's ninth resolution stipulated that "Congress will assume complete jurisidiction of such vacated territory where such unconstitutional and illegal things have been attempted, and will proceed to establish therein republican forms of government under the Constitution" (*Globe*, 37th Cong., 2nd sess., 737).

5. The *Evening Post*'s 13 March article stated that only Congress *and* a state legislature acting jointly could, under the Constitution, "terminate" a state.

6. The *Evening Post* declared that CS's plan "prostrates our whole peculiar political organization in order to save the poor slaves."

7. In an editorial (22 March 1862:2) the *Evening Post* reiterated its distinction between the state as a permanent entity and its transitory officials. The editorial stated, "There is no occasion for resorting to doubtful theories of state existence, or to anti-constitutional means, to reach every practicable end that Mr. Sumner contemplates."

To Francis Lieber

Washington 29th March '62

My dear Lieber,

I was penetrated with joy when I found that it was only the left arm that yr brave boy had lost.[1] Only! but this is a great loss. And yet last evng at a restaurant there was a young man, of most gentleman-like appearance, who had lost his left arm & I watched him with constant interest, so that I could hardly eat my dinner. He was gay & easy, & made his single arm do the work of two. His hand when he entered was gloved; but he contrived to unglove it, &, then, with a friend of his own age enjoyed his Champagne & dinner, beginning with oysters. I do not know who he was.

Assuming that our military success is complete, & that the rebel armies are scattered—What next? Unless I am mistaken,—the most difficult thing of all—viz. the re-organization. How shall it be done? By what process? What power shall set a-going the old govts? Will the people co-operate enough to constitute self-govt? I have positive opinions here. If successful in war we shall then have before us this alternative (1)—separation —or (2) subjugation of these states with Emancipation. I do not see any escape. Diplomatists here & abroad think it will be separation; I think the latter, under my resolutions, or something like.[2]

Ever yours,   Charles Sumner

ALS MH-H (64/207, PCS)

1. Hamilton Lieber (1835–76) had been wounded at Fort Donelson (Frank Freidel, *Francis Lieber* [1947], 324–25).
2. Lieber replied on 1 April 1862 from New York advising CS and other U.S. policymakers to ignore the diplomats, for the ministers from Britain and France "know very little indeed." Lieber wrote, "Regarding slavery I repeat, let us compress it as much as we can"; freeing slaves through war conquests would eliminate the need for a special emancipation proclamation (75/552, PCS).

To Horace Gray, Jr.

Senate Chamber
5th April '62

Dear Mr Gray,

I had not heard of Lothrop's illness. I trust it is not serious. But I can hardly let you off from the revision of that Slave-trade bill.[1]

I concur entirely in yr views about the Dred Scott case.[2] You will pardon my troubling you on the point. But, in the multiplicity of subjects which I must consider, how can I avoid referring to those who are especially familiar with them? I knew you to be a master of that case, & that you would be able to tell me promptly, if there was any thing in the way of legislation, or Congressional declaration, what ought to be done against it.

I return the papers, which I sent to you as professional curiosities.[3]

Ever yours,   Charles Sumner

ALS (photostatic copy) DLC (75/562, PCS)

1. CS had written Horace Gray, Jr. (1828–1902), reporter for the Massachusetts Supreme Court and later U.S. Supreme Court justice, asking his advice on a treaty

between the U.S. and Britain abolishing the Atlantic slave trade (27 February 1862, 75/484, PCS). Gray replied that the illness of Thornton K. Lothrop (1830–1913), a Boston lawyer, had kept him from addressing CS's concerns (Boston, 2 April, 25/286).

2. In his letter Gray answered CS's earlier query about the Dred Scott decision, which CS wrote he hoped to get Congress to "set aside." Gray doubted that Congress could "overrule an opinion of the Supreme Court. . . . [A] judicial usurpation is not to be addressed by a legislative usurpation."

3. Gray had enclosed papers (unidentified), fearing that, since CS had not included a note, they had been sent to him by mistake.

To John Andrew

Senate Chamber
22nd April '62

My dear Andrew,

Not so fast!—The Senate felt strongly on the District Bill, & longed to speed it.[1] We adjourned on Friday at 5 o'clk till Monday—not knowing then that the Bill would pass the House that day. It did not pass till after 6 o'clk, when the House promptly adjourned till Monday. The Bill was not enrolled or signed by the Speaker, so that had the Senate come together on Saturday, it could not have received it. In point of fact, the Bill, though hastened did not reach the Senate till Monday evng *after 5 o'clk* when it was promptly despatched to the President.

I regretted that the Presdt. held the Bill back for two days[2]—making himself, as I told him, for the time being, the largest slave-holder in the country. During all this time poor slaves were in concealment, waiting for the day of Freedom to come out from their hiding places.

After six weeks of animated discussion I carried the Hayti Bill through my committee. It was opposed there most bitterly by Garrett Davis,[3] as a "social question," while so good a man as Doolittle sought to overlay it with a scheme of Colonization, & so important a man as Collamer avowed that he "had lost his interest in the question." Anxious for the Bill, I was unwilling that the debates of the Committee should be transferred to the Senate; if this occurred, the Bill, though it passed the Senate, might be damaged in the House, or, possibly it might be postponed even in the Senate. Therefore, it seemed to me advisable to put the Bill under the lea of the District Bill, which has more intrinsic political strength. The Colonization question & the social question have both been discussed on the District Bill, thus clearing the way for the Hayti Bill on its own exclusive merits. On my motion it has been made the special order for tomorrow at ½ past 12 o'clk.[4] In this course, I have been governed by motives of prudence, founded on my ample knowledge of the actual condition of the question here. I know that I am generally charged with making too much haste on this class of questions.

Private & Confidential.

I have no reason to believe that there was any foundation for the report that Stanton was to leave the cabinet. The President will be very—very—slow to make any change in his cabinet. It is true that he has very little confidence in McLellan & that he was not disposed to send the re-inforcements which he desired. These were sent by the order of the Presdt. himself.

The expedition to Yorktown is a failure, with two chances of escape. (1) [by?] a diversion on the side of Washington, & (2) by the arrival of the Galena, & the destruction of the Merrimac.[5]

All that we hear of our officers at Pittsburg Landing is most painful. Some of them ought to be shot —according to all the laws of war.[6]

Major Lecomte, the accomplished Swiss officer, of McLellan's staff, tells me that Yorktown cannot be taken without a siege of 6 weeks or two months. According to him it will take 3 weeks to dig the ditches. So we are to have a Sevastapol.[7] But I trust to some new move.—But when we have overcome the military power of the rebels, *what then?* How shall peace be organized? Good bye!

As ever yours,   Charles Sumner

ALS   MHi   (75/590, PCS)

1. The Senate took up the bill to emancipate slaves in the District of Columbia on 12 March 1862 and passed it, 29–14, on 3 April (*Globe*, 37th Cong., 2nd sess., 1191, 1526).

2. The bill passed the House, 92–39, on 11 April (ibid., 1648), and Lincoln signed it on 16 April.

3. On 4 February CS reported from the Senate Foreign Relations Committee a bill to send diplomatic representatives to Haiti and Liberia (ibid., 619). Committee member Garrett Davis (1801–72) was U.S. senator (Unionist and Dem., Ky.) from 1861 to 1872.

4. CS spoke on 23 April supporting his bill, "Independence of Hayti and Liberia" (ibid., 1773–76).

5. McClellan's siege of Yorktown, begun 5 April, was still under way. CS hoped that the *Galena* or some other U.S. ironclad would destroy the former U.S. ironclad *Merrimac*, now the C.S.S. *Virginia*, which was attacking U.S. vessels off the Virginia coast.

6. Rumors were circulating that the Federal army at Pittsburg Landing (Shiloh, Tennessee), under the command of Brigadier General Ulysses S. Grant had been unprepared for the Confederate attack on 6 April.

7. Sebastopol, the Russian port, was under siege from the British and French for a year during the Crimean War.

To Francis Lieber

Senate Chamber Friday—
[*25 April 1862*]
Exec. Session

Dear Lieber,

The question of Confiscation drags its slow length along. No action of the House can conclude the Senate. How long our debate will last I can not tell. But if you can send me any jottings *at once* I shall value them.[1]

Laus Deo! Yesterday by special pertinacity I carried through the Slave-trade with Great Britain,[2]—a great event in two aspects; (1) it puts an end to the slave-trade & (2) it is a pledge of good will & friendship between U.S. & England. I hurried from the chamber to Seward who was asleep on his sofa at the Department. He leaped, when he heard the news—especially that it was done unanimously—"Good God! The Democrats have disappeared. This is the greatest act of the Administration." In the evng Ld Lyons, to whom I sent the news, came to me in great joy, happy that his name was signed to a treaty of such importance—perhaps the last slave-trade treaty which the world will see. He overflowed with gratitude & delight.

On the same day I carried the acknowledgt. of Hayti & Liberia. Rarely has the Senate done so much in a single day.

Ever yours,   Charles Sumner

ALS   MH-H   (64/215, PCS)

1. The Senate had been considering intermittently since 15 January 1862 the issue of confiscating conquered Confederate property, including slaves. In his letter to Lieber of 20 April, CS requested advice on the extent of confiscation. Should it be applied only to "official leaders"? Should personal property and land be confiscated also? (64/213, PCS). Lieber asked on 24 April whether, since the confiscation bill had been defeated twice in the House, his views would still be useful to CS (75/596). In a later letter Lieber wrote that he thought all leaders' property must be confiscated but warned that determining exactly who was a leader would be difficult (29 April, 75/609). CS argued for congressional control over confiscation in his Senate speech "Rights of Sovereignty and Rights of War," 19 May (*Globe*, 37th Cong., 2nd sess., 2188–96).

2. On 24 April the Senate approved CS's motion to ratify the treaty suppressing the slave trade (*Executive Proceedings*, 12:256).

To John Andrew
Private

Washington Sunday—
[*27 April 1862*]

Dear Andrew,

I had supposed that Genl. Doubleday had communicated with you. He called upon me last evng & assured me that he would.

I am sorry—& grieved—that my course about Hayti has displeased you.[1] I acted as seemed to me best; & having the responsibility of conducting the matter, I was more sensitive, perhaps, than others to the difficulties which were to be avoided. The Bill has passed the Senate, & I am assured it shall be put through the House promptly—perhaps without debate.[2] A month ago it would have been overlaid by a Colonization discussion & other things.

I wish I could send cheerful news. I cannot. The Presdt. told me yesterday, that McL. had gone to Yorktown very much against his judgt., but that he did not feel disposed to take the responsibility of overruling him. McDowell will not go further than Fredericksburg,[3] probably,—as it is feared, that Washington would then be exposed to the enemy. Seward expects a battle immediately at Yorktown. It may come; but I doubt.

I found Stanton yesterday—dull. He considered that an incalculable folly had been perpetrated in quitting Manassas, where we had a broad country, to go to Yorktown & meet the same forces. M. Blair was with me the other evng till after midnight. I will not write all that he said. But he criticises Stanton, & speaks kindly of M. L. [*McClellan*]—although not with perfect confidence.

I agree with yr message[4]—entirely. The Constitutional law was perfect, & so was your mode of stating it. What did the legislature mean? But we are threatened with Hunkerism. God bless you!

Ever yours,   Charles Sumner

ALS   MHi   (75/603, PCS)

1. Unrecovered is a letter from Andrew to CS apparently criticizing CS's procedure regarding the Haiti bill and containing a reference to Abner Doubleday (1819–93), Civil War officer. Andrew wrote CS 30 April 1862 that he regretted his criticism of CS but had an "awful fear that the old negro phobia wd postpone" the bill. He was glad his fears were unfounded (25/436, PCS).

2. The bill recognizing Haiti passed the Senate 24 April, 32–7, and the House 3 June, 86–37 (*Globe*, 37th Cong., 2nd sess., 1815 and 2536).

3. The forces under Major General Irvin McDowell (1818–85) originally were to join McClellan's for the assault on Richmond.

4. On 7 April Andrew had sent to the Massachusetts Senate his message explaining his veto of the Senate bill that would have divided the commonwealth into congressional districts for the purpose of electing representatives. The Senate overrode Andrew's bill on 14 April (*Boston Daily Advertiser*, 8 April 1862:2; 15 April 1862:1, 2).

To Wendell Phillips

Senate Chamber 22nd May '62

Dear Phillips,

Yr letter to Stanton came yesterday morng. Knowing that I was to meet him at dinner that evng I put it in my pocket, & before soup put it into his hands, explaining its contents. He promised to read it carefully; but it has arrived too late to be felt with regard to Hunter's order.[1]—I deplore what has been done; so does Chase sincerely & nobly. Stanton wished that Genl. Saxton[2] had been allowed to set free the slaves without talking about it.

But my faith is fixed. Emancipation or separation is the inevitable alternative.

Give me a hint at any time. God bless you!

Ever yours,   Charles Sumner

ALS   MH-H   (75/631, PCS)

1. On 9 May 1862 Major General David Hunter (1802–86), commander of the Department of the South, ordered that slaves be freed in Florida, Georgia, and North Carolina. On 19 May, however, Lincoln overruled Hunter's order, stating that such powers were reserved for the president (CWL, 5:222–23). Phillips's letter to Stanton apparently supported Hunter's order; Phillips's note to CS asked him to pass a letter on to the secretary of war if CS approved. Phillips wrote he was "profoundly impressed with the risk we run *in the direction* my *note points* out, if Hunter be countermanded" (c. 19 May, 25/657, PCS).

2. Brigadier General Rufus Saxton (1824–1908) had just left for Beaufort, South Carolina, to become military governor of the Department of the South, which included all of Hunter's command (*New York Times*, 16 May 1862:8).

To Orestes A. Brownson

Washington 25th May '62

My dear Dr,

I still hope for yr son's commission, which I have not in any way neglected. The absence of Mr Stanton has prevented my bringing it to a decision. Please say this to him. But there is a "hitch," which I can speak of when I see you, having no relation, however, to you or yr son.

I feel proud of yr good opinion.[1] The distinction, which I elaborated in my speech, seems to me to save us from all these constitutional scruples by which people have been disturbed. It is vain to resort to [War?], if we have not all the Rights of War.

I see a cloud in the East—from foreign nations. Nothing but great triumphs, & a positive policy on Slavery can save us from some form of intervention. It may be what is called "moral"; but, whatever it may be, its effect in strengthening the Rebellion will be complete.

It seems to me clear that, if we do not remove Slavery, we shall be compelled to acknowledge the independence of the rebels. That is our alternative. And I fear that history teaches that protracted contests for dismemberment lead to foreign intervention. *Vide* Holland— U. States—Spanish Colonies—Greece—Belgium—Italy. But give us Emancipation & the terrible strife will be glorified.

I can not thank you enough for yr powerful article on State Suicide.[2]

Ever sincerely yours,   Charles Sumner

ALS InND (75/635, PCS)

1. Brownson praised CS's Senate speech "Rights of Sovereignty and Rights of War," 19 May 1862, stating he had not seen until then the difference between "the rebels as criminals & the rebels as enemies." He believed CS had shown that rebels as enemies must help pay the expenses of the war (Elizabeth, New Jersey, 21 May, 25/ 571, PCS). In his speech CS had stated that Confederates were "enemies whose property is actually within the territorial jurisdiction of the United States, so that, according to the Supreme Court, it only remains for Congress to declare the rights of war which shall be exercised against them. . . . *Every rebel in arms is directly responsible for his conduct*; as in international war the Government or prince is directly responsible; so that on principle he can claim no exemption from any of the penalties of war. And since public law is founded on reason, it follows that the rule which subjects to seizure and forfeiture all the property, real as well as personal, of the hostile Government or prince, should be applied to all property, real and personal, of the rebel in arms" (*Globe*, 37th Cong., 2nd sess., 2193).

2. "State Rebellion, State Suicide," *Brownson's Quarterly Review*, April 1862, is reprinted in *The Works of Orestes A. Brownson*, ed. Henry F. Brownson (1884–1902), 17:228–53.

To John Andrew
Private

Washington 28th May '62

My dear Andrew,

I have read the article to which you call my attention in the *Advertiser*.[1] It is absolutely false. I was with the Presdt & the Secy of War

Sunday evng, & had from their own lips the precise state of the case. *The late movements have all been under the orders of the Presdt.* Of this be assured. But this is not all.

This whole trouble is directly traceable to McLellan, who took away to Yorktown an amount of troops beyond what he was authorized to do, *so as to leave Washington defenceless.* When the Presdt. became aware of this, he was justly indignant. I have seen his letter of rebuke to Mc-Lellan in his own autograph under date of 9th April,[2] to which M. L. has never deigned to reply. Should this letter ever see the light it will reflect honor upon the calmness, sagacity, & firmness of the Presdt. If published now it would crush McL.

But it became the duty of the Presdt to rally a defence for Washington, & he ordered the transfers of troops which the Advertiser criticises.

The temper of the press in Boston is wicked, & the Advertiser, from all that I hear, is almost as bad as the Courier. But these spirits are doomed to disappointment. The cause of Emancipation cannot be stopped. We shall begin soon to fire at the magazine.[3] *Stanton told me this morning that a decree of Emancipation would be issued within two months.* I say nothing of the time; but I know that it must come. Chase, with whom I dined alone this evng, agrees with me that the war can be ended only through Emancipation. If we do not declare Emancipation we must make up our minds to acknowledge the independence of the rebels. This is fixed. Thus far I have not hesitated to take the responsibility of my position as a senator of Mass, & I shall continue to the end. Mass. shall not be in the back-ground.

There is a diabolism in Mass. I sometimes think that, if I were out of the way it would be less rampant. They seek to injure me.[4] Very well. I shall go forward; & so will you, I know, & [Henry] Wilson also. God bless you!

Ever & ever Yours, Charles Sumner

ALS   MHi   (75/633, PCS)

1. In his letter of 25 May 1862 from Boston, Andrew referred CS to a *Boston Daily Advertiser* article (26 May 1862:2) that criticized Stanton first for "having ruined the campaign in the York peninsula" and then for ordering Banks "to sacrifice all the fruits of his advance" up the Shenandoah Valley and to join McDowell on the Rappahannock. Andrew criticized the paper's "acrimonious spirit . . . united with a pretentious candor," which he feared would have an "injurious effect" on the public (25/605, PCS).

2. In his letter to McClellan, Lincoln asked, "And now allow me to ask 'Do you really think I should permit the line from Richmond, *via* Mannassas Junction, to this city to be entirely open, except what resistance could be presented by less than

twenty thousand unorganized troops?' This is a question which the country will not allow me to evade." Lincoln continued, "It is indispensable to *you* that you strike a blow" (CWL, 5:184–85).

3. CS repeats here a metaphor for freeing the slaves that Andrew used in his public letter of 19 May to Stanton. In it Andrew complained that Massachusetts soldiers were not permitted to "fire at the enemy's magazine," that is, fight for the real goal of the war, emancipation. Andrew stated that if the president would endorse Hunter's order to free slaves in states under U.S. martial law, then New Englanders "would pour out to obey your call" for additional infantry regiments (*New York Times*, 25 May 1862:8).

4. In his letter of 10 May Wendell Phillips warned CS of decided Massachusetts opposition in some quarters to his reelection and urged CS to "*stump the state*" on the emancipation issue (25/502).

To Richard Henry Dana, Jr.
Private

Washington Sunday—
[*1 June 1862*]

My dear Dana,

I congratulate you upon the prompt success of yr cousin.[1]—

I think that a professorship of German *will* be established at West-point.[2] That others think so too is attested by the number of applications I have had with regard to it.

There is no *exclusive* responsibility for last Sunday's panic, or rather for the orders which exhibit it. About 5 o'clk that afternoon, Trumbull & myself, on our way to dinner at Hooper's, met near the War Office, Fessenden & Grimes,[3] who, told us the news—that Banks was flying[4]—that Washington was menaced, & then they rallied me on my chances of an early execution—among the first. After dinner, I saw the Presdt & Stanton together, & was with them for sometime. Seward was there also, dejected that the proclamation he had written, & also his flowing despatch to Europe, must be kept back.[5] There also were 3 or 4 generals. It was a council—of war, if you please. I addressed myself at once to the Presdt. & from his lips learned what had occurred—he described it vividly—& said among other things that Banks's men were running & flinging away their arms, routed & demoralized. To which I added simply—"another Bull Run." I was then told that despatches had gone to Govr. Andrew for help. From this little glimpse, you will see that Govr. Andrew, if not Stanton, is exonerated from any special responsibility.

I first heard of Andrew's letter which you say "*no one* approves," from Stanton, the day he received it.[6] We were dining together in a small company & before going to the table, he mentioned the letter, without any disapproval, or regret. The next day at the Senate, I heard of it through Grimes, one of our ablest & most solid senators, who had seen the letter. *He admired it much*, & desired Wilson & myself, & other senators to write in a telegram to Andrew, thanking him, which I gladly did. He wished similar letters to be obtained, if possible, from other governors. The next day, I obtained a copy of the letter, & taking it to the Senate, handed it about. It was generally read, & much admired. I did not hear any disapproval of it. Of course nobody supposed that it expressed loyalty with a *proviso*; but we all felt that it told the Govt. truth, which ought to be sounded in its ears, with frankness & power. In short it was a most patriotic letter, where the Govr. took a personal responsibility to do an act of noble patriotism; destined to be historic.

There is a diabolism now in the Boston press, &, if I can judge from one or two numbers in the *Advertiser* as much as in any.[7] Good men ought to insist upon a change.

I see no cheerful omens. Victory is possible; but not success—at present. There must be more suffering, debt & bloodshed—to be followed by a famine throughout the slave states. God bless you!

Ever Yrs   Charles Sumner

From Europe bad omens!

If you have no objection, I wish you would let Judge Sprague know the way in which I introduced his name in a recent speech—which I send.—page 3.[8]

ALS MHi (75/645, PCS)

1. Having asked CS earlier about a commission for Captain James J. Dana, in his letter of 29 May 1862 Dana wrote that his cousin had received one from Governor Andrew and was now in Washington (29 May, 25/635, PCS).

2. Dana also hoped that a friend, Schmitt of the Massachusetts 20th Division, who had been wounded at Ball's Bluff, might become professor of German at West Point (see also 4 May, 25/678).

3. Lyman Trumbull (1813–96), U.S. senator (Rep., Ill.), 1855–73. Samuel Hooper (1808–75), U.S. congressman (Rep., Mass.), 1861–75. James Wilson Grimes (1816–72), U.S. senator (Rep., Iowa), 1859–69.

4. On 25 May Major General Nathaniel P. Banks's Union forces were defeated by Major General Thomas "Stonewall" Jackson's troops at Winchester, Virginia, fifty miles from Washington.

5. Seward's "flowing despatch" may be that of 28 May to Charles Francis Adams expressing the hope that, in the light of Northern victories, Europe would not recognize or favor the Confederacy (*Foreign Affairs*, 1862:101–5).

6. Dana complained about Andrew's letter to Stanton of 19 May: "Which is crazy, Mr Stanton or Gov. Andrew?" He thought Andrew's insistence on emancipation as a war aim a "grave mistake." It implied "Massachusetts is loyal *provided*, while Md, Ky, & Missouri must be loyal unconditionally."

7. The *Boston Daily Advertiser* criticized Andrew's letter to Stanton as well as Andrew's precipitous summoning of the state militia to defend Washington (26 May 1862:2; 27 May 1862:2; 28 May 1862:2).

8. In "Rights of Sovereignty and Rights of War," CS quoted Peleg Sprague's statement in a recent prize case that the Confederates had "'added the guilt of treason to that of unjust war'" (*Globe*, 37th Cong., 2nd sess., 2189).

To John Andrew
Private

Washington—5th June '62
Thursday evng.

My dear Andrew,

On getting yr good long letter, I went at once to the War office. The Secy had just left. But I spoke to the first Assistant about the cadets.[1] *That must be changed*

McL. calls constantly for more troops. That was the call at Yorktown; & now at Richmond. Fortress Munroe was put under him, so as to put 10,000 more well-disciplined men within his call; but, as Wool would be his superior in rank (so they say) Dix was transferred to F. Munroe, & the veteran was transferred to Baltimore.[2] That is all.

We are all indignant with Stanley, whose course is explained when you consider that he was selected by Seward, & doubtless took his cue from the Secy of State, whose policy is too faithfully carried out.[3] It is *Sewardism*.

I have already spoken once on this abomination—two days ago, & I shall offer other resolutions, unless I hold back on account of Stanton.[4] The country cannot stand such infamy.

Yr letter on "firing into the magazine" will be one of the best of yr many claims to public gratitude. It must be done, or we must make up our mind to separation. I regret infinitely that the necessity was not foreseen by our Govt, & prompt preparation made to meet it. *That would have been Statesmanship*. Alas! we have not had any such thing. How long! Oh how long must we wait! God bless you for yr quickening words,

Ever yours,   Charles Sumner

ALS   MHi   (75/649, PCS)

1. Andrew's letter is unrecovered, but apparently he objected to Northern cadets waiting upon rebels in some manner (see CS to Andrew, 6 June 1862, 75/652, PCS).

2. Major General John E. Wool (1784–1869), now in command of the Middle Department of the Department of Virginia. Major General John Adams Dix (1798–1879), later minister to France, 1866–69, and governor of New York (Rep.), 1872–74.

3. Edward Stanly was appointed military governor of North Carolina on 2 May and soon thereafter declared his opposition to schools for black children, stating such institutions were forbidden by North Carolina's state laws. In his letter of 4 June, Andrew protested Stanly's appointment. Did the administration "wish to drive our N.E. troops out of the field & disgust mankind"? (Boston, 25/675).

4. CS offered a resolution on 2 June requesting that the Senate be provided with copies of all orders regarding appointments of military governors. On 6 June he asked that the president revoke Stanton's appointment of Stanly because such an appointment subordinated civil governments to military authority (*Globe*, 37th Cong., 2nd sess., 2477, 2596). The first resolution was passed, the second postponed.

To the Duchess of Argyll

Washington 9th June '62

My dear Duchess,

If I have not written lately, it has been because my time has been too much occupied to leave me even a moment for correspondence, &, then each day seemed to be producing events which would report themselves. But I was happy to have yr pleasant note.

It seems pretty certain that the *military power* of the rebellion will be soon broken. What then? That is the great question. Seward assured me yesterday that it would "all be over in 90 days." I do not see it so. But there is no sign any where of a willingness on the part of the U.S. to abandon one foot of territory. I think that you must take this into yr calculations, & also the power of the Govt.[1]

Should any body propose a separation, where should the line be run? Should it concede all the slave states? or only the cotton states? or the cotton states & some others? The difficulties of determining such a line seem to me insuperable. Then, what should be the condition of slavery? Should we continue the surrender of fugitive slaves? Whatever may be the difficulties & burthens of the contest they are less perplexing than any attempt at separation. Indeed, I have long regarded the latter as a practical impossibility. The war, therefore, must go on, &, unless the slave states submit, Slavery will be directly abolished by military decree. From this result I have long seen no escape—except by the surrender of the South. Thus far we have no sign of such surrender. There are some who expect it. I [do?] not dogmatize on this point. But it seems hard to believe that men, who have made such professions & declarations, & whose pride is terribly enlisted, will submit. But just in proportion to their continued resistance is Slavery endangered. M. Mercier, who saw the leaders at Richmond, is satisfied that they will never submit.[2]

Who can have quizzed Mr Dizraeli? Never were two diplomatists better friends or more cordial in their relations with each other than M. Mercier & Ld Lyons. They are together daily, I often see them together, & often hear them speak of each other. Ld Lyons is happy in his *Congé*.[3]—We rejoiced together in the Slave-trade Treaty. The same day on which I carried through the Senate the recognition of Hayti & Liberia, I moved the ratification of the Treaty & to my astonishment, it was ratified without a dissenting voice. God bless you!

Ever Yours,   Charles Sumner

ALS   CSmH   (75/658, PCS)

1. The duchess warned CS, in her note of 18 May 1862 from Kensington, not to think it "unfriendly" that the British could not see "the necessity of having the *whole* South again" (25/537, PCS).

2. In April Henri Mercier (c. 1816–1886), French minister to the U.S., was given permission by the Lincoln administration to visit the Confederacy in order to explore possibilities of ending the war (Glyndon Van Deusen, *William Henry Seward* [1967], 318–19).

3. The *New York Times* (5 June 1862:2) reported that in the House of Lords on 19 May Disraeli mentioned a report regarding a "want of accord" between the British and French ministers to America. Palmerston denied the report. Lyons was about to take a leave of absence in England.

To Sydney Howard Gay[1]
private

Met. Hotel Saturday
[*26 July 1862*][2]

My dear Sir,

I am about to take the train for Boston.

It seems to me the time has come when Mr Seward's early despatches to Adams & Dayton ought to be analysed & exposed critically.[3] There is the official statement of that policy which has turned Europe against us & still keeps 4 millions of slaves the invaluable allies of our enemies.

Read these papers carefully. There is much in them.

Ever Yours,   Charles Sumner

ALS   NNCB   (76/028, PCS)

   1. Sydney Howard Gay (1814–88), editor, *National Anti-Slavery Standard*, 1842–56; managing editor, *New York Tribune,* 1862.

   2. The letter is tentatively dated by CS's travel from Washington to Boston after the adjournment of Congress on 17 July 1862.

   3. Seward's 1861 dispatches abroad had been printed with the president's annual message in December 1861. The *New York Times* published excerpts soon thereafter and highly praised the diplomacy reflected in Seward's correspondence (9 December 1861:4, 8 December 1861:8, 16 December 1861:4). The dispatches to which CS objected most strenuously are likely Seward's instructions to Charles Francis Adams, 21 May 1861 (see CS to Seward, 12 June 1861), and Seward's instructions to Adams and to minister to France William L. Dayton (1807–64), 10 April and 22 April 1861. In the instructions to Adams, Seward emphasized that "disunion" and not slavery had caused the war; in his dispatch to Dayton, Seward stated explicitly that slavery had not caused secession: "the revolution is without a cause; it has not even a pretext" (U.S. Senate, *List of Papers Relating to Foreign Affairs*, Senate Ex. Doc. no. 1, 1861, serial set 1117, 72, 77, 197–98).

To John Bright

Boston 5th Aug. '62

Dear Mr Bright,

I wish I could sit by the seashore & talk with you again. It is hard to write of events—& of persons, with that fullness & frankness which you require.

The letters which I enclose from Mr [*Edward*] Atkinson, a most intelligent & excellent person, will let you see the chance of cotton from the South.[1] *Do not count upon it*. Make yr calculations as if it were beyond reach. His plan of opening Texas reads well on paper, but thus far we have lost by dividing our forces. We must concentrate & crush. The armies of the South must be met & annihilated. If we start an expedition to Texas there will be another diversion. Climate too will be for the present against us.

The correspondence between Genl. Butler & Mr Johnson will shew you that Govt. puts no restraint upon the sale of Cotton.[2] It is the perverseness of the rebels that does it all.

Congress has adjourned. After a few days in Washington, to see the Presdt & cabinet, I have come home—glad of a little rest, but to find new cares here. Our session has been very busy; I doubt if any legislative body ever acted on so many important questions. You who follow our [fortunes?] so kindly, doubtless know what has been done for freedom—for reform generally, &, also in the way of organizing our forces & providing means. There have been differences of opinion on questions of policy—especially on Slavery. This was to be expected. But the Bill of Confiscation & Liberation, which was at last passed, under pressure from our reverses at Richmond, is a practical Act of Emancipation.[3] It was only in this respect that I [valued] it. The Western men were earnest for reaching the property of the rebels. To this I was indifferent except so far as it was necessary to break up the strongholds of slavery.

I wish that the Cabinet was more harmonious, & that the Presdt. had less *vis inertia*. He is hard to move. He is honest but inexperienced. Thus far he has been influenced by the Border States. I urged him on the 4th July to put forth an edict of Emancipation, telling him he could make the day more sacred & historic than ever. He replied—"I would do it if I were not afraid that half the officers would fling down their arms & three more States would rise." He is plainly mistaken about the officers & I think also with regard to the States. In the cabinet, Chase, who enjoys & deserves public confidence more than any other member, also the Secy of War & Secy of the Navy, are for this policy.—The last call for 300,000 men is recd. by the people with enthusiasm, because it seems to shew a purpose to push the war vigorously.

There is no thought in the cabinet or the Presdt. of abandoning the contest.[4] *Of this be sure.* It will be pushed to the full extent of all the resources of the Republic *including, of course, the slaves.* Strange, it seems to me, that I, who so sincerely accept the principles of Peace, should be mixed up in this terrible war. But I see no way except to go forward; nor do I see any way in which England can get cotton speedily except through our success. England ought to help us with her benedictions; for she is interested next to ourselves. But her adverse sympathies help put off the good day. All here are grateful to you, for yr strong & noble words. God bless you! I say with all my heart.

Ever Yrs, Charles Sumner

The Army of the Potomac once 160,000 men is reduced by death & casualties to 85,000. Yr Walcheren expedition[5] on a larger scale.

ALS GBL (76/040, PCS)

1. Writing from Rochdale, 14 July 1862, Bright expressed hope that, with New Orleans now under Federal control, some cotton could be shipped to Britain: "if 100 000 Bales or 200 000 could come, it would greatly alter opinion here with many people" (26/177, PCS).

2. Soon after assuming command of occupation forces in New Orleans, Major General Benjamin F. Butler had seized funds and goods belonging to consuls and foreign merchants. To investigate complaints, Seward sent Reverdy Johnson (1796–1876; U.S. senator [Whig, Md.], 1845–49, [Dem., Md.], 1863–68)) to New Orleans in July (Hans Trefousse, *Ben Butler* [1957], 126–27). On 21 July, Butler assured Johnson that no cotton would be "confiscated by U.S. authorities here"; on 28 July Johnson informed Butler that the U.S. was willing to ship cotton to Europe (*Private and Official Correspondence of General Benjamin F. Butler* [1917], 2:94, 120).

3. The confiscation bill passed the House 11 July and the Senate 12 July. Besides authorizing the president to confiscate property of Confederate officers and government officials, the act declared that slaves of any person in insurrection against the U.S. were free; that no fugitive slaves should be returned to their masters; that the president could employ "as many persons of African descent as he may deem necessary and proper for the suppression of this rebellion" (*Globe*, 37th Cong., 2nd sess., 3267–68, 3276, appendix, 412–13). McClellan's army had been repulsed on every attempt to take Richmond. On 3 August General Halleck ordered him north to defend Washington.

4. The British press, Bright wrote, still predicted that the U.S. would not "overcome the insurrection—& it is this feeling only,—that you are engaged in a war for an unattainable object,—that withdraws so much sympathy from you, & destroys faith in you."

5. In 1809 the British, in attempting to take Antwerp, left 15,000 men on Walcheren Island, where 7,000 died of malaria.

To Abraham Lincoln

Boston 29th Aug. '62

My dear Sir,

That you may be sure to see it in its correct form, I send you a Boston paper, containing Genl. Fremont's speech last evng.[1] I think that I do not err when I call it one of the most remarkable ever made on this continent; complete in statement & argument; elevated in sentiment—exquisite in language; constituting in itself an event & a victory. I understand that it was received by the immense audience with undescribable asent & enthusiasm.

Our country must be saved, & I see no other way than that which Genl. Fremont has so nobly declared. *Recruits will not do it. A draft will not do it.*

Believe me, my dear Sir,

Ever Sincerely Yours, Charles Sumner

ALS DLC (76/068, PCS)

1. Frémont, who had recently resigned from the U.S. Army, spoke 28 August 1862 at Tremont Temple in Boston. He defended his Missouri proclamation of 30 August 1861 freeing slaves there and urged immediate emancipation of all slaves (*New York Times*, 29 August, 1862:8).

To Orestes A. Brownson

Boston 1st Sept. '62

My dear Sir,

I like yr distinction. Emancipation is a War measure. Colonization a Peace measure. To take up the latter now is to carry weight.[1]

Like all that you say this speech is most powerful & instructive. But did you leave the Presdt without moving him forward?[2] Or is he stolidly inert?—I am curious to know yr last impression.

It is hard to read of all this blood & sacrifice, & to think that it might have been averted—which I most solemnly believe.

Ever Sincerely Yours,   Charles Sumner

ALS InND (76/075, PCS)

1. Brownson had given a speech 26 August 1862 at Willard's Hotel in Washington in response to a serenade. In his remarks, he urged immediate emancipation of all slaves of rebels as a war measure. He stated that he agreed with Lincoln about the need for colonization of blacks, but thought that such an activity "from its very nature, is a matter more properly reserved to peaceful times" (*New York Times*, 27 August 1862:5).

2. Lincoln discussed colonization and emancipation with Brownson on 24 August (*Lincoln Day by Day*, ed. Earl S. Miers [1960], 3:135).

To John Quincy Adams Griffin

Boston 11th Sept. '62

My dear Sir,

I cannot thank you enough for the clear, firm, & able way in which you maintained our cause at the Worcester Convention, especially in its association with my name.[1] I have perused the debate with admiration.

At last Massachusetts will settle down upon *hard pan*. This will be an epoch.

It was with a pang that I gave up the idea of going to Worcester; for I recognized completely the importance of the occasion. You did not exaggerate it in the note you kindly wrote me.[2] But my instincts were strongly against going where my name was to be brought in question, &, reviewing the day I feel satisfied that I was not there, especially when I think of my able defenders. Besides—"all is well that ends well."

Believe me, my dear Sir, with much regard,

very faithfully Yours,   Charles Sumner

P.S. I hope to deliver my views at length—very soon.

J. Q. A. Griffin Esq

ALS   MWelC   (76/090, PCS)

1. John Quincy Adams Griffin (1826–66), a journalist and Republican party leader, had on 10 September 1862 at the party's state convention introduced a resolution nominating CS for reelection. After some parliamentary maneuvering, Griffin's resolution was adopted (*New York Tribune*, 11 September 1862:5).

2. Griffin wrote CS from Charlestown, Massachusetts, on 8 September urging him to attend the convention and deliver "bold words that will at once admonish the government at Washington and cheer the hearts of us at home" (26/352, PCS). Instead of attending, CS sent a letter to the Republican State Committee that was read to the convention, calling for unity on the part of all Massachusetts citizens behind the war effort (9 September, Wks, 9:187–90. For analysis of moderates' opposition to CS and CS's delicate political position, see DD, 2:67–78).

To Francis Lieber

Boston 16th Sept. '62

Dear Lieber,

I enclose yr M.S. notes, which are clear & good. But I wish you would treat exhaustively two points—(1) That under the laws of war slaves coming within our lines are freed & (2) The policy of enforcing this rule.[1]

I do not think any thing was said at the time on Mr Adams's diplomatic correspondence.[2] Of course, the slave-holders who then had the Govt. were pleased with it.

I despair of any thing definite or final until the Genl. Govt. boldly strikes Slavery. Then the whole Rebellion will tremble to its centre. Of this I have no doubt, & I do not speak as Abolitionist or philanthropist but simply as statesman, so far as I may claim that character. This is the only way in which there can be an *end* to our calamity.

You speak mysteriously about Norman. Where is he now?[3]

The part which the army menaces to play makes even success gloomy.[4] Alas! poor country! But a vigorous ruler might have saved it. God bless you!

Ever Yours,   Charles Sumner

ALS CSmH (76/094, PCS)

1. Lieber had sent CS on 23 August 1862 (New York, 76/064, PCS) notes on emancipation that CS had apparently requested. Replying 20 September to CS's latest request, Lieber wrote that he was organizing more materials, which he would soon send (76/099).

2. Lieber wrote CS 6 September that he was collecting information to show that John Quincy Adams erred in saying, when he was secretary of state, that it was "usage of war not to receive runaway slaves," and asked CS if he knew of any "good and sound" criticism of Adams's statement (76/084).

3. In his 6 September letter, Lieber stated that his son Norman was "safe as to body" but bemoaned his unnamed fate. On 20 September Lieber explained that Norman had not been promoted to captain and was now with Banks in Washington.

4. The Union forces were preparing to counter the Confederate advance into Maryland.

To Benjamin: Perley Poore[1]

Boston 23d Sept. '62

Dear Major,

I see nothing of the bag of speeches or *Globes*.[2] Both will be welcome; so also a bag or two of Patent Reps.

At last the Proclamation has come.[3] What say the Hunkers?

The Presdt. told me weeks ago that I was the first person who suggested the proclamation of the Acts of Congress. I have always regarded this as an effective edict of Emancipation. But it will be necessary to provide promptly for the employment of the slaves who come within our lines.

Entre nous, what about the Count,[4] & his dismissal?

Faithfully yours,   Charles Sumner

ALS ICHi (76/101, PCS)

1. Benjamin: Perley Poore (1820–87), Washington correspondent for the *Boston Daily Journal*.

2. In his letter to CS from Washington, Poore stated he had forwarded all copies of CS's speeches he could locate and other material CS had requested (11 September 1862, 26/364, PCS).

3. On 22 September Lincoln released the preliminary Emancipation Proclamation, which declared that if the states rebelling against the U.S. were still in rebellion on 1 January 1863, slaves residing there were free. Evidently CS did not expect a proclamation to be issued in September; as recently as 17 September he had complained to Congressman John Fox Potter of "fatal irresolution" in the Lincoln administration (76/096; see DD, 2:80–81).

4. Adam Gurowski had been dismissed from the State Department for, among other causes, publishing a diary containing criticisms of administration officials (Henry G. Pearson, *The Life of John A. Andrew* [1904], 2:25). In his letter to CS, Poore, noting Gurowski's dismissal, wondered, "what black pages must that journal contain?"

To John Bright
private

Boston 28th Oct. '62

Dear Mr Bright,

I wish that I were at Landudno where for a day I could talk on our affairs, & enjoy a little repose.

The Presdt. is in earnest.[1] He has no thought of any backward step. Of this be assured. Since I last wrote you I have been in Washington, where I saw him daily, & became acquainted precisely with his position at that time. There is nobody in the cabinet who is for "backing-down." It is not talked of or thought of.

The Presdt. was brought slowly to the Proclamation. It was written six weeks before it was put forth, & delayed, waiting for a victory; & the battle of Antietam was so regarded.[2] I protested against the delay, & wished it to be put forth—the sooner the better—without any reference to our military condition. In the cabinet it was at first opposed strenuously by Seward, who, from the beginning has failed to see this war in its true character, & whose contrivances & anticipation have been those merely of a politician, who did not see the elemental forces engaged. But he countersigned the Proclamation, which was written by the Presdt himself, as you may infer from the style.

The old Democracy (more than half of which is now in armed Rebellion) are rallying against the Proclamation. At this moment our chief if not only danger is from the division which they may create at the North. The recent elections have shewn losses for the Administration;[3] but these may be explained by the larger proportion of Republicans who have gone to the war. I regret these losses; but I do not think it possible that we can be without a determined working majority in the House, who will not hearken to any proposition, except the absolute submission of the rebels.

The hesitation of the Administration to adopt the policy of Emancipation led democrats to feel that the President was against it & they have gradually rallied. I think a more determined policy months ago would have prevented them from shewing their heads. The President himself has played the part of the farmer in the fable who warmed the frozen snake at his fire.

But from this time forward our whole policy will be more vigorous, & I should not be astonished to see the whole Rebellion crumble like yr Sepoy Rebellion,[4] which for a while seemed as menacing to yr Indian Empire as ours has been to our Republic. I believe that I have avoided in my letters any very confident predictions. I have never seen our affairs with Mr Seward's eyes. But I have from the beginning seen that our only chance against the Rebellion was by striking Slavery, &, it seemed to me that these mighty armaments on both sides & their terrible shock were intended to insure its destruction. It is time for it to come to an end.

I am grateful to you that you have kept yr faith in us, & I pray you to persevere. I write to you sincerely, as I feel, & I beg you to believe that I would not excite any confidence which I do not believe well-founded.—Of course, we have before us the whole reconstruction of Southern Society. I have seen it so from the beginning. But I have hope that our people will rise to the grandeur of the occasion. The Colonization delusion is from Montgomery Blair, Post-Master Genl. who has made a convert of the President.[5] But thus far I have thought it best to allow it to have a free course & thus to avoid a difference with the Presdt. Our generals are inefficient; but our troops are excellent. I have loved England, & now deplore her miserable & utterly false position towards my country. God bless you.

Ever Yrs   Charles Sumner

ALS   GBL   (76/132, PCS)

1. Regarding the Emancipation Proclamation, Bright wrote from Llandudno on 10 October 1862, "If the 'proclamation' means anything, it means that you will preserve the Union even tho' it involve a social revolution in the South, & the transformation of 4 millions of slaves into as many laborers & peasants." A defeated South, wrote Bright, would result in "a population deeply exasperated & disloyal." The "Black nation" must be made a "population *for the Union*" in order to restore the entire South. "Is the north prepared for all the hazards, & for all the confusion which, for a time, such a course may render inevitable,—& will the Govt be thoroughly supported by all the free States in such a policy?" (26/504, PCS).

2. After the battle of Antietam, 17 September, a virtual standoff, Confederate forces under Robert E. Lee withdrew from Maryland.

3. Elections on 14 October in Ohio, Indiana, and Pennsylvania gave Democrats additional congressional seats.

4. The revolt of Indian soldiers was put down by the British in 1858.

5. On 14 August, when Lincoln met with a deputation of blacks to discuss colonization in Central America, he stated it was "better" for the white and black races to be separated, that there existed in the U.S. "an unwillingness on the part of our people, harsh as it may be, for you free colored people to remain with us" (CWL, 5:370–75).

To Sydney Howard Gay

private

Boston 7th Nov. '62

My dear Sir,

When on 27th Oct. Mr Weed entreated the people of Mass. not to elect Mr Sumner & denounced him as "impracticable," he did not think much of Union among Republicans.[1]

He has done more than any body else to prevent this Union so much desired.

Mr Sumner was "impracticable" because he never would hearken to any of Mr Weed's schemes of Compromise.

I suppose the authority in Washington for the private letter on the relations between B. & S. is Judge Black.[2]

I am pained inexpressibly by the result in New York. Seward's miserable letter to the Wadsworth meeting disgusted me by its heartlessness.[3] When you wanted a bugle-note he gave you a riddle.

Ever Yours,   Charles Sumner

ALS NNCB (76/151, PCS)
Enc: Clipping to "Gov. Seward and Mr. Buchanan"

1. Until the announcement of the Emancipation Proclamation brought CS's and Lincoln's goals together, conservative Republicans posed considerable threat to CS's reelection (DD, 2:78–86). The *Boston Courier* (30 October 1862:1) printed from the *Journal of Commerce* an article praising the *Albany Evening Journal's* criticism of the "impracticable Mr. Sumner," which stated that radicalism in Massachusetts was as threatening as in New York. The article exhorted good "Union-loving men of Massachusetts" to elect a "practical" senator, not CS. The election of a solidly Republican Massachusetts legislature on 4 November 1862, however, ensured CS's reelection to the Senate. In his reply, Gay congratulated CS on the "certainty" of reelection (New York, 12 November, 26/645, PCS).

2. CS attached a letter from the *New York Times* (6 November 1862:4) signed

"T.W.," which complained about an unsigned letter dated 3 November from "a friend from Washington" (New York *Evening Post*, 5 November 1862:3). The *Evening Post* letter stated that Seward had collaborated continually with President Buchanan in 1861. Jeremiah Black, anonymously cited in the *Evening Post* letter, was then U.S. Supreme Court justice.

3. Democrats won the New York governorship and additional congressional seats on 4 November. Seward's one-paragraph letter to a Republican rally on 30 October for the New York gubernatorial candidate James S. Wadsworth (1807–64) carried no endorsement but said only that Republicans must be "active, vigilant, and persevering" (*New York Times*, 31 October 1862:1). According to Glyndon Van Deusen, Seward and Weed were lukewarm about Wadsworth's candidacy because of his support of emancipation (*William Henry Seward* [1967], 327).

To Abraham Lincoln

Boston 8th Nov. '62

My dear Sir,

I send you Mr Livermore's Memoir on the employment of slaves & Africans during our Revolution, & call your especial attention to the last half.[1] You will find it learned, thorough & candid.

Its author is a conservative Republican, & his paper was read before the Mass. Historical Society, which is one of the most conservative bodies in our country.

I deplore the result in New York. It is worse for our country than the bloodiest disaster on any field of battle. I see only one way to counteract it; & this is by the most unflinching vigor, in the field & in council. Our armies must be pressed forward, & the proclamation must be pressed forward; & the country must be made to feel that there will be no relaxation of any kind, but that all the activities of the country will be yet further aroused.

I am sanguine yet of the final result, although I fear further disaster; but I am sure of two things, first, this grand Republic cannot be broken up & secondly, Slavery in this age cannot succeed in building a new Govt. Believe me, my dear Sir,

very faithfully Yours,   Charles Sumner

ALS   DLC   (76/161, PCS)

1. George Livermore delivered his paper, "An Historical Research Respecting the Opinions of the Founders of the Republic on Negroes as Slaves, as Citizens and as Soldiers," to the Massachusetts Historical Society in July and August 1862. Livermore had compiled statements from various U.S. authorities to show that blacks were entitled to U.S. citizenship and had served well in the Revolutionary War (*Proceedings of the Massachusetts Historical Society* [1862–63], 6:86–248).

To Lord Lyons

Boston 12th Nov. '62

Dear Lord Lyons,

Let me welcome you back to the great duty of keeping the peace between our two countries, & to all possible satisfaction & pleasure.[1]

Ever sincerely Yours,   Charles Sumner

ALS   GBWSR   (76/169, PCS)

1. Replying to CS's "kind" note, Lyons added, "To promote peace and goodwill between our two countries is indeed an object dear to us both" (Washington, 16 November 1862, 26/662, PCS).

To John Bright
Confidential.

Boston 18th Nov. '62

Dear Mr Bright,

The elections will doubtless encourage the Rebellion; but their *contre-coup* on the Administration has been good. The President is immensely quickened, & the War Department is harder at work than ever. It seems as if the machine was beginning to bear at last. Chase writes me from Washington more cheerfully than since the war began.[1]

There is this consolation even in our disasters, that they have brought the Presdt to a true policy. A wise, courageous & humane statesman, with proper forecast might from the begining have directed this whole war to the suppression of Slavery, & have ended it by this time. I cannot doubt this. But with Lincoln as Presdt, & Seward as Secretary this was impossible. Another agency was necessary & Providence has interposed delay & disaster, which have done for us more than argt. or persuasion. How many dreary interviews I have had with the Presdt where the future seemed so dark! As for S. he has neither wisdom or courage. He fraternizes with Thurlow Weed, who is only a politician, & whose influence from the election of Lincoln has been disastrous. He did not understand the crisis. His diagnosis was utterly wrong, & his nostrums ever since have been injurious. He & Seward set themselves against Emancipation, & they both began with Compromise; & with the idea that by some patch-work this great question could be avoided.

I find myself writing with great freedom; but yr true friendship for my country entitles you to know the truth. Seward has talent & prodigious industry, but little forecast, & a want of seriousness. He has been one of the protectors of McLellan, who has been the author of our delays. But we must be grateful to him; for only in this way has the Presdt. been overcome.

I am not sure that Burnside[2] is capable. Can you send us an English-man who will handle completely two hundred thousand men? The work is not small. Time is required to bring out the true talent.

I am sad & mortified that English sentiment has jumped so com-pletely on the wrong side. This will be a dishonorable page of yr history. England helping a Govt, whose inspiration, life & whole *raison d'etre* is Slavery![3] Bah!—The Carib & Feejee chieftains are extinct; or I would commend her to them. Let her set them on their legs again & give them a cannibal feast. But how foolish to seek our confusion;—as if our prosperity was not best for England. I start this week for Washington.

Ever sincerely Yours,   Charles Sumner

Cobden at Rochdale was himself.[4]

ALS   GBL   (76/176, PCS)

1. Although he lamented the loss of some "noble fellows," Chase wrote CS that he was not discouraged about midterm elections (9 November 1862, 26/639, PCS). Replying to CS's letter on 6 December, Bright stated that he thought the Republican losses had not "much influence on opinion here." The British had concluded "that the war will go on till something like exhaustion takes place, & then that something will be patched up, & that in the meantime slavery will have recd a severe, if not a mortal blow" (Rochdale, 27/031).

2. On 5 November Lincoln ordered Major General Ambrose E. Burnside (1824–81) to replace McClellan as commander of the Army of the Potomac.

3. Bright replied that, despite such examples of British support for the Confed-eracy as a "Southern Club" in Liverpool and the construction of the cruiser *Alabama*, England was "not *more*, but is really *less* hostile than she was some time ago. . . . To me it seems that mediation, or intervention, is less likely & less possible than ever, & that recognition will be a thing not even talked about by any sane man, if you once obtain possession of your Atlantic & Gulf Ports."

4. In a speech to Rochdale constituents, 29 October, Cobden said he opposed recognizing the Confederacy. Although uncertain of the war's outcome, Cobden stated he disagreed with Gladstone and Lord Russell and believed that the Union would not break up (London *Times*, 30 October 1862:5).

To Wendell Phillips
private

Washington 4th Dec '62

My dear Phillips,

Yr nephew Mr Walley[1] has, I trust, received his commission. The Secy, to my inquiries called for his list, & read the name "charged to

Mr Sumner;" so he called it. Consider this appointment as made by yourself, & do not say that you have no influence.

I have tried to put Mr Grover on the way to his desires.

Stanton is hopeful, & determined. Burnside says he has men enough. He seemed to me cheerful, if not confident.

The last paragraph of the message is every thing. That is the operative part, declaring & vindicating Emancipation. All the rest is surplusage.[2]

I wish I could see you. The Message is a curiosity, & its Confection was a curiosity. It is the Presdt's exclusive & unaided work. Seward was not in his counsels.

[*Benjamin F.*] Wade is bitter & most denunciatory. I am not. Good bye!

Ever yours,   Charles Sumner

ALS   MH-H   (76/209, PCS)

1. Henshaw B. Walley was appointed paymaster in the army (Walley to CS, 23 December 1862, Boston, 27/143, PCS).

2. Lincoln ended his annual message to Congress, 1 December, with the statement: "In *giving* freedom to the *slave*, we *assure* freedom to the *free*—honorable alike in what we give, and what we preserve. We shall nobly save, or meanly lose, the last best, hope of earth." In his message, Lincoln also proposed two constitutional amendments that would provide for colonization and compensation to slaveholders in loyal states (CWL, 5:537, 530).

To Henry W. Longfellow

Washington Sunday
[*21 December 1862*]

Dear Longfellow,

I lost no time in making the proper inquiries with regard to yr nephew.[1]

I understand that you already know the result by telegraph. His wound appears to have been slight, & he is doing well.

Our losses at Fredericksburg are less than was at first supposed. But the whole affair was a charge of the Light Brigade on a much larger scale. There has been a terrible depression here & I recognise it throughout the country.[2]

We are now in the midst of what in Europe is called a "ministerial crisis."[3] It is difficult to see how it will end. I have been much with the Presdt., & profoundly pity him. He wants to do right & to save the country.

Many talk & write to me about going into the cabinet.[4] Of course, I should not shrink from any duty required of me by my country at such a moment of peril. But I much prefer my present place.

Where in all history has there been any thing more transcendant in interest than this war?

God bless you!

Ever yours,   Charles Sumner

ALS   MH-H   (76/263, PCS)

1. Longfellow wrote CS on 18 December 1862 from Cambridge requesting more information on Stephen Longfellow, wounded at Fredericksburg (76/256, PCS).

2. The Federal army, defeated in the battle of Fredericksburg on 13 December, failed to drive the Confederates southward. Casualties of killed, wounded, and missing totaled at least 12,000.

3. On 18 December a committee of nine Republican senators (Collamer, Fessenden, Grimes, Ira Harris, Jacob M. Howard, Samuel C. Pomeroy, Trumbull, Wade, and CS) called on Lincoln to request cabinet changes, with most criticism directed at Seward. Seward promptly submitted a letter of resignation. Meeting on 19 December with the cabinet, Lincoln informed them of these events and asked them to meet again in the evening with Republican senators. At the evening meeting Lincoln announced the cabinet's support of Seward and asked if the Republican committee still advocated his resignation. Five senators agreed with Lincoln that Seward should not resign and only Grimes, CS, and Trumbull strenuously dissented (*New York Times*, 21 December 1862:1; 22 December 1862:1; 23 December 1862:1; *The Diary of Edward Bates*, ed. Howard K. Beale [1933], 269–71).

4. Both journalist James C. Welling and Treasury auditor Thomas L. Smith so urged CS (20 and 21 December, 27/123, 125). Congressman James M. Ashley, however, begged CS to remain in the Senate (20 December, 27/122).

To John Andrew

Washington 28th Dec. '62

My dear Govr,

Stanton is fixed, that our action should be Executive, rather than Legislative.[1] Of course, I am indifferent—so it shall be had.

His commissioners were to be H.[*orace*] Binney, Agassiz, & Bishop Simpson, of the Methodist Church;[2] hoping by the fame & character of these men to secure for their work great acceptance. Mr Binney has declined, on account of age.

A live working commission ought to have [*Frank B.*] Sanborn, & men with their hearts in the cause. How would you constitute the Commission?

He proposes that the *formula* of appointment shall be so broad as to allow them to inquire into every thing past & present on Slavery.[3]

But he is now at a stand-still.

Shall I take it up in the Senate? My judgment says—no. If I could leave my place & go on the Commission,—it is a service I should like. But I must stay here.

Stanton will have 200,000 negroes under arms before June next.

Good bye! A happy new year to you!

Ever yours,   Charles Sumner

ALS   MHi   (76/283, PCS)

1. Apparently CS had written Andrew on 23 December 1862 asking his advice about a commission to oversee the needs of slaves who would be freed as of 1 January 1863. In his response to CS's inquiry, Andrew stated that an *"executive* investigation & report" would be more expedient; it would avoid lengthy debate in Congress (Boston, 25 December, 27/156, PCS).

2. Louis Agassiz (1807–73), professor of natural history, Harvard, 1848–73. Matthew Simpson (1811–84).

3. Andrew advocated a "broader inquiry" than that recently undertaken at Fort Monroe on freedmen; he suggested that the commission look at the "whole history & workings of emancipation."

To John Murray Forbes

Washington 28th Dec. '62

My dear Forbes,

Last evng I handed to the Presdt. a memorial from clergymen, calling on him to stand by his Proclamation, *reading it to him aloud.*

I then handed him yr slip *Andax,*[1] which he commenced reading.

Then a slip from a Boston paper, advertising a musical celebration in honor of the Proclamation 1st Jan, with all the names,—yours among the rest.

Then the unsigned Address from the Electors, *which he proceeded to read aloud.*[2]

I then read to him Mr. Chapman's letter,[3] which I enforced by saying that he was now a very able judge of our Sup. Ct., once a Hunker & not much of my way of thinking in times past.

I then proceeded to dwell on the importance & grandeur of the act & how impatient we all are that it should be done in the way to enlist the most sympathy & to stifle opposition. On this account I urged that it should be a military decree, *counter signed by the Secy of War,* & that it should have something in it shewing that, though an act of military necessity & just self-defence, it was also an act of justice & humanity which must have the blessings of a benevolent Govt.

The Presdt. says that he could not stop the Proclamation if he would, & would not if he could. Burnside was present at this remark.

I find Stanton unusually sanguine & confidant. He says that he shall have 200,000 negroes under arms before June—holding the Mississippi River & garrisoning the ports, so that our white soldiers can go elsewhere. The Presdt. accepts this idea.

Let the music sound, & the day be celebrated.

Ever yours,   Charles Sumner

ALS   MHi   (76/285, PCS)

1. Forbes wrote CS on 18 December 1862, concerned that no apparent efforts were under way to enforce the Emancipation Proclamation. He wanted CS to know he would do whatever he could to rouse the president and enclosed an article signed "Andax," setting forth his "general views" on the proclamation (Boston, 27/110, PCS).

2. On 26 December Forbes sent CS a copy of a letter endorsing the proclamation signed by as many members of the Electoral College as Forbes could locate (27/166).

3. With his letter of 26 December Forbes also sent an endorsement of the proclamation by Reuben A. Chapman (1801–73).

To John Murray Forbes

Washington 30th Dec. '62

My dear Forbes,

If yr letter of 27th is for the Presdt. very well. I will read it to him.[1] But you seem anxious to convince me that the Proclamation is on the ground of military necessity.[2] I believe that I am the first, who, *in our day*, called for this exercise of power. There are at least half a dozen speeches where I have argued it & vindicated as a military act.

But while I put it on this constitutional & legal ground, I am anxious that it should have all possible elevation in its tone, its form & associate ideas, so that it shall at once command & captivate the universal assent.

The Presdt. thank God, is now for the employt. of the negroes.[3] A new epoch is at hand.

Ever yours,   Charles Sumner

Stanton does not seem to think the old Procltn worth circulating.[4] He says that he is for the new one; or both may be put together. But he evidently was not interested by the idea.

ALS   MHi   (76/294, PCS)

1. Forbes's letter to CS is in the Lincoln Papers at the Library of Congress (76/274, PCS).

2. Forbes argued that the "ground of *'military necessity'* should be even more squarely taken than it was on 22 September." In order to secure the widest public support for the proclamation, Forbes thought that emphasizing it as a necessary war measure would persuade many who cared nothing for the slaves but wanted to win the war.

3. Forbes wrote he hoped the proclamation would now enable blacks to serve in the Northern army.

4. On 23 December Forbes had suggested that copies of the 22 September proclamation be printed as well (27/140).

To John Meredith Read

Washington 1st Jan. '62 [*1863*]

My dear Sir,

I fear that I have not duly acknowledged yr complete & conclusive argt on the power to suspend the Hab. Corp.[1] It is clear & well-founded.

But *ex necessitate rei—ut res magi valeat quam pereunt*[2] for the sake of *the safety of the Republic*—it seems to me that in vacation of Congress the President may exercise this transcendant power.[3]

But thus far our Govt. has been acephalous.

Accept my best wishes for a Happy New Year & may better fortunes attend our country!

Ever faithfully Yours,   Charles Sumner

ALS   PHi   (76/304, PCS)

1. Prompted by Lincoln's proclamation 24 September 1862 suspending the writ of habeas corpus to all those arrested for "resisting militia drafts, or guilty of any disloyal practice" (CWL, 5:436–67), CS wrote Judge Read 4 December asking for "a sketch of a Bill to meet the Hab. corp. question" (76/211, PCS). Read sent CS two reports on the British view of the suspension of habeas corpus (16 and 17 December, 27/103, 107) and stated that most scholars were "against our practice," and that all his research showed that grounds and crimes must be clearly specified. The U.S. should give "ample indemnity for the past and if possible for the future."

2. "From the necessity of the situation—in order that it may be a greater good than that which is lost."

3. On 27 January 1863 the Senate approved a bill to indemnify the president for suspension of the writ of habeas corpus; CS briefly argued that the protection of the president should apply in both criminal and civil cases and voted for the bill. After much debate in conference committee and both houses, the bill (known as the Indemnity Act) was approved on 3 March (*Globe*, 37th Cong., 3rd sess., 529–54, 1494; James G. Randall, *Constitutional Problems Under Lincoln* [1964], 130–31).

To Orestes A. Brownson
private

Washington 4th Jan. '63

My dear Sir,

I wish that I could converse with you; I can not write.

Our country, great & glorious, is acephalous And yet my faith is so strong, that I believe it must triumph.

Our Potomac army is where it can do nothing but dissolve, decompose & die. There must be some speedy extrication, or its present encampment will be a Golgotha.

There is an injunction of secrecy upon our doings with regard to the Cabinet. I have insisted upon its removal. If all were known, the relative positions of certain persons would be altered.

But let me confess, that I see great difficulties in organizing a true & strong Cabinet. Who will you take? Some at least that you would select would ⟨not⟩ object, especially if in the Senate.

My own idea would be Chase as Secy of State & a New Yorker for the Treasury; & let the whole Cabinet be Anti-Slavery, & have this inspiration—teach one *omnis in hoc.*[1]

Butler returns chafing at his removal, which under the circumstances, he regards as a surrender to European bullying.[2] Banks seems to be wavering. There are many who begin to predict his failure, Genl. [*David*] Hunter knows New Orleans well; he takes a gloomy view.

Ever sincerely yours,   Charles Sumner

Where is yr Jany no?

ALS   InND   (76/311, PCS)

1. "The whole in this."
2. On 16 December 1862 Major General Nathaniel P. Banks replaced Major General Benjamin F. Butler as head of the Federal Department of the Gulf. Butler's repressive rule in New Orleans had been criticized in the British press (e.g., London *Times*, 29 October 1862:6), and CS had written Butler "that the French government has forbidden the papers to mention yr name" (5 December 1862, 76/214, PCS).

To Benjamin F. Butler
private

Senate Chamber, 8th Jan. '63

Dear General,

Mr Stanton assured me last evng that had he known yr real position with regard to the Proclamation, he would have cut off his right hand before he would have allowed any body to take your place; that his fixed purpose was that on the 1st Jan a General should be in command at New Orleans, to whom the Proclamation would be a living letter, &, that in this respect, it was natural, after the recent elections in Pa. & N.Y. that he should look to a Republican rather than to an old Democrat.

I mention these things frankly that you may see the precise motive of the recent change.

I afterwards saw the Presdt, who said that he hoped *very soon* to return you to New Orleans.[1] He added that he was anxious to keep you in the public service & to gratify you, as you had deserved well of the country.

I do not know that you will care to hear these things; but I trust that you will appreciate the sympathy & friendly interest which dictate their communication.[2] Believe me; dear General,

very faithfully Yours,   Charles Sumner

ALS   DLC   (76/321, PCS)

1. Apparently Butler had enlisted CS's help in retrieving his command in New Orleans. Lincoln considered returning Butler to New Orleans on 23 January 1863, but never sent the order (Dft, CWL, 6:73–74).

2. In previously asking CS's help to get more troops, Butler had written on 15 November 1862 that, despite some differences in their "political relations," Butler felt justified in writing because both had a "common desire" to do their "best for the Country's service" (New Orleans, 26/649, PCS).

To George Livermore

Senate Chamber 9th Jan. '63

My dear Livermore,

I read to the Presdt. yr letter on the Pen, & then handed it to him.[1] He said, he would accept it as yr answer, so that you need not trouble yourself to write again.

The Proclamation was not signed till after three-hours of hand-shaking on New Year's Day, when the Presdt. found that his hand

"Emancipation Day in South Carolina," from Frank Leslie's Illustrated Newspaper, *24 January 1863. "[T]he act will be firm throughout time" (to George Livermore, 9 January 1863). Courtesy of the Boston Athenaeum.*

trembled, so that he held the pen with difficulty. The enemy would say—naturally enough, in signing such a doct. But it is done, & the act will be firm throughout time.

The last sentence was actually framed by Chase, although I believe that I first suggested it both to him & to the Presdt.[2] I urged that he should close with "something about *justice & God*." Those words must be introduced. The sentence which I suggested,—without, however, writing it down—was this;—"In proclaiming freedom to the slaves, which I now do as an act of military necessity, for the sake of the Constitution & the Union, I am encouraged by the conviction, that it is also an act of justice to an oppressed race, which must draw down upon our country the favor of a beneficent God."

I then added, as I was leaving him, that there must be something about "justice" & "God."

Ever yours,   Charles Sumner

ALS   MHi   (76/330, PCS)

1. Livermore wrote CS on 29 December 1862 asking him to buy a gold pen at Livermore's expense and have Lincoln use it for signing the Emancipation Proclama-

tion. He then asked to have the pen returned to him "fit for perpetual preservation" (Boston, 27/188, 187, PCS). Livermore's letter of 5 January 1863 to CS, now in the Lincoln Papers, informed him that the pen had arrived safely and stated that no trophy, sword, or plaque was more appreciated than "this instrument which will forever be associated with the greatest event of our country and our age" (76/314). The pen is now at the Massachusetts Historical Society.

2. The final paragraph of the proclamation reads: "And upon this act, sincerely believed to be an act of justice, warranted by the Constitution, upon military necessity, I invoke the considerate judgment of mankind, and the gracious favor of Almighty God" (CWL, 6:30).

To Francis Lieber

Senate Chamber 23d Jan. '63

My dear Lieber,

There can be no armistice—although Greeley has favored mediation to which an armistice must be an incident. You may have observed the prompt way in which I despatched Jewett's two petitions.[1]

The war will go on. The storm prevented a great battle last Tuesday.[2] I found Stanton last evening cheerful; confident that we should soon have Vicksburg. The army at Fredericksburg is now 180,000 men; 68,000 horses & mules, for which there is daily forage; including 16,000 cavalry; & 6,000 wagons. Where in history was such a force thus appointed, gathered together. Stanton says it ought to be able to go on its belly to Richmond.

I do not understand yr anxiety about protection in New England.[3] Wilson & myself are not its partizans, & I am ready to move in any policy which is liberal & just,—especially to the West.

Is it not wicked in McDougal to bring forward these resolutions about France & Mexico.[4] He has intreated me to let them be taken up & discussed. I shall stop the discussion, if I can, & so told him.

There is another bill authorizing Letters of Marque,[5] which I shall stop, if possible.

Good bye!

Ever yours,   Charles Sumner

The pressure for the expulsion of Seward increases—by letters, & fresh arrivals.

ALS   MH-H   (64/233, PCS)

1. Talk of an armistice had been raised by the *New York Tribune*'s editorials and Horace Greeley's communications with the French minister Henri Mercier regarding French mediation in the war (*New York Tribune*, 22 January 1863:4; *New York Times*,

29 January 1863:4). On 16 January CS had moved that the Senate once again postpone indefinitely the petition from William Cornell Jewett (1823–93; a Philadelphia publicist) seeking mediation, and the motion carried (*Globe*, 37th Cong., 3rd sess., 348). Lieber wrote CS on 22 January that an armistice would be "a suicide and a peculiarly disgraceful one"; he hoped all senators were opposed to it (New York, 76/354, PCS).

2. Burnside tried to cross the Rappahannock on 21–22 January, but mud and rain forced the Army of the Potomac back to their winter quarters in Fredericksburg.

3. Lieber wrote several times, most recently on 20 January, protesting a high protective tariff (76/350).

4. On 19 January James A. McDougall (1817–67; U.S. senator [Dem., Calif.], 1861–67) introduced resolutions that the U.S. should aid Mexico in repelling the French from that country. The Senate agreed to lay them on the table (*Globe*, 37th Cong., 3rd sess., 371). CS spoke against the resolutions on 3 February, and the Senate once again agreed to table them (ibid., 694–95).

5. On 7 January CS moved that a bill authorizing the president to issue letters of marque, which would allow private U.S. vessels to capture Confederate vessels at sea, be referred to the Committee on Naval Affairs; the motion carried (ibid., 220–21). Lieber replied on 24 January that CS should "reflect very calmly and long" before opposing letters of marque (76/358).

To Samuel Gridley Howe

Washington Sunday—
[*1 February 1863*]

My dear Howe,

I have been disabled for several days, so that I have hardly been able to keep about. Of course I have gone to the Senate, but have been obliged to lie down there. The trouble is, I think, a cold which has settled especially in the lower part of the bowels, giving me pain & breaking my rest.

I mention this—as my excuse for not having seen the Secy, & closed our proposed commission.[1]

Pray tell me how you find George. My clerk who saw him last week thought he had lost ground visibly since he saw him in the autumn.[2]

It seems to me a little singular that the *Cwlth* should print an article, with a conclusion like that on "the First election of Mr S."[3] I know that I have many failings; call them—"serious faults." But I doubt if it be just to allow such a statement from the lips of a disappointed office-seeker, whose complaints all who know them regard as insane; but put forth as they are in a friendly paper they are calculated to give the idea that I have been guilty of something very different from what even he would charge me with.

Ever yours,   Charles Sumner

ALS   MH-H   (64/237, PCS)

1. On 16 March 1863 Edwin M. Stanton appointed Howe, James McKaye (1805–88; a New York City antislavery activist), and Robert Dale Owen (1800–77; U.S. congressman [Dem., Ind.], 1843–47) members of the American Freedmen's Inquiry Commission to "investigate the condition of the colored population emancipated by acts of Congress" (*War of the Rebellion*, series 3, 3:73–74).

2. As early as April 1862 CS had written Howe about George Sumner's deteriorating health and offered to cover all medical costs (5, 7 April 1862, 75/564, 64/209, PCS). Howe replied to CS's present concern that George's disease (Howe described it as a probable deterioration of the spinal tissue) was presently at a "standstill" (Boston, 3 February, 76/382).

3. An article, "The First Election of Mr. Sumner," in the Boston *Commonwealth* (31 January 1863:2) stated that the Free Soil Party had concluded in 1851 that CS was its best candidate, although there were others "of larger political experience, . . . who had made greater sacrifices, both social and political." The writer ("A. G. B."), probably Albert Gallatin Browne, a Boston businessman and in 1863 U.S. Treasury agent, concluded that while CS had "serious faults," he was "sincere in his Anti-Slavery principles, pure and irreproachable in his morals."

To James W. White[1]
private

Washington 1st March '63

My dear Sir,

I have never conversed on the topics to which you refer in yr letter except *confidentially*.[2] I was willing that you should know certain points for yr own advisement, but I never uttered a word with regard to them except on the condition above-mentioned.

Of course, I must reserve to myself the power to determine when I will enter into a personal controversy. You know that, from the beginning, while I have had positive opinions, I have not seen the way clear to any effective action; least of all have I seen that any thing was to be gained to the cause, worthy of the sacrifice, if I should enter into a personal contest with certain parties.

I have always been frank with the President; very frank. But what has passed between us I have never communicated in any way to the public.

I am pained by the controversy in which you are involved. But I do not think it fair to involve me in it personally. There are seven other Senators—eight in all—who know the fact as well as I.[3]

I am astonished that the despatch of 5th July 1862 to Mr Adams on p. 124 has not been reproduced with comments & the question asked, if that is merely a formal despatch?[4]

Faithfully Yours,   Charles Sumner

ALS   ICUJR   (76/429, PCS)

1. James W. White (1807–67), New York superior court judge.

2. White had written CS 19 February 1863 (New York, 27/561, PCS) criticizing, among other faults, Seward's failure to refuse the French offer of mediation more emphatically. White thought the *New York Tribune* would support a cabinet change in order to obtain more "action in the prosecution of the war." He asked CS to send him an account of what CS considered to be Seward's "most important diplomatic failures and follies," which White hoped to publish in the *Tribune*. Apparently CS did not comply, but White on 22 February wrote a letter signed "Truth and Courage" that was published in the *Tribune* (25 February 1863:5). In his letter, besides describing Seward's conduct as full of "soulless dodging, inconsistencies and political heresy," White stated that he could declare "as a fact" that Seward did not show all dispatches to the president. "A Senator," wrote White, had called Lincoln's attention to an 1862 dispatch that Lincoln declared he had never read. After the *New York Times* (27 February 1863:4) repudiated White's charges, White wrote CS on 27 February, reminding CS of his statement about Lincoln and Seward's dispatches. White asked CS's permission to state publicly that Lincoln told CS he had not seen "a certain dispatch" (27/605).

3. In his 27 February letter White wrote that he had heard elsewhere that when the Republican caucus of senators called on Lincoln on 18 December 1862, Lincoln said he had not seen Seward's dispatches to which the committee referred. In a letter to all members of this caucus, 6 March (28/025), White asked for confirmation of Lincoln's statement, since the "truth, I believe, has never been fully given to the public."

4. In this dispatch Seward commented to C. F. Adams that both "extreme advocates" and "vehement opponents" of slavery seemed to be "acting together to precipitate a servile war," the opponents of slavery by "demanding an edict of emancipation" (*Foreign Relations* [1862], 124).

To John Jay

Senate Chamber
2nd March [*1863*] Monday night

Dear Jay,

Yr draft was very valuable.[1]

My resolutions were discussed in Comttee. three days—2 hours each day—.[2] The first day, all was confusion, & Mr Garrett Davis said he would not sanction any thing which had Slavery in it. I despaired. But at last, after some modifications, chiefly with regard to Slavery as the origin & main-spring of the Rebellion, the resolutions were, unanimously adopted. I was surprized at the result. It seemed as if the millennium was at hand.

Seward came to me to-day & expressed the desire that I should press them to a vote, which I hope to do tonight.[3] The Presdt, I understand, is pleased with them.

My hope was to do something to lift the tone of our foreign relations.

I beg you to believe me grateful for the kind & good help which you gave me.

It looked as if Clay would be rejected. He pressed his case, & interested the Presdt till at last on Saturday Seward came to me with a most urgent message from the Presdt. to let him pass.[4] Other members of the Comtee. were spoken to also. So I was authorized to report him; but I have not yet done it. Meanwhile it is said he has been posting Raymond.[5] Alas!

Ever Yours,   Charles Sumner

ALS   NNCB   (76/434, PCS)

1. Jay professed doubts in three letters to CS from New York (22 and 26 February, 1 March 1863, 27/571, 594, 621, PCS) as to the merits of his draft (requested by CS) protesting foreign intervention in the Civil War. Jay wrote that he desired to keep the tone moderate, "to avoid [expression?] that might reasonably give offence," and apologized for not bringing in the slavery issue satisfactorily.

2. The resolutions, which CS offered to the Senate 28 February on behalf of the Senate Foreign Relations Committee, stated (1) that Congress would look upon any interference by foreign powers in the war to put down the rebellion as an "unfriendly act," (2) that the U.S. "regret that foreign Powers have not frankly told the chiefs of the rebellion that the work in which they are engaged is hateful," and (3) that the U.S. would continue its war "until the Rebellion shall be overcome." Slavery was twice referred to as "the corner-stone" of the rebellion, and a government founded on it was described as "so far shocking to civilization and the moral sense of mankind that it must not expect welcome or recognition in the commonwealth of nations" (*Globe*, 37th Cong., 3rd sess., 1359–60).

3. The Senate passed the resolutions, 31–5, on 3 March (ibid., 1498).

4. The nomination of Cassius M. Clay as minister to Russia was reported to the Senate on 10 March, and confirmed 11 March, with CS voting against confirmation (*Executive Proceedings*, 13:273, 284). Jay replied he was concerned that Clay's recent, strongly worded criticism of Britain had damaged Anglo-American relations (4 March, 28/006). Of Clay's confirmation CS wrote Hamilton Fish, "the chief argt. in his favor was that, all things considered, it would be better to have him out of the country. On this ground Garrett Davis & the Democrats voted for him" (30 March, 76/502).

5. Clay wrote Henry J. Raymond, *New York Times* editor, on 24 February protesting a recent *Times* charge that Clay was capricious, opinionated, and demanding. Clay stated on 5 March that he was preparing "an article of self-defence" for the *Times* (*New York Times*, 23 February 1863:4; 26 February 1863:4; 9 March 1863:5).

To William Lloyd Garrison
private

Washington Sunday
[*8 March 1863*]

Dear Mr Garrison,

It seems to me that George Thompson, if he continues his blows, will drive the author of the Fug. Sl. Bill out of England.[1] Let him strike again; & do not forget. (1) Slave-breeding in Va, which may be portrayed so as to excite disgust at its "[vigintical] crop," & (2) the story of Mrs Douglass, imprisoned for teaching slaves to read the Bible.[2] Let it all be told.

This further can be said, that, when a Senator was struck down on the floor of the Senate, Mason wrote a letter *publicly approving the act*; — so also did his chief Jeff. Davis while his colleague at Paris [*John Y. Mason*] approved it by speech, & so also did Robert Toombs;[3] & thus this Rebellion is the continuance of that act.

I write this for yr private eye; but hope that you will prompt yr friend in yr own way.

Ever yours,   Charles Sumner

ALS   MB   (76/442, PCS)

1. Garrison at this time was raising money for George Thompson (1804–78), British abolitionist and then chairman of the London Emancipation Society (see Garrison to Theodore Tilton, 10 March 1863, *The Letters of William Lloyd Garrison*, vol. 5, ed. Walter M. Merrill [1979], 139–40). Confederate emissary James M. Mason was still seeking British recognition.

2. Margaret Douglass, a white seamstress of Norfolk, Virginia, was sentenced in 1854 for breaking a law that forbade teaching black children to read and write (*The Life and Writings of Frederick Douglass*, ed. Philip S. Foner, 5 [1975], 315–16).

3. For example, Jefferson Davis expressed his "sympathy" with South Carolina citizens and described Preston Brooks as "a brother, who has been the subject of vilification, misrepresentation, and persecution, because he resented a libellous assault upon the reputation of their mother" (Washington, 22 September 1856, *The Papers of Jefferson Davis*, vol. 6, ed. Lynda L. Crist and Mary S. Dix [1989], 44). Robert Toombs, speaking about the details of the Brooks assault, stated that he told "some gentleman present" that he "approved it" (27 May 1856, *Globe*, 34th Cong., 1st sess., 1305).

To Montgomery Blair

Senate Chamber 12th March '63

My dear Blair,

You are prudent, & would not needlessly embarass our country. For God's sake, do not issue Letters of Marque. They will be mischievious & discreditable; & all the good they can do can be better done in some other way.

I have thought of this policy carefully, & feel that it will be a folly, if not something worse. Do—stop it.[1]

Ever sincerely Yours,   Charles Sumner

ALS DLC (76/447, PCS)

1. The subject was discussed in the Cabinet on 13 March 1863, but since Chase and Seward were absent, a decision was postponed. According to Attorney General Edward Bates (1793–1869), Blair was first opposed to issuing letters but was later convinced by Lincoln that the U.S. "would have to come to it, in some form" (*The Diary of Edward Bates*, ed. Howard K. Beale [1933], 284).

To Horace Greeley

Washington Sunday—
[*15 March 1863*]

My dear Greeley,

Yr last letter to T.W. is admirable—although I regret that any hospitality is given to the idea of mediation.[1] T.W. is an enormous mischief-maker, &, since this war began, has added much to our troubles. Through his policy Copperheadism has become strong.

I fear that T.W. is not without reptives. in the Senate.

I observe that the Chamber of Commerce will consider again on Wednesday what shall be done to catch the Alabama.[2] Will you not help save the country from the scandal of Privateers when they can do no good? Let your tool be adapted to yr work. Now, it is obvious that a Letter of Marque is not the tool needed.[3]

Let Govt. hire any good merchant-ship, & then offer a bounty for catching one of our hostile sea-rovers.—But do not let us take the odium of *Privateering* when all that you propose can be better done in some other way.

Nothing but mischief can come from the revival of this discarded system now, & we shall make a precedent to be used against us, perhaps, hereafter. Besides, it is barbarous & uncivilized.

Ever yours, Charles Sumner

ALS NN (76/424, PCS)

1. Greeley wrote a letter to the *New York Times* 13 March 1863 refuting accusations from Thurlow Weed, which the *Times* had published. Greeley denied Weed's assertion that Greeley had sought to negotiate with the Confederates; he insisted the North could win the war without "further concessions." Greeley also declared he was "not adverse to peace through mutual submission to the arbitration of our differences" (*New York Times*, 14 March 1863:8). Replying to CS, 16 March, Greeley defended arbitration and criticized CS's rigidity. He informed CS that at any time he would have "gladly arbitrated all questions at issue between us and the Rebels before a competent, impartial European tribunal" (New York, 28/076, PCS).

2. The C.S.S. *Alabama*, built in Liverpool in 1862, had already destroyed a number of Federal ships.

3. In a one-paragraph editorial, the *New York Tribune* opposed letters of marque (17 March 1863:4).

To John Bright
private

Washington 16th March '63

Dear Mr Bright,

At last the Senate has adjourned *sine die*. Congress ended on the 4th March, but we have been detained to consider nominations, chiefly military.

The session beginning in Dec. has been very laborious. If I have not written you often & fully it has been because my duties compelled me to forego every thing else. You will note (1) our provision of means to carry on the Govt—being the largest money-bill ever voted; (2) our conscription law which places all citizens between 20 & 45 at the call of the Govt, & refuses to exempt clergymen or members of Congress;[1] (3) the Indemnity Bill, authorizing arrests & (4) our declaration of Foreign Policy, or rather our declaration of what we expect from civilized nations.

Besides these important measures, there have been innumerable details—with regard to our army, the navy, iron-clads, police, discipline, the enforcement of the laws, & even the organization of our courts, so that we leave the Govt. invested with ample authority, & with our machine reasonably complete.

I doubt if any legislative body ever did more memorable work; certainly none except, perhaps, the Long Parliament & the Constituent Assembly of France.[2] The only measure which failed was the Emancipation Appropriation for Missouri.[3] The two Houses disagreed on the terms & amount, & there was not time to arrange the difference. But there was careless management, so much so that I predicted the result. I regret this sincerely, because it would have made Emancipation in Missouri sure, & thus would have begun the work in the Border States. But it must go on.

A difficulty, amounting almost to calamity, is the want of confidence in Mr Seward. There is not a senator—not one—who is his friend politically, & the larger part are positively, & some even bitterly against him. It is known that from the beginning he has had no true conception of our case; that he regarded this tremendous event with levity; that he has filled his conversation & his writings with false prophecies; that he has talked like a politician, & that he has said things & kept up relations, shewing an utter indifference to his old party associations. There are some who attribute to him a purpose of breaking down the Republican Party, even at the expense of his country, to revenge his defeat at Chicago. I do not share this judgment, &, when I have heard it pressed upon the Presdt, I have presented a milder theory which is simply this: that he failed at the beginning to see this event in its true character & that, blinded by an illimitable egotism, he has never been able fully to correct his original misapprehensions.

In the House of Reps. he has no friends; nor among his colleagues of the cabinet, not one of whom regards him with any favor.—I have mentioned before the *vis inertia* of the Presdt—& his indisposition to change. Then there is a fear of his friends in the press & in business, lest they should make war on the Administration, if he were dismissed.

I mention these things reluctantly; but feeling that yr generous support of our cause justifies this confidence.—In foreign questions, I find him speculative & imprudent, while he failed to state our case at the outset in the only way in which it could expect sympathy abroad.

This revival of Letters of Marque is his work. I have protested to the Presid against their issue; but I fear that I shall not entirely succeed, although he does not like the idea & will limit it as much as possible.

There is a slight "hitch" at Charleston,[4] but I am assured that in a fortnight this case will be decided. The place has been made a Sevastopol. With Charleston ours, then our national ships can be released from the blockade so that there will be no apology for Privateers.

The feeling towards England runs high, & I hear it constantly said that war is inevitable unless those ships now building are kept from preying on our commerce.[5] As a peace-maker, I am troubled. Pray, do all you can to save us from any such provocation.

The resolutions on Foreign Intervention had the *unanimous* support of my Comttee, although when I first laid them before the Comttee, the Border State Senators were positive & one of them furious against them; but at last they were accepted & passed both Houses by unprecedented majorities. How honest Britons can fraternize with the author of the Fug. Sl. Bill & the emissary of slave-dom is passing strange. Good bye! God bless you!

Ever yours,   Charles Sumner

ALS   GBL   (76/454, PCS)

1. The Congress passed apppropriations for the army and navy on 28 January and 19 February and approved the conscription law on 28 February 1863 (*Globe*, 37th Cong., 3rd sess., 561–65, 1097–1101, 1391).

2. Dissolved by Charles I, the British Parliament continued to meet from 1640 to 1660; the Constituent Assembly met from 1789 to 1791.

3. CS tried to persuade the Senate to pass a bill promoting immediate, not gradual, emancipation in Missouri, but his substitute motions were defeated. The bill to recompense the state of Missouri for freed slaves passed the Senate, with CS supporting it (ibid., 12 February, 897–903).

4. Federal ships did not leave Hilton Head, South Carolina, for Charleston until 25 March.

5. In Liverpool, British shipbuilders were at work on two Confederate ironclad rams.

To Richard Cobden

private

Senate Chamber 16th March '63

My dear Cobden,

Yr letter was most cheering & instructive. With what joy I hail returning English reason.[1] But I am anxious—very anxious—on account of the ships building in England to cruise against our commerce. Cannot something be done to stop them? Our people are becoming more & more excited, &, there are many who insist upon war. A very important person said to me yesterday—"we are now at war with England, but the hostilities are all on her side."

I know the difficulties of yr laws, & how subtle & pertinacious is the temptation of money-making; but, it would seem, as if there should be a way to prevent the unparalelled outrage of a whole fleet built expressly to be employed against us. Of course, in this statement I assume what is reputed & is credited by those who ought to be well-informed. A comttee. from New York waited on the Presdt yesterday, & undertook to enumerate ships now building in English yards professedly for the Emperor of China but really for our rebels. The case is aggravated by the fact, that their armaments are supplied also by England, & their crews also, for it is not supposed that there will be a rebel sailor on board.

To-day the cabinet consider whether to issue Letters of Marque under the new statute. I have seen the Presdt. twice upon this question, which I regard as grave, for it is intended as a counter-movement to what is done in England. Even if no mischief ensue, I am sure it will be a bad precedent which I deplore with my whole soul. I found myself powerless against it in the Senate, for there was a "war fever," &, you know how irresistible & diabolical that becomes.[2] But the Presdt is prudent & pacific, & has listened most attentively to my objections. The original idea is Seward's, who drew the first Bill. I said to Grimes, the senator who urged the measure—"how can you push so zealously a measure of S, whom you dislike"—To which he replied—"the substitute I shall move is drawn by Genl Butler."

I read to the Presdt. yr last letter, which deserves a better acknowledgment than this scrawl. He enjoys the change in English sentiment, but was astonished that yr public meetings[3] were not called under this device—"No fellowship with a new Govt. founded on the perpetuity of Slavery."

The Democrats are becoming patriotic, & all are now hopeful. The authorities predict the speedy fall of Charleston. Every thing is ready.— I owe you & John Bright a full account of recent affairs & of the present position of our Cabinet. I wish I could talk with you.

Ever Yours,   Charles Sumner

ALS   GBWSR   (76/460, PCS)

1. On 13 February 1863 Cobden wrote from London that the Emancipation Proclamation had evoked much popular support in Britain; moreover, "Recognition of the South by England, whilst it bases itself on negro slavery, is an impossibility,— unless indeed after the Federal Government has recognized the Confederates as a nation" (27/488, PCS).

2. CS spoke twice against issuing letters of marque, on 14 and 17 February. The bill authorizing the president to proceed passed the Senate on 17 February and the House on 4 March (*Globe*, 37th Cong., 3rd sess., 960–61, 1020–22, 1027–28, 1488).

3. Among the public meetings praising the Emancipation Proclamation were two mass meetings at Carlisle and Liverpool on 19 February. In his letter Cobden described another pro-emancipation meeting in London, which "without one attraction in the form of a popular orator" filled Exeter Hall "with an enthusiastic audience."

To Abraham Lincoln

212 F St.   18th March '63

My dear Sir,

I send you two slips from important papers —both strongly *against Letters of Marque.*[1]

I hope you will let me again most earnestly entreat you to abandon the idea. If it did not seem to me essentially injurious to our best interests I should not occupy your time against it. Here are my reasons;

(1) It is not *practical*. It is not the agency best calculated to do the required work.

(2) It may *possibly* involve us with Foreign Nations.

(3) It is counter to the opinions & aspirations of the best men in our history.

(4) It is condemned by the civilization of the age.

(5) It will give us a bad name.

(6) It will do this—without any corresponding good.

(7) It will constitute a precedent which we shall regret hereafter & the friends of Human Progress will regret every where.

(8) It will pain our best friends in Europe.

The rules regulating Letters of Marque, which it is proposed to issue, will be a monument of an effort, which I believe will fail, but which will leave a stigma upon our country.

I am proud of my country & wish it to be successful & glorious; but Letters of Marque can do nothing for us now. They cannot save any thing. *There is no economy in them*, but waste.

Ever Sincerely Yours,   Charles Sumner

ALS DLC (76/468, PCS)

1. CS enclosed two editorials from the New York *Evening Post* and the *New York Tribune*, 17 March 1863, both arguing that the U.S. Navy, not privateers, should be responsible for capturing rebel ships (Lincoln Papers, Library of Congress). On 17 March the cabinet again discussed issuing letters of marque, with Seward and Chase favoring, and Welles opposing, their issuance (*Diary of Gideon Welles*, ed. Howard K. Beale [1960], 1:247–49).

To Richard Cobden
private

Washington 24th March '63

My dear Cobden,

Letters of Marque make no head-way. I have labored earnestly with the Presdt. & also with the press against them. It is an absurdity, coined by S.[*eward*], which ceasing to be folly is wickedness.

The North promises now to be united. The Democrats are for the war. The Mississippi will soon be open.

Our preparations at Charleston are enormous; 9 Monitors & a large fleet & army, with contrivances, which left New York 6 days ago against torpedoes, & also to clear out obstructions. The delay has been caused by the extent of preparations. The rebels are confident there; so also is our Navy Department. There has been a disappointment in the effectiveness of the Monitors *against earth-works*;—in the experiments of firing at Fort McAllister.[1] They cannot be fired fast enough. Good bye!

Ever sincerely Yours,   Charles Sumner

We are still anxious about the young pirates now fledging in England. Stop them, pray, stop them.—That is our only anxiety now.

ALS GBWSR (76/493, PCS)

1. On 4 March Federal ironclads (monitors) abandoned their attack, begun the preceding day, on the Georgia fort (*New York Times*, 14 March 1863:8).

To John Bright
private

Washington
7th April '63

Dear Mr Bright,

I have passed an anxious & unhappy week; for all the signs are of war—more surely than in the time of the Trent. I have read Ld Russell's letters.[1] They are bad & mischievous, & seem intended to provoke.

I must believe that the number of ships building is exaggerated; but, if there be any, &, if they are allowed to sail, & to depredate upon our commerce, so far as any now remains, you must see at once the exasperation which will ensue. The question has been considered in our cabinet.[2] There is no difference of opinion; not the least. And it is now thought by many that the British Ministry mean war, since every body is supposed to mean the natural consequences of his conduct.

Seward has wished at once to issue Letters of Marque *against the rebels*. I have opposed it, that we might not have any new complication, & thus far I have prevailed. The Secy of the Navy has sided with me strongly.[3] But all look forward to action of the most decisive character, should those ships come out.

England will then have thrown herself into the arms of Slavery, & our war will assume new proportions, involving perhaps all Europe. *There will be no hesitation here.* Our purpose now more fixed than ever is to prevent the establishment of a disgusting slave-empire on our borders, & we shall continue our efforts against all the allies it may enlist, & make our appeal to the civilized world.

We have bad news from Vicksburg,[4] & the Presdt expects bad news from Charleston; but we are not disheartened. These are the vicissitudes of war. Our people are now more than ever united & determined. The rebels are enfeebled & famished. There is no person in the Administration who doubts the results. Our only present anxiety comes from England. If England were really "neutral" our confidence would be complete.

But this is no contest for "neutrality"; & here is the mistake made at the beginning. It belonged to England, as a leader of Civilization, to declare at once, that a disgusting slave-empire, ready for the slave-trade itself, could not expect fellowship. But the *moral element* has been ignored, & Ld Russell writes irritating letters against those who are in deadly struggle with Slavery. —I hear but one sentiment, whether from the Presdt, his cabinet or members of the Senate (so far as any are here now). I try to tranquilize the sentiment; but I clearly see that, as events now tend, all who talk peace, will be powerless.

The Trent affair was not in this age a *casus belli*. I never so regarded it, & was always convinced that it must be adjusted. But I cannot see our present difficulties in this light. If English vessels are permitted to destroy our commerce, so that it will cease to exist, there is an event which in itself must have great consequences; among which will be the inevitable *contre-coup*. That of England will disappear next, & this world of ours will be topsy-turvy. Whatever may be the vicissitudes I am sure that at last Freedom must prevail. And this is my consolation, as I cast this gloomy horoscope. —

Let me hear from you fully, & believe me dear Mr Bright,

Ever sincerely Yours,   Charles Sumner

ALS   GBL   (76/525, PCS)

1. Two letters from Lord John Russell to Charles Francis Adams on 9 March 1863 stated that no evidence existed that the Liverpool shipbuilding was "in direct hostility to the United States" and that Great Britain "entirely disclaim all responsibility for any acts of the Alabama" (*Foreign Relations* [1863], 1:143–45).

2. On 8 March Lincoln approved a memo from Seward to Lord Lyons protesting further British shipbuilding of Confederate ships (*Lincoln Day by Day*, ed. Earl S. Miers [1960], 3:172).

3. Welles prepared on 31 March a letter to Seward stating his objection to issuing letters of marque and discussed his objections with Lincoln on 2 April (*Diary of Gideon Welles*, ed. Howard K. Beale [1960], 1:252–59).

4. In a dispatch dated 6 April from Vicksburg, the *New York Times* correspondent reported that the U.S. forces were "as far from taking possession of Vicksburg as when we landed here" in January (16 April 1863:1).

To Samuel Gridley Howe

Washington 9th April '63

My dear Howe,

(1) The Secy liked the idea of letting the freedmen here be guarded by men of their own color, in uniform, & he proposed to request Genl. Dix to put uniforms on a hundred at Fortress Munroe.

(2) He thought that any superintendent, who did not do all he could to encourage & elevate the freedmen should be dismissed, especially if he seemed to nurse them for emigration.

(3) It is impossible to give your Comrs. the power to require copies of papers. This would enable them to interfere with public business. I think this is reasonable.

The Secy wished to know when you would all be ready for work. I said—"next Monday."[1]

I have yr letter this morng. The Presdt. since you left has been absent with the army.[2] Meanwhile another arrival from England shews no change.—I have written this week very earnestly to important quarters. I am determined to keep the peace, if possible, & then, if war must come, to appeal to the Civilized World.

God bless you!

Ever Yours, Charles Sumner

ALS MH-H (64/244, PCS)

1. Howe replied from Boston 14 April 1863 that although there had been some delays, the American Freedmen's Inquiry Commission was working on framing questions and securing staff. He continued, "When we shall, to any considerable extent, trust blacks; uniform them; arm them; pay them, & trust them altogether as *free* men,—they will believe that our war is to result in their good,—& they will make those in slavedom believe it" (76/546, PCS).

2. Lincoln was in Fredericksburg conferring with Major General Joseph Hooker (1814–79), now in command of the Army of the Potomac.

To John Bright
private

Washington
12th April '63

Dear Mr Bright,

I took yr speech of the 26th to the Presdt yesterday,[1] & found with him the Secy of the Navy & the officers of the Keokuk, just arrived from Charleston. He had already read it with delight & gratitude, & so I gave my copy to "old Neptune" as he calls Mr Welles.

The iron-clads stood very well the English shot directed upon them by the slave-mongers at Charleston. The captain of the Keokuk says that there never before in the history of war was such a storm of shot, of unprecedented force, all fresh from English manufacturers.[2] If the slave-mongers gained anything on that day from shot, give the credit to England.

The difficulty was in the obstruction of the harbor, which kept the vessels in the fiery focus. Had these been removed they could have pushed forward.

I have just come from the Presdt, *who is more hopeful* now than a fortnight ago. He thinks the quality of the ships is now known, & that the obstructions can be removed.

But what power can remove the obstructions interposed by yr Govt. to justice when asked by the U. States? We have read the debates of the 26th. Ld Palmerston makes me despair.—Ld Russell's previous speech was in the right direction.[3] To that [complexion?] they must all come at last. The slave-mongers cannot be admitted as a *new State*; & let this be declared at once, & then the doom of Slavery will be fixed. It seems to me that this is the single point, &, if the discussion be held close to this point, not even Palmerston can escape. But why do I deal in such suggestions to you, my master—*maestro mio*—Good Bye!

Ever sincerely Yours,   Charles Sumner

ALS   GBL   (76/535, PCS)

1. In "The Struggle In America," given to the Trades' Unions of London 26 March 1863, Bright called the Civil War a stuggle between "freedom or slavery, education or ignorance." He vowed that, despite certain leaders who were "hostile or coldly neutral," working men of Britain would support the Union cause (John Bright, *Speeches on Questions of Public Policy*, ed. James E. T. Rogers [1878], 124–28).

2. After heavy bombardment from both sides, the U.S. Navy abandoned its attempt to take Charleston on 7 April. The *Keokuk*'s commander was Alexander C. Rhind (1821–97).

3. On 27 March Palmerston declared that the British government had "done all that the law enabled or permitted us to do" and thus could not seize the *Alabama* before it left Liverpool. Palmerston also stated, "Wherever any political party, whether in or out of office in the United States, finds itself in difficulties it raises a cry against England, as a means of creating what in American language is called political 'capital.'" On 23 March Russell said that, although he was not certain the North would succeed, it would "be a failure of friendship on our part if at this moment we were to interpose and recognise the Southern States." He advised against

any European intervention in the struggle, stating the U.S. and the Confederacy should settle their conflict themselves (*Hansard's Parliamentary Debates*, 3rd series, 170:90–94; 169:1734–41).

To John A. Stevens, Jr.
private

Washington 19th April '63

My dear Sir,

Do with my letter what you please—in whole or in part.[1] I have no desire to express. But events since it was written, in which I have taken a part, give an additional interest to the discussion.

The subject has been much considered here, & for sometime I saw the Presdt upon it daily, & at his request members of his cabinet. My counsel was to hold England to her duty, not to let the pirate ships leave her ports, & in this sense I have written private letters to England, setting forth the inevitable consequence of her continued madness.

But the essential complement of this policy was that we should carefully avoid any step that might give England an apology for her outrageous conduct. On this account especially I deprecated at this moment the whole idea of Letters of Marque.

I have no recollection of the passage to which you refer,[2] except that I alluded to what seemed to me a happy omission in yr pamphlet; but I am at a loss to conceive that I could have said any thing which could disturb a single commercial feather. But do with this & all the rest as you please, & believe me always earnest for our country's rights[3] & also

very faithfully yours,   Charles Sumner

ALS   NNHi   (76/565, PCS)

1. John A. Stevens, Jr. (1827–1910), a New York City financier and member of New York's Chamber of Commerce, wrote CS on 17 April 1863 (New York, 28/239, PCS), agreeing to print "in some of our journals" a letter CS had written him on 17 March opposing letters of marque (76/557).

2. In his 17 April letter Stevens had suggested that a paragraph in CS's original letter be "modified"; in the paragraph CS had stated it was a "good omen" that reference to the Chamber of Commerce's support for letters of marque was omitted from the chamber's pamphlet. CS agreed to the deletion (to Stevens, 22 April 1863, 76/586) and his letter was published in the New York *Evening Post* (22 April 1863:1; also Wks, 11:313–15).

3. Responding on 25 April, Stevens informed CS that many New Yorkers agreed with CS that it was essential not to give Great Britain "the least pretext for that intervention which she seeks occasion for" (28/270).

To Richard Cobden

Washington 21st April '63

My dear Cobden,

I have yr letter of 2nd April. We are more tranquil now than when I wrote before & are settling down in the assurance that England will not be guilty of the madness inconceivable of making war for slave-mongers.[1] Her course has been bad—very bad. I write frankly; I can not help it.

I did not fail to note the needless complication in Mr A's despatch,[2] & had already called attention to it.

Meanwhile our policy is pacific & prudent. The folly of Letters of Marque has recd its quietus at least for the present. Mr Seward was its author & trumpeter. But he never saw all its bearings.

Some of our Govt. were against any further action by our officers or agents in Europe for the arrest of the guilty ships, feeling that the English Govt. was bound to stop them; that evidently it was not intended to stop them; that we ought not to expose ourselves to further insults; & that the English Govt should be left to take its own course, with all the responsibilities incident to it. On the other hand I insisted, that, while I could not doubt the obvious duty of the English Govt, yet, in a question of peace or war, I would not stand on any form, & that I would employ agents, & attorneys, & set in motion the judicial tribunals, & in short do what we did not doubt it was the duty of the English Govt to do in order to arrest the ships. This policy has been substantially adopted. Mr Evarts,[3] who stands at the head of the bar, is sent to London, in order to put himself in communication with the Law Officers of the Crown, &, in other respects to act professionally, according to his discretion for the U. States. I hope that his visit will help the relations between our countries. God knows they need help enough!

I shall give him a letter to you. He is a friend of Seward's, & aspire, with the favor of the latter, to be his successor in the Senate. But he has never been in public life & is only known professionally.

Our news from Vicksburg is good. It is understood that our fleet has run by the batteries where it can effect a junction with the fleet ascending. The Secy of the Navy does not give up the idea of taking Charleston. There is another assault in contemplation.

I have sent you through our Legation the *Congressional Globe*—5 vols. 4to (don't be frightened!)—our *Hansard*—containing the debates of the called session of July '61 & the long session of 61 & 62. I shall send you the two vols for the session just closed, as soon as they are printed.

You will find the materials there for the history of the propositions which have occupied the attention of this important Congress.

But never tolerate the idea of recognition for a Nation of Slave-Mongers. On this I stand!

Ever sincerely Yours,   Charles Sumner

ALS   GBWSR   (76/576, PCS)

1. Cobden wrote from London that upon receiving CS's letter of 16 March 1863 he had urged Lord Russell to "be more than passive in enforcing the law respecting the building of ships for the Confederate Government. I especially referred to the circumstance that it was suspected that some ships pretending to be for the Chinese Government were really designed for that of Richmond,—& I urged him to furnish Mr Adams with the names of all the ships building for China & full particulars of where they were being built.—This Lord R. tells me he had already done, & he seems to promise fairly" (28/174, PCS). On 6 April Russell ordered that the Confederate warship *Alexandra* be held in Liverpool, not released to the Confederates.

2. Cobden wrote that while the British government could stop the sale of a ship built for another government, it could not prevent arms being sold from one private British business to a private Confederate one. Thus he regretted Adams's protesting these transactions in his dispatch of 30 December 1862 to Lord Russell (*Foreign Relations* [1863], 1:38–44). Cobden advised CS, "Do not let it be supposed that you have any grievance against us for selling *munitions of war*. Confine the question to the building of ships."

3. William Maxwell Evarts (1818–1901), a New York attorney, later U.S. attorney general, 1868–69.

To William E. Gladstone

Washington

21st April '63

My dear Mr Gladstone,

I cannot forget yr kindness to me nor the pleasant hours which you gave me down to that last moment when you left me in the Hansom cab on the night before I started for home.

You are much occupied, but I trust that you will be able to see Mr Evarts, who visits England, at the request of our Govt, & with the good will of Ld Lyons, to contribute his professional knowledge to the removal of difficulties which seem to beset the relations of our two countries. At our bar he is without a superior, &, I am sure that he will do all in his power for that Peace which you value so truly.

I fear that I have not thanked you for the little book which you sent me. Both for itself & as a souvenir I value it much.

You will pardon me if I add, that, amidst all the seeming uncertainties of our affairs here, I cannot doubt that Peace will at last be established on the overthrow of Slavery. It is Slavery that is our only Disunionist. Believe me, with much regard,[1]

Ever sincerely Yours,   Charles Sumner

ALS GBL (76/581, PCS)

1. Gladstone did not reply until 5 November 1863, stating he had earlier considered CS's letter as only an introduction to Evarts, but on rereading it, he saw it was "more." Referring to CS's last paragraph, Gladstone wrote that in Britain "nearly all consider war against slavery unjustifiable: but all without exception will rejoice, if it should please God that by the war slavery shall be extinguished." He added, "I could go farther & say it will please me much if by the war the Union shall be reestablished," but he regarded such a sentiment "only a shabby way of currying favour with you." Gladstone still feared that the Union's goal was "wholly unattainable" (Hawarden, 29/539, PCS).

To Richard Cobden
private

Washington 26th April '63

My dear Cobden,

We are for the moment tranquil—& confident; not doubting the result.

The Secy of War told me yesterday that he had 800,000 men, on his rolls—all paid to 28th Feb—well clothed & well-fed; also powder & saltpetre housed sufficient for 3 years, even if our ports were closed; 500,000 muskets in our arsenels, & also 50,000 produced monthly. But better still we have a *policy*, from which there can be no retreat— *Anti-Slavery in every respect*; (1) in the Presdt's Proclamation[1] (2) in the Resolutions of Congress adopted with unequalled unanimity (3) in the speech of our Adgt Genl, an old pro-slavery man, calling upon the Army to welcome negroes to the service.[2] (4) in our communications with Foreign Govts, as all our Ministers have been instructed to read the Congress. Resolutions to the Govts where they reside (5) in the establishment of a Commission, composed of 3 excellent & able men, with secretaries, stenographers &c to visit the seats of Slavery, including the West Indies, & to report what can be done to make the freedmen useful to themselves & to the State. Thank God! our policy is at last fixed.

Meanwhile the feeling towards England has an intensity without bonds, & it is strongest precisely where it was once most sympathetic. The most intelligent, the wealthiest & the Anti-Slavery, are now filled with indignation at the coarseness of her conduct. Nobody here regards it as neutral. Old Mr Binney, the head of our bar, is in the habit of speaking of England—"walking about just now in her neutrality *surtout*."[3] But there is an arrogance in her tone, whether in speech or writing, which is most maddening. I say nothing now of myself. I record the impressions which I note. And yet I do not hesitate to say that, unless Ld Russell meant war, I think his letters most unhappy.— I am tempted to tell you how our imperturbable Presdt felt on reading the Letter about his Proclamation.[4] As he knew nothing of Ld Russell personally & very little of him as a public man, he was not able to make the apologies for him which I could. And yet it was hard. The case was very bad. I doubt if all history shews an instance of a question of such magnitude being treated with such mingled levity & ignorance; for I am sure that he did not intentionally misstate.

A day or two ago, talking with the Presdt on the exasperation which had arisen towards England, I remarked that when the Rebellion was put down, we should have a still more difficult piece of statesmanship to keep from instant war with England. He agreed with me; but he is well-disposed. Besides 500,000 Irishmen said to be enrolled for a war with England, there would be the old Democrats, & now the best people exasperated, embittered, & smarting under a sense of unpardonable wrong. God knows I have tried hard to arrest this. But Ld Russell by his letters & Ld Palmerston by his speeches, renders all who love peace powerless.

I see but one course for England. Let her act upon her Anti-Slavery history, & let the Slave-mongers know that they can expect nothing from her. Say it frankly & openly—the sooner the better. Their only hope is England. It is England that keeps them on their legs. Such a declaration, besides its perfect consistency with the traditional policy of England, would be glorious for her, & I am sure, that it would do more than any thing else to bring back that temper of peace which ought to prevail between our two countries. Perhaps all this is too much to expect. But I will not give it up.[5]

The idea of Letters of Marque has been abandoned.

The *Peterhoff case*[6] is a new trouble. In that I was for leaving it all to the court, there to await judgment without any interference from Govt. I think I am right when I say this was the view of all the Cabinet, except the Secy of State, & of the Presdt too. The Secy, in his reckless ignorance of such things had committed himself to Ld Lyons, & the surrender of the mails was his act. It is much discussed in the papers & has caused feeling in the Cabinet. The Presdt by a duplicate note has invited the Scties of Navy—& of State to furnish him their written opinions on the matter. The former, who is much incensed, has written a very positive paper, which will be in the Presdt's hands to-day. He had intended to push it at the Cabinet tomorrow. Meanwhile Seward has gone on an excursion to *Fortress* Munroe. It is a pretty quarrel, & is only an illustration of what occurs when the helmsman cannot steer.

Adgt Genl. Thomas's speech is an event. He is an old man & useless here. But that speech, from an old Army man, bred in Slavery, is worth every thing.

I hope to leave here soon. We expect the opening of the Mississippi <very soon> immediately—also a victory between here & Richmond;[7] & we are sure that the Rebellion will be crushed. Have faith,

Ever yours,   Charles Sumner

ALS   GBWSR   (76/600, PCS)

1. On 20 April 1863 Lincoln issued a proclamation admitting West Virginia into the Union now that it had fulfilled the requirements for gradually abolishing slavery (CWL, 6:181).

2. The address was given on 8 April to Union soldiers at Lake Providence, Louisiana (Prc, 4:137). Adjutant General Lorenzo Thomas (1804–75), originally from Delaware, had been sent by Secretary of War Stanton to the Mississippi Valley to organize black regiments.

3. "As an overcoat."

4. In his letter of 17 January to Lord Lyons, Lord Russell had stated that the Emancipation Proclamation "makes slavery at once legal and illegal" and called it "a measure of war, and a measure of war of a very questionable kind" (*British Documents*, part 1, series C, 6:137–38).

5. Cobden replied on 22 May, "I called on Ld Russell & read every word of your last long indictment, against him & Ld Palmerston, to him. He was a little impatient under the treatment, but I got through every word" (28/421, PCS).

6. The British ship *Peterhoff*, bound for Mexico, had been captured on 25 February by the Union and taken to New York, where a prize court had been established to deal with matters of restoration and claims. Disagreeing with Welles, Secretary of State Seward had acceded to Lord Lyons's demands that the captured mails be forwarded to their destinations. The Union would thus lose any proof that this mail, as well as other supplies, was ultimately destined for the Confederacy (Stuart L. Bernath, *Squall Across the Atlantic* [1970], 64, 70, 72; *The Diary of Gideon Welles*, ed. Howard K. Beale [1960], 1:266–67, 269–86).

7. On 16 April a Union fleet of eleven vessels had successfully passed Vicksburg, thus strengthening preparations for the land assault on that city. Meanwhile in Virginia, Hooker had moved his troops across the Rappahannock toward the confrontation with Lee's forces.

To Samuel Gridley Howe

Washington 29th April '63

My dear Howe,

I think that it must be well for the commission to work together at first—perhaps in La,—so as to concert a system of operations, & a method of inquiry, which cannot be fixed at once.[1] But after a while, I should think it easy for them to divide into 2 or 3 separate parties, & thus to traverse a wider field. By beginning together you will be able to work separately, because each will have the experience of all.

Major Poor is very earnest that you should have Mr Lord as stenographic clerk. He was with our comttee. on the Conduct of the War[2] more than a year & made himself very useful. He is much in earnest, & understands the importance of a record & how to keep it; also how to take down & write out testimony.—God bless you!

Ever yours,   Charles Sumner

ALS   DLC   (76/621, PCS)

1. Howe wrote CS from Bordentown, New Jersey, on 26 April asking his opinion about expanding the Freedmen's Inquiry Commissioners' responsibilities to different sections of the country. He told CS his view would "have weight" with Howe's colleagues on the commission (76/607, PCS).

2. Established in December 1861, the Joint Committee on Conduct of the War (CS was not a member) was authorized to investigate causes for Federal military defeats.

To Henry W. Longfellow

Washington 29th April '63

Dear Longfellow,

Dante finished![1] "What next?"—Print. There will be work & solace in that to carry you through the war & away from unhappy thoughts. Yes! Print. Don't leave it to yr executor.

You & I have been younger than we are now. Life to me is often very wearisome & dark. All my sunshine is little more than moon-shine.

Therefore, print!

I fear that George's case required the Hospital.[2] It is hard to think so. I hope his friends will be able to visit him there frequently.

The servt. with the horses reported to me again to-day.[3]—But there must be something decisive very soon. Hooker is [nearing?], full of battle.

Ever yours,   Charles Sumner

ALS MH-H (76/625, PCS)

    1. Longfellow wrote CS from Cambridge 27 April 1863 that he had finished his translation of Dante, and asked his friend, "What next?" (76/611, PCS).

    2. Reporting on his recent visit to George Sumner, Longfellow regretted that he needed to be hospitalized.

    3. Charles Appleton Longfellow (1844–93), Longfellow's oldest child, was then serving with the Army of the Potomac on the Rappahannock, and Longfellow wrote that he had sent Charles, thanks to CS's assistance, a servant and two horses.

To Francis Lieber

Washington 3d May '63

My dear Lieber,

    Of course I always listen to you—especially on any topic within the domain of history or public law—with the disposition to assent at once. You conquer as soon as you come upon the ground. And Mr Binney has an authority peculiar to himself also.[1] You know that I have always regarded him as the first lawyer our country has produced. Others may have had as much law; but none have had as much of every thing which makes the consummate lawyer.

    And yet I must say frankly that I think you are both mistaken in yr judgment of Ld Lyons. If you had expressed regret that the British Minister had not openly & magnanimously declared his sympathy with our cause, I should agree with you. I regret it much.

    But you speak of him as "tampering with our enemies"—& "holding covert intercourse with disloyal men"; & this very serious charge is founded on his receiving New York Democrats, perhaps John Van Buren & Horatio Seymour,[2] immediately after their triumph at the polls last autumn, while he listened to their complaints & theories. If these men at that time talked of peace & of mediation, they did nothing more than they had done at public meetings, & in newspapers, with the acquiescence if not sympathy of many calling themselves Republicans. This is melancholy; but it is the fact. Our Govt. has never proceeded against them; nor has any body suggested such proceedings.

    But any well-founded criticism of Ld Lyons must assume that these Democrats were guilty of something beyond political obliquity.

I take it that no publicist will now question that a Foreign Minister may cultivate relations with a Constitutional Opposition—in countries where constitutions exist; that he may listen to its opinions & its plans, &, through its leaders, inform himself. This at least has been the habit in France, England & the U. States. From the time I took my seat in the Senate, when I was almost alone, & in the Administration journals often denounced as a traitor, I had such relations with the Foreign Ministers here, especially of England & France. I think that they were more intimate with me than with any supporters of the Administration, &, I assure you, I never failed to talk my treason to them. But I never supposed that they in this way made themselves obnoxious to censure.

Had I been a revolutionist—an "enemy"—or "disloyal," they could not have listened to me; but so long as my conversation was on topics, which entered into the differences of party, they were free to listen, as I was free to talk.

Last autumn the opponents of the Administration reached the verge of disloyalty. Just at that moment, when a popular election had seemed to sanction their ideas, Ld Lyons arrived, & he listened to them, & reported what they said.

Do you remember that old Wiquefort[3] says of the Perfect Ambassador, that he has two characters, first that of Minister of Peace & secondly, that of an Honorable Spy? I doubt if it can be said that his lordship was not a little of both at this time. But I am at loss to see how it can be said that he transgressed.

When the *revolutionists* of Rome called upon the French Ambassador, Joseph Bonaparte,[4] in 1797, to announce the revolution at hand, he replied—que la place que j'occupais auprès du souverain de Rome, ne me permettait point d'entendre tranquillement une semblable ouverture. Ils reprirent, qu'ils voulaient avoir mon conseil, et savoir si le gouvernement français protegeait leur revolution, une fois faite. Je leur dis;—*que spectateur impartial des événemens, je rendrais compte à mon gouvernement de ce qui se passait; je ne pouvais avoir autre chose à dire dans le moment.* etc—que comme ministre français je leur enjoignais de ne plus se présenter chez moi avec de telles intentions." It seems to me that this incident, which you will find in the last of the *Causes Celebres* of Charles Martens's Collection,[5] exhibits two points clearly; (1) not to listen to revolutionists (2) to report to his Govt. what as an impartial spectator the Minister may obtain.

There are old privileges which are now abandoned; for instance, the right of asylum, which made the Embassy a retreat for revolutionists or criminals. Nor would any one claim now what is made the subject of a whole chapter by Wiquefort, with this frank title, *Il est permis à l'Ambassadeur de corrompre les Ministres de la Cour ou il negocie.*[6] But I do not think you can deny the Minister frank intercourse with all persons, not really disloyal, on questions of public policy, that he may acquire the means for informing his Govt. at home.

It is not fair to say in reply, that the course of the Democrats was fatal to the Republic. You & I think so, & history will record it; but I doubt not that many sincerely thought our course fatal. It is enough that the difference between us, owing to our public calamities, had become a *party difference.* Thank God! this day has passed.

But there is another piece of Statesmanship, difficult as any we have had;—*to keep from war with England.* For success here, we must avoid dropping any new ingredients into the cauldron. And this is why I trouble you with my dissent.[7]—Bon jour!

Ever Sincerely Yours, Charles Sumner

P.S. Suppose the Duc de Noailles,[8] the French Ambassador in London, before France acknowledged our Independence, had recd. the visits of the Marquis of Rockingham, Ld Chatham, Mr Burke, Mr Fox, & Mr Wilks, I can well imagine the anger of George 3d, who knew little of law or Constitution; but I doubt if Lord North[9] would have complained.

Of course, in entertaining such relations, the Minister expresses himself to the dislike of the Govt. in power, &, it will be for him a question of tact & policy, to determine how far he can go without impairing the influence which he ought to preserve. But no constitutional Govt. will deny him this intercourse.

private

P.S. no 2—I do not differ from you with regard to the State Department. The present incumbent wants good sense & also a knowledge of International Law. His course about the Peterhoff has been a most wretched blunder of ignorant egotism, ready to sacrifice his country to save his own consistency. There is a history here which I may, perhaps, give you, when we meet.

I have always thought McLellan incapable as a general, & without any sentiment for Liberty. This is his mystery. Both were needed.

There is no doubt here about Hooker. He told Judge [*Edward*] Bates, at the time of the visit with the Presdt, that he did not mean to drive the enemy "but to bag him." It is thought he is now doing it.

ALS   MH-H   (64/252, PCS)

1. Lieber wrote CS several times criticizing Lord Lyons's conduct, for Lieber believed that Lyons should have refused to meet with leading Democrats and listen to criticism of the U.S. war efforts. In his letter of 19 April 1863 Lieber stated: "This occurrence belongs to the large class of facts which show, and have shown for the last 250 years, that monarchies always treat republics as incomplete governments, unless guns and bayonets and commercial advantages prevent them from doing so." With his most recent complaint he enclosed a letter from Horace Binney agreeing with Lieber's view (see letters of 19, 24, and 25 April, 76/561, 588, 592, PCS).

2. Horatio Seymour (1810–86), governor of New York.

3. Abraham van Wicquefort (1606–82), *L' Ambassadeur et ses Fonctions*, 1681.

4. Joseph Bonaparte (1768–1844).

5. "That the place that I occupied in the service of the Roman sovereign did not permit me to listen calmly to such an overture. They went on to say that they wished to have my advice and to know if the French government would protect their revolution, once accomplished. I told them that as an impartial spectator of events I would render an account to my government of what was happening; I could not say anything more at the moment, etc.—that as French minister I enjoined them to come to me no longer with such intentions." Karl von Martens (1790–1863), *Causes célèbres du droit des gens*, 2nd ed., 1858–61.

6. "The ambassador is allowed to corrupt the court ministers or he negotiates."

7. Lieber replied after reading CS's "long, kind and disagreeing letter" that he was "far from grumbling with your dissent" (7 May, 77/011).

8. Emmanuel Marie Louis de Noailles (1743–1822).

9. Frederick North (1732–92), prime minister under George III.

To William H. Seward

F St—9th. May '63

My dear Secretary,

I seem to have offended you. If so, most unintentionally.

After conversing at some length on our relations abroad, while you spoke with freedom & listened to me kindly, I turned to speak of the latest incident, affecting our relations with France, whose Govt. I had special reason to believe felt wounded.[1] Believing most sincerely that the quicker the question was settled by a frank explanation, without any delay, I said so. It was with true pleasure that I learned that you thought so too, & had already acted accordingly.

I then remarked that it seemed to me important for us at Paris & at London to have new Secretaries of Legation; that I had no personal interest in any candidates for the place, but that I spoke simply for the public interest, which would be promoted at each place by an accomplished, substantial Secretary, who would do credit to the country in social & business intercourse, & be a friend & companion of the minister. From your manner, & the nature of yr criticism, I inferred that, in yr opinion, I erred in making the suggestion; especially as I did not take into view the political claims of the two Secretaries.[2]

Perhaps I exaggerate the importance of good Secretaries at Paris & London; but knowing something of both those places, I think not.

At all events, I pray you to consider that, in making the suggestion, I supposed that I was saying nothing in any way unwelcome to you, or inconsistent with those habits of conversation which had prevailed between us.[3]

Faithfully Yours,   Charles Sumner

ALS   NRU   (77/o15, PCS)

1. The French government expressed concern over Charles Francis Adams's granting of a letter of credit to an American adventurer, General Zirman, to ship arms to Mexico, interpreting this act as encouragement to the Mexican resistance to France. The American minister in France, William L. Dayton, described the concern in a letter to Seward of 24 April 1863, and Seward answered it 8 May (*Foreign Relations* [1863], part 1:659–60, 665–66).

2. Gideon Welles recorded that CS told him that "Seward flew into a passion" when CS mentioned replacing the present secretary, Charles L. Wilson, who had reportedly abused the British publicly (13 May, *Diary of Gideon Welles*, ed. Howard K. Beale [1960], 1:300–301).

3. Seward's reply reads as follows: "I shall very cheerfully explain to you the cause of the impatience which I betrayed on the occasion to which you allude. Perhaps it may turn out that there was something of fault on both sides" (Washington, 12 May, 28/361, PCS).

To the Duke of Argyll
private

Washington
10th May '63

My dear Duke,

I was glad of yr letter, because I know that you could not have written it, if yr Govt. meant war with us. I am sure of you, as a peace-maker, & I know no better title.

If I answer frankly some of yr suggestions, it is from no purpose of controversy, but simply in the interest of that cause which made you write.

There are two general propositions in your letter, which have my cordial assent, & I doubt if any body here differs from me.

One of these is where you say, that the moment a war becomes *hopeless*, it becomes wrong.[1] For myself, I tremble to assert that war is not wrong, unless in a case of *strict self-defence*. But our war is not *hopeless*; nor has any thing been done beyond the requirements of *self-defence*.

I know intimately all the members of Govt., & have conversed with them often on their inmost convictions, & I assure you that there is not one who entertains any doubt of our success; & this confidence is not impaired by any reverses yet experienced. We all believe that, there can be but one end to the war,—sooner or later; & that is the triumph of the Govt., & the establishment of Peace on the extinction of Slavery. Adverse influences from Europe may postpone this day; may multiply our trials & increase bloodshed. But the great result will not be changed. *Therefore*, the war is not *hopeless*. ["*no reason given*"][2]

The other general proposition of yr letter, which has my cordial assent, is where you say that we must keep ourselves within the recognized limits of International Law.[3] Nobody here questions this duty. Our only desire is that England may be as true to International Law as Mr Cobden has shewn the U. States to have been,[4] & as we now most sincerely mean to be. Bring our acts, one or all, to this touch-stone, & we shall abide the result. If our cruizers now seem to disturb yr commerce, I ask you to look at the six vols of Robinson, & the two vols of Dodson[5]—to say nothing of other sources—& see how cautious & moderate they have been compared with the juridical scourge upon our commerce which is there recorded. Nothing is done now without the sanction of British precedents, which Ld Russell tells us will not be disowned.

But I cannot forget that International Law is too often like the shield which is read differently on the two opposite sides, & with equal honesty in the two. ["*quite true*"] For instance, England considered the taking of two men from the Trent, as a *casus belli* according to International Law, & made preparations for war. Nobody here, who had studied International Law, had for a moment this idea. To most it seemed monstrous, that, according to International Law, an accident, founded on an honest interpretation of the Law, & really involving no question of *self-defence* (the only apology for war) but simply a question of law, should be made a *casus belli*. A case for a demand, followed, if the demand were denied, by an arbitration; but not a case for bloodshed. Such is our view of International Law, & any other view seems to us a bad example & sad for civilization. But the English Govt. thought differently.

Amidst these differences something is gained if each party will sincerely avow its purpose to follow International Law; but I pray that it may be this law interpreted generously, humanely & in the spirit of Peace. Otherwise it is only a phrase which we use.

And now, passing from these observations on the general propositions of yr letter, let me say, that, when I said that the inevitable
tendency of our relations with England was to war,[6] it was precisely
because it seemed, to us here that England had flung aside all regard
for International Law, & all disposition to cultivate International amenities, as shewn in the building [*"not built by 'England' tho' by Englishmen"*]
of pirate ships to cruize against our commerce, & in the tone of Ld
Russell's letters.

Of course, I never supposed that the mere building a ship for a
belligerent was a violation of Law; but this is not the present case. *Ships
of war* [*"How defined? She was not armed in England"*] have been built in
England; this is something, but not all. These ships have been manned
by Englishmen, who have been enlisted [*"not with knowledge or consent of
Govt."*] in England; & have then sallied forth to destroy our commerce.
You will see at once the difference between a *commercial venture* [*"But it
was a [purely?] commercial venture on the part of the shipbuilder"*] & *a hostile
act.* And it was because Ld Russell shewed a complete indifference to
this *hostile act*, &, public report said that this *hostile act* was to be
repeated ten or twenty times, even indefinitely, that I felt our relations
to be most critical.

Of course, I asked no question about yr Enlistment Act.[7] That is
your affair not ours. It was enough, that you were violating International Law, which both of us recognize. [*"I agree that it is an international
obligation to prevent such acts—if we can—"*] The sailing of those ships
would be on yr part a Declaration of War against us, as much as [*"not
quite"*] the bombardment of Copenhagen or the seizure of the Spanish
galleons. Assuming that they are what public report says, & considering the amount of commerce involved, they would be more deadly than
either of these acts, &, I think, full as much open to condemnation.

If one nation can allow its ports & dock-yards to become the nurseries
of belligerent activity against a friendly power, & all for the sake of
Slavery, it seems to me we may as well renounce International Law, &
all its gathered justice & wisdom, & adopt the code of the Feejee Islands. [*"I entirely agree in this"*]

You allude also to what I said about the "tone" of Ld Russell's letters.[8]
A letter can never justify war; no matter how rude. But you know well
that letters unhappily written may add to bad feelings at a moment
when international relations are in a painful condition. Read for instance Mr Canning's[9] despatches of 1808 & 9—as brilliant as any he
ever wrote; but honest history is obliged to class them among the
influences, which produced that exasperation that ended in the war of
1812 between England & the U. States. They did not shew their fatal

fruit for several years. Admiring Lord Russell, as I did, it was with amazement that I perused his correspondance. It seemed to me that it shewed a desire to provoke war or a conviction that war had already come. An acute foreign diplomatist here tells me that I should have thought of "Buncombe"; but I did not. To me it is inconceivable that a statesman, guarding the peace of nations, should scatter words, which may produce or quicken international strife.

Lord Russell for some time has been in the position of a person pledged against our success. This was unfortunate, & its influence naturally gave an *unneutral* character to his correspondance. What he has said latterly, especially the speech in reply to Ld Clanricarde[10]—bating the exaggeration about the *accident* of the certificate—has been unexceptionable in its tone.

There are many here who have felt these things keenly, & none more keenly than the true friends of England. You have increased the difficulties & responsibilities of our position, & helped to make us powerless. ["*powerless as regards what?*"] There are men who keep a "bill of particulars" of all that is done or said by England, which ought not to be done or said, &, sooner or later, they will insist upon a complete liquidation of the account. For God's sake, &, in the name of Peace, let the items be kept as few as possible. I do not now enter into the question of British liability for every ship captured or burned by the Alabama. I note that learned Professors in England bravely assert the liability of their country.[11] Read their noble speeches & then read Ld Russell's correspondance, including his yet unpublished note,[12] where the denial is repelled with a sting. When the sum-total of her havoc is known, & the mists of passion have ceased to obscure those principles of justice which are to nations of perpetual obligation, I shall be glad to listen to Ld Russell's judgment upon this question.

This Rebellion will be crushed. But I look to a more anxious day, when, in the consciousness of power, our people shall review the conduct of England, while 500,000 Irishmen, & all the Democracy insist upon war. I can fight against Slavery; but I have no heart for a war with England. Before that evil hour, let my days be ended. And now the best service which I can do to my own country & to that other country where I have so much of friendship garnered up, is to warn you, who can exert so much influence, of the danger which needs yr care.

There is one way, in which a true friendship can be secured. *Let England simply recover her natural, traditional & instinctive position against Human Slavery*, & our two countries will be together. I hope that this may be done before the war is ended, so that our people may be warmed by the sympathetic action. Should our Peace at home find England still sullen & unaccommodating, or sympathetic with slave-mongers, I know not where to look for the safeguards of our future relations.

Ld Russell's [23 March] speech makes it impossible for England to recognize the slave-monger State, & introduce at Court a new slave-monger Minister. If this declaration were made as explicitly as the earlier declaration, that separation was inevitable, involving the establishment of a slave-monger Power, there would be little occasion for further anxiety. But you will see that, if England cannot *recognize* the slave-monger State, she cannot of course, accord to it belligerent rights—on the sea, which is the only place, where she can be brought in contact with it. [*"This is pure nonsense. The recognition of Belligerency is quite a separate thing—from the recognition of Independence the U.S. Govt. itself has recognized the belligerent character of the Rebels"*] There was the first mistake. It is not only because the slave-mongers have no port, *but because they are slave-mongers*, that they can have no recognition, as a nation, & *a fortiori* as a *naval belligerent. It is wrong to accord belligerency* unless you are willing to give them welcome into the Family of Nations. *Ce n'est que le premier pas qui coute.* [13]

You will see that I write you frankly—as you kindly wrote to me—& as I have always written. There must be no war between us. *There cannot be unless you make it.* Our Govt. is fixed for peace. But we entreat you to *adhere closely to International Law, in those requirements which make for peace.* Stop the ships. Let any correspondance between our two Govts. be as if we were friends, & not as if we were enemies or expected soon to be.

I do not suggest any *arbitrary* acts on yr part, but simply a compliance with International Law. [*"There is truth in this—"*] If yr municipal statute is not strong enough, Parlt. can make it stronger. Mr Cobden has shewn that our Congress did not hesitate to do as much for you.

If I were not anxious for harmony between our two countries, I could not have written what I have. I pray you if there is any thing said which ought not to be said, to consider it as *unsaid.* If at any time you think I can be of service in promoting a correct understanding, write to me plainly, & you know that I shall write to you plainly in reply. [14]

I think of you always with affection & beg you to believe me, my dear Duke,

Ever sincerely Yours,   Charles Sumner

P.S. I say nothing of the Peterhoff or any other ships, because these are cases for the Courts, & Ld Russell does not intimate doubts of our tribunals. The writers on International Law testify to their character & authority.

On the receipt of yr letter I saw the Secy of the Navy & proposed a change of Admiral Wilkes.[15] He liked the idea, & said that he had never been in favor of employing him. In the evng, while I was with the Presdt., the Secretary entered, & proposed to him the change. The Presdt. at once assented. It was suggested that an exchange be made between him & the Commander of the Pacific Squadron. I presume it will be done at once.—But you see the Admiral in a strange light. He is a learned, bookish, & gentlemanlike sailor, who means simply to do his duty.

"Europe[16] has had her errors, her hesitations, for which we are paying dearly today on both shores of the Atlantic. *What blood would have been spared to you*, what industrial suffering avoided by us had European opinion declared itself with that force *which you have the right to hope for.*"

"Wonder is expressed that Slavery is abolished in the revolted States & yet preserved in the loyal States!—

"We look with suspicion upon that pretended Abolitionism whose unfriendly exactions were first put forth on the very day illumined in America by the dawn of Abolition.

ALS   CSmH   (77/018, PCS)

1. In his letter from London (24 April 1863 28/251, PCS), Argyll, a member of the British cabinet, had stated, "the moment a war becomes *hopeless*, it becomes wrong; but I have no means of judging when hopelessness can be predicated of it. That responsibility rests with you. I regard your undying confidence with astonishment. But I shld. rejoice to see that confidence justified by the event."

2. Argyll's formal reply to CS is noted below. His penciled marginal comments to CS's arguments are incorporated here in brackets as they occur in CS's letter.

3. Argyll had written CS: "You have no right to expect neutral nations to submit to any infringements of those limits. You will give a handle, and a lever, to the secret aiders and abettors of the Slave cause, if you extend *arbitrary* action beyond the sphere of yr. own municipal law."

4. Speaking in the Parliament 24 April for strict enforcement of Britain's Foreign Enlistment Act, Cobden praised the U.S. for passing its own Foreign Enlistment Act in 1794 and for continuing to uphold the principle of neutrality (*Hansard's Parliamentary Debates*, 3rd series, 170:723–36).

5. Christopher Robinson (1766–1833), *Reports of Cases Argued and Determined in the High Court of Admiralty* (1799–1808), and John Dodson (1780–1858), *Reports of Cases Argued and Determined in the High Court of Admiralty, 1811–22* (1815–28).

6. In his 7 April letter to the duchess of Argyll, to which the duke alluded in his reply of 24 April, CS had written, "On their character & the inevitable tendency of our relations with England, there is but one opinion in the cabinet" (76/519). The duke replied, "if you mean that your Government has any just cause of quarrel against ours,—to justify such acts,—then I must declare my conviction that there is no shadow of such cause, and that if war arises, the blood will be upon the heads of your Govermt. and your People" (28/251).

7. The British government had thus far stated that the recent shipbuilding did not violate their Foreign Enlistment Act, which prohibited the building and arming of warships for any belligerent power.

8. Argyll stated in his 24 April letter, "I am certain there is not one of them which wd. justify even an official protest—far less, hostile acts tending to 'inevitable' war."

9. George Canning (1770–1827), British foreign secretary.

10. In replying to Hubert Burgh Canning, second marquess of Clanricarde (1832–1916), Russell advised caution in dealing with the U.S. over the *Peterhoff* seizure: "let us discuss the circumstances with a wish to do justice to each other. Do not let us be led by passion into anything which is not founded on justice" (23 April, *Hansard's Parliamentary Debates*, 3rd series, 170:560–66).

11. So stated Goldwin Smith (1823–1910; law professor at University College, London) at a meeting in Manchester, 6 April (James Ford Rhodes, *History of the United States from the Compromise of 1850* [1900], 4:370).

12. Probably Russell's letter to Charles Francis Adams of 2 April, in which he stated that the British government could not interfere in commercial dealings between British subjects and the Confederacy (*Foreign Relations* [1863], part 1, 205–7).

13. "It is only the first step that is the most difficult."

14. In his reply from Balmoral, 30 May (28/462), Argyll asked CS, "But has it never occurred to you that the Government as such—your nation as such, is not entitled to hold the same language,—that its object in the war—however legitimate—is inferior to *your* object, as claiming the sympathy of mankind? This is no question in dispute. It is a *fact* that the Govt. fights, not against Slavery—but against rebellion. Quite right to do so, but *this* fight does not claim in the same degree the special sympathies of the world." He closed his letter saying, "We must be *neutral*—but it does not follow that we shld. be *indifferent*. I trust & believe that Peace will be kept."

15. Acting Rear Admiral Charles Wilkes, of *Trent* fame, had ordered the seizure of the *Peterhoff*.

16. The following paragraphs are on a separate page as an enclosure.

To Samuel Gridley Howe

Washington 15th May '63

My dear Howe,

The Secy. says that he has no authority to constitute a new Bureau; but that sometime ago he offered to Fremont the *headship* of the freedmen, to be gathered in camp at Harper's Ferry, where John Brown began.[1]

The Secy has sometime ago adopted the idea of sending Regimental officers, constituting a skeleton, to the South—to be filled by freedmen.

Good bye! God bless you!

Ever yours,   Charles Sumner

ALS   MH-H   (77/040, PCS)

1. Talk of John C. Frémont's heading a regiment of black troops circulated in Washington at this time.

To the Duchess of Argyll

Washington 19th May '63

My dear Duchess,

Yours from Inverary reassures me. I am happy that you are not displeased by my plainness;[1] but I am happier still at the tokens of peace between our two countries.

It has seemed here that the English Govt. meant war, or at least was utterly indifferent to it. And the letters of Ld Russell seem still to shew him utterly *intractable.* For instance, how can one explain that of April 20th about sailors?[2] Nobody has suggested that the U.S. have *enlisted English sailors against England.* A few stragglers may have come among us. The complaint of our Govt is that a "Navy," according to Mr Gladstone,[3] is equipping in England, which supplies ships, guns *& sailors,* to be employed *against our Govt.* for the sake of Slavery.

As I read this letter I feel uncertain with regard to the future. I do not believe in sarcasms between nations or flings. They can do nothing but mischief. If they please certain persons for a moment they must make the judicious grieve.

A wise statesmanship will prevent points or differences between our two countries, which may rise hereafter. My aim is not only to keep the peace now; but to prevent any thing which can be stored up as material for future strife & bitterness. You know enough of human nature to know that unkind words are treasured, & sooner or later, are repaid. Ld Russell teaches our Govt. how to write hereafter,—when our power is again established. There are many who will rejoice to say back all that he now says with interest.

Our Govt. never wished to order ships at Liverpool. The whole story is a fabrication. I have to-day sent to Mr Cobden a letter from our Secy of the Navy denying it point blank.

But I come back to the place where England will yet be. *Suppose we had.* It is one thing to supply ships to an organized Govt. fighting for Civilization & Freedom & to put down a slave-monger State crawling into existence; & a very different thing to supply ships to help build this slave-monger State. One must forget that God is God, not to see the difference; & it has been a fatal mistake that this difference was not at once recognized.

The reports from the South West are cheering. The army of the Potomac is said to be strong & confident.[4] But I look calmly to the Future, rather than to any battle. Other disasters I expect; but *that the Rebellion will be put down I am sure.*

God bless you!

Ever yours,   Charles Sumner

ALS   CSmH   (77/058, PCS)

1. The duchess had written 29 April 1863, "Friendship wd. be a poor thing if it did not make frankness a *necessity*. I have never shrunk from telling you what may have been very disagreeable." She went on to say that the British government "wd be free from any guilt" if war between the two countries resulted. She saw Britain's neutrality policy as a "necessity" (28/290, PCS).

2. Lord Russell wrote Adams 20 April responding to the latter's complaint about British sailors enlisting in the Confederate service; Russell stated that the U.S. had not prevented British subjects from serving in U.S. forces and that, before protesting, Adams should furnish proof that all British subjects had been discharged from U.S. forces (*Foreign Relations* [1863], part 1, 232–33).

3. CS refers to Gladstone's Newcastle speech of 7 October 1862, when the chancellor of the Exchequer said, "There is no doubt that Jefferson Davis and other leaders of the South have made an army; they are making, it appears, a navy; and they have made what is more than either—they have made a nation" (London *Times*, 9 October 1862:7).

4. Having closed in on Vicksburg, Grant's and Banks's armies had begun the siege of the Mississippi River port; in Virginia, the Union army had failed to defeat the Confederates at Chancellorsville, 2–4 May, and Hooker moved his army back across the Rappahannock.

To Richard Cobden

Washington
19th May '63

My dear Cobden,

There seems to be a better feeling on both sides. We begin to feel that you do not mean war with us. But why does Ld Russell write such letters? Can he not be made to see that every one of these letters must be treasured, as so much material for future animosity & all to be repaid with fearful interest like *post-obit* bonds? It may not be in his day; but every new letter adds to the account.[1]

It is not enough to keep the peace now. We must see that there are no occasions of difference left out-standing, no sarcasms which will be remembered only to be hurled back. This is our duty. But yr Foreign Minister makes me sad with regard to the Future. I know too much of public opinion, & of individual opinion, not to see danger ahead. To

Ld Lyons, I say—"Avoid making questions, if possible, & if they must be made, put them in such a form as to leave behind the least possible record or souvenir."

There have been conflicting opinions about our Potomac Army. The latest report from those who have visited it is most encouraging. The army is strong & confident. I think there will be a movement soon. But the rough & wooded character of Va. makes difficulties unknown in Europe. Military men doubt if there can be a decisive battle, where there is no field on which the troops can be marshalled. Happy country, where there is no battle-field!

But I cease to watch very closely single events in this war. It is the result which I keep in view *& this is sure*. I expect further disaster, & now deliberately make up my mind to it. But this can only postpone without changing the final day. Perhaps it is needful in order to carry out the transition which is now in progress.

I send you a letter from Mr Welles, contradicting the statement of Mr Laird, that our Govt. has ordered any war-ships in England.[2] You are welcome to use it in any way you think best. It is thought advisable to bring Commdre W.[*ilkes*] home instead of sending him to the Pacific.

The mail question is still under discussion. The letter of 31st Oct. on which Ld Russell relies was never acted on by the Secy of the Navy, who did not suppose that Mr Seward had any authority on the matter.[3] No instructions on the subject have been given to the Navy. There are some persons who feel that a question very simple & easy of arrangement has been confused by mismanagement. Under our Constitution & laws, it was a question for the court, or for Treaty. I doubt if any body connected with the Govt. has a different opinion, unless it be Mr S.

It seems to me that Maritime Rights must gain by late discussions, & the practical development of hardships. Seward said to me the other day—"This is our last blockade."—I hope so.

Goodbye!

Ever sincerely Yours,   Charles Sumner

It begins to be too hot here & you are tranquil. So I leave in a few days for Boston.

I do not write to Bright by this Steamer, but I owe him a letter.

ALS   GBWSR   (77/060, PCS)

1. Cobden had tried to reassure CS in his letter of 2 May 1863, stating, "If Lord Russells despatches to Mr. Adams are not very civil he may console himself with the knowledge that the Confederates are still worse treated" (London, 28/317, PCS).

2. In the letter CS enclosed (19 May 1863, copy, 77/065) Welles wrote that ship-builder John Laird (1805–74) stated "what was not true" in his Parliament speech of 27 March; neither Welles nor the U.S. Navy had authorized anyone to have ships built abroad for the U.S.

3. Regarding the *Peterhoff* seizure, in a Parliament speech Russell quoted a letter from Seward to Welles, 31 October 1862, which stated that the "public mails of any friendly or neutral Power" discovered on captured merchant vessels would be sent on unopened to their destination. Russell thus contended that the U.S. Prize Commission investigating the *Peterhoff* seizure should comply with Seward's dictum (27 April, *Hansard's Parliamentary Debates*, 3rd series, 170:765).

To Abraham Lincoln

212 F St.   20th May '63

My dear Sir,

I have been horror-struck by the menace of Slavery to our colored troops & of death to the gentlemen who command them, should they fall into the hands of the rebel enemy.

It seems to me that the time has come, when it should be declared to the world, by Presidential Proclamation, in the most solemn form possible, that these officers & soldiers of the U. States will be protected by the Govt. according to the laws of war, & that not one of them shall suffer without a retaliation, which shall be complete; not vindictive but conservative.

Such a Proclamation would give encouragement to the army; it would gratify the country, & it would teach foreign nations the difference between a barbarous foe & the upholders of Human Liberty. Besides, it would be intrinsically an act of justice.

I venture to ask you to think of these things[1] & to believe me, my dear Sir,

very faithfully yours,   Charles Sumner

ALS   DLC   (77/068, PCS)

1. On 30 May 1863 CS presented to the president a committee, which included William Cullen Bryant and Horace Greeley, asking that Frémont be given a command of black troops. In reply Lincoln stated his willingness to receive "not ten thousand but ten times ten thousand" black troops and his wish "to protect all who enlisted." Lincoln said that he "looked to them for essential service in finishing the war" (*New York Tribune*, 1 June 1863:4; CWL, 6:239). Privately Lincoln wrote CS that he "would cheerfully send [*black troops*] to the field under General Fremont," but he could not spare enough white troops to make up a new department (77/107, PCS).

To John Jay
private

Washington 3d July '63

My dear Jay,

I am always glad to hear from you.

I wish you knew our Presdt better. You would then see that we must make the most of what we have.[1]

The Conscript Law has been put in operation in R.I.—Vt & Mass. *The evidence shews that there has been no opposition to enrolment in N.Y.*

Are there not patriot citizens in N.Y. who would speak to Govr Seymour & enlist his good will? Will he let his country be sacrificed.[2]

I do not think there is any disposition to employ McLellan even in drilling troops.[3] I think that the Secy of War would consider such a humiliation of the Govt to the companion of a cashiered officer as the beginning of the end, & that it would only remain for us to settle the terms of separation. Has this major Genl ever uttered a single patriotic voice since our troubles began? I ask for information.

A great battle is now raging,—as I presume. Meade telegraphed his purpose to bring it on.[4]

Hooker asked to be released on account of a difference with Halleck about the evacuation of Harper's Ferry.[5] Meade's first order was for its evacuation, as Hooker had desired.—

I hope to leave here Sunday evng.

Ever yours,   Charles Sumner

ALS   NNCB   (77/167, PCS)

1. Jay wrote CS twice from New York suggesting that Benjamin F. Butler replace Halleck as general of all U.S. armies (29 and 30 June 1863, 28/645, 653, PCS).

2. In his 30 June letter, Jay suggested trying to get Seymour to issue a statement supporting the draft in order to obtain its "quiet enforcement."

3. Jay also recommended recalling McClellan to serve, stating that his name "would assist immensely in making the draft popular."

4. George Gordon Meade (1815–72), who had replaced Hooker as commander of the Army of the Potomac on 27 June, was now leading that army at the Battle of Gettysburg.

5. On 16 June Hooker requested permission to move his army north of Washington to try to stop Lee, but Halleck ordered him to follow Lee and protect Harper's Ferry as well.

To James A. Hamilton

Washington 4th July '63

My dear Sir,

I wish that I could have the opportunity of conversing with you on the topics of yr letter.[1]

I doubt if our condition would be improved by any probable change. We must be careful not "to fly from evils that we have to those we know not of."[2]

Mr Stanton is determined to put this Rebellion down & Slavery also. I believe there have been times when "he has held the bridge" against the enemies of the Republic in the guise of false friends.

As you have left yr letter to my discretion I have thought it best not to speak of it to the Presdt. I fear that no good would come from it.

The news seems to be good.[3]

I shall leave for home at the beginning of the week, glad to be in another atmosphere.

Believe me my dear Sir,

very faithfully Yours,　　Charles Sumner

ALS　NN　(77/171, PCS)

1. James A. Hamilton (1788–1878), a New York lawyer and son of Alexander Hamilton, wrote CS 30 June 1863 from Nevis, New York, asking if CS could initiate the removal of Stanton. He noted how upset the "working classes" were over the draft; they did not want to be "driven into the army to be . . . slaughtered" by administration policies (28/651, PCS).

2. ". . . rather bear those ills we have / Than fly to others that we know not of?" (*Hamlet*, 3.1.81–82).

3. On 3 July Union forces won at both Gettysburg and Vicksburg.

To the Duchess of Argyll

Washington—6th July '63

My dear Duchess,

Our papers are printing extracts from Mrs Butler.[1] There is one thought that haunts me as I read them. Behold the system with which England coquets—to which England accords "*rights*"!!—which England lifts to an *equality* with an established govt. *Neutrality*—that is the English word. Oh! no. There can be no neutrality in such a case. It is all a frightful misapplication of a just principle.

I have been reviewing English history, diplomatic & other, on this subject, going far back. The beautiful form "ends in a fish." I was not aware before how great a departure there has been. I am saddened as I see it; for I have no pleasure in any short-coming or backsliding by England. But my present trust is that the Ministers will review their relations to this war from the beginning. They or at least Ld Russell—have already moderated much with regard to the pirates. Why not more still? They have contributed infinitely to the strength of the Rebellion, &, therefore, of course, to the battle-fields where our people have been mowed down. When will they see the duty of telling the slave-mongers that they are accused & can expect nothing from the British people?

I give to all with whom I correspond the assurance that this war can have but one end; that there can be no hesitation on the part of our Govt, that not a member of it could consent to any separation; & that, therefore, every act or word of encouragement to the rebels tends to bloodshed on a still more colossal scale. Read the daily accounts of battles. Never before did the world sup so full of horrors. Amidst all delays & reverses the cause advances—like the tide against the refluent wave.

The *Times* dwells on Fernando Wood's interview with the Presdt.[2] I tell you what is not known here, but what I had from the Presdt himself, that he *assured the Presdt that he would sustain every appropriation for the prosecution of the war.*

I have not yet read the article on Ld Canning. It will be the *bonne bouche* for my first hour of leisure.[3] At last my *paquets* are made, & I quit Washington tomorrow.

Will Tennyson print soon? And how is Mrs Norton?[4] Do not be offended by my plainness. But I do long to have English people see the war aright. To this end I am willing almost to be rude. God bless you!

> Ever sincerely yours & the Duke's   Charles Sumner

ALS CSmH (77/173, PCS)
Enc: unidentified newspaper clipping

1. CS had attached to his letter a clipping, apparently an excerpt from Fanny Kemble's *Journal of a Residence on a Georgia Plantation in 1838–39*, which had just been published. He underlined the sentence, "Think, E——, how it fares with slaves on plantations where there is no crazy Englishwoman to weep, and entreat, and implore, and upbraid for them." Underneath CS wrote, *"Mrs Butler,"* and beside the clipping wrote "Oh! for a few 'crazy Englishwomen' at home in England!" Replying to CS's remark on Fanny Kemble's protestation against slavery, the duchess wrote, "Whatever happens remember your Union *did* uphold it; thank God for the loosing

of those chains upon your necks, and trust Him to do more in his own way" (London, 23 July 1863, 28/725, PCS).

2. Peace Democrat Fernando Wood (1812–81; U.S. congressman [N.Y.], 1863–65, 1867–81) had met with Lincoln on 5 June. The London *Times* interpreted this meeting as a sign that the peace and compromise movement was gaining support with the administration, that Lincoln would favor peace "if he knew how to reach it. Perhaps this meeting may show him the way," wrote the *Times*, and both sides could agree to "reasonable terms of separation" (19 June 1863:9).

3. The duchess had recommended in her letter of 26 March (Kensington, 28/130) that CS read "India under Lord Canning" by her husband in the April 1863 *Edinburgh Review* (117:229–57). *Bonne bouche*, "tidbit."

4. Caroline Sheridan Norton (1808–77), poet.

To the Duchess of Argyll

Boston 14th July '63

My dear Duchess,

At last I am away from Washington—glad enough for I am very weary.

The papers report our battles, which seem never to end. Alas! England has just again blown her bellows. The papers to-day give a telegraphic report of the debate of 30th June.[1] Of course every word in that debate, which did not pronounce the rebel slave-mongers accursed & not to be tolerated in the Family of Nations is a fresh encouragement to a hideous crime—take it all in all the greatest of history. That every Englishman does not see it so is incomprehensible.

As I stopped in New York I saw several whose devotion & love to England have known no bounds. They all feel bitterly what she has done & left undone. We have all been obliged to give up some of our most cherished illusions. But there is a Providence shaping these mighty events, & I believe justice will be done. How sadly I read the [mere?] abstract of Mr Gladstone.[2] He is one whom I cannot resign. But all these debates & prophesies have but one result; they cause more slaughter, quicken the work of death, rob our mothers of their children & elevate for yet a little longer the crime of Slavery. *They cannot prevail.* They are impotent except to aggravate our trials. But what a calamity!—

I notice that Ld Russell has again spoken unhappily. He has a fling at our Prize Judges.[3] Now, at this moment, there is no person on the bench in England who brings to that class of questions as much aptitude & talent as Judge [*Peleg*] Sprague of Boston. I do not except Dr [*Stephen*] Lushington, for Sprague is his equal in talent & is still in the freshness of his powers.

I await with anxiety the full report of the debate of 30th June,—to see how Justice & Liberty fared on that day. Reviewing minutely as I have latterly the course of England & Englishmen, I have found more than ever occasion for sorrow. The case looks worse the more you look at it.—But it is hard for me to write these things. And yet I desire you to see how we cannot help seeing England. I enclose a letter from an *Anglomane*, which contains a parenthetic allusion to England shewing how we feel.—Good bye!—

Ever sincerely Yours,   Charles Sumner

Thanks for yrs of 21st June. How Channing would have sorrowed for England![4]—

ALS   CSmH   (77/188, PCS)

1. The *New York Times* (13 July 1863:1,2) carried an account of the parliamentary debate over John A. Roebuck's motion to recognize the Confederacy; his motion failed.

2. Gladstone opposed recognition but stated he did not believe restoration of the Union was possible (ibid.).

3. Speaking on the *Peterhoff* case, Russell said in Parliament, 15 June 1863, that he regretted that the case would not be tried directly by the highly respected U.S. Supreme Court but instead by lower courts; "it is to be lamented that there should be a considerable delay" until the case could be appealed to the Supreme Court (*Hansard's Parliamentary Debates*, 3rd series, 171:882–83).

4. In her letter the duchess asked CS what William Ellery Channing would have thought of the struggle to preserve the Union; she believed that the Fugitive Slave Law would have made the Union "intolerable to him" (London, 28/597, PCS).

To John Bright

Boston 21st July '63

dear Mr Bright,

I have read the debate of 30th June. Yr last words[1] touched the whole question to the quick. The guilt of this attempt is appalling; but next to the slave-mongers is England, with a grinning neutrality.

My friend Mr Gladstone[2] dealt with the whole question as if there was no God.

Englishmen may doubt. I tell you, *there can be but one end to this war.* I care not for any temporary success of the slave-mongers; they must fail. But English sympathy is a mighty encouragement. Even doubts tell for them. There can be no doubt.

You will note our successes in the South West.[3] Every thing there is against the Rebellion. There is pretty good reason to believe that Charleston will soon be ours. Lee's army has lost 30,000 men; & I am inclined to think now must be much demoralized. *We are too victorious.* I fear more from our victories than our defeats.

If the Rebellion should suddenly collapse, democrats, copperheads & Seward would insist upon amnesty & the Union & "no questions asked about Slavery." God save us from any such calamity. If Lee's army had been smashed, that question would have been upon us. Before this comes, I wish 200,000 negroes with muskets in their hands, & then I shall not fear compromise. *Time is essential.* So great a revolution cannot come to a close at once.

By next Steamer we send you Mr Whiting, an admirable lawyer *in the full confidence of the Presdt*, & my personal friend, agreeing with me positively in policy & object—to take the place of Mr Evarts,—to advise our Minister, to confer with yr Crown lawyers & govt, & to state our case. *Nobody in England from here* has known so much of the intimate opinions of our Govt. or of its policy. He has been the legal adviser of our War Depat. I send you a pamphlet by him.[4] I hope that he may have good opportunities. Pray announce his visit to Cobden & Forster.[5] He is amiable, social & true as steel on Slavery, determined that the war shall end only with Slavery.—I long to write you about our cabinet, in reply to yrs of 27th June.[6] I wish we could sit together on the sea-shore.

Ever Yours,   Charles Sumner

The Presdt promised to take care of yr Birmingham boy.[7]

ALS   GBL   (77/196, PCS)

   1. In his speech Bright stated that the goals of the Civil War were still in God's hands; no one now knew if the war would "give freedom to the race which, for generations past, white men have trampled in the dust." He concluded, "I beseech this House, that my country may lift nor hand nor voice in aid of the most stupendous act of guilt that history has recorded in the annals of mankind" (*Hansard's Parliamentary Debates*, 3rd series, 171:1826–38).
   2. Gladstone described the South as offering a "resistance as heroic as ever has been offered . . . on the part of a weaker body against the overpowering & vastly superior forces of a stronger" and expressed his sympathy with the "exalted visions" of those forming the Confederacy (ibid., 1800–1812).
   3. The Mississippi River, completely under Federal control, was open to navigation.
   4. William Whiting (1813–73), a Massachusetts lawyer and solicitor in the War Department. CS may have sent Whiting's recent work, "The Return of the Rebellious States to the Union," a document containing Reconstruction proposals similar to CS's (John Niven, *Gideon Welles* [1973], 467–68).
   5. William E. Forster (1818–86), British M.P. and antislavery activist.

6. Bright wrote that the Americans in Great Britain had a "great want of confidence in your Cabinet"; he feared that "great losses of men & means, & long delays, & apparent mis-management, must have the effect of creating a disgust with the war, or a disgust with those who are responsible for its failures" (28/631, PCS).

7. Bright had asked CS to help get a pardon for Alfred Rubery (15 May 1863, 28/373). Rubery had been charged with conspiring to seize a ship in San Francisco and use it as a privateer on behalf of the Confederacy (George M. Trevelyan, *The Life of John Bright* [1913], 296).

To John Bright

Boston 4th Aug. '63

Dear Mr Bright,

I do not write to you of victories or reverses; for all these you will read in the newspapers. Whether victory or reverse—I know well that there can be but one end to the war. The Rebellion will be put down.

There are two things which make me anxious. First, I fear [that?] devil of Compromise. I do not think the danger is great; but any such danger is terrible. The longer our triumph is postponed, the more impossible this becomes. With 200,000 negroes under arms I shall not fear it.

Our present policy is therefore. (1) 200,000 negroes under arms (2) the admission of a Gulf State with an altered Constitution abolishing Slavery. Florida is ready to take this step. It may be in 6 or 8 weeks. This will be a controlling precedent. & (3) to insist that there can be no talk of admission into the Union except on the basis of *the actual condition at this moment, with Slavery abolished by the Proclamation.*[1] We fear the Secy of State may intrigue the other way.

The second cause of anxiety is in our relations with England. Yr Govt. recklessly & heartlessly seems bent on war. You know how the democracy, which it now courts, will tear & rend it, while Irish have at last their long sought opportunity. A leading merchant said to me this morning that he would give $50,000 for a war between England & Russia, that he might turn English doctrines against England. The feeling is very bitter. When we are disengaged, who can arrest it?—A just policy of kindness & good will might do something to win back the true relations. But it ought to be adopted at once.—*The draft will be enforced.* Those rioters[2] are the present allies of the London Times.

Ever Yours,   Charles Sumner

I enclose a slip[3] & will write about Russia another time.

ALS GBL (77/217, PCS)
Enc: unidentified newspaper clipping.

1. Responding to CS's letter, Bright agreed: "the Union is only good & great, when a Union of Freedom" (Rochdale, 11 September 1863, 29/117, PCS).

2. Rioters, mostly immigrants and other laborers, protested the draft in New York City, 13–16 July, until put down by U.S. troops and state militia.

3. The clipping concerned Copperheads' opinion of Massachusetts. Citing the Washington correspondent of the New York *World*, the writer stated that Copperheads believed that Massachusetts was about to start a foreign war with Britain and France to benefit cotton manufacturing, although "Mr. Sumner has been hard at work hitherto to prevent this."

To Abraham Lincoln

Boston 7th Aug '63

My dear Sir,

The *London Star*, from which the above passage comes, is edited by a son-in-law of John Bright.[1]

I find every where consternation at the idea that the Proclamation can be forgotten or abandoned. Of course, Mr Seward's speech has had a tendency to excite distrust,[2] which has been increased by reports that some of the Cabinet wished the Govt. to turn from the Proclamation.

Mr Thurlow Weed has increased these anxieties by the overtures which he has made in the *Evening Journal*.[3]

For myself, I have seen but one way from the beginning, & that way becomes brighter as we proceed. It is by doing justice to the black man. Then shall we deserve success.

But I did not intend a sermon. My object was simply to call attention to the extract from the London paper which stands by us always.

Sincerely Yours,   Charles Sumner

ALS DLC (77/220, PCS)
Enc: newspaper clipping

1. CS attached a clipping from the 23 July 1863 issue of the London *Morning Star* stating that the Emancipation Proclamation was considered by some, even those in the U.S. cabinet, as a "*trick to be revoked*" (CS's emphasis). The writer went on to state that the *Morning Star*, however, did not doubt Lincoln's commitment "to the wedded cause of the Union and of Emancipation." Samuel Lucas (1811–65), editor of the London *Morning Star*, 1856–65, was a brother-in-law of Bright.

2. Speaking 7 July on the fall of Vicksburg, Seward repeated a statement he had made at the war's beginning: "The country shall be saved by the Republican party if it will, by the Democratic party if it choose, without Slavery if it is possible, with Slavery if it must" (*New York Times*, 9 July 1863:5).

3. For example, the *Albany Evening Journal* stated that once the Confederate army had surrendered, citizens loyal to the U.S. should not be prohibited from "enjoying and exercising all their former privileges and immunities." The *Journal* declared, "It would require the erection of no new machinery to put the old Union cogs in motion" (28 July 1863:2).

To Abraham Lincoln

Boston 21st Aug. '63

My dear Sir,

I send you two recent letters—one from Bright & the other from Cobden. They both relate exclusively to our affairs & touch strongly the questions of "reconstruction." Each insists that the Proclamation must be maintained at every cost.[1]

When you have read them will you be good enough to put under an envelope & return them to me?—[2]

I hope you bear the heats of Washington better than I bear those of Boston. I detest hot weather.

Meanwhile the good cause advances. The Future is sure, if we are only firm.

Ever sincerely Yours, Charles Sumner

From other English sources I learn that the idea is still maintained in important quarters that our Union cannot be restored. We will let them see.

ALS DLC (77/236, PCS)

1. The letters that CS sent on to Lincoln were almost certainly Bright's letter of 31 July and Cobden's of 7 August 1863 (29/007, 030, PCS). Bright's letter, prompted by news of recent Union victories, dealt almost entirely with Reconstruction policies, based on the Emancipation Proclamation, which he accepted "as a fact not to be undone or reversed." He saw the future of freedom "full of difficulty" and recommended that the U.S. assume "not a farthing of the Southern Debt." Regarding readmission of rebel states, Bright asked, "Would it be possible to declare that, in accordance with the Proclamation, Slavery was legally at an end, & that anything in the Constitution & laws of the states which legalized & enacted Slavery must be repealed & abolished to give them a right to their ancient position in the Republic? Unless something definite & resolute is done," warned Bright, "you may have the states repealing their ordinances of Secession, & announcing their old position in the nation, & electing members to Congress &c and then beginning a fight with the central Govt. in the Supreme Court as to the legality of the Proclamation, & insisting on the retention of Slavery. The Govt. would be powerless under such circumstances—all the base pro-slavery party in the North would unite with the South & possibly your next Presidential election may be made to turn on this vital question,

& your whole nation may be dishonored for ever by the repudiation of the Proclamation which the existing Administration has failed to sustain." Cobden stated in his 7 August letter, "To restore the old Union, slavery and all, will be to cover with shame the partisans of the North throughout the world, and justify the opponents of the war everywhere.—It would leave the question still to be settled by a similar process of blood by another generation.—However, I do not see how this compromise can be accomplished."

2. On 24 August John Hay, Lincoln's secretary, returned the letters to CS and, on behalf of the president, "expressed the gratification with which he has read them" (29/060).

To Salmon P. Chase

Boston 30th Aug. '63

My dear Chase,

I have just read yr reply to O'Connell's paper. It is worthy of you & of the subject.[1] Of course I read it at the time, & yet it reads like something fresh,—it is so true & vital. I wish the President could read it.

That idea of the constitutional impossibility of Slavery within the exclusive jurisdiction of Congress has salvation in it.

I use it in an article which I have in the October Atlantic on "Our Domestic Relations or How to treat the Rebel States."[2]

I shall treat "Our Foreign Relations" in a speech at New York—perhaps the most elaborate I ever made.[3]

Meanwhile I am sure the good cause becomes stronger. Retreat is now impossible.

But how is Florida?[4] Have you ever made medicines "contraband"? Englishmen criticize us on this account. The Navy Dep. has done nothing that way. How is this?

Ever Yours,   Charles Sumner

How Louis Napoleon's wickedness is unmasked.[5] I rejoice that I suspected him from the beginning.

ALS   DLC   (77/241, PCS)

1. "Liberty or Slavery? Daniel O'Connell on American Slavery. Reply to O'Connell" (1863). Chase's pamphlet, written in 1843, had been recently reprinted. In it Chase stated, "No person, under any act of Congress, can be constitutionally held as a slave for a single moment anywhere within the range of exclusive national jurisdiction" (11).

2. In his article, CS stated this point, adding that "Mr. Chase, among our public men, is known to accept it sincerely" ("Our Domestic Relations," *Atlantic Monthly* [October 1863], 12:527).

3. Delivered before the Young Men's Republican Union at Cooper Institute 10 September 1863.

4. Chase recorded in his diary 6 September a visit from a Treasury agent who said Florida was within the Union army's grasp and could be "restored as a Free State by the first of December" (*Inside Lincoln's Cabinet*, ed. David Donald [1954], 190).

5. A French force had been in Mexico since May 1862 and on 10 June 1863 the new French-dominated body, the Assembly of Notables, offered the Mexican crown to the Austrian archduke Ferdinand Maximilian.

To Richard Cobden

Boston 4th Sept. '63

My dear Cobden,

Yr letter of 7th August is my last news from England. You seem tranquil. Gold is beginning to rise here, & a few days ago the agent of the Barings came to consult me about our Foreign Relations, saying that he was so anxious that he hesitated to give credits. But his anxiety was put on the uncertainty about the ironclads. We hear nothing authentic with regard to them. Evarts was here a few days ago anxious, but with the impression that they would not be allowed to sail.[1] But, I think, the public generally is more excited about L. Nap., who has put himself in a direction which must eventually bring him in collision with us.[2]

Meanwhile the war goes on—not as fast as the public expected, but full as fast as I expected. In the military counsel which ordered the present attack on Charleston last June the Chairman Genl. Halleck "doubted the result but thought there was no harm in trying." The others were confident. I do not think success will come early or easy.— It is not proposed to move against Mobile until cool weather.—The movement of Rosecrantz[3] is very important. His army is excellent, & he is a good officer.—A movement in Texas is preparing.

I accept the idea of delay & even of reverse; *but the end is sure*; & I have so regarded it ever since the Presdts Proclamation. But I am inclined to think that "time" is an essential element of a conflict which has become a social revolution.

I do not differ from you when you say, that you never would have counselled a war for Emancipation. Nor I.[4] Indeed, I have done nothing but accept the conditions inposed by the other side. Of course, I would not surrender to Slavery. There was a *moment* when, perhaps, it was possible to let the states go; but I doubt. Since then the thing has been morally impossible. The war must be fought out. This is sad enough to me. It costs me a pang to give up early visions & see my country filled with armies, while the military spirit prevails every where. Every where soldiers come forward for offices of all kinds—from the Presidency to the post of constable, & this will be the case from this time during my life.

You will read the Presdt's letter.[5] It is like him—unique & characteristic; but he states the case very well. It has given assurance that there is no chance of Compromise—Of course not—Every day makes the end of ⟨the war⟩ Slavery more certain.—I wish I could talk with you.[6] I would ask you among other things about Louis Napoleon? He cannot be wise—this intermeddling. Good bye!

Ever sincerely Yours,   Charles Sumner

I shall say something at New York next week on "Our Foreign Relations" & shall review the policy of England & France towards us—also the absurdity of conceding *Ocean Belligerency* to rebels without a Prize Court.

ALS   GBWSR   (77/259, PCS)

1. On 8 September 1863 Russell informed Adams that he had ordered the detention of the two ironclad rams in Liverpool (*Foreign Relations* [1863], part 1, 368).

2. The *New York Times* (1 September 1863:2) reported that Maximilian, the choice of Napoleon III, had accepted the Assembly of Notables' offer to rule over the new Mexican empire.

3. Federal naval forces continued to fire on Fort Sumter in Charleston harbor, but could not capture it. In Tennessee, Major General William S. Rosecrans (1819–98) was moving his army toward a confrontation with Braxton Bragg's Confederate forces at Chattanooga.

4. In his 7 August letter from Midhurst Cobden wrote, "Though *I* would not have begun the war for the emancipation of the negroes, & though I cannot urge its continuance for that object, yet I have always felt that the only result which could justify the war was the manumission of every slave on the Northern Continent of America" (29/030, PCS).

5. On 26 August Lincoln responded to James C. Conkling, who represented a delegation of Illinois's Unconditional Union men. In his letter, Lincoln assured the delegation that he would make no secret compromise; in fact he doubted that "any compromise, embracing the maintenance of the Union, is now possible." To the delegation's criticism of the Emancipation Proclamation, Lincoln said, "The war has certainly progressed as favorably for us, since the issue of the proclamation as before. I know as fully as one can know the opinions of others, that some of the commanders of our armies in the field who have given us our most important successes, believe the emancipation policy, and the use of colored troops, constitute the heaviest blow yet dealt to the rebellion; and that, at least one of those important successes, could not have been achieved when it was, but for the aid of black soldiers" (CWL, 6:406–10, 423, the last sentence inserted by Lincoln on 31 August). CS wrote Lincoln 7 September, thanking him for "yr true & noble letter, which is an historic document. . . . It cannot be answered" (77/271).

6. Cobden had written on 7 August, "Though we have given you such good ground of complaint on account of the cruisers which have left our ports, yet you

must not forget that we have been the only obstacle to what would have been almost a European recognition of the South.—Had England joined France they would have been followed by probably every other State of Europe, with the exception of Russia.—This is what the Confederate agents have been seeking to accomplish.—They have pressed recognition on England & France with persistent energy from the first."

To the Duchess of Argyll

Boston 8th Sept. '63

My dear Duchess,

We are all very anxious here. Does Ld Russell mean war against the U.S.? That is the question. Has the time come for him to throw himself unreservedly & beyond recall into the arms of Slavery? Nobody can answer. But he pronounces our doom in speeches & then does more than any Rebel Army to bring it about. His course seems a continuation of George Grenville[1] & Lord North—the same misconception with regard to us, which unless arrested can have nothing but disaster.

But, perhaps, I should not write this; & yet it is in my heart & my deepest convictions. The fatal mistake was when the British Cabinet forgot the essential question of *morals* in this war & then declared "Neutrality." I have read Mr Gladstone's speech in the Commons with pain unspeakable. It was more guarded than former utterances, but it seemed to be a speech which said "There is no God." Alas! alas!

Meanwhile our war proceeds—slowly of couse; but none the less surely. The President's letter confirms the Proclamation in unmistakable terms.[2] It has been very much liked—even admired for its quiet firmness & its quaint individuality of style.

But a predominant topic in conversation is the conduct of England & France towards us. From the beginning I have suspected L.N. I am not disappointed by his course. It is over England that we grieve. Meeting lately an excellent friend of England, I asked his feelings. He held up both his hands, & said "Who could have believed it; & yet they don't see what they are doing." He added that in his opinion England was responsible for "at least two years of our war, with its losses in treasure & blood." And all this—"simply by forgetting her past history & the obligations of moral duty."—But again I come back to my refrain. Another friend, who knows & loves England well writes—"Have patience with England. She is always wrong at first about every thing; but the old galleon gets her head round in the right direction. A great change in popular opinion has already taken place & every day she understands us better. It will be all right between us at last—despite her obstinancy & wrong-headness"—

I do not expect immediate success at Charleston. There will be no attempt at Mobile immediately. So great a war, with such energies aroused, cannot be put down without time. But when we come out of it purified, our nation will begin to live. There will be no Slavery; & with its fall here, it must fall every where. What a sublime Revolution!

If I could reach the English Govt. I would appeal to it, with all the fervor of love & piety, *to change absolutely its policy* to the Rebellion—; for the sake of peace between us; of Freedom & of Civilization.

We have been touched by the death of Col. Shaw, a refined brave youth, son of my friends, who fell on the parapet of Fort Wagner at the head of his colored troops.[3] I send you his portrait that you may see the ⟨youth⟩ stuff that is sacrificed in this war. And now pardon me. God bless you! & believe me

Ever very sincerely Yours,   Charles Sumner

ALS   CSmH   (77/274, PCS)

1. George Grenville (1712–70), British statesman responsible for the Stamp Act of 1765.
2. See CS to Cobden 4 September 1863.
3. Robert Gould Shaw (1837–63) died 18 July, commanding the 54th Massachusetts Colored Infantry.

To Francis Lieber

Boston 15th Sept. '63

My dear Lieber,

I was sorry not to see you. But especially should I have been glad, could I have had the advantage of yr counsels on the many topics of fact, law & history, which I undertook to treat.[1]

I spoke on two accounts, first, because it seemed to me that the country needed light; that people were groping from ignorance of what England had done, & also from ignorance of law & history applicable to our case. And, secondly I spoke in the hope of reaching France & England,—people & cabinets. To the latter, I am personally known as a lover of peace, so that my austerity will mean more than the N. York *Herald*.

Of course, I shall be brutally attacked.

The speech is stereotyping & the plates will be all cast to-day—to be published in New York.[2]

Several of the points, I think are new. I ask yr particular attention to that about Ocean Belligerency,[3]—where I think I am impregnable. But if I am right—what a *blunder-crime* do I throw upon England!—

Seward writes me that he has read my speech "without once stopping"—& that I have "performed a very important public service" &c &c.[4]

I had intended to speak without notes; but I found my brain, exhausted perhaps by labor, did not grapple with the text; so I read—for the first time before such an audience.

I was recalled to Boston to be near my poor dying brother. [*George Washington*] Greene is here—to be with him.

Ever yours,   Charles Sumner

ALS MH-H (64/282, PCS)

1. Lieber wrote CS that he had to leave the Cooper Institute during CS's "great speech" of 10 September 1863 because of illness and found CS had already left his hotel when he called the next day (New York, 13 September 77/283, PCS).
2. Believing that CS's speech must be read "to be fully understood and digested," Lieber asked where he could obtain more copies to distribute around the country.
3. In his speech CS argued first that the Confederacy was not entitled to rights of ocean belligerency since it had no open port to which it could take captured ships. Second, all Confederate ships had been built in Great Britain and British ports "constitute their *naval base of operations and supplies.*" The cruisers went forth "*never touching the pretended government*" in whose name they rob and burn" ("Our Foreign Relations" [1863], 71).
4. Seward wrote that CS was right to "rouse the nationality of the American People. It is an instinct upon which you can always rely, even when the conscience that ought never to slumber is drugged to death" (Washington, 12 September, 29/137). CS included Seward's letter, along with many others, in an appendix to his speech (Wks, 10:152).

To Horace Greeley
private

Boston 21st Sept. '63

My dear Greeley,

Besides public opportunities of information with regard to the demands of our cause in Europe, I have had from the beginning of the war, a private correspondance, which has been full of instruction. What I saw instinctively has been confirmed by all that I have heard—that our special strength, *almost our only strength*, in Europe was in the Anti-Slavery sentiment there.[1] But I know well that our cause can be presented, even without referring to Slavery. But the argt. of international

law & of policy I believe needs re-enforcement from the other sentiment.

I aimed, in the first place, to make our cause impregnable on the law
& the fact. But I was satisfied that if I stopped there, I should not reach
the European conscience. Besides, I was able to shew how completely
England was committed against Slavery, so that all logic & consistency
required her to set her face as flint against any paltering with Slavery.

The first great wrong to us was lifting rebel Slavemongers to an
equality with the National Govt. One of my best correspondents in
England reminds me at times that "the National Govt has had *full as
much* in the way of arms &c as the Rebels."[2] What of that? The Rebels
should have had nothing. I have been glad to find that Mr Evarts thinks
our first great item against England is this concession to the rebels. Our
friends in England are not prepared for this position; but, as the discussion proceeds, they will be obliged to adopt it.

I am for peace now—as always, & recognize Mediation as one of the
refinements & triumphs of Civilization.[3] I shall be unhappy if I have let
fall a word which can stand in the way of a cause which has so much of
my heart & reverence. Like you I loathe & detest war, & one of my
visions on the Future is that our Country, emancipated & without a
slave, may institute a disarming of the nations. Nor am I less confident
in this Future—now that so many men are mustered in arms. It must
come & I hope to help its coming.

Pardon my homily. You wrote of me so kindly, that I could not
forbear sending you—not a reply—not a criticism—but simply a token that I had read you gratefully.[4]

Ever Yours,   Charles Sumner

ALS   NN   (77/302, PCS)

1. "Mr. Sumner on Intervention" by Greeley appeared in the New York *Independent*
17 September 1863:1. While generally praising CS's speech, Greeley advanced two
criticisms. First, he stated that the U.S.'s "case against the Western Powers of Europe
. . . is perfect, apart from any question of Slavery." CS's charge against Britain and
France based on violations of international law, wrote Greeley, was sufficient and
compelling. But when CS introduced the argument that, because the government
was based on slavery, the Confederacy should be denied recognition, he lost support
from some quarters.

2. CS possibly refers to Bright's letter of 2 May 1863: "since the South were
admitted as belligerents, in respect of the sale of arms, you have been treated as two
nations equal in the sight of our Govt, & one as much in their favor as the other"
(London, 28/313, PCS).

3. Greeley's second criticism was that CS had not stressed the possibility of me-

diation: "our statesmen *should make* precedents in favor of Arbitration instead of resting content upon those which make against it."

4. Greeley replied to CS 24 September, again pleading for arbitration and objecting to the conditions raised by the U.S. that prevented such a solution (New York, 29/231).

To John Bright

Boston 22nd Sept. '63

Dear Mr Bright,

The news from Rosecrantz is not all that we desire: but I have great confidence in his military ability, & in his "hold fast" character.[1] And yet I confess that to my military eye—so far as I may judge such things—his position does not look right. But what then? His defeat would only postpone—not change—the result.

At Charleston Genl. Gilmore has done all that for the present he can do.[2] He now waits for the navy. This is stopped—not by batteries or fire—but by ropes under the water, which are contrived to foul the screws of the monitors, by which they would be rendered unmanageable, so as to drift ashore. I am astonished that means have not been devised for the removal of this net-work. But thus far they have not succeeded. I think, however, the necessary contrivances will not be long wanting. With that, I understand there will be nothing serious to prevent the iron-clads from going to Charleston.

You will observe that the elections, as they have occurred are for the Administration. Chase writes me from Washington that "things look better & better" there.[3]

Our only anxiety is from England & France. Nobody can measure the complications which either of these Powers may cause. The feeling towards England, among those who have been most Anglican, is of intense disappointment & sorrow. The Irish & Democrats are naturally against England. They need no excuse. But the merchants & the educated—those who depend upon English books & enjoy the thought of English life—are now thoroughly aroused. I doubt if any Ministry since Ld North's has made such a mistake as Ld Russell's. It might have buckled this great & growing Power in perpetual amity; but it has pushed it aside, with insult. I long for England *thoroughly to reconsider* her course towards us. She must take a new start, or all who love peace here will be powerless.

Meanwhile the prosperity of the North is great. Travel is immense. Every conveyance, whether the largest steamer or the largest train, is crowded to repletion. Incomes are large. Mr Stuart of N.Y.[4] said that his income had been at least *4 millions of dollars*, & he paid as income tax $200,000. This is the largest that I know of.

I shall send you by next steamer a *corrected copy* of my recent speech,[5] from stereotype plates, printed in New York. If by accident there should be any disposition to reprint it in England, I hope it may be from this copy.

Ever sincerely Yours,   Charles Sumner

ALS   GBL   (77/308, PCS)

1. In the Battle of Chickamauga, 18–20 September 1863, the Confederates decidedly stopped Major General William S. Rosecrans's advance.

2. Major General Quincy Adams Gillmore (1825–88) was in charge of the X Corps and the Department of the South.

3. Republicans had won in Vermont and the Unionists in California (*New York Times*, 2 and 5 September 1863:5). Chase wrote optimistically from Washington 16 September, "though some anxiety I hear is felt in military quarters." He wished the Federals had a "great general, honest & faithful and inspired by our cause" (29/179, PCS).

4. Possibly Robert L. Stuart (1806–82), a sugar refiner.

5. Of "Our Foreign Relations" Bright wrote 23 October from Llandudno that from the U.S. standpoint "it is reasonable enough—from that of Englishmen generally, it is thought to be too severe." However, he believed the speech had "forced Lord Russell to a more distinct statement" of British neutrality. He cautioned CS and his compatriots not to "excite yourselves," for Bright believed Britain was now truly neutral (77/360).

To Orestes A. Brownson

Boston 5th Oct. '63

My dear Dr,

I have just read yr last number.

I am glad you consider again the terms of re-union.[1] I have taken up again the subject, & was struck by the concurrence between us. *It is important to secure for Congress the control of the Rebel Region.* Let this be done, & all the rest will follow.

I believe that the moment any territory lapses under the *exclusive jurisdiction* of Congress, Slavery ceases;—because of its essential incompatability with the Constitution of the U. States.

But, without relying upon this postulate, it is clear that, if the territory is under the jurisdiction of Congress, then Congress may affix terms of restoration, or, if it please, by special legislation trample Slavery out & keep the territory in pupilage until the discipline is finished.

Our people need education on this head, & I am glad that you have given it to them so clearly.

I enjoyed much the passage in another article on the letter of the Pope & the position of the Archbishop.[2]

Ever sincerely Yours,   Charles Sumner

ALS   InND   (77/320, PCS)

1. In "Return of the Rebellious States" (*Brownson's Quarterly Review*, third New York series [October 1863]: 481–511), Brownson stated that no concessions should be granted to Confederate states. They should become territories, with the question of their readmission left to Congress, a body which had been too timid in asserting its prerogatives in the past.

2. The article "Catholics and the Anti-Draft Riots" (ibid., 385–420) criticized a letter of October 1862 from Pius IX to the archbishop of New York urging peace at any price.

To Arnold B. Johnson

Boston 5th Oct. '63

Dear Johnson,

The "water-closet" is one of the gifts of modern civilization, & must always be taken into account, when you select a house.

Ever Yours,   Charles Sumner

ALS   ViWWL   (77/326, PCS)

To John Bright
private

Boston 6th Oct. '63

Dear Mr Bright,

If Ld Russell wants cotton, let him withdraw all support, material & moral, from the Rebellion; & let him begin by withdrawing his prophecies *against us*.[1] Nothing is clearer than this, that the policy of the British Govt. has prolonged the contest, & thus put off the day when the mills & operatives of Lancashire can count upon a supply of cotton. It is this Govt. which has been their greatest enemy. Every blockade runner, & all talk of mediation or recognition is a coquetry, which gives encouragement to the Rebellion.

I am always sure if my feet are planted on a *moral principle*, that I cannot be permanently defeated. Such is not the Providence of God. And I am sure that those whose feet are not planted on a *moral principle* cannot stand permanently. But pray where are the feet of England? They should have been planted at the outset on the principle, that Slavery is wrong, &, that, therefore, in harmony with her past history, she would have nothing to do with it. There should have been no paltering with it—no encouragement to this wickedness.

At this moment, I am more solicitous about France & England than about our military affairs. In the latter there is a temporary check,[2] &, you know I said long ago, that I was prepared for further disaster; but this can only delay & not change the result. Foreign Intervention will introduce a new, vast & incalculable element. It would, probably, provoke a universal war.[3]

You will observe the hobnobbing at New York with the Russian Admiral.[4] Why is the fleet gathered there?—My theory is that when it left the Baltic war with France was regarded as quite possible & it was determined not to be sealed up at Cronstadt. If at New York, they could take the French expedition at Vera Cruz.

The Emperor of Russia h[as?] done well in emancipating the serfs,[5] &, I doubt not, himself & his empire are both elevated by the act & better prepared for good things. *But I am not a Russian.* I believe yet in Western Civilizaton. But England & France must retrace their steps.

Ever Yours,   Charles Sumner

ALS   GBL   (77/331, PCS)

1. In his letter of 11 September 1863 from Rochdale, Bright asked, "Can you say anything about Cotton? If the great river is open, surely something should come down—we want it sadly here" (29/117, PCS).

2. The Union forces had been stopped at Charleston, at Chickamauga, and in Texas.

3. Bright wrote, "You must quarrel with nobody while the rebellion continues—& then hereafter forgiveness will be nobler than revenge."

4. The *New York Times* devoted page 1 of its 2 October edition to an extensive description of the warm welcome extended to the Russian fleet and Admiral Lisovsky.

5. Alexander II had abolished serfdom in 1861.

To Samuel Gridley Howe

Hancock St—Wednesday—
[7 October 1863]

My dear Howe,

I had expected—& hoped for you last evng—& then again to-day. I fear that you are ill.

Poor George is at-last released from his trials & we shall bury him from my mother's house tomorrow (Thursday) at *2 o'clk precisely*.[1] Let Mrs Howe know this.

The funeral will be *private*, but his friends can never be otherwise than welcome, & my mother spoke to-day especially of Dr & Mrs Howe as having been kind good friends to him.

This change afflicts me more than I had anticipated. It reminds me again of my loneliness in the world. God bless you!

Ever yours,   Charles Sumner

ALS CSmH (77/338, PCS)

1. George Sumner died 6 October. CS wrote similar letters to John Andrew and his old friend the Unitarian clergyman Robert C. Waterston (77/333, 342, PCS).

To Louis Agassiz

Boston 20th Oct. '63

My dear Agassiz,

On looking over the scraps to which I referred in our conversation, I found that they seemed to fall into the province of Prof. Cook, &, therefore, I send them to him.[1]

Instead, I send to you a box of *St Georges*, recd. direct from Mr Gordon,[2] who is the owner of the choicest vinyard of this name, near the village—rough, stony & unpromising to a common eye, but producing the best wine. Montesquieu in commending his wine to some of his English correspondents said that they would receive it "just as he received it from the good God,"—& I think I may say the same of this St Georges.

Last evng Mr Gardner Brewer, who is rich & generous, called upon me. I told him fully of yr necessities—I mean the necessities of yr noble Museum—& expressed a desire to enlist Mr Thayer.[3] He said that for the present it would be difficult, as there was a disposition to confine donations & charities to the war. But I do not despair.

Ever Yours,   Charles Sumner

The wine will go by express.—

ALS MH-H (77/353, PCS)

1. CS sent a box of minerals to Josiah Parsons Cooke (1827–94), Harvard professor of mineralogy and chemistry (Cooke to CS, Cambridge, 24 October 1863, 29/464, PCS).

2. In his letter to CS, Richard Gordon, the son of CS's late friend in Montpellier, said he hoped CS would find the wine "an excellent 'table or dinner tipple'" (Montpellier, 1 September, 29/074).

3. Gardner Brewer (1806–74), Boston merchant. Agassiz sought financial backing for a scientific journey to Brazil; support was provided by Nathaniel Thayer (1808–83), a benefactor of Harvard (HWL, 4:480).

To Francis Lieber

Boston 24th Oct. '63

Dear Lieber,

I have yrs of 23d.

It has not gone in England much differently from what I expected.[1] I knew too well (1) the prejudices of country & (2) the prejudices of party to suppose that I could speak as plainly as I did without giving pain &, perhaps, exciting anger. All supporters of the Govt. must be against me—*at present*, while the fit is on them.

Of the Independent Liberals I was doubtful. Some I supposed would be with me & some against me. Professor Newman, personally a stranger, writes me full of thanks & predicts that the speech must do great good.[2] So also writes an eminent business man of Manchester. But you tell me that G. Smith is the other way.[3] I am sorry; for I admire & honor him much, & should be proud of his sympathy.

But I feel that the *whole question*, in all its hearings, was one which I was more competent to decide than my critics. I know England & America well, &, better than most any body, I know the tendencies of my own country. On my conscience, after a constant & minute private correspondance on all the topics of my speech, I felt that the time had come when the case should be plainly stated to England *by a friend* who meant peace & not war. My speech was a warning—with a pleading for peace. But misconception & misrepresentation have planted in many persons a false idea of it.[4]

Ever Yours,   Charles Sumner

ALS   MH-H   (64/288, PCS)

1. The London *Times* editorial on CS's "Our Foreign Relations" concluded: "We believe our readers have by this time had enough of the logic of Mr. Sumner. It is based neither on law nor on fact, but upon his own sympathies and antipathies, which he is pleased to assume must also be ours,—on the supposition, which we do not admit, that the North are obviously in the right, and on the inference, which we refuse to draw, that, even if the North are in the right, we are bound to violate the

laws of neutrality in order to assist them" (28 September 1863:6). The *Economist* expressed disappointment that the well-informed senator had "apparently" decided "to exacerbate all the violent passions and prejudices now entertained against us by the most ignorant and ill-disposed of his countrymen" (3 October 1863:1093).

2. Francis E. Newman (1805–97, British writer and brother of John Henry Newman) wrote CS approvingly, stating that CS's recent speech was appropriate and not likely to "inflame" Americans against Great Britain (London, 30 September, 29/283, PCS).

3. Lieber reported in his letter of 23 October that Goldwin Smith "deeply regrets your speech" and feared it would give "renewed power to the oligarchy" in Britain (New York, 77/363).

4. Lieber replied that the British had evinced "such a supercilious disdain of others, and especially of Northerners here that they get angry when a man shows how grossly wrong they are" (26 October, 77/389).

To the Duchess of Argyll

Boston 26th Oct. '63

I have been happy even in yr somewhat impatient patience with me, my dear Duchess. I knew I must have given you pain, & I supposed I should be misunderstood. But I could not do otherwise.[1] There was the cause of Freedom,—& of Peace between our two countries—both put in jeopardy by the uncertain, irritating & offensive policy of Ld Russell. *The time had come to tell him so plainly.* I had written so in private again & again. But this last public letter had quibbled about the evidence of the iron-clads, & it was only on the 9th Sept.[2] that you were able to write me that at last they were to be stopped; *while it was on the 10th that I spoke in New York.*

I had become heart-sick over the painful abandonment, as it seemed to me, of what was pure & glorious in English history. Even at the last days of the session of Parlt. Ld Palmerston repelled Mr Cobden, & gave us to understand that the question of recognition was one of *time*; —as if such a piratical continuation could be recognized at any time, without unspeakable disgrace to the English name & covering this reign with infamy.[3] Ld Palmerston did not seem to see the difference between continuing relations, with a Power already in the Family of Nations, & "recognising" a new Power which openly makes Slavery its cornerstone—as if the latter were not shocking to logic, morals & humanity. But why argue this question anew—at least in private letters? It is now stated before the world, & the truth will at last prevail.

You say "was the fire not hot enough already." Yes—too hot; & I wished Ld Russell to stop feeding the flames. I wished him to give us peace—to stop the sacrifices which he has so cruelly promoted—&

frankly offer assurances that would enable us to live in peace together hereafter.

You have said "that Ld Russell would hate war with all his soul." Then why has he done so much to arouse it? Why has he written so recklessly? Why has he prophecied so hostilely? You allude to his last speech in parlt.[4] which with good ideas stopped short of that assurance in which peace could be founded.

You allude to the "Trent." I cannot doubt how history will record that. M. de Gasparin, & Mr Henri Martin,[5] the two eminent French writers tell us. It was a part of the terrible mistake that England has made since the slave-mongers rebelled.

You speak of the "disgraceful cheer," in the House of Commons as caused by the statement of Mr Laird that he had recd. offers from the U. States. On the day of the date of yr letter Mr Forster confessed in public speech at Leeds,[6] that he never rose on the American question without feeling that the House was against him.

Of course, the criticism upon us in the House of Lords—must be accepted as an illustration of that feeling, which constituted in itself a "peril."

I do not judge the French course as more favorable than the English.[7] On the contrary my language was most decided when I spoke of the Emperor. Candor compelled me to admit that he had not been "un-amiable" in form; nor had he been "illogical."

Of course Texas is now a part of this Republic—as much as Ireland of Great Britain.[8]

Thus have I glanced at the points to which you call my attention;— I wish it had been for agreement rather than disagreement. Meanwhile this great cause, on which from the beginning Ld Russell has scowled goes on—not as rapidly as men desire, but according to the Providence of God who shapes the great ends. But Providence expects men to do their duty—especially that England shall not forget her vows; & when she seems about to forget them, all who truly love her & enjoy her greatness must tell her so plainly.

We have just heard of Ld Lyndhurt's death.[9] I believe he has stood by us during the last year. At least his letters here have been friendly. I saw Mr [*Josiah*] Quincy a few days ago—3 mos. older; inferior as a speaker, but superior as a writer & as a character. He is very happy—enjoys his years, & especially the triumph of our cause, which he foretold long ago. He loves England, &, therefore, enjoyed my speech. He said to me; "I see Ld Russell is angry—very angry—I am glad of it. That is a sign I like. *He will change now.*" It was when I returned from my poor brother's funeral that I heard of the ebullition of Ld Russell in Scotland.[10] I think it has done great good for it has produced a conviction that he will stop his tormenting system. I have already told you that I have been here the defender of Ld Russell. The prevailing opinion is that he is "false" & "tricky." The President says, that no true man could have written what he has. I reply; you mistake; he is reckless, self-confident & unhappily committed himself early against us.

Of course, I am abused. I expected it. I expected a sheaf of spears in my own bosom. But I rejoice in the good which has been done here at home, & also in the good which impartial minds assure me has been done in England & in France.

I am weary, & have been sad from my affliction, or I should have answered Ld Russell at once, exposing what he has failed to answer & the "illogical" doctrine that Slavery is "a great crime," & yet that he will "recognise" a nation of Slave-mongers with Slavery as the "corner-stone."—a nation built on crime! Alas! Alas! for England's Minister! But Good bye! & God bless you!

Ever sincerely Yours,   Charles Sumner

ALS CSmH (77/384, PCS)

1. The duchess wrote CS 22 September 1863 upon receipt of his speech, "Alas, that it has come to this—that you should have felt it right to charge England as you have done in a public assembly. . . . I could not read your speech without much pain" (Inverary, 29/219, PCS).

2. On 13 August Russell replied to a letter from the Emancipation Society in Britain, which protested the Liverpool shipbuilding. He stated the government needed evidence to detain the rams, evidence that the Society had not supplied (New York Times, 15 September 1863:5). The duchess wrote CS 8 September (29/099).

3. On 13 July Palmerston described Cobden as being "too high-minded" to take a salary when on a diplomatic mission to Paris; on 10 July he stated that because "events of the utmost importance are about to take place in America," Parliament should not at present consider Roebuck's motion to recognize the Confederacy (Hansard's Parliamentary Debates, 3rd series, 172:671, 556).

4. The duchess criticized CS for failing to comment upon Russell's "noble" speech in Parliament, apparently that of 23 March (see CS to Bright, 12 April 1863). It was "as emphatic against recognition as you could desire."

5. Agénor de Gasparin (1810–71) and Martin were strong Union supporters and correspondents of CS's.

6. Forster's speech of 21 September was reprinted in the New York Times, 6 October 1863:1, 8.

7. CS criticized Napoleon III's policy of conceding belligerency to the Confederacy, receiving its emissaries, attempting mediation in the Civil War, and invading Mexico ("Our Foreign Relations" [1863], 21–24). But he also said, "the Emperor, though acting habitually in concert with the British Cabinet, has not intermeddled so illogically or displayed a temper of so little international amiability" (21).

8. In his speech CS had compared the partition of Poland to the possible absorption of Texas by the French (ibid., 24–25). The duchess wrote, "How you can com-

pare your hold of Texas—a state annexed the other day, in defiance of your own best Men with the possession the Poles had of Poland is a mystery."

9. 12 October.

10. At Blairgowrie, 26 September, Russell said, "if I look to the declarations of those New England orators—and I have been reading lately, if not the whole, yet a very great part, of the very long speech by Mr. Sumner on the subject, delivered at New York,—I own I cannot but wonder to see these men, the offspring, as it were, of three rebellions, as we are the offspring of two rebellions, really speaking, like the Czar of Russia, the Sultan of Turkey, or Louis XIV himself, of the dreadful crime and guilt of rebellion." He went on to state he had respect for Seward's fairness as contrasted with CS's one-sidedness regarding Britain (*New York Times*, 13 October 1863:1). CS discussed with Lieber the possibility of answering Russell publicly, but Lieber dissuaded him (CS to Lieber, 15 October, Lieber to CS, 17, 23, 26 October, 64/284, 77/351, 363, 389).

To Montgomery Blair

Boston 28th Oct. '63

My dear Blair,

It does seem to me that you have fallen into a complete mystification.[1]

There are several things which I desire:

(1) The complete suppression of the Rebellion, so that there can be no further trouble from it; & this involves necessarily the end of Slavery.

(2) The restoration of our system to perfect harmony under the National Govt.

(3) The protection of the Union-men & the freedmen during the *transition period*, so that they shall not be oppressed by the old rebels

(4) The most effective & constitutional process by which all this is to be accomplished.

Now, I take it that you agree with me in desiring these four things. Then where is the difference between us?

If you will shew any way in which these can be accomplished surely, completely & *constitutionally* without the agency of Congress, I shall not oppose it.

Of course, this cannot be done *constitutionally* by military or presidential power. At least, such a course is not in harmony with the genius of our institutions.

But I follow the simple paths of the Constitution, & cannot follow in yr extravagant concessions to military power or to the conglomerate of chance. And yet I am for *any system* by which the good we both seek can be accomplished. Put forth yr system. Let it work, if it will constitutionally.

Of course, you do not recognize Pickens & his crew as the constitutional govt of S. Carolina.[2] There is no constitutional govt, in that unhappy state except the U. States. This is the indisputable *fact*; & this is all. Let us look at the *fact* in the light of common sense & proceed harmoniously to provide the *best agency* for the establishment of a new govt. This is all.[3]

Ever Yours,   Charles Sumner

ALS   DLC   (77/391, PCS)

1. On 3 October 1863 Blair delivered a speech at Rockville, Maryland, criticizing the "ultra-Abolitionists" generally and Reconstruction policies specifically as laid out by the unidentified writer of the October *Atlantic Monthly* article "Our Domestic Relations." Blair attacked CS's state suicide concept (see CS to Parke Godwin, 23 March 1862), arguing that the people, not separate states, were the source of support to the federal government and that loyal citizens in returning Confederate states should not be deprived of their rights. He feared the "ultra-Abolitionists" were "equally despotic" as the rebels, and advised Lincoln to "steer a course" between the Confederates and the abolitionists, both of whom threatened the Union (*New York Times*, 17 October 1863:11). Blair wrote CS 11 October stating his Rockville speech was not a personal attack and that, although he suspected it, he had not been certain CS was the author of "Our Domestic Relations" (29/378, PCS). In answering Blair's letter on 21 October, CS stated he wished Blair's speech had been "better confined to the *principles* involved" and that he failed to see any great difference between them (77/357). Blair replied that he *did* see many differences, because CS's resolutions of February 1862 would in effect "enslave the white people, beginning with the abolishments of the Constitutions of ⅓ of the states" (Washington, 24 October, 29/460).
2. Francis W. Pickens (1805–69), Confederate governor of South Carolina, 1860–62.
3. Blair replied 28 November that he agreed with CS's four propositions, but thought CS's plan for carrying them out was unconstitutional in that Congress should not interfere "in the resuscitation of the States." He wished CS could look at Reconstruction "from my Jackson stand point. . . . You will then have no occasion to go into the Imperialism involved in the State annihilating doctrine.—I will quote for you some of these days what Jefferson says of the tendency of New England ideas on this head. Rely upon it he understood your people and he understood better than any man who ever lived the true harmonies of our system" (29/652).

To Richard Cobden

Boston 6th Nov. '63

My dear Cobden,

I have yr letter on my speech.

Not for controversy but for statement, I reply to yr *cui bono?*[1]

(1) As regards my own country. People here had a right to expect from me a statement of the case. There was a feverish & indignant feeling against G.B., without much knowledge. The facts which I set forth—, none of which can be questioned, are now accepted as an exhibition of what yr Govt has done. The effect has been excellent; for

the people now understand the points in discussion. Instead of exciting them, I think that speech allayed existing excitement—followed as it was by a change in England.

(2) As regards England. It was important that yr govt & people should know how those in our country most friendly felt with regard to their conduct. For months we have done all that could be done—& Ld Russell down to the 9th Sept (I spoke the 10th Sept) gave no hint that we should not have war; *indeed, the inference from his course was that we should have war*; for the departure of those rams would have been tantamount to a declaration of war by G.B. against the U.S.

For weeks before I spoke, bankers & leading business men had revealed to me their anxieties, & the agent of a great English house had told me he could not venture to open credits. It was time, that something was said openly & plainly. I knew too well the prejudices of country & of party not to see that such an exposition would draw down upon me abuse & misrepresentation. But it seemed clearly my duty,—& I am glad I did it.

I know England well, & I know my own country. Being somewhat behind the scenes too, I felt that I could judge what was needed—not to sooth for the moment—not to gratify personal feelings—; but to secure the great object of my heart solid peace between our two countries. I have often told you that the tendency here will be to war, just as soon as our Rebellion is suppressed. My hope is that England will so far reconsider her course, & fraternise with us that war will be impossible. But there can be no hope of this, unless the truth is put before her plainly.

It is painful to me on such a grave occasion to lose the sympathy of English friends—especially of those who have stood by us so well; but all that has occurred, & especially the smart of Ld Russell, shews the good that has been done. People who resent my accusations & deny even their truth, will think twice before they give occasion for their repetition. Ld Russell will change his war policy; *I call it such; for it tended inevitably to war.*

But I have said too much on a personal matter. Let me add in reply to yr suggestion, that the frankness which the occasion required did not allow me to make the distinction which you suggested between England & France.[2] *Both were offenders,*—& it was necessary to tell them so.

Meanwhile our elections are for Emancipation & the Union.[3] Our armies are moving slowly—too slowly. But no reverse can change the inevitable result, which is just as sure as the multiplication table;—how soon I know not.

[*William*] Whiting has returned to cheer us with good news from England,—that no more Alabamas will be allowed to make England a *naval base*. He enjoyed his day with you. I wish that I were there. But Ld John & the Atty Genl.[4] insist upon defending the Concession of Belligerency on the Ocean to rebel-slavemongers, without a prize court. That folly shews that there is more work to be done. *We are all agreed* that, here is the first great offence. Evarts puts this as No. 1. To take back this bloody folly will be bad for yr Cabinet; but sooner or later, in some way or other, it must be done.—Good bye!

Ever sincerely Yours, Charles Sumner

ALS GBWSR (77/400, PCS)

1. Cobden wrote CS from Midhurst 8 October 1863: "The admiration which I feel for the masterly ability of your speech at the Cooper Institute cannot suppress a certain amount of resistance to it on the score of *policy*. I was, I confess, rather beset with the feeling of *cui bono* after reading your powerful indictments against England & France, *together*. . . . [W]as it politic to array us in hostile attitudes just at a moment when the hopes of the South were mainly founded on the prospect of a rupture between yourselves & Europe?" (29/336, PCS).

2. Cobden criticized CS for his "indictment" against England as well as France: "would it not have been better to have shown, in the most favourable colours consistent with truth, the strength of the alliance between the masses in England, led by so much of the intellect & the moral and religious worth of the kingdom, & the Federals, & to have demonstrated the impossibility of the aristocracy, with all their hostility, drawing us into a war with each other."

3. Republicans and War Democrats united to elect governors in Indiana, Iowa, Ohio, and Pennsylvania.

4. William Atherton (1806–64), British attorney general, 1861–63.

To Salmon P. Chase
private

Boston 8th Nov. '63

My dear Chase,

Pray read the enclosed letter from John Bright.

But my special object is to ascertain from you,—so far as you know—what answer can be given to his inquiry on the 2nd page. I should like to give him as much information as possible.[1]

In writing to a member of the English cabinet I had said freely, that, *in my opinion*, the equipping in English ports of several ships like the Alabama, & especially rams for a hostile expedition against the U. States would *ipso facto* be a declaration of war by G. Britain, as much as the seizure of the Spanish galleons or the bombardment of Copenhagen.[2] I let Seward know that I had written this; but I have never known what precise attitude he adopted.

This note will arrive, perhaps, at the wedding of yr daughter—for whom be all happiness & love.[3] My benedictions I offer with a warm heart.

Ever Yours,   Charles Sumner

ALS   DLC   (77/406, PCS)

1. CS sent Chase Bright's letter of 23 October 1863 (77/360, PCS). Bright sought more information about what exactly had brought the British government "more right on the question of the rams." He wondered if the story were true that Russell had hesitated only when presented with Adams's ultimatum stating that if the rams left Liverpool, the U.S. "would consider it an act of war." Bright hoped CS could supply him with "any particulars you are at liberty to give me," for he wanted to compare the American version with the British.
2. See CS to the duke of Argyll, 10 May 1863.
3. Kate Chase married Senator William Sprague on 12 November.

To the Duke of Argyll

Boston 10th Nov. '63

My dear Duke,

I was glad to have yr frank letter.[1] I knew that you would be pained. But it is not the first time that speaking against Slavery & its abettors & for the cause of peace, I have been obliged to give pain. It was a duty to be done, & I am glad to have done it. The dissent & anger which I have encountered in England are not more than I expected. Of course, you will not do again the things which I charge.

Ld Russell will stop writing pert notes; he will stop unfriendly criticism; he will stop unneutral speeches; he will stop most unneutral prophecies; he will stop offensive allusions to courts that will compare favorably with any in England; he will stop future Alabamas;—he will stop all refusal to pay for the damages which he has already caused;—he will cease the ignoble dalliance, into which he insists upon carrying the govt. with slave-mongers, by planting himself on the moral principle, to which England is bound by history, that it cannot help into being a new Power whose object & inspiration are Slavery.—Of course, if I did England injustice when I presented this dismal list—if I exaggerated—if I misrepresented—then will there be no occasion in the future for any such story. All hail! The very criticism to which I am subject is an earnest that these things cannot be repeated. Willingly do

I make the sacrifice of what is dear to me,—even of good name—if I can help my country in maintaining Liberty & in securing Peace.

You say, my dear Duke, that my "attack on Ld Russell about the Prize-Courts is not a just one." But his very speech shews that it was just. I understand the subject better than he does. He thinks & you seem to join with him, that praise of the Supreme Court would justify him in disparaging our "Prize Courts." I do not. He did belittle those courts. It was in ignorance & recklessness. Now, in fact, our "local" judges are better in prize causes than the Sup. Ct. itself. Ware at Portland[2] is beyond question the finest living scholar in Admiralty,— & [*Peleg*] Sprague at Boston, take him for all in all, has not his superior on the English bench; but these are the men that the British Foreign Secy chooses to toss on his rash pitchfork. No—no—he made a mistake; &, perhaps, I shall take occasion to tell him so again. *For this system must be stopped.* Earnestly, sincerely, do I plead for peace, & therefore, protest against Ld Russell pricking & goading my country into war.

You say that I "condemn the expression of individual sympathy with the South as inconsistent with real neutrality."[3] I condemn Ministers of State who make unneutral speeches & prophecies.

You say that "there are no two opinions in England as to the inevitable necessity of the recognition of the South as Belligerents." Now it so happened the mail which brought yr letter brought me three letters from strangers to me[4]—one from a Glasgow laborer—another from a gentleman who described himself as living in the neighborhood of Blairgowrie—& another from one of the finest minds in England;—all three thanking me warmly for my speech & the latter dwelling with especial satisfaction upon my exhibition of the great mistake of England in endowing rebel Slave-mongers with the privileges of Belligerency. But even if every Englishman were against this exhibition, it could not alter my appreciation of it—any more than if they got angry against the decalogue or the multiplication table. England made a terrible mistake & I know that this will be yet seen. You are improving. Look at the *Times* & the speeches of yr Ministers.[5]

You say that "the distinction between a new Slave Power & an old one is not logical."—For years this distinction has entered into our politics, &, therefore, I am naturally more familiar with it, than you can expect to be. The first speech I ever made was against the admission of Texas "as a Slave State";[6] & a political principle which I have always maintained has been "No more Slave States." This has often been called abolitionist & fanatical; but never till now "illogical." Of course it is sternly *logical*. If a Nation may exercise a discretion in its conduct, & in its relations with other nations—then is it bound morally to exercise this discretion, so as best to promote good morals, freedom & peace.— Nothing shews how completely the English mind has ⟨been corrupted⟩ back-slided than the fact that this conclusion is not gladly adopted. It furnishes a noble & historic answer to the rebel slave-mongers, calculated to give them a *quietus*. Had this been given at the beginning this war would have been over long ago,—& blood & treasure would have been saved.

You do not see "what good the speech can possibly do in America." The people here naturally look to me for an explanation of their Foreign Relations, & the speech produced at once an excellent effect. The people saw their case & understood it. The fever was changed into calm assurance. It was felt that England never could go to war against us, linking herself with slave-mongers, with such a plain statement given to the civilized world.

You say that the speech "can do nothing but harm" in Britain. Of course on this point I do not like to argue with a Briton. But it ought to be settled what is meant by "harm." I can imagine that any complicity with the fatal policy I felt it my duty to arraign must create a sensitiveness under the arraignment. But if I helped warn Ministers, & the British people against doing certain things, then my speech has done good.

And now, dear Duke, I have been plain & frank. Let me add, that I made that speech singly & sincerely in the interest of peace between our two countries. God knows how truly I have it at heart. There are few who know the whole field better than I do. *I know the dangers*, & I tell you Ld Russell was carrying England to certain war with the United States;—if not immediately by letting loose rams or Alabamas, then at last just so soon as our Rebellion is suppressed. I have written in private, very frankly. I felt that the time had come to make an appeal before the world. *My hope was to bring about such a change of British policy, as would restore good feeling between our two countries & take away from our war-party here all excuse for war.* In this hope I spoke.

I have said too much—& perhaps too plainly. But I write always in the sincere desire of helping the cause which I know you & the Duchess have truly at heart. God bless you—

Ever Sincerely Yours,   Charles Sumner

ALS   CSmH   (77/408, PCS)

1. Argyll wrote from London on 30 September 1863, "I read yr last speech with sorrow—not seeing what good it cd possibly do in America & feeling sure that it wd do nothing but harm here" (29/277, PCS).

2. Ashur Ware (1782–1873), judge of the U.S. district court in Maine.

3. Argyll wrote, "if it is inconsistent with neutrality to express this feeling, it must be equally inconsistent in me & others to express sympathy with the Govt. of the U.S., which I have felt myself free to do. You have confounded *indifference of opinion* with neutrality of action."

4. "A Labourer," 5 October; Thomas Bayly Potter, Dunkeld, 29 September; and Francis E. Newman, London, 30 September, 29/316, 265, 283.

5. CS may have referred to Parliament's defeat of Roebuck's motion to recognize the Confederacy. Recently the London *Times*, while regularly pessimistic about the North subduing the South, did state that British recognition of the Confederacy at this stage of the war "would probably be almost fruitless" (23 September 1863:8).

6. Not CS's first speech but his first on antislavery, 4 November 1845. In "Our Foreign Relations" CS had distinguished between Britain's proper relations with Spain and Brazil, which allowed slavery, and improper relations with a "*new* power, with Slavery as its declared 'corner-stone'" (1863, 66).

To Abraham Lincoln

Boston 30th Nov. '63

My dear Sir,

You have seen, perhaps, that the London *Post*, which is sometimes called Ld Palmerston's organ, menaces "recognition" of the rebel slave-mongers, in the event of any reverse to the national arms. The *Times* has also thrown out the same menace in a very recent article.[1]

Now, I have no fear that there can be any arrest of the judgment which Providence has entered already against Slavery & its abettors. But I am anxious that the case should be stated, so that Civilization shall gain as much as possible. And this will be accomplished, if the British people can be made to see that it will be immoral on their part to recognize such a combination. Why cannot the discussion be changed to this ground?

Congress already by its resolutions, which Mr Seward has communicated to Foreign Powers, has declared its regret that Foreign Powers did not at once tell the chiefs of the Rebellion that they could not expect "recognition" for the State which they were trying to build. If this point could be pressed on the Foreign mind, there would be two good results.

(1) The talk of "recognition" would stop, & our people would not be disturbed by reports that it was at hand.

(2) If "recognition" would be wrong—then, of course it was wrong to concede "belligerency," which is a semi-independence; & our argument against England on this head would be strengthened immensely by shewing that "recognition" was a moral impossibility.

This is a long introduction to a suggestion, which I desire to make. It is that, in yr message, you should refer to the resolutions of Congress,

& mention that they have been sent to Foreign Govts;—& then add to this statement, the enunciation of the principle you so well expressed in the memdum. you gave to me last spring[2]—to the effect that, while in times past there have been Nations where Slavery was an incident, now, for the first time in human history, a new Power presents itself & asks "recognition" in the Christian Family, whose only declared reason of separate existence is the support of Slavery—& that no such Power can expect any such "recognition," but that Christian States are bound to set their faces against it.

Let this statement be made in the message & it will reach *the people* of Europe. Its essential truth will vindicate it every where. But it must be stated so that the people can know it.

If our cause in Europe could be put openly on this ground, the Rebellion would receive a death-blow. Nor is this all. Slavery every where would tremble before the judgment of the civilized world.

Let us get as much as possible for our own country & also for mankind out of all our bloodshed.[3]

Ever sincerely Yours,   Charles Sumner

ALS   DLC   (77/431, PCS)
Enc: Concurrent Resolutions of Congress Concerning Foreign Intervention in the existing Rebellion, Senate Document No. 38, 28 February 1863.[4]

1. The London *Morning Post* (11 November 1863:4) stated that Britain should recognize the Confederacy immediately in order to preserve British hegemony and to prevent a "gigantic democracy" in the West. In another editorial the London *Times* (14 November 1863:8) saw no military resolution of the Civil War and wondered whether "enough has not been done to prove that the Confederates are determined on independence and strong enough to maintain it."

2. "Resolutions on Slavery," [15 April 1863], CWL, 6:176–77.

3. Lincoln did not incorporate CS's suggestion in his presidential message of 8 December 1863. Instead he stressed the positive course international relations had taken: "Questions of great intricacy and importance have arisen out of the blockade, and other belligerent operations, between the government and several of the maritime powers, but they have been discussed, and, as far as was possible, accommodated in a spirit of frankness, justice, and mutual good will" (CWL, 7:36).

4. CS underlined passages in the fourth and fifth resolutions. In the fifth, where the text reads "until the Rebellion is suppressed," CS substituted "overcome."

To Thomas Wentworth Higginson

Senate Chamber 12th Dec. '63

My dear Sir,

I have always been of the opinion, that, in point of law, the colored troops, enlisted as "soldiers," are entitled to the same pay as the whites,

& I have so insisted at the War Department. If the blunder is not corrected there, Congress must do it.[1]

I am proud of the colored troops. From the beginning I have had faith in them & I rejoice that my anticipations have been so nobly fulfilled.

The Govt. cannot make any discrimination against such meritorious soldiers, who are helping us in our need.

I have just recd. yr letter with regard to W.P., which I shall attend to with pleasure.[2]

Congress is tranquil—beyond all precedent. Never before since I have been here have the signs of a quiet session been so positive. The battle of "ideas" was fought in the last Congress. It remains now only to assure the victory, & this we shall do.

Ever sincerely Yours,   Charles Sumner

ALS   NjMo   (77/472, PCS)

   1. Higginson, colonel in command of the First South Carolina Volunteers at Beaufort, South Carolina, wrote enlisting CS's help in obtaining payment for Higginson's black troops. He said they had not received any wages since the end of February (24 November 1863, 29/633, PCS).

   2. Higginson sought a pass for Wendell Phillips in order that he might address the troops on the first anniversary of the Emancipation Proclamation. Higginson wished all "the great advocates of Freedom" could come to speak at Beaufort (5 December, 29/707).

To John Bright

Washington. 15th Dec. '63

Dear Mr Bright,

Rubery's pardon[1] will issue as soon as the papers can be prepared. It was my desire that it should take effect months ago on yr first suggestion & before the trial. But the Presdt thought that it would be better to wait. At the same time he was most anxious to carry out yr desires. Your full-length photograph is on the mantle in his office, where the only other portrait is of one of his predecessors Andrew Jackson.

There is much feeling in California against the crime of Rubery & his associates. But the judge who tried him & both the Senators[2] say that every body will be satisfied if it be known that Mr Bright, the good friend of our country, desired the pardon.

The sentence is imprisonment for 10 years & a fine of $10,000— which will be remitted.

I have just recd the Manchester Examiner, containing the speeches at Rochdale, which I have read gratefully & admiringly. Cobden's positive testimony must tell for us.[3] And let me add that I like him the better the nearer he gets to the position that recognition is a *moral impossibility*. If this were authoritatively declared, the case would soon be closed. It is because the gate is still kept open, that the public is vexed by constantly recurring reports, that, in the event of Federal reverses, there will be recognition. No Federal reverse can be an apology for such a crime. But to talk of it is criminal.

Mr Seward is printing two large vols. of despatches—a collection as large again as that of last year. I hope to be able to send a portion of it to the Star in advance of its communication to Congress.[4]

The reports of Heads of Dep. for this year were communicated at once to the press here,—so that I could not anticipate the publication.

Never before since I have been in Congress has it come together in such tranquility. The Opposition is powerless. Our friends are confident. There are no doubters. Besides, the battle of "ideas" has been fought—in the last Congress. It only remains that we should carry forward the "ideas" that have been adopted.

The Presdt's proposition of reconstruction has *two* essential features—(1) The irreversibility of Emancipation,—making it the "corner-stone" of the new order of things, (2) the reconstruction or revival of the States by *preliminary process* before they take their place in the Union.—I doubt if the details will be remembered a fortnight from now.[5]

Any plan which fastens Emancipation beyond recall will suit me. All that I have proposed has been simply to secure this result. And thank God! this will be done. The most determined Abolitionists now are in the slave-states—& naturally for with them it is a death-grapple!— But how great & glorious will be this country when it is fully redeemed, & stands before the world without a slave—an example of Emancipation! Pardon my exultation!

Ever sincerely Yours,   Charles Sumner

ALS GBL (77/486, PCS)

1. In his most recent letter, 20 November 1863 (Rochdale, 29/606, PCS), Bright asked CS not to forget Alfred Rubery, who had been convicted of piracy on 12 October.

2. The *New York Times* on 17 December announced Lincoln's pardon; it is printed in CWL, 7:71. California senators were James A. McDougall and John Conness (1821–1909; U.S. senator [Rep., Calif.], 1863–69).

3. Bright had written that although both he and Cobden would speak at Rochdale on 24 November, he would not speak about the U.S. because he regarded "your question in safe hands; that is, in the hands of the people of the United States— where I am willing to leave it." Speaking on nonintervention and free trade, Cobden declared that the Confederacy's war aims were solely "to establish a slave empire" and that it would be defeated. He praised the "fortitude, self-respect" of the Lancashire workers while the cotton mills had been inoperative and predicted that cotton would once again come from the South, a product of "African free labour" (*Manchester Weekly Times*, 28 November 1863:2).

4. Bright had requested this favor of CS in his letter of 6 November and CS forwarded Bright's letter to Assistant Secretary of State Frederick Seward on 1 December (77/443, 442).

5. On 8 December Lincoln issued his Proclamation of Amnesty and Reconstruction (CWL, 7:53–56). The proclamation stated that whenever one-tenth of the voters (calculated by votes cast in the 1860 election) would take the oath of allegiance and would establish a "republican" government, that government "shall be recognized as the true government of the State" and the state would thereupon receive the protection of the U.S. government. Bright had written CS 20 November, "it is remarkable that in this country, all parties have a high respect for Mr. Lincoln—so much does a real integrity gain upon the minds of all men."

To George Bemis[1]

Senate Chamber 18th Dec. '63

Dear Bemis,

I send you a letter from Dr Sargent which you will be glad to read. Please do not forget to return it. I am glad that he continues to occupy himself with our question.[2]

How is Mr Loring proceeding with his answer to Historicus?[3] I have had a search for precedents at the Dep. of State, & there are none where we paid for captives not brought into our ports. The case must be argd, therefore, without any such help. But I believe the liability for the Alabama can be sustained.

I hear G. S. Hale[4] is also studying the question.

Every thing here is very tranquil. Never before was Congress so quiet. All have the assurance of success. And yet shall I tell you that I have had a visit of three hours from the French Minister, in which he told me plumply that he thought now as at the beginning that the war must end in "separation," & that France was ready at any time to offer her "good offices" to bring about peace!!—When he said this—I snapped my fingers. But does not this help explain the perverse policy of the Emperor? What news have you?

Ever Yours,   Charles Sumner

Seward thinks that Mercier has changed—he told me so on my arrival—& that his return to Paris would be advantageous to us—as he would enlighten the Emperor![5]

ALS   MHi   (77/496, PCS)

1. George Bemis (1815–78), Boston lawyer.
2. Fitzwilliam Sargent (1820–89), father of the painter John Singer Sargent, wrote CS from Nice 23 November 1863 encouraging his emancipation efforts (29/631, PCS). Sargent's pamphlet *England, the United States and the Southern Confederacy* was published in 1863.
3. Charles G. Loring was preparing an answer to the British legal scholar William Harcourt (1827–1904), who wrote under the pen name "Historicus" in the London *Times*. "Historicus" had stated that the British government acted under the principles of international law when it allowed the *Alabama* to sail. "A subject of the Crown may sell a ship of war . . . to either belligerent with impunity; nay, he may even despatch it for sale to the belligerent port," but he cannot make "overt" war against any who are not declared enemies ("On the Foreign Enlistment Act," *Letters by Historicus on Some Questions of International Law* [1863], 168). Bemis wrote that he thought Loring's argument contained some weaknesses and worried that the pamphlet "will not produce much effect on those to whom it is addressed."
4. George Silsbee Hale (1825–1927), Boston lawyer.
5. The French minister Mercier sailed for France on 30 December (Daniel B. Carroll, *Henri Mercier and the American Civil War* [1971], 354). CS wrote Lieber 28 December, "Mercier leaves Washington to-day. *Inter nos*, he will tell the Emperor that the Mexican Expedition is a mistake & that he ought to withdraw it; but that the national cause here is hopeless & that the war will end in separation! This I have from his own lips" (64/292).

To Orestes A. Brownson

Washington 27th Dec. '63

My dear Dr,

It seems to me you have done wisely—although I offer an opinion on such a matter with diffidence.[1]

I wish you would tell me any way in which I can help;—by letter or by word of mouth any where—& it will be much at yr service.

The Presdt's recent message & Proclamation has 2 points that are important & will be memorable

(1) He makes Emancipation the corner-stone of reconstruction.

(2) He treats the rebel states as now "subverted" & as practically out of the Union, & provides for their reconstruction out of the Union before they shall be recd. How this differs from what is called "the territorial theory" I am at a loss to perceive, except that it is less plain & positive.

In short the Presdt's theory is identical with ours, although he adopts a different nomenclature. But my single object is to settle the question permanently by the obliteration of Slavery, & I am ready to accept any system which promises this result.

I note Mr McKeon's slander. I believe that I have more openly & frankly defended the Catholics than any other person in public life— especially when Know Nothingism scoured the land. I stood out against it & at Faneuil Hall protested against any question on account of religion or birth.[2]

Ever sincerely Yours,   Charles Sumner

ALS InND (77/515, PCS)

1. Brownson wrote 20 December 1863 that he was changing his *Review* from its Roman Catholic emphasis to a "National Secular Review," addressed to both Catholics and Protestants (Elizabeth, New Jersey, 30/080, PCS).

2. In a speech before the New York Court of Common Pleas John McKeon (1808–83; U.S. congressman [Dem., N.Y.], 1835–37, 1841–43) accused CS of aiming to rid the country of Catholicism as well as slavery (*New York Times*, 21 December 1863:4). CS referred to his 2 November 1855 speech, "Political Parties and Our Foreign-Born Population," in which he denounced the Know-Nothing Party for its attacks on Catholics (Wks, 5:63–82).

To Henry C. Wright

Washington. 27th Dec. '63

My dear Sir,

You ask me if in the Reconstruction Policy of the Administration the Federal Govt will be made to assume the Rebel Debt?[1]

I have never heard any such policy proposed by any member of the Administration or by any of its friends.

To me the idea is absurd & revolting. Of course, I shall oppose it wherever it shews its head.

It would be hard that we should pay the murderers who have filled our land with mourning.

I have never been fixed against compensation, as a way of getting rid of slavery—on the principle of a Bridge of Gold for the retreating fiend. But this is very different from a proposition to pay for carrying on the war against us. The person who stands up in Congress to make it ought to be photographed in the act, that mankind may see precisely how he looks.

Meanwhile the good work proceeds. *The end is certain.* I wish I knew as well *when* as *how*. But Slavery will disappear, & this land of ours will be grand & glorious beyond any imagination to conceive.

Accept my best wishes & believe me, dear Sir

Very faithfully Yours,   Charles Sumner

ALS   MB   (77/522, PCS)

1. Henry C. Wright (1797–1879), an abolitionist of long standing, wrote CS that whenever Wright lectured, he was asked this question. He sought CS's permission to quote him as confirming that the U.S. would not assume the Confederate debt; such an answer "would allay the anxiety of many—with whom this—next to the Abolition of Slavery—is an all absorbing question" (Cape Ann, Massachusetts, 20 December 1863, 30/084, PCS).

To the Duchess of Argyll

Washington 29th Dec. '63

A Happy New Year to you! my dear Duchess—although this will not reach you till the Day of Benediction has passed. I trust also that it may deal gently with yr Mother, for whom I feel anxious.

I thought of you often on Xmas day, while I was visiting hospitals. Here are some thirty buildings, hastily constructed, but thoroughly comfortable, beyond any Parisian hospital, where are our poor soldiers, with occasional wards of their rebel enemies. One hospital had in every ward an Aquarium—also a large room with a stage & scenery, where the convalescents enacted farce & comedy. There were also libraries of several hundred volumes, where I observed Macaulay's Essays, Hume's England, Scott's novels, the Caxtons.[1] The Xmas dinner was bountiful & I send you a Bill of Fare at one of the Hospitals.

I went through a rebel ward with some 80 invalid prisoners, treated precisely like our own soldiers. Never before did I notice so great a contrast in so large a number of human beings. After observing our soldiers, as they lay in their beds or sat in their chairs, the rebels seemed in a different scale of existence. They were mostly rough, ignorant, brutal, scowling. I talked with several, &, by inquiries about their health & hopes that they might enjoy their dinner, softened them into a smile. When they knew who I was they seemed uncertain whether to scowl *extra* or to be civil.

Nothing has occurred to disturb the tranquil confidence which prevails here. The result is certain—sooner or later.

The Presdt. shewed me last evng a paper just recd. from Gasparin, Laboulaye, Martin & Cochin,[2] which it made me sad to think was not written by Lord Russell. Such a paper from him would have made our two countries strong in international good will. And why was it left to Frenchmen? Of course, it expressed absolute trust in the result—gave good counsel—regretted the course of Europe—criticised Ld Russell's sayings without, however, naming him. I send you two or three sentences which these good & great men write.

I hear from Vienna, where there is an American who loves England;[3] but it is just in proportion to our love, that we are unhappy at the course of England. The speech which you & the Duke condemn he regards as containing what ought to be said. But I do not allude to him, except to let you see that the best friends of England are those who are most pained. But why do I tumble upon this topic again? I began on hospitals; but the *thought of what might have been*, had England simply stood aloof from Slavery & had nothing to do with its support, haunts me. But enough.

Our Chief Justice is at the point of death.[4] Chase will probably be his successor. I found the Presdt. last night studying how to meet these exigencies.

God bless you!

Ever sincerely Yours, Charles Sumner

ALS CSmH (77/526, PCS)

1. Translations by William Caxton (c. 1421–91).
2. "Reply of Messieurs Angénor de Gasparin, Édouard Laboulaye, Henri Martin and Augustin Cochin and other Friends of America in France, to the Loyal National League of New York" (1863). Not previously identified is Cochin (1823–72), political scientist and also a correspondent of CS's. Commenting on CS's criticism of Britain, the duchess asked him why he thought her country "has not given you as much as France has" (London, 2 February 1864, 30/315, PCS).
3. Motley, then minister to Austria, wrote CS 2 December (29/691).
4. Taney did not die until 12 October 1864.

To William E. Gladstone

Washington 1st Jan. '64

Dear Mr Gladstone,

I begin the year with my acknowledgments of the kindness of yr letter[1] & with my best wishes.

A happy New Year to you & to yr family!

A happy New Year also to all England: for my heart is always with England.

Winter has come, & our soldiers are preparing their huts for winter-quarters. So it is hereabout at least. But I learn that Gen. Grant will not go into winter-quarters.[2] He means to trouble the Rebellion without giving it time to rest. This is more practicable in the milder climate where he is than in Virginia which is on the isothermal line of Crimea.

But our politics seem to have something of the tranquility of our neighboring army. Never since I have been in public life has there been so little excitement in Congress. The way seems at last open. Nobody doubts the result. The assurance of the future gives calmness.

Some who come direct from Genl. Grant declare that the war can be ended on the 4th July next. For myself, I have never seen *when* this war would be ended; for I was unable to estimate the courage & force the resistance might derive from foreign nations. But it has been clear to me always that there was but one way in which it could end; & I have felt sure that could foreign nations see it in its true light there could be no difference on the question.

The Rebellion is simply *Slavery in arms*, making pretensions utterly without precedent in history, revolting, indecent, impious. If the Rebellion could in any way be distinguished from this crime,—then it might have a chance of success. But I do not believe—I cannot believe that in this 19th century—a just Providence will allow such a crime to flourish, or will continue to it the favor of Foreign Powers. No reverse of arms, no failure or national misfortune can shake this firm conviction. There have been gloomy days, & it has been hard to see friends cut off,—so many victims to Slavery supplied & encouraged from Europe; but my confidence has not been disturbed.

It has often seemed to me that if we had failed, there must have been at the last moment a shudder in England at the awful responsibility of taking by the hand a bloody Power the co-mate of Dahomey,[3] & that the English heart would have said—"No"—"In the name of Heaven—No."

Meanwhile our own efforts have relieved England from any such final responsibility. But my heart yearns to see the country that I love pronounce the word which will hasten the end of our domestic war & make any foreign war impossible—all of which is in her power. Rarely in history has any nation been so situated as to do so much for another nation, & for civilization—to say nothing of the infinite profit to herself.[4]

I hope I do not write to you too frankly. I should not write so, if I had less confidence in yr sincerity & goodness.

I have been pained to learn that the Duchess of Sutherland—whose kindness to me enabled me to see you whom I already honored much— is still ailing. I hope that her generous nature may be spared yet longer to soften & quicken our social life. I am sure that she will rejoice when *Slavery now in arms* is cast down never to rise again. I think she would be glad to help at this overthrow.

The date of yr letter "Hawarden" reminds me of a pleasant day, which I can never forget.[5]

Believe me, dear Mr Gladstone,

Ever sincerely Yours,   Charles Sumner

ALS   GBL   (77/550, PCS)

1. Hawarden, 5 November 1863 (29/539, PCS); see CS to Gladstone, 21 April 1863.

2. Grant was then in Chattanooga, planning further Federal penetration into Georgia.

3. West African kingdom that had been the center of slave trade.

4. Gladstone replied from London 1 February 1864, "no good can now be done I think by egging on the combatants from our safe position in Europe. That might be done, I think while there was a hope that European opinion was so formed as to be in a condition to speak with moral force, and with a prospect of usefulness. But the contest has long passed that phase; if indeed it ever was in it. And I am bound to say that as far as I can see European opinion is a good deal bewildered, if not divided. I have therefore only two things to wish: that the issue may come soon, and that it may be beneficial to America, whatever be its form" (30/306).

5. CS had visited Gladstone at his home 4 November 1857 (CS's journal, Prc, 3:554).

To Richard Cobden

Washington 25th Jan. '64

My dear Cobden,

I hope you will receive by this steamer at least the 1st vol. of the Diplomatic Papers for the last year. You will read them with interest, but wish there were not so many. The English Correspondance occupies more than 700 pages.

But read;—& you shall see why I made my speech on 10th Sept. Ld Russell's letter of 1st Sept,[1] seemed to leave small loop-hole for peace. War was imminent.

I was determined to try to reach certain persons, &, then, if Ld Russell would have war, there was to be a statement of our case.

The new vol. makes me feel more than ever how right I was in my determination.

There is the repose of winter-quarters almost in our Congress. Never have I known our politics so tranquil.[2]

The diplomatists here are becoming more reasonable & friendly. This shews progress.

Our papers have noticed extensively yr pressure upon Mr Delane,[3] which seems now to be ended. It seems to me that you gained two important points.

(1) You brought Delane to light.

(2) You exhibited his recent misrepresentation so clearly & put it under such a calcium light that all England saw it. There is an end to it. Speech & argt. would have failed to do what you did by those few impassioned words.

Bon jour! Ever Yours,   Charles Sumner

ALS   GBWSR   (77/619, PCS)

1. On 1 September 1863 Russell wrote Adams that, since no firm evidence had been uncovered to indicate that the rams were intended to serve as Confederate cruisers, "her Majesty's government could not properly direct a prosecution or action under the foreign enlistment act" (*Foreign Relations* [1863], part 1, 362–63).

2. Cobden wrote CS 7 January 1864 from Midhurst, looking ahead to the presidential election: "I hope you will re-elect Mr Lincoln.—He is rising in reputation in Europe,—apart from the success of the North. He possesses great moral qualities which in the long run tell more on the fortunes of the world in these days than mere intellect.—I always thought his want of enlarged experience was a disadvantage to him. But he knows his countrymen, evidently, and that is the main point.—And being a stranger to the rest of the world, he has the less temptation to embark in foreign controversies or quarrels. . . . I say all this on the assumption that he has irrevocably committed himself to 'abolition' as the result of the war" (30/176, PCS).

3. In December 1863 Cobden had carried on a sharply worded correspondence with John T. Delane (1817–79), editor of the London *Times*. On 3 December the *Times* had criticized Bright for proposing, in his Rochdale speech, new land distribution to the disadvantage of the British aristocracy. Cobden charged that the *Times* misrepresented Bright and broadened his attack to criticize the paper's consistent defense of the privileged classes. Excerpts from the correspondence are printed in John Morley, *The Life of Richard Cobden* (1879), 887–98; see *New York Times*, 26–30 December 1863; 8 January 1864.

To Francis Lieber

Washington 31st Jan. '64

My dear Lieber,

(1) Did I write to you, asking your opinion on introducing the system of Competitive Examination for minor offices in our civil department?[1]

I have such a bill drawn, but I am not sure if Public Opinion will sustain me.

(2) The Academy of Science, created by Act of Congress, seems to have been successful.[2] Agassiz thinks it a great success & the beginning of a new Power in Science.

But should we stop here?

What say you to two Academies

(*a*) Sciences Morales et Politiques

(*b*) Belles Lettres.

If these were constituted, we might have our Institute.

The names must be changed somewhat to *Americanize* them. "Moral & Political Sciences"—would not do. Every body would see vulgar politics in such a designation—What say you to—"Social Sciences"? Or what is the proper term?

The other should be simply—"Academy of Literature."

Now, dear Lieber, please think of these things. Is there any thing practical in them? If the exact sciences can have an Academy, why not the other sciences & literature?

If you are favorably impressed by these hints, then help me to two lists of 12 or 20 to go into two Bills constituting these different Academies.

I can at least make the effort. But petty jealousies may interfere with immediate success. But I am not easily disheartened.

Write me frankly on all the points involved.[3] Meanwhile do not speak *aloud* on a subject which if started would pique the curiosity of the public.

(3) England & Ld Russell soften towards us. L. Nap. continues the same sphynx. Meanwhile I am sad to see the cloud of war gathering over the continent, just ready to break. Is not war inevitable?[4]

Ld Lyons said to me the other day—"*you do* take good care of my treaties."—But his chief at home charges me with disturbing the peace.

Our consul at Liverpool has written out for 1000 copies of my New York speech,[5] & the League at Phila. has voted to supply the edition.

Ever yours,   Charles Sumner

ALS   MH-H   (64/294, PCS)

1. Lieber replied on 2 February 1864 that CS's plan was "most desirable," yet "most difficult." However, he urged CS to go ahead, for wasn't his plan "one of those cases in which the mere breaking the ice is of importance?" (New York, 77/642, PCS).

2. The National Academy of Sciences was founded in 1863 as a private organization with selected membership.

3. If two academies were formed, wrote Lieber, he would like one to bear the "time-honored name" of political science. He would soon send CS a list of proposed members and promised to be "very impartial."

4. The British courts had recently decided to take no further action on the ironclad *Alexandra*, which had been in British custody since April 1863; thus the ship would not be released to the Confederates. On the continent, Denmark stated it would fight Prussia to retain the duchy of Schleswig, half Danish, half German. Both countries began preparing for war (*New York Times*, 31 January 1864:3; 25 January 1864:1).

5. In the only recent recovered letter, Thomas H. Dudley (1819–93; consul 1861–72) requested "20 or 30 copies" of "Our Foreign Relations," stating, "The speech has done us much good here. It tells them the truth this they do not like to hear" (26 December 1863, 30/105).

To the Duchess of Argyll

Washington 8th Feb. '64

My dear Duchess,

I know not if I have spoken to you of a Comttee. raised in the Senate on my motion, to take into consideration the whole subject of Slavery & the treatment of freedmen.[1] Only a short time ago such a Comttee. would not have been authorized. A few years ago the proposition would have created a storm of violence.

As chairman of this Comttee. I find myself with work enough. I wish daily for ten times the strength I have—especially as my other duties in the Senate, & as Chairman of the Comttee. on For. Relations are very onerous.

But the appointment of the Slavery Comttee. marks an epoch of history. I hope very soon to report a bill sweeping away all Fug. Slave Bills—also an Amendment of the Constitution abolishing Slavery throughout the U. States.[2]

Alas! alas! as I think of these measures, I say how strongly England has thrown herself in their way.

There is a claim of an Englishman now pending on account of the action of one of our ships. I have held the bill back for sometime. It is a just claim; but I have marvelled that Ld Russell could present a claim for a penny against this govt—when his conduct has driven our commerce from the sea & created so many claimants. What a piece of work is man!

I may, on moving its passage, take occasion to review the topics suggested by such a claim. But I am weary & much occupied, & would gladly avoid any effort which is not required in the discharge of duty.

I have ventured to acknowledge the message of the Bishop of Oxford[3] in a note which I leave unsealed for you to read & drop into the post-office, if you do not think me too bold in writing it.

I hope yr mother the Duchess is strong again. I know how anxiously she must watch the bloody currents of this fearful war.

Europe too seems volcanic.[4] I do not see how war can be prevented. If it ends in the fall of the French Emperor I shall have no grief.

Ever Yours & the Duke's   Charles Sumner

P.S. The photographs of Slavery came as prompt as a letter. But I was astonished to find Freedom at last beneath the English flag. I do not so read events. If English statesmen had been indulged, & Ld Russell's prophecies fulfilled, the English flag would have been intertwined with the flag of the Slave-monger Nation. But the drawings are very interesting, & I value them much from you.

ALS   CSmH   (77/651, PCS)

1. The Senate unanimously adopted CS's resolution that a select Committee on Slavery and Freedmen be formed on 13 January 1864, and on 14 January he was appointed chairman (*Globe*, 38th Cong., 1st sess., 174, 197).

2. CS presented his bill abolishing fugitive slave acts on 29 February; the seventh of his resolutions, "Guarantees and Safeguards Against Slavery and for the Protection of Freedmen," 8 February, called for a constitutional amendment "to prohibit Slavery everywhere within the limits of the Republic" (ibid., 864, 523).

3. The duchess wrote CS 30 December 1863 that she thought Samuel Wilberforce (1805–73) "entirely in the wrong" when he said he thought emancipation "would come sooner, and safer" after the South had won its independence (Roseneath, 30/122, PCS). CS's message to the bishop, 5 February, stated that the war could end only in the abolition of slavery and that he thanked God "the cloud which hung over England" seemed to be lifting (Prc, 4:174).

4. The *New York Times* carried more talk of mobilization on the part of Prussia and Denmark (31 January 1864:3; 4 February 1864:1).

To Francis Lieber

Senate Chamber 10th Feb. '64

My dear Lieber,

I think your point is in the last speech of Calhoun in Senate—read by Mr Mason—& to be found in his works, which must be in yr College Library.[1]

I send another *souvenir*, for the glimpse it gives of life at the Exec. Mansion.[2]

The vote on my proposition to amend the Constitution was wonderful—31 to 8; & yet no New York paper noticed it. This is history.[3]

Slavery will be abolished by amendment of the Constitution; but time will be required. Much else must be done.

I am tired. At this moment I have two important foreign questions, first, the removal by capitalization of the dues paid by our commerce on the Scheldt,[4] on which I expect to speak to-day in Exec. session; & secondly, a Bill to pay 5 millions for French spoliations on which I am now drawing a report. To these add business of all kinds, & the various questions of Slavery—& of England—& I wish for a day of rest.

Ever yours,   Charles Sumner

ALS   MH-H   (64/300, PCS)

1. Lieber asked CS for the citation to Calhoun's speech in which he argued that the U.S. should always admit a free and a slave state together in order to maintain an equal representation of both in the Senate (New York, 8 February 1864, 77/655, PCS).

2. From time to time CS sent his correspondents letters to him from his friend Mary Todd Lincoln (1818–82), although this particular one has not been recovered. Lieber did not specifically respond to CS's "souvenir" in his letter of 12 February, but did comment on Mrs. Lincoln's extravagance, abetted by William S. Wood, Commissioner of Public Buildings in Washington: "she has not done much good to the President" (77/657).

3. On 8 February, when CS introduced, as a joint resolution, his proposal for emancipating all slaves, he requested that it be referred to his committee on slavery and freedmen; however, when Lyman Trumbull, chair of the Judiciary Committee, said the proposal was more appropriately the responsibility of his committee, CS acquiesced. The Senate voted down, 8–31, the motion to postpone indefinitely consideration of CS's proposal, and it was referred to the Judiciary Committee (Globe, 38th Cong., 1st sess., 521–22).

4. After some consideration, the Senate ratified the commercial and navigation treaty between the U.S. and Belgium on 26 February (Executive Proceedings, 13:423).

To Francis Lieber

Senate Chamber 19th Feb. '64

Dear Lieber,

Yr missives have been speeded.[1]

É pur si muove![2] And this is an illustration.

Last evng at dinner with Judge Holt,—Seward sitting opposite me—& the venerable Judge Wayne on my side,[3]—the latter said—"I wish, Mr S. that you would move a Comttee of 10 in the Senate to consider amendments to the Const. & to have them made before the rebel states are admitted back. The Constitution is a failure"—

"But, Judge" said I, "this seems new language. I have never said that the Constitution was a failure."

"But" said the Judge "it is a failure, & I wish to see it thoroughly revised."

Considering the age & character of the Judge—a judge of the S.C—from the South—I thought this language an illustration of the change of sentiment, which seems now to be moving like a Bay of Funday tide.

I hesitate whether to report a Bill to ratify the Presdt's Proclamation of Emancipation; but I shall brush away all Fug. Sl. Acts, & give the reasons in a report which the Comttee. has approved.

Ever yours,   Charles Sumner

ALS   CSmH   (77/669, PCS)

1. Lieber had enclosed an unidentified message for Major General Halleck in his letter to CS of 17 February 1864 (77/663, PCS).
2. "And then it is moving!"
3. Joseph Holt (1807–94), a War Democrat from Kentucky, had been appointed judge advocate-general of the army in 1862. James M. Wayne (c. 1790–1867) was associate Supreme Court justice, 1835–67.

To Francis W. Bird
private

Senate Chamber 22nd Feb. '64

My dear Bird,

You do not understand Wilson's point.

By accepting the suggestion of 1st Jan. when all were to be equal, black & white, he obtained a certain advantage.[1]

But he sustained positively my proposition. He saw from the opposition developed against it that it would not pass *on that bill* & felt that it must be attempted in some other way.

If you look over the yeas & nays, you will see what *New England senators* voted against it.[2]

One of the most common devices of opposition is to say "This is not the Bill for yr proposition"—"Bring in a separate Bill & we will vote for it"—Humbug!—

My amendment ought to have passed on that Bill. *It was the very place for it.*

But, when the Chairman of the Finance Comttee. {*Fessenden*}, from New England, lead off against it, its fate was doubtful. There is a squad ready to follow him, while all Hunkers, whether calling themselves Republicans or Democrats naturally voted against the proposition.

The two Iowa senators surprized me; but they feared trouble on account of certain negro troops enlisted in Iowa at $10.[3]

The whole debate was discreditable. But it grew out of a false inter-

pretation of the statutes by a Massachusetts officer, & it was instigated
by a New England senator?

Have I told you that Mr Chase says there will be no Appraiser vacancy
in Boston? Mr [*Oliver*] Dorrance will not be continued in New York.

I am sorry, for I had hoped to see Darragh[4] in the place.

Ever yours   Charles Sumner

I write this without any hint from Wilson & without his knowledge.[5]

ALS MH-H (77/671, PCS)

1. The Senate considered on 10 and 13 February 1864 Henry Wilson's bill to pay
black and white soldiers equally and CS offered an amendment that the pay be retroactive to the black soldiers' enlistment. During the debate on 13 February, Wilson
stated he would vote for CS's amendment but in order to get his bill passed, he would
also accept a different amendment providing for retroactive pay only from 1 January
1864 (*Globe*, 38th Cong., 1st sess., 562–66, 632–643). In an editorial, the Boston
Commonwealth (19 February 1864:2) stated its "surprise" that Wilson "seems to have
requested Mr. Sumner to withdraw the amendment, that he might offer one making
the full pay date from January 1."

2. Senators Collamer, Fessenden, and Foot voted against CS's amendment, as did
Senators Grimes and James Harlan (1820–99; [Rep., Iowa], 1857–65, 1867–73)
(*Globe*, 38th Cong., 1st sess., 643).

3. Fessenden spoke on 10 February against what he considered special favors that
CS's amendment would grant to black troops. On 13 February he remarked that
Massachusetts should take responsibility for paying its troops according to its promise
(ibid., 564, 636).

4. Robert K. Darrah (c. 1815–85).

5. Bird answered on 24 February, expressing regret for his "hasty paragraph" on
Wilson, and assured CS he would "put it right." He still thought Wilson should have
supported CS's amendment more emphatically (Boston, 30/396, PCS).

To Relief Jacob Sumner[1]

Washington 22nd Feb. '64

My dear Mother,

I wish you would look at the Mining Stocks, & find the Dana scrip
& send it to me. I have no recollection of it.

Please return the notice also.

It has been very cold here; but it now comfortable.

I have just completed a Report, brushing away all Fug. Slave Laws.

I hope you are strong & well.

Ever Yours   C. S.

ALS MH-H (64/304, PCS)

1. Only eighteen letters from CS to his mother have been recovered and none from her to him.

To Susan B. Anthony

Senate Chamber 2nd March '64

Dear Madam,

I return the slip with one or two corrections[1]

I regretted at the time that the debate on yr petition was not reported at length in the N.Y. papers. It would have been an advertisement of the movement, which would have acted powerfully on the country.[2]

But the press is now occupied by military matters, & I infer that the public is less interested in debates.

Franks can be used only where the Senator or M.C. happens to be.[3] They could not be made & sent for use in N.Y. If they were despatched from Washington, they could be easily obtained.

Meanwhile the work goes on. Slavery is doomed. But much remains to be done.[4]

Accept my best wishes & believe me, Madam,

very faithfully Yours,   Charles Sumner

ALS CSmH (78/008, PCS)

1. Susan B. Anthony (1820–1906), working on behalf of the National Woman's Loyal League, had sent a petition with 100,000 signatures asking for the emancipation of "all persons of African descent." This petition CS had presented to Congress 9 February 1864 with a brief speech (*Globe*, 38th Cong., 1st sess., 536). Anthony now asked CS to look over the *Globe* account because she wanted the speech to be printed with the new round of petitions the National Woman's Loyal League intended to circulate (New York, 1 March, 30/427, PCS).

2. Anthony was indignant that the "stupid *Washington* Correspondent" for the *New York Tribune* had not reported CS's speech in full.

3. Because of her concern about expenses of gathering signatures on the 25,000 additional petitions, Anthony asked if CS could get franking privileges for the league. She informed CS that the new petitions carried a request for a constitutional amendment abolishing slavery "to kill the *cause* of our national troubles."

4. Thanking CS for his help, Anthony also endorsed a recently formed "*Freedom & Fremont* Club" which "asserts the right to examine & pronounce upon *the administration*" (New York, 6 March, 30/451).

To Mary L. Booth[1]

Senate Chamber 7th March '64

Dear Miss Booth,

I learn on inquiry that the Comttee. of the Senate has determined to recommend the confirmation of yr excellent brother. He will beyond question be confirmed.[2]

Don't trouble yourself on this point.

I admire Laboulaye always. He has the knowledge, instinct & firmness of a statesman. I fear that our noble friend Gasparin has not meditated enough the injunction "*First* pure, *then* peaceable."[3]

There is a time for all things. And now is the time sternly to put down the Rebellion, & Slavery; for the two are mated, so that they will stand or fall together. Accept my best wishes, & believe me,

very faithfully Yours,   Charles Sumner

ALS   NcD   (78/021, PCS)

1. Mary L. Booth (1831–89), writer, editor, and translator, had been a friend of George Sumner's.

2. The Senate approved Charles A. Booth's appointment as assistant adjutant general on 8 March 1864 (*Executive Proceedings*, 13:439).

3. Booth had recently translated several essays and tracts by the pro-Union French writers Augustin Cochin, Laboulaye, and Gasparin.

To Francis Lieber

Senate Chamber 14th March '64

My dear Lieber,

The day I recd. your letter which recognises Slavery in the fugitive clause of the Constn, Bertinatti the Italian Minister, a most accomplished jurist, steeped in the Roman law & the principles of interpretation, came bounding into my room, saying that he had read the report carefully from beginning to end—that as a question of interpretation it was clear that Slavery cannot be established on inference;[1]—that the rule—*impius et crudelis qui libertate non foret*—must govern the question;—that the *cour de cassation*[2] of France, & every Supreme Court of Europe would apply that rule as I applied it.

I was led to my confidence in this conclusion by the remarkable argt of Granville Sharp, who drove Ld Mansfield to declare that Slavery could not exist in England.[3] In his researches he found that "Slave" & "Slavery" was not mentioned any where in the British Constitution. He next gathered together the commanding rules, requiring that for the sake of Liberty we must "take hold even of a "twine-thread," & that, if certain words are susceptible of two significations that must be adopted which is not "odious."

Unhesitatingly I lay it down as a rule, that such is "Slavery" it cannot be legalized *indirectly*. If you would legalize this enormity you must name it "positively"; for the court will be bound to save the instrument from any such criminal character if it can be shewn to be applicable to any thing else. The moment words were adopted which meant or might mean *two things*, it was impossible to make them mean Slavery.[4]

Harvey[5] said that no physician *over 40* accepted his invention of the circulation of the blood. The lawyers *over 40* will be against me. But I did count upon your testimony.

The appropriation bills drive my repeal out of sight. But I shall press it.

But where are your two lists?[6] And what titles for the Academies? Will it do to say "political"? People will suspect that it is a caucus.

Ever Yours,   Charles Sumner

ALS   MH-H   (64/306, PCS)

1. Regarding CS's recent report, *Wrong and Unconstitutionality of Fugitive Slave Acts*, Lieber wrote that, although it was "significant" that the word *slave* did not appear in the Constitution, he believed that the phrase in article 4, section 2, paragraph 3, "'persons held to labour' meant chiefly slaves" (New York, 12 March 1864, 78/031, PCS). Joseph Bertinatti (1808–81) served as Italian minister to the U.S., 1861–66.
2. "Liberty will not permit that which is unscrupulous and cruel." *Cour de cassation*, "the highest court of appeal."
3. Granville Sharpe (1735–1813), antislavery activist who founded an abolition society in Great Britain in 1787. CS cited Sharpe's argument in his report (U.S. Senate, Select Committee of Slavery and Freedmen, *Wrong and Unconstitutionality of Fugitive Slave Acts*, Senate Report no. 24, 1864, 3, serial set 1178).
4. Lieber had written CS, "let us abolish Slavery and no discussion about Fugitives will be necessary."
5. William Harvey (1578–1657).
6. Lieber suggested that CS propose two academies, one of "Moral and Political Science and History" and another of "Literature," possibly including fine arts. He also sent CS some names of prospective members (20 March, 78/044).

To Francis Lieber

Senate Chamber—
22nd March [1864]

P.S. The question is not what the authors of the fug. Clause really at the time *intended*, but what they *succeeded in declaring*.[1] Now, they did

not use words which *mean Slavery*, & you cannot go outside of the words
they used. How often a will breaks because the testator did not use fit
terms!

But your argt. overthrows Somersett's case,[2] Ld Mansfield & Granville Sharp. On these I stand.

—

But pray send me *two* lists. I have not preserved the lists I sent you.
Give me the lists complete. I have no time to devise them.[3]

Ever Yours,   Charles Sumner

ALS   MH-H   (64/314, PCS)

1. In his letter of 20 March 1864, Lieber repeated to CS his argument of 12 March regarding terminology in the Constitution and stated his belief that if CS's bill to abolish fugitive slave acts passed the Senate, it would fail in the House. "Until the Constitution is changed—and it must be changed—it would have been safer to ask trial by jury for fugitives, or to let the matter rest at present, since no one will claim a fugitive now" (New York, 78/046, PCS).

2. James Mansfield argued in 1772 that the slave James Somersett could not be returned to his native Virginia because he was free once he had landed in Great Britain.

3. On page four of CS's note Lieber wrote the following names: "Binney, Lieber, Bancroft, Dr {*Daniel B.?*} Smith, Everett, Ticknor, Motley, P. Godwin, Howe, {*Fitzgreene*} Halleck, S.{*amuel*} Tyler, Woolsey."

To Nathaniel Niles

Senate Chamber, April 2nd, 1864.

Dear Sir:

Thanks for the suggestions of your letter.[1]

Starting from your premise that the Franco-Austrian Empire in Mexico is a fixed fact, I should come to your conclusions, were it not for a doubt, of the weight of which I leave you to judge, whether such a course as you propose would not impress the Emperor with a sense of our weakness and so hasten the very thing we wish to avoid.

The disadvantages of a contiguous Empire are so great that we should not waive our right to object to it unless by so doing we could count upon great advantage. I admit that a cordial relation with French Mexico, cutting off all hopes of the secessionists from that quarter, would be such an advantage as might pay us for the sacrifice, but could we count upon obtaining it?[2] Would not our friendship be hollow?

It is a very difficult subject and I am glad of any light upon it. Believe me dear Sir,

faithfully yours,   Charles Sumner

N. Niles Esq. 122, 2nd Av. New York

P.S. The more I reflect upon it, the more impossible I find it to make any concession to this new-fangled imperialism.[3]

LS   NcD   (78/057, PCS)

1. Nathaniel Niles (1791–1869), a physician and former diplomatic representative in Europe, wrote CS 25 March 1864 recommending that the U.S. recognize the Maximilian government (New York, 30/561, PCS). Niles had recently written a letter to the *Journal of Commerce* in which he called a prospective House motion criticizing the Maximilian government "demogogic and futile" (clipping, CS Papers, Duke University).

2. Unconvinced by CS's arguments, Niles replied that the U.S. should avoid any quarrel with a neighbor that might weaken the Union cause. He saw in CS's letter "a struggle . . . between your *opinions* as a statesman responsible to the country for the effect of your acts, and your *sentiments* in hostility to monarchy" (11 April 1864, 30/628). CS replied on 21 April, "You are entirely mistaken in supposing that feeling has anything to do with my views on this question. It is with me as it undoubtedly is with you merely a question of what is right and what is expedient" (78/109).

3. The P.S. is in CS's hand.

To George William Curtis

Washington 13th April '64

My dear Curtis,

I send you at Govr. Morgan's hint a copy of the *Globe* of Saturday containing the closing debate on the Constitutional Amendment.[1]

The *Globe* shows substantially what was said; but it does not show the impatience of the Senate towards the close of the discussion. Senators wished to vote & get their dinner. Yielding to this impatience I forebore to press my substitutes.[2] I regret now my forbearance.

I wish especially that I had brought the senate to a vote by *Ayes & Noes* on the question whether Slavery should be allowed as "a punishment of crime."[3] But there is a chance that the House will amend our proposition, which is as poor in form as possible.

I owe you an apology for not answering yr letter about the Albany outrage;[4] but it found me in the midst of a most laborious report from the Comttee on Foreign Relations, which left me no time even for rest. At the same time I was engaged with the Slavery Comttee.

At last I have made a report of a new bill to organize a Bureau of Freedmen. The *Tribune* does me injustice, of course;—as is its habit.[5] In an article yesterday, it makes "Mr Sumner" responsible for not accepting the House bill. This is a mistake. I have tried to get the House

Bill through the Comttee., & have presented to the Comttee. every consideration urged by the *Tribune*. My heart is in this matter, as much as the *Tribune's*, & I have no personal opinions or prejudices in the way. *I seek the best that is practicable*. But the *Tribune* likes a fling at me.

But the Comttee. consists of *seven*, all with opinions of their own.[6] Charles 5th[7] could not make his clocks go alike, & I have had a similar experience with the Comttee.—until day before yesterday they united cordially in the new bill which I had drafted.

I keep the House Bill still in Comttee.—to be reported, if the other bill fails. This was the best thing I could do. But when I attempted to press the House Bill, I was met by an inflexible opposition. There was only one other member who was willing to unite with me in reporting the House Bill. Pray let Mr Shaw[8] know these things.

Of course, what passes in Comttee. is not for the public. Therefore, I must bear the ungenerous imputations to which I am exposed.

This is a long story—for a busy man. Pardon.

Ever Yours,   Charles Sumner

I send you two reports from my comtee. (1) to repeal all fugitive slave acts (2) all exclusion of colored testimony.[9] The last is essential to the protection of the new made freedmen.

ALS   MH-H   (78/082, PCS)

1. Edwin D. Morgan (1811–83), governor of New York, 1859–62, was a U.S. senator (Rep., N.Y., 1863–69). During the debate on 8 April 1864 CS delivered his speech ("No Property in Man") supporting the Thirteenth Amendment to the Constitution (*Globe,* 38th Cong., 1st sess., 1479–83).
2. CS proposed a substitute stating that "All persons are equal before the law, so that no person can hold another as a slave; and the Congress may make all laws necessary and proper to carry this article into effect everywhere within the United States and the jurisdiction thereof," but withdrew it. The Senate passed the Thirteenth Amendment, 38–6 (ibid., 1483, 1488–90).
3. CS spoke in favor of the proposal of John B. Henderson (1826–1913; U.S. senator [Dem., Mo.], 1862–69), which contained this wording (ibid., 1487–88).
4. Curtis had written CS on 21 March protesting the Albany Young Men's Association's decision to deny blacks admission to future lectures (Staten Island, 30/537, PCS). CS wrote the organization's secretary on 16 April, stating he could not speak before "an audience too delicate to sit beside a black citizen" (Wks, 11:228).
5. The House bill on a freedmen's bureau was referred on 2 March to CS's Committee on Slavery and Freedmen. CS's bill was reported on 12 April (*Globe,* 38th Cong., 1st sess., 1559). The *New York Tribune*, stating that the issue was too important to squabble over trivial differences, criticized CS for opposing the House bill (12 April 1864:4).
6. Committee members were Benjamin Gratz Brown (1826–85; U.S. senator [Dem., Mo.], 1863–67), Charles R. Buckalew (1821–99; U.S. senator [Dem., Pa.],

1863–69), John S. Carlile (1817–78; U.S. senator [Union, Va.], 1861–65), John Conness (Calif.), Jacob M. Howard (Mich.), and Samuel C. Pomeroy (Kans.).

7. Charles V (1500–1558), Holy Roman Emperor.

8. Jacob M. Howard joined CS (DD, 2:175). Francis George Shaw (1809–82), a New York merchant, Curtis's father-in-law, and father of the late Robert Gould Shaw, wrote CS 11 April (New York, 30/636) about the work of the National Freedmen's Association.

9. CS presented his report, *Exclusion of Colored Testimony,* in the Senate 29 February (*Globe,* 38th Cong., 1st sess., 864).

To Edward L. Pierce

Senate Chamber April 22nd. 1864

Dear Sir,

I do not see the difficulty which you seem to see in giving the commissioners authority to decide as to who are rebels,[1] of course they would make such decision only in the first instance and subject to the revision of the Courts. It seems to me that the owner of an actually abandoned estate would be presumed to be a rebel so that a provision authorizing the occupation of all abandoned estates in addition to the provision of the bill is not necessary. The design of the provision as it stands is to cover lands liable to sale for taxes, or to which the U.S. has any title whatsoever.

The change of Department was made because there was found to be all ready in the Treasury the machinery for such a bureau,[2] and because Secretary Chase objected to having abandoned plantations withdrawn from his jurisdiction, unless he were also relieved of responsibility as to the collection of direct taxes, commercial intercourse &c, in the rebel States.

Faithfully yours,   Charles Sumner

E. L. Pierce Esq. 16 Summer St Boston

This subject is environed with difficulties. [Outside?] criticism will, probably, defeat the whole effort. *The House Bill* could not be got through the Senate Comttee. It was voted down *five* to *two;* I being in the minority. The only chance now is to push the Senate Bill; but if that is defeated, then the question is lost. It has cost me much trouble & anxiety. Gratz Brown was so strong against the House Bill, that he would *speak & vote* against it in the Senate. He considered that it handed over the freedmen to a 2nd slavery. You will observe that the Senate Bill provides against any such fate.[3]

Pray help us sweep away the fug. slave Bill.[4]

LS   MH-H   (64/318, PCS)

1. Pierce wrote from Boston 18 April 1864 about differences between the House and Senate proposals to establish a freedmen's bureau. He thought that the Freedmen's Commission would have difficulty in determining exactly what property was subject to sale or confiscation, and raised the question of abandoned real estate (30/659, PCS).

2. Pierce favored the House bill, which put the bureau under the aegis of the War Department, at least while the war lasted, because military cooperation would be available.

3. The Senate bill provided for careful freedmen's bureau supervision of both the treatment and wages paid to freedmen to guard against what CS called "enforced labor or apprenticeship" (see CS's speech on the bill, "A Bridge from Slavery to Freedom," 8 June, *Globe,* 38th Cong., 1st sess., 2798–2800).

4. The last two paragraphs are in CS's hand.

To William Lloyd Garrison
private

Senate Chamber 23d April '64

Dear Mr Garrison,

You will see what has occurred in the Senate.

We were on the point of passing a "little bill repealing all "acts or parts of acts" for the surrender of fugitive slaves, when John Sherman of Ohio interfered to keep alive the old act of 1793; & Foster of Conn has followed with an elaborate speech vindicating the atrocity.

The vote in favor of slave-hunting stood 24 to 17, including *ten* republicans in the majority.[1]

If the Anti-Slavery sentiment had not become so sluggish, this could not have taken place. Cannot you help to revive it?[2]

The *practical measures* are to clean the statute-book of all support of Slavery.[3]

Ever Yours,   Charles Sumner

ALS   MB   (78/113,PCS)

1. On 19 April 1864 CS moved and spoke for the repeal of all fugitive slave acts. John Sherman amended the bill to except the Fugitive Slave Act of 1793 and after debate the Senate approved, 24–17, Sherman's amendment. Republican senators voting for the amendment were: Collamer, Edgar Cowan, Garrett Davis, James Dixon, Doolittle, Foster, Ira Harris, Timothy Howe, Sherman, and Trumbull (*Globe,* 38th Cong., 1st sess., 1709–15). Lafayette Foster (1806–80; U.S. senator [Rep., Conn.], 1855–67) spoke on 20 April in support of the Act of 1793, with frequent interruptions from CS (ibid., 1746–52).

2. CS wrote a similar plea to Parke Godwin of the New York *Evening Post* (23 April, 78/115, PCS).

3. The *Liberator* (29 April 1864:70) printed a one-column extract of CS's report describing it as "touchingly expressed," and included the report's close, a call for repeal. However, the writer described as "fallacious" the arguments in the report trying to prove that article 4, section 2, of the Constitution did not refer to fugitive slaves.

To John Andrew
private

Senate Chamber 30th April '64

Dear Andrew,

At last we see day-light. Yesterday was the opinion of the Atty. Genl,[1] & on the same day the House Military Comttee. reported back the Senate Bill doing justice to colored troops,[2] & the House Comttee. of Ways & Means agreed to report the Appropriations Bill on which the Senate had fastened its Bill of Justice.

I recd. your telegram asking for copy of the opinion just as the Senate was adjourning. Shortly afterwards while at dinner in company with Stanton, the Presdt suddenly entered in pursuit of his Secretary. Seeing me, he said "I have something good for you;" & he then referred to the opinion of the Atty Genl. I then read yr despatch, asking for a copy. He said "you shall have mine." During the evng he sent it to me, & I now forward it to you. It is the opinion of the Atty. Genl, signed by him & transmitted to the Presdt.

God be praised!

Ever Yours,   Charles Sumner

ALS   MHi   (78/124, PCS)

1. Andrew had been exercised over the case of a black chaplain, Samuel Harrison, of the Massachusetts 54th regiment, whom Stanton had denied the regular $100 a month chaplain's pay. Stanton argued that Harrison merited only the pay of $10 a month as provided by the law of 17 July 1862 for those "of African descent" employed in the armed services. In his opinion of 23 April 1864, requested by Lincoln, Bates distinguished between blacks who were "employed" to perform menial tasks and those who "enrolled" in the armed services and thus stated Harrison was entitled to the regular chaplain's pay (*New York Times*, 8 May 1864:6; Lincoln to Bates, 4 April, CWL, 7:280).

2. Andrew had also written CS about general inequities to black troops and criticized the "false decision" of the War Department as well as congressional "neglect," which was "more stupid than wicked" (Boston, 23 April, 78/111, PCS).

To Charles Eliot Norton
private

Senate Chamber 2nd May '64

My dear Norton,

I regret very much that the Baltimore Convention is to be at so early a day.[1] I see nothing but disaster from mixing our politics with battle & blood. The Presidential Question should be kept back as long as possible—at least until the end of summer. On this point I have no doubt.

Do not regard me as dogmatical. I should not write on this point, if you had not expressly asked my opinion.

Unless the Convention is postponed,—the future seems to me uncertain.

Of course, I say nothing about candidates. *That question ought not to be touched now.* I say nothing upon it here, & take no part in any of the controversies. My relations with the Presdt are of constant intimacy, & I have reason to believe that he appreciates my reserve.

As to the Bill for Freedmen, on which you propose to express a positive opinion[2] let me ask yr attention to *three* questions;

(1) Should this Bureau be placed in the War Department or the Treasury? The House put it in the War.

(2) The House Bill separates the care of freedmen from the care of plantations. Some who are most familiar with the subject from practical knowledge, say that this is "worse than nothing, & cannot work." How is this?

(3) Gratz Brown insists that the House Bill furnishes no protection to the freedmen,—so as to keep them from being made serfs or apprentices. On this account he announces that he would vote & speak against it. What say you?[3] I mention these as points on which we are obliged to act.

The whole question is embarassing from essential differences of opinion, & the peculiar character of the House Bill.

For myself, I am ready to take any bill & trust to the corrective of good sense in its administration & future legislation.

Ever yours,   Charles Sumner

ALS MH-H (78/134, PCS)

1. Charles Eliot Norton (1827–1908), then a writer for the Loyal Publication Society, wrote CS 29 April 1864 from Cambridge about a movement in the society

to urge postponement of the Republican convention scheduled for 7–8 June in Baltimore. Norton opposed such a change because he believed it would only breed dissension and favor "Fremont, Butler & other impossible candidates" (30/714, PCS).

2. Norton sent CS a draft (now unrecovered) of an article he had written to answer the *New York Tribune*'s criticism of CS's bill. If CS approved, Norton planned to publish the article immediately.

3. Responding, Norton wrote he thought CS's bill "far superior" to the House bill but was concerned about the Senate bill's success. He now believed it better to "take the House bill, with all its defects." He considered highly crucial the person chosen to administer the Freedmen's Bureau (7 May, 31/039).

To Francis Lieber

Senate Chamber 4th May '64

My dear Lieber,

I have both yr letters of 2nd & 3d May. I am much pressed by work, but always read what you write with much interest.

I think that Banks's military character has suffered very much—hardly more than he had suffered as a statesmen by his proceedings for reconstruction.[1]

The sentiment in Louisiana among the earnest Anti-Slavery men is very strong for Butler. The Presdt. some time ago sent for me to show me private letters from Banks on reconstruction;[2] but I have not exchanged a word with him on Banks's military character, &, considering that he is a Massachusetts man, I do not wish to interfere against him. For the present I stand aloof

I was glad that you thought so well of my speech.[3] I know of no proposition to reprint it. Indeed, there is very little disposition now to print or reprint any thing that does not describe a battle. How would you change the passage to which you refer? That grew out of a discussion a few days before between Reverdy Johnson & myself, where the former vindicated the Dred Scott decision, & I branded it as an outrage.[4]

Important. Tell me what you think of our duty now with regard to Mexico & France. You notice that the House Resolution has already caused an echo in Europe. I have kept it carefully in my committee-room where it still sleeps.[5] My idea has been that we were not in a condition to give L. Nap. any excuse for hostility—or recognition—or breaking the blockade. At another time I should be glad to speak plainly to France or rather to its ruler; but I would not say any thing now which cannot be maintained—nor which can add to our present embarassments. What say you? Let me have yr views on this question.

Should Congress speak? If so, how? Should the House Resolution be allowed to sleep? Or be adopted?

Ever yours,   Charles Sumner

ALS   MH-H   (64/321, PCS)

1. Lieber's letter of 2 May 1864 concerned a possible move to replace Banks as commander of the Department of the Gulf (New York, 78/132, PCS). Banks was then in the process of organizing elections in Louisiana that would send free-state representatives to Congress. He sought to continue the former plantation system, and Radicals feared that what Banks called a transitional stage in granting freedom to blacks was only another form of slavery (Eric Foner, *Reconstruction* [1988], 54–56).

2. Two of the letters to which CS refers may be those of 22 January and 26 March on Reconstruction details (CWL, 7:162, 186–87).

3. Writing on 3 May, Lieber asked CS for a dozen copies of his "No Property in Man" speech and about possibilities of having it printed as a pamphlet (78/139). Lieber thought the speech "so noble" that he felt moved, as a close friend, to suggest a change in CS's passage referring to the judiciary: "Let the appeal be made to the courts. But, alas! one of the saddest chapters in our history is the conduct of judges, who have lent themselves to the support of slavery. . . . Courts which should have been asylums of liberty have been changed into *barracoons,* and the Supreme Court of the United States, by final decision of surpassing infamy, became the greatest *barracoon* of all" (*Globe,* 38th Cong., 1st sess., 1481). Lieber recommended "equally strong but less bitter language." The passage was modified in later versions of the speech.

4. On 31 March, in debating the nature of a territorial government for Montana, Johnson cited the Dred Scott decision to argue that blacks were not citizens. CS called the decision "as absurd and irrational as . . . a reversal of the multiplication table, besides shocking the moral sense of mankind" (ibid., 1363–64).

5. The House had passed unanimously on 4 April a joint resolution criticizing the Mexican government. The resolution called for the U.S. to declare its disinclination to recognize "any monarchical Government erected on the ruins of any republican Government in America under the auspices of any European Power" and was referred to the Senate Foreign Relations Committee on 5 April (ibid., 1408, 1416). Lieber did not advise CS until 20 May, when he wrote that CS's problem was "somewhat knotty." He suggested CS wait to learn more details from Thomas Corwin, then ambassador to Mexico, soon to arrive in Washington (78/190).

To Francis Lieber

Senate Chamber 17th May '64

Dear Lieber,

Winter Davis has just come to press me about his Mexican Resolution.[1]

Goldwin Smith's pamphlet is excellent. I doubt if it would interest the Presdt, who reads very little.[2] Seward said to me two days ago, "There was a great cry last year on the question whether the Presdt.

reads despatches *before they are sent*; but I am sure he never reads a d—nd one which we receive."[3]

Ever Yours,   C. S.

ALS MH-H (64/332, PCS)

1. Henry Winter Davis (1817–65; U.S. congressman [Union, Md.], 1863–65) had sponsored the House resolution on U.S. policy toward Mexico.

2. Lieber had recommended Smith's 23 May 1864 "A Letter to a Whig Member of the Southern Independence Association" and asked CS to show the heartily pro-Union document to the president (New York, 8 May, 78/161, PCS).

3. Lieber replied, "what you write about P's not reading is dreadful. It makes one's head hang" (20 May, 78/190).

To Henry W. Longfellow

Senate Chamber 21st May '64

My dear Longfellow,

I have just seen in a paper the death of "R. J. Mackintosh at London, 26th April." Is this so? It makes me unhappy. Tell me about it. Had he been ill? And what becomes of his family?[1]

I hear also that Hawthorne has gone. One by one;—almost in *twos,* they seem to go. We shall be alone soon. I forget. I shall be alone. You have your children.[2]

Life is weary & dark—full of pain & enmity. I am ready to go at once. And still I am left.

Hawthorne was a genius. As a master of prose, he will come in the first class of all who have written the English language. He had not the grand style; but who has had a delicacy of touch superior to his?

Have you recd. my report on French Spoliations? There is work in that.[3]

God bless you!

Ever Yours,   Charles Sumner

ALS MH-H (78/192, PCS)

1. Longfellow replied on 23 May 1864 that Mackintosh had died of "dropsy and heart-complaint" (Cambridge, 78/201, PCS).

2. Hawthorne died on 18 May. Longfellow wrote, "do not be disheartened. You have much work of the noble kind to do yet. Let us die standing."

3. U.S. Senate, Committee on Foreign Relations, *Claims on France For Spoliations of American Commerce Prior to July 31, 1801*, Senate Report no. 41, 1864, serial set 1178. Running to 147 pages, the report eventually concluded that the U.S. should pay the claims, which it had assumed from France, to descendants of U.S. citizens. The report was presented to the Senate 4 April (*Globe,* 38th Cong., 1st sess., 1402).

To John Jay

Washington Sunday
[c. 28 May 1864]

My dear Jay,

I wish that you would let me have a copy of Chief Justice Jay's charge at Richmond on Neutrality;[1]—or at least send it to me for perusal.

It ought to be printed now. Recent discussions & still pending questions in England make it important.

We are all anxious here. I believe that we must conquer. I am sure of it. But these delays are distressing, & the bloodshed is appalling.[2] More than ever, I am a peace-man; but I wish that no effort should be spared to put down the Rebellion.

I wish that our political future looked fairer. But there seem so many divisions among our friends—so little concord—that I know not how to cast the horoscope.

For weeks I have tried in vain to press the Freedmen's Bill;[3] but thus far without success. Other measures are in the way. And, then, there is the ever-recuring discord among our friends.—I doubt if any thing will be done. This makes me very sad.

Ever yours,   Charles Sumner

ALS   NNCB   (77/104, PCS)

1. Jay's charge, presented at the opening of the circuit court at Richmond, 22 May 1793, declared that neutral countries should maintain a "strict impartiality" toward both warring powers (*The Correspondence and Public Papers of John Jay,* ed. Henry P. Johnson, 3 [1891], 478–85).

2. Lt. General Grant, now in command of the Armies of the U.S., fought Lee in the battles of the Wilderness, Spotsylvania, and North Anna 5–26 May 1864, without any real resolution. Federal losses in these battles totaled over 32,000.

3. CS finally gained Senate consideration of the Freedmen's Bureau bill on 8 June (*Globe,* 38th Cong., 1st sess., 2798).

To Francis Lieber

Senate Chamber 2nd June '64

Dear Lieber,

The resolution to which you refer was introduced on my own responsibility; but it represents, I think, the opinions of a considerable majority of the Senate.[1] To this conclusion senators have come slowly.

You will find it two years ago in resolutions & speeches of mine; also in the article of the Atlantic Monthly. From the beginning it has been opposed—at first brutally & offensively,—but comparatively little now.

A House caucus has affirmed, with only one dissenting vote, the principle of my resolution. This was last week.

The question becomes immensely important, in view of the Presidential question; for if reptives & senators in Congress are admitted, we must also admit their votes in the electoral college or, it may be, in Congress should the election come there.

The resolution was inaccurately reported in the *Times*;—a rough telegram. But the *Times* is always glad to attack me.[2]

The case of Fishback will compel senators to show their hands.

Last evng at dinner Chase pressed me very [*MS incomplete*]

———————————

AL   MH-H   (64/342, PCS)

1. On 27 May 1864, when the Senate considered whether William M. Fishback (1831–1903) should represent the newly formed government of Arkansas, CS introduced a resolution stating that a rebel state was subject to military rule and no person could be received by Congress until his state was duly readmitted to the Union by a vote of both the Senate and House (*Globe,* 38th Cong., 1st sess., 2512). Lieber wrote that he agreed with CS's resolution, for "who else should decide?" He warned CS, however, that he would have "all theorists against you; and every political wrongdoer in America is a theorist" (New York, 1 June, 78/218, PCS).

2. The *New York Times* reported CS's resolution as stating that a state "pretending to secede from the Union and battling against the Government was not entitled to a representative" until both the Senate and House agreed on readmission (28 May 1864:4).

To Francis Lieber

Washington Sunday.
[*12 June 1864*]

Dear Lieber,

I return the proof-sheet with a few corrections. I hope it is not too late.

I like the looks of this page.

Can I have 30 or 40 copies—chiefly to send abroad.[1]

I was perplexed yesterday on the long pending question of the back pay of colored troops, which has been so much discussed. At last I consented that the question should be submitted to the Atty Genl. This takes it from Congress.[2]

The Arguelles case is as bad as can be. I told the Presdt, the moment I heard of it, that it was utterly indefensible[3]

I do not like to see the commutation clause in the Conscription law abolished. Tomorrow we decide it.[4]

My bill for a Bureau of Freedmen is also under discussion. I hope to send you my speech tomorrow.[5] This too is perplexing.

Then comes the question on Arkansas. I shall speak elaborately on that—perhaps tomorrow.[6]

I hope the House will pass the bill repealing all fug. slave acts tomorrow. *E pur si muove.*[7]

I have yr notes on the Academies. My purpose is to introduce the two bills at the same time. Should they pass, the three Academies may be combined by a subsequent act. But I regard the present proceeding as a *tentative process.* The other bill slipped through without debate & unnoticed. But this cannot be done again. Of course, there will be something said, & debate, I fear, will be fatal. But I shall try.[8]

Ever Yours,   Charles Sumner

P.S. Genl. Grant declines to receive our French visitors.[9] I have spoken to Stanton & Halleck on the subject, & they assure me that every facility possible shall be afforded.

ALS   MH-H   (64/339, PCS)

1. Lieber had arranged for the Loyal Publication Society of New York to print CS's Senate speech on the Thirteenth Amendment, "No Property in Man" (Lieber to CS, New York, 11 May, 7 June, 14 June 1864, 78/171, 225, 242, PCS).

2. After much debate and amending, on 11 June the Senate passed an amendment that entitled all free black soldiers to the same rights and pay as whites. "Any question of law" resulting from the provision would be referred to Attorney General Bates (*Globe,* 38th Cong., 1st sess., 2879).

3. A Spaniard, José Arguelles, who was living in New York City, was arrested by U.S. authorities for selling slaves he had captured. Since no treaty of extradition existed between Spain and the U.S., Secretary Seward had delivered him to Spain under what he called, in a report to the Senate of 30 May, an act of "comity" (CWL, 7:370; *The Diary of Edward Bates,* ed. Howard K. Beale [1933], 374; *Foreign Relations* [1864], part 2, 60–61).

4. On 13 June Wilson moved to repeal a clause that would exempt from the draft those paying $300 for a substitute; the Senate agreed only to print Wilson's motion, and he later withdrew it in favor of a similar amendment (*Globe,* 38th Cong., 1st sess., 2907, 3088).

5. "Creation of the Freedmen's Bureau: A Bridge from Slavery to Freedom," given 8 June (ibid., 2798–2800).

6. CS spoke against recognizing the government of Arkansas on 13 June (ibid., 2898–99).

7. "And then it is moving."

8. CS and Lieber exchanged frequent lists on CS's proposed academies and on 2 July CS introduced the bill, with a list of prospective members of both a National

Academy of Literature and Art and a National Academy of Moral and Political Science. CS wrote Lieber 2 July (64/350), "I fear madness for adjournment will prevent me from getting them up. I shall try." Indeed, the Senate declined to consider CS's bill (ibid., 3492–93).

9. Lieber had recommended his friend François Victor Adolphe de Chanal (1811–82), who had been sent by the French government to inspect the Union military system (21, 22 May, 78/191, 197).

To Ralph W. Emerson

Senate Chamber 18th June '64

My dear Emerson,

I do not know if I ever reported to you that the Presdt. told me, that Genl. Stone was dropped at the order of Genl. Grant just before he commenced his march on Richmond. This is an answer to the suggestion of yr correspondant.[1]

I am weary & disappointed,—& wish I could have a day's ramble with you in the woods of Concord, to get refreshment of body & soul.

If it be true that Petersburg is really taken, the French Commissionair here—a military critic of distinction—tells me that the war is ended.[2] God be praised!

Ever yours,   Charles Sumner

ALS   MH-H   (78/245, PCS)

1. Emerson had written CS from Concord on 7 May 1864 concerned about the dismissal of General Charles P. Stone, who had earlier been imprisoned for six months (see CS to Andrew, 10 January 1862) and was now dismissed from service in General Banks's army. Emerson enclosed a copy of a letter supporting Stone sent to him by a friend on Banks's staff (78/153, PCS).

2. Grant's assaults on Petersburg were then under way. If Petersburg fell, he then planned to march on Richmond. The "French Commissionair" is possibly François de Chanal.

To Thomas Wentworth Higginson

Senate Chamber 22nd June '64

My dear Col.

Be assured that I have never for one moment lost sight of yr regt.[1] The debates in the *Globe* down to the last moment when the report of the Conference Comttee. was accepted will show that I did not forget it.

I accepted that report with reluctance & under protest, with a conviction, that the opinion of the Atty Genl—if we ever get it—adjudging pay to the Mass regts. would practically rule yr case also.

If there be any distinction in our military laws it is not between "free black" & "slave black," but between "black" & "white." If the Atty decides that the "free blacks" of Mass are entitled to a soldier's pay it must be on grounds which will support yr case also.[2]

It is hard that our trouble in this matter should come from New England. (1) A Mass. functionary at Washington gave an erroneous opinion & stuck to it. When did a lawyer or judge ever give up an opinion once given?—(2) A New England senator thwarted all action in the Senate.[3]

I have been pained by this denial of justice, & have remonstrated against it constantly in debate, & also with the Secy of War & the Presdt. I have offended the Secy by my plainness of speech. He has lost his temper.

I hope that you will recover strength for the contest that still remains.

Ever Sincerely Yours,   Charles Sumner

ALS NjMo (78/263, PCS)

1. Higginson wrote 20 June 1864 (Pigeon Cove, Massachusetts, 31/250, PCS) asking CS to remember his "defrauded regiment," the 1st South Carolina Volunteers. He was concerned that the bill to equalize pay for black soldiers stated that retroactive pay would be given only to "*free* colored regiments," while Higginson's regiment, made up of fugitive slaves, had been "earlier in the field" and had had Stanton's assurance they would be paid.

2. Bates's opinion, delivered 14 July, stated that since no law prohibited the "enlistment of free colored men into either branch" of the U.S. armed services, any black enlisting between December 1862 and June 1864 was entitled to the same pay and supplies as a white soldier (*War of the Rebellion*, series 3, 4:490–93).

3. William Whiting, then solicitor of the War Department, had rendered an opinion on 4 June 1863 that blacks in the U.S. Army should be paid the wages of laborers, not soldiers (Henry G. Pearson, *The Life of John A. Andrew* [1904], 2:98; see *War of the Rebellion*, series 3, 3:252). On Fessenden's role, see CS to Bird, 22 February 1864.

To Henry W. Longfellow

Senate Chamber 23d June '64
10 minutes before 4 o'clk PM

My dear Longfellow,

All fugitive slave Acts were to-day expunged from the statute-book.[1] This makes me happy.

Ever Thine,   Charles Sumner

Thus closes one chapter of my life. I was chosen to the Senate in order to do this work.[2]

ALS   MH-H   (78/269, PCS)

1. The House had passed CS's motion to repeal all fugitive slave laws on 13 June 1864; the Senate vote on 23 June was 27–12 (*Globe*, 38th Cong., 1st sess., 2920, 3191).

2. Longfellow replied, "Your hour of triumph has come at last! . . . This will compensate you for all your toil and patience and long-suffering with evil-doers!" (Cambridge, 28 June, 78/298, PCS).

To Mary Peabody Mann

Senate Chamber 27th June '64

My dear Mrs Mann,

I have a complete set of the Pacific R.R. vols—13—a real contribution to science, which I wish to give to some worthy student of science. Does Horace possess these vols? If he does not, then I shall send them to him.[1]

This last week was fruitful—(1) all fug. acts repealed (2) my proviso, prohibiting the exclusion of colored persons from any car, adopted—so that now all three of the rail-roads in the District are thus treated. (3) the coast-wise slave-trade prohibited & the acts of Congress regulating it repealed (4) &, best of all, the exclusion of colored testimony in U.S. courts prohibited.[2] The latter provision is of immense practical importance.

You strangely imagine that speeches are read now. *You* do not even know the speeches I have made this session, for no newspaper prints them. I make no complaint; but this is my reply to what you say about "thunder."[3] Nothing is read now which does not concern the army, blood & battle.

I shall try to send the docts which Horace's friend desires.[4]

Ever Sincerely Yours,   Charles Sumner

ALS   MHi   (78/294, PCS)

1. Mary Mann had written CS 25 June 1864 about obtaining congressional documents. Her son, Horace Mann, Jr. (1844–68), had written her from San Francisco asking for some 1858 government reports for an old friend. She added that Horace would like any documents that she could gather (Concord, 31/284, PCS).

2. CS's proviso was attached to the bill amending the charter of the Washington and Georgetown Railroad Company and passed the Senate 17–16, 22 June. On 25 June CS offered as amendments to the Civil Appropriation Bill the prohibition of both coastwise slave trade and exclusion of black testimony, which passed by votes of 23–14 and 29–10, respectively (*Globe,* 38th Cong., 1st sess., 3137, 3264).

3. Mary Mann wrote that she hoped to "hear a little more of your thunder—I am told you could frighten the world by disclosing all you know of iniquity in high places."

4. In her response of 30 June Mann wrote that her husband had said that CS "knew more of every interest of the country than any other man in Congress. . . . [H]ow near he must be to you oftentimes!" (Concord, 31/332).

To Elizabeth Cady Stanton

Washington, June 28, 1864

Dear Mrs. Stanton:

I am afraid that you do not appreciate the extent to which a public mind is preoccupied by the war. Speeches are neither reported, nor read when reported. Interested as you are in the subject, I yet am daily speaking words against slavery which you do not and have not the opportunity to read.[1]

Faithfully yours,   Charles Sumner

TTR[2] NjRD (78/300, PCS)

1. Elizabeth Cady Stanton (1815–1902), president of the National Woman's Loyal League, had sent CS another 85,000 signatures supporting the Thirteenth Amendment. She asked CS to speak on the petitions before the Senate adjourned and "please take some pains to have what you say reported" (New York, c. 21 June, 23 June 1864, 31/269, 275, PCS).

2. No holograph letter has been recovered.

To Lydia Maria Child

Boston 7th Aug. '64

Dear Mrs Child,

You always make me feel happy by one of yr letters—although I know well that I do not deserve all that you say.[1]

Among all the measures concerning Slavery which have prevailed at the late session, I regard as first in practical value the overthrow of the rule excluding colored testimony. For this result I have labored two years.

The repeal of all fugitive slave acts is of immense importance for us abroad; but its practical importance at home is not great, except that every blow at Slavery is practically important, so that it is difficult to measure it.

Into the darkness of the Presidential contest I am not prepared to enter.[2] It was a great mistake—to make a nomination so early. The whole subject might have been postponed till Sept. when we should have seen more clearly who ought to be the candidate.

This war ought to have been ended long ago, & Slavery extinguished.

Remember me kindly to Mr Child, & believe me, dear Mrs Child,

> Very Sincerely Yours,   Charles Sumner

ALS   I   (78/336, PCS)

1. Lydia Maria Child, CS's long-time correspondent, wrote him 31 July 1864 from Wayland, Massachusetts, thanking him for his "consistent and persistent advocacy of Justice and Freedom" (31/419, PCS).

2. Child was concerned about the chances of reelecting Lincoln, "with his slow mind and legal conscience, forever pottering about details and calculating chances." She regretted that his "fear of God is unfortunately secondary to his fear of the Democratic Party." Still, she respected Lincoln's honesty and thought him a stronger candidate than Frémont, the candidate a splinter convention of Radical Republicans had nominated at Cleveland on 31 May.

To Francis Lieber

Boston 19th Aug. '64

My dear Lieber,

I have been a week with Longfellow on his piazza at Nahant. He is recovering his original nature which has been sadly overcast. Last night he dined with our club at a dinner for Chase—where Curtis Noyes assisted also.[1]

Tom Appleton was to arrive last evng. Mrs Wadsworth is already here after a long absence.[2]

It has been very hot, & every body is away. I was surprized yesterday by a gay visit from the French Minister [*Mercier*]. This evng I run down to Newport for a day or two. These are the only vacations I have had since the war began.

—since the war began! If a proper energy—"action"—"action"— "action"—had inspired the Govt, it would have been already ended.

I do not as yet see the Presidential horizon. I wait for the blue lights of Chicago, which will present the true outlines.[3]

I have not read Adml Napier, but am obliged by yr hint.[4]

I have sent Martin's articles to the Duchess of Argyll.[5]
Goodbye!

Ever Yours, Charles Sumner

ALS MH-H (64/354, PCS)

1. On 30 June 1864 Lincoln accepted Chase's resignation as secretary of the Treasury. Chase had recently been touring New England with William Curtis Noyes (1805–64), a New York lawyer, and exploring the possibilities of Chase's becoming a replacement for Lincoln as the Republican presidential nominee. According to his diary, he dined at the Union Club on 18 August (*Inside Lincoln's Cabinet,* ed. David Donald [1954], 247).

2. Longfellow's brother-in-law returned from Europe on 18 August. Emmeline Austin Wadsworth (1808–85) of Geneseo, New York, had also been in Europe (HWL, 4:428, 215).

3. The Democratic convention was scheduled to meet in Chicago 29–30 August.

4. Elers Napier, *The Life and Correspondence of Admiral Sir Charles Napier* (1862). Lieber wrote CS that Napier's study contained examples of how Great Britain regarded its own foreign enlistment act (New York, 10 August 1864, 78/343, PCS).

5. Lieber wrote CS that J. Sella Martin (c. 1825–76), a black clergyman and ex-slave, had written a series of articles, "Our Friends in England," which appeared in the New York *Evening Post* (15 August, 78/346). Martin sent CS copies of his articles (New York, 22 August, 31/470).

To Abraham Lincoln

Boston 20th Aug. '64

My dear Sir,

I have recd. from the Emancipation Society of London a protest against certain acts of Genl. Banks, which are supposed to have a tendency to support Slavery. In a communication from the Secy I am requested to lay this protest before you.[1]

I regret very much that I have not the opportunity of conversing on this subject. But I content myself now with laying this document before you.

Faithfully Yours, Charles Sumner

ALS DLC (78/349, PCS)
Enc: Minutes, Emancipation Society of Great Britain

1. Frederick W. Chesson (1833–88) served as secretary of the London Emancipation Society in the 1860s. The society's membership included Bright, Cobden, John Stuart Mill, Francis W. Newman, and George Thompson (Ralph Korngold, *Two Friends of Man* [1950], 287). In its communication the committee praised Lincoln's

administration for its emancipation measures, but regretted that Banks's "ordinances establishing a system of serfdom in the state of Louisiana, have apparently been sanctioned by the authorities at Washington." The committee asked that Lincoln abolish the "regulations and ordinances which perpetrate the substance of slavery in whatever form or prevent the colored race in the South from enjoying the rights of citizenship" (78/350, PCS).

To John Andrew
Private & *Confidential*—

Boston 24th Aug. '64

My dear Andrew,

I had hoped to be in New York Tuesday; but cannot.[1]

Of course all who wish to preserve the Union & to overthrow Slavery *must act together.* There must be harmony, & to this end there must be *self-abnegation* every where from the highest to the lowest.

But I see no way of meeting the difficulties from the candidacy of Mr Lincoln, *unless he withdraws patriotically & kindly, so as to leave no breach in the party.* Will he do this?

I can imagine a patriotism, which setting aside all personal considerations, & looking singly to the good of the country at this trying moment, should insist upon another appeal to the people in Convention.[2] The other Convention was premature & out of time. The country needs a maturer birth. But I seem to speak in enigmas.

You know well that I have always regretted that the Republican Convention was called at so early a day. Its action seemed to me ill-considered & unreasonable[.] If it were regarded as merely temporary, then its errors might be corrected by another Convention, which, with the concurrence of Mr Lincoln, might nominate a candidate who would surely be elected.

Let me know by telegraph if I can be of service & I will try to meet you.[3]

Ever yours,   Charles Sumner

ALS   MHi   (78/335, PCS)

1. Andrew was part of a group organizing a meeting at David Dudley Field's in New York City on Tuesday, 30 August 1864, to discuss a plan to replace Lincoln as the Republican nominee. Other organizers were Horace Greeley, Henry Winter Davis, William Cullen Bryant, and Benjamin Butler (Henry Greenleaf Pearson, *The Life of John Andrew* [1904], 2:155–63).

2. The group was considering calling another convention in Cincinnati on 28 September to nominate a new presidential candidate.

3. In his letter to CS of 31 August Lieber described the meeting at Field's, which he had attended the previous day. The group decided to have a delegation call upon Lincoln and ask him to withdraw his candidacy. The group agreed, wrote Lieber, that Lincoln could not be elected unless the U.S. won some battles soon. Lieber wrote that although he had not signed the group's manifesto he doubted if Lincoln could be elected (New York, 78/361, PCS). CS replied, 3 September, "I have declined to sign any paper or take any part in any action, because I was satisfied that nothing could be done except through Mr L. & with his good will" (64/356). The fall of Atlanta on 2 September negated the anti-Lincoln movement, as Andrew wrote Greeley 3 September: "the mistakes" of the Lincoln administration "may be more easily borne than to attempt a remedy" (Pearson, 2:163).

To Andrew Johnson

Boston 10th Sept. '64

My dear Sir,

If you can find time to visit the North, I am sure that you will have a true welcome in Providence.[1] You would cheer & strengthen us. Perhaps you would be cheered & strengthened also by the patriotic fervor which I am sure yr visit would inspire.

Faithfully Yours,   Charles Sumner

Hon. A. Johnson

ALS   DLC   (78/368, PCS)

1. Johnson had been nominated vice president at the Republican convention in May. CS's invitation accompanied a letter from Providence manufacturer Amos Barstow (b. 1813) inviting Johnson to speak to the Providence Association of Mechanics and Manufacturers on 2 November. However, Johnson did not campaign in New England (*Papers of Andrew Johnson*, ed. LeRoy P. Graf, 7 [1986], 152).

To John Bright
Confidential

Boston 27th Sept. '64

Dear Mr Bright,

The enclosed letter from Mr Harrington the Assistant Secy of the Treasury answers the inquiries of yr friends[1]—I trust satisfactorily.

The Chicago platform & our victories have settled the Presidential election beyond question, & we all see the beginning of the end.[2] In the large towns, especially New York, the enemy are strong. But elsewhere our majorities will be decisive.

Before the Chicago Convention, Mr Lincoln's case seemed almost hopeless. There was a profound discontent in his own party & especially among those who have been in the way of knowing him most. There was a distrust of his capacity. It is a general impression that with a Presdt. of ordinary vigor & practical sense, this war would have been ended long ago. But the Chicago platform was too [bad?]. Greeley who had stood out at once came in; so did Bryant.[3] Wade & others have followed.

From the beginning I declined to have any thing to do with any *adversary* proceeding, partly on the ground of my personal relations with the Presdt but more because I was satisfied that it would only endanger the result. I should have been satisfied with any one of 100 names—with any one of half the Senate, & I think any such person, *if nominated with the good will of the Presdt* could have been elected. But our candidate long ago set his heart on a re-election, & he will have it. Perhaps it is useless to go into reasons or details.

Chase at first was very bitter & went so far as to doubt the Presdt's loyalty to the Anti-Slavery cause. I never have *so far as he understands it*. But he does not know how to help or is not moved to help. For instance, I do not remember that I have had any help from him in any of the questions which I have conducted—although a word from him in certain quarters would have saved me much trouble. It is hard to tug at questions day after day, when govt. support might supersede all labor. But he has no instinct or inspiration. I write to you frankly for yr own *private eye*.

You will note our military successes. I do not expect the surrender of Mobile immediately. It is not in the programme. *But Grant says he can take Richmond now*. He must strike before long.

Ever Yours,   Charles Sumner

There is a movement to carry Chase back to his place in the Treasury. The appointment of Dennison from Ohio blocks this.[4]

ALS GBL (78/398, PCS)

1. In his letter of 3 September 1864 Bright asked CS's help in persuading the U.S. Treasury Department to revoke import duties on goods a British group planned to send to freedmen. George Harrington (1815–92) held his Treasury post from c. 1861 to 1865.

2. Besides the fall of Atlanta, the Union enjoyed other victories when Major General Philip Sheridan's troops defeated the Confederates near Winchester, Virginia, on 19 September, and at Fisher's Hill on 22 September.

3. Democrats at Chicago adopted a platform calling for "immediate efforts" to end

the war and the preservation of all states' rights "unimpaired." Greeley ran editorials in the *New York Tribune* attacking the Democratic nominee, McClellan, and his running mate, George H. Pendleton (20 September 1864:4, 23 September 1864:4). Bryant's New York *Evening Post* endorsed Lincoln (21 September 1864:4).

4. Another Ohioan, William Dennison (1815–82), a former governor, was appointed postmaster general 24 September to replace Montgomery Blair, who resigned at Lincoln's request on 23 September.

To Salmon P. Chase

Boston 24th Oct. '64

My dear Chase,

I have yours of 19th Oct. & am glad that you approve my course.[1]

I confess strongly the feeling of friendship; but in my relations with the Administration I have acted always with reference to the best interests of my country, & of the cause in which we have labored together.

You ought to be C.J., & I do not doubt that you will be; for I cannot believe that the Presdt. will allow himself to be pushed from his original conclusion.

It has been said that Judge [*Ira*] Harris wished to be an Associate, &, to carry out this idea Judge Swayne was to be made C.J.[2] I do not think this possible. It so happened that the Presdt. last spring mentioned Judge Swayne to me as the ablest of the new judges & a candidate for C.J. I spoke very frankly of the effect of such an appointment, & insisted that he had not the elements required for the head of the bench now. It was after this conversation that he said that he would tender the place to you, & I understand he has repeated this determination since, especially to the Senate Comttee. when it visited him to know the occasion of yr resignation. He then confessed that you & he could not get along together in the cabinet, but that he should be glad to make you C.J. John Sherman knows about this conversation.[3]

I have written again to the Presdt. renewing my recommendation & insisting that the sooner it was done the better.

Ever Yours,   Charles Sumner

ALS   DLC   (78/447, PCS)

1. On 12 October 1864, the day of Chief Justice Taney's death, CS wrote Lincoln that the new chief justice should be "an able, courageous & determined friend of Freedom" and saw these qualities in Chase. CS expressed thanks that "Providence" had given the country "a victory for liberty & for the Constitution" in Taney's death (Boston, 78/424, PCS). On 14 October CS wrote that he was certain Chase would be

nominated and urged him to accept. Chase replied from Cincinnati on 19 October that although he had heard "nothing from Washington of a definite character," he agreed that Lincoln "remains of the same mind expressed to you last spring" (78/430, 438).

2. Noah Swayne (1804–84), Supreme Court justice, 1862–81.

3. Sherman was a member of the Senate Finance Committee, which met with Lincoln 30 June to discuss whether Chase might be kept in the cabinet (*Lincoln Day by Day*, ed. Earl S. Miers [1960], 3:268).

To Abraham Lincoln

Boston 24th Oct. '64

My dear Sir,

I do not like to trouble you; but I do not write long letters, nor do I write, unless I think I have something to say.

It seems to me that there is a feverishness in the public mind with regard to the Chief Justiceship. Anti-Slavery men are all trembling, lest the opportunity should be lost of appointing a Chief Justice, who, in his interpretation of the Constitution & of the War Powers, would deal a death-blow to Slavery. They do not think that any old-fashioned lawyer, who has accepted for years pro-slavery glosses can do this. Our new Chief Justice must believe in Liberty & be inspired by it.

I think the nomination of Mr Chase would cause a glow of delight throughout the country among all the best supporters of the Administration, & according to my judgment, the sooner it is made the better.

You will pardon my earnestness; but I long to secure a just interpretation of the Constitution. No personal friendship could induce me to intrude upon you, if I did not feel that I was consulting the best interests of my country.

Believe me, my dear Sir,

very faithfully Yours,   Charles Sumner

P.S. I have to-day recd. a letter from Mr Chase which contains a passage, that I venture to transcribe.

S. P. Chase to Charles Sumner   Cincinnati—19th Oct. '64

"It is perhaps not exactly *en régle* to say what one will do in regard to an appointment not tendered to him; but it is certainly not wrong to say to you that I should accept. I feel that I can do more for our cause & our country & for the success of the next Administration in that place than in any other. Happily it is now certain that the next Administration will be in the hands of Mr Lincoln from whom the world will expect great things. God grant that his name may go down to posterity with the two noblest additions historian ever recorded—*Restorer & Liberator.*[1]

ALS DLC (78/449, PCS)

1. CS's transcription is faithful (see 78/438, PCS); he also underlined *Restorer* and *Liberator*.

To Abraham Lincoln

Boston 20th Nov. '64

My dear Sir,

I venture to call yr attention to a speech which I send entitled "Slavery & the Rebellion, One & Inseparable"[1] & especially pp. 24 & 25, where I have endeavored to show that, not only by the Proclamation, but by principles of Constitutional & public law every slave in the rebel states is now *de jure* free. This is my last speech against Slavery. Here I close this chapter of life.

There is a movement among certain democrats & slave-holders at the North to substitute *prospective* Emancipation for *immediate*. They say that this would give the rebels an opportunity of making terms. But I have replied, promptly, when approached on this point, that freedom once given could not be reclaimed, & that the country was solemnly bound to the immediate present freedom of every slave in the rebel states.

Something is said in the newspapers about negotiations, terms of peace, & commissioners.[2] I do not know that any such thing is seriously entertained; but I venture to suggest that there is no power in the rebel states with whom we can deal—surely not with Jefferson Davis, & his associate traitors. It only remains that the rebel armies should be broken. Let this be done, & the Unionists of the South can then show themselves.

I venture to suggest, whether the whole subject of "terms" & of "reconstruction" does not properly belong to Congress, according to the analogies of our govt, if not according to the terms of the Constitution. I make this remark with no other object than to secure that harmony & unity in our public counsels, which will render the Govt. irresistible.

Next to the Rebellion itself I most dread a premature State Govt. in a rebel state, placing at hazard, as it must, these two things which we so much desire, Peace & Liberty.[3]

I notice that the Chief Justiceship is not yet filled. Meanwhile the patter in the newspapers goes on, & the country is anxious. I know that my excellent friend Govr Morgan thought it advisable to postpone the nomination till after the election. I differed from him. I thought it ought to have been made on the evening of Taney's funeral. The promptitude of the nomination would have had an inspiring effect. But I can see no ground of delay now, even if the pendency of the election furnished one.[4]

To me it is of inconceivable importance that the Constitution hereafter should be interpreted *always for Freedom*, & I long to have that assurance which can be found only in the appointment of a Chief Justice, whose position on this great question, in all its bearings, is already fixed & who will not need argts of counsel to convert him.

I am sorry for the question with Brazil. Why did not Capt. Collins scuttle the Florida & save us the question about surrendering the ship?[5]—But I rely upon the friendly sentiments of the Brazilian govt. not to make any demand which we can not comply with.

Believe me, my dear Sir, with much regard,

Very faithfully Yours,   Charles Sumner

The President.

ALS DLC (78/476, PCS)

1. At the end of his speech "Slavery and the Rebellion," given 5 November 1864 at the Cooper Institute, New York, CS exhorted his audience to fight slavery by supporting the Republican ticket (Wks, 11:443–83). Lincoln was reelected 8 November.

2. The *New York Times* (20 November 1864:4) reported from Washington that, instead of sending peace commissioners to Richmond, Lincoln would deal with the subject of peace negotiations in his annual message to Congress. In this message, 6 December, Lincoln stated, "no attempt at negotiation with the insurgent leader could result in any good. He would accept nothing short of severance of the Union—precisely what we will not and cannot give" (CWL, 8:151).

3. CS left a large space here, perhaps for pasting in some news clippings.

4. CS also wrote Chase on 20 November telling him to ignore rumors of other appointees and reassuring him that he would be nominated chief justice; perhaps Lincoln was waiting until Congress reconvened on 5 December. On 3 December Chase sent CS an editorial from the Cincinnati *Gazette* that urged Chase's nomination. Chase wrote: "I would not have the office on the terms of being obliged to [seek?] for it; nor would I send you this paper, if I did not know your interest in the subject, & that you wd. naturally be pleased to know that it is shared as this paper shows it to be" (78/474, 498, PCS). Lincoln nominated Chase chief justice on 7 December.

5. Captain Napoleon Collins (1814–75) had seized the C.S.S. *Florida* on 7 October while the Confederate vessel was in Brazilian waters at Bahia.

To Abraham Lincoln

Boston 24th Nov. '64

My dear Sir,

The enclosed letter from Professor Lieber seems to me so interesting, & important in its ideas, that I forward it to you.[1] I think it will repay perusal.

Prof. Lieber, you will remember, was for 20 years Professor at Columbia, S.C. He has two sons in our armies.

very faithfully Yours,   Charles Sumner

ALS   DLC   (78/490, PCS)
Enc: Francis Lieber to CS, 22 November 1864.

1. Lieber was concerned about an address by Benjamin F. Butler on 14 November in New York which offered, said Lieber, "*the Olive Branch* . . . to the South," a gesture many believed was supported by the Lincoln administration. Lieber asked, "What Olive Branch? What have we been fighting for all this while?" He insisted Lincoln had been elected to restore the Union and abolish slavery and that there should be no olive branches now. "The Election is an immense *trust*" (78/490, PCS).

To Francis Lieber

Sunday
[*Washington, 18 December 1864*]

Dear Lieber,

What say you to Dix's order?[1] There can be no question that any general on the frontier might follow invaders back into Canada, if the Canadian govt. should fail in its duties. But a deliberate order *in advance* to invade neutral territory is a grave step.

I have presented to the Presdt. the duty of harmony between Congress & the Executive. He is agreed. It is proposed to admit La (which ought not to be done)[2] & at the same time pass the Reconstruction Bill for all the other states, giving the electoral franchise to "all citizens," without distinction of color. If this arrangement is carried out it will be an immense political act.

I have great questions for the Comttee—(1) the termination of the reciprocity treaty (2) armament on the lakes. (3) the Canadian complications. (4) Mexico (5) Arguelles case (6) claims of England growing out of the war. (7) Florida case. (8) Question of belligerent rights. &c &c Any thing on any of these matters will be welcome.[3]

We expect to pass the Constitutional Amendment by (1) Secession Democrats & (2) 5 votes from La.[4]

Ever Yours,   Charles Sumner

ALS   MH-H   (64/368, PCS)

1. On 19 October 1864 a Confederate band had crossed over from Canada to St. Albans, Vermont, robbed three banks, and killed one U.S. citizen. After fourteen of the Confederates had been captured by the Canadian government, Seward requested on 25 October their extradition to the U.S. On 14 December General John A. Dix, commander of the Military District of the East, ordered that any future Confederate raiders should be pursued into Canada and, if caught, not surrendered to Canadian authorities but returned to the U.S. However, on 17 December Lincoln countermanded the portion of Dix's order regarding pursuit of raiders across the Canadian boundary (*Foreign Relations* [1864], part 2, 752–53; *New York Times*, 15 December: 1864:8, 18 December 1864:4). Lieber responded to CS's inquiry on 21 December, stating that, while he "liked" Dix's order, he completely supported Lincoln's action (New York, 78/543, PCS). In Senate remarks on 19 December, CS argued against any "hasty action" by the U.S. that could bring about a war with Britain and stated that Dix's order was not supported by Halleck's *International Law: or, Rules Regulating the Intercourse of States in Peace and War* (*Globe*, 38th Cong., 2nd sess., 58–62). Privately, CS wrote Hamilton Fish 15 December that any captured raiders would be "an 'elephant' on our hands. . . . As it is, their discharge binds the Canadian & the British govt to extra exertions to keep the peace; & peace we must have" (78/529).

2. On 6 December the Senate referred to the Judiciary Committee a report from the provisional government of Louisiana, recommending that two delegates be received as U.S. senators from Louisiana (*Globe*, 38th Cong., 2nd sess., 5). The Louisiana constitution abolished slavery but did not extend suffrage to blacks.

3. Of these eight items on CS's agenda, Lieber commented 29 December on the proposed termination of the Reciprocity Treaty between the U.S. and Great Britain, which had governed commercial relations between the U.S. and Canada: "I see the very worst consequences which would naturally result from establishing the harsh, and I think, semi-barbarous line of prohibition between us and Canada—*the harsher*, the less feasible the thing will be" (New York, 78/529).

4. The House passed the Thirteenth Amendment, which the Senate had approved in April, on 31 January 1865 with the necessary two-thirds vote (*Globe*, 38th Cong., 2nd sess., 530–31). The Louisiana delegates had not yet been declared official representatives and did not vote.

To Salmon P. Chase

Senate Chamber 21st Dec. '64

My dear Chase,

Please read the enclosed letter & let me know what I shall do with regard to it.[1]

Mr Rock is an estimable colored lawyer, who, as you will see, is cordially recommended by Govr. Andrew & others in the public service. He is one of several colored lawyers in Mass. who practise in all our courts, & are always received with courtesy.

Before I came into the Senate, now several years ago, I was counsel in a case before our Mass. Sup. Ct, in which one of these colored lawyers, was my associate, & I remember well the very great kindness & attention with which he was received by Chief Justice Shaw[2] & all the bench.

I mention these things that you may see something of Mr Rock's title to admission to the Sup. Ct. of the U.S.

I know not how far the Dred Scott decision may stand in the way.

Of course, the admission of a colored lawyer to the bar of the Supreme Court would make it difficult for any restriction on account of color to be maintained any where.[3] Street cars would be open afterwards.

Ever Yours,   Charles Sumner

ALS PHi (78/541, PCS)

1. John Rock (1825–66) of Boston had for at least a year been seeking admission to practice before the U.S. Supreme Court, and in December 1863 reminded CS of a "conversation at your house" (Philadelphia, 30 December 1863, 9 February 1864, 30/127, 355, PCS). CS probably enclosed a letter of 17 December to him from Rock in which Rock wrote, "We now have a *great* and *good* man for our Chief Justice, and with him I think my color will not be a bar to my admission." Rock asked CS to consult with Chase and enclosed a page of recommendations from Massachusetts officials (32/129).

2. CS and Robert Morris argued the Roberts case in 1849 with Lemuel Shaw presiding.

3. CS wrote Chase a note on 5 January 1865 about Rock to which Chase replied "not forgotten" (64/372). After he had been presented by CS and formally admitted to practice on 1 February 1865, Rock wrote CS a note thanking him for his "unceasing kindness" (Washington, 32/463; see also Wks, 12:97–100). No letters from CS to Rock have been recovered, but CS's handwritten account of his presentation of Rock to the Supreme Court is in the John Hay Papers, Library of Congress.

To James Freeman Clarke

Senate Chamber Dec. 31st. 1864

Dear Mr Clarke,

My going to France is out of the question. I hope you are not among those who wish to see me out of the country![1]

All things considered is not Mr Everett the best man?

Putting aside his past political shortcomings, and taking into view his social rank, his admitted intelligence, his extensive knowledge of history and international law, his experience above all, it seems to me that he could do us more good at a European capital than any other man.

For Mr Curtis I have the sincerest admiration and the warmest personal regard.[2] I have long thought he ought to have a foreign mission and have so said. There are few that I put on an equality with him. Paris at this moment is a place where we ought to bring to bear as much influence as possible.

Ever sincerely Yours, Charles Sumner

Rev. James F. Clarke

LS   MH-H   (78/564, PCS)

1. The minister to France, William Dayton, died suddenly 1 December 1864. Clarke wrote CS from Boston that if there were a chance CS would be Dayton's replacement, "that would be the very best thing of all" ([December 1864], 32/217, PCS).

2. In his note to CS, Clarke had also sent another letter, now unrecovered. Presumably it contained a recommendation for George William Curtis. CS wrote the duchess of Argyll 27 December, "I cannot abandon my post here, which is much more important" (Washington, 78/554).

To John Bright

Washington
1st Jan. '65

Dear Mr. Bright,

I wish you a happy New Year; but even before this, let me assure you of my sympathy in yr recent bereavement.[1] There are many here who have suffered with you.

I wish I could give you good news from Wilmington. Thus far the expedition has failed.[2] The Navy is indignant, insisting that Genl. Butler is at fault. He insists that the failure was on the other side. The Navy has the advantage of being first before the public with a report. Officers who have come from the fleet cry out bitterly. They say that the fort was ready to fall into our hands. Mr Stanton tells me that the trouble was from having two men who had never learned that there could not be two suns in the heaven.

But while unfortunate at Wilmington our arms seem to prevail elsewhere. I have not doubted Sherman's success from the beginning.[3] His army is the best we have & is 60,000 strong. The rebels have no force to stand against it. He telegraphs that he can march through the two Carolinas into Virginia. Whether he will stop for Charleston & Wilmington, I know not.

Meanwhile the questions of statesmanship press for decision. The Presdt. is exerting every force to bring Congress to receive Louisiana under her Banks govt. I do not believe Louisiana is strong enough in loyalty & freedom for an independent state. The evidence on this point seems overwhelming. I have discussed it with the Presdt. & have tried to impress on him the necessity of having no break between him & Congress on such questions. We must go together. Much as I am against the premature recognition of La, I will hold my peace, if *I can secure a rule for the other states*, so that we may be saved from daily anxiety with regard to their condition.

Our good Baron Gerolt, the dean of our diplomatic corps, said to me, on reading the correspondance about the Florida,[4] "Can we hold G. Britain to the immunity of neutral water?" That is a question—especially in view of the several violations as late as 1860. The only difficulty in the Florida case has been with regard to the ship. Regarding that ship as we do, I have hoped that Brazil would never raise any question with regard to it. To this end I wrote an article on the subject sometime ago, which Goldwin Smith misinterpreted;[5] but I sympathize so entirely in his desire for peace between our two countries & also the advancement of International Law, that I pardon his hasty judgment.

You will observe that the recent correspondance leaves to Brazil the necessity of making a special demand with regard to the ship. I trust that she will be advised to let the matter drop. No good can come of it.

The Canadian storm has for the present passed, & I think there is a disposition there to keep the peace. But Ld Russell insists upon keeping up ill blood. His letter of 25th. Nov. is in his worst style.[6] Does he mean war? Or is it a general *cantankerousness*, to adopt an expression of Mr Canning's, that governs him?

The feeling against Canada was very strong. But the discharge of these offenders has doubtless had the effect of making the Canadians more cautious & putting them on their good behavior.[7] The chief trouble, however, comes from across the ocean. If England were right, there would be little trouble here, & our war would soon be at an end. When will Ld Russell be Englishman enough to say openly, that people engaged in founding a new Slave-State, must not expect recognition? Let this be done, & the war ceases. Now it is *Anglo-rebel*.

I was sorry that the *Star* committed itself[8] on the claims we have for the Alabama piracies.

We have lost a faithful reptive in Mr Dayton, who seems to have inspired respect in Paris. The Presdt. originally destined him for London, & gave up his idea reluctantly. I am pressing Mr Everett for the vacancy. His character & abilities would help us in Paris.

Ever sincerely Yours   Charles Sumner

ALS   GBL   (78/578, PCS)

1. Bright's son Leonard died in November 1864.
2. In the assault on Fort Fisher near Wilmington, North Carolina, 23–25 December 1864, Major General Butler commanded the army, while Rear Admiral David Dixon Porter led the fleet. Butler's plan to blow up Fort Fisher failed, as did Porter's fleet bombardment, and the entire expedition was withdrawn.
3. Major General William T. Sherman (1820–91) occupied Savannah, Georgia, on 21 December.
4. On 12 December Ignacio de Alvellar Barboza da Silva, Brazilian chargé d'affaires in Washington, protested the U.S. violation of neutrality in the capture of the *Florida*, which had sunk off Hampton Roads 28 November, and demanded an explanation and reparation. Seward replied 26 December that the U.S. assumed responsibility for the *Florida*'s capture and would court-martial Captain Collins, but that the U.S. government admitted to no treachery (*New York Times*, 4 January 1865:2).
5. CS's article, signed "Americanus," appeared in the *Boston Daily Advertiser*, 29 November 1864:2, and is reprinted in Wks, 12:11–34. In it he argued that the U.S. was not obliged to return the ship to Brazil because the *Florida* was "lawless in origin and conduct," owned by a body "not an independent power." In a letter to the *Philadelphia Press* (n.d.), Goldwin Smith, then touring the U.S. (he had met CS in Boston in October) argued that none of CS's examples of British violation of neutrality was recent and that "moral sentiment" in Britain had advanced substantially since the Napoleonic wars. He urged the U.S. to stop dwelling on past wrongs (*New York Times*, 18 December 1864:3).
6. Replying to Confederate representatives Mason, Slidell, and A. Dudley Mann regarding their request for recognition, Russell reiterated Great Britain's "strict and impartial neutrality." He also stated that the British government had, since the war began, "continued to entertain sentiments of friendship equally for the north and for the south" (*Foreign Relations* [1865], part 1, 9). About Russell, Bright replied from Rochdale 26 January, "I sometimes suspect he says things he would rather not say that he may not *appear* to take sides with the North" (32/402, PCS).
7. The Canadian cabinet "unanimously denounced" the decision of the Canadian judge presiding over the case of the St. Albans raiders to discharge the Confederates (*New York Times*, 16 December 1864:1).
8. In an editorial, the London *Morning Star* (9 December 1864:4) criticized the U.S. seizure of the *Florida* and drew a parallel between it and the British destruction of a privateer (built in the U.S. and sailing under the flag of a small South American republic headed by Artigas) in a Portuguese harbor. In the Artigas case, Portugal presented claims against the U.S. for damages committed by the privateer. The U.S. disallowed the Portuguese claims and, wrote the *Star*, "American people can understand that such is the kind of precedent we are likely to follow." The *Star* concluded that surely the U.S. "will be convinced of the impropriety of urging a demand to which we could not justly accede." Bright responded on 26 January, "The *Star* assumes that *culpable* negligence against our Govt. cannot be proved, & that therefore

your claims cannot be supported—for it would be absurd to suppose that, after our laws had been *evaded*, in spite of *proper efforts* to prevent it, we should be called upon to compensate you for the damage done by a ship which had sailed from an English port."

To Peleg W. Chandler

Washington
Sunday [*8 January 1865*]

Dear Chandler,

You will note the correspondance about the Florida. It ends by mentioning the destruction of the ship,—leaving [it?] to Brazil to make further claim, if it sees fit.[1] But *I say to you*, no further claim will be allowed.

The settlement is, therefore, precisely according to what was foreshadowed in the article of Americanus. The Brazilian *Chargé* here seems content; but he is not in a condition to know the final views of his Govt.

I note the bad temper of *Privatus*, who evidently is glad to strike at me, & his swift adhesion to Goldwin Smith's inconsiderate assertion, that Great Britain has changed since the Crimean War.[2] No such thing. There are instances as late as 1860—& I think later also, where her cruizers have seized a ship in neutral waters. Oh! for a little less of personal spite, & more knowledge!

A leading lawyer of N.Y. whom I met at dinner last evng expressed surprize when I told him that Evarts had been pressed for Chief Justice. He inquired—"Who pressed him?"—I said he was pressed from Mass. "Ah! I was not aware of it."

Ever Yours,   Charles Sumner

ALS   ICUJR   (78/601, PCS)

1. Seward ended his letter of 26 December 1864 to the Brazilian chargé d'affaires Barboza da Silva by declaring that the sinking of the *Florida* had been determined to be "an unforeseen accident," not the fault of the U.S. (*New York Times*, 4 January 1865:2).

2. Writing as "Privatus" in "'Americanus' and the Florida Case" (*Boston Daily Advertiser*, 13 December 1864:2), Henry W. Torrey (1814–93), Harvard history professor, stated that "Americanus" overreacted to British statements on the *Florida* seizure. "Privatus" agreed with Goldwin Smith that "Americanus"'s argument suffered because he had not cited any recent precedents in his discussion of international maritime law. Chandler wrote CS from Boston on 2 February 1865 that illness had caused his delay in publishing CS's "Supplement" on the *Florida* affair. In his "Supplement" (*Advertiser*, 17 January 1865:2, Wks, 2:35–41) CS cited more recent British violations of neutrality.

To Francis Lieber

Senate Chamber 20th Jan. '65

My dear Lieber,

What say you to the resolutions reported by our Military Comttee. on Retaliation about prisoners? I shrink from them. But I shall value yr careful judgment.[1]

In terminating the Reciprocity Treaty, you will observe that we have a full year in which to negotiate a substitute. You will see at once that it was essential to the success of any new negotiation that we should be released from the old treaty. We are now "masters of the situation."[2]

My "supplement" on the Florida was accidentally delayed nearly 3 weeks—until it is out of season. I flatter myself that it is an answer to G.[oldwin] S[mith].

Ever yours,   Charles Sumner

I have just recd yours of 18th Jan—. The motion to insert "republic of" before Mexico was ill-advised; but I was left to decide with regard to it at once.[3] If passed it would stick a pin in Louis Nap.; if rejected or if contested, there would be a pin stuck in the American people. I said to myself that "the least said the soonest mended," & held my tongue.

Sherman started Jan 15th on his march Northward through Carolina. Mr Blair has left for Richmond with a letter from the Presdt![4]

Ever yrs   C. S.

ALS   MH-H   (64/375, PCS)

1. These resolutions, reported to the Senate 18 January 1865, called for similar retaliation to that suffered by Union prisoners of war at the hands of Confederates (*Globe,* 38th Cong., 2nd sess., 307). Lieber replied 22 January from New York, "I am unqualifiedly against the retaliation resolutions concerning prisoners of war. The provision that the Southerners in our hands shall be watched over by national soldiers who have been in Southern pens is unworthy of a great people or high-minded statesmen." CS quoted most of Lieber's letter when he spoke against the resolutions on 24 January (78/632, PCS; *Globe,* 38th Cong., 2nd sess., 381–83).

2. CS spoke for ending the treaty on 11 January (ibid., 206–7).

3. Benjamin F. Wade had moved to call Mexico a "republic" when the Senate approved appropriations for consular and diplomatic expenses 13 January (ibid., 250). In his letter of 17 January Lieber wrote that Mexico was not a republic but an empire, and the Senate must "adhere to *Fact*" (78/624).

4. Francis Preston Blair met in Richmond with Jefferson Davis on 12 January asking the Confederates to abandon slavery, make peace, and join with the U.S. to put down the French in Mexico. After conferring with Lincoln, Blair returned to Richmond on 21 January with an offer from Lincoln to meet with Confederate rep-

resentatives to discuss possible peace negotiations (Elbert B. Smith, *Francis Preston Blair* [1980], 365–67; CWL, 8:220–21, 243).

To Hamilton Fish

Senate Chamber, 25th Jan. '65

My dear Fish,

While talk is proceeding I take my pen to gossip in reply to yr note.

Mr. Blair's visit is of his own motion. He was recd. the first time cordially, & actually embraced by Mrs. Davis[1] who flung herself into his arms saying—"You dear old rascal"!

I asked the Presdt. a day or two ago if he had made up his mind on the French mission. He said—"not quite." I had urged Mr. Everett for the place until his death took him from the list of candidates.[2] I think the Presdt. is keeping the place as a make-weight in political arrangements—& in some way to be used for Hamlin's benefit. He is very anxious to provide for H. Last week it seemed as if [*Lot M.*] Morrill would accept the District Judgeship & thus leave another chance for Hamlin in the Senate; but that arrangement has fallen through.

Nothing here is known with regard to Seward's plans. My neighbor in the Senate, Gov. [*Edwin D.*] Morgan, has no hint on the subject. Greely when here was very earnest for Morgan as Secy of the Treasury.[3] The Presdt. last week had another person in view, but was not decided. He is so reticent that nobody can speak confidently on any of these points.

It is rumored that Mr. Adams would like to return home, but I have no information on the subject. There are several candidates from Mass. for the cabinet—Andrew, Boutwell, [*Samuel*] Hooper, Butler, Banks, [*John*] Wiley Edmands &c.—a long list—longer I think than the New York list.

My excellent friend John Jay is very earnest for a foreign mission. I am told that he looks to London.

I am sorry to hear of yr illness; but I hope that you are well again. I am weary. Remember me kindly to all yr house & believe me,

Ever sincerely yours,   Charles Sumner

TTR[4]   DLC   (78/638, PCS)

1. Varina Davis (1826–1906), wife of Jefferson Davis.
2. Everett died 15 January 1865.
3. Fessenden, who had been secretary of the Treasury since 5 July 1864, had recently been reelected to another Senate term and planned to resign his cabinet post.

4. No holograph letter has been recovered. A note in the Fish papers states that this transcription was made by John Bassett Moore, international law scholar.

To Benjamin F. Butler

Senate Chamber 11th Feb. '65

My dear General,

Until the Department is created, I have not thought it advisable to consider the question of who should be its head. Indeed nothing has been said about it.[1]

You will note the small vote by which the report was accepted in the House.[2] There is a disposition in the Senate to delay action on it; but I shall press it, & I think that I have the votes.

Very sincerely Yours,   Charles Sumner

Thanks for yr good speech.[3]

———————

ALS   DLC   (79/019, PCS)

1. Butler had been removed from command of the Department of Virginia and North Carolina on 7 January 1865. He wrote CS from Boston 5 February about a position heading the Freedmen's Bureau. He noted rumors that both Banks and he were candidates, but wondered if they might "excite such bitter hostility" that neither would be chosen. He asked CS to see the president about "the *possibility* of my selection" (32/490, PCS).

2. The House had approved the Conference Committee's report on the bureau on 9 February, 64–62; the Senate approved the report without debate on 3 March (*Globe*, 38th Cong., 2nd sess., 694, 1348).

3. Butler spoke in Lowell, Massachusetts, 28 January defending his conduct at Cold Harbor and Fort Fisher (*New York Times*, 30 January 1865:1).

To John Bright

private

Washington 13th Feb. '65

Dear Mr Bright,

I am glad of yr assurance, in harmony with Mr Cobden's, that intervention is played out.[1] I hope so. I am glad also of yr speech.[2] It amuses me to read the criticisms, which I can appreciate at their value, as I have been exposed to the same. For years it was said that I was governed by hatred of the slave-masters, & did not care at all for the slaves. Oh no! not at all.

You will read the report of the conferences.[3] It appears that the Presdt. was drawn into them by the assurances of Genl. Grant, who was led to expect something. Perhaps the country sees now more clearly than ever, that the war must be pushed to the entire overthrow of the rebel armies. The interview was pleasant. Seward sent the Commdrs. on their arrival three bottles of choice whiskey, which, it was reported, they drank ⟨greedily⟩ thirstily. As they were leaving he gave them a couple of bottles of Champagne for their dinner.

Hunter, who is a very experienced politician, & has been all his life down to the Rebellion in Washington, said, after the discussions were closed, "Governor, how is the capitol? Is it finished?" This gave Seward an opportunity of picturing the present advanced condition of the works, with the dome completed, & the whole contributing one of the most magnificent edifices of the world.

Campbell, formerly of the Sup. Ct. of the U.S. & reputed the ablest lawyer in the slave states, began the conference by suggesting peace on the basis of a Zollverein,[4] & continued free trade between the two sections, which he thought might open the way to something hereafter; but he could not promise any thing. This was also the theory of the French Minister here, Mr Mercier, now at Madrid, who insisted that the war must end in that way.

It was remarked that these men had nothing of the haughty & defiant way which they had in Washington formerly.

Mr Blair, who visited Richmond, still insists that peace is near. He says that the war can not go on *another month* on their side, unless they have help from Louis Nap. But here the question of a monarchical govt. may arise. Jeff. Davis, whom he describes as so emaciated & altered, as not to be recognized, sets his face against it. He said to Mr Blair that "there was a Brutus who would brook the eternal devil as easily as a king in Rome," & he was that Brutus in Richmond.

Meanwhile the war goes on with converging forces. Mr Stanton was with me yesterday, & gave me fully his expectations. He thinks that peace can be had only when Lee's army is beaten, captured or dispersed; & there I agree with him. To that end all our military energies are now directed. Lee's army is 65,000 men. Against him is Grant at Petersburg—a corps now demonstrating at Wilmington—& Sherman marching from Georgia. The latter will not turn aside for Augusta or Charleston, or any fortified place, but will traverse the Carolinas until he is able to co-operate with Grant. You will see from this statement something of the nature of the campaign. Mr Stanton thinks it ought to be finished before May.

I have for a long time been sanguine that, when Lee's army is out of the way, the whole Rebellion will disappear. While that is in fighting condition, there is still a hope for the rebels, & the unionists of the South are afraid to show themselves.

I am sorry that so good & great a man as G. Smith, who has done so much for us, should fall into what Mr Canning would call *cantanker*.[5] He rushed too swiftly to his conclusion. But I hope that we shall not lose his powerful support for the good cause.

I have felt it my duty to say to the British *chargé* here,[6] that nothing could be done to provide for British claims on our govt arising out of the war, which are very numerous, until Ld Russell took a different course with regard to ours. He tosses ours aside haughtily. I am sorry; for my system is peace & good will, which I shall try, in my sphere, to cultivate. But there must be reciprocity.

I have not time to write to Cobden. If you see him, you can shew him this letter.

Goodbye!

Ever sincerely Yours,   Charles Sumner

ALS   GBL   (79/030, PCS)

1. Bright wrote CS 26 January 1865 that there was no danger of war: "we seem never to have been so far from it, or from wishing it." In his letter of 11 January, Cobden stated that he did not believe "there is the remotest risk of anything of the kind" (32/402, 288, PCS).

2. Speaking to residents of Birmingham on 18 January, Bright declared that the great historical issues, such as parliamentary reform, could never be buried, and used the example of slavery in the U.S. The black was "every day becoming more and more a free man" (London *Times*, 19 January 1865:9).

3. On 2–3 February Lincoln and Seward met with Confederate emissaries Senate President *pro tem* Robert M. T. Hunter, Vice President Alexander Stephens, and Assistant Secretary of War John Archibald Campbell (1811–89) at Hampton Roads, off Fort Monroe.

4. German states united loosely for free trade among themselves and a common tariff on imports.

5. Writing from Oxford on 6 January to the *Boston Daily Advertiser* (26 January 1865:2), Smith objected to what he considered unwarranted anti-British feeling from Americans, and used CS's article on the *Florida* case as an example. He wished "the good to be taken with the evil. Mr. Sumner's 'political ethics' may be high; but I am not disposed to admit that they are higher . . . than those of Canning or Sir Robert Peel."

6. Joseph Hume Burnley.

To George Bancroft

Senate Chamber—28th Feb '65—

My dear Bancroft,

I gave notice tonight that I should move the rail-road bill on the Post-Road Bill, one of the general bills which must go through & cannot be postponed.[1] It may be voted down; but there will be a vote.

You are right in yr appreciation of the La question.[2] Perhaps, it is the greatest of our history. In rejecting the application of this state during this session we obtain the vacation for the discussion of the question & the appeal to the sober 2nd thought of the people. Already the agitation has begun, proceeding of course from Mass. We shall insist upon the Decltn of Indep. as the foundation of the new State govts; & the argt. will be presented, not merely on the grounds of Human Rights, but of self-interest. It will be shewn that we shall need the votes of the negroes to sustain the Union, to preserve tranquility & to prevent the repudiation of the national debt. You are right in calling it a stupendous question.

But let it be ⟨established⟩ decided, & the pledges of the Decltn of Indep. redeemed, & our country will be very grand & glorious. And, believe me, all this will be done. To this consummation every thing tends.

Ever Yours, Charles Sumner

ALS   NICO   (79/084, PCS)

1. *Globe*, 38th Cong., 2nd sess., 1183. Bancroft had written CS on 21 February 1865 from New York, regretting that a bill permitting unregulated railroad shipment and travel in all the states had been postponed (32/584, PCS). The Senate on 3 March voted not to consider it (*Globe*, 38th Cong., 2nd sess., 1394).

2. Regarding the admission of Arkansas and Louisiana, Bancroft wrote that he saw "great difficulties either way." He asked CS, would not "rejection of the new constitutions bring with it the establishment of the old ones?" Bancroft added, in his letter of 27 February, that the "public's mind is at present fixed in the idea, that 27 states [*three-quarters of loyal plus returning rebel states*] are required to amend the Constitution" (32/618). CS had on 4 February introduced resolutions declaring that the Thirteenth Amendment would be valid when three-quarters of the states *de facto*, not including states in rebellion, ratified it (*Globe,* 38th Cong., 2nd sess., 588).

To Francis W. Bird

Senate Chamber 1st March '65

My dear Bird,

I send you the *Globe* of Friday last, giving our first day on Louisiana. I have made some corrections which I wish transferred, should the debate be quoted.[1] In one place the reporter makes nonsense. In another he did not get my full idea.

From this time forward the *mot d'ordre* must be the organization of the rebel states on the basis of the Decltn. of Independence. That was the idea of my resolutions,[2] & I think that during the summer & autumn, before the next Congress, the country can be rallied there, especially as the argt. of self-interest will be so strong.

The vote on La. Monday was *final*.[3]

There has been a whisper that it may be moved on an Appropriation Bill; & also Taney's bust.[4] Then the bill will be lost.

The question will come up in another form at the Extra session of the Senate on the credentials of Mr Hahn. Can you send me the evidence of his having held office under the Rebellion?[5] I have seen a statement if not affidavits on that subject. Let me have these docts. at once.

Ever yours,   Charles Sumner

ALS   MH-H   (79/093, PCS)

1. Debate as to when the Senate would consider readmission of the state of Louisiana began 24 February. CS's debate with John B. Henderson that the present government of the state of Louisiana was antirepublican because it did not give suffrage to blacks (*Globe*, 38th Cong., 2nd sess., 1066–69) is printed in Wks, 12:180–83, with CS's changes, made in 1865 or possibly later. In one instance CS removed the *Globe*'s account of CS's exceptions to his contention that "no act of secession can take a State out of this Union"; in another he amended the *Globe*'s statement that "No government that does not guaranty these things can be recognized as republican in form, according to the theory of the Constitution of the United States, if the United States are called to enforce the constitutional guaranty" (*Globe,* 38th Cong., 2nd sess., 1067) to "No Government failing to guaranty these things can be recognized as republican in form, when the United States are called to enforce the constitutional guaranty."

2. CS's resolutions, introduced 25 February, were originally intended as a substitute for the resolution admitting Louisiana. They declared that all reentering states should be based on the "consent of the governed," that "all men shall be equal before the law," that "proper safeguards for the rights of all the citizens" be established, and that without the votes of blacks, "the cause of human rights and of the Union itself will be in constant peril" (ibid., 1091).

3. The Senate voted 34–12 on 27 February to postpone consideration of the Louisiana question (ibid., 1129).

4. Both houses were considering funding for a bust of the late Chief Justice Taney. CS spoke against the bill on 23 February (ibid., 1012–13).

5. On 2 March the credentials of Michael Hahn (1830–86; U.S. congressman [Union, La.], 1862–63; governor of Louisiana, February 1864–March 1865) were presented. The Senate postponed consideration 9 March (ibid., 1278, 1434). Bird replied he had not found the information CS sought, but had referred CS's request to William L. Burt (d. 1882), judge advocate general on Andrew's staff. (Burt wrote CS 4 March from Boston that Hahn had been a notary public in the Confederacy.) Bird hoped CS would succeed in rejecting Hahn: "a Senator without a state is of very little account" (32/700, 701, PCS).

To Wendell Phillips

Washington 12th March '65

My dear Phillips,

A movement should be started at once in La, making the Decltn of Indep. the guide.[1]

Chase C.J. has just given an opinion of Sup. Ct.—of immense importance—declaring the Banks govt. void *ab initio*[2] &, I am assured, affirming every fundamental principle in the condition of rebel territory which I have ever held. This is important for the future.

You see that we have sent off the claimants from La & Ark. without their mileage.[3] I thought it our duty to discourage such applications. They will see that there is a power in Liberty which cannot be neglected, & I profess humbly to be one of the reptives. of that power.

Earnestly, & most persistently I labored to bring the Senate up to action in order to redeem the national name, & republican institutions, & to save the country on account of the intemperance of the Vice-Presdt; but unsuccessfully.[4] The bitter spirit has come back to thwart every thing good & liberal. But I did prevent yesterday the confirmation of a drunkard & negro-hater as general—much to the rage of certain senators.[5] I said to them—"for 24 hours I have the veto, & I shall exercise it."—

Ever yours,   Charles Sumner

ALS   MH-H   (79/119, PCS)

1. Phillips wrote CS twice in March congratulating him on the defeat of the admission of Louisiana and assuring him Massachusetts supported its senator (1, 10 March 1865, 32/667, 738, PCS).

2. In U.S. v. Alexander, Chase on 10 March ruled for the U.S., stating that the cotton Mrs. Elizabeth Alexander claimed the Union forces had stolen from her Louisiana plantation belonged to the U.S. and should have been turned over to the U.S. Treasury, not a local military government. Chase stated that all residents of a state or district rebelling against the U.S. "must be regarded as enemies, until by action of the Legislature and the Executive or otherwise" (*United States Supreme Court Reports*, Lawyers Edition, Book 17 [1884], 915–21).

3. On 10 March (*Globe*, 38th Cong., 2nd sess., 1439).

4. CS wrote Lieber on 8 March that Andrew Johnson's behavior at the inauguration was "frightful . . . he has continued in the most unhappy condition ever since" (Johnson did not preside over the special session of the Senate 7–10 March). CS regretted that, because the House was not in session, Johnson could not be "impeached & removed from office." CS had tried to get a Senate Republican caucus to demand Johnson's resignation, but told Lieber, "the *drags* are against me" (64/400).

5. Thomas H. Redfield's promotion was rejected in executive session on 11 March. In full session, Senator Sherman protested adjournment before all Senate business was

concluded, stating he was "not willing to yield to the will of one member" (*Executive Proceedings*, 14:298; *Globe*, 38th Cong., 2nd sess., 11 March, 1440).

To John Bright
private

Washington 13th March '65

Dear Mr Bright,

I have yr good & most suggestive letter. I concur in it substantially.[1] A practical difficulty is this; can Emancipation be carried out without using the lands of the slave-masters. We must see that the freedmen are established on the soil & that they may become proprietors.

From the beginning I have regarded confiscation only as ancillary to Emancipation. The great plantations, which have been so many nurseries of the rebellion, must be broken up, & the freedmen must share the pieces.

It looks as if we were on the eve of another agitation. I insist that the rebel States shall not come back except on the footing of the Decltn of Indep. with all persons equal before the law, & govt. founded on the consent of the governed. In other words there shall be no discrimination on account of color. If *all* whites vote, then must all blacks; but there shall be no limitation of suffrage for one more than the other.

It is sometimes said "what—let the freedmen yesterday a slave vote?" I am inclined to think that there is more harm in refusing than in conceding the franchise. It is said that they are as intelligent as the Irish just arrived.

But the question has become immensely practical in this respect. Without their votes, we cannot establish stable govts. in the rebel states. Their votes are as necessary as their musquets. Of this I am satisfied. Without them, the old enemy will reappear &, under the forms of law, take possession of the govts.—choose magistrates & officers—&, in alliance with the Northern democracy, put us all in peril again, postpone the day of tranquility, & menace the national credit by assailing the national debt. To my mind, the nation is now bound by self-interest—aye, *self-defence*—to be thoroughly just.

The Declaration of Indep. has pledges which have never been redeemed. We must redeem them, at least as regards the rebel states which have fallen under our jurisdiction.

Mr Lincoln is slow in accepting truths. I have reminded him that if he would say the word we might settle this question promptly & rightly. He hesitates.

Meanwhile I felt it my duty to oppose his scheme of govt. in Louisiana, which for the present is defeated in Congress. Chief Justice Chase yesterday pronounced an opinion of the Sup. Ct declaring the whole scheme "illegal & void" from the beginning; so that it fares no better in court than in Congress. Mr Chase & myself have always concurred in opinion on this question. With the habit of deference here to the Sup. Ct. I anticipate much from this opinion.[2] Substantially it affirms the conclusion which I adopted three years ago, sometimes called "the territorial theory."

That has been much misunderstood in Europe. It has been supposed sometimes as a menace of subjugation. Nothing further from my mind—at least in any offensive sense. I felt that the rebel region must for a while pass under the *jurisdiction of Congress*, in order to set up the necessary safeguards for the future; & I have labored to this end.

Nothing has been heard of Sherman for weeks,[3]—but Mr Stanton has no anxiety about him. He will re-appear in North Carolina. Grant is very cheerful. But for the moment the curtain is down. It may lift any day.

I send you the Resolutions on Reciprocity & Lake Armaments, as they passed the House, & as amended by me. The Italics are mine; & that is the form adopted.[4]

You will see from the date of the House Resolution on Armaments how long I held it back. I was unwilling to take the step, until the outrages on the Lakes seemed to shew its necessity.[5]

I came into the proposition to give the notice to terminate the Reciprocity Treaty, because I was satisfied that we could not negotiate for its modification, on a footing of equality unless our hands were untied. You will see this in my speech. I make this remark in reply to yr suggestion on the subject.[6]

Congress has separated in good humor, without anxiety for the future, & indeed confident that we are on the verge of peace. My desire is that England should do something to take out the bitterness from the American heart—before the war closes[.] Help. I owe Cobden, & shall write him next.

Ever Yours,   Charles Sumner

ALS GBL (79/121, PCS)

1. In his letter to CS from London 17 February 1865 (32/559, PCS), Bright laid out five points for Reconstruction: (1) abolition of slavery; (2) amnesty to almost all Southerners except a dozen or so Confederate leaders; (3) U.S. retention of lands already captured, but for the rest "*a large generosity & mercy*"; (4) denial of any federal or state office to Confederate leaders; and (5) nullification of all Confederate debts.

He added, "nothing should be done or conceded that lessens the idea of the *crime* which the slaveholders have committed. . . . [I]f the leaders of this rebellion are recd. into the bosom of the State, & if the sums they have expended in the effort to destroy the Govt. & the country are repaid to them by that Govt. & that Country, there will be held out to future aspirants for 'independence' no small encouragement & support."

2. CS wrote Bright on 18 March that CS had overreacted to Chase's ruling. Chase explained to CS that the court had not ruled on "the validity of the La. govt, but only on the validity of proceedings in certain parts of the state" (79/133).

3. News of Sherman's whereabouts later surfaced; he was in Fayetteville, North Carolina, 11–14 March.

4. CS enclosed H.R. 91, joint resolution of 18 January terminating the Treaty of 1817 between Great Britain and the U.S. governing navies on the Great Lakes. CS underlined a passage that stated that since the present border was now threatened by "lawless persons," a greater naval force was needed.

5. CS underlined the dates "1864 June 20" and "1865 January 17," with a note, "Which passed. Please see." The "outrages" to which CS refers were the Confederate attempts, 19 September 1864, to rescue prisoners from Johnson's Island on Lake Erie and the St. Albans raid.

6. In his letter Bright said, "I think you are quite *right* about having more force on the lakes, & *wrong* about the Reciprocity Treaty—but this last you will find out in time."

To Francis Lieber

Washington 13th March '65

Dear Lieber,

I have no purpose of going North before May.[1]

The Presdt's speech, & other things augur confusion & uncertainty in the future—with hot controversy.[2] Alas! Alas!

Ever yours,   Charles Sumner

ALS   MH-H   (64/402, PCS).

1. Lieber wrote CS 7 March 1865 inviting him to New York on his way back to Boston (New York, 79/105, PCS).

2. CS probably refers to Lincoln's closing paragraph, conciliatory to the South, in his Second Inaugural Address.

To Louis Agassiz

Washington 20th March '65

My dear Agassiz,

It is a beautiful expedition that you are about to commence[1]—in contrast with the deeds of war. And yet you are going forth to conquer new realms & bring them under a sway they have not yet known. But science is peaceful & bloodless in her conquests. May you return victorious! I am sure you will.

Of course, you will see the Emperor of Brazil, whose enlightened character is one of the happy accidents of govt. If he gives you an opportunity, I hope you will not fail to let him know that there are good friends of Brazil here who think that a grave mistake was made when this Power, naturally friendly to the United States, consented to follow the lead of Lord Russell in elevating our rebels to the condition of lawful belligerents on the ocean. It is difficult to see all the consequences of this act.

Of course, Lord Russell adopted at once the conclusion that the Rebellion must triumph, &, therefore, made the concession which he did. The effect of this concession has been infinitely mischievous. Without it, the rebellion would have been crushed long ago.

I wish that the Brazilian govt. could see the mistake that has been made, & cancel it. The better way would be to recognize the mistake *ab initio*, as made on a misunderstanding of the actual facts. How there can be any hesitation to withdraw the concession now, at this stage of the war, when obviously the rebels have no prize courts, I am at a loss to understand. But, as I have said, it would be better still to let it be known that the original concession was made under a misapprehension,—caused by the great maritime powers.

You are a naturalist; but you are a patriot also. If you can take advantage of the opportunities which you will surely enjoy, & plead for our country, to the end that its rights may be understood, & the hardships it has been obliged to endure, may be appreciated, you will render a service to the cause of international peace & good will.[2]

You are to have great enjoyment. I imagine you already very happy in the scenes before you. I too should like to see nature in her most splendid robes; but I must stay at home, & help keep the peace. Good bye! *Bon voyage*!

Ever sincerely Yours,   Charles Sumner

ALS   MH-H   (79/139, PCS)

1. Agassiz wrote CS that he was leaving 21 March 1865 on a scientific expedition up the Amazon. He asked if there were any way he could "help the cause of our country" (Cambridge, 14, 17 March, 33/028, 042, PCS).

2. Describing his interview with the Brazilian emperor Don Pedro II (1825–91), Agassiz wrote of the emperor's hopes that slavery "would soon be every where abolished" (Rio de Janeiro, 21 June, 33/648).

To Richard Cobden
private & confidential

Washington 27th March '65

My dear Cobden,

I begin by answering yr inquiry.[1] Ld Lyons, when he left Washington, was very ill. I doubted if he could recover. But I think he was tired of his work here & of an uncongenial life. He was just & loved peace, but he had no facility in business or intercourse—so that his heavy work told on him. The Foreign Office was his absolute guide. Therefore, every letter that he recd —& the whole spirit of Ld John—entered into him. But he never said that we could not succeed. He was too discreet for that. My relations with him for much of the time were intimate; but after my speech in New York we saw each other only accidentally. He did not call on me, & I did not call on him; & yet when we met it was in the most friendly way. I always think of him with great respect. He is a sincere, truthful person. And yet I think that his successor[2] has an experience of the world & an ease which will give him great advantages in the transaction of business.

It is time that the relations between G.B. & the U.S. were on a better footing. From the beginning of the war they have been at the extremest tension always.[3] I doubt if the history of diplomacy can show such a succession of pestilent letters as Ld Russell has felt it his solemn duty to address to us. A bad page of British history! This ought to stop. It could hardly be otherwise, when Ld Russell had first mis-represented our contest & then, prophecied our defeat. Had he supposed we were to be successful, he would have spoken & written less. How will it read hereafter, that the British govt. took advantage of our imagined weakness to say what it would not have said had we been strong.

The only point on which there can be any positive difference is the ill-omened alliance with the Rebellion, by the concession of belligerency & the opening of British work-shops, involving, of course, the whole case of the Alabama. If Ld Russell insists that our claims shall not be heard, he takes the responsibility of keeping alive this difference. Of course we must follow his example, & refuse to hear any British claims. Mr Seward sent Mr Burnley to me last winter with the British claims, which are not few in number or small in amount. I told him that it was impossible for us to make any provision for the consideration of these claims, so long as Ld Russell refused to consider ours. I did not pretend to say by what proceeding or tribunal our claims should be determined; but I insisted that they should be considered, & that until this was done it would be useless for him to present any British claims;

& I requested him to communicate this answer to Ld Russell. So the case stands. Of course, the longer the claims are allowed to remain without some provision for their consideration, the more deep-seated will be the heart-burning & anger which they will excite.

It is foolish & immoral, as I believe, for any power to put itself in the position of refusing to consider claims made in good faith by another power, & thus challenging war. It is because I am so sincere for peace that I regret this course. There are Americans who are glad of it, because they wish to keep alive a cause of war. There are others, who think that upon the whole it is the best policy to say little about our claims now but "to wait until England is in a tight place." An able foreign diplomatist said to me lately—"don't try to convince the English govt. that it is wrong, but wait till a European war occurs, & then practice on her precedents, & sweep her commerce from the seas." Now, I am against all this. I wish a settlement at once, so that there can be no old score for either side to use. And let it be approached in a spirit of good will—as two neighbors would act, who had not got so angry as to lose their balance—& I am sure it can be settled. If we are wrong, I hope that we shall have the good sense to confess it. But our case must be heard.

I do not fear any immediate trouble with England; but I am pained by the tone of our diplomacy. This must be changed. Sir Frederick Bruce must turn over a new leaf.

Do not commit yourself to the Artigas correspondance, brought forward by Historicus.[4] It will be shewn at the proper time to be a falsification, where dates have been suppressed, & a despatch of Mr Adams has been put forward as a reply to what was never answered. I wonder at Historicus whose character must be compromised.

France is more of a tinder-box than England, & the Mexican question may possibly furnish a chance for combustion. If our rebellion should be suddenly crushed, what will become of the two armies? Grant thinks that many of our officers & men will insist upon driving Maximilian out of Mexico. It is very easy to imagine the rebel forces pouring in the same direction. Old Mr Blair, in his interview with Jeff. Davis, submitted a plan by which the latter was to be allowed to withdraw, carrying his army & immediate followers into Mexico & he was authorized to offer Commissions from Juarez.[5] I do not doubt that this proposal tempted Jeff. Davis to the Peace Conference at Fortress Munroe, where the "continental question" was presented by the rebels as furnishing an opportunity for union; but the Presdt. did not hearken to it. You may be certain that our govt. did not give the rebels any reason to hope on that question. We mean to have peace, domestic & foreign.

Such is the purpose of our govt. And yet our people are so sensitive with regard to the establishment of a monarchy in Mexico, that I know not what chapter may be in reserve for us. Some think that England will look with complacency upon the chance of complications with Louis Nap.—

Meanwhile the question occurs at home, how shall we treat the rebel states? I felt it my duty to oppose the President's policy as shewn in the case of Louisiana. Too much blood & treasure have been spent to allow these states to come back again until they are really changed. The whole social & political system must be remodelled.[6] *Union govts. cannot be organized with out the* blacks. Of this I am sure, & on this I mean to act. The question before us is *suffrage without distinction of color.* So that out of the death of Slavery arises another question still. The Presdt. took the defeat of his plan very kindly. I think that his mind is undergoing change. In our foreign affairs, he is thoroughly pacific; but he does not understand Ld Russell, nor how he can write such letters.

I notice that the termination of the two Treaties has caused discussion in England—Our act has been much misunderstood, & especially my connection with it. Perhaps you have seen my remarks on the Reciprocity Treaty. I was satisfied that it was best to give the notice, that the Treaty might be revised. Public Opinion on our side seemed to require it; our relations with Canada did not justify any sacrifices on our part; & the very Treaty seemed to anticipate its revision at the end of ten years. If you will look at the terms of the notice—the case of armaments on the lakes, you will see that the resolution passed the House *June 20th 1864,* & that in its terms, it contemplated the establishment of "one or more navy yards." I did not think proper to act on it at that time. Indeed, I told the comttee. that it looked too much like war. Afterwards the rebel agents seized a steamer on the Lakes, & St Albans was robbed. Mr Seward, of his own notion gave the notice. I then called up the resolution in my commttee as late as *Jan 17, 1865* & submitted a substitute which recited, as the reason for the notice that "the peace of our frontier is now endangered by hostile expeditions against the commerce of the lakes & by other acts of lawless persons, which the naval force of the two countries, allowed by the existing treaty, may be insufficient to prevent." My substitute was adopted in Committee & afterwards by both Houses of Congress,—so that my agency was to moderate & limit the terms of the notice. In point of fact, Mr Seward has already let yr govt. know that we should not act upon it. *Cessante ratione cessat et ipsa lex.*[7]

Do you do justice to our finances?[8] I doubt we have acted under the necessities of our case; but not in such ignorance as you seem to suppose. Our case has been with out a paralell, & thus far we have been reasonably successful. Of course, there will be trouble. Such immense transactions, in the *transition-period*, must cause trouble. But pray do not by public prophecy increase our load. Pray hold back Goldwin Smith, who is too good & great to do any thing willingly by which we can suffer. You say nothing of yr health.[9] How are you?

Good bye!

Ever sincerely Yours   Charles Sumner

I send a letter from Mr Hooper, who has exercised much influence over our finances & who understands them well. The Presdt has thought of him for Secy of the Treasy. The extract from the *Tribune* was read to me by Seward a fortnight ago, as from a person at Richmond in the secrets of the Rebellion.

ALS   GBL   (79/163, PCS)
Enc: Samuel Hooper to CS, 26 March 1865, ALS

1. In his letter of 2 March 1865 from Midhurst (32/680, PCS), Cobden asked, "Is there any other reason besides ill-health for Lyons's resignation?" (in February 1865). CS wrote Lord Lyons a farewell letter 11 December 1864 (Prc, 4:204, 64/366).

2. Frederick Bruce (1814–67) became minister to the U.S. 1 March 1865.

3. Cobden had written, "There is no denying the fact that your terrible struggle has demonstrated an amount of hostility on the part of the ruling class here, & the ruling powers of Europe generally, towards your democratic institutions, for which none of us were prepared. Still it must not be forgotten that the common people of England were true to the cause of freedom. . . . I know you are greatly & justly angered at the conduct of our upper classes,—but do not forget the attitude of the workers" (Midhurst, 32/680).

4. In an article in the London *Times*, 22 December 1864:6, William Harcourt ("Historicus") criticized Lincoln's assertion in his presidential message that the Confederacy did not merit the status of a belligerent. Harcourt drew a comparison similar to that raised by the London *Morning Star* (see CS to Bright, 1 January 1865) between Portugal and the U.S. In 1816 Portugal claimed from the U.S. damages from cruisers outfitted in the U.S. and flying under Artigas's flag. Harcourt, giving no dates, quoted letters from the Portuguese minister at Washington and suggested that these were the "models" for Charles Francis Adams's and Seward's protests to Britain. He also quoted John Quincy Adams's letter, 14 March 1818, in which the U.S. denied Portugal's claim.

5. Benito Juarez (1806–72), former president of Mexico, who had been driven into exile by Maximilian's forces.

6. In his 2 March letter Cobden congratulated CS on Congress's passage of the Thirteenth Amendment and John Rock's admission to practice before the Supreme Court: "In all these proceedings at Washington, *you* ought to be allowed to indulge the feelings of a triumphant general.—You served as a volunteer in the forlorn hope when the battle of Emancipation seemed a hopeless struggle.—*Your* position within the walls of Congress was very different from that of the agitators out of doors, meritorious as were their labours.—I have served in both capacities, & know the

difference between addressing an audience of partisans at a public meeting & a hostile parliamentary assembly."

7. "When the reason for the law ceases, the law itself ceases."

8. Cobden wrote of the "serious task" the U.S. would confront after the war: "The country is revelling in a Saturnalia of greenbacks & government expenditure, & is under the delusion that it is a genuine prosperity. It is destined to a rude disenchantment, & this will test the statesmanship of the republican party." With his letter CS enclosed a letter to him from Samuel Hooper, who had included with *his* letter an undated clipping from the *New York Tribune* on Cobden's concern about the U.S. debt.

9. Bright had written CS 17 February (32/559) that, although Cobden's health was better, he was unable to attend Parliament.

To William Lloyd Garrison

Washington 29th March [*1865*]

Dear Mr Garrison,

I expect to be here till May. Please do not cut me off from the *Liberator*, & let me have the back numbers since you stopped sending to the Senate.

Our last battle approaches. Its countersign will be Equality before the law—without distinction of color. The good cause must triumph. Then at last will come *reconcilation*; & not before.[1]

Ever sincerely yours, Charles Sumner

ALS MB (79/178, PCS)

1. The *Liberator* (24 March 1865:46, 47) announced it would cease publication in December 1865. According to editor Walter M. Merrill, Garrison believed his goal, the abolition of slavery, had been accomplished; the paper was also in financial straits (*The Letters of William Lloyd Garrison*, 5 [1979], 248–49).

To John Bigelow

Washington 4th March [*April*] '65

My dear Minister,

Here is the final answer of Little & Brown. What can I do? I will write to New York.[1]

If the solicitude of the French Legation here is a reflection of Paris, you must have anxious people about you. Mexico causes much serious thought. Ld Palmerston's sommersault of the 13th March is not calculated to calm French sensibilities here.[2]

The feeling yesterday, when it was known that Richmond was ours, broke forth every where with regard to England & France. Much that was said has been suppressed. There was a general expression that "our little bill," as it was called should be presented forthwith to England, & that Louis Napoleon should be worried to leave Mexico. Moderation & peace; these are my watchwords; & the Presdt. agrees.

There are generals in our army ready to join Benito Juarez. I suppose the rebel generals will be too happy in such an opportunity.

Ever Yours,   Charles Sumner

ALS   NSchU   (PL, 79/199, PCS)
Enc: Little, Brown & Company to CS, 28 March 1865

1. On 24 February 1865 Bigelow wrote CS from Paris about possible publication of the speeches of the British diplomatist Sir Henry Bulwer (79/075, PCS). CS enclosed the publishers' rejection of Bigelow's proposal.

2. Bigelow had on 24 December 1864 been made chargé d'affaires at Paris (*Retrospections of an Active Life*, 2 [1909], 249); he wrote asking CS to give a speech urging that the U.S. not interfere with French policy in Mexico. Palmerston's "sommersault" of 13 March was his Parliamentary speech stating that the British government had "no complaint" against the U.S. and that he expected "most friendly relations" between the two countries (*Hansard's Parliamentary Debates*, 3rd series, 177:1633–37).

To Salmon P. Chase

Washington Monday
[*10 April 1865*]

My dear Chase,

The report in the papers of what passed at Richmond is substantially correct. But the Presdt has to-day sent for Govr. Pierpont.[1]

On the main question he is reticent.[2] But he saw with his own eyes at Richmond & Petersburg, that the only people *who showed themselves were negroes.* All others had fled or were retired in their houses. Never was I more convinced of the utter impossibility of any organization which is not founded on the votes of the negroes.

The Presdt. is full of tenderness to all & several times repeated "Judge not that ye be not judged." This he said—even when Jeff. Davis was named as one who should not be pardoned.

I hope that the complication at Richmond may be got rid of,[3] or, rather, that the whole proceeding may fail so completely, that he will be without any embarasment in adopting a just & safe system.

I wish you were about him to exercise yr influence. The Atty. Genl. is excellent.[4] He & I agree entirely, & he is ready to do all that he can.

Ever Sincerely Yours,   Charles Sumner

Why not write directly to the Presdt? I think it would be well.

ALS   CSmH   (79/217, PCS)

1. Lincoln toured the vacated capital on 4 April 1865. CS, at the invitation of Mary Lincoln, accompanied her in a small party, joining the president at City Point 5–9 April (2 April, 33/116, PCS). On 10 April Lincoln met with Francis H. Pierpont (1814–99), organizer of the West Virginia state government, 1861–63, and head of the loyalist government in Virginia in 1865.

2. Chase wrote CS a note on 10 April stating that the government headed by Pierpont "must be recognized & maintained as the true & legal govt." He urged that *all* loyal people, "colored or not colored," should form the new governments in the returning states (Washington, 79/220).

3. On 6 April Lincoln notified Major General Godfrey Weitzel (1835–84), the Union commander at Richmond, that he should give permission and protection to "gentlemen who have acted as the Legislature of Virginia, in support of the Rebellion" to convene in order to organize the dispersement of Virginia troops. Weitzel was to show his order to Confederate emissary John A. Campbell but not to "make it public" (CWL, 8:386, 389).

4. James Speed (1812–87), U.S. attorney general, 1864–66, had been with the Lincoln party at City Point.

To Salmon P. Chase
private

Washington 12th April '65

My dear Chase,

I am very unhappy;—for I see in the future strife, & uncertainty for my country, & another hot controversy for myself.

I have not recently shared yr sanguine hopes. I have never seen in the Presdt. the disposition to accept general principles & to follow them logically & courageously.

His interview with Campbell was two days before we reached there.[1] Genl. Weitzel told us that the Presdt. had authorized him to convene the Va legislature.

Stanton telegraphed to Genl. Weitzel that he must not hold any intercourse with Campbell. The General replied that he was instructed to do so by the Presdt. Here is discord.

I found Stanton yesterday very much disconcerted & feeling that we might lose the fruits of our victories.

The more I have seen of the Presdt. the more his character in certain respects has risen, & we must all admit that he has said some things better than any body else could have said them. But I fear his policy now.

What shall we do? What can be done?

I was invited to the White House last evng,[2] but was unwilling to put myself in the position of opposing him on his own balcony or assenting by silence.

Ever Yours,   C. S.

ALS   DLC   (79/225, PCS)

1. Lincoln met with Campbell on 4–5 April 1865 and notified him (1) that no peace could be made until federal authority was restored throughout "all the States," (2) that slavery must be abolished, and (3) that all rebel armies must be disbanded. He stated that "all propositions coming from those now in hostility to the government; and not inconsistent with the foregoing, will be respectfully considered, and passed upon in a spirit of sincere liberality."

2. Mary Lincoln invited CS and his friend, the French political writer Marquis Charles Adolphe de Chambrun (1831–91), to a victory celebration at the White House (11 April, 33/170, PCS).

To Salmon P. Chase

Washington 13th. April '65

My dear Chase,

I like yr letter, & think it must do much good.[1]

I find Stanton much excited. He had a full & earnest talk with the Presdt. last evng & insisted that the proposed meeting at Richmond should be forbidden.[2] He thinks that we are in a crisis more trying than any before, with the chance of losing the fruits of our victory. He asks if it was not Grant who surrendered to Lee, instead of Lee to Grant. He is sure that Richmond is beginning to govern Washington.

The Presdt. is very anxious.

So far as I can see, his speech has fallen very dead.[3]

Ever Yours,   Charles Sumner

ALS   I   (79/233, PCS)

1. Chase wrote Lincoln two letters on Reconstruction, 11 and 12 April 1865; CS probably refers to the first, in which Chase urged Lincoln to recognize the Pierpont

government in Virginia and to organize other returning state governments "under constitutions securing suffrage to all citizens" and not to exclude the "colored loyalists of rebel states" (CWL, 8:399).

2. Lincoln telegraphed Weitzel on 12 April that, in issuing orders for Confederate Virginia leaders to convene, he did not intend to recognize them "as a *rightful* body" but only "as men having power *de facto* to do a specific thing" (ibid., 406–7).

3. In what is now termed his "Last Public Address," 11 April, at the White House, Lincoln defended his Reconstruction policy in Louisiana and described as a "pernicious abstraction" the question of whether Confederate states had actually seceded from the Union. He stated that although he would have "prefer[red]" that suffrage in Louisiana had been granted to "very intelligent" blacks and those who had been soldiers, he thought Louisiana should be admitted into the Union under its present plan. As for the other states, Lincoln declared that such were the "great peculiarities" in each state that "no exclusive, and inflexible plan can safely be prescribed as to details and colatterals" (ibid., 399–405).

To John Jay

Washington 13th April '65

My dear Jay,

I am not indifferent to the good will or confidence of my fellow citizens, especially when they think of me for a high position. But my single desire is to serve my country, & the cause in which you & I have so long labored. I doubt if I could be as useful in the place you name as where I am.[1]

I am not a candidate for any office, & do not look to any change. Let me add, that I doubt very much the expediency of any action or recommendation with regard to such a place as you name. Count me out, if you please, & say so to my excellent friend Mr Hall, & believe me,

Ever yours,   Charles Sumner

ALS   NNCB   (79/235, PCS)

1. Jay wrote CS from New York 11 April 1865 that William A. Hall, a New York merchant, and others wished to start a movement in that city supporting CS for secretary of state. Would CS "disapprove" of such an action (33/169, PCS)?

VI
THE
JOHNSON
YEARS

April 1865 – December 1868

I<small>N FEBRUARY</small> 1862,
when he thought the war would soon end, Sumner offered nine Reconstruction resolutions in the Senate, providing for territorial governments in former rebel states. From this time, Sumner consistently argued that Congress should assume control over these states, and he sought to "guaranty a republican form of government" in them (to Parke Godwin 23 March 1862; to George Bancroft, 3 February 1866). Now that Republican dominance in the government offered hope for national social change, Sumner reversed himself regarding its sovereignty: states had "certain powers," he wrote Lieber, but "there is no power to interfere with the National Govt. which in its orbit is supreme" (2 May 1865).

When Sumner realized that abolition was imminent, he began to press for black male suffrage in returning states (to Francis Lieber, 18 December 1864), a privilege, Sumner wrote Bright, that was as crucial practically as it was morally: "Their votes are as necessary as their musquets" (13 March 1865). Sumner expressed some willingness to compromise on Reconstruction terminology, for he wrote John Hurd that he had abandoned the state "suicide" phraseology because the phrase "gave rise to discussion & diverted attention from the fact" (27 December 1865). In addition, he wrote the conservative Montgomery Blair (28 October 1863) that the two did not disagree on goals; Sumner was for "*any system* by which the good we both seek can be accomplished." (However, as Blair pointed out, Sumner insisted on congressional intervention as both necessary and constitutional.) He wrote Orestes Brownson on 27 December 1863 that Lincoln's Reconstruction plan differed from Sumner's only in "nomenclature." He wished to make permanent "the obliteration of Slavery," and would "accept any system which promises this result." However, Sumner would not accept Lincoln's "system" for the admission of Louisiana without black suffrage. Although Sumner wrote Bright on 1 January 1865 that on Lincoln's Louisiana plan he would "hold my peace if *I can secure the rule for the other states,"* on 24 February he argued against Louisiana's readmission (see to Francis W. Bird, 1 March 1865); the Senate postponed consideration of Lincoln's plan on 27 February.

At first Sumner believed he and Andrew Johnson agreed on granting the franchise to blacks. However, Sumner's disenchantment came swiftly and rudely when on 9 May 1865 Johnson recognized a Virginia government that did not provide for black suffrage. By 5 June Sumner was writing that he now believed Johnson would oppose Republicans' plans for Reconstruction, even though "only a few weeks ago it seemed as if we should succeed without a contest" (to John Bright). Sumner worried about Johnson's "usurpation" of the executive office and his exclusion of blacks in reconstructed governments. The senator's letters in the summer of 1865 reveal his efforts to get both allies like Thaddeus Stevens and critics like Gideon Welles to persuade the president to change his policy and to allocate more responsibility to Congress. A comparison of letters to Carl Schurz before and after Schurz's tour of the South shows Sumner's rapid disillusionment. In June he urged Schurz to see Johnson and "make one more effort to arrest" the president's policy; in October Sumner realized that pleas to Johnson were fruitless and that Schurz should instead widely publicize his report stressing the need for federal supervision of Reconstruction (22 June, 20 October 1865). Johnson's veto of the Civil Rights Bill (see to the duchess of Argyll, 3 April 1866) antagonized moderates who joined with Radicals to bring about Sumner's long-cherished goals. In a letter to Bright of 27 May 1867, Sumner described in gleeful detail the passing of the Reconstruction Act of 1867, which required all rebel states to grant universal male suffrage. Although he would have preferred different, provisional governments for former Confederate states, Sumner was satisfied: "It is in politics, as in life; we rarely obtain precisely what we desire."

Sumner's life can be seen as a series of stormy personal relationships with many men—Andrew, Felton, Fish, Howe, Lieber, Seward—and one woman. One wonders why twenty-eight-year-old Alice Hooper was attracted to the arrogant, humorless Sumner, supposedly at fifty-five a confirmed bachelor. Since so few of her letters to him have been recovered, all that is clear is her admiration for his Radical leadership. Although politics may have initially been enough of an attraction for Alice Hooper, she evidently became quickly disillusioned. Many a Victorian wife would have dutifully remained with her prominent husband; Alice Sumner did not. Sumner's reaction to their separation reveals the same pattern as his breaks with male friends, but here the sole cause was personal, not political, incompatibility. Typically, Sumner saw himself as the completely wronged victim, who had only tried to please and accommodate. Even Sumner's natural reticence on such matters gave way after five discreet months to emotional outbursts to his longtime friend Samuel Gridley Howe: "Enough if I say that my home was hell," he wrote on 17 November 1867. Before and after his marriage, Sumner described his idealistic approach to the institution (to Lieber, 22 September 1866; to Anna Cabot Lodge, 21? August 1868); a failed marriage and separation had no effect on Sumner's unrealistic notions. About marriage he wrote Anna Lodge, "I have seen it through visions, & I gave myself to it with a complete surrender; when I was rewarded by the most unpardonable conduct."

Sumner's general arrogance does not seem to have carried over to friendship with black people. Blacks rightly regarded Sumner as their hero for his struggles to secure their freedom and civil rights; letters of tribute and gratitude poured into Sumner. Blacks looked to Sumner for guidance. For example, Hiram Revels sought Sumner's advice before speaking in the Senate (March 1870, 9 April 1870, 50/302, 351, PCS). Unfortunately, few of Sumner's letters to black friends and colleagues have been recovered (none to Frederick Douglass, for example), so that we cannot adequately document Sumner's personal relations with them. In the few recovered letters, Sumner's tone is no different from that in those to his white associates. He privately chastised Joshua B. Smith for blacks' lack of initiative; because blacks in the District of Columbia appeared to be cowed by white politicians, Sumner wrote Smith, "I am disgusted with the colored people in Washington" (19 May 1867). Yet writing abroad a week later to the duchess of Argyll, Sumner praised blacks' "gentleness and intelligence," as well as their growing assertiveness. "At their meetings some of them come forward at once as orators" (27 May 1867). In public and private letters, Sumner urged blacks to show more pluck and aggressiveness, "to insist upon Equal Rights & not to stop until they are secured," as he wrote black cashier Charles N. Hunter (29 December 1871). It appears that, unlike many antislavery leaders who did not care for blacks as individuals, Sumner regarded them as people, not as political pawns.

To Francis Lieber

Washington 17th April '65

Dear Lieber,

Have I told you that, while on board the steamer coming up from City Point, I put into Presdt Lincoln's hands yr letter on lists of persons to be doomed & to be saved?[1] He read it with much interest.

I passed an hour with the new Presdt last evng. I insisted that none

Mr. J. Ulke.   Mr. H. Ulke.   Mr. G. Welles.   Mr. Farnsworth.   Mr. Petersen, Jr.   Chief-Justice Chase.   Mr. Colfax.
                                                                                                             Surgeon Stone.

THE DYING MOMENTS OF PRESIDENT LINCOLN, AT WASHINGTO

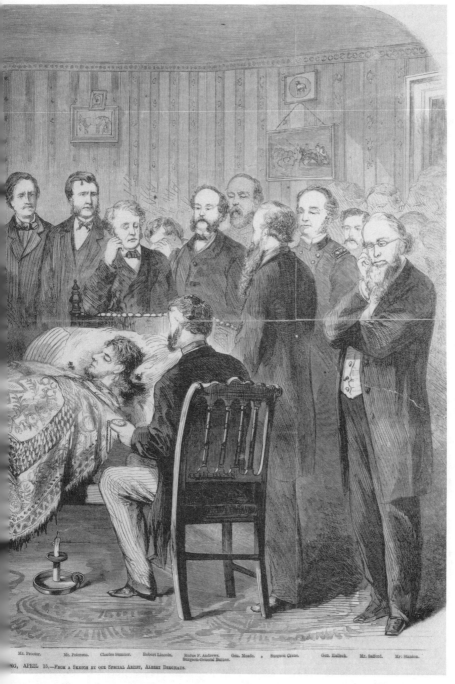

Mr. Procter. Mr. Peterson. Charles Sumner. Robert Lincoln. Rufus F. Andrews. Gen. Meade. . Surgeon Crane. Gen. Halleck. Mr. Safford. Mr. Stanton.
Surgeon-General Barnes.

NG, APRIL 15.—FROM A SKETCH BY OUR SPECIAL ARTIST, ALBERT BERGHAUS.

From Frank Leslie's Illustrated Newspaper, *29 April 1865. "I stood by Presdt Lincoln's bed, & left only when his heart ceased to beat" (to Francis Lieber, 17 April 1865). Courtesy of the Boston Athenaeum.*

of the old traitors should be allowed to take part in establishing new govts; &, still further that our officers should be reminded that treason was a crime disgrace, which must attach to all who have borne arms against their country, especially those who have left the flag. He is of this opinion strongly.

I proposed that we shall frighten out of the country as many as possible, & that we should begin with Campbell & Hunter. I think you will find prompt action in this respect.

The recent tragedy will strengthen those who wish strong measures.[2]

I found the new Presdt. discreet, properly reserved, but firm & determined.

Ever yours,   Charles Sumner

There are 6 persons in Seward's house suffering from that single assasin with wounds differing in degree.[3]

From ¼ before 11 o'clk till ½ 7 oclk in the morng I stood by Presdt Lincoln's bed, & left only when his heart ceased to beat. He was senseless from the beginning.

ALS MH-H (64/410, PCS)

1. Lieber had sent CS his list 1 April 1865. He recommended that Lee "&c" be pardoned, but that Davis, Judah P. Benjamin, Alexander Stephens, and generals Breckinridge and Beauregard be "excluded" from amnesty (79/185, PCS).

2. Lieber wrote that "the South must be literally swept with the sword, all the fiends ought to be driven out or hanged" (15 April, 79/237).

3. Besides Seward, his sons Frederick and Augustus and Seward's nurse were wounded in the attack on 14 April. His wife, Frances Seward, died on 21 June of causes indirectly related to the attack. A black doorman was also present during the attack (Glyndon Van Deusen, *William Henry Seward* [1967], 413–16).

To the Duchess of Argyll

Washington 24th April '65

My dear Duchess,

I have recd. yr good letter of 5th April, with the Duke's[1] They came in the midst of our unprecedented sorrow.

At last belligerent Slavery, defeated in battle, has taken to assassination; indeed it took to assassination always. This was a part of itself. But the world will now see the crime that civilized nations have invested with *rights*, under the sanctions of International Law. As I stood by the bed-side of our dying Presdt from ¼ before 11 o'clk in the evening to ½ after 7 o'clk in the morning, I could not think of the humble criminal. He was very little in the agencies that directed the fatal bullet. It was easy to see that if the Rebellion had been left to itself without external alliance & support, there would have been peace long ago without assassination.

The Presdt. was absolutely unconscious from the moment the ball entered his head till his heart ceased to beat. His death was, therefore, sudden, but not unprepared for. Down to the last he had been gentle & forgiving. I had been with him for several days at the front only a week before, breakfasting, lunching & dining in one small family party. The Atty Genl. & other members of the Cabinet were of the party. He said nothing harsh even of Jefferson Davis & when one of the party insisted that he must not be spared, the Presdt said he must repeat the words quoted in his late Address, "Judge not that ye be not judged," &, when still further pressed on this point, he repeated these words again.

In all my intercourse with the late Presdt I have never known him speak harshly of but one man, & this was an eminent Englishman who has so misstated him & our cause; & with regard to him he spoke solemnly as the voice of history.[2] The four terrible years of our war cannot be understood or written without depicting the part which has been performed by this Englishman. To my mind it is one of the most unhappy places in all history.

The new Presdt. has glided quietly into his duties, with a simplicity & modesty which are admirable. I have seen him daily to transact public business, & find him easy, sympathetic, calm, with proper caution & reserve. The first business I had with him was with regard to the reception of Sir Fred. Bruce. It was on the evening of Presdt Lincoln's death that I had this interview. He gave me a message of courtesy & good will for yr Minister. You will see by his speeches that he is very determined that treason shall be punished.[3] Already the question is asked, how many must be executed in each state? My anxious hope has been that the war might be closed without a capital punishment— although if ever men deserved this fate it is those who have been the inhuman instruments of Slavery in this last dying struggle.

The Sewards, father & son, have rallied to-day & seem to be doing very well. The conspirators will be caught.

Perhaps you will not be offended if I let you know that I showed the late Presdt. at his request yr letter of March 2nd, in which you express the confidence in him, & speak of the distrust of me.[4] I was at the theatre with him—the last time he had been there before his assassination. I mentioned to him the purport of yr letter. He at once said—"I wish you would shew me that letter." I sent it to him & he returned it in an envelope on which he had written yr name, & under cover to my address, with his frank in the upper right hand corner, where with us the frank is written. I send them as autographs, which may interest some of yr friends.

Presdt Lincoln had determined not to convene Congress before next autumn. I was glad of this—because this will give time to get the Alabama case out of the way, if Ld Russell does not mean to bring about war. I believe that I have already written that if Congress were in session I did not doubt there would be a peremptory demand for the payment of English liabilities on account of the Alabama, adopted by the House of Reps nearly unanimously. I trust that the good sense of all who are connected with this question will see that it is settled. *Every day that it is kept open is a mistake.* But why write of this? Have I not written for years?—always anxious for peace, & never indifferent to the honor or renown of England. I owe the Duke a letter. I wish he would look at the recorded opinions of Ld Granville in 1794 on the question of damages in the case of the Alabama.[5]

Ever sincerely Yours,   Charles Sumner

ALS   CSmH   (79/260, PCS)

1. Both the Argylls expressed their good will toward CS on 5 April 1865 (33/136; 32/707 [misdated 5 March], PCS).

2. The duchess responded to CS's criticism, saying "I suppose you mean Ld. Russell as the man who misunderstood him. He did—and it grieves me bitterly that he did." But she reminded CS that it was Russell's "impatience" for the "Cause of Freedom" that made it difficult for him to understand "Lincoln's own view of his position at the time of the Emancipation Proclamation" (12 May, 33/417).

3. On 18 April Johnson told an Illinois delegation that the assassination could be traced directly "to that source which is the spring of all our woes. . . . [T]reason is a crime and must be punished." He declared to a Vermont delegation that "the wealthy traitor" must "pay the penalty" (*New York Times*, 19 April 1865:4, 23 April 1865:4).

4. Along with expressing the "great confidence" the British had in Lincoln, the duchess assured CS of Britain's equal confidence in him, despite his speech on the Reciprocity Treaty, a speech "some who wd. not wish to think so—think very hostile to England" (Kensington, 2 March, 32/673).

5. In his 5 April letter the duke asked CS for an example of a case when the U.S. had ever "admitted the principle of its being held liable for the depredations" to neutrals by raiders that had illegally escaped from U.S. ports. William Wyndham Grenville (1759–1834), British foreign secretary, 1791–1801.

To John Bright

Washington 24th April '65

Dear Mr Bright,

The more I think of yr great loss in England the more I make it mine, & my country's. Mr Cobden's death is a calamity for civilization. We needed him in the questions which approach. I read the account of his funeral, & was glad to see that Mr Gladstone was there.[1] I remember his home well; for I was there several days, which I enjoyed much.

Our country is still moved by the great tragedy. It is plain that Mr Lincoln has a hold on the public heart, such as few men have had in history. Meanwhile with our victories come unexpected complications. Sherman's conduct is that of a madman.[2] Stanton was disposed to recall him & send him before a court-martial; but Grant was full of tenderness for his lieutenant & undertook at once to go down & relieve him, thus breaking his fall. He started at an hour's notice, taking little more than a saddle & bridle.

Public opinion insists upon executions. Stanton thinks there must be 3 or 4 in each state. I have told him to hesitate before he commences these assises. And yet I do not venture in the present uncertain condition of things to *dogmatize* on our policy, except that I wish it to be as generous & magnanimous as is consistent with national security.

There is no sign that Congress will be called together; or that the Alabama case will have a reprieve, when I trust the sober second thoughts will prevail over Ld John's temper. Presdt. Lincoln never expressed himself with bitterness about any body, except the British Minister for Foreign Affairs. Alas! what a chapter for history, that of Lord John's persecutions of this Govt. during three years!

Our new Presdt. makes a good impression. Of this be sure. His chief topic thus far has been that treason is a crime; but I am satisfied that he is the sincere friend of the negro, & ready to act for him decisively. He has conversed with the Chief Justice & myself on this important subject.

It is supposed by many that Sherman was lured by the idea of being democratic candidate for the Presidency, with two planks State Rights & War with England. But he is Ichabod. His military name cannot save him. The Democrats are looking round to find some way of righting themselves & getting on the side of their country. A foreign war would be their ally. Don't let them have it. —I wrote a long & *confidential* letter to Mr Cobden, which must have arrived after his death.[3] I hope it will not go where it should not. Will you not take it?

Ever Yours,   Charles Sumner

P.S. When I mentioned to Presdt Johnson, that Mr Bright's portrait was in the office of his predecessor over the fire-place, he said—"We'll keep it there."

ALS   GBL   (79/263, PCS)

1. Cobden died in London 2 April 1865; his funeral was held at Midhurst 7 April. In his letter to CS of 14 April Bright described his last long conversation with Cobden ("much on America, & on the Canadian defences question") and the asthma attack that killed him (Rochdale, 33/185, PCS).

2. On 18 April at Durham Station, North Carolina, Sherman signed an armistice with the Confederate general Joseph E. Johnston. The agreement provided for a general amnesty, restoration of property rights to Confederates, and speedy recognition of state governments.

3. CS's letter of 27 March. Bright wrote Catherine A. Cobden, 14 May, asking permission to see the letter and then return it if Mrs. Cobden wished (Cobden Papers, West Sussex Record Office). CS's letter is now with the Bright Papers, British Library.

To Wendell Phillips

Washington 1st May '65

My dear Phillips,

I *do* admire yr speech on our late President. You have anticipated mine at the summons of the Mayor of Boston, & have said it all inimitably. Emerson too was exquisite.[1]

Private & Confidential

But I should not write now except to tell you how our course looks for the future. Never so grand, & fair & beautiful. The end is coming & just as you & I desire. I have had several conversations with the new Presdt. on the new role for the rebels. The Chief Justice was with me on one occasion. The other was last evng when, after going over the question, he said "there is no difference between us."

Without going into details it is enough to say, that I avowed my object to be the elective franchise for the colored race as essential to stable govts. in the rebel states; that to secure this result modes & forms were immaterial, although I had my own idea as to the best mode of proceeding; but that I was comparatively indifferent to this branch of the question; that I would accept even La. if the franchise was secured without distinction of color. He has his plan, which I have advised him to foreshadow in a speech.

Meanwhile the Chief Justice has started on a visit to the two Carolinas, Georgia, Florida, New Orleans, where unofficially he [may?]

exert himself for the good cause. The Presdt. knows of his journey & has authorized him to set on foot movements for reorganization by all loyal citizens without distinction of color. *All this I confide to you*, not to be used at present. Meanwhile cannot our friends bring influence to bear in all the rebel states by travelling agents? The Presdt's idea is that the movement should seem to come from the people. I have told him that this could not be successful unless it was known that it was his desire. He has authorized the Chief Justice to speak for him, &, I think, will soon speak for himself. Is not this good news?[2]

Ever Yours,   Charles Sumner

ALS MH-H (79/282, PCS)

1. Phillips spoke on Lincoln in Boston 19 April 1865 ("Lincoln's Assassination," *Speeches, Lectures and Addresses*, second series [1891], 446–53), and Emerson on 19 April at First Parish Church, Concord (*The Complete Works*, ed. Edward W. Emerson [1903–04], 11:329–38).

2. Phillips replied on 5 May assuring CS he would keep his letter confidential. He urged CS to tell the president "to give us time" to rally the people for universal suffrage. He advised CS to come home to Boston and organize one or two conventions for people there who "wish a leader whom they feel is *safe to follow*" (33/370, PCS).

To Francis Lieber

Washington 2nd May '65

My dear Lieber,

I enclose letters for Mr Blodgett, which please give him with my complts.[1]

I read to Presdt. Johnson Col. Baker's letter with yr introduction.[2] He said at once that he accepted every word of it; that colored persons are to have the right of suffrage; that no state can be *precipitated* into the Union; that rebel States must go through a term of *probation*. All this he had said to me before.

Ten days ago the Chief Justice & myself visited him in the evng to speak of these things. I was charmed by his sympathy, which was entirely different from his predecessors.[3]

The Chief Justice has left for the two Carolinas, Georgia, Florida & New Orleans, & is authorized to say wherever he is what the President desires & to do any thing he can to promote organization without distinction of color.[4] The President desires that the movement should appear to proceed from the people. This is in conformity with his general ideas; but he thinks that it will disarm party at home.

I told him that, while I doubted if the work could be effectively done without *Federal authority*, I regarded the *modus operandi* as an inferior question, & that I should be content, provided *Equality before the law* was secured for all without distinction of color. After a protracted conversation he said, "there is no difference between us."

I said during this winter that the rebel States could not come back, except on the footing of the Decltn of Indep. & the complete recognition of Human Rights. I feel more than ever confident that all this will be fulfilled. And then what a regenerated land!

I had looked for a bitter contest on this question, but with the Presdt. on our side it will be carried by simple *avoir du pois*.

It remains to get our question with England settled. This Power must see that she has done us wrong. I do not despair here.

You are right in yr judgment of our lawyers, & Judge Washburne is no exception.[5] Unhappily he too wrote a pamphlet last autumn in which he exalted the states. I did not agree with him then; nor do I now. Unquestionably there are certain powers reserved to states with Executive & Legislative functions, including punishment, pardon; but there is no power to interfere with the National Govt. which in its orbit is supreme. I have sometimes thought the States might be likened to the "isles of the sea," which Neptune, according to Milton in his Comus,

> By course commits to several governments
> And gives them leave to wear their sapphire crowns
> And wear their little tridents:[6]

but their "tributary Gods" are all under the God of the Sea.

There is a letter from Washington to Jay different from the one you quote, which is, if possible, more to your purpose. I quoted it in the Senate last February. It was written in '87.[7] Pray look at it.

Yr pamphlet will do good. The hydra of State rights must be beaten to death. Thanks for what you have done.

I hope to leave here at the end of this week or beginning of next, & hope to see you in New York.

Ever yours,   Charles Sumner

ALS   MH-H   (64/412, PCS)

1. Lieber asked CS for letters of introduction to John L. Motley in Vienna for Lieber's friend William T. Blodgett, a New York merchant (New York, 30 April 1865, 79/276, PCS).

2. Lieber enclosed, with his letter of 19 April, a letter to him from a former pupil and Confederate soldier who, now swearing allegiance to the Union, had asked Lieber about Reconstruction. Lieber asked CS to show it to the president (79/255).

3. Lieber asked in his letter of 26 April how CS regarded Johnson: "Is there *confidence* between you?" (79/273).

4. Chase left Washington 1 May. According to Frederick J. Blue, although Chase did not have explicit orders from the president, Chase made the trip with Johnson's full knowledge and support (*Salmon P. Chase: A Life in Politics* [1987], 250–51).

5. In his 30 April letter Lieber complained to CS of lawyers' criticism of his recent pamphlet, "Amendments of the Constitution" (1865) (*The Miscellaneous Writings of Francis Lieber* [1881], 2:137–79). He wrote that lawyers "go by 'their books.' I go by *the* book . . . *History*." He noted that Harvard law professor Emory Washburn (1800–1877) was "dead against" Lieber's statement that allegiance to both state and federal governments was impossible (166–67).

6. Line 47 of *Comus* reads "And weild their little tridents."

7. CS quoted Washington's letter of 12 September 1787 on the necessity of the "consolidation of the Union" in his speech 14 February, "Railroad Usurpation in New Jersey" (*Globe*, 38th Cong., 2nd sess., 790–93).

To Thomas Gaffield

Washington 6th May '65

My dear Sir,

Do as you please. The names you mention are excellent.[1]

If I could choose one it would be Revd Mr Grimes, the colored preacher.[2] It was for his race that Presdt. Lincoln died. If Boston adopted him as chaplain on the day when we mourn, it would be a truer homage to our departed Presdt, than music or speech. I can say nothing that could promise to be so effective on earth or welcome in Heaven. Think of this, & believe me, my dear Sir,

very faithfully Yours,   Charles Sumner

ALS   NNCB   (79/303, PCS)

1. Thomas Gaffield, chairman of the committee on services to commemorate Lincoln, wrote CS from Boston 4 May 1865 about program arrangements. He was pleased CS would deliver the eulogy on Lincoln, and asked whom CS would suggest as chaplains (33/361, PCS).

2. Gaffield replied 15 May that the committee had voted unanimously to invite the antislavery activist Leonard A. Grimes (d. 1873) to participate. At the ceremony, 1 June, Grimes delivered the benediction (33/435; *Boston Evening Transcript*, 2 June 1865:2).

To Wendell Phillips

Washington 11th May '65

My dear Phillips,

Your speech at New York was full of truth & beauty.[1]

The course about Va is a miscarriage. I tell the Presdt. that the time of shams has passed, & the Pierpont govt. is nothing but a sham.[2] My hope now is to save the rest. *I have been an hour to-day with the Presdt, & am to see him again tomorrow by appointment,*—when I set my face homeward.

I have written to the City Comttee to invite a colored chaplain for 1st June.

Twenty years ago I spoke for Boston. Not since then till now could I have spoken again. This period was required to bring us together.

Ever Yours,   Charles Sumner

ALS   MH-H   (79/324, PCS)

1. Phillips spoke at the Church of the Puritans 9 May 1865 on granting suffrage to blacks (*Liberator*, 19 May 1865:78).
2. On 9 May President Johnson recognized the Pierpont government, which did not give blacks the franchise, as the rightful Virginia government.

To John Bright

Washington 18th May '65

Dear Mr Bright,

Just before starting for Boston, I acknowledge yours of 29th April.[1]

The feeling in England is not greater than I anticipated. I hope that it will make yr govt. see the crime with which for four years it has fraternized.

Mr Seward's disability causes a suspension of our diplomatic discussions, which I think he is anxious to resume. He was aroused to great indignation when he heard that the British authorities at Nassau had been receiving the pirate Stonewall.[2]

A proclamation was read to him yesterday, in the draft, which concluded with something about the "peace & *safety* of the U. States." He speaks with difficulty, but he stammered forth not "safety" but "dignity"; "The U. States are safe enough."

I have been pained by seeing him, as he shows so many signs of the terrible hazards he has passed.

I am sorry that J. D. is caught.[3] If not shot in pursuit, I wish he had escaped. Grant was anxious to keep him out of Mexico.

I have but a moment & write illegibly, but

Ever Yours, Charles Sumner

ALS GBL (79/331, PCS)

1. Bright asked CS to convey condolences to Mary Todd Lincoln and best wishes to Seward for his recovery. Regarding Lincoln's assassination he wrote, "The whole People positively mourn, & it would seem as if again we were one nation with you, so universal is the grief & the horror" (Rochdale, 33/309, PCS).

2. The C.S.S. *Stonewall* surrendered to Spain, which turned it over to the U.S. at Havana 10 May 1865.

3. Jefferson Davis was captured at Irwinville, Georgia, 10 May.

To John Bright
private

Boston 5th June. '65

Dear Mr Bright,

I thank you for yr letter pleading so wisely & well for the humane course towards our traitors.[1] I agree with you entirely, & have already enforced the same views. There has been a perceptible change in the public feeling, & I do not despair to see it right, if time is allowed. It was Stanton who wished to hang 3 or 4 in a state. I think that even he is more moderate now.

I regretted that J. D. had not been shot, like Booth in the attempt to capture him. Then there would have been no discussion at home or abroad. He is no better than Booth. He is an assassin. The evidence against him seems to increase. It looks as if the Judge Advocate would be sustained in his original assertion to the Presdt that "the evidence was overwhelming."[2] A man who serves Slavery must be an assassin. If Ld Russell had kept on much longer, he would have been one.

But while giving the rebels their lives, I must insist upon confiscation. Otherwise, how can we get lands for the freedmen? They ought to be allowed farms where they have been accustomed to work.

There has been immense disappointment in Johnson's Proclamation for the re-organization of North Carolina,[3] excluding the colored persons. This is madness. But it is also inconsistent with his sayings to the Chief Justice & myself. I have to-day a letter from him in Florida,[4] where he had sworn in a Mayor of Fernandina chosen by white & colored

votes—*all the loyal citizens* voting. Johnson will insist that he is in favor
of the colored suffrage; but that he must leave the decision to the States.
Here again we have State Rights in the way of Equality, as they were in
the way of Liberty. But there is prodigious unanimity of sentiment for
the colored suffrage. It is felt that it is needed to counter-balance the
rebels. I am very sanguine that we shall succeed; but not without a
contest. Only a few weeks ago it seemed as if we should succeed without
a contest.

There is great tranquility in the public mind with regard to our
Foreign Relations, & a disposition to peace. But knowing as I do the
sentiments of leading politicians, I wish to get every pending question
out of the way; I mean by this, that it must be put in such train of
settlement as to be taken out of the sphere of Congressional action—if
that be possible. Therefore, Ld Russell's letter repelling our claims must
be reconsidered.[5] A resolution calling upon the govt to demand the
settlement of our claims & to follow the British precedent in the case of
the Trent, would pass the House of Reps. almost unanimously. But the
House is not in session, & when I left Washington the Presdt had no
idea of calling it together.—Sherman has one of his paroxisms, arising
from an excitable organization, & is ruining himself by wild talk.[6]—
Seward wishes to stay in the cabinet long enough "to finish his work";
but he is very feeble. The centers of life have not been touched, but he
speaks only a few words & with great difficulty.—There is a pressure
against Stanton, in which the Blairs, & the ring of cotton speculators
are very active. When I left Washington, there was not the least sign
that the Presdt would listen to them.

There are but two questions now that interest the public—(1) the
question of reconstruction, including of course the question of the
suffrage & (2) the execution of J. D.

I notice the cry for J. D. in England.[7] This is the present form of
sympathy with the Rebellion. He does not deserve it. And yet I wish
that his life should not be touched.—It was painful to read what was
said in parlt on the Presdt's death, except Disraeli. Derby was wicked,
Russell was drivel.[8]—It was a beautiful & masterly speech which Stansfeld made at the public meeting. That speech, if made by Russell,
would have been as good as the payment of our claims. I have not the
pleasure of knowing him; but I wished to thank him, as I read it.[9] The
case was stated admirably.

As often as Ld Russell speaks on belligerency, he seems to say "My
Lords, 2 & 2 make 5. Such was the early declaration of her Majesty's
govt—after communicating with her Majesty's Law Advisors, & with
the late Ld Campbell.[10] The *necessity* of making this declaration was

apparent when the United States Govt. declared by solemn Proclamation that 2 & 2 make 4." When will he remember that no Proclamation of the U. States could justify complicity with Slavery?—

Good bye!

Ever sincerely Yours,   Charles Sumner

I have used yr letter where it will do good.

ALS   GBL   (79/345, PCS)

1. In a lengthy letter to CS, 16 May 1865, Bright urged CS not to allow execution of Southern leaders, even Davis and Lee: "the whole proceeding would shock your own Country & would astonish & disgust the world." Bright argued that since slavery had been a "legal Institution" in prewar years, "an attachment to it cannot by your law be reckoned a crime. We must consider the case of the Rebel leaders entirely apart from our hatred of the cause for which they have made war" (Rochdale, 33/441, PCS). Bright contined, "Banish the most guilty if you will,—break up your pestilent plantation oligarchy, make a signal example of the class which has conspired & made war upon your Govt. & Country—but do not grant one victim to the gallows on the ground of treason & rebellion."

2. John Wilkes Booth had been killed 26 April. In Washington, D.C., as Judge Advocate Joseph Holt presided over the trial of others in the assassination plot, the prosecution produced evidence of a plan for a raid on the North that Davis had endorsed (*New York Times*, 19 May 1865:1).

3. On 29 May President Johnson appointed William W. Holden provisional governor of North Carolina, and asked him to organize a convention to form a government in preparation for North Carolina's reentry into the Union. Johnson's proclamation stipulated that voter qualifications would be the same as before secession, i.e., no black suffrage.

4. Chase to CS, 20 May, Jacksonville, 79/333.

5. Russell wrote Adams a long letter, 4 May, stating Great Britain's case for refusing to pay damages incurred by British-built Confederate raiders (*Foreign Relations* [1865], part 1, 356–60).

6. Sherman had recently censured generals Halleck and George Stoneman about their criticism of his negotiations with Confederate general Joseph E. Johnston (*New York Times*, 14 June 1865:4). In May he had testified before the Committee on the Conduct of the War that his lenient peace terms to Johnston were in accordance with Lincoln's views (James M. Merrill, *William Tecumseh Sherman* [1971], 299).

7. The London *Times* editorial (29 May 1865:8) argued that Davis, "the chosen ruler of a people," should not be executed for treason.

8. In approving a parliamentary resolution of sympathy toward the U.S. on 1 May, Disraeli spoke of the U.S.'s promising future; Lord Derby stated that he was certain the South had no part in the assassination. Lord Russell praised Lincoln, who was "perfectly justified" in delaying emancipation, and alluded to the "temper and moderation" both countries had exhibited during his presidency (*Hansard's Parliamentary Debates*, 3rd series, 177:1245–46, 1223–26, 1219–22).

9. Speaking at a meeting of the Emancipation Society in London, 30 April, M.P. for Halifax James Stansfeld (1820–98) stated that the North had not fought for an empire as Lord Russell contended, but for a "common country" (London *Times*, 1 May 1865:5).

10. John Campbell, first Baron Campbell (1779–1861), advised the British government to concede belligerent rights to the Confederacy.

To Lot M. Morrill

Boston 15th June '65

My dear Colleague,

I shall send you my Eulogy in pamphlet—corrected, & revised by the author.[1]

I tried to determine the late Presdt's place in history, & I have photographed my own impressions, strictly & honestly, without any exaggeration.

I knew him well, & saw much of him. I think his delays tended to prolong the war. Indeed, if ever the account is impartially balanced he & the Secy of State must answer for much treasure & bloodshed. But the victory was won at last, & Emancipation secured. History dwells on results rather than the means employed.

The despatches of the Secy during the first year of the war are deplorable. I have never thought our case was properly stated to Foreign Powers.

But the late Presdt. put his name to Emancipation—made speeches that nobody else could have made—& early dedicated himself to the support of Human Rights as announced in the Decltn of Indep. Therefore, we honor him, & Fame takes him by the hand.

Ever sincerely Yours,   Charles Sumner

Can't you do something to arrest the Presdt's reconstruction policy[2]— which is *dividing the North*, encouraging the democrats, & postponing the day of tranquility & reconciliation. Alas! alas!

———————————

ALS   MeHi   (79/365, PCS)

1. Senator Morrill wrote CS from Augusta, Maine, on 12 June 1865 congratulating him on his eulogy of Lincoln (33/596, PCS): "It was truly most difficult to speak candidly of the elements of his character without offending the public sense at this time so keenly sensitive from memory of great events."

2. CS wrote Morrill another letter on 22 July again complaining about Johnson's leniency toward the South (79/462). Morrill replied ([July 1865], 34/093) that the North should now avoid criticism of Johnson in the interests of "harmony." Although Morrill deplored the president's inclination toward restoring states' rights, he wrote that the American people would protest this policy and "It will fail of course."

To Gideon Welles

Boston 15th June '65

My dear Sir,

I cannot conceal from you my anxiety on account of the North Carolina & Mississippi Proclamations.[1] Of course, their first effect is *to divide
the North*, & to give the democrats an opportunity to organize. Then
they postpone indefinitely the day of tranquility & reconciliation.

If the Presdt. can create a govt. in a State, which is contrary to law
& usage, surely he can recognize loyal people as voters, in conformity
with the Declaration of Indep., which insists that govt. must stand "on
the consent of the governed."

The true course seems to be so easy & natural, that I am astonished
there could be a mistake. Now, in this work of reconstruction, let us
adopt the *rule of justice*. Build on this, & our foundations will endure
forever. But it is proposed to build on an *outrageous injustice*.

I write to you freely, as I have always been in the habit of conversing
with you.

Nothing since Chancellorsville has to my mind been so disastrous to
the national cause, & to the cause of peace. Alas! that this blow should
be struck by our own Administration!

Very Sincerely yours,   Charles Sumner

ALS   DLC   (79/369, PCS)

1. On 13 June 1865 Johnson appointed William L. Sharkey, a planter who remained neutral during the war, provisional governor of Mississippi and called for a
convention of all loyal white citizens to set up a new state government.

To Thaddeus Stevens

Boston 19th June '65

My dear Sir,

We must speak & act.[1]

I hope you will write a letter, if you do not make a speech. There
must be as many voices as possible to arrest this fatal policy.

I have written to Washington in protest against it.[2]

I hope you will write to the President;—better still, see him & tell
him plainly what you think.

The North was ready for the true doctrine & practice.
It is hard—very hard to be driven to another contest.

Very truly Yours,   Charles Sumner

ALS   Stevens Papers,   DLC

1. Upon learning of Johnson's recognition of the Pierpont government in Virginia, Stevens wrote CS 10 May 1865 from Philadelphia that he feared the president would have "so be-deviled matters as to render them immovable" before Congress convened (33/401, PCS). Again on 3 and 14 June Stevens wrote CS about stopping Johnson. On 14 June he asked if CS could organize a protest in Massachusetts: "I have thought of trying it at our state convention—if something is not done the President will be crowned King before Congress meets—; How about his interfering with the internal regulations of the States, and yet [considering?] them as "States in the Union" (Caledonia, Pennsylvania, 33/539, 610).

2. On 7 June CS sent Johnson a petition from freedmen of North Carolina who sought "'the enrollment of our loyal men without regard to color.'" CS wrote, "I venture to express my entire sympathy with the prayer of the petition, & I hope that it is not too late to consider it" (Boston, 79/355).

To the Duchess of Argyll

Boston 20th June '65

My dear Duchess,

I have not yet seen the Duke's letter to the Scotsman, & I have only found an abstract of his valuable speech at the Freedmen's meeting.[1] I was at a loss to understand why I was excluded from assent or sympathy. So far as the report enabled me to follow him, I agreed entirely. I am not unreasonable; but I am in earnest. You know I have always insisted that our war was to be seen in two aspects

(1) In what we proposed.

(2) In what the rebels proposed.

Now we proposed to save our country—& to put down the Rebellion which was Slavery in arms.

The Rebels proposed to destroy our country & *to build a new Power* on the corner-stone of Slavery & with no other declared object of separate existence.

Therefore, from the beginning, it was morally impossible for any foreign Power to invest such wickedness with rights or to concede to it Belligerency.

There I stand. I cannot see it otherwise. But I do not now argue.—

I long to see the Duke's letter. Perhaps tonight or tomorrow it will come.

Since I wrote you last Lord Russell has spoken twice on our affairs. It is strange that he should make such mistakes. There was a mistake in every thing that he said about Presdt. Lincoln. Not one sentence correct, according to the report which I read. Then came the speech about Belligerent Rights.[2] I am so much of an Englishman, that I am unhappy at such displays. As often as he speaks, he seems to say, "My Lords, it is my duty to declare to you that two & two make five. This is the solemn opinion of her Majesty's legal advisers. The *necessity* of this declaration is apparent when yr lordships consider the declaration of the late Presdt. Lincoln that two & two make four. The moment the latter Proclamation was issued her Majesty's govt had no alternative. It was their duty to declare that two & two make five."

How does it happen that France, or rather L. N., who has wished to hurt us from the beginning, has cultivated the amenities with us so much more than Ld Russell?

We have another class of trials now. There is a strong pressure in important quarters to employ our discontented spirits in Mexico. I hope that the French Emperor will listen to the counsels of M. Thiers & withdraw his troops.[3] Then *there is the question of reconstruction.* On this the Presdt. seems to be failing. He does not carry out what he said to the Chief Justice & myself, with regard to the colored suffrage. And so we have before us another controversy. I see no chance of tranquility or reconciliation, except through the support of the late freedmen. In one word,—be just to them, & they will help you; & their help will be better than a standing army.

Ever sincerely yours,   Charles Sumner

P.S. Can you send me a *carte* of yr mother? I have several engravings of her, but no *carte*. Perhaps she will send me one.

ALS   CSmH   (79/377, PCS)

1. In a speech to the British Freedmen's Aid Meeting in London, 17 May 1865, the duke of Argyll argued that abolition of slavery was the Northern aim in the Civil War. He stated that CS might consider Argyll's version of Northern antislavery sentiment "to some degree unjust" because CS was even more vehemently against slavery than many of his compatriots ("Speech to the National Committee of British Freed-Men's Aid Societies" [1865], 9–13). In his letter to the Edinburgh *Scotsman*, published 5 June 1865:7, Argyll again argued that the Civil War was fought to end slavery. The British should believe, wrote Argyll, that more than "evil passions or sheer politics" initiated the war.

2. Speaking in Parliament on 15 May on the issue of whether Great Britain should now withdraw the concession of belligerent rights to the Confederacy, Russell stated that the U.S., by proclaiming a blockade of Southern ports, had forced Britain's move

in 1861. "Her Majesty did not concede belligerent rights, but recognized the state of facts which the President of the United States himself declared, and followed this by a proclamation of neutrality in the war which was then being carried on" (*Hansard's Parliamentary Debates*, 3rd series, 179:287–89). Responding to CS's assertion, the duchess wrote on 4 July, "I wish you would not dwell so much (to *yourself*) on those belligerent rights." She contended that no one in the British cabinet "thought that the giving of belligerent rights could be avoided—they believed it was a necessity. . . . I protest again against your supposing it a proof of Ld. Russell's ill-will, when it was a Cabinet measure" (London, 33/714, PCS). The duke wrote CS 7 July, "It is no use now disputing about belligerency. I don't see the force of your 'therefore' when you say that because the cause of the South was a bad and even an immoral cause, *therefore* we had no right to recognise them as belligerents. It was a *fact* that they were belligerents. We recognised a fact, and we cd not have recognised your own proceedings unless we had done so" (London, 33/730). CS sent these letters to Seward on 25 July (79/467).

3. Louis-Adolphe Thiers was then a leading anti-imperialist in the French legislature.

To Carl Schurz

Boston 22d June '65

My dear General,

I have recd. both yr letters. The last is very interesting.[1]

Of course the policy of the Presdt. *must break down*. It cannot succeed. I am pained that he commenced it.

I am glad that he has invited you to journey in the rebel states. You *must go*. Let me know the *extra* premium on yr policy. The friends of the cause here will gladly pay it. I write this in earnest & as business. Send me the bill; & do you go at once on the journey.[2]

But before you go, make one more effort to arrest the policy of the Presdt. Every step that he takes is a new encouragement to (1) the rebels at the South (2) the democrats at the North & (3) the discontented spirits every where. It is a defiance to God & Truth.

Of course, we shall fight this battle, &, I know, we shall prevail. It cannot be that this great & glorious Republic is to sink to such an imbecile & shameful policy

Ever Yours,   Charles Sumner

ALS   DLC   (79/383, PCS)

1. Carl Schurz (1829–1906), a German emigrant and most recently brigadier general of volunteers in the U.S. Army, wrote 5 June 1865 about his recent visit with President Johnson and Schurz's subsequent disappointment in the North Carolina proclamation. At his meeting, Schurz wrote, he tried to persuade Johnson not to take any irrevocable steps in formulating his policy. He thought Johnson "would heed my advice" when Schurz urged the president to extend suffrage to blacks, but "I fear he has not that clearness of purpose and firmness of character he was supposed

to have." He thought both Johnson and the cabinet were unduly influenced by the Southern Unionists pouring into Washington, men who had not changed their prejudice against blacks since the war. Schurz advised CS to go to Washington to counter this influence (Bethlehem, Pennsylvania, 79/350, PCS).

2. Schurz agreed to make an inspection tour of the Southern states but was worried about his present financial situation. He wrote CS 27 June that he would "certainly accept the Presidents proposal. . . . I shall endeavor to do my duty to the best of my ability, although the trip is indeed no pleasure excursion" (Bethlehem, 79/392). He began his tour 12 July (Hans Trefousse, *Carl Schurz* [1982], 154).

To Salmon P. Chase

Boston 25th June '65

My dear Chase,

I do not know where you are, but I hope that this may find you in Washington. *You are needed there.*

The President's course on reconstruction causes painful astonishment. It is positively inconsistent with what I understood him to say to me during repeated interviews after you left. Thus far there is a disposition to treat him tenderly & to avoid a break; but some of my correspondents anticipate a break. I trust there will be prudent counsels on both sides. He is our Presdt, & we must keep him ours unless he makes it impossible to go with him.

I am more than ever satisfied that the Presdt. ought to give up all idea of reconstruction by *Executive action*. I doubt his power constitutionally, & I am clear that a question of such transcendent magnitude should be referred to Congress.

But even if I recognized the Executive as proper to lead in this business I am clear that *he has no right to begin by establishing a discrimination of color*. If he acts at all *he must act according to the requirements of the Declation of Indep*. On this I stand, & I insist that any other course is unconstitutional,—as it is under the circumstances indecent.

I hope it is not too late to arrest this fatal policy. I have reason to believe that the President has lately shown a disposition to treat what he has done as an experiment. He has invited Carl Schurtz to visit the rebel states & report to him on his reconstruction policy.

Yr letter from Florida gave me an interesting glimpse of yr wanderings.[1] I should have written you at once, if the letter had not come so tardily, that I was not sure I could hit you, while on the wing.

Since the Presdt's policy of reconstruction has been declared officeholders & newspapers have hastened round to him. In some cases the [charge?] is ignoble. But here in Mass. the people stand solid for the suffrage. Old conservatives help swell our ranks—feeling that the suffrage is essential in self-defence.

I never cease to regret that Jeff. Davis was not shot at the time of his capture. I do not wish to see any trial by a civil tribunal, unless he might be tried for some *special crime* which would distinguish him from the crowd.

Let me know how you find *the* question in Washington.

Ever Yrs,   Charles Sumner

ALS   DLC   (79/386, PCS)

1. Chase's letter from Jacksonville (20 May 1865, 79/333, PCS) described the progress in that area, under the direction of Major General Quincy A. Gillmore, in establishing suffrage, schooling, and compensated labor for blacks. Chase expressed concern, however, that military officials in Georgia and other parts of Florida were "far from sound on the reorganization question."

To Andrew Johnson

Boston 30th June '65

My dear Sir,

I have received the enclosed petition from three hundred colored citizens of Georgia with the request that I would present it to you.[1]

The petitioners humbly ask that they may be allowed to exercise the right of suffrage. Profoundly convinced, as I am, that they have a right to the suffrage—& that the peace & tranquility of the country require that *they should not be shut out from it*, I present their petition & most sincerely unite in its prayer.

Faithfully Yours,   Charles Sumner

ALS   DLC   (79/397, PCS)

1. CS enclosed a printed petition affirming Georgia blacks' loyalty to the U.S. and their request for suffrage (Andrew Johnson Papers, Library of Congress).

To Salmon P. Chase

Boston 1st July '65

My dear Chase,

I was glad to have yr letter from Cincinnati. But I wish you were at Washington—even in its heats, where you might help save the President,—rather than in the sea-breezes of Narraganzet.[1]

There is madness in the Presdt.—His policy is already dividing the

party & drawing the praises of the copperheads. Of course, if he perseveres he will become the temporary head of the latter, to be cast aside
at the proper moment.

The people were ready to accept the true principle. Never before were
they so ready. Business-men see how clearly their welfare is associated
with its establishment.

The Blairs have triumphed.[2] I see their influence, not only here but
in other things. When I left Washington Mr Johnson had assured me
that on this question "there was no difference between us."

He has appointed Carl Schurtz to visit the rebel states & report on
the reconstruction policy & has said that, if the present policy did not
work well, he was ready to change it. Alas! that the country should be
subjected to this uncertainty, where from the beginning our rulers
ought to have been clear & positive.

I was born too early. I wish that I had come into the world 30 years
later. How beautiful this world will be 30 years from now.

Ever Yours,   Charles Sumner

What are your plans?

ALS   PHi   (79/409, PCS)

1. Chase wrote CS 25 June 1865 (79/388, PCS) that he would soon be at the farm
of his son-in-law, William Sprague, at Narragansett Beach. He bemoaned Johnson's
"moral, political, & financial mistake" in refusing to recognize black citizens in returning states: "The vanquished rebels were ready to accept, though of course reluctantly, universal suffrage; a large portion of the loyal whites regarded it as essential
to their own safety; the whole body of the colored citizens were anxious for it, & will
never be satisfied or work contentedly without it."

2. Francis Preston Blair and his son Montgomery Blair, friends of Johnson, believed that Southern whites should determine suffrage in their states (Eric Foner,
Reconstruction [1988], 218–19).

To Gideon Welles

Cotuit. Port—Mass.
4th July '65

My dear Sir,

Yr kind letter[1] has followed me to this retreat by the sea-shore where
I am for a few days with Mr [*Samuel*] Hooper.

What you say of the policy of the Administration, although not new
to me, is indescribably painful. Of course, this policy, if carried out,
inevitably breaks up the Republican party, & carries the President into

the arms of the copperheads, who already praise him & lure him on to destruction. Can not the Cabinet save him & thus save the country?

Never since I have been in public life has there been any question on which public opinion was so prompt & spontaneous. The President had only to say the word, & he had the whole country at his back. All were ready to follow him in the path required by the Declaration of Independence. How he could go in the opposite direction is incomprehensible.

The question is naturally asked, where does the Presdt. get the power to re-organize a State? It would be difficult to say where. But, if he undertakes to exercise this power, he must proceed according to the requirements of the Declaration of Independence.

His present course in reviving the old Oligarchy of the skin & attempting to build *reformed* governments upon it[2] is offensive (1) to the national safety which it endangers; (2) to national justice which it shocks; (3) to the Constitution, *which it sets aside* & (4) to God Almighty, Whom it insults. —

Seeing this policy thus, I can not recognize it as "within constitutional limits." It defies the highest principles of the Constitution, which are found in the national safety, national justice, & the requirements of a republican govt. *It openly sanctions a govt which is not founded on "the consent of the governed" &, therefore, cannot be republican in form.*

Nor can I consider such a policy as any thing but the worst kind of "aggression." It is flagrantly "aggressive" on Human Rights.

Of course it utterly "incompatible with that harmony which it is desirable to maintain among those who have been faithful to the cause of the Union."

As to the power of the Federal Govt. over this subject in the rebel states, it is the same as the power to suppress the Rebellion, to carry on the war or to decree Emancipation, with that larger untried power superadded "to guarantee a Republican form of govt.," which at this moment it is bound to enforce in the rebel states.

It is because the difficulties of reorganizing the rebel states are so great, that the Govt. must proceed according to the rules of justice & the natural laws. We must have nature & God on our side.

There is no right reserved to any State, inconsistent with the national peace & security—especially can there be no right, according to the language of Burke, "to turn towards us the shameful parts of the Constitution," & insist that these—& these only—shall be recognized.

There is no question of "forfeiture," but simply *a question of fact. The old state govts. are vacated.* This is enough. Of course, *for the time being*, the power is with the Federal Govt., represented by Congress, which must proceed to set up republican govts.

The complications & antagonisms sure to come from this ill-considered policy are already apparent in the inability of the Provisional Governors to take the oath of office prescribed by Congress without perjury. It is idle to say that their office is not included within the Act of Congress. (1) It is a national office, under the national govt; paid by the National Treasury, (2) It is clearly within the spirit, if not the letter of the statute, (3) It is a notorious fact, that the object of Congress was to prevent any men who could not take that oath of office from having any thing to do with the great work of re-organization, *all of which must be put into the hands of men who have been loyal always*.

But I have faith in my country. The right will prevail. The present policy will come to shame & disaster; & the true principles will at last be recognized. I tremble to think how much of agitation, trouble & strife the country must pass through, in order to recover from the false move which has now been made.

I write to you plainly, as I have always been in the habit of speaking on public questions. The question is too serious for hesitation. *The discussion has begun, & it will not stop* until Human Rights are recognized & the Providence of God is vindicated.[3]

Believe me, my dear Sir,

very sincerely Yours,   Charles Sumner

ALS   DLC   (79/421, PCS)

1. Writing from Washington (30 June 1865, 33/694, PCS), Welles defended Johnson's Reconstruction policy, stating it was "within consitutional limitations" and essential to the "harmony . . . so desirable to maintain among those who have been faithful" to the Union. Welles declared that returning states had not legally seceded or "forfeited their civil, territorial or political rights," which included the right of suffrage. He admonished Radicals not to become "denunciatory and intolerant" of the administration's course.

2. Another recent Johnson appointment was that of James Johnson (1810–91), a neutral during the Civil War, as provisional governor of Georgia.

3. No reply from Welles has been recovered until that of 13 July (34/009) to a later complaint from CS about pro-Southern appointments in the Norfolk navy yard (9 July, 79/438). Welles repeated the need for "cultivating harmony" between Republicans and Southern Unionists and concluded, "Let us not persecute the whole of the Southern people."

To Hugh McCulloch[1]

Boston 12th July '65

My dear Sir,

I send you a letter from Mr Brewer, who is not unknown to you as one of our most successful merchants. His large moneyed interests make him an authority on any question affecting the financial affairs of the country.[2]

You will observe how positive he is that we must be just to the colored race,—if for no higher reason,—because it is the "best policy." He sees danger to the national credit, if we continue to deny these people equality before the laws.

You can, of course, see this danger in certain aspects much better than I can; but I confess that the counsels of history & reason are vain, if we can proceed in the present course without much suffering. Two months ago the whole South was ready to accept the *rule of Justice*, prescribed by the Declaration of Independence. Now it is perverse, recalcitrant & rebellious.

I have heard the mischief of the present policy estimated by a very able person, whom you *honor* much, fresh from a visit to the rebel states, at not less than 500 millions of dollars.[3] I should put it at more. *What the country needs is tranquility*, so that people will work steadily & contribute the results of their industry. Clearly Financial prosperity is linked with obedience to God's law.

It is also painful to see that this destructive system is pushed forward (1) in violation of a solemn act of Congress & (2) in violation of the Constitution itself.

Congress has prescribed an oath of office, which the newly appointed governors cannot take without perjury; & it is well-known that the precise object of Congress was to exclude that very class of persons from having any thing to do with the processes of reorganization. And yet these persons are entrusted with the supreme power in rebel states.

I doubt if the Presdt. has any power to appoint a Provisional Governor. There is nothing in the Constitution or any act of Congress authorizing him; & the Constitution seems to require that "appointments not herein provided for *shall be established by law*." He might send a major general to command there; but I am at a loss to see how he can empower a civilian to be Governor & invest him with such enormous powers.

But, however this may be, there is another point on which the system of the Presdt. is clearly & flagrantly *unconstitutional*. He insists upon recognizing a *discrimination of color*; in defiance (1) of the express words of the Constitution, which says that repstives shall be chosen "by the *people* of the several states," leaving to the states only the determinating of the "qualifications," under which head may be included property, payment of taxes, education; *but not color*, because from the nature of the case the latter cannot be a "qualification," (2) in defiance of the Declaration of Indep. which insists on the equality of all men, & the consent of the governed as the only just foundations of govt.; & (3) in defiance of the Constitution again, which requires that we shall guarantee a "republican form"; but when called to enforce this guarantee clearly we must follow the Declaration of Independence which gives us the definition of a republican govt.

But my object was simply to send you Mr Brewer's letter. Pardon me. Pray help save us from the calamity of a protracted contest *which can end only in one way*. The Declaration of Independence is stronger than President or cabinet.[4]

Faithfully Yours, Charles Sumner

ALS DLC (79/444, PCS)

1. Hugh McCulloch (1808–95), U.S. secretary of the Treasury, 1865–69.
2. Gardner Brewer wrote CS from Newport, Rhode Island, 7 July 1865 about the need for black suffrage on grounds of both justice and political necessity. If blacks were denied the vote, Southerners would unite with Northern Democrats to produce a "long train of evils" including "a great reduction of the Tariff doing away with its protective features" and finally *"Repudiation."* Thus the South could ruin the North economically, for European bonds would be withdrawn from U.S. markets, the price of gold would rise, and specie payments postponed (33/734, PCS).
3. Chase to CS, 25 June (79/388).
4. McCulloch returned Brewer's letter to CS on 15 July and stated he would answer CS at length later (Washington, 34/014).

To Henry L. Dawes
private

Boston 20th July '65

Dear Mr Dawes,

My attention has been called to a recent speech of yours in the *Advertiser* to-day where you are reported as saying;

> "There was absolute unanimity in the last cabinet council; & the result was a plan for the restoration of civil govt in Va & N.C.— *then agreed upon & reduced to writing."* [1]

I think that I have conversed with every member of the cabinet on the transaction of that afternoon, & I am sure that I have never heard from any one anything to sustain yr statement.

The main discussion that afternoon related to Presdt. Lincoln's orders to Genl Weitzel & his dealings with Judge Campbell. There the Presdt.

confessed his error & all was harmony. Mr Stanton then opened the question of reconstruction with some very impressive remarks, & concluded by reading two drafts of Executory Orders, one for Va & the other for N.C., *which without discussion were postponed*. So far from being "agreed upon," nothing was done about them.

Afterwards Mr Stanton himself amended the .N.C. order, in conformity with the Constitution of the .U.S. requiring the voters to be the whole "people." So it stood for three weeks, during which not a word was said in the cabinet on the subject, when Mr Stanton introduced the orders again as amended. A motion was made to strike out the words applicable to the whole "people," & insert "the voters before the act of secession." A discussion for two days ensued, during which the Presdt. said nothing & the cabinet which you represent as so "unanimous" stood 3 to 3.—Stanton, Speed & Denison one side— Welles (alas! for New England) Usher[2] & McCulloch on the other. This occurred before I left Washington.

I had every reason to believe that Presdt. Johnson would incline to the side of Equal Rights. His conversation with the Chief Justice & myself was positive that way. The Atty Genl. was confident that it would be so.

I was astonished & pained that he had departed from his promises.

I cannot believe that Presdt. Lincoln, if alive, & seeing the anarchy & insecurity which it entails & its defiance of just principles, would have given his name to any such policy. But my object is simply to set before you certain facts which may not have reached you.[3]

Faithfully Yours,   Charles Sumner

ALS   DLC   (79/455, PCS)

1. Henry L. Dawes (1816–1903; U.S. congressman [Rep., Mass.], 1857–75) had delivered a Fourth of July speech at Pittsfield, Massachusetts, defending Johnson's Reconstruction policy and stressing its consistency with Lincoln's. He stated that criticism of Johnson's Virginia and North Carolina proclamations was "criticism of the wisdom of President Lincoln and his Cabinet." CS quotes from Dawes's remarks about the cabinet meeting on 14 April 1865 (*Boston Daily Advertiser*, 20 July 1865:1).

2. John Palmer Usher (1816–89), U.S. secretary of the Interior, 1863–65.

3. Dawes replied from Pittsfield, 23 July (34/044), that his source of information was "one who could not be mistaken." He could not explain the discrepancy other than "ascribing them to different periods. [Others?] opinions even those of Cabinet officers do sometimes undergo a change."

To William Lloyd Garrison
private

Hancock St—22nd July '65

Dear Mr Garrison,

Has not the time come for yr voice?[1]

This criminal & cruel experiment of the Presdt. must be exposed. I would not break with him, but let him know frankly the opportunity he has lost, & the mischief he has caused.

Ever sincerely Yours,   Charles Sumner

ALS   MB   (79/459, PCS)

1. No reply from Garrison has been recovered. The *Liberator* ran an editorial, "The Renovation of the South" (18 August 1865:130), stating that recent reports about treatment of freedmen would not continue to be discouraging. Readers could expect "a careful and decided course of action soon" that would provide for blacks: "We hope the jubilee is near at hand." For Garrison's subsequent disillusionment in Johnson, see his letter to Henry C. Wright, 2 October 1865 (*The Letters of William Lloyd Garrison*, vol. 5, ed. Walter M. Merrill [1979], 298–99).

To Edwin D. Morgan

Boston 22nd July '65

My dear Governor,

I was glad to hear from you.[1]

To my mind the *case* was clear—very clear.

But the Presdt. has adopted a policy, which if not stopped will divide our party—exalt copperheads—perplex the country—& postpone the glad day of peace & reconciliation. Of course, it must fail miserably. The good cause cannot be lost.

But meanwhile the country suffers.

I think that some of our friends have failed in frankness with the Presdt. Do not break with him. *He is our Presdt*; but precisely on this account, in the devotion of friendship & truth, tell him plainly the blunder he has made, compromising all that has been done. There is but one man in our history who has made an equal blunder, & that was James Buchanan.

I hope you will tell him plainly that this country must not be sacrificed.

Ever yours sincerely,   Charles Sumner

ALS   N   (79/460, PCS)

1. Replying to a previous entreaty from CS (12 July 1865, 79/449, PCS), Morgan wrote from New York on 21 July urging Republicans to be "calm and conciliatory" with the president. Morgan thought Republicans could at the same time be "firm, in our purpose to carry in to effect measures necessary for the honor and safety of the country." Morgan also stated his belief that it would be "more acceptable generally" if universal male suffrage be written into the new state constitutions (34/036).

To Francis Lieber

Boston 2nd Aug. '65

My dear Lieber,

I have from the beginning desired the exile of a considerable number of the leading rebels, say 100, or, better still, 500. So long as these people remain at home, even though shut out from office, they will be so many centers of influence, through correspondance, conversation & the subtle free-masonry of kindred ideas. Let them all go with their lives, & learn abroad how to appreciate the crime they have committed.

I told Mr Lincoln on the Sunday before his death, that if I had the control of the telegraph, I would keep it going, so that at least 500 should be frightened out of the country.

I hope [*Robert M. T.*] Hunter will be exiled; but at the same time I would exile at least 99 others. *This ought to have been done at once*; two months ago. I urged it upon Mr Stanton, who was for hanging.[1]

Ever yours,   Charles Sumner

ALS   MH-H   (64/424, PCS)

1. From New York Lieber wrote, "strict justice, that is death, for say 10 of the worst" was "out of the question," even though he favored it. "As to exile we must not forget that we can only get at it by way of conditional pardon—not by a law— whence arises immediately the difficulty, what will you do with the traitors who do not apply for pardon, or who decline accepting it" (4 August 1865, 79/488, PCS).

To Benjamin F. Wade
private

Boston 3d Aug. '65

My dear Wade,

I was glad to hear from you.[1]

The course of the Presdt. is so absurd that he cannot force it upon Congress. It must fail.

Even Fessenden, I hear, says that we must not let any state back until it has established the suffrage of negroes in its constitution. Morrill is very strong.

I think we shall be able through Congress to accomplish our purposes & save the country; but at what cost? Meanwhile the rebels are all springing into their old life, & the copperheads also. This is the President's work.

I do not understand the Presdt. He said to me—"I agree with you on this question. There is no difference between us. We are alike." Whose influence has brought about the change?

We must let him know frankly, that we will not follow his fatal lead. Here the cabinet has failed. There is nobody to talk plainly to him.

We must also let the country know that we will not consent to this sacrifice. Every man should raise his voice. We have done well in Massachusetts. I wish you would write a letter or speak somewhere. Yr bugle ought to be heard.

Ever sincerely Yours,   Charles Sumner

ALS   DLC   (79/486, PCS)

1. Wade wrote CS a discouraging letter on 29 July 1865 from Jefferson, Ohio (34/083, PCS); Johnson's policy was "consigning the great union, or Republican party, bound, hand and foot, to the tender mercies of the rebels we have so lately conquered in the field and their copperhead allies of the north." Expressing no hope that Johnson would or could redirect his course, Wade wrote, "the salvation of the country devolves upon Congress and against the Executive, will they be able to resist the downward tendency of events?" He feared that Congress could not, and the "great, victorious union party" would "pass again under the yoke."

To John Bright
private

Boston 8th Aug. '65

Dear Mr Bright,

My early prophecy in 1862 will be fulfilled, & nobody will be hanged for treason.[1] So it looks. There is uncertainty with regard to Jeff. Davis, & there is talk now of a trial for complicity in the assassination or in the cruel treatment of our prisoners. There is little doubt of his guilt under both these heads; but I do not know if it can be proved in a court of justice. I come back constantly to my original regret that he did not escape, unless shot like Booth in the attempt to capture him.

You have doubtless seen in the papers that Burnley, in whom Prof. G. Smith was interested, was not convicted, as the jury did not agree.[2]

The policy of the Presdt. in reconstruction is failing wretchedly. Meanwhile the day of tranquility & reconciliation is still further postponed. Some of our friends are in great despair. I am not. The good cause cannot be lost. My counsel has been to put off the question. Neither party is ready to accept in proper spirit any final settlement. The former masters are as little ready for Equality as the freedmen; but the latter are the better prepared. I think Congress will be disposed to settle the great question on proper principles. Thus far there is more agreement among us than I have ever known at any other state of our protracted controversies.[3]

Genl. Grant was here last week.[4] He told me that he had mustered out 800,000 men, leaving about 200,000 still on the rolls, of whom 130,000 were ready for the field. On our foreign policy he was very positive. He regarded the French invasion of Mexico as "a part of the Rebellion," which ought now to cease. He kept 25,000 men in Texas beyond police necessities on this account, making an annual cost of 25 millions of dollars, which we must charge to L. N. He cared little whether England paid "our little bill" or not;—upon the whole he would rather she should not as that would leave the precedent of her conduct in full force for us to follow, & he wished it understood that we should follow it. He thought that we should make more out of "the precedent" than out of "the bill," & that Boston especially would gain. Of course Genl. Grant has no official connexion with our foreign Relations, but his weight in the country gives value to his opinion. I need not say that I dissented from his policy most resolutely. I told him, that our true object should be to bring the two countries into relations of harmony & good will—that this could not be done, if one nation was watching an opportunity to strike, & if the other was standing on guard—that the [truest?] statesmanship was to remove all questions, & to that end I wished the precedent rejected. But I do not see how this can be done, with Lord Russell in his declared moods. Thank God, he is less supercilious. His last letter[5] had a tone of Equality which I hail as a harbinger of better days.

I have come to the end of my sheet without one word on yr election.[6] I had thought the liberals would prevail even more than they have. I note losses & gains which surprize me.

It is well for the country & for himself that Gladstone is now a *freedman*. You may remember that I once told you he was nearer to you than you seemed to be aware.

Ever sincerely Yours,   Charles Sumner

I had thought that Goldwin Smith might go into Parliament to swell yr powerful cultivated, philosophical & learned Opposition.

ALS GBL (79/491, PCS)

1. Bright wrote CS from Rochdale that the British viewed the postponement of Jefferson Davis's trial as a sign "in his favor—but the sudden execution of the [Lincoln] Conspirators has again excited the fears of his friends" (24 July 1865, 34/048, PCS).

2. Bennett Burley, a Scotsman and one of the Confederate participants in the raid on St. Albans, Vermont, was recommitted and later escaped to Canada (Robin W. Winks, *Canada and the United States: The Civil War Years* [1960], 291–92).

3. In his reply of 22 September Bright wrote that CS's "proposition for delay seems very wise." Bright thought that President Johnson's pro-South policy "may be wise as far as the White people are concerned, but I doubt it much in reference to the interests of the negro" (34/307).

4. Grant and his entourage made a public visit to Boston 29–31 July (*New York Times*, 29 July–1 August 1865, passim).

5. Published in the *New York Times* (25 July 1865:8), Russell's letter of 6 July to Sir Frederick Bruce stated that any former Confederate vessel would now be regarded as the property of the U.S., and that no further belligerent rights would be granted to such ships. The British government was "gratified" that the U.S. would "no longer claim" belligerent rights against Britain, and "normal relations of the two countries are practically returned to the condition in which they stood before the civil war."

6. Both Liberals and Radicals gained seats in the British general election 18 July. Bright wrote, "With a system of representation so bad, it is wonderful that a Parlt. can be returned that in any degree represents liberal opinions" (34/048). Gladstone lost his seat as M.P. for Oxford, but was reelected to represent South Lancashire, a constituency regarded by his Liberal colleagues as less conservative. CS wrote Gladstone a congratulatory note, 8 August (79/494).

To Francis Lieber

Boston 14th Aug. '65

My dear Lieber,

All my first impressions were for the writing & reading qualification, but on reflection it seemed to me impracticable.

Of course any rule must apply to the whites as well as blacks. *Now, you cannot get votes* of Congress to *disfranchise*, which you must do in imposing this qualification. Providence has so arranged it, that the work shall be done completely;—*because it must be done.*

Besides, there are very intelligent persons, especially among the freedmen, who cannot read & write.

But we need the votes of all & cannot afford to wait. And we shall have them.

History smiles derisively at this Presidential plan of jumping rebels at once into the partnership of govt. I know no absurdity equal to it. Thirty years were passed in training for the rebellion. How long it will take to train out of it I know not; *but time is necessary*.

Could you ask Mr Binney to send me a set of his pamphlets on Hab. Corpus. I should like also his argt. on the Charity case;[1] his memdm on children of Am. citizens born abroad; his speeches in Congress? I have already the Eulogies, & should like to make a vol. for the binder.—I have given away my copies of the Hab. Corp. pamphlet. You know I have always placed him at the head of our profession in the U. States. He is our Sergt. Maynard[2]

Ever Yours,   Charles Sumner

I will send you a note for Genl. Howard.[3]

ALS   MH-H   (64/427, PCS)

1. *The Privilege of the Writ of Habeas Corpus under the Constitution* (1862); *Argument of Horace Binney in the Case of Vidal v. the City of Philadelphia* (1844).

2. John Maynard (1602–90), British judge and legal scholar.

3 In a P.S., probably to his letter of 11 August (Washington, [before 21 August 1865], 79/512, PCS), Lieber asked CS for a letter of introduction to Freedmen's Bureau chief Oliver Otis Howard (1830–1909).

To Thaddeus Stevens

Boston 20th Aug. '65

My dear Sir,

The 3d & 4th resolutions of yr Convention are excellent.[1] Such a voice from Pennsylvania has salvation in it.

Pray what was the feeling of yr Convention? Give me a hint about yr State. Can any thing be done to stop this wretched experiment which the Presdt. is making?[2]

Faithfully Yours,   Charles Sumner

ALS   DLC   (79/518, PCS)

1. The Union State Convention met in Harrisburg 17 August 1865 and unanimously adopted its committee's resolutions, among them (3) that the Southern states "cannot safely be entrusted with the political rights which they forfeited by their treason" until they showed willingness to adopt constitutional provisions that guar-

antee to all men the "inalienable right to the life, liberty and the pursuit of happiness" and (4) that the laws concerning readmission of rebel states "should be referred to the law-making power of the nation, to which it legitimately belongs" (*Boston Evening Transcript*, 21 August 1865:2). Stevens replied from Lancaster, Pennsylvania, on 26 August that "our views" had been adopted "amidst much chaff." Although he regretted that the black suffrage issue had been "passed over as heavy & premature," Stevens stated that if the rebel states were delegated to a "territorial condition," suffrage could be "easily dealt with" in Congress (34/197, PCS).

2. Stevens had earlier advised CS that Radicals should "try and keep out of the ranks of the opposition—the danger is that so much success will reconcile the people to almost any thing" (17 August, 34/153). In his response of 26 August Stevens stated that he was gratified with CS's efforts "to arrest the president's fatal policy—I wish the prospects of success were better—I have twice written him urging him to stay his hand until Congress meets—Of course he pays no attention to it."

To Hugh McCulloch

Boston 21st Aug. '65
Monday

My dear Sir,

Since my letter of Saturday I have seen the note of Genl. Kilpatrick's remarks, where he says that it is "*unreasonable* to suppose that the reptives. of the South will be reconciled to the *national debt*."[1]

A widely circulated journal also remarks on "the copper head papers as breaking ground for repudiation."

Another article, entitled "Capt. Save the ship" is written by one of our most distinguished lawyers.

I call attention to these, & again I supplicate you, as one of our pilots, to keep the ship from the rocks. For the sake of our country—for the sake of those national finances of which you are the guardian—I pray you to help arrest this irrational, most costly & every way dangerous experiment which the Presdt. in an unhappy moment has commenced.

You will think me importunate, but I have been thought so before; you may think me mistaken, but I have been told so often before. Think of me as you please, *but help save our country*.

You are so situated as to speak with power. Among the counsellors of the Presdt. you can utter the decisive word. Say to him frankly that his policy, if continued, is fatal to the national credit, & to the reestablishment of security & reconciliation—that it is a policy of discord & protracted strife, & *entreat him to refer the whole subject to Congress where it belongs*.

very sincerely Yours,   Charles Sumner

ALS DLC (79/522, PCS)

1. McCulloch had not replied at length to CS's letter of 12 July 1865 until 16 August. Then he wrote that he was "greatly alarmed" at the tendency of Radicals to argue that the president was fomenting a union of former Confederates and Northern Democrats that would repudiate the war debt. "It will not do to make the faith of the nation dependent upon any such issue; and I entreat you as a leader and a creator of public sentiment, not to encourage this idea" (Washington, 34/147, PCS). No letter from CS to McCulloch of 19 August has been recovered. A farewell speech 25 July by Hugh Judson Kilpatrick (1836–81), major general in the U.S. Army, was published in the *Boston Evening Transcript* 18 August 1865:2. In these remarks Kilpatrick urged his troops to "crush out every semblance of discord and disloyalty throughout the land, and perpetuate forever universal freedom and the unity of the States," but made no mention of the debt.

To Hannibal Hamlin

Boston 22nd Aug. '65

My dear Hamlin,

It seemed to Wilson & myself that, before determining yr course, you ought to know the history of the recent change at our Custom House, & we hoped for an opportunity of speaking of it freely in a personal interview. As you may not be here very soon, I will give the narrative.[1]

Sometime ago Mr Hooper received a letter from the Secy. of the Treasury, stating that the Administration desired to change the three officers at the Custom House, whose salaries were large, & he asked him to confer with the two Senators & with Mr Rice,[2] & send him the names which we should agree upon for the places. We concluded not to confine the conference to those indicated, & I invited the whole delegation to meet at my house for this purpose.

At the meeting of the delegation, I stated, that, on general grounds, I was against a change—that I doubted its policy—but that I should co-operate cheerfully with the delegation in making the desired recommendation. I then proceeded to propose Mr Hamlin for Collector. It was evident at once that there was a strong disposition in all the delegation towards Mr Hamlin; but it was remarked that the naval office was easier in its duties & with absolutely the same emoluments as the collectorship;—that the naval officer might be absent for weeks without any inconvenience at the office, while the collector ought to be at his office constantly;—&, further, that the collectorship was to a certain extent a political office affecting our local Mass. politics, &, therefore, most properly filled by a Mass. citizen. These topics were discussed at length, when the delegation overruled my proposition, & recommended, Mr Gooch for Collector & Mr Hamlin for Naval Officer. Mr Hooper & myself were appointed a Comttee. to communicate this result to the Secy of the Treasury.

Some days later Mr Hooper received a letter from the Secy, stating that the Presdt. wished to offer Mr Hamlin the alternative of these two offices.

This all we know. I am not informed with regard to yr personal desires. The newspapers announce the nominations, but with the programme of the delegation changed.[3] Since then Mr Claflin, the chairman of our State Comttee. has called upon me to urge the argt. that the collectorship properly belonged to a Mass. citizen. Others who take a strong interest in our politics have pressed the same argt.

Such is the narrative which I have thought I ought to submit. I have done it with hesitation; but, considering our relations & my position in the delegation, it seemed to me that you would not misconstrue my frankness.

Of course, whatever conclusion you may adopt, you may count upon the cordial support of the delegation & especially of myself.[4] Let me add that Govr. Andrew was warmly in favor of yr nomination.

Ever sincerely Yours,   Charles Sumner

ALS MeU (79/526, PCS)

1. Hamlin telegraphed Wilson and CS on 21 August 1865 from Bangor, Maine, that, although he would like to meet with the two senators, he was unable to get to Boston (34/180, PCS).

2. Alexander H. Rice (1818–95), U.S. congressman (Rep., Mass.), 1859–67.

3. The *Boston Daily Advertiser* (19 August 1865:1) announced the appointment of Hamlin as collector for the port of Boston and Daniel W. Gooch (1820–91; U.S. congressman [Rep., Mass.], 1858–65) as navy agent for the port.

4. Hamlin accepted the appointment and served until 1866. The *Advertiser*'s editorial (21 August 1865:2) praised Hamlin as one who would serve the Massachusetts business community well, although it regretted the government had declined to consider a Boston merchant.

To John Hutchins

Boston 28th Aug. '65

My dear Sir,

I have just read yr admirable speech at Warren.[1] I know not where the whole important question has been presented with more force or clearness.

The argt. is complete, & the illustrations are apt. I had noted Satan for use myself in my next speech.[2] It is a case in point.

To my mind nothing is clearer than this; the Constitutional Amendmt. is already adopted by "the *legislatures* of ¾th of the states."[3] If states have no "legislatures" shall the ratification of an amendment be indefinitely postponed? I will not make this concession to the Rebellion.

We need *time*. This is the great point now. It will then be seen that Congress must assert jurisdiction of the rebel region & mould it into republican states. To this end yr speech is a positive help, & I hope it may be extensively circulated.

I mourn that so respectable a character as Genl. Cox should have made such a mistake.[4] It makes one distrust his judgment, for I suppose his fidelity is beyond question.

very faithfully Yours,   Charles Sumner

ALS   OCLWHi   (79/531, PCS)

1. John Hutchins (1812–91), U.S. congressman (Rep., Ohio), 1859–63, and now a Warren lawyer, spoke at an Ohio Union rally 15 August 1865 in favor of striking the word "white" from the Constitution (*Cleveland Daily Plain Dealer*, 16 August 1865:2).

2. In his speech to the Republican State Convention, 14 September, "The National Security and the National Faith: Guarantees for the National Freedman and the National Creditor," CS, quoting from *Paradise Lost*, declared "the spirit of Satan" had fueled the rebellion and the war was still not extinguished (Wks, 12:320–21).

3. By 28 August twenty-three states of a possible thirty-six (counting seceding states) had ratified the Thirteenth Amendment. However, some of the ratifying legislatures (e.g., Virginia, Tennessee, Arkansas) were provisional bodies organized in former Confederate states.

4. In his "Oberlin Letter" of 24 July, Republican gubernatorial candidate Jacob D. Cox (1828–1900) opposed black suffrage and argued for separation of the races in the South by means of black colonization in the southern U.S. (Eugene H. Roseboom, *History of the State of Ohio*, 4 [1944], 450).

To Hugh McCulloch

Boston 28th Aug. '65

My dear Sir,

Yours of the 22nd is now before me.[1] I dislike to take yr time, & I beg to assure you that I write in no spirit of controversy. I write in earnest desire to do what I can for my country at a critical moment;— as after Bull Run or before Gettysburg.

The Opposition could never have triumphed on negro suffrage in any Northern State, if the Administration had not pointed the way, & encouraged it. The whole country was ready to accept the principles of the Declaration of Indep.—until all at once & unexpectedly these principles, which should have been a beacon, were set at naught by the Administration. This was more strange, because adherence to these principles was plainly essential to the national security.

You say—"rebels & enemies will not be permitted to take possession of the Southern States or to occupy seats in Congress or to form coalitions with the northern Democracy for the repudiation of the national debt or the restoration of Slavery." Good! I like this. I see safety in this avowal. The sooner the Administration act upon it, the sooner we shall feel secure for the future. But thus far the Administration has openly set aside an Act of Congress, passed to meet this very case, & appointed "rebels & enemies" as Provisional Governors.

You say that "the policy now being tried is approved by a large majority of Union men of the North." I do not think so. It is regarded with sorrow & dismay. I know none of the friends of the Administration from Maine to Iowa who do not deplore it, although they may for the moment be silent.

You say that "the Treasury cannot stand the expense of a large standing army." For this reason, I entreat the Secy of the Treasury to abjure a policy which postpones the day of reconciliation & entails untold expense upon the Treasury, with danger to the national credit.

Let me also protest against the whole suggestion of Colonization, as disastrous.[2] We cannot spare the labor of the ex-slave. He is needed.

My policy is all expressed in one word, "Security & Reconciliation for the Future." To my mind the policy of the Administration might be entitled "Danger & discord for the Future." If not arrested these are certain.

Accept my best wishes & believe me, my dear Sir,

very faithfully Yours,   Charles Sumner

ALS   DLC   (79/533, PCS)

1. McCulloch wrote from Washington that he failed "to see that the preservation of the public faith depends upon the enfranchisement of the negro" (34/189, PCS). He begged CS to be "patient, and not despondent." He acknowledged Johnson's plan to be "but an experiment. If it fails, it will not be the fault of the President; and he will then be at liberty to pursue a sterner policy, and the country will sustain him in it."

2. McCulloch closed his letter, "Slavery will cease to exist. The negro will at no distant day be removed to a country further South which the Almighty intended him to occupy, and this great nation will be the home of a homogeneous people."

To Carl Schurz
private

Boston 28th Aug. '65

My dear General,

I fear that you will make yr journey too short.[1] Should you not prepare for the future by gathering details & proofs?

The Presdt. seems determined on his "experiment," but it is announced that it is only an "experiment." The Secy of the Treasury calls it so. But there seems an infatuation among certain persons.

You note Genl. Cox's demonstration in favor of a separation of the races. Absurd! I have reason to believe that this idea prevails at Washington. The Secy of the Treasury avows it; & you know the Presdt. launched it early.

Of course, we must work on. I see but one solution of the case. This will be found in *Time & Justice.* Time is needed. No rebel State is ready now. Meanwhile it must continue under the National Govt. When at last recognized, it must be with Justice as the foundation of all its institutions.

The Presdt. disappointed the Chief Justice, who had reason to believe that he would not act until after his return to Washington. The recent interview between the Presdt & Ch. Justice was solicited by the former, to counsel about J. D.'s trial.[2] The Ch. Justice did not think it proper to confer with the Presdt. on that question. The idea of a civil trial for J. D. seems to me the *ne plus ultra* of folly.[3] I never cease to regret his capture alive.

Ever sincerely Yours,   Charles Sumner

P.S. I have promised to preside at our State Convention 14th Sept, when I shall speak plainly.

ALS   DLC   (79/536, PCS)

1. The most recent letter recovered from Schurz to CS is that of 2 August 1865 from Savannah (79/479, PCS). In it Schurz advised that military rule continue, for "things here are very far from being ripe yet for the restoration of civil government." He saw the need for "sensible, clearheaded people here to superintend the affairs of the colored people. A great many indiscretions are being committed that do much mischief."

2. Writing from Washington 20 August, Chase described his recent meeting with the president, who seemed "less cordial than before I went South." The meeting produced little of consequence, wrote Chase, for Johnson "evidently did not wish to discuss other questions & [hinted?] there was not time" (79/516).

3. To Cincinnati lawyer William Greene CS wrote about a possible trial for Jefferson Davis, "There is nothing for a jury to try. To reduce this gigantic omnipresent

guilt to the proportions of an offense cognizable by a jury from the *vicinage* is to deprive it of its historic character" (7 July, Boston, 79/431).

To James G. Blaine

Boston 6th Sept. '65

My dear Sir,

Too tardily I acknowledge yr kindness.

I have read yr good speech carefully. It touches a very important question, destined to grow in importance. I think we ought to act upon it.[1]

An export tax upon cotton would be a great "benevolence" to the Treasury.

If people would come to their senses about the Constition, & see that "the legislatures of ¾ths of the states" cannot mean to embrace states which *de facto* have no legislatures, we can amend the Constition promptly. I do not doubt that the Amendt. abolishing Slavery is already adopted.[2]

Do not fail to read *Bishop on Criminal Law* 3d edition, *just published*, & especially chapters on "Martial Law"—"Trial of J. D."—"Treason" "Constitutional Amendment" &. Mr Bishop is an authority on the Courts.

Faithfully Yours,   Charles Sumner

ALS DLC (79/551, PCS)

1. In his letter from Augusta, Maine (19 May 1865, 33/468, PCS), James G. Blaine (1830–93; U.S. congressman [Rep., Maine], 1863–76) called CS's attention to a speech he had made on 2 March. Blaine proposed a constitutional amendment giving Congress the power to tax exports, specifically citing cotton, which in time of peace could be taxed five cents per pound and still be competitive (*Globe*, 38th Cong., 2nd sess., 1313–15).

2. CS presented this same argument at length in a letter to the New York *Evening Post*, 28 September 1865 (Wks, 12:357–60), citing *Commentaries on the Criminal Law*, 3rd edition (1865), by Joel Prentiss Bishop (1814–1901).

To Hugh McCulloch

Boston 16th Sept. '65

My dear Sir,

I hope you will pardon my delay in not sooner acknowledging yr favor of 11th. Sept. I should have answered it at once, had not our State

Convention at Worcester occupied me for the time to the exclusion of other affairs.

Let me say that our Convention is regarded as the largest & most powerful political assemblage ever held in Mass. It was *thoroughly harmonious & united*. Two ideas predominated, first, a conviction of the mistake already made by the Administration, & secondly, the duty of saving the country from the impending calamity, if this mistake was not corrected. We were encouraged to frankness by the thought, that Massachusetts had given 70,000 majority to make Andrew Johnson Vice-Presdt, & that our zeal for the success of his Administration cannot be called in question.

Goodwill & support were pledged to the Presdt. "in his efforts to re-establish govt *on the basis of equal & exact justice to all men*." [1] The following resolution obviously points at the open disregard of the Act of Congress on "reconstruction" by the Presdt, &, as it seems also by the Treasury Department; [2]

The latter resolution expresses my own judgment, & is an answer to yr last letter, so far as I understand it. You say that "when Congress convenes there will be found in the Revenue & other offices of the govt. *some persons who gave aid to the Rebellion*." [3] Obviously no such persons can be appointed except in violation of the Act of Congress. [4]

But you proceed to intimate a doubt of the Constitutionality of this act. Allow me to remind you that the discussion of this act in the senate was protracted; that it was assailed at the time by the philo-rebels, like Mr Powell of Ky, & Mr Johnson of Md. as unconstitutional. In the face of their assault, the act was affirmed by a very large majority. [5] Afterwards it was extended to all persons practising in the courts of the U. States, & since then it has been embodied among the rules of the Sup. Ct of the U. States. Surely in the face of this confirmation, no department of this Govt. will undertake to set it aside as unconstitutional.

You then say, that "certainly it was not intended for such a condition of things as now exists." To this I reply, most certainly & undeniably it was intended for this very condition of things. *Its supreme object was to prevent all persons who could not take the oath, from having any thing to do with reconstruction, until Congress chose to relax it.* It was aimed at the very men you now recognize.

In reply to yr last inquiry, as to the validity of proceedings, where the incumbent is not able to take the oath, I content myself with quoting the words of the statute; "Hereafter every person elected *or appointed to any office of honor or profit under the govt. of the U.S.* either in the civil, military or naval departs. of the public service, excepting the Presdt. of the U.S. *shall before entering upon the duties of such office & before*

being entitled to any of the salary or other emoluments thereof, *take &
subscribe the following oath*." I understand you to admit that persons, who
cannot take this oath, cannot receive compensation. Pray, how then can
they "enter upon the duties of such office"? To my mind, it is clear that
all such persons are intruders, & it is the duty of the Department to
treat them as such.

But this very question of the oath seems to reveal the radical difference between the Administration & the great bulk of its supporters.
The Administration, in defiance of Congress, *is determined to employ rebels
in reconstruction*. The people insist upon the employment of loyal men,
or the postponement of all action until loyal men can be found. But the
people in this respect merely ask that a simple act of Congress, whose
meaning is very plain, shall be followed.

Let me confess again the anxiety which I feel on account of the policy
of the Administration. So far as I can tell, this anxiety is very general.
With many it is intense. If this policy is not arrested, nothing can save
this country from destruction but a good Providence, & that star which
will yet light the way. It will be arrested. But meanwhile what a golden
opportunity has been lost. Many cannot estimate the loss already to the
country.

Again, therefore, Mr Secretary, I entreat you, give us peace; above
all, do not let the national credit be sacrificed. *And for the present be
willing to follow a plain Act of Congress*.

I write earnestly. I cannot help it. When I see a great calamity
brought upon my country by the direct agency of our own rulers, I
cannot but cry out. This was done by Mr Buchanan & his cabinet. But
the failure was not greater then than it has been now.

I write *currente calamo*.[6] I have no clerk, & have no copy of any thing
I write; for I write simply in the hope of inducing you to help produce
a *right-about-face* in the present policy.[7]

Believe me, my dear Sir,

Very truly Yours,   Charles Sumner

ALS   DLC   (79/563, PCS)

1. According to the *Boston Evening Transcript* (14 September 1865:3), the resolution read, "good and exact justice to all."

2. Four lines are blank in the letter, where CS apparently appended the resolution,
which read in part: "we agree with the Republicans of Pennsylvania, who, in their
recent State Convention, expressed the conviction that the people, lately in resolution
[*revolution*] cannot safely be entrusted with the political rights which they forfeited
by their treason, until they have proved their acceptance of the results of the war by

incorporating into their Constitutional provisions, and securing to all men within their borders the inalienable right of liberty and the pursuit of happiness; and we call upon Congress, before whom must speedily come the whole question of re-organizing the Southern communities, to see to it that the loyal people, white and black, shall have the most perfect guarantees for their safety before any final steps are taken toward restoring the revolted people of the South to their forfeited rights" (ibid.).

3. McCulloch had continued, "but who are now cooperating with the Administration in its efforts to restore the Federal authority throughout the South, and are as loyal as any in the loyal states" (Washington, 11 September 1865, 34/257, PCS).

4. Two lines are blank here.

5. On 23 June 1862 the congressional act requiring all prospective officeholders to swear they had never been disloyal to the U.S. government passed the Senate by a vote of 33–5, with Lazarus W. Powell (1812–67; U.S. senator [Dem., Ky.], 1859–65) opposing (*Globe*, 37th Cong., 2nd sess., 2873); it became law 5 July 1862. Reverdy Johnson was not sitting in Congress at that time.

6. "Without deep reflection; offhand."

7. In a brief note dated 22 September McCulloch stated that he believed CS was "mistaken both in regard to the temper and intentions of the people at the South, and the sentiments of the Northern people in regard to Mr. Johnson's policy of Reconstruction" (Washington, 34/311).

To John Bright

Boston 26th Sept. '65

Dear Mr Bright,

Mr Watkin has been here. Mr Kinnaird is here now. The former will come to us from Canada again.[1] I have been glad to see them both. The latter is an old abolitionist & seems to sympathize with us in our new trials.

Nothing has made me so happy & grateful latterly as Mr J. S. Mill's letter,[2] just published in our papers, where he grasps our case so well. I hope it may be felt where it ought to be felt. It is masterly in its treatment of the question. If you see him, I wish you would let him know that I am only one of many among my countrymen, for whom he has spoken, not forgetting all the freedmen. I am tempted to write to him directly.

The Presdt. makes us very unhappy. His scheme is folly. He says now that it is "only an experiment," & that he will leave the whole question to Congress. But why did he undertake it? Of course he has set on foot the old rebels & their Northern allies. His appeal is to the disloyal element, converted by amnesty, & rejoicing to find the way so easy.[3]

The evidence is complete, that for one month after the surrender of Lee, the rebels confessed themselves ready to accept the terms which the National Govt. chose to impose. *The Presdt has changed all this*; & now these old rebels are in full scamper back to their old alliance with Northern democrats. The *Herald*, you will observe, praises the policy of the Presdt. & couples with it a violent foreign policy.[4] Alas! alas! I have never felt more anxious. And yet my faith in the Republic is infinite. It is a life-boat, which wind & wave cannot sink; but we shall be beaten about sadly.

Mr Mill has led the way. I hope that the friends who have stood by us thus far will not desert us. Good bye! God bless you!

Ever sincerely Yours, Charles Sumner

I do not mean to break with the Presdt. unless it becomes absolutely necessary. Seward has failed us—of course.[5]

ALS   GBL   (79/591, PCS)

1. Edward Watkin (1819–1901), railroad developer and British M.P. Arthur Fitzgerald Kinnaird (1814–87), philanthropist and British M.P.

2. Writing to William M. Dickson, 1 September 1865, regarding Jacob Cox's colonization proposal, the philosopher John Stuart Mill (1806–73) expressed his fear that Southern blacks would likely be no better off under Johnson's present Reconstruction policy. Each rebel state had "forfeited its [*Union*] privileges" and should not be automatically readmitted. He urged the U.S. to "give guarantees to freedom" for blacks (*The Later Letters of John Stuart Mill*, ed. Francis E. Mineka and Dwight N. Lindley [1972], 16:1098–1101).

3. Bright responded on 20 October (Rochdale, 34/412, PCS) that although Johnson's policy of "mercy" might be beneficial in "outwardly restor[*ing*] the Union sooner," it neglected the "interests of the Negro, & the fundamental principles of your Constitution." Bright saw "some difficulty" in granting universal suffrage: Johnson might "join Congress in shutting the South out from Congress unless the law in every point is the same for white & black—but, most unfortunately for this course, even in a majority of the Free States, the suffrage law does not appear to be the same for the two races—how then could he insist on doing that in the South which he cannot enforce in the North? Can this be done except by another amendment of the Constitution? & if not, could such an amendment be carried? I think not."

4. The *New York Herald* (25 September 1865:4) applauded the efficient restoration of rebel states, and the "statesmanlike policy and able management of the President." The *Herald* looked forward to the next Congress with "every State being represented, and there being a complete reunion of all the members of this former happy family of States." At the same time the *Herald* criticized Seward's "laissez-faire" policy toward England and France and stated that the U.S. should demand "security against such hostile interference," specifically the withdrawal of France from Mexico.

5. According to Glyndon Van Deusen, Seward believed Southerners professing loyalty to the U.S. should be speedily assimilated into the Union, and he helped secure pardons for many ex-Confederates (*William Henry Seward* [1967], 424–27).

To Francis Lieber

Boston 8th Oct. '65

My dear Lieber,

This Republic cannot be lost. Therefore the policy of the Presdt. must fail.

The Presdt. promises not to interfere with Congress—to adopt the principle *laissez faire*. I doubt if this is possible;—because the two parties will become heated. Each will commit itself more & more. But I insist that the Presdt. shall break with us & not we with him.

Of course we shall be obliged to define "a republican govt." This question is directly before us. I shall insist upon its definition, according to American institutions, & so as to be an example to the world.

Inter nos, I have had a full conference with Govr. Morgan & we agree entirely.[1]

Never was so great an opportunity lost, as our Presdt. has flung away.

You know well that I have carried through Congress the rule admitting colored testimony *in all courts of U.S.* It must be fixed by guarantees.[2]

Ever yours, Charles Sumner

I have *precise information* of the position of the Presdt.

ALS   MH-H   (64/435, PCS)

1. After his meeting with CS in New York, Edwin D. Morgan wrote Lieber that he believed the Republicans could find some points of agreement and would support the president (6 October 1865, quoted in James A. Rawley, *Edwin D. Morgan* [1955], 215).

2. Lieber had advised CS not to make the black suffrage issue "a test question for the Union party. It would weaken you and our side altogether." But he urged CS to "do your utmost to expose the truculency and ruffianism—yes ruffianism in still disqualifying negro testimony" (Washington, 5 October, 79/618, PCS).

To Francis Lieber

Boston 12th Oct. '65

My dear Lieber,

Send me the reference to yr article on "republican govt";—also any other references to history or discussion explaining its meaning.[1]

Words receive expansion & elevation with time. Our fathers builded wiser than they knew.

Did they simply mean a guarantee against a king? Something more, I believe, all of which was not fully revealed to themselves; but which we must now declare in the light of our institutions.

We know more than Montesquieu[2] on this question.

The time has come to fix a meaning upon those words. We cannot avoid it. Let us affix a meaning which will make us an example, & will elevate mankind. To this end I spoke in my eulogy of Mr Lincoln,[3] & I find from all parts of the country an echo. If the Presdt. had not set himself the other way there would have been one universal voice. What one man in the same time ever did so much to arrest a great cause!

My point is that Liberty, Equality before the law, & the consent of the governed are essential elements of a republican govt.[4]

Of all failures none has been more unexpected than the Evening Post, whose course is most painful. It wars on "centralism."[5] À la bonne heure! When Human Rights are secured, then we will join in this warfare.

Bigelow writes me from Paris[6] that he expects Bulwer there very soon, & he wishes to tell him the condition of his Speeches. What say you? What shall I write to him?

You have one or two long letters to me from the Orleans Princes, which I have not answered, partly because I wished to read them again, & partly because one of them had something about you which I thought you might like to answer.[7]

The list of books on Laws of War in my hand-writing was an addition of my own to that furnished by the Duc de Nemours. I took it from my recent Brunet.[8]

The author of Charles the Bold is Kirk, for many years & to his death amanuensis & private secy to Prescott.[9]

Ever yours,   Charles Sumner

At last the sorry farce of a jury trial for J. D. is abandoned.[10] It ought never to have been entertained. Expect soon _____.

Our relations with France tend to a diplomatic rupture.

ALS   MH-H   (64/437, PCS)

1. Lieber had written on 11 October 1865 about his article published "long ago" on constitutional guarantees of a republican government (New York, 79/627, PCS).

2. In *Spirit of the Laws* (1750) Montesquieu had discussed a republican government.

3. "It is the Republic, which to-day, with one consenting voice, commemorates the murdered dead. The same Republic, prompt to honor him, must require that his promises to an oppressed race be maintained in all their integrity and completeness, in letter and in spirit, so that the cause for which he became a sacrifice may not fail" ("The Promises of the Declaration of Independence" [1865], 64).

4. Lieber replied 18 October: "there is a passage in my Civil Liberty, in which I speak of the fact that the republican form of government had nothing to do with liberty, directly and intrinsically, and that there is far more liberty in monarchical England than in republican South America, or ever was in any French republic. I think I speak of this also in my Pol. Ethics. Universal suffrage does not constitute the essence of a Republic—witness France at present. . . . But res publica, like

commonwealth, was used for common weal, the totality of public affairs considered as one coherent thing, or system" (79/642).

5. In an editorial, "The Political Situation" (11 October 1865:2), the New York *Evening Post* called for a political realignment. The Union party was too "diverse," stated the *Post*, and in pursuing its war aims had been forced "to exercise extraordinary and almost unwarrantable powers"; the party had accustomed itself to a "dangerous centralization." Men like CS were "urging and stimulating this congestive tendency" in calling for federal interference with states.

6. 21 September (34/300).

7. Henri Eugène d'Aumale (1822–97), a writer and son of Louis Philippe, wrote CS thanking him for sending Lieber's letter (Twickenham, Great Britain, 18 August, 34/155).

8. In thanking CS for this list, Lieber had mistakenly concluded that additions in CS's hand were copies from that made by Louis-Charles-Philippe-Raphaël, duc de Nemours (1814–96), another son of Louis Philippe also in England. No letters from him to CS have been recovered. The Frenchman Jacques-Charles Brunet (1780–1867) compiled bibliographical guides.

9. John Foster Kirk (1824–1904). Lieber had asked CS whether he knew the author of *Charles the Bold* (79/627).

10. The *New York Times* reported later that rumors that there would be no jury trial for Jefferson Davis had been unfounded; judicial details were being discussed by Chase and Johnson (10 November 1865:1).

To Lot M. Morrill

Boston 14th Oct. '65

Dear Governor,

What we need now is *time*. These rebels must be put off. With time they will come to their senses & our people will be united. Therefore, *delay* must be our first effort.[1]

With a President, who would *infuse* correct ideas into those who approached him the work would be easy. If the Presdt. perseveres in his present policy I see gloomy days. I do not say, as a very quiet & intelligent friend of mine said to me lately, "then the country is ruined"; for I believe that no rebellion & no perverse Presdt. can ruin this country. It is too strong & vital. But I do see difficulty & darkness.

The course of the Presdt. seems unaccountable. There is nothing like it in all history. Its nearest paralell is J. B's course after Mr Lincoln's election.[2] But be of good cheer. It is a great battle to fight, but a great cause is at stake.

Ever yours,   Charles Sumner

ALS MeHi (79/631, PCS)

1. Morrill wrote CS in early October (n.d., 34/472, PCS) about correct legal procedures in restoring states' rights. "We must not go to Congress thinking to head off 'restoration' without some plan of our own. . . . [W]e ought to be ready to state [definitely?] the terms on which they [*Southern states*] can be restored to Union."

2. In his 14 September speech, "The National Security and National Faith," CS criticized Buchanan for stating that the federal government had no constitutional power over seceding states (Wks, 12:305).

To Carl Schurz
private

Boston 20th Oct. '65

My dear General,

It is as I expected. It was so with the Chief Justice, who visited the South, by arrangement with the Presdt., & who wrote to him from different places until at Mobile he encountered the proclamations when he stopped. When he saw the Presdt. on his return nothing was said of his observations. It seems it was so with you.[1]

I did not think the Presdt. in earnest when he invited you to make yr tour. Since then he has been pushing forward his "experiment," &, I doubt not, will push it further, if Congress does not assume jurisdiction of the whole subject.

Of course, you will make yr report. But you ought as soon as possible to make a speech.[2]

Govr. Andrew says he can meet you in N.Y. a week from tomorrow (Saturday) I fear that I cannot.[3]

I wish you could give me briefly an outline of yr impressions. My own convictions are now stronger than ever with regard to our duty. *The rebel states must not be allowed at once to participate in our govt.* This privilege must be postponed. Meanwhile all parties will be prepared for the great changes in their political relations. *There must be delay.* The Presdt. does not see this, & every step that he takes is toward perdition.

Never was the way so clear or the opportunity so great. The Presdt. might have given peace to the country & made it a mighty example of justice to mankind. Instead of this consummation, he revives the old Slave Oligarchy, envenomed by war, & gives it a new lease of terrible power.

This Republic cannot be lost; but the Presdt. has done very much to lose it. We must work hard to save it.

St Louis is a central place. But I long to see you in Congress, where you can act directly by public speech on the country.[4] But less than any body, do you need Congress. You have already the public ear.

I hope you will speak soon.

Ever sincerely Yours, Charles Sumner

ALS DLC (79/646, PCS)

1. Writing from Bethlehem, Pennsylvania, on 17 October 1865 (79/639, PCS), Schurz described his meeting with President Johnson on 14 October: "He received me, not indeed without civility, but with great coldness, asked me no questions about the results of my investigations and seemed to desire not to have any conversation about them at all. . . . That the views expressed in my letters to the President were radically at variance with his policy, is quite probable, but I do not see how, as a sensible and fair minded man, he could make that the occasion for a personal rupture. In one word, I am completely in the dark."

2. Schurz replied on 24 October that he expected the report of his tour to be finished soon. "I cannot think of composing a speech before that is accomplished, and I have some doubts as to the propriety of delivering one before my report has seen the light" (79/652).

3. In his 17 October letter Schurz asked CS if he and John Andrew, in his capacity as president of the Emigration Society (an organization investigating Northern investment prospects in the South), could meet him in New York and on 24 October again asked CS to meet with him in order to discuss certain recommendations in his report.

4. Schurz informed CS on 17 October of his plans to start a newspaper in St. Louis if enough capital could be raised. Regarding running for Congress, Schurz wrote on 24 October that he needed "to work for a living" and sought an "activity which will give me an influence upon public opinion and be remunerative at the same time."

To Theodore Tilton
private

Boston 2nd Nov. '65

My dear Sir,

I have read B's sermon with inexpressible pain, even to tears.[1] It is a mistake to cry over. Freedom must have "shrieked" at that fall. It reminds me very much of Moses Stuart's defense of the Fug. Slave Act, with a declared sympathy for the negro & yet surrendering him to his enemies.[2] It is sad—very sad that such a career so grand & beautiful,—should have such a close—at this moment when a little more constancy would secure peace & reconciliation on everlasting foundations.

Pray, in yr demands, do not forget the national debt. I notice that the *Herald* now insists that there must be guarantees *against* the rebel debt & *for* the national debt. This is something. In my Worcester speech these were demanded.[3]

Look also at the Russian experiment, which is worthy of example.[4]

This cause can not be lost.

Knowing history somewhat & accustomed to search its examples, I find no instance of such a mistake as has been made by our Presdt. Next to it is that of Buchanan in Dec. '60; but this was more natural & even pardonable than Johnson's.[5]

Ever Yours,   Charles Sumner

ALS   NBu   (80/001, PCS)

1. In his sermon "Conditions of a Restored Union," 29 October 1865, Henry Ward Beecher argued for black suffrage in the returning states, but also declared that the U.S. needed now to "save the self-respect of the South," and should trust Southerners applying for restoration of their rights. He praised Johnson's "auspicious wisdom" and stated the U.S. should leave freedmen's rights to the care of individual states (*Patriotic Addresses* [1887], 713–35).

2. Moses Stuart (1780–1852), professor at Andover Theological Seminary, had supported the Fugitive Slave Act in his 1850 pamphlet "Conscience and the Constitution" (Wilson, 2:318).

3. The *New York Herald*'s editorial (31 October 1865:4) called the assumption of the national debt by returning states one of the "essential conditions of re-organization." For CS on the debt, see "The National Security and the National Faith," Wks, 12:326.

4. In his Worcester speech CS praised the Russian experiment that granted suffrage and the right to hold office to freed serfs (Wks, 12:312–14).

5. Tilton agreed with CS in his reply from New York on 17 November (34/535, PCS). He intended to "remain every week at my Editorial post" and urged CS to continue to denounce publicly Johnson's Reconstruction measures as he had done in a letter to the New York *Independent* of 29 October (Wks, 12:368–70); wrote Tilton, "No man's letters give me more satisfaction than your own."

To John Bright
private & confidential

Boston 5th Nov. '65

Dear Mr Bright,

For the present domestic questions are uppermost. I am very anxious, more than ever before. At no time of the war has our peril seemed so vast. It comes from the Presdt. himself. I write to you frankly, as I feel.

He has held a long conversation with a person, who has reported it to me, on the next Presidency, & the possible candidates. He relies upon the returned states to support himself. My colleague, Genl. Wilson, assures me that the Presdt. also entered into secret negotiations with the Democrats of New York, who promised him that state by an immense majority, if he would get rid of the "radicals." It is undeniable that he has held long conversations with their leaders, & that, though pressed during the recent canvass, he declined to say a word in public favoring the Union party. Such are some of the facts, which show the uncertainty of his political relations.

Then his policy has been to set the old rebels on their feet again. I have letters daily from Unionists in the rebel states saying that they cannot continue to reside there, unless this policy is changed.[1] Of course, the poor freedman is exposed to brutality & cruelty.

My first point is that the Unionists & freedmen there must be protected. This is a sacred debt. Then also we must have assurance that the national debt will not be repudiated. If we admit 84 reptves. from the rebel states to Congress, they will very soon find allies enough from the copperheads of the North to control Congress on this question.

It is doubtful how Congress will stand. Those who are associated with the Presdt. in his policy think it will unite with him. Others, who have considerable opportunities of information, feel sure that it will be firm the other way, at least to the extent of obtaining time. I know many who I am sure will not yield. I shall not. I have a letter from an able Western Senator,[2] who has been much attached to the Presdt, but who now writes: "His course has done more to jeopardize the liberties of the country, than the war with all its rebel leaders combined. We have a greater & more perilous fight on our hands than we have had at any other period." If the Presdt. perseveres the Union party is broken up.

The Presdt. is a person without statesmanship & with very little real humanity. What could you expect from an old slave-master & an old democrat?

I have said enough of domestic questions. The foreign add to my anxieties. Here the Presdt. is disposed to be positive, in the hope of diverting attention from domestic questions, & there are some about him who press this view strongly. I see no danger of war; but grave complications must ensue both with England & France. Ld Russell seems to have made a case,[3] which necessarily closes the door to amiable relations between the U.S. & England. How idle, if not insulting to offer a commission for English claims, when ours are treated as out of court. Such a commission, if accepted, might be under an act of Congress, or a Treaty. It is probable the latter course would be attempted. But even if Seward should consent, it could not obtain the *⅔ds vote* of the Senate required for the ratification of a treaty. So that proposition may be dismissed. The Reciprocity Treaty also falls. The game that Ld Russell begins will doubtless be followed on this side.

Let me say to you, that to me this is inexpressibly painful. I believe in peace, & I long to see it established sincerely between our two countries.

There is more present danger from the Mexican question.[4] Our people already clamor for the withdrawal of the French troops. I think the House of Reps. will address an instant summons to Louis Nap., which will embarass the question much. *He will not move.* I fear that this question may turn us away from guarding the poor freedmen.

If our Presdt. were properly inspired, he might *impel*, or *infiltrate* correct principles into the South, without a proclamation or an act of Congress. But he is not. Do you wonder that I am unhappy?

Let me hear from you soon. My letters are poor returns, I know.

Ever sincerely Yours, Charles Sumner

I was glad to see yr nephew & his friend. They called while I was reading yr last most interesting letter.[5]

ALS GBL (80/008, PCS)

1. The CS correspondence does not contain "daily" letters from such Unionists, but for examples see R. F. Lehnran from New Berne, North Carolina, 21 October 1865; Joshua Webster from Corinth, Mississippi, 26 October; and T. P. Atticus Bibb from Richmond, 3 November (34/420, 453, 484, PCS).

2. Benjamin F. Wade to CS, Jefferson, Ohio, 1 November, 34/477.

3. In his letter of 30 August to Adams, Russell laid out historical and legal precedents for Britain's refusal to pay damages to the U.S. incurred by British-built ships. He concluded that his government would not "make reparation and compensation for the captures made by the Alabama, or refer the question to any foreign state," but would agree to a commission to which all claims could be submitted (*Foreign Relations* [1865], part 1, 536–45).

4. The liberal forces in Mexico had recently lost a battle to the Imperialists at Matamoras. In an editorial the *New York Times* deplored Maximilian's presence in Mexico, which, it stated, was counter to the Monroe Doctrine (2 November 1865:1, 30 October 1865:4).

5. Bright had introduced his nephew, Frank Bright, to CS in his letter of 22 September (Rochdale, 34/307). For Bright's "interesting letter," 20 October, see CS to Bright, 26 September.

To Edwin M. Stanton
private

Boston 5th [*8th*] Nov. '65

My dear Sir,

I made haste to call on Govr. Parsons, who seemed to be intelligent & amiable.[1] After conversation with him, I was led to doubt if his influence in the State of Alabama could be otherwise than pernicious.

He *volunteered* to say to me, that rather than allow negroes to vote he would emigrate. I did not give the reply which was natural, "that if he is unwilling to accept the principles of the Declt. of Indep. he ought to emigrate." To my mind such a man must be a bad example.

What can we expect for the future when such a spirit leads?

At the club in the evng.[2] Govr. P. made an address which seemed to me & many others truly Pecksniffian.

I write this, thinking you will be glad to have a report of the impression he produced on some persons.

His conversation has added to my anxiety with regard to the future, unless this policy of giving power to rebels is arrested. The mischief already done seems to me incalculable.

Very truly Yours,   Charles Sumner

ALS   DLC   (80/013, PCS)

1. Although CS dated this letter 5 November 1865, it is probably a slip for 8 November. Lewis E. Parsons (1817–95; provisional governor of Alabama, June–December 1865) arrived in Boston 7 November (*Boston Evening Transcript*, 7 November 1865:2). Stanton telegraphed CS 6 November recommending Parsons as a "loyal & patriotic man entitled to respect and confidence." Stanton thought CS would be "gratified with his acquaintance" (Washington, 34/497, PCS).

2. Parsons spoke at the Union Club 7 November (*Boston Evening Transcript*, 7 November 1865:2).

To Andrew Johnson

4:40 P.M.
Boston 11 November 1865

The President of the U.S.

As a faithful friend and supporter of your administration I most respectfully petition you to suspend for the present your policy towards the Rebel States. I should not present this prayer if I were not painfully convinced that thus far it has failed to obtain any reasonable guarantee for that security in the future which is essential to peace & reconciliation [T]o my mind it abandons the freedmen to the control of their ancient Masters & leaves the National debt exposed to repudiation by returning Rebels. The declaration of Independence asserts the equality of all men & the rightful government can be founded only on the consent of the governed. I see small chance of peace unless these great principles are practically established by our Government [W]ithout this the house will continue divided against itself.

Charles Sumner   Senator of US.

TEL   DLC   (80/018, PCS)

To John Andrew

Hancock St Friday afternoon
[24? November 1865]

Mr Sumner asks pardon for not sooner acknowledging Govr. Andrew's letter, & begs to say that he rejoices in the many generous acts which the Governor has done, & especially in the recent testimony to our national duty which he narrates.[1]

Mr S hopes that the Governor will not cease that watchfulness which has done him so much honor. He ventures to suggest that first & foremost "among the arts & methods of peace,"[2] which the Govr now wishes to cultivate, is justice to the oppressed, & he entreats the Govr. not to allow any negro-hater, with his sympathizers, to believe him, at this crisis, indifferent to the guarantees of Human Rights or disposed to postpone his efforts in their behalf.

AL   MHi   (80/035, PCS)

1. Andrew, who was retiring as governor of Massachusetts in January, had endorsed Johnson's Reconstruction policies. During Parsons's visit to Boston, Andrew defended the Alabama governor against CS's criticism (Henry G. Pearson, *The Life of John A. Andrew* [1904], 2:272–73). Shortly thereafter in an undated note, CS sent Andrew a letter from an Alabama resident that, said CS, reported "the actual condition of society there" (21? November 1865, 80/049, PCS). Responding on 21 November (Boston, 34/548), Andrew wrote he was not surprised at the conditions described, but he believed President Johnson was truly trying to secure "safety and

progress" for the freedmen. Andrew advocated conciliation toward the South. "As to the reception of Senators and Representatives into Congress from the Seceding States, I expressed my opinion to the Faneuil Hall meeting, that the Presidents experiment would not succeed. I still think it will not. But I hope he will get all the good out of it, possible to it. The right position for *New England* is one of friendliness, not antagonism."

2. In his letter Andrew stated, "we have got rid of War. We now can take hold of the arts and methods of Peace."

To Francis Lieber

Washington Sunday
[3 December 1865]

Dear Lieber,

I was sorry to miss you,[1] as I wished much to confer with you quietly on history & philosophy. Of course, Holland was called a Republic. Bodin,[2] whom I have just read, calls the govt. of Nimrod a Republic. I have been through every thing on this question, & see my way clearly. Never before more clearly.

The debate which approaches on the meaning of a "Republican govt." will be the greatest in our history. I shall launch it tomorrow.[3]

On my arrival last evng I went at once to the Presdt, with whom I was 2½ hours. He began the interview warmly & antagonistacally; but at the close thanked me for my visit. He does not understand the case. Much that he said was painful, from its prejudice, ignorance & perversity.

I had my hat on the floor at the side of my chair. In his ardor the Presdt. unconsciously used it as a spitoon!—

You ask about my relations with Mr Welles. I am on excellent terms with every member of the cabinet. With him I had special relations, so that he was in the habit of appealing to me to carry some things with Presdt. Lincoln. He has latterly written me complaining that I exercised on one occasion too much influence with the latter against something which the Depart. had at heart. I have been disgusted with Mr Welles's course on reconstruction, &, we have had considerable correspondence on the subject, which was always amiable in manner. This is my answer to yr inquiry.

Ever yours,   Charles Sumner

Launch Gasparin promptly.[4]

ALS   MH-H   (64/443, PCS)

1. Lieber wrote 1 December 1865 that he had hoped to see CS when he passed through New York but was otherwise engaged (New York, 80/054, PCS).

2. Jean Bodin (1530–96), French jurist and political economist.

3. On the first day of Congress, 4 December, CS introduced three groups of resolutions proposing Reconstruction policies, one of which asked Congress to guarantee that every reentering state maintain "a republican form of government," and that no government could be considered republican "where large masses of citizens who have always been loyal to the United States are excluded from the elective franchise" (*Globe*, 39th Cong., 1st sess., 2).

4. Lieber wrote CS that he would soon decide under what auspices to print a recent letter from the French publicist Angénor de Gasparin to President Johnson on black suffrage and would send CS "a quantity" (1 December, 80/056).

To Carl Schurz

Washington Xmas-day
[*25th December 1865*]

Dear General,

I am in the midst of yr Report,[1] which I find all that I expected; very able, elaborate, complete, full of facts & ideas. Let me suggest that in yr speech, you present a vivid vigorous portraiture of the condition of things in the rebel states. Of course, this will not preclude a presentment also of the ideas involved.

Meeting Sir Fred. Bruce at dinner Sat. evng, I found he had been prodigiously impressed by the power of Stevens's speech. He evidently put it before Raymond's.[2]

Until the Committee[3] give us the facts Congress will occupy itself with the ideas. This discussion will go on for months. I do not see how it can be stopped; nor do I think it desirable to stop it. At last the evidence, as reported will show the necessity of interference by Congress. Now, to my mind the single point to be reached is *the assertion of jurisdiction by Congress*.

One person will reach this point by one road & another by another road. Provided it is reached, it is not of much importance how this is accomplished. Therefore, I hope that all will speak & ventilate their theories; for though differing, I feel sure that a large majority will concur in asserting Congressional jurisdiction; & this is the main thing.

Meanwhile the Presdt & Seward press their policy. Alas! alas! unhappy country. Good bye!

Ever sincerely Yours,   Charles Sumner

ALS   DLC   (80/079, PCS)

1. CS requested on 12 December 1865 that a copy of Schurz's "Report on the States of South Carolina, Georgia, Alabama, Mississippi, and Louisiana" be furnished to the Senate, and President Johnson duly complied. When the report was presented on 19 December, CS moved that it be read aloud, but the effort was soon disbanded (*Globe*, 39th Cong., 1st sess., 30, 78–80).

2. Thaddeus Stevens spoke 18 December and Henry Raymond 21 December (ibid., 72–75, 120–25). Stevens termed the rebel states "dead carcasses lying within the Union" waiting for readmission. He stated that Congress was empowered to establish standards for this process and should not permit "a white man's government" in the South. Raymond disagreed with Stevens, stating that not all matters of Reconstruction were the responsibility of Congress; Congress should work in conjunction with the president.

3. The Joint Select Committee on Reconstruction was proposed in the House on 4 December; the Senate concurred on the committee's formation on 19 December (ibid., 7, 78).

To the Duchess of Argyll

Washington 26th Dec '65

My dear Duchess,

A merry xmas to you & yours! I owe you two letters, each of which was very pleasant—although I am pained by the reports you give of yr mother. But I trust that she is better.

Poor Lilly Motley—now Mrs Ives—reached the home of her husband's family in Providence only a fortnight ago.[1] He became ill three days after the marriage in Vienna, & on their arrival at Paris the doctors pronounced the case hopeless. They started for America; but he died at Havre. Her parents came to her there; but she made up her mind to return to America & to see his mother, who, I understand, is a very interesting person.

I knew Capt. Ives slightly. He looked like an invalid, but had shown a noble character. His means were very ample, say a million of dollars, but he volunteered at once in the war, & received a commission in the navy for which he had natural proclivities. I understand that his services were valuable; I know that he was much regarded. This early premature widowhood is a sad incident in the life of a young person, & I understand that she is now much depressed, although calm.

From this sorrow I turn to other scenes. Sir Fred. Bruce is agreeable, & social. I like him, & also his niece. He is very interesting in talking of China, & our Minister there Mr Burlingame, who is now at home, agrees with him. I wish that Chinese civilization could prevail to banish the ideas of war. The new French Minister, M. de Montholon, who was not long ago a rebel & secessionist, now talks very softly. He tells me that I am right in my policy. He is anxious to keep the peace & encourages us to believe that there will be some declaration in the Emperor's speech to the Chambers which will smooth our relations. He assures me that the Emperor desires to withdraw his troops from Mexico. À la bonne heure! Let him do it. Meanwhile I shall try to prevent any definitive action by Congress until he has an opportunity.[2]

The intelligence from our Southern States is of the most painful character.[3] In most places the freedmen are worse off than when slaves; being exposed to the brutality & vindictiveness of their old masters, without the old check of self-interest. The sentiment of disloyalty is intense. Of all this I have no doubt. The President, who is hide-bound in prejudice, is painfully insensible to the real condition of things. I have had an interview of several hours with him & found him in a very unhappy frame of mind. Congress, thank God! is resolved to apply the corrective. But this opens an unwelcome chapter. The power of the Presdt, through his patronage, is enormous, extending into every village. I still hope that a conflict may be avoided. But it is a terrible calamity, that now, at this crisis, the chief of the nation fails us. He has no sentiment or heart for the poor freedman;—& he forgets also the white unionist who has kept his faith to the flag. In his whole policy he is sustained by Mr Seward. This again is very painful. Two others of the cabinet are with him, Mr Welles, Secy of the Navy & Mr McCulloch, Secy of the Treasury. The rest are the other way, one or two very strongly. With all of these I confer freely. This little recital will give you a glimpse of present anxieties, which at times make me very unhappy.

I suppose you must be now at Kensington. At least I shall address you there.

I think you will enjoy Bryant's translation of the parting of Hector & Andromache, which is an exquisite poem. I took up the other day Milnes' Poems, which I have always liked for their kindly sympathies & their culture, with a certain flavor of poetry; so that I read them with pleasure. I have on my table now Ld Milton's tour, which I shall read with an interest derived from my knowledge of his family & my reverence for his grandfather, who was a most estimable person. I have not yet finished Mr Gladstone's Edinburgh Exercitation,[4] which is very learned & suggestive. But I have little time for these things.

I suppose the next bag will bring me the book which you announce.[5] I hope the Duke is well. Tell him that he must not slacken his sympathies for the freedmen. They will need all. I tremble for them now. Good bye!

Ever sincerely Yours,   Charles Sumner

ALS   CSmH   (80/082, PCS)

1. In her letter of 24 November 1865 (34/561, PCS) the duchess had expressed her grief at the Motley family's loss and sought more information. Elizabeth Cabot Motley, daughter of John Lothrop Motley, had married Thomas Poynton Ives in October (*John Lothrop Motley and His Family*, ed. Susan St. John Mildmay and Herbert St. John Mildmay [1910], 28, 248).

2. The Marquis de Montholon, former minister to Mexico, had been appointed minister to the U.S. 15 March (*Foreign Relations*, part 2, 242). On 11 December the Senate asked President Johnson to furnish all correspondence regarding the French occupation of Mexico (*Globe*, 39th Cong., 1st sess., 17). Meanwhile, more French troops were arriving in Mexico, and the *New York Herald* stated that recent intelligence from Matamoras testified that the French there expected a war with the U.S. (18 December 1865:1).

3. For example, an ex-Union soldier now living in Nashville wrote CS protesting Johnson's leniency to ex-Confederates (no signature, 23 December, 34/739).

4. Bryant's translation of the *Odyssey*, book 6, *Atlantic Monthly* 16 (December 1865): 657–59. *Selections from the Poetical Works of Richard Monckton Milnes, Lord Houghton* (1863); *The Northwest Passage by Land* (1865), by William Fitzwilliam Milton (1839–77); Gladstone, "Address on the Place of Ancient Greece in the Providential Order of the World: Delivered before the University of Edinburgh, on the Third of November, 1865" (1865).

5. The duchess did not identify the book but promised CS he would find in it "very reverential mention made of Dr. Channing."

To John C. Hurd

Washington 27th Dec. '65

My dear Sir,

I am obliged by yr attention in sending me yr letter to the *Times*, which seems to me unanswerable.[1]

To my mind a state is a corporate body all whose officers are bound by oath to support the Constitution of the U. States. Of course at the close of the war no such body existed in the rebel region. Latterly I have said nothing about *suicide*, because this was a phrase which, of itself, gave rise to discussion & diverted attention from the fact. Now the *fact* was that in the rebel states there were no govts. that we could recognize. Nobody can question this *fact*. Very well. But the Constitution of the U. States was never displaced. This continued to overarch every acre of the region. Therefore in the Constitution or under the Constitution the powers of govt. were to be found for this abnormal condition.

Perhaps some persons are frightened by the phrase "territory" or "territorialize." Very well. I willingly renounce this. Strictly speaking, this rebel region is not "territory" of the U. States. It is only by analogy that we call it so.

The point at which I have aimed from the beginning is to *establish the jurisdiction of Congress over this region*, & I accept any theory which accomplishes this most desirable & necessary result. Call it "territory"; say that we must exact security for the future; declare that we must require republican govts; in each of these cases the power of Congress cannot easily be disputed.

If at any time there has been a seeming inconsistency in my views,[2] it has been, because I was more disposed sometimes to dwell on one argt. than on the other;—most sincerely believing each to be unanswerable & all to be consistent with each other.

Accept my thanks & believe me, my dear Sir,

very faithfully Yours,   Charles Sumner

ALS   NNHi   (80/085, PCS)

1. John Hurd (1816–92), a Boston publicist, enclosed his letter appearing in the *New York Times* (26 December 1865:3) in his to CS of 26 December (New York, 35/018, PCS). In his public letter, Hurd discussed the relationship between individual states and the federal government; he argued that the Confederate states, by seceding, gave up their stake in the national government as well as local sovereignty.

2. Hurd did not criticize CS for inconsistency. Hurd stated that Orestes Brownson's theory of state suicide in *The American Republic* (1865) seemed inconsistent in that Brownson would require seceded states to return "identical and unchanged in all matters of political law, when they shall have ceased to be held as territory" (35/018).

To John Bright

Washington 1st Jan '66

Dear Mr Bright,

I have just read yr magnificent speech[1]—I need not say with perfect sympathy.

I wish I had good news from our side. The Presdt. is perverse, & not well-informed. He is also fired with the idea of carrying through his "experiment," which thus far is a terrible failure.

It is very hard that we should have this new controversy. But I have no doubt with regard to my course. The way was never clearer.

Affairs with France are very *tendues*; but M. de Montholon thinks that with "time" the question can be arranged. He expects that the Emperor will make some statement in his address to the Chambers, which will open the way to a good understanding. I hope so.

Sir F. Bruce is very amiable & excellent; but he can do nothing. Ld Russell has sent him on an impossible mission. It is time that yr Ministry should consider the old rule that "Whoso would have equity must do equity."

I write in great haste & merely to wish you a Happy New Year.

Ever Yours,   Charles Sumner

Seward assures me that his voyage is solely for health & to avoid holidays.[2]

———————————

ALS   GBL   (80/110, PCS)

1. Bright spoke 13 December 1865 in Birmingham on electoral reform. He proposed the eventual suffrage of five million British subjects and the immediate suffrage of one million (London *Times*, 14 December 1865:9).

2. Seward planned a trip with his family to Havana; rumors that the secretary would travel to Mexico in order to get in touch with the Juarez government were unfounded, stated the *New York Times* (30 December 1865:4).

To Peleg W. Chandler

Washington
3d Jan. '65 [*1866*]

My dear Chandler,

You have influence over the *Advertiser*. Don't let it fail the Union cause at this moment. There is especial need of firmness & frankness. The Presdt. has made a fearful mistake, & perseveres in it. Any body who sees him familiarly knows this painfully.

He is impenetrable. After a conversation of 2½ hours with him I felt saddened. He was stolid, & without any sympathy for the freedman. I give you a specimen.

"*Presdt*   Mr S. Do murders ever occur in Mass?
Mr S.   "Unhappily yes, Mr Presdt—"
Presdt—"Do people ever knock each other down in Boston—"
Mr S.   "Unhappily yes Mr Presdt, sometimes."
Presdt.   "Would you consent that Mass. should be excluded from the Union on this accnt.
Mr S.   "No, Mr Presdt; surely not."—

The difficulty is that people do not talk to him frankly; & the newspapers are silenced.

The case is plain as day. The evidence accumulates daily. The condition of unionists & freedmen in the rebel states is wretched. The Presdt's policy if not arrested hands them over to their rebel foes. Of this be assured.

We must not break with the Presdt. unless as a last resort, & then he must be left to break with us. But all is lost, if we fail in frankness.[1]

You told me to send you hints, & I send you now what is of immense practical importance. I have been in this warfare long & know how to conduct it.

I am amused at the Boston trepidation.[2] Do you remember in history when a person in place was supposed to be about to fall, that those who owed places to him made haste to detach themselves from his fortunes? Alas! for human nature, which is the same now as always.

You will be glad to know the position of Mr [*Samuel*] Hooper. The Atty Genl [*James Speed*] said to me the other day "If yr Mr Hooper were a speaker he would be the most powerful man in Washington; he has such excellent sense." Of course he is influential with the Presdt.

I suppose that you know that Fessenden is as strong as I against the Presdt's policy.[3]

Ever Yours,   Charles Sumner

ALS   ICHi   (80/114, PCS)

1. Chandler, in a delayed reply due to illness, wrote CS 12 February 1866, "There is a very feverish dread" in both Boston and Philadelphia of "any *breach with the president.*" He cautioned CS, "If we cannot have all we need, we must take what we can get" (Philadelphia, 35/366, PCS).

2. No reference has been identified. CS may have referred to a Massachusetts official criticizing John Andrew, outgoing governor.

3. Fessenden had been selected to chair the Joint Select Committee on Reconstruction. He voted with CS on two matters concerning organizational details of the committee. In Senate remarks Fessenden declared that although he respected President Johnson, he did not believe that Congress should necessarily follow all aspects of his Reconstruction policy (12 December 1865, *Globe*, 39th Cong., 1st sess., 26–29). To a cousin Fessenden wrote that CS had desired to serve on the Reconstruction committee, but since he was "committed to the most ultra views, even his friends declined to support him" (to Elizabeth F. Warriner, 24 December 1865, quoted in Eric McKitrick, *Andrew Johnson and Reconstruction* [1960], 277).

To William H. Claflin
private

Senate Chamber 11th Jan. '66

Dear Governor,[1]

We must do all that we can for the circulation of our docts. The country must be carried & can be carried for the ideas now in issue. Never was greater question presented for decision.

But we need help from Massachusetts. Govr. Boutwell has called this morning particularly to urge that we should unite in asking for it. I offered at once to write to you in his behalf & my own.

In one word we need funds to pay for the printing of speeches. The country must be flooded under our franks. Of course, every body here contributes out of his own pocket, but there are few among us whose means are not limited. For instance I have already circulated at my own expense 3000 copies of the pamphlet entitled Bills & Resolutions, & also 3000 copies of the other on the Condition of the Rebel States.[2] I subscribe also to the speeches of others. As the debate goes on these calls will be more & more onerous.

Will you see if there can not be a fund placed at our disposal here to help in this work?

Ever sincerely yours,   Charles Sumner

Those concluding sentences of Bullock[3] were pearls of truth & diction.

ALS   OFH   (80/135, PCS)

1. Claflin had recently been elected lieutenant governor of Massachusetts.
2. CS's speech 20 December 1865 (*Globe*, 39th Cong., 1st sess., 90–95).
3. In his inaugural speech, 6 January 1866, newly elected Massachusetts governor Alexander H. Bullock stated that readmission of rebel states should be "conditioned upon emancipation in fact as well as by name, upon their full and solemn recognition of the equality of all men before the law" and he trusted Massachusetts senators and representatives to see that these conditions be met (*Boston Evening Transcript*, 6 January 1866:2).

To George Bancroft

Washington 21st. Jan. '66

My dear Bancroft,

I send you the note you desire. Use it as you please.[1]

There is great anxiety here as to the course of the Presdt. & the most painful rumors.

Meanwhile the tidings from the South are most distressing. I have a long letter from the Govr of Texas[2] & from the Atty Genl. appealing to us to stand firm in Congress against the policy of the Presdt, by which peace & safety there are sacrificed. They say that if it is not arrested they will be obliged to flee from the State.

If you can approach the Presdt, I entreat you to induce him to stay his hand.[3] Thank God! Congress will stand firm against his madness. But should he persevere, I see nothing but peril.

Ever yours,   Charles Sumner

ALS   NICO   (80/145, PCS)

1. Bancroft was preparing a eulogy on Lincoln, to be delivered in the House of Representatives 12 February 1866. He wrote CS on 17 January seeking CS's recollection of Lincoln's statement criticizing Lord Russell's letter on the Emancipation Proclamation (New York, 35/159, PCS).

2. Andrew J. Hamilton (1815–75), a Union officer in the Civil War, military governor of Texas, 1862, and provisional governor, 1865.

3. Bancroft had been in close contact with Johnson since his inauguration, and it is now known that Bancroft had helped write Johnson's first annual presidential message.

To George Bancroft

Washington 3d Feb. '66

My dear Bancroft,

I value yr suggestions always. It is possible you have some information about Tennesee which I have not. I confer often with one of her senators, & sometimes with our Comttee. now engaged in considering her condition.[1] Perhaps, you are not aware that the testimony is very black. But there are two inquiries on which I should like yr instruction. (1) In what way do you propose to assure protection to the unionists of Tennessee, black & white, so as to save them from the returning tide of rebels?

(2) How do you reconcile the exclusion of 285,000 loyal citizens from the ballot-box with the idea of republican govt. which we are bound to guarantee. Taxation without representation is tyranny, & yet here is a large population subject to this tyranny. Can the State which does this be regarded as republican under the guaranty of the Constitution? Clearly not, & I shall insist tomorrow that Congress must say so.[2] I propose to review our colonial history to illustrate the inevitable Conclusion. Thank God Congress grows stronger every day.

We expect a generous word from you the 12th

Ever yours,   Charles Sumner

ALS   NICO   (80/161, PCS)

1. Bancroft wrote CS on 27 January 1866 urging him to "come forward *yourself* & ask that the Senators from Tennessee be *at once* received into the Senate." Bancroft argued that those states abolishing slavery should receive congressional representation (New York, 35/221, PCS). The two Tennesseans aspiring to be favorably considered by the Select Joint Commission on Reconstruction then reviewing the admission of Tennessee were David Patterson and Joseph S. Fowler.

2. In his speech "The Equal Rights of All," delivered 5 and 6 February, CS argued against the Reconstruction Committee's constitutional amendment (the apportionment amendment), which proposed that if a state denied suffrage to any citizen be-

cause of race, "all persons therein of such race or color shall be excluded from the basis of representation." CS declared that no state government could be considered "republican" if it excluded any "favored class" from the franchise: "What I ask especially is impartial suffrage, which is, of course, embraced in universal suffrage" (*Globe*, 39th Cong., 1st sess., 534, 673–87).

To Richard Henry Dana, Jr.

Senate Chamber 8th Feb. '66

My dear Dana,

I have never used the Prize Cases, except on one occasion, as an authority for the phrase "territorial civil war." I knew too much of Prize Law, not to know my ground.[1]

I have never said that states were "territories"; but I have said that, from the *necessity of the case*, as with territories, Congress must enter in & govern them until new govts. can be fashioned.[2] This view harmonizes with the other power coming from War.

There are still other grounds of jurisdiction, one of which is the guaranty clause, & the other is the 2nd clause in the Constitutional Amendment.[3] It is under the latter clause, that we have just decreed equality of *civil rights* every where in the U. States.[4] *A fortiori*, we may decree political rights.

The clouds lower at the White House.

Ever Yours,   Charles Sumner

ALS   MHi   (80/172, PCS)

1. Commenting on Henry J. Raymond's recent speech in the House of Representatives, 29 January 1866, urging prompt admission of rebel states (a speech CS had sent Dana), Dana wrote that "'Enemy's territory' in the meaning of Prize Law, in a civil war, is a *shifting line of bayonets*." No conquered property could be considered the enemy's and thus condemned by the conqueror (Boston, 5 February, 35/263, PCS).

2. Dana asserted that the Supreme Court had "*decided nothing* as to the political status of the rebel territory or its inhabitants. To attempt to make the decision subserve our purpose now, would be to pervert the truth."

3. In "The Equal Rights of All" CS had declared that the "guaranty clause" of the Constitution necessitated that a state which "sets aside 'the consent of the governed'—which imposes taxation without representation—which discards the principle of Equal Rights, and which lodges power exclusively with an Oligarchy, Aristocracy, Caste, or Monopoly, cannot be recognized as a 'Republican government,' according to the requirement of American Institutions" (*Globe*, 39th Cong., 1st sess., 675–76). Section 2 of the Thirteenth Amendment stated, "Congress shall have power to enforce this article by appropriate legislation."

4. The Civil Rights Bill granted such rights as making contracts and initiating lawsuits to all U.S. citizens except Native Americans, and empowered the U.S. government to enforce these rights. It passed the Senate 2 February, 33–12 (ibid., 606–7).

To Gerrit Smith

Senate Chamber 12th Feb. '66

My dear Mr Smith,

I hope you have sent copies of yr letter to every member of the two Houses, & especially the Senate.[1]

The measure will be defeated, I trust. To my mind it is the meanest & wickedest proposition ever brought into Congress. Its baseness is colossal.

I have already exposed it in my speech,[2] which I hope to send you; but I shall consider it again.

Ever Yours,   Charles Sumner

ALS NSyU (80/174, PCS)

1. Smith wrote CS 8 February 1866 from Peterboro, New York, thanking him for his "noble speech," "The Equal Rights of All," against the apportionment amendment. He informed CS that he had "taken the liberty to address a public letter to you" (35/326, PCS). In that letter, 5 February, Smith asked that the Senate refuse to ratify the House's vote for the apportionment amendment. Smith called the amendment a "Disgraceful, if not, indeed a fatal, blot on the Constitution," and a measure that would give Southern states "certain and absolute" governance of the freedmen (*New York Times*, 15 February 1866:2).

2. In "The Equal Rights of All" CS told Congress that the apportionment amendment would be "a present renunciation of all power under the Constitution to apply the remedy for a grievous wrong, when the remedy, even according to your own recent example, is actually in your hands." It would also "hand over wards and allies, through whom the Republic has been saved, and therefore our saviors, to the control of vindictive enemies to be taxed and governed without their consent; and this you will do for a consideration 'nominated in the bond,' by virtue of which men may do a great wrong, provided they will submit as a *quid pro quo* to a proportionate abridgment of political power" (*Globe*, 39th Cong., 1st sess., 674).

To Horatio Woodman

Washington 18th March '66

My dear Woodman,

The power of Atty from Mr & Mrs H.[*astings*] is to settle the estate of G[*eorge*] S[*umner*] & to make any needful conveyances. I think it is complete. It is in the hands of F. V. Balch, my old secy, & atty.[1] I will ask him to hand it to you.

My mother is very feeble. I think Dr John Homans,[2] who is her attending physician could probably take her acknowledgment.

I am glad to know that Andrew agrees with me in opposing the Amendment.[3] I know that I am right. People will sometime or other thank me for having resisted it. Many will think it the best thing of my life.

Ever yours,   Charles Sumner

ALS MHi (80/212, PCS)

1. Horatio Woodman (1821–79), a Boston lawyer, and Francis V. Balch (1839–98) handled legal affairs for the Sumner family (Balch to CS, 8 January, 24 March 1866, 35/100, 209, PCS).

2. John Homans (1793–1868) sent CS reports from Boston on his mother's condition every week or ten days (ibid., reels 35 and 36, passim.).

3. The Senate defeated the apportionment amendment 9 March. Woodman did not mention John Andrew in his letter of 10 March (Boston, 35/653), but he agreed with CS that passage of the amendment would have meant that Southern states could frame a constitution denying suffrage to blacks.

To the Duchess of Argyll

Washington 3d April '66

My dear Duchess,

This morng just before the courier leaves for the packet I have yr good letter of 20th March. I was sure how you would be, but I am glad to know it under yr hand.

These are trying days for us. I am more anxious now than during the war. The animal passions of the Nation aided the rally then. Now the appeal is to the intelligence, & to the moral & religious sentiments. How strangely we are misrepresented in the *Times*.[1] I read it always, & find nothing true in its portraiture of our affairs.

Believe me, the people are with Congress. When it is considered, that the Presdt has such an amazing part, it is extraordinary to see how the conscience of the masses has stood firm. Congress is misrepresented in England. I speak of the Lower House now. In my opinion it is the best that has ever been since the beginning of our govt. It is full of talent & is governed by patriotic purpose. There is no personal or party ambition, which prompts its course. It is to save the country, that it takes its present responsibilities.

You say "Why not urge the Abolition of the Black Codes"?[2] This I have done from the beginning. There are several speeches of mine, which you have never seen, three years ago, against any exclusion of witnesses on account of color; also an elaborate report. A partial measure I carried. Since the cessation of hostilities this subject has occupied me constantly. In my speech at Worcester I dwelt on the Black Codes; then again in a speech early this session. At last we passed a Bill known as the Civil Rights Bill. It went through both Houses by unprecedented majorities. The Presdt. refuses to sign it. By our Constitution it requires a vote of ⅔ds to pass it over his Veto. It is still uncertain, if we can command this large vote. The division will be very close. The loss of this Bill will be a terrible calamity. It leaves the new crop of Black Laws in full force & gives to the old masters a new letter of license to do any thing with the freedman short of making him a chattel. A new serfdom may be substituted, & this is their cruel purpose.

But after most careful consideration I see no substantial protection for the freedman except in the franchise. He must have this (1) for his own protection (2) for the protection of the white Unionist & (3) for the peace of the country. We put the musket in his hands, because it was necessary. For the same reason we must give him the franchise. Unionists from the South tell me that unless this is done they will be defenceless. And here is the necessity for the universality of the suffrage. Every vote is needed to counter-balance the rebels.

It is very sad that we should be tried in this way. For our country it is an incalculable calamity. Nobody can yet see the end. Congress will not yield. The Presdt. is angry & brutal. Seward is the Marplot. In the cabinet, on the question of the last Veto, there were 4 against it to 3 for it; so even there among his immediate advisers the Presdt. is left in a minority. Stanton reviewed at length the Bill, section by section, in the cabinet & pronounced it an excellent & safe bill every way from beginning to end. But the Veto Message was already prepared & an hour later was sent to Congress.[3]

You hear that I do not bear contradiction.[4] Perhaps not. I try to bear every thing. But my conscience & feelings are sometimes moved, so that I may show impatience. It is hard to meet all these exigencies with calmness. I hope not to fail.

I despair of the Presdt. He is no Moses, but a Pharoah to the colored race, & they now regard him so. He has all the narrowness & ignorance of a certain class of whites, who have always looked upon the colored race as out of the pale of Humanity.

I am glad to hear what you write of yr son.[5] Sir Frederick Bruce & myself sometimes talk of the prospect of seeing him here. I fear he will find us much preoccupied; but it will be a good experience for him. Seward will be kind to him. I wish he would let me know at once when he reaches New Orleans.—I am sorry that yr mother has suffered again. Give her my kindest regards. And God bless you!

Ever Sincerely Yours,   Charles Sumner

Fenianism[6] is to us only a noisy shadow, without reality. I never saw a Fenian.

My excellent friend Schleiden is much mistaken in his present views of our affairs.[7] He follows the London *Times*.

ALS   CSmH   (80/229, PCS)

1. In a letter from the U.S. (12 March 1866:12) the London *Times* correspondent compared Johnson to William Pitt the Younger in that both encountered legislative "antagonism" yet enjoyed popular support. Johnson's Reconstruction policy was described as "sound and self-consistent." Joel Cook (1842–1910), financial editor of the Philadelphia *Public Ledger and Times*, was probably the *Times* American correspondent in the late 1860s.

2. In her letter from London (20 March, 35/716, PCS) the duchess wrote, "I do not understand the *degree* of Importance you attach to Negro Franchise, when it seems to us from old experience that it may be worth very little to such an entirely dependent class as they must be,—and the political awkwardness of forcing it on the South *before* the North gives it, seems very great. Why not urge the abolition of the black Codes—the equal rights in Courts of Law, as the great necessity?"

3. Johnson returned the Civil Rights Bill to the Senate on 27 March, declining to sign it. In his veto message the president criticized the bill because it would "establish, for the security of the colored race, safeguards which go infinitely beyond any that the General Government has ever provided for the white race" and in fact favored the black race (*Globe*, 39th Cong., 1st sess., 1679–81).

4. In his Washington's Birthday address Johnson denounced congressional Radicals. He stated, "I look upon them . . . as much opposed to the fundamental principles of this Government, and believe they are as much laboring to prevent or destroy them as were the men who fought against us." When asked to be specific, Johnson named Stevens, CS, and Wendell Phillips (*New York Tribune*, 24 February 1866:4). Characterizing Johnson's speech as "that savage outbreak of Feb. 22," the duchess wrote on 20 March, "I am told by some that my Friend does not bear contradiction calmly. If so he has gone thro' some fierce discipline."

5. The Duchess's eldest son, the marquess of Lorne, was then traveling in the West Indies.

6. The Fenians were a secret Irish nationalistic movement active in Ireland, Britain, and the U.S., planning a rising against British rule. Recently, prompted by the British suspension of the Habeas Corpus Act in Ireland, rumored raids into Canada by New York–based Fenians had caused Canada to call out troops in defense (*New York Times*, 10 March 1866:4, 11 March 1866:5; *British Documents*, part 1, series C, 3:125–29.

7. The duchess wrote she had recently met Rudolph Schleiden (1815–95), Hanseatic League minister to the U.S., 1853–64.

To the Duchess of Argyll

Washington 9th April '66

My dear Duchess,

I forgot to say last week that Mrs Sprague & her sister [*Janet Chase*], daughters of Chief Justice Chase, have sailed for England. They are young & clever. I have given them a letter to you. I think they can tell you much about affairs here that will interest you. Mr Sprague is a senator & the youngest we have. He is detained here by public duties.

The Act securing Civil Rights has been carried over the Presdt's Veto by the ⅔ds vote required by the Constitution.[1] You will infer from this vote how strong our cause is in Congress. The Presdt. is supported by the old Democrats & half a dozen back-sliders of our party. That he should obtain so few recruits shows how objectionable his policy is. Under ordinary circumstances his immense patronage, & the prestige of his position would counterbalance large numbers in Congress.

What a calamity is such a President! I have made no allusion to him any where since last December. Then I let fall the word, which caused such sensation, that his message about the condition of the rebel states was "a white-washing doct."[2] I said this purposely in order to bring home to the public mind the character of this message & to discredit it. I had made up my mind then that his course would be hostile to us, & that he ought to be unmasked. Our friends generally still deluded themselves with an idea that our differences might be bridged over. My full conversation with him on my arrival had satisfied me that this was impossible. I found him stolid, impenetrable, & utterly without sympathy with the freedman.

You must not believe of me all that newspapers say.[3] I see so much that is absolutely false in fact or idea about me, that I despair of the truth being generally known. I shall persevere,—whatever may be said. But I fear that I am at times impatient. It is sometimes said that I am "impervious" & "dogmatic" in debate. Perhaps so. I try not to be. But at times the way seems to me so clear, that I cannot but press forward earnestly. I make these remarks in reply to yr kind hint. So far as the Presdt. is concerned, I do not need it. I have never for one moment thought of replying to him. It may be my duty to discuss again his policy; but I shall make no allusions to any thing he has said about me.

Our future is uncertain. There is a dead-lock, & nobody can yet see the way out of it.

I hope yr Mother is better. Remember me to her kindly. Why does not Sir John Acton make a mark in Parlt? I thought he would. I wish you would ask him to send me his study on Human Sacrifices by the Romans.[4] I have Ld [*Philip Henry*] Stanhope's pamphlet & should like his. Good bye! God bless you.

Ever Sincerely Yours,   Charles Sumner

ALS CSmH (80/245, PCS)

1. The vote on 6 April 1866 was 33–15 (*Globe*, 39th Cong., 1st sess., 1809).

2. CS stated that Johnson's message on the condition of the Southern states was similar to "the white washing message of Franklin Pierce with regard to the enormities in Kansas" (ibid., 19 December 1865, 79).

3. Commenting on Americans' reaction to Johnson's 19 February veto of the Freedmen's Bureau Bill, the London *Times*'s American correspondent wrote that people feared the "evils and disasters" of the Civil War would continue "if the policy of Mr. Sumner and his followers is to prevail" (6 March 1866:5).

4. "Human Sacrifice" (privately printed, London, 1863) by John Acton (1834–1902), historian and moralist.

To Edward Atkinson

Senate Chamber 10th April '66

My dear Sir,

I fear I erred in taking the liberty I did. I sent to you because you were the only person with whom I occasionally corresponded who was connected with the Nation & I felt sure of yr candor.[1] Of course, I had no purpose of controversy. I have no time for it.

I know something of misrepresentation by the press. Probably no person in our country has ever had so much of it. I am very little touched by it. If I were, my life would be sorry enough. But it is very rarely that I have read any thing about myself, which to my mind, & I may add to that of others, was more absolutely in the nature of misrepresentation—&, as the French would say, *brutalement* so, than the article to which I refer in the Nation. I call it a misrepresentation, positive, open & bare-faced. Some two months later there was an apology, for which there should have been no occasion.[2] If you look at the article you will see that I do not characterize it too strongly.

I said of a doct that it was "whitewashing" & then added that I intended no impeachment of the "honesty" or "patriotism" of the Presdt. Of course I had a write to give my own definition, & yet in the face of this definition this paper arraigns me for charging the Presdt. with what I plainly said I did not charge him with. Curiously another article in the same paper called the message "rose-colored."[3] What is the difference between this & "white-washing"?—Others at the time found in the article on me a personal vindictiveness. For what I am at a loss to understand. Of course the Spectator never could have admitted an article so coarsely false.[4] So it seems to me. But I write too much. Pardon me. It is yr letter that tempted me.

Very faithfully Yours, Charles Sumner

ALS MHi (80/251, PCS)

1. In an editorial, "Mr. Sumner on Whitewashing," the *Nation* (28 December 1865:806–7) criticized CS's use of the word *whitewashing* in his 19 December remarks on the president. Stating that the word could be defined only as connoting "a charge of moral turpitude," the *Nation* characterized CS's remark as "unseemly" and unjustified. In his letter of 9 April 1866 from Boston (36/129, PCS) Atkinson responded to articles from the *Nation* that CS sent him periodically with marginal comments. Atkinson wrote he failed to see anything "*brutal*" (a term CS had used) in the *Nation*'s "whitewashing" article. Atkinson assured CS that the *Nation*'s editors (E. L. Godkin, 1831–1902, and Wendell P. Garrison) had no "personal animosity" to him; they considered him "one of the great leaders of the party of freedom."

2. The *Nation* (15 February 1866:194) stated it would stand by its interpretation of the meaning of *whitewashing*, but since CS had denied he intended to impugn Johnson, "we are bound to acquit him of all blame in the matter except for carelessness, or lack of judgment."

3. In another editorial, 28 December 1865:806, the *Nation* stated, "This rose-colored view from the White House has been applauded and defended by all newspapers and politicians whose business it is to sneeze when the President takes snuff."

4. In his letter Atkinson noted that he and other founders of the *Nation* had modeled it after the London *Spectator*.

To Theodore Tilton
private

Senate Chamber 12th April '66

Dear Mr Tilton,

I am sorry you have gone home—at least without giving me the promised opportunity of conversing with you.[1] Perhaps, I might have communicated something about public affairs. At all events, I flatter myself had you known my habits more accurately you would not have held me up as "rhetorician"—"elaborating sentences before delivery."[2]

It so happens that since you have been here, I have spoken on nearly every important question, & on at least two what I said had some weight in determining the result. There are speeches in the *Globe* of 2 or 3 columns during this period. Now not one word of any thing I said was "elaborated before delivery." You have it there just as it came to me at the time. Of course I had studied the question, as I study every question before the Senate.

There are speeches for the Senate, & speeches for the country; — different in character, &, in preparation. If, in making a speech intended for the country, I give to it that Study, without which such a speech must fail, I do not think that my whole senatorial life should be described as that of a "rhetorician." If there is any person in the Senate who works more hours on public business than I do, with less relaxation or vacation, I do not know him.

But pardon me. I write this for *yr private eye*. I am a worker, & with me life is earnest. Therefore,——but I stop. I have said too much. Sometime or other, perhaps, you will think better of me. But I shall always think well of you

Ever sincerely Yours,   Charles Sumner

ALS NBu (80/255, PCS)

1. Tilton replied he had not seen CS when visiting Washington because he deemed the senator "too *busy* to talk to a man who had no *business*" (New York, 16 April 1866, 36/183, PCS).

2. In his "Editorial Correspondence" from Washington in the New York *Independent* (12 April 1866:4), Tilton speculated on the real leader of the Senate. Although "properly speaking, no one" led the Senate, Tilton wrote that "Fessenden has more continuous influence in the Senate than belongs to any other senator" and praised his integrity, debating ability, and range of knowledge. "Sumner is the rhetorician of Congress. . . . He elaborates his sentences with great diligence before delivery, and accordingly his speeches tell less on the Senate than on the country." In his letter of 16 April Tilton professed regret that his remark "made in the hurry of letter-writing" had offended CS. CS had "no warmer friend" than himself.

To William H. Claflin

Senate Chamber 4th May '66

My dear Lieut.,

If Mass speaks it must be for those principles which are essential to the peace & stability of the Republic. The report of the Reconstruction Comttee. contains no such principles. It is grossly inadequate to the occasion.[1]

But there is nothing in it positively offensive, as in the Constitutional Amendment which I helped defeat. How lucky that defeat! Who is there now to regret it? And yet you do not forget how I was abused.[2]

It is said the Presdt. will veto the Colorado Bill.[3] What madness to pass such a bill & brave such a veto, where Congress is in the wrong! Fessenden, Grimes & myself—to say nothing of others—will sustain the veto, when it comes. Thus the politicians, who engineered Colorado, will fail in their purposes, while they injure their influence inconceivably in sustaining the just cause with regard to the rebel states. How can they insist upon impartial suffrage in any rebel state when they refused to require it in a state over which at the moment they had jurisdiction? Alas! alas! Poor short-sighted man!

Follow principles. Do this & you cannot err. Above all keep Mass. firm for justice.

Ever Yours,   Charles Sumner

ALS   OFH   (80/294, PCS)

1. On 30 April 1866 Thaddeus Stevens introduced the Reconstruction Committee's proposed constitutional amendment. Besides (a) declaring that all persons born in the U.S. were citizens and (b) repudiating any Confederate debt, the amendment stated that the basis of representation would be reduced in a state if it denied suffrage to any citizens (*Globe*, 39th Cong., 1st sess., 2286; U.S. House of Representatives, Joint Select Committee on Reconstruction, *Report of the Joint Select Committee on Reconstruction*, House Report no. 30, 1866, part 1: 22, serial set 1273). Claflin wrote CS 1 May to inform him of plans for a Massachusetts meeting to endorse the amendment and inquired if such an endorsement would be in direct opposition to CS's stand. Claflin himself supported the amendment as the only legislation possible this session, but he wrote CS that an endorsement meeting had been delayed in order to "learn your views, as to the proper course to pursue" (Boston, 36/251, PCS).

2. After the defeat of the apportionment amendment, the *Boston Daily Advertiser* (12 March 1866:2) criticized CS's opposition to it because, the *Advertiser* alleged, such opposition only made way for another amendment even more repugnant to the Radicals. In a letter to the *Advertiser* of 15 March (Wks, 13:375–76), CS stated that he had opposed the amendment not because, as the *Advertiser* stated, "'it fell short of what was needed,'" but because it would have "carried into the Constitution by express words the idea of inequality of rights." Second, wrote CS, the amendment would have "lent the sanction of the Constitution to a wholesale disfranchisement on account of race or color."

3. CS's attempts to insert a passage guaranteeing universal suffrage in the bill to admit Colorado as a state were defeated, and the bill passed the Senate 19–13 on 25 April, with CS dissenting (*Globe*, 39th Cong., 1st sess., 2180). Johnson vetoed it 15 May and the bill was postponed.

To John Bright

private

Washington 21st. May '66

My dear Bright,

I was very glad to hear from you & to find you so cheerful. Of course I note day by day all that you say & do. I see how you are the selected mark.[1] À *la bonne heure!* That will not hurt. I speak from a little experience of my own.

I am sure that there will be no tranquility or security here until complete justice is rendered to the negro. Perhaps your question is not so urgent, yet I confess I can see nothing but agitation & unrest until the franchise is extended. It seems to me that you consent to accept a very small installment.

Our dead-lock continues with no chance of relief. The people sustain Congress, which stands firm. But there is no hint that the Presdt. will give way. He is indocile, obstinate, perverse, impenetrable, & hates the education & civilization of New England. Seward encourages him. McCulloch is bitterly with him. Dennison sometimes with him & sometimes against him. Wells is with him. Stanton, [*James*] Harlan &

[*James*] Speed are against his policy. So that his cabinet is nearly equally divided. When I speak of the opinions of these men, I speak according to my personal knowledge from conversation with each of them. I do not think that they are always frank with the Presdt.

Seward is rash & visionary, with a most wonderful want of common sense. For instance, only a week ago he told me that he had drawn a message for the Presdt., asking for proceedings *vs.* Equador, because this puny Republic had failed to pay the first installment on an award of our claims, & that he had had a Bill drawn, which he hoped I would report, giving to the Presdt. the authority to make reprisals. I made a mild protest at the time, shrugged my shoulders & said—"If we must do this thing, let us take one of our size." Since then the message has been recd. & is now before my committee, where it is safe enough. Meanwhile I have ascertained the sum for which war was to be waged. The award was for $94,799, payable in 9 installments, the first installment due Feb. 17th 1866 being $10,533, for which we were to launch the bolt. Was there ever an enterprize more ridiculous.[2] Yr Don Pacifico case was nothing to it.

On Protection & Free Trade there does not seem to be any general feeling. This question will be settled for some time by the necessities of our position without much reference to principles. My own people, originally strong protectionists, are silent now. It is Pennsylvania which is clamorous, & the balance of parties in this important State makes the question one of political power.

I read the *Times* constantly. The perversions of its correspondant about our affairs are as great now as during the war, only in a different way. Nothing he says is true. I never see my own name without saying "what false hood."[3] The correspondant writes like a Presidential hireling.

I am pained to see that you are not well. I hope you will tell me that you are better. Curiously, I too have fallen into the Dr's hands. He finds my brain & nervous system over-tasked & suffering from my original injuries as a predisposing cause. I long for rest, & yet every day I grind in my mill. Good bye! Let me hear from you soon.

Ever sincerely Yours, Charles Sumner

ALS   GBL   (80/309, PCS)

1. On 12 March 1866 Gladstone, leader of the House of Commons, introduced a bill to reduce the property qualifications for suffrage in Britain, and Bright spoke in favor of this bill. The London *Times* criticized Bright's speeches as "senseless railing"

and chastised Bright for being "absolutely single-minded" in his efforts to gain suffrage for Britain's working class (6 April 1866:6; 25 April 1866:11).

2. Johnson's message on Ecuador on 9 May was sent to the Senate on 15 May, at which time CS moved that the request be forwarded to the Senate Foreign Relations Committee (*Globe*, 39th Cong., 1st sess., 2609). Bright responded in his letter of 3 July that CS's account of Seward and "the small Republic" was "something wonderful." He wrote that he had not hitherto agreed with Cobden's unfavorable judgment of Seward, "but I now begin to think he was right" (Rochdale, 36/505, PCS).

3. The London *Times*'s American correspondent wrote (30 April 1866:10) that Democrats throughout the U.S. were in the ascendancy and Republicans were losing influence. Earlier, the correspondent stated, regarding public criticism of Johnson's veto of the Civil Rights Bill, that the people "have still the tremendous bitterness stirred up by the war ready to the hands of skillful politicians, and Mr. Sumner and his party have proved themselves expert in playing upon them" (23 April 1866:9).

To Relief Jacob Sumner

Washington 26th May '66

My dearest Mother,

The Dr writes me that you are not so well.[1] I trust that this is only for a day, & as I have not heard from him since, I am encouraged to think so.

Something has been said of my not being very well, & that you may not have any concern about me, I write that I am somewhat overworked, but there is nothing serious.

Mr Balch wrote me that he had seen you on business.[2] You can rely on him absolutely. He is of excellent judgment & perfect integrity.

I wish I had good news to send you about public affairs. The President is obstinate & perverse. Nobody can see how this difference between him & Congress will end.

Good bye! God bless you always.

Ever yr affectionate   Charles—

ALS   MH-H   (64/456, PCS)

1. Two recent bulletins from John Homans informed CS that Mrs. Sumner was gradually growing weaker "both in body and mind" (20 and 24 May 1866, 36/331, 357, PCS).

2. Balch sent CS on 8 May an accounting of CS's holdings in bonds and treasury notes and described a recent visit with Mrs. Sumner to "make out her income return" (Boston, 36/291).

To George Bancroft

Senate Chamber 30th May '66

My dear Bancroft,

At last our little Bill, the curb of rail-ways, has passed the Senate; with certain amendments, which do not touch N. Jersey, but which I hope the House will refuse to accept. It has been contested as if it were rebellion. On the last day of the debate Cowen of Penn. said that the bill was the most important of all the important bills of this Congress.[1]

I enjoyed yr correspondance with Ld Russell, which was conclusive.[2] There was a later letter sometime in '64, addressed to Mason, which was very impertinent in its assertion of our Union being "late."

I trust you will be content with what we have done for free commerce between the states.

Ever yours,   Charles Sumner

ALS   NICO   (80/320, PCS)

1. Bancroft wrote CS on 7 May 1866, praising him for his "consistency" in voting against the admission of Colorado. He asked CS about the status of a bill providing for federal regulation of interstate commerce, advising CS to sponsor it: "it is just such a measure that you need, to show those who count, that you can frame & [press?] & carry a business measure" (New York, 36/284, PCS). On 29 May the Senate approved the bill, 22–19, but an amendment gave each state the authority to forbid the building of any new railroad or connection within its boundaries. Edgar Cowan (1815–85; U.S. senator [Rep., Pa.], 1861–67) argued against the bill as illegal interference by the federal government (Globe, 39th Cong., 1st sess., 2870–76).

2. In a letter to Adams of 23 March Bancroft defended his assertions that the British had failed to support the North in the Civil War. Bancroft stated that Lord Russell had indeed referred to the U.S. in 1861 as "the late Union." The pertinent letters and Bancroft's supporting documents were published in the New York Times (7 May 1866:4–5).

To the Duchess of Argyll

Washington 4th June '66

My dear Duchess,

I hear this morning through Mr Thompson that Lorne is in Canada, just in season to witness the puncture of Fenianism.[1] I did not see so much of Mr Thompson as I desired; but he impressed me favorably. I have an excellent letter from him this morning on the metric system. I am chairman of a special Committee of the Senate on this subject &

hope to go as far at least as you have done. Yr Duke made an excellent speech when it was under consideration in the Lords.[2]

I infer from yr letter, that you do not quite understand my position.[3] Of course I am against the inequality of representation, which is a relic of Slavery, & am ready to do any thing to repair this evil. The measure which I opposed was an attempt, which, while repairing this, actually grafted onto the text of the Constitution inequality & caste on account of color, & tied the hands of Congress against any exercise of power to remove it. But that measure was defeated—after passing the House by a large vote. Of course, on this occasion I took a great responsibility, but I could not do otherwise.

I do not think you feel the *necessity*, as I do, of the colored vote, not only for the protection of the freedmen, but of the white unionists. Without it I see small chance of repose or even ordinary security.

I am glad that yr Mother is doing well. I know the interest with which she must follow our affairs, especially as they concern the welfare of the race for which she has done so much.—Europe is on the verge of great events.[4] I am glad that my country cannot be drawn into that vortex.

Ever sincerely yours,   Charles Sumner

I enjoyed Gladstone's speech & always enjoy Ld Russell, except when vindicating his policy towards us.[5] On other things I like to praise him.

ALS   CSmH   (80/333, PCS)

1. Henry Yates Thompson (1838–1928), a book collector from Liverpool, was then touring North America. Recently, bands of Irish revolutionaries had attemped raids from the U.S. into Canada near Niagara, but most had been arrested or disarmed by both U.S. and Canadian authorities (*New York Times*, 4 June 1866:1).

2. CS had been named chair of the Select Committee on Coins and Weights and Measures, 23 May 1866 (*Globe*, 39th Cong., 1st sess., 2760). The duke of Argyll spoke in favor of a dual system of measurement 21 July 1864 (*Hansard's Parliamentary Debates*, 3rd series, 176:1784–85).

3. In her letter of 17 May the duchess wrote, "Tho' I have read your speech I cannot enter into your reasons against the proposal to change the counting of the South. It seems to me quite preposterous to continue the ⅗ counting, & that the South must know it is unreasonable. But for the sake of the Negroes themselves I cannot wish Negro Suffrage forced on—. . . Their social position is the thing to be most anxious about, and I cannot think the suffrage wd. help them, socially" (Kensington, 36/321, PCS).

4. As war among Prussia, Austria, and Italy threatened, Britain, France, and Prussia planned an international congress to arbitrate the differences (*New York Times*, 4 June 1866:8).

5. Speaking for the Reform Bill on 27 April Gladstone stated that Lord Russell's name had been associated for forty years "with every measure of beneficent legislation" (*Hansard's Parliamentary Debates*, 3rd series, 183:128–29). Commenting on Gladstone's speech, the duchess had written CS that it "was very fine," but "I fear you wd not much care" for Gladstone's praise of Russell.

To Wendell Phillips
private

Senate Chamber 7th June '66

My dear Phillips,

I am touched by yr beautiul note, but am glad to let you know that I am much better than I was some weeks ago. I have been disturbed in my condition. Powerful medicines & comparative repose—such as I can find in a certain abstinence from some of my labors—seem to have had an influence.

I am sorry to let this debate pass without taking part in it.[1] There are things I wish to say. I hope to find another opportunity before the session comes to an end.

I shall never vote to receive any State until it establishes impartial suffrage or this is established by Congress. Meanwhile I am willing to do other things which do not tie our hands for the future.

I do not despair. Important men from N.C. are here to know our real *ultimatum*. I have told them that it is impartial suffrage, & that if their Convention now in session will establish this, I will move the admission of their senators.[2] They think seriously of it. If others would speak positively I think they could be brought to the point.

I told them that the State which led in this act of justice would have at once the favor of the country, political, commercial & social. "Now is yr chance" said I; "put yr State at the head of the line."—I do not despair. Ten men thoroughly devoted to the idea of impartial suffrage & not impressed by timid counsels, could press it through Congress—as the Civil Rights Bill was pressed. But in some form or other it shall be done. Such is my vow. Thanks & God bless you.

Ever sincerely Yours,   Charles Sumner

ALS   MH-H   (64/462, PCS)

1. The Senate debated the joint resolution on Reconstruction (the Fourteenth Amendment) on 7 and 8 June 1866 (*Globe*, 39th Cong., 1st sess., 3010–11; 3026–

42). On 8 June CS voted in favor of an amendment to the resolution and the resolution itself, but he did not speak.

2. According to Roberta Sue Alexander, North Carolina delegates convening in Raleigh in May 1866 to draw up laws governing freedmen were more liberal than those in the preceding convention (*North Carolina Faces the Freedmen* [1985], 50–51).

To Theodore Tilton
private

Senate Chamber
6th [7*th*] June '66

Dear Mr Tilton,

My argt. is that whatever Congress was able to do for Civil Rights it can do for Political Rights.[1] To my mind the argt. is stronger, if possible, for the latter than the former. It is enough to say that it is as strong in one case as in the other. Here I stand, & with me is the Chief Justice, who accepts this conclusion conditionally. So also do all the best Anti-Slavery lawyers of the country. Thinking so, & seeing this road open, I deem it my duty to press Congress to try it. I do not despair. If not this year, then next year or some other year this will be done.

I see little chance except through the action of Congress in some form or other. The Veto was used against the Civil Rights Bill & failed. If Congress could pass a Bill establishing impartial suffrage, it would pave the way at least for triumph. As an old soldier, always studious of my duty, I claim a certain experience, which gives me sometimes an advantage over a fresh recruit. My experience admonishes me not to despair; & it teaches me still further to carry our flag loftily & confidently. Let me assure you it shall not drop while I bear it. Pardon me & believe me

Ever sincerely Yours,   Charles Sumner

ALS NBu (80/344, PCS)
Enc: article from the New York *Independent* 7 June 1866:4.

1. The clipping attached to CS's letter criticized his proposal for universal suffrage. The article stated, "Few men, we presume, even among the radical members of Congress, believe that such a law would be constitutional," and argued that even if a bill passed Congress, Johnson would veto it.

To George S. Boutwell

Boston 15th [*16*] June '66
Saturday

My dear Govr.

I do not see that my bill to revise the statutes has been reported from yr Comtee. Pray give your excellent Chairman a hint. I should be very sorry to have it lost when it has got so far on the road. For 15 years I have worked at that. Do give it a helping hand.[1]

I reached home in season to be with my mother during her last hours.[2] I think that my own health is better. I was able to see in New York my old Paris physician, Dr Brown-Séquard.

I do not expect to be in Washington until the end of next week. Meanwhile I watch yr doings with something more than interest.[3]

Sincerely Yours,   Charles Sumner

ALS   MWA   (80/357, PCS)

1. Boutwell replied from Washington on 17 June 1866 (36/465, PCS) that the committee would probably "report your bill" in the next two weeks. When Frederick E. Woodbridge (in the absence of Judiciary Committee Chairman James F. Wilson) brought up the bill on 22 June, it passed the House (*Globe*, 39th Cong., 1st sess., 3360).

2. Relief Sumner died 15 June.

3. Boutwell observed that there had never been more "uncertainty" in the House than on the bills for readmission of rebel states: "We must never permit the passage of an act pledging the country to the admission of rebel states when amendments are ratified. Better that Tennessee be admitted at once; which, however, I hope will not happen."

To Henry W. Longfellow

New York 24th June '66
Sunday.

Dear Longfellow,

I cannot forbear expressing my anxiety about yr health.[1] The symptoms which you mentioned haunt me. The Bromide of potassium will be certain to secure sleep, &, I think it will act favorably on the other symptoms. But you should take more of it.

I wish you could see Dr Brown-Sequard. He expects to be at the Tremont House in Boston about 2nd July, in search of cooler weather. He is very sensitive to the heat.

I longed, before I left,—for a long talk with you about myself; but the moment was not propitious. When we meet again, I may have something to tell you;[2] & certainly I shall have much on which to seek yr communion. I have come to an epoch in my life. My mother is dead. I have a moderate competency. What next?——

Meanwhile I hurry to my duties nearer to the sun. When you read this note I shall be in Washington.

Good bye!

Ever & ever Yours,   Charles Sumner

ALS   MH-H   (80/363, PCS)

1. Longfellow wrote CS 4 July 1866 that he should not worry, "I am better now, and sleep like a top" (Cambridge, 80/377, PCS).

2. Longfellow replied that he too hoped "to discuss with you the future, and what you are to do in it." CS indirectly mentions here, for the first time, his thoughts of marrying Alice Mason Hooper (1838–1913), widow of William Sturgis Hooper and daughter-in-law of Samuel Hooper.

To Richard Henry Dana, Jr.

Senate Chamber 27th June '66

My dear Dana,

The sheets of yr notes have not yet come to hand. I trust you will not forget them.

I was sorry that our last interview was so hurried. I never believed that you & I would be on opposite sides, although at one time you seemed to think so. I knew my own purposes & I was persuaded that in the end you must have substantially the same. We might differ in methods; but I was sure that you, like myself, would seek the security & repose of the govt. on the fundamental principles of justice. My anticipations have not be disappointed; but I was happy in the assurance that you also recognized a substantial agreement.

My considerable experience teaches me candor & indisposes me more & more to personal controversy. I hope never to have a personal question again. I will not, if I can prevent it. It is enough for me to state argts. & conclusions in public & there to rest.

But I do not intend a homily, & I close at once by wishing you & Mrs Dana a pleasant voyage & a happy tour[1] Good-bye! & believe me, dear Dana,

Sincerely Yours,   Charles Sumner

ALS   MHi   (80/369, PCS)

1. Dana and his wife, Sarah Watson Dana, sailed for England in early July (Long-fellow to CS, 4 July 1866, 80/377, PCS). After Dana returned, he resigned as U.S. district attorney because he found himself "unable to accord that sympathy and co-operation" necessary to carry out the president's Reconstruction policies (letter of resignation, 29 September, quoted in Charles Francis Adams, *Richard Henry Dana* [1891], 2:336).

To James T. Fields

Senate Chamber 7th July '66

My dear Fields,

I am now more than ever disposed to prepare a complete & revised edition of my speeches in some 5, 6 or 7 vols. When I mentioned this before you thought the time not propitious.

How is the time now? Should the edition be like L & B's edition of Burke[1]—large 12 mo?—or 8 vo ?

How can this be accomplished? And at what expense?[2]

Ever Yours,   Charles Sumner

ALS   CSmH   (80/379, PCS)

1. Edmund Burke, *Miscellaneous Works*, five volumes (1851), published by Little and Brown.
2. No response from Fields has been recovered. According to Donald, Fields again told CS the time was "not propitious" (DD, 2:329). Ticknor and Fields did not publish a volume of CS's speeches.

To Moncure D. Conway
private

Washington 30th July—[1866]

Dear Mr Conway,

If I have not written to you before it was because my engagements left me no time, & now that Congress has closed I can do little more than make my apologies.

I thank you for yr vigilant testimony to the good cause,[1] which has suffered infinitely, first through the terrible tergiversation of the President, & secondly, through the imbecility of Congress, which shrank from a contest on principle. If Congress had willed it we could have carried a bill for *political* rights as well as for *civil* rights, & on precisely the same argument—that it was needful in the enforcement of the prohibition of Slavery. I tried hard, but could not bring Congress to this duty.[2] But I do not give it up.

The Presdt. is singularly reticent: but his prejudices are strong. With Seward as counsellor nobody can tell what he will forbear. His policy has been arrested by Congress; but this has been by a dead-lock, rather than by establishing a contrary system. Meanwhile all true unionists from the South testify alike. Unless something is done they will be constrained to leave their homes. On this the testimony is concurring, whether from Texas or N. Carolina. Govr. Hamilton has left Texas[3]— but cannot return. Other Unionists are following his example.

I have succeeded during this session, in creating a commission for the revision & consolidation of the statutes of the U.S. I have also carried through the Senate, bills, that had already passed the House, for the introduction of the metric system of weights & measures.[4] Add to these I stopped in the Senate that bad Banks Bill repealing our Neutrality Statute, after it had passed the House *unanimously*.[5] These are incidents of the session which I mention with personal satisfaction. And now for the future! God is with us. I shall fight the battle to the end. You will also

Ever sincerely Yours, Charles Sumner

I leave for Boston tomorrow where I shall be glad to hear from you

---

ALS   NNCB   (80/404, PCS)

1. Moncure D. Conway (1832–1907), a former abolitionist clergyman now preaching and writing in England, wrote CS from London 2 May 1866, "We are all rejoicing over the grand success of Congress in the Civil Rights matter." He asked CS for more news on rights for blacks and hoped rumors he had heard that Johnson would "relent" were true (36/260, PCS).

2. On 21 July CS argued that Tennessee's constitution was not "republican in form" since it denied suffrage to blacks. On similar grounds, he protested the admission of Nebraska 27 July. The Senate voted to admit both states into the Union with CS voting against in both instances (*Globe*, 39th Cong., 1st sess., 3997–98, 4007; 4207, 4222).

3. Andrew J. Hamilton had sided with Republican critics of Johnson. By order of the president, Hamilton was relieved of his duties (Henry Stanbery, acting secretary of state, to Hamilton, 11 August, *New York Times*, 22 August 1866:2).

4. The Senate and House approved the final bill to appoint a commission to revise and consolidate all U.S. statutes on 25 June, but CS apparently took no part in the public deliberations (*Globe*, 39th Cong., 1st sess., 3382). He did seek to confer with Seward, however, on the commission appointments (CS to Seward, 28 June, 80/372). CS spoke in favor of the metric system 27 July (*Globe*, 39th Cong., 1st sess., 4217–19).

5. The Banks bill, which passed the House 26 July, sought to modify penalties for U.S. residents or citizens engaged within the U.S. in assisting a foreign power against another foreign power and to permit U.S. citizens to sell ships to belligerents in any war in which the U.S. did not take part. It was referred, by motion of CS, to the Senate Foreign Relations Committee 27 July (*Globe*, 39th Cong., 1st sess., 4217–19, 4197, 4206). See CS to Lieber, 29 December 1866.

To John Bright

Boston 17th Aug. '66

Dear Mr Bright,

I am yr debter for an excellent letter. Meanwhile on both sides of the water affairs have moved rapidly. I am glad that England keeps out of continental war.[1] She is wise in this & will increase in means for any future emergency. If I could admire battle, I should confess the singular brilliancy of that victory by which Austria has been driven from the German Confederation. Of course I rejoice in the result. It seems as if German unity must be established, & as this is normal & natural I am sure that it must be for the welfare of mankind.

Two days ago I was much disturbed by the cable news that France insisted upon going to the Rhine. In this claim I saw nothing but terrible war. All Germany would rise as in 1813. I am glad to learn to-day that the claim is abandoned.[2]

Our Presdt. goes on from bad to worse.[3] He is another James 2nd with Seward as his Sunderland.[4] His apostacy is complete. People now see that I was right at the beginning of the late session when I declared the breach irreparable. I had seen him under such circumstances as to draw him out, so that I knew his system.

The Philadelphia Convention, now in session, has no constituency behind, except the Democracy.[5] The Republican party stands unmoved, losing very few here & there, but, I think, not weakened materially. The West is very firm. I think the autumn elections will vindicate Congress.

I represent now what I have said constantly, that I see small chance of peace & security so long as the freedmen are denied Equality of Rights. I have insisted upon *impartial*—not universal—suffrage; in other words there must be only one rule for the two colors. All this might have been easily established had the Presdt. gone with Congress. Now we have before us terrible strife, & perhaps, war again.

Among the practical measures of the last Congress was one for the revision & consolidation of our statutes, which I have long had at heart; also another, following British example, with regard to the Metric

System. On the main question of Equal Rights Congress did much, but not all it ought to do.

Yr new ministry seems softening towards us.[6] Is it not? I was glad to arrest in the Senate that mad vote of the House upsetting our Neutrality system. I gave notice tha[t] if they attempted to pass it, I should speak till the close of the session, so that nothing else could be done. It was then abandoned.—I was glad to know that yr health is good. Mine is much improved.

Ever Sincerely Yours,   Charles Sumner

ALS   GBL   (80/416, PCS)

1. After a brief war in which Austria was defeated, Prussia and Austria agreed to an armistice stipulating that Austria take no part in the German confederation (*New York Times*, 15 August 1866:1).

2. A cable from Paris, 15 August 1866, stated that France had abandoned the idea of claiming German provinces on the Rhine (ibid., 16 August 1866:1).

3. Bright had written CS 3 July, "I hope Congress & people may stand firm, & that the President may have to yield. He will probably be obstinate till the fall elections determine the will of the nation, & then, if against him, he will give way" (Rochdale, 36/505, PCS).

4. Robert Spencer, second earl of Sunderland (1640–1702), secretary of state and political intriguer during James II's reign.

5. The National Union Convention, made up of Democrats and conservative Republicans, met 17–19 August, produced a platform uncommitted to the Fourteenth Amendment, and ratified Johnson's policies (Eric Foner, *Reconstruction* [1988], 264; *New York Times*, 20 August 1866:1).

6. Lord Edward Henry Stanley (1826–93; foreign secretary in the Tory government, 1866–68) stated in Parliament 23 July that he hoped "to remove any feeling of irritation or of soreness" between Great Britain and the U.S. as a result of the Civil War. Although he could not commit the British government to any change regarding the *Alabama* claims case, officially closed, he hoped to "lessen the probability" of future differences by requesting that a special commission be established to investigate Britain's neutrality laws (*Hansard's Parliamentary Debates*, 3rd series, 184:1280).

To Francis W. Bird
<u>private</u>.

Centre Harbor [New Hampshire]
17th [22?] Aug. '66[1]

My dear Bird,

I have thought much of what you said yesterday. I cannot comprehend those spirits who seek to misrepresent me with Andrew.[2] What do they seek to accomplish?

I have known Andrew for years & have never thought of him, except

From Harper's Weekly, 3 November 1866. "Our Presdt. goes on from bad to worse. He is another James 2nd with Seward as his Sunderland" (to John Bright, 17 August 1866). Cartoon by Thomas Nast. Courtesy of the Boston Athenaeum.

with affection & respect. I was one of the earliest & most determined to press him for Govr. & I have ever since sought to serve him. The speech which you say, is attributed to me, was impossible. I never said it or thought it.

I have often said that whenever Andrew desires my place I shall not be in his way.[3] There are reasons why I might be glad to exchange it for another service. And yet there are two objects which I should like to see accomplished before I quit. One is the establishment of our govt. on the principles of the Declaration of Independence & the other is the revision of international maritime law. But I would give up readily opportunities which I value, if I could in this way gratify an old friend & a valuable public character like Andrew. I mention these things that you may see the absurdity & wickedness of those who seem so constantly attributing to me something which is not in me. Should I quit the national service I should find employment with my pen or as lecturer, after a visit to Europe.

Ever Sincerely Yours,   Charles Sumner

A bad pen & bad ink appear in this profusion of blots.

ALS   MH-H   (80/414, PCS)

1. CS did not reach the White Mountains until 21 August 1866.
2. David Donald states that CS intended that Bird show this letter to Andrew (DD, 2:343). The letter was printed in Henry G. Pearson's *Life of John A. Andrew* (1904), exemplifying, in the opinion of Pearson, "the last word in the history of their friendship" (2:317). As set forth in Andrew's valedictory address, 5 January, Andrew espoused a more moderate Reconstruction policy than CS's. In the address Andrew affirmed his support of Johnson's course, particularly in allowing most Southerners to assume positions in state governments (ibid., 284).
3. There had been talk earlier in 1866 that Andrew might try to oppose CS in the 1868 senatorial elections (DD, 2:244–47).

To Abigail Brooks Adams

Boston 2nd Sept.—'66

My dear Mrs Adams,

An event which was often the subject of conversation between us, as a possibility or an impossibility, has at last arrived, and I am unwilling that you should hear of it from any other person than myself. In memory of pleasant days in the past, I write now to tell you that I am engaged to be married.[1] Do not be too much surprised.

At such a moment I naturally go back in my thoughts to old friends, & the associations of Quincy & Mt Vernon St. are revived. Be good enough to accept for yourself & husband the assurance of the good wishes with which I am, dear Mrs Adams,[2]

Yours Sincerely,   Charles Sumner

ALS   MBApm   (80/428, PCS)

1. CS wrote similar letters about his engagement to Alice Mason Hooper to other friends and colleagues, including the duchess of Argyll, Edwin D. Morgan, and Henry Wilson, 31 August–4 September 1866 (see 80/426–45, PCS).

2. Mrs. Adams repied from London, sending congratulations from her husband as well. "You bid me not to be too much surprised!! I am not so I assure you, my surprise has always been that you did not secure to yourself that happiness many years ago" (19 September, 36/715).

To John Bright
private.

Boston 3d Sept. '66

Dear Mr Bright,

In my last letter I anticipated several of yr inquiries in the letter just recd.

Before the adjournment of Congress many persons were satisfied that the Presdt. contemplated a *coup d'état*.[1] This was discussed in one of our confidential caucuses. Several senators wished to make some provision against it. I did not see how it could occur—without revolution & another civil war, & I did not think the Presdt. would dare to commence such proceedings. But there is a painful uncertainty with regard to the future. He is perverse, distempered, ignorant, & thoroughly wrong. You may judge him by the terrible massacre at New Orleans.[2] Stanton confessed to me that the Presdt. was its author.

I think this recent journey—not yet finished—& the speeches of the Presdt. & of Seward, have done them no good.[3] People are disgusted. Seward seems to have lost his wits, as well as principles. The Presdt., of course, is driven into close relations with the latter; but it is only a short time ago that he said of him to a member of the cabinet—"Mr S. seems to have no cardinals."—

The French Minister [*Montholon*] was with me last evng. I am satisfied that he expects the substantial withdrawal of the French troops from Mexico before next winter.[4] It was on this assurance given by me in my committee that Congress was kept still; & I have let M. Drohyn de l'Huys know this.

I agree with you about our neutrality statutes.[5] I think that in my last I let you know something of what passed on that head. Mr Bemis is preparing an elaborate article on our statutes & Mr Banks's madness.

Meanwhile peace seems to be prevailing in Europe. I thank God for this; but I am also grateful for the changes wrought by the war. I am for German unity, as well as Italian unity. Indeed I see little chance of permanent peace until these nations are established in their natural relations. Austria is an abnormal unreal nation & ought to cease.

I follow yr excitements in England & look forward to the next session of Parlt. as of great importance.—New York is the only state where we have anxiety as to the elections. It remains to be seen what Seward & Weed can accomplish.

Ever sincerely Yours,   Charles Sumner

P.S. Shall I tell you at the end of this letter that I am to be married? This is not political.[6]

ALS GBL (80/435, PCS)

1. In his letter of 16 August 1866 Bright commented on news that Radicals had accused President Johnson of "the desperate intention of playing the game of a 'Coup d'etat' during the recess. Your politicians are accustomed to language much more violent than that we indulge in, but I can hardly think eminent men would thus speak unless they had some shade of foundation for their charges or their fears" (Rochdale, 36/632, PCS).

2. On 30 July, as a constitutional convention with the express intention of granting suffrage to blacks tried to meet, fighting ensued between delegates and New Orleans police, who were mainly former Confederate soldiers. Federal troops finally subdued the conflict, which resulted in thirty-seven dead, all blacks or Radicals. According to Eric Foner, Johnson and Stanton were not sufficiently concerned about potential violence to have federal troops available immediately (*Reconstruction* [1988], 263).

3. Beginning 27 August, Johnson and Seward toured Eastern cities and the Midwest, speaking in support of the administration's Reconstruction plan.

4. On 5 April Napoleon III had announced the gradual withdrawal of French troops in three detachments, beginning in November (Alexander De Conde, *A History of American Foreign Policy* [1978], 244).

5. Bright wrote 16 August, "I am sorry to see an attempt made to lessen the force of your neutrality laws. You should, as heretofore, set us an example of some thing better, instead of coming down to our level."

6. Responding to CS's announcement, Bright wrote that he hoped marriage "would add to your happiness, without lessening your usefulness. My wife sometimes complains reasonably that my public life interferes with domestic comfort, but she is compensated to some extent by the belief that my public labors have a great purpose & are not wholly without result. I hope Mrs. Sumner may have her consolation in the same way, if she is ever disposed to complain" (Rochdale, 14 December, 37/292).

To Francis Lieber

Boston 22nd Sept. '66

My dear Lieber,

I wish you to know directly from myself that I am engaged to be married. I am not sure if you have ever met the beautiful lady of 28, who sometime this latter season presided at Mr Hooper's house in Washington.[1] I hope you will meet her this winter, if not before, at mine. Tell this to Mrs Lieber from me.

I write this gaily, & yet I cannot withold from an early friend the solicitude which I feel at this great change in my life. I am an idealist & I now hope to live my idea. But I cannot forget that I am on the earth where there is so much of disappointment & sorrow. But I have said enough.[2]

Good bye!

Ever sincerely Yours,   Charles Sumner

ALS   MH-H   (64/464, PCS)

1. CS's letters to Alice Hooper have apparently not survived. In December 1865 she acknowledged his "note," as well as a pamphlet by Agénor de Gasparin, a letter to CS from the duchess of Argyll he had sent, and a copy of his recent Reconstruction resolutions (Boston, 16 December, 22 December 1865, 34/704, 736, PCS). In the three recent surviving letters to CS, Alice Hooper wrote about mutual friends and encouraged CS in his Reconstruction efforts. She wrote CS c. 21 November quoting a compliment Fessenden had made when calling on her: "'Mr Sumner's views have modified down to *just* the right point.'" Alice Hooper continued, "I was also charmed to find that Mr Fessenden was going to as 'firmly oppose' admitting the Southerners as you are—" (Boston, 34/553). She closed her 16 December letter about her prospective visit to Washington, "Hoping that I shall not find you gloomy by that time—& wishing you a happy Christmas, believe me, very truly yours, Alice M. Hooper."

2. Responding on 8 October 1866, Lieber wished CS and his bride "the choicest happiness." He told CS, "I think of her when I write to you" (New York, 80/467).

To Julia Kean Fish

Boston 17th Oct. '66

Dear Mrs Fish,

A certain lady has received a beautiful present with yr card. She is very busy with infinite packing for Newport—Washington & elsewhere,—& all that is needful in leaving one house & preparing for another. So I said at once, that I would write our acknowledgments.

I assure you of my pleasure in having a souvenir of you in my new house.

To-day at 3 o'clk we shall be in the presence of the Bishop at the house of Mrs Charles Appleton. At 4½ o'clk we shall be on the way to Newport—with her little daughter Bell & her dog Ty.[1] So I begin with a little family. We shall be at Newport 2 or 3 weeks.

Again I thank you, dear Mrs Fish, for all yr kindness to me for many years. Accept my best wishes for yourself & all yr family, & believe me,

Ever sincerely yours,   Charles Sumner

ALS   DLC   (80/484, PCS)

1. CS and Alice Mason Hooper were married at the home of her sister, Isabella Mason Appleton (1835–69), with Episcopal bishop Manton Eastburn (1801–72) performing the ceremony. Isabella Hooper (m. Edward Balfour, 1879) was then eight years old.

To Anna Cabot Lodge

Newport R.I. 1st Nov. '66

My dear Mrs Lodge,

Yr note of congratulations was most welcome. It was very kind.[1]

It was received just before our marriage, which took place 17th Oct. at 3 o'clk P.M. Bishop Eastburn was very imposing. That evening we came to Newport where we have been ever since. But there must be an end to all things—even to this enchantment. We return to Boston, where we shall be in my obscure home, which you remember in Hancock St,—until we start for Washington sometime in the 3d week of Novbr.

Thus I begin to live. I have a house in Washington, where I hope to be very happy.[2] Tardily I begin.

Meanwhile you are seeing foreign sights, looking upon Alps & upon art. I should like this much.—My winter will be busy enough. The great question of "reconstruction" on which I have labored so much, must be advanced. Of course I shall insist upon the Equal Rights of All. When that cause is won one great part of my work will be accomplished.

Think of me, helping furnish a house—considering glass & china—ordering coal—& even inquiring about a one horse Brougham. But I

have said enough. Good bye! Remember me kindly to your family &
believe me, dear Mrs Lodge,

Ever sincerely Yours, Charles Sumner

ALS   MHi   (80/499, PCS)

 1. Anna Cabot Lodge, widow of John Ellerton Lodge, wrote from Geneva, Switz-erland, 23 September 1866 (36/735, PCS), "You have chosen well & wisely." Al-though she regretted her acquaintance with Alice Sumner was so "slight," Mrs. Lodge wrote she had had "a peculiar fancy for her whole style, bearing & manner from her girlhood."
 2. The Sumners rented a furnished house at 322 I Street (DD, 2:275).

To George Bemis

Senate Chamber 12th Dec. '66

My dear Bemis,

 Yr pamphlet so far as I have seen it looks well—very well. I shall study it.[1]

 [*Henry J.*] Raymond has asked me if you would give him sheets to use in the *Times*. He will print from it largely.[2]

 You noticed the allusion to the neutrality laws in the Presdt's mes-sage. Bad enough. He seemed to invite the repeal.[3] *Per contra*. To-day I laid the subject before my comttee. The feeling was strong to stand on the antient ways. The prevailing idea was that we had better bury the bill in the comttee.-room, & not call attention to it by a report. What say you?[4]

Ever Yours, Charles Sumner

Has Mr L's admirable discussion of Reconstruction been printed in a pamphlet?[5] I wish it much, if you can send me a copy.

ALS   MHi   (80/536, PCS)

 1. Bemis wrote CS from Boston on 8 December 1866 (37/237, PCS) that he was sending CS proofs of three-fifths of his pamphlet "American Neutrality: Its Honorable Past, Its Expedient Future" (1866). In it Bemis argued against any changes in present neutrality laws.
 2. The *New York Times* did not print Bemis's 211-page pamphlet, but reviewed it favorably (*New York Times*, 4 January 1867:8).
 3. Johnson's annual message to Congress, 3 December, discussed U.S. neutrality laws in light of the Fenian raids into Canada and the subsequent capture of some

U.S. citizens. He stated that these laws should be more lenient; "if they operate harshly, unjustly, or oppressively, Congress alone can apply the remedy, by their modification or repeal" (*Globe*, 39th Cong., 2nd sess., appendix, 4).

4. Bemis replied 13 December that holding back the House neutrality measure "would *do it good*." He thought CS should try to maintain the "*status quo*" in the committee, especially if the *Alabama* claims case reopened (Boston, 37/284).

5. Charles Greeley Loring's *Reconstruction: Claims of the Inhabitants of the States Engaged in the Rebellion to Restoration of Political Rights and Privileges under the Constitution* was published in Boston in 1866.

To Anna Cabot Lodge

Washington 16th Dec. '66

My dear Mrs Lodge,

There was a scene in our house when a large box arrived with an indubitable London look. After a proper interval of suspense during which the imagination had full play, axe & hammer did their work. Then appeared in a bed of paper & hay a most comely case made to open very much like an altar, & inside a marvel of beauty in silver & glass. Mr Dana had already announced it, & so we knew that it was your gift.[1]

Alice thinks it lovely, but when shall we use it?—It will shine like the sun in our little world. Really, dear Mrs Lodge, you have sent us a most beautiful souvenir of yr friendship. I wish you were here to see it in its proper place.

I imagine you now in Rome, where there will be only one drawback to pleasure, & that is the crowd of travellers, so that it will be difficult to be tranquil. At Rome it is pleasant to give oneself to the genius of the place, & to look art & antiquity in the face, without interruption from fashion or social duties. But the ancient city is now filled with English & American colonies.

You will witness Rome with the French troops withdrawn.[2] I hope this will be followed by the quiet disappearance of the temporal power of the Pope, & the annexation of this venerable capital to the new nation of Italy. Then will Italy be a unit.

You will be glad to know that I have a house of my own here in Washington, where we live very quietly,—seeing one or two persons at dinner & such as call in the evening. Thus far there have been no parties or entertainment, much to my satisfaction, as I am happier at home than any where else. Meanwhile Congress is doing its duty. We have just passed by very large votes an act conferring the suffrage upon all colored persons in the District, so that here at least my ideas have prevailed.[3] I think you were in Wash last winter when I vindicated them in a speech of two days. The Presdt. will, probably, veto the bill;

but we shall pass it over his veto.[4] What next? I shall try to have the govts. organized by the Presdt. in the rebel states *superseded* so that we can begin again & build on the loyal element.—Congress is in good spirits & courageous. A leading reptve. who was here last evng. was confident that the Presdt. would be impeached. Perhaps, but on this point I say nothing, as I should be one of his judges.—The Presdt seems to be much isolated. Very few republicans call on him. We have dined with Mr Seward, who is amiable—but fallen! His dinner table makes a great shew with a service of silver where all the plates are silver & another service of Sevres. I wish his politics were half as good as his *Sèvres!* Alice joins me in kind regards. Remember me to yr children, & believe me, dear Mrs Lodge,

Ever sincerely Yours,   Charles Sumner

ALS   MHi   (80/540, PCS)

1. Mrs. Lodge wrote CS from Paris 6 November 1866 that she was sending the Sumners an épergne as a wedding gift. Samuel T. Dana (1810–77), a Boston merchant, on 11 December sent CS details of the gift's shipment (37/132, 261, PCS).

2. According to the September Convention of 1864 between Napoleon III and the Italian government, France was to withdraw her troops from Rome in two years provided that Italy not try to capture the city from the pope (Harry Hearder, *Italy in the Age of the Resorgimento, 1790–1870* [1983], 242).

3. The bill passed the Senate 13 December by a vote of 32–13, and the House on 14 December, 118–46 (*Globe*, 39th Cong., 2nd sess., 109, 138).

4. As CS predicted, both houses overrode Johnson's veto on 7 and 8 January 1867 (ibid., 313–14, 344).

To Francis W. Bird
private

Senate Chamber 22nd Dec. '66

My dear Bird,

You will note what has passed on Nebraska. Time has been obtained.[1] Now let yr voices be raised. Let the *Cwlth* speak, & insist that no state shall be admitted with the word "white" in its Constitution.[2]

Will not the colored persons speak by petition?—

Wade seems to have lost his head &—his heart too. Wilson came out well & put himself substantially with me.[3]

Ever yours,   Charles Sumner

ALS   MH-H   (80/551, PCS)

1. On 14 December 1866 the Senate renewed consideration on the admission of Nebraska. As before, CS objected to Nebraska's constitution because it granted suffrage only to white male citizens, and he argued for a delay in debate on the bill. After three days of debate, on 20 December the Senate adjourned until 3 January 1867 (*Globe*, 39th Cong., 2nd sess., 121–30, 191–99, 215–24).

2. The Boston *Commonwealth* (29 December 1866:2) endorsed CS's protest against Nebraska's admission: "No such State should be admitted. . . . No more white men's governments!"

3. On 14 December Wade, chairman of the Committee on Territories, argued that the Fourteenth Amendment bound Congress to admit any states that met all the amendment's conditions. He accused CS of inconsistency because he had voted for the Fourteenth Amendment and would now refuse Nebraska's admission (*Globe*, 39th Cong., 2nd sess., 121–30). On 19 December Henry Wilson stated that he had changed his mind since the debate on Colorado's admission, which he had supported. Now that the fall elections ensured a substantial Republican majority in Congress, Nebraska's votes in Congress were not needed; hence, said Wilson, he could reverse his earlier stand, based on political expediency (ibid., 191).

To Henry W. Longfellow

Washington 22nd Dec. '66

Dear Longfellow,

I wish you a merry Xtmas—with much happiness for yr children. Give them my love.

This morning came yr letter with its valuable suggestions. The subject of Copyright is before my Comttee. I hope to do something for it.[1]

Can you not make us a little visit?[2]—I have a French cook & good wines.—The dining-room servt. was for 13 years with Chief Justice Taney who died in his arms. Such are the vicissitudes of life—from T to S!—Do—come. It would please my wife very much.

If you are curious about my life here—let me say, that I have somebody to dine every evng—1, 2, 3 or 4. Last evng Thad. Stevens— Baron Gerolt—Sir Fred Bruce & Miss Cabot of Boston. To-night we dine out. Once we have dined with the Sewards. But come & see. We will talk copyright & every thing else.

Alice was charmed with yr kindness in sending the photographs which seem to interest her much.[3]

Good bye!

                                   Ever Yours,   Charles Sumner

I have just had an old-fashioned battle to defeat a Constitution with the word "white" in it.

ALS MH-H (80/553, PCS)

1. Longfellow wrote CS 18 December 1866 (Cambridge, 80/549, PCS) what he termed a "business letter" asking CS to introduce copyright legislation providing for mutual copyrights in Great Britain and the U.S. According to Pierce, CS repeatedly tried to bring about an international copyright treaty but never succeeded (Prc, 4:293–94).

2. Longfellow thanked both the Sumners for their separate invitatons but declined (1 January 1867, 80/591).

3. On 18 December Longfellow wrote that he had already heard from Alice Sumner and was gratified the photograph (unidentified) pleased her.

To George Bemis
Confidential

Washington 24th Dec. —'66

My dear Bemis,

Sir F. Bruce has been to see me several times on the present relations with our country. He tells me that he has left with Mr Seward informally for his perusal, without giving him an official copy, a despatch from Ld Stanley accepting arbitration in the Alabama case.[1] As he has not left any official copy Mr Seward has nothing as yet to answer. —Sir Fred. wishes to know of me, whether if the Alabama case is put in [train?] of settlement, we will then proceed to a general settlement of reciprocity, Fisheries & every thing else. He thinks that one motive for advances on the Alabama claims would be that there was to be a sincere restoration of good relations.

Talking with Seward, I find him watching the signs of public opinion, & to this end he says he reads the *Herald*.[2]

I think I have already explained to you that our diplomatic relations with England are merely formal. No questions are discussed between us, & no negotiation is opened. Ld Russell's refusal of our offer in the Alabama case is the reason. —I should like to put an end to this abnormal condition, if possible.

There are claims of Prussia which my excellent friend Baron Gerolt is pushing with ardor. He hoped to sign a Convention for a joint commission; —but Mr Seward retreated, after the Convention had been drawn up & was ready for signature. The Baron feels sore. The Secy says that he must leave it to Congress. Of course, this adds to my work.

Genl. Baez, the deposed Presdt. of Dominica[3] has been here to obtain help of some kind. Seward would not see him. I listened to his bad French by the hour.

There is also the Cretan question, which is becoming interesting.[4]

Seward wishes us to sanction a Minister to Greece. But I fear a political job.

Give me yr views especially about our relations with England, & confer with Mr [*Charles G.*] Loring & our excellent Judge [*Richard Fletcher*].

Ever yours,   Charles Sumner

ALS   MHi   (80/566, PCS)

1. Answering on 30 November 1866 a request from Seward to reopen the *Alabama* claims negotiations, Lord Stanley instructed Bruce to agree, ruling out only discussion of Britain's concession of belligerent rights to the Confederacy. Bruce forwarded Stanley's letter to Seward on 7 January 1867 (*Foreign Relations* [1867], part 1, 183–88).

2. The *New York Herald* had recently praised Johnson's "vigorous foreign policy" in general, and "the diligence and the tenacity" of Seward specifically in seeing that the French evacuated Mexico (2 December 1866:4, 7 December 1866:4). However, the *Herald* subsequently criticized Seward's role (12 December 1866:6) and stated that Congress should assume control of U.S. policy toward Mexico.

3. Buenaventura Báez (1810–84), ruler of Santo Domingo, 1849–53, 1856–58, 1865–66.

4. Cretans sought independence from Turkish rule; CS introduced a resolution on their behalf on 19 July 1867 (*Globe*, 40th Cong., 1st sess., 727).

To Francis Lieber

Washington 29th Dec. '66

My dear Lieber,

I return Motley's interesting letter, as you desired.[1]

I thought that I had told you the fate of the Neutrality Bill of Banks,[2] which Bemis has so thoroughly riddled. It passed the House unanimously & came to the Senate Friday afternoon, when the end of the session had been fixed for 4 o'clk Sat. afternoon. It was at once referred to the Comttee. of Foreign Relations. I made up my mind to let it sleep there without calling the Comttee. together for its consideration. Of course this was a grave responsibility for me to take; but I felt justified in it.

In the afternoon a plan was formed among the heated heads to discharge the comttee. by special vote & to pass the bill in the Senate, as in the House. Taking advantage of the recess from 5 till 7 o'clk in the evng I got together the old statutes on the subject, & examined the new bill. At 7 o'clk I came to my desk with an armfull of books & announced to all about me that I was "good for 5 hours at least" if the neutrality bill were called up. Very soon Wade tried to move it, but did not succeed.

From 7 o'clk in the evng till 7 o'clk in the morning I kept my seat on the watch. At last at 11 o'clk on the forenoon of Saturday Chandler actually made the motion to take up the bill. I gave notice that I should speak all the remainder of the session, if necessary to defeat it.[3] This was the end of the effort, & the bill now sleeps the sleep of death in my Comttee.-room. Such is the fate of a measure which began so loftily.

Ever yours,   Charles Sumner

When shall we see you again at our table?—I enclose a letter from Bemis which may interest you.[4] His pamphlet is first-class.

ALS   MH-H   (64/473, PCS)

1. In his letter to CS, 25 December 1866, Lieber asked CS to return Motley's letter (New York, 80/571, PCS); Motley's letter from Vienna contained his observations on European politics (3 December, Lieber Papers, Huntington Library).

2. On 27 July; see CS to Moncure Conway, 30 July. Lieber wrote CS that he had seen no Senate action on the Banks bill. Favoring retention of the present neutrality statutes, Lieber told CS he had advised George Boutwell in the summer of 1866 "not to touch so noble a law."

3. Zachariah Chandler (1813–79), U.S. senator (Rep., Mich.), 1857–75. Apparently these exchanges took place off the record, or in one of the many executive sessions the Senate held in the last two days of the first session of the 39th Congress.

4. Bemis to CS, 13 December, on which CS had written "to be returned" (37/284). See CS to Bemis, 12 December 1866.

To Gerrit Smith
private

Washington 29th Dec. '66

My dear friend,

Our excellent Wade has strangely failed us on the question of refusing to receive a new-state with the word "white." Can you not address him one of yr letters; plead & remonstrate with him & keep him true to his history.[1]

Ever sincerely Yours,   Charles Sumner

ALS   NSyU   (80/581, PCS)

1. CS had written Smith 22 December 1866 asking for Smith's help in rousing the public against the Nebraska admission. Smith's noncommital reply on 26 Decem-

ber stated that he hoped neither Nebraska nor Colorado would become states "with their infamous Caste Constitutions" (80/557; Peterboro, New York, 37/350, PCS). CS sent similar pleas to Wendell Phillips, Charles W. Slack, and Theodore Tilton (80/555, 556, 564).

To Francis W. Bird

Senate Chamber 10th Jan. '67

My dear Bird,

I think it best to adopt the Amendment; but since a question has been made as to its character as an offer to the rebel states, I would in a report or resolution declare that it is in no respect an offer, which, if accepted by them, will bind Congress to receive them back.[1] In one word, it is only an installment & not a finality.

I think you will be satisfied with the result on Nebraska & Colorado.[2] The declaration, that there shall be no exclusion from the elective franchise on account of color, is not in the form which I preferred; but you have the declaration, which to my mind is a great gain. Is it not? And thus ends a long contest, where at first I was alone [*part of letter missing*]

P.S. Mr Stewart of Nevada, who is sitting near me says that "it cannot be said now, that the Republican party is not committed to negro suffrage." You have (1) The District Bill (2) The Nebraska Bill (3) The Colorado Bill & (4) The Territorial Bill passed to-day declaring that in the Territories there shall be no exclusion from the suffrage on account of color.[3]

The report of my remarks in the *Journal* is a jumble.[4] Paragraphs were out of place; so that the argt. was confused. It was clear enough.

AL   MH-H   (80/601, PCS)

1. The Massachusetts legislature was then considering ratification of the Fourteenth Amendment, which it approved on 20 March 1867, Bird dissenting (*New York Times*, 23 March 1867:2).

2. CS voted for the admission of these two states after the Senate passed George F. Edmunds's amendment stipulating that "there shall be no abridgment or denial of the exercise of the elective franchise or of any other right to any person by reason of race or color, excepting Indians not taxed" (9 January, *Globe*, 39th Cong., 2nd sess., 360).

3. William M. Stewart (1827–1909), U.S. senator (Rep., Nev.), 1864–75. The Territorial Bill declared that the vote could not be denied to male citizens because of "race, color, or previous condition of servitude" (ibid., 382).

4. The *Boston Daily Journal* (9 January 1867:4) printed ("verbatim," it claimed)

CS's speech criticizing the Nebraska constitution (8 January, *Globe*, 39th Cong., 2nd sess., 329–30) with two paragraphs misplaced.

To Henry W. Longfellow

Senate Chamber 15th April '67

My dear Longfellow,

I hear nothing from you; but the papers announce yr Dante. Is it yet published?[1]

I have been tried a good deal by the Russia Treaty, which has given us a new world, with white foxes & walruses not to be numbered. At last I made up my mind that I could not take ground against it. My course had a decisive influence. I feel the responsibility, & am now trying to write out the speech which I made. I spoke 2 hours & ¾ths[2] How I envy yr quiet days of beautiful labor. But how is Dante?

Erny, of course, is very happy—& well, I trust.[3] Good bye!

Ever & ever Yours,   Charles Sumner

ALS   MH-H   (81/041, PCS)

1. In his reply, 30 April 1867 (Cambridge, 81/059, PCS), Longfellow informed CS that book 1 of his translation of *The Divine Comedy of Dante Alighieri* was printed and that CS would soon receive a copy.

2. CS spoke in favor of annexation of Alaska on 9 April ("The Cession of Russian America," Wks, 15:1–169), and the Senate ratified the treaty on 9 April, 37–2 (*Executive Proceedings*, 15:675–76). CS had not learned about the treaty until Seward notified him 29 March (38/575; CS to Seward, 29 March, 81/024). For an analysis of CS's decision to support Seward's treaty and the Senate Foreign Relations Committee deliberations, see DD, 2:304–8. No reporters were permitted in the Senate's executive session; hence CS prepared his own version of the speech.

3. Longfellow's letter to CS of 18 March (Cambridge, 81/014) announced the engagement of his son Ernest to Harriet Spelman.

To John Bright

Senate Chamber
16th April '67

Dear Mr Bright,

I am much yr debtor. Day by day I have hoped to write you at length on our affairs. We have gained a good deal—almost all. Meanwhile the South, seeing the power of Congress, is more & more submissive.

Had the Presdt. been right at the beginning all would have been well & peace established. He has postponed the good day.

Yr young friends called this morng. I was glad to see them. I write now simply to confess my seeming remissness. The Senate will rise this week when I shall write you at once.

The Russian Treaty tried me severely. Abstractly I am against further accessions of territory unless by the free choice of the inhabitants. But this question was perplexed by considerations of politics & comity & the engagements already assumed by the govt. I hesitated to take the responsibility of defeating it.

I think you will like a recent act of Congress declaring that our Foreign Ministers shall not wear any uniform "unless previously authorized by Congress." [1] Of course Congress will not authorize any; so our ministers must appear in plain clothes—to the dismay of some who are afraid of being taken for "upper servants."

Good bye!—In great haste.

Ever sincerely Yours,   Charles Sumner

The suffrage has already helped colored people infinitely. One told me that the other day that he was treated better now than before—that people who once called him "Syphex" now addressed him as "Mr Syphex!"

ALS   GBL   (81/044, PCS)

1. The act passed the Senate 20 March 1867 (*Globe*, 40th Cong., 1st sess., 216–17).

To Theodore Tilton
Private

Senate Chamber 18th April '67

Dear Mr Tilton,

The objection to yr proposed amendt. [1] is two-fold.

(1) It is superfluous & needless. The Constitution with its two supplementary amendments gives the power amply & triply. Three times over you have it. If there is any sound lawyer, who, after examining this question, thinks otherwise, I do not know him. The Chief Justice does not question the power. The civil rights bill is applicable to the whole country. A political rights bill is the proper complement; & one is just as constitutional as the other.

(2) We cannot wait for the slow process of a constitutional amendt. The change should be *at once*. Last year when senators ⟨insisted on⟩ proposed a constitutional amendt. to reach the suffrage question in the

rebel states, I insisted that it must be done by act of Congress—that
the power was ample—& only in this way could the work be done in
season. Very well. The act of Congress has been passed.[2]

The same argt. is applicable to the Northern States. The change must
be made before the Presdtial. election. In Congress we have a large
majority. Let it act,[3] & the question is settled in every state, without an
infinitude of local Contests. Every Northern state will move into line
with the colored vote to strengthen the Republican cause. Ind & Delaware will be saved—to say nothing of Kentucky. One vote in Congress
& the work is done!

Do you say that these rights must be placed under the protection of
the Constitution? They have it. Instead of patching & tinkering more,
simply read the Constitution. *The right of suffrage once given can never be
taken away*. It will be immortal.

Help! if you please![4]

Ever sincerely yours,   Charles Sumner

ALS NBu (81/050, PCS)

1. The New York *Independent* (18 April 1867:4) proposed a Constitutional amendment, mandating black suffrage in all U.S. states. Its editorial stated that the "new
amendment . . . shall establish the negro's political rights throughout the North as
well as throughout the South."

2. Among the provisions of the Reconstruction Act of 1867, passed by Congress
on 2 March, was one stating that no rebel state could be considered for readmission
until all male citizens "twenty-one years old and upward, of whatever race, color, or
previous condition" were granted suffrage (*Globe*, 39th Cong., 2nd sess., appendix,
197–98).

3. CS introduced a bill in the Senate on 26 March to enforce the Constitution in
guaranteeing suffrage for blacks in all states. CS brought the bill up several times,
but the Senate decided on 12 July not to consider it (*Globe*, 40th Cong., 1st. sess.,
345, 614–15).

4. Tilton responded 19 April by asking CS to write a public letter for the *Independent*, and stated he would "advocate your bill heartily." He did not care how black
suffrage was to be established "if only it be *done*" (New York, 39/007, PCS). CS's
letter of 20 April appeared in the *Independent* (2 May 1867:1) with Tilton's emphatic
support (see Wks, 15:176–80).

To Joshua B. Smith[1]

[Washington] 19th May '67

Dear Mr Smith,

I enjoyed much the account of the dinner or supper at the opening of
the Boston branch of the *Smithsonian* Institution. But why have you not
sent me my bill?

I shall need you very soon, but how can I ask you, if you do not send me a bill?—

We shall be in Boston for a little while at the beginning of June at the "old stand" in Hancock St, & I shall be obliged to look to you for help.

I am disgusted with the colored people in Washington. I wished them to nominate one or two of their own number, as an example to the freedmen at the South. I thought it very important. They allowed themselves to be frightened by politicians who said that "it would not do"—"that it would have a bad effect on the elections at the North"— precisely what certain persons have always said to every generous proposition. Though in one of the wards they had a majority, they have not nominated one of their own color.

Wormley[2] told me a day or two ago that they meant to give me a serenade before I left. I told him at once, that I would not take it—& that I did not want any thing of the kind from people who abandoned in this way their own cause.

Very truly Yours,   Charles Sumner

ALS   MH-H   (81/073, PCS)

1. Joshua B. Smith (1813–79), black caterer and antislavery activist living in Boston.
2. James Wormley (1819–84), black caterer and owner of Wormley's Hotel in Washington, D.C.

To the Duchess of Argyll

Washington 27th May '67

My dear Duchess,

It seems long since I have heard from you. Meanwhile yr house has bloomed with authorship—a morning glory & a myrtle, if the latter blooms. Lorne's book has the disadvantage of leaving out, probably, his best things, because they were free or personal. It is hard in these days for a traveller who has seen to write. Yr Duke's book[1] I have not seen, but Mr Bancroft tells me that it is "very remarkable," & "entirely the best book ever written by a cabinet minister."

You are having yr trials. I am mystified by the everlasting wrangle about "compound householder"[2]—a term which the unaided reason cannot unravel. I delight that for the present at least peace has been assured[3] & that Europe has been saved from the terrible war that lowered.

May not the success of France at her Exhibition[4] have its effect in teaching her that there is something better for her than military glory? That would be a profitable lesson; & how true it is. If France could keep out of war another ten years she would never consent to another war. Meanwhile her industrial advance would be incalculable. All France would become one immense *article de Paris*, with every art & aptitude developed.

Perhaps yr interest in our affairs is less now than it was.[5] —All our best hopes of the colored people are sustained. They are showing gentleness & intelligence. At their meetings some of them come forward at once as orators. Mr Wilson, who has just traversed the whole country,[6] has been astonished by *speeches* from negroes. I wish to see some of them in Congress. Then their rights will be fixed beyond recall.

The spirit of the old rebels is generally reactionary & stiff-necked. Some of our friends, returning from the South, are much disheartened & think there is little chance of change during the present generation. Nothing but the colored vote there can save society. Otherwise there would be nothing but traitorous anarchy.

There was the usual attempt in the House of Reps. to pass foolish resolutions on foreign questions, including Fenianism & Ireland, which I stopped in the Senate—so that they sleep tranquil enough.[7]—Thus far the Alabama claims have not been discussed. The publication of the recent correspondance—should it see the light—will start it again, if the question is not settled before the meeting of Congress.—How are you? & how is yr mother? Remember me kindly to her & yr Duke.

Ever sincerely yours,   Charles Sumner

ALS   CSmH   (81/084, PCS)

1. *A Trip through the Tropics and Home through America* (1867) by the marquess of Lorne; *The Reign of Law* (1867) by the duke of Argyll.

2. The new Tory government initiated a second Reform Bill in Parliament in February 1867, and debate on it continued through the spring. One issue raised was whether suffrage should be granted to renters, who did not pay taxes directly ("compound householders") but did so through their landlords.

3. The *New York Times* noted (10 April 1867:1) that war seemed likely between Prussia and France because Prussia opposed Holland's selling the Grand Duchy of Luxembourg to France. However, European diplomats gathered in London in May for a peace conference to settle their territorial differences (*New York Times*, 24 May 1867:1; Gordon A. Craig, *Germany 1866–1945* [1978], 17).

4. The Paris International Exhibition opened 1 April (*New York Times*, 3 April 1867:1).

5. In her letter of 19 February [1867, misdated 1866] (35/449, PCS), the duchess asked CS, "*On the whole* do you think the accts. of the Freedmen as good as can be expected?"

6. Henry Wilson toured the South in April and May (Richard H. Abbott, *Cobbler in Congress* [1972], 186–91).

7. CS argued that a proposal permitting the sale of U.S.-made ships to friendly belligerents be referred to the Senate Foreign Relations Committee, and the bill was deferred (*Globe*, 40th Cong., 1st sess., 23 March, 25 March, 291, 328–30).

To John Bright
private

Washington 27th May '67

Dear Mr Bright,

I am about to leave Washington for Boston, although I expect to return here in the beginning of July; but before I go, I send a line to you.

I follow you in the *Times*;[1] —not a very friendly guide; but a full newspaper. How it misrepresents! I judge it from what it says about affairs here, & occasionally in allusion to myself;—almost uniformly erroneous or positively false. I do not suppose it better when it speaks of you. But it prints yr speeches, & thus you have the opportunity of stating the case before an immense audience.

Yr reform discussions are a perpetual mystification. You seem to be splitting hairs, instead of asserting principles. It cannot be that so important a question as whether a citizen shall have a voice in the govt. can depend on such narrow considerations & technicalities of property. Who but the learned" can ever know how to define a "compound householder"? It seems to me that the present success of D'Israeli[2] will drive you to place the suffrage question on absolute principles, where I am sure it belongs.

For a long time I was perplexed by the subtlety, so often presented, that the suffrage is a "privilege" & not a "right," & being a "privilege," it was subject to such limitations as the policy or good will of the legislature chose to impose. The more I think of it, the more it seems to me, an essential right, which govt. can only regulate & guard, but cannot abridge. All *just* govt. stands on "the consent of the governed." Starting with this principle from our Declaration of Independence, I see no other conclusion, than that every citizen, having a proper residence, must be a voter. If it be said that, then, the ignorant man has the same electoral weight as the intelligent, I reply; "No; each has the same vote; but the other exercises an influence over the result, in other words over other votes, *in proportion to his intelligence*." In the vote itself all are equal. This is another instance of Equality before the law.

I cannot but think that you will be driven in England to discuss the question on higher grounds. Parties will then arrange themselves anew. Until then, "there will be no repose. Nothing short of this will be *hard pan*. As our discussion has proceeded here, the hard pan has prevailed. In Mass. we have what is equivalent to a small rating. Every voter before his name can be registered must pay a poll-tax, which is usually $1.50, or about 6 shillings.

Thus far our great change at the South promises well. Without the colored vote, the white unionists would have been left in the hands of the rebels. Loyal govts. could not be organized. The colored vote was a *necessity*. This I saw at the beginning, & insisted pertinaciously that it should be secured. It was on this ground, rather than principle, that I relied most; but the argument of principle was like a re-inforcement.

I do not know that I have mentioned to you how the requirement of universal suffrage in the new Constitutions came to be adopted in our reconstruction bill. The bill, as it came from the House, was simply a military bill. In the Senate, several amendments were moved in the nature of conditions of restoration. I did not take much interest in these, as I preferred delay, &, therefore, was content with anything that secured this, believing that Congress must ultimately come to the true ground. In the confusion which ensued a caucus of republican senators[3] was called. There Mr Sherman moved that all the pending propositions be referred to a commttee of 7. Of this comttee he was chairman. I was a member. In the committee, I insisted that the existing govts. should be declared invalid. Adopted. Then the states in question be designated simply "rebel states." Adopted. Then that in the new constitutions there should be no exclusion from suffrage on account of color. This was voted down. Only one other member of the comttee. sustaining me,— Mr Sherman being strongly adverse. When the committee reported their bill to the caucus, I stated my objection, & moved my amendt in an enlarged form, to the effect that in the new constitutions all citizens with a proper residence should be voters. In moving it I simply said, that it was in our power to decide this question & to supersede its discussion in the Southern states; that, if we did not decide it, every state & village between here & the Rio Grande would be agitated by it. It was dinner-time, & there was impatience for a vote, which was by the ayes standing & being counted, & then the noes. There were two counts; 17 ayes to 15 noes; so this important requirement was adopted. Mr Sherman, as chairman of the committee, was directed to move the amended bill as a substitute for the pending measure. & It was passed by the usual republican majorities.[4] That evng. in caucus some few saw the magnitude of the act, & there was corresponding exultation. Wilson wished to dance with somebody.

I have given you this narrative, because it concerns an important event, & will show you how business with us is sometimes conducted.

Could my way have prevailed, I would have provided Provisional Govts. of a civil character, which should have shaped the rebel states into their new political forms, & superintended the transition. I am entirely satisfied now that this would have been the better course. But we were obliged to sacrifice to the impatience of politicians, who thought that the Presdt. could be met only by promptest reconstruction. It is in politics, as in life; we rarely obtain precisely what we desire.

I have just perused the correspondance between Mr Seward & Ld Stanley on the Alabama claims.[5] There is a dead-lock, the legacy of Ld Russell. The British govt. offers arbitration, but insists upon excluding the fundamental questions on which our claims rest, namely the rightfulness morally & legally of the recognition of the rebels as belligerents on the ocean. We are willing to arbitrate, provided the whole case is submitted. I think that the correspondance, when published will rally the whole country. Great Britain erred in the fatal concessions of the Queen's Proclamation. Had the rebellion succeeded, her policy might have been vindicated; at least some may think so. But the Queen's Proclamation went down with the rebel flag. So it seems to me. I cannot see it otherwise. You know I have seen it so for a long time. Thus far I have avoided saying any thing on this question in the Senate, because I was anxious to secure time for an amicable adjustment. The next congress will debate it fully, unless mean while in some way it is settled. I was glad that Ld Derby was able to speak as confidently as he did about the future.[6] I fear that on this question we may not have the sympathy of some of our good friends in England.

You have had a hard battle, but seem to stand it well. I trust that your health is firm. Mr Stansfield's[7] death is a great loss. His speech on the duties of England to the U. States was a model of completeness & elegance. I know nothing in the same space which at the time struck me so favorably. I always had a longing to thank him.

Do you remember my previsions with regard to Mr Gladstone? I thought that you & he would ultimately act together. I expect to see him on the higher platform of principle. In the honesty of his nature he cannot avoid it. —

You can have very little time for correspondance; but I shall always value any thing you write.

Ever sincerely Yours,   Charles Sumner

ALS GBL (81/086, PCS)

1. The London *Times* supported an extension of the franchise, but warned against giving the vote to so many of the lower classes as to cause "a subversion of Parliamentary Government" (15 April 1867:8). About Bright, a *Times* editorial lamented that all he could do was produce "more petitions and more meetings" that accomplished nothing (14 May 1867:11).

2. On 13 April the Disraeli government defeated Gladstone's amendment (which Bright supported) to give the vote to compound householders as well as property owners. In May Parliament debated another amendment to enfranchise all those who paid taxes.

3. When the Senate on 15 February began consideration of what would become the Reconstruction Act of 1867, CS's amendment that only "valid" state legislatures were eligible to ratify the Fourteenth Amendment was defeated. The caucus that CS describes took place 16 February (*Globe*, 39th Cong., 2nd sess., 1392–96, 1448).

4. CS was not present at this vote later in the evening of 16 February. He later explained that ill health forced him to leave, "knowing that the great cause was assured" (ibid., 1469; 41st Cong., 2nd sess., 640–41).

5. Seward's letter to Adams of 12 January gave him instructions to Stanley and defended "such of my former statements as Lord Stanley has disallowed." Once again Seward stated that Britain had responded too quickly to the Confederacy's request for a concession of belligerent rights. He wrote that the U.S. would agree to arbitration but "would expect to refer the whole controversy" to a commission. Responding to this letter via the British minister Bruce on 9 March, Lord Stanley again ruled out consideration of the belligerency question and stated he would agree only to arbitration on claims for damages (*Foreign Relations* [1867], part 1, 45–54, 191–93).

6. Speaking in Parliament 21 May, Prime Minister Derby stated that the *Alabama* negotiations had thus far "been carried on in a spirit which was likely to lead ultimately to a satisfactory termination" (*Hansard's Parliamentary Debates*, 3rd series, 187:862).

7. No Stansfield of CS's description died in the spring of 1867. Possibly CS or a telegraph news dispatch confused Sir James Stansfeld with the British painter Clarkson Stanfield, who died 22 May.

To [Simeon Corley?]

private

Boston 30th July '67

My dear Sir,

Of course, you are aware, that, there is no objection from the Constitution or any existing law to the choice of colored men as senators or reptives in Congress. As you are in S.C. I hope you will see that this is understood.[1]

No incompetent person, white or black, must be sent. But would it not mark the era of reconciliation, if a colored person should receive the commission of S. Carolina as senator? There should also be one or two in the House of Reps. Their presence would make any retreat from our present position impossible. It would be more than an act of Congress.

I do not know the colored citizens of S.C. Are there not among them some who could receive these trusts?—All this I foreshadowed in my speech of 14th Sept. 1865, a copy of which I send.[2]

Faithfully Yours,   Charles Sumner

ALS SCUC (81/157, PCS)

1. The recipient is tentatively identified as Simeon Corley (1823–1902; U.S. congressman [Rep., S.C.], 1868–69, and a frequent correspondent of CS's) because of his letter to CS from Lexington, South Carolina, of 5 July 1867 (39/335, PCS). In that letter Corley described a forthcoming Union Republican State Convention to which he had been elected. He told CS he looked forward to a *"proper, loyal construction"* of the South that was more stringent than Johnson's plan. Apparently Corley wrote CS another letter about black officeholders (unrecovered) after the convention on 24 July.

2. In his speech "National Security and National Faith" CS had held up the Russian czar's emancipation of serfs as "the lesson of the great Empire to the great Republic." The proclamation not only freed the serfs but gave them civil and political rights, including the right to hold office (Wks, 12:312–14). Hiram Revels (1827–1901; U.S. senator [Rep., Miss.], 1870–71) was the first black to serve in the Senate; the first black congressman was Joseph Rainey, a representative from South Carolina, elected in 1869.

To Peleg W. Chandler

Hancock St—17th Aug. '67

My dear Chandler,

The Presdt. is neither crazy or drunk;—he is simply himself, as he has been for months—essentially perverse, pig-headed, bad.[1]

Stanton reached Hooper's yesterday morng, & this morng left for Cotuit, where he will be for sometime. He seems worn & indifferent to newspapers. His wife does not wish him to see a newspaper.[2] He regards the adjournment of Congress as a "simple betrayal" of the country to the Presdt. On this he speaks stronger than I ever did.

Nothing is clearer to my mind than this; the country has lost every way by the tardiness of Congress in bringing a bad Presdt. to justice; business has lost millions; reconstruction is postponed. Besides the immediate good from such an energetic proceeding, the Republic would show an example & establish a precedent of incalculable value in history. Liberal ideas every where would have been advanced. Shortsighted men! But most who opposed proceedings were enmeshed with the Presdt—by visiting him—by asking office from him—by receiving office—& then by open committal in his favor. But all hastens to the great result, which is inevitable.

I have not seen Andrew;[3] but I cannot believe that he will go with the Presdt,—although he strangely keeps aloof from old friends & old lines of travel.

Ever yours,   Charles Sumner

Tell Miss Dana that her father gave us a perfect dinner of fish & game at Taft's! My first experience!—

ALS   NBHi   (81/174, PCS)

1. Chandler wrote CS on 15 August 1867, "Is the president crazy, or only drunk?" (Brunswick, Maine, 39/534, PCS). Johnson had recently removed military officers in the South and on 5 August tried to dismiss Stanton, citing as a reason "considerations of public interest." Stanton replied on 6 August that "considerations of public interest" convinced him that he should remain as secretary of war, at least until Congress convened in the fall. Meanwhile, the press debated whether Johnson's removal of Stanton violated the Tenure of Office Act passed by Congress February 1866, an act designed to safeguard Republican appointees (*New York Times*, 7 August 1867:4, 8 August 1867:4; Eric L. McKitrick, *Andrew Johnson and Reconstruction* [1960], 494–96).

2. Ellen M. Hutchison, married Edwin M. Stanton, 1856.

3. Chandler wrote CS that he feared that Johnson's latest actions would "make us all favor impeachment. Is it possible that [*John*] Andrew favors those things?"

To Anna Cabot Lodge

Hancock St Saturday
[*31 August 1867*]

Believe me, dear Mrs Lodge, I have appreciated all the kindness & friendship of yr note.[1] I was touched more than I can tell by knowing your interest for me in that matter.

All that I meant was that I did not see very well how I could say any thing about it.

There is a French saying, which often comes to my mind. Give an office to a man & you make *un ingrat et dix ennemis*. I have known something of this verity; but it is only partially true in the present case. I have made at least one enemy,[2] who was for a long time a valued & devoted friend. How many others I know not.

I am not indifferent to these things, for I count much on my friends, &, amidst the asperities of life & some of its disappointments, turn to them.

Of course to you I look always.

Ever sincerely yours,   Charles Sumner

ALS   MHi   (81/242, PCS)

1. George W. McCrackin, a New York Democrat traveling in Europe, had written Seward that Motley, from his post as minister to Austria, had publicly denounced the Johnson administration. After denying such charges, Motley resigned. During January 1867 CS repeatedly asked for publication of the letter on which Seward had based his charges that Motley had shown open hostility to Johnson (Glyndon Van Deusen, *William Henry Seward* [1967], 466–67; *Globe*, 39th Cong., 2nd sess., 540, 854, 960–61). CS had shared with Anna Lodge Motley's letter of 1 July to CS (Vienna, 39/300, PCS), in which the former minister wrote that he believed the handling of his recall "quite unexampled in the diplomatic history of our country or of any other." In her 31 August 1867 letter Mrs. Lodge suggested to CS that he inform Motley that his appointment had been brought about not by Seward but by CS (Nahant, 39/673).

2. CS wrote Mrs. Lodge on 29 August that he was "always . . . sorry" that he lost John Jay's friendship when he recommended Motley as minister to Austria in 1861; Jay "has always insisted that, if I had not favored Motley, his nomination was sure" (Boston, 81/188). On 6 April 1864 Jay drafted a letter of complaint to CS (78/072), but did not send it.

To Edward L. Pierce

Hancock Street
Tuesday—[*c. September* 1867][1]

My dear Pierce,

I return the letter you kindly sent me.

I always thought that Chase never understood or appreciated the indignities which I have recd. from F. He knew something of those shown by the old slave-masters. But nothing from them was so constant, elaborate & complete;—nothing so vindictive, so disorderly, & utterly in defiance of all rules of the Senate—or of good breeding. Read Conness's testimony in the letter which you have seen; but he has come into the Senate recently, & does not know the beginning. Consult Hamlin, or Morrill, both colleagues of the offender. The latter has often spoken to me of the unjustifiable conduct of F.

Grant that I have been positive & peremptory in debate. That is the worst said of me. I have never left my seat ostentatiously when F. rose to speak;—I have never sought to disturb him in debate; I have never talked in abusive terms to him while he was on the floor; I have never made an allusion to him; unless in direct reply.

I adopted my present relations reluctantly, but at the dictate of self-respect. Often before I took this course, I said to him; "I know you in yr talents & opinions, & always listen to you with interest & respect. Why will you maltreat me?"—

It is a mistake to suppose that there are any "two sides" to the case. I have always been ready for kindness—have always said so—& have been deeply sensible of the shame to the Senate of conduct such as I was exposed to. There has been no quarrel, but only a constant attack——ubi tu pulsas, ego vapulo tantum.[2] This is the exact truth.

Chase thinks there is a "misconception on both sides." None on my side. I am not insensible to the good opinion of my associate; but I do not complain that he thinks ill of me. I complain of acts. He treats me badly.[3] See the *Globe* passim; consult any person on the floor of the Senate. If he chooses to continue this conduct,—which, I believe, is without a precedent in parliamentary history, let him do it. I have borne it in times past. I can bear it yet longer.

But when before did an eminent leader of debate resort to such petty spite against one whom he disliked? Answer in debate. Very well. But personal indignities to attract the attention even of the galleries & of strangers, I think are without example. For the honor of the Senate I trust they will be stopped.

The very words which Chase says I ought to say, I said years ago,—& I have repeated them ever since in conversation with friends.

But why do I write this? I have never written it before.

Ever Yours,   Charles Sumner

I hope that Chase has seen the Conness report.

ALS   MH-H   (64/388, PCS)

1. This letter is tentatively dated September 1867 because CS's relations with Fessenden seemed especially acrimonious in the recent Senate sessions. In an interview CS conducted 30 August with a *Boston Daily Advertiser* correspondent, CS used some language almost identical to that describing Fessenden in paragraph 3 of this letter. He also called Fessenden "a drag on reconstruction" (reprinted *New York Times*, 5 September 1867:1). Apparently Pierce sought to reconcile the two senators and had sent CS a letter from Chase (unrecovered) on their differences.

2. "Where you strike, I cry out greatly."

3. In the spring and summer of 1867 CS and Fessenden exchanged barbs and criticisms on CS's supplemental Reconstruction bill (*Globe*, 40th Cong., 1st sess., 50–51, 467, 523). They also argued in February 1867 about the alleged partisan appointments made by Secretary of the Treasury McCulloch. CS charged that McCulloch had pressed his preferences on the Sixth Auditor; McCulloch had "whispered in his ear or let him well understand that members of the Johnson Departmental Club were the men to be preferred in securing this extra compensation. . . . He is notoriously an intense partisan." The exchange continued:

> Mr. FESSENDEN.   I will ask the senator if he has any proof that the Secretary of the Treasury is a man who goes about whispering these things into the ears of others?
> Mr. SUMNER.   I have ample proof that he is what I called him, an intense partisan.

Mr. FESSENDEN.   So is the Senator an intense partisan. Does the Senator judge the Secretary of the Treasury of his own heart, that he would do such things?
Mr. SUMNER.   When the Senator addresses me a personal remark I prefer not to answer it.
Mr. FESSENDEN.   I will not address the Senator. Now I disclaim for the Senator anything of that kind. I know that he would not; I know that he could not; I know that it is contrary to his whole nature, I know him so well; but I hint to my friend that where things of that sort are suggested with regard to others without proof, they may lead those who do not know the Senator to infer that he judges of the acts of others by what he would do himself. [*Globe*, 39th Cong., 2nd sess., 7 February 1867, 1051–54.]

To Henry W. Longfellow

Albany—4th Oct. [*1867*] '3

My dear Longfellow,

Thus far on my journey since 2 o'clk yesterday, when I left the old house not to return.[1] None of my family have left it so dead.

My eyes moistened as I shook hands with the good domestic, & I went away alone & homeless. The journey was sad, & my eyes often filled with tears, as I thought of the unhappy waif that I am & must be.[2] Good bye! God bless you & yours!

Ever Yours,   Charles Sumner

ALS   MH-H   (81/245, PCS)

1. CS had left Boston on a speaking tour, delivering his "Are We A Nation?" (Wks, 16:3–65) in six midwestern states. Regarding CS's former home on 20 Hancock Street, Longfellow wrote George Washington Greene, "Sumner has sold his house; and sits there gloomily like Marius on the ruins of Carthage" (Cambridge, 22 September 1867, HWL, 5:179).

2. Rumors that the Sumners had separated were just surfacing. Alice Sumner had left for Lenox, Massachusetts, in mid-June, and the two never met again. Apparently Longfellow and CS had discussed the separation at length before CS embarked on his speaking tour. "He is in great sorrow," Longfellow wrote Greene 5 October in response to Greene's question about "Sumner's relations to his wife" (ibid., 181). CS had also discussed his marital problems with Samuel Hooper, Alice Sumner's former father-in-law, for Hooper wrote CS 16 September that Alice had told Hooper that it was "useless" for Hooper "to say anything in regard to any change of her plans" (Lenox, 39/636, PCS). As late as 1 September, however, CS was still not generally acknowledging any break, because he wrote Lieber, "Mrs S. is at Lenox in mountain-air" (64/496).

To Samuel Gridley Howe
private

Providence R.I. Sunday—
[*17 November 1867*]

Dear Howe,

I am at a loss to know what I can say in self-defence without impeaching another which I am unwilling to do. She will have enough to bear in her experiment.[1]

That Mrs H.{*ooper*} should befriend her is natural. As Mr H. says — "if she does not, who will?"[2] But she does not know the case, & acts, I think, from feminine sympathy. I have never spoken with her on the intolerable life, with constant dishonor, for 3 months, which determined my course. Here I purposely avoid details. Enough if I say that my home was hell. During all this time I bore & forebore, saying & doing nothing.

——But I have written too much already. I do not know how freely Mr H. will talk with you; but he knows more than any body.

All that Mrs H. knows relates to matters subsequent to the long offending. Of course, if a husband absents himself from a wife without cause, there is a natural sympathy with her; but in order to judge the case you must know the antecedents.

Tonight I leave for N.Y. I know that in this terrible trial I have been careful, considerate, kind & gentle. Good bye!

Ever Yours,   Charles Sumner

ALS   MH-H   (64/503, PCS)

1. Upon returning from Europe, Howe wrote CS that he was "deeply concerned" about rumors there concerning CS's "domestic relations." Howe wrote CS that he was sure the senator had done "nothing inconsistent with your deserved character for integrity, honor & generosity" and that CS had done everything possible "to avoid a separation" (Boston, 28 October 1867, 40/036, PCS). CS had already written Howe asking for sympathy and support (10 November, 64/501).

2. Samuel Hooper kept CS informed of his wife's whereabouts and plans. Alice Sumner returned from a brief trip to Europe on 31 October, and soon thereafter went to Lenox with Hooper's wife, Anne Sturgis Hooper. In his letter of 4 November Hooper described a letter Alice Sumner wrote him, showing what Hooper hoped was "a new heart that will appeal to your manly strength and magnanimity" (Hooper to CS, Boston, 31 October, 4 November, 9 November, 40/052, 75, 92). Hooper defended his wife in a later letter to CS; Mrs. Hooper was "convinced" from being with Alice Sumner that the two should permanently separate (Washington, 28 November, 40/178).

To Henry W. Longfellow

Senate Chamber 2nd Dec. '67
Monday

My dear Longfellow,

This is the first day of the new session, & we are in idleness waiting for the [*presidential*] message, which, probably, will not come till to-morrow.

You have doubtless seen Dickens.[1] I hope he is well & prosperous. Tell me something of him;—also of yourself & yr plans.

My house is now ready, & before me is still the question—shall I furnish & occupy it? Shall I furnish a few rooms?[2]—Or shall I go on where I now am in my suite of 4 rooms? If Mr H.[*ooper*] were not so positive & pressing, I should not think of the house.

To furnish a couple of rooms on the lower floor & the first chamber floor would take $5000. Then there would be the expense & responsibility of a household. Why can I not see this question more clearly? Ah! why have I been obliged to see it at all?

I took this house for another. I have no heart about it or any thing else. I am afflicted & unhappy. What can I do?—Would that I were in some far-off land?

Good bye

Ever & ever yours,   Charles Sumner

ALS   MH-H   (81/276, PCS)

1. Charles Dickens arrived in Boston 1 November 1867 on his second American tour. From the Parker House Hotel he wrote CS 28 November, hoping the two could meet before the novelist returned to England in the spring. About his return to Boston Dickens wrote, "The last five and twenty years would seem to me but so many months, were I not sometimes reminded of their sweeping changes" (40/174, PCS).

2. The Sumners had earlier planned to move into a new house at Vermont and H Streets in Washington. Longfellow advised CS to remain instead in his lodgings: "Why go into an empty haunted house? You would only feel your loneliness the more" (Cambridge, 8 December, 81/287).

To John Bright
private

Senate Chamber
10th [*and 16th*] Decbr. '67

Dear Mr Bright,

Long ago I should have written you, but I have been much on the wing & when at rest much occupied; & now I write at my desk while a debate is dinging in my ears.

I was much interested in yr October letter & yr views on our claims.[1] Meeting Seward lately at dinner, he told me that Adams had reported to him the inclination of yr opinions, which the former regretted much. When I mentioned that I had a letter from you on the subject he expressed a desire to see it. With some hesitation I let him have it. He has returned it with a letter which I now enclose.[2] Let me observe, that it must not be thought peculiarly formal, because it is not in his handwriting. He dictates always & only signs his letters.

You will see how he looks upon our question; or rather you will see here his familiar & unofficial views, in which I am sure he is much in earnest. He is anxious for the settlement of the claims question. As long as it continues unsettled it is in the way of your claims & also of all other foreign claims.

——*16th Decbr.*——I was interrupted in this letter, & now return to it after a week. I cannot disguise my anxiety on this question. You will see that it is now referred to Congress,[3]—which is what I have always deprecated. I have hoped that in some way it would be settled by diplomacy, so that Congress would have no occasion for action. Mr Seward thinks the claims will be paid, sooner or later; & now he abandons the idea of arbitration.

I had hoped that the proposition for arbitration would have been adopted. This is the way of civilization. Any refusal of arbitration seems to be a lapse into barbarism. I cannot understand a willingness to submit a part of the case only to arbitration. If we think ourselves injured by another power there are two remedies;—one by war—to be avoided always, the other by arbitration. I understand England to consent to arbitration on a part of our injuries; but on another part, where we think ourselves right, she is so entirely satisfied that she is right, that she will not let her conduct even be drawn in question. If she is right, then why hesitate to leave the question to a disinterested tribunal?—But the *point of honor* is invoked. This is always invoked by [*parls?*] looking to war rather than to more peaceful substitutes.

It seems to me that Ld Stanley made a great mistake in not frankly accepting our proposition.[4] He might have said generously & wisely—

"if England has done wrong to the U.S. in the judgment of a disinterested tribunal, then she must pay the damages awarded; nor can there
be any limitation to her liabilities, except in justice thus administered."
Surely if one part of our case is proper for such a proceeding, the whole
must be. It may seem unreasonable to an Englishman; but the very
object of arbitration is to adjudicate by *reason* rather than by *war*. Let
us try our case by reason, & forbid the thought of war. But just in
proportion as you reject the arbitrament of reason, you invite war in
some of its forms, if not in the field, then at least by a constant menace—all of which I deplore immeasurably.

Again I say, the very fact that we deem ourselves wronged is a sufficient reason for the arbitration, unless you are resolved to be judges in
your own case, which is the way with Ld Stanley when he insists that
England is so clearly right that he will not even allow her conduct to
be drawn in question.

I am not disposed to go into the question, whether we are right or
wrong. It is enough that our govt believes itself in the right.

I have never understood that we make any claim for damages, except
where proved to proceed directly from malfeasance or nonfeasance of
the English govt. But one link in the Alabama chain is the Queen's
Proclamation, which, as we insist, opened ship-yards & armories to our
rebels, & lifted them from the condition of pirates & criminals to be
belligerents. In a general sense, I cannot doubt that this act of Great
Britain was the main cause of the prolongation of the war, with all its
terrible cost of blood & treasure. For all this there can be no compensation. But we do not feel willing to abandon this part of our case in
fixing the British govt. with responsibility for cruisers fitted out in
British ports & welcomed afterwards by British authorities.

I long to have this question settled. There are others who would be
better pleased to keep it open, that we may use the precedent. *I do not
wish to use the precedent*. I desire it trampled out.—A senator came to
me the other day to say—"we cannot afford to accept from G. Britain
pay for the Alabama depredations," & this is the opinion of others who
exercise much influence.

I wish I could write cheerfully about our affairs at home. The Presdt.
is exercising a terrible influence adverse to reconstruction & for the
oppression of Union men. But the work proceeds. Though conducted
under immense difficulties, I am sanguine that it must measurably
succeed. With a Presdt. on our side its success would be a triumph of
civilization, brightening the age.

It looks now as if Grant would be the Presidential candidate; but
there is a very strong feeling that he must say more on our side.

As I look at Europe I tremble for Italy, where Louis Napoleon exercises a perverse influence. The cable tells us daily of disturbance in Ireland or England.[5] Why not settle all pending questions with us? Why nurse a cause of trouble? Let us have an "imparlance."

I hope that I have not written too strongly. You know how much I am for peace.—Let me hear from you soon.[6]

Ever sincerely Yours,   Charles Sumner

ALS   GBL   (81/298, PCS)

1. Bright wrote CS 26 October 1867 from Rochdale that he thought that Britain should compensate the U.S. for "not only the harm done you by the ships built here, but the injury you sustained by the mistake of our Govt in believing that you could not conquer the South." Bright stated, however, that while he considered Britain's concession of belligerent rights to the Confederacy "a foolish act—an unfriendly act—at the moment an unnecessary act," he did not deem it as "a breach of international law." Britain's concession was, he wrote, "a matter wholly different from the 'Alabama' question, in which I fear & believe there was a distinct breach of a well known international law." He asked CS, "Who can estimate the harm done you by the admission of the belligerent right of the South? . . . [H]ow can it be reckoned in dollars or pounds sterling?" Bright told CS that the British generally approved Stanley's offer to refer the *Alabama* claims to arbitration but that no one "thinks our Govt can concede what Mr Seward is understood to demand." He feared the U.S. would suffer in world opinion by refusing the British proposal (40/026, PCS).

2. In his letter to CS (Washington, 6 December, Bright Papers, British Library; copy, 81/283), Seward expressed the wish that Bright were "as logical in international politics as in domestic politics." Seward reiterated his view that the U.S. could not negotiate on only part of the claims issue, because damages incurred by the *Alabama* were a direct result of the "unfriendly and injurious proceedings of the British government in regard to belligerent rights."

3. CS called for publication of the diplomatic correspondence between the U.S. and Great Britain on both countries' claims and on the belligerent rights issue (4, 10 December, *Globe*, 40th Cong., 2nd sess., 19, 98). The *New York Times* noted that Secretary Seward would soon furnish this correspondence to Congress and request from it "a formal expression of opinion on the subject" (16 December 1867:5).

4. In his dispatch of 16 November Stanley once again stated that the British government would not refer the belligerent rights matter to a tribunal. He hoped the U.S. would accept Britain's offer for arbitration of the *Alabama* and other ships' claims (*Foreign Relations* [1867], part 1, 209–11). In his annual message, 3 December, President Johnson devoted one paragraph, which CS wrote George Bemis (6 December, 81/281) was written by Seward, to the *Alabama* claims. Johnson stated he had turned down Stanley's proposal "because it has hitherto been accompanied by reservations and limitations incompatible with the rights, interest, and honor of our country" (*Globe*, 40th Cong., 2nd sess., appendix, 6).

5. Napoleon III returned French troops to Rome in October 1867 when Garibaldi's forces threatened it (Harry Hearder, *Italy in the Age of the Risorgimento* [1983], 244). Fenians desiring Irish independence from Great Britain had recently blown up a prison in London in hopes of rescuing a prisoner there (*New York Times*, 14 December 1867:1).

6. Bright wrote on 11 January 1868 that he would soon respond to CS's letter in detail: "I am not quite sure that we are writing on the same thing" (40/533).

To Thomas Nast

Senate Chamber
Dec. 16th [*1867*]

Dear Sir

I have your note of the 13th in reference to your "Caricaturama," and am sorry to hear that it is not so successful as you expected.

I cannot say whether it would be more so here or not, but if you try, I hope you will find it so.[1]

Yours truly   Charles Sumner

Th. Nast Esq.
New York W. 125th St.

LS   DLC   (81/304, PCS)

1. Thomas Nast (1840–1902), the political cartoonist for *Harper's Weekly*, had written CS 13 December 1867, sending him a catalog from Nast's recent New York exhibit of political cartoons. It had been considered "too radical" in New York, but Nast wished to continue it, perhaps in Washington. "I think it would at least create some sensation among the members of congress, as there are a good many of them represented" (New York, 40/300, PCS). According to Albert Bigelow Paine, Nast dismantled his exhibit after exhibits in New York and Boston proved unprofitable (*Thomas Nast: His Period and his Pictures* [1904], 118).

To Horatio Woodman
private

Senate Chamber 17th Decbr. '67

My dear Woodman,

I had nothing to do in any way, directly or indirectly with the recall of Baron H.[1] I never made any suggestion or gave any hint on the subject to a human being. The whole story of my agency is a pure invention,—or imagination;—as is every thing else reported about me in relation to another person. I hope this is explicit enough.

Sometimes it seems strange to me that I should be exposed to such virulent calumnies, as if character were nothing. Nor does there seem any appreciaton of that forbearance, which cultivates silence rather than defend myself at the expense of another.[2]

Ever sincerely Yours,   Charles Sumner

ALS MHi (81/306, PCS)

1. Friedrich von Holstein (1837–1909), German statesman, had been frequently in Alice Sumner's company during the winter of 1866–67, when he was an attaché at the Prussian embassy. He was recalled to Berlin in April 1867 (DD, 2:291–95). An allegation that CS had engineered Holstein's recall, written by a New York *Express* correspondent, was reprinted in the New York *World*, 22 October 1867:8. The correspondent concluded, "the *basis* of the report in Boston is such as I send you. What I have written is in everybody's mouth." Woodman wrote CS c. 15 December, "If it is utterly untrue, that you ever, directly or indirectly, sought to procure the recall of the Baron Holstein are you willing to say so in a line to me. . . . I wish to be able to contradict it." He concluded, "Your friends don't know enough to answer the many pertinacious and detailed slanders. Your side stands entirely un-stated" ([Boston], 40/423, PCS).

2. Woodman thanked CS for his denial of the charge, one which he had known "on instinct was as false as all the rest. . . . *Don't let any or all the advice of mistaken and hopeful friends and relatives, or your own generosity, induce you, against your better instincts and judgment*, to resume relations which will make a daily bitter draught of life. You have known the worst already" (18 December, 40/328).

To Samuel Gridley Howe
private

Senate Chamber 18th Dec. '67

My dear Howe,

I will send you a note for Mr Warner.[1] But who is he? What shall I say of him?

My reply to Woodman, enclosed to you yesterday, has already answered yr inquiry or suggestion. You will see that the allegation against me, such as it was, had no foundation, like every thing else said against me in my calamity.

I am unwilling to be thought only "in the main right."[2] I know that there cannot be "two sides" to the question. Reviewing the whole case I find nothing but too great forbearance & tardiness on my part. Mrs Eames tells me that her husband,[3] who dined with me in December, came home saying—"poor Sumner; he has married a devil." This was before her whole nature was poisoned by her intimacy with a foreigner. My house soon became an *Inferno*, & my name was dishonored. So completely was I overcome by this conduct, that I let her know, that, if I were not in public life I should take the first steamer for Europe & there hide myself; that I thought seriously of resigning my post in order to do this. This was in the spring. All that summer I passed alone in Boston, never breathing a word of my distress to a human being—not to a solitary person—hoping for some change, but despairing & very unhappy, when she suddenly determined to leave for Europe.

Down to her determination to leave for Europe I never wrote or spoke to any body in Washington or elsehwere, nor did I ever give a hint with regard to her conduct; not to H.[*ooper*] in Washington or L.[*ongfellow*] in Cambridge. I bore it all in silence, & I have continued my silence since, except that I sought the sympathy of one or two friends. Not a word has gone to the public from me. During this time I have been exposed to the most cruel & brutal imputations. But I have said too much. I confide this to yr friendly heart.

Ever yours,   C. S.

P.S. At last I have yielded to Mr Hooper, whose heart was set on my going into my house.[4] He says that when I am once in it I shall never be willing to give it up. But I think he has been strongly influenced by a desire that I should not openly advertise to the world that I shall always live alone, which might be implied if I went into lodgings. I resisted as long as I could, until I thought he was unhappy in my refusal. This imposes an expense which oppresses me.

I confess the satisfaction in the idea of a house of my own, so that I need not pack & unpack at the begining & end of every session. At my time of life I naturally seek repose—such as I can hope to find in my solitude. After the terrible experience of last year my solitude is happiness.

I expect to sleep in my own house at the end of this week. I shall have room for a friend. Come & occupy it. I shall also give a room to my secretary.[5]

ALS MH-H (64/508, PCS)

1. In his letter of 15 December 1867 Howe asked CS to supply a letter of introduction for [N.?] J. Warner, who, Howe informed CS in a later letter, was CS's former neighbor in Boston (Boston, 40/305, 412, PCS).

2. Howe told CS that "Society seems to be settling down to the belief that you were, in the main, right" and that CS had had "a difficult & painful part to play." The only criticism he had heard, wrote Howe, was that CS wrote about Alice Sumner's behavior "in a complaining way" (40/305).

3. Charles Eames (1812–67) was a lawyer and former diplomat who had settled in Washington until his death in March; his widow, Fanny (d. 1890), was a confidante of CS's.

4. Besides Longfellow and Howe, Anna Cabot Lodge advised CS to remain in lodgings (Howe to CS, 30 December, Lodge to CS, 20 December, 40/412, 349). Hooper, however, assured CS that he and Mrs. Eames agreed that there was "no cause for apprehension" that Alice Sumner would return to CS's large house, and "silence on the subject, so far as the public is concerned, was best" (28 November, 40/178). See Hooper to CS 6 October, 39/702, for details of CS's house.

5. Moorfield Storey (1845–1929), secretary to CS, 1867–69; lawyer and writer.

To Edward Atkinson

Washington 3d Jan. '68

My dear Sir,

I read all that you write, whether for the public or for myself personally.[1]

I am with you thoroughly in every effort for the national credit. It must not be drawn into suspicion in any way. It is one of our best possessions.

I am not sanguine that any thing of substantial value can be done, before reconstruction is finished; & this must be postponed till after the administration of Johnson is finished. It is sad to see this long period, so important to the business of the country, sacrificed.

Meanwhile we must do what we can. Had better councils prevailed we might have been close upon specie payments now.

I return Dr Howe's letter, which is excellent.

On second thoughts I prefer to keep the Dr's letter for further perusal. Congress will not consent to free banking; nor will it consent to substitute interest paying bonds for legal tenders, which it must do if new banks are created in order to absorb the legal tenders.[2]

Very truly yours,   Charles Sumner

Dr Lieber lives at 48 East 38th. He will be glad to see you.[3]

ALS   MHi   (81/341, PCS)

1. Atkinson wrote CS 24 December 1867 (Boston, 40/372, PCS) informing him that he would soon receive extra copies of Atkinson's public letter to CS of 4 December, which appeared in the New York *Evening Post* (20 December 1867:1). In that letter Atkinson argued that gold contracts should be legalized and that, after the government had stepped in to resume specie payments, the banking system should remain unregulated "under the action of the natural laws of trade." Atkinson feared that the price of gold would rise and paper money depreciate "if General Butler and Mr. Stevens succeed in the nefarious attack upon the honor and credit of the country."

2. In his *Evening Post* letter Atkinson proposed that as of 1 January 1870 only gold should be legal tender and that a series of 10-40 (10- to 40-year maturity) bonds be issued beginning 1 July 1868.

3. Atkinson asked CS for Lieber's address in hopes he could see him when in New York.

To William H. Claflin
private

Senate Chamber 13th Jan. '68

My dear Claflin,

Whither? O! whither? Where are we going? Reaction here; & even in Mass. Of course, T's confirmation would be aid & comfort to the old pro-slavery rebel spirit.[1] The Govr. could not have seen this. Cannot something be done to smooth this incident?[2] Pardon my freedom.

Ever sincerely Yours,   Charles Sumner

ALS   OFH   (81/358, PCS)

1. John Murray Forbes wrote and telegraphed CS on 9 January 1868 urging him to try to stop the nomination of Benjamin F. Thomas (1813–78; U.S. congressman [Conservative Unionist, Mass.], 1861–63) as chief justice of the Massachusetts Supreme Court. Forbes wrote that although he realized CS did not "like interfering in state politics," he saw Governor Bullock's choice as an "insult" to Republicans. In his telegram Forbes asked CS to "reach the council thro' Claflin or otherwise it will split our party" (40/690, 516, PCS). According to Donald, Bullock sought to test CS's power in Massachusetts with this nomination (DD, 2:344).

2. On 17 January the Executive Council of Massachusetts rejected Bullock's nomination and Claflin informed CS that his letter had been successful (*New York Times*, 18 January 1868: 1; Boston, 1 February, 40/695). Edward L. Pierce wrote CS 20 January that CS's friends (Francis W. Bird, Edward Kinsley, W. S. Robinson, and Claflin) had "worked hard" to defeat Thomas and "this success settles the question of your reelection. It shows that the old Free Soil fervor and vigor lives" (40/582).

To John Bright

Senate Chamber
18th Jan. '68

Dear Mr Bright,

I recd. the enclosed from the War Depart. on the morng after Genl. Grant ceased to be its head.[1] It is one of his last orders.

Of course, there is no payment of any kind.

We are looking for Mr Thornton now as the bearer of peaceful tidings. It is pleasant to see [that?] on the naturalization question, there will be no serious difference.[2] But the sooner it is out of the way, the better it will be for our two nations. Would that the Alabama question could follow!—

Mr Stanton will continue in his office, if the Senate desire.[3] Thus far the opinion is strong that he should stay. His presence there will prevent the employment of the influence & opportunities of this office on the side of the Rebellion. A. J. is now a full-blown rebel, except that he does not risk his neck by overt acts; but in spirit he is as bad as J. D.

Ever sincerely Yours,   Charles Sumner

I enclose one of the ballots in South Carolina, with the head of Abraham Lincoln, as a sign to the former slaves that it was the "true ticket."[4]

ALS   GBL   (81/370, PCS)

1. Grant had been secretary of war *ad interim* since Stanton's removal in August 1867. On 14 January 1868 Grant resigned upon learning that the Senate's Committee on Military Affairs had recommended that Stanton be reinstated under the terms of the Tenure of Office Act; the Senate approved the committee's recommendation on 13 January (Grant to Andrew Johnson, 25 January, printed in the *New York Times*, 5 February 1868:1; *Executive Proceedings*, 16:128–30).

2. Sir Edward Thornton (1817–1906) succeeded Sir Frederick Bruce (who had died in September 1867) as British minister to the U.S. British and U.S. negotiations on the rights of American immigrants concerned most particularly Irish who had become naturalized citizens. The U.S. argued that naturalized U.S. citizens abroad should enjoy the same rights as native-born citizens. Seward, writing to Charles Francis Adams on 13 January, considered the matter one that could be negotiated with Britain "so a comprehensive settlement might be attempted" (*Foreign Relations* [1868], part 1, 141–42).

3. The *New York Times* (17 January 1868:1) reported that Stanton had resumed his duties at the War Department on 16 January.

4. The ballot (Bright Papers, British Library) bore the inscription "Union Republican Ticket of Lexington District for the Convention" with the names of Lemuel Boozer and Simeon Corley.

To William H. Seward

Monday morng
[*3 February 1868*]

My dear Seward,

I make haste to say this morning that Mr Stanton & Mr Dickens did not finish their cigars till it was too late for a visit—Mr D. said he should call on you.[1] But he has no other evng for society.

Ever Yours,   Charles Sumner

He does not go out while he is reading.

ALS   NRU   (81/419, PCS)

1. Charles Dickens arrived in Washington 31 January 1868. CS wrote Seward three notes on 2 February trying to arrange a meeting between the two (CS to Seward,

81/414, 415, 416, PCS). Dickens asked CS to dine on 5 February. Refusing, because of his cold, CS's invitation of 7 February, Dickens wrote CS, "To bring me to the Capitol would be superfluous and dangerous" (Washington, 40/725, 744).

To John Bright
private

Senate Chamber 4th Feb '68

Dear Mr Bright,

I wish I could answer yr inquiry directly & without explanation.[1]

Evidently the idea of paying 5-20s in green-backs has made an impression, especially at the West, destined to predominate in the approaching Presidential election. I say this of the West, & not of the idea, for I trust that this will never predominate. But I do not disguise my anxieties at times. And yet, as I reflect upon the question, & confer with my associates, I am encouraged to believe that the Public Faith will not be tarnished.

There can be no declaration of Congress that the 5 20s must be paid in coin; but I do not think there can be any declaration that they shall be paid in greenbacks. The question will be postponed, or, if dealt with, settled without deciding the meaning of the original obligation.

It may be settled by the arrival of specie payments, when every obligation will be payable in coin.

Another solution, which is now under the consideration of our Finance Committee, is the creation of a new stock,[2] principal & interest declared to be payable in coin—probably at 5 per cent,—into which the 5-20s will be convertible as they become due at the option of the holders. In other words, the holder of the 5 20s can have these coin bonds, if he will take them, even if specie payments have not arrived.

The more I reflect upon the situation, the more I feel the impossibility of any act of repudiation. And yet any thing short of payment in coin is, I fear, in the nature of repudiation. I wish I could write more positively. You will see that I write frankly.[3]

So much do I trust to the public faith, that, although sometimes disturbed by adverse menaces, I cannot bring myself to believe that there is any real danger. My only sister, who is in California, has all her small means in 5-20's, but I have not counselled any change.—I fear that this is a very unsatisfactory letter.—Mr Thornton has arrived. We have exchanged calls, without meeting. I hear him called amiable & interesting.

Ever sincerely Yours,   Charles Sumner

P.S. I cannot cease to deplore the blow at Arbitration dealt by the English Govt, through whose reptve. it was recognized at the Congress of Paris[4] as the proper mode of deciding questions between nations.

ALS   GBL   (81/421, PCS)

1. Bright asked CS, in his letter of 11 January 1868, whether the U.S. intended to repudiate its debt, i.e., to pay its 5-20 bonds in paper currency (U.S. Treasury bonds with a maturity of twenty years but redeemable after five years at 6 percent interest were known as 5-20 bonds; *Globe*, 40th Cong., 2nd sess., 1464). He feared that the "foolish talk" of redeeming these twenty-year maturity bonds, sold during the Civil War, "may make a panic." He asked CS to write him what was *"certain,"* i.e., whether the bonds would be paid in gold or greenbacks (Rochdale, 40/533, PCS).

2. CS used the British term for government bonds.

3. On 7 March Bright responded to CS's letter, "I grieve to think that you are only able to speak in an uncertain manner. . . . [Y]ou must borrow in some shape to pay off those whose debt you will partly repudiate—& in future nobody in Europe will trust you, & all your securities of every kind will suffer some taint" (41/272).

4. Peace conference of the European powers in 1856.

To Oliver Otis Howard

Senate Chamber Feb. 8th. [*1868*]

Dear Sir

I return herewith the report you were kind enough to send me, and have read it with attention.[1]

It is hard to believe that one who wrote so fully and elaborately, and made such professions of virtue, as Mr. Hitchen, can be the character he is described to be,[2] but I do not question the accuracy of the report. I am much obliged to you for the attention you have given the matter.[3]

Faithfully your's   Charles Sumner

Maj Gen O. O. Howard
Office of Freedman's Bureau

LS   DNA   (81/430, PCS)

1. Among the several petitions from black Southerners sent to CS at this time was one from George Hitchen of Natchez, Mississippi. Hitchen wrote CS on 23 January 1868 of a plan for blacks to buy the A. K. Farrar farm with money granted by the Freedmen's Bureau. He complained that the bureau had given blacks "next to nothing, while the whites will come in their carriages to draw the very supplies that we ought to have." He begged CS to use his influence with Howard, "or we will die off

like rotten sheep" (Natchez, 81/400, PCS). On 24 January Hitchen wrote that Mississippi blacks sought "the sound satisfaction of showing to the world, and to you that we can bring this business to a successful issue . . . by our own Ingenuity, Intuitiveness, and business qualifications" (81/398). CS wrote Freedmen's Bureau chief Howard several times in January and February pressing Hitchen's request, and enclosing letters from Hitchen as well as a formal petition with approximately 270 names requesting funds to purchase the Farrar farm (81/397, 402, 427).

2. Replying to CS's earlier entreaties, Howard wrote on 4 February that his agent in Mississippi reported that Hitchen was "not to be trusted," for, among other offenses, he was known to sell whiskey to other blacks. Howard reported that Hitchen had, moreover, exaggerated the value of the farm, and if his "scheme" were carried out, the freedmen would lose all the money they had pledged for the farm's purchase (Washington, 81/423).

3. Hitchen continued to ask CS for various forms of assistance through March of 1869 (see letters of 26 March, 8 July 1868, 20 and 24 March 1869, 41/402, 42/610, 45/601, 641).

To Samuel Gridley Howe
private

Senate Chamber 18th Feb. '68

My dear Howe,

In yr note you say that people say that she made "a mistake in leaving."[1] This theory proceeds in ignorance. Her misconduct was complete in the spring, & my course was then determined, subject always to a declared change in her. I did not see precisely when or how the separation would finally take place. When during the summer I forebore going to Lenox, she saw that she was compromised, & that at the end of the season, she must decide whether to return or not. In a tempest of passion, she resolved to go to Europe & then launched her pretexts.

There are details which ought not to be consigned to paper shewing the indecent untruthfulness of her statements.[2]

Of course my present liberation is an immense improvement on my condition of last year. But this is a terrible blow under which I stagger; & the reports & calumnies to which I have been exposed increase my trials. I have desired to shield her—for her own sake—her daughter's sake—& for her family. I was willing that all should be left to smoulder in darkness; but she & her friends have willed it otherwise.

Genl. Burt[3] made a curious revelation to me with regard to her first husband, who, it seems, away in New Orleans, remembered her misconduct at home & dreaded to return there. He says that he communicated this to you before my marriage.—She is a bad woman.

Ever yours,   Charles Sumner

ALS MH-H (64/548, PCS)

1. Howe wrote CS on 14 February 1868 with the most recent Boston gossip about CS's separation from Alice Sumner: "Ladies of standing do not call upon her. All her own connexions say she made a mistake in leaving you" (Boston, 41/073, PCS).

2. Howe reported a rumor which he described as "cunning & apparently incapable of being disproved." The story, as Howe phrased it, was "that what coarse natured women consider a just drive, was not fully granted;—& that, when by means of that denial she desired separate apartments—that too was denied." He assured CS that "the woman who under any circumstances could be governed by such feelings is not worthy to be the wife of any man of delicacy."

3. Probably William L. Burt, postmaster for Boston, 1867.

To Edward Atkinson

private

Senate Chamber 27th Feb. '68

My dear Sir,

Sherman has just finished his speech, which I heard with pain.[1]

In reply to yr letter just recd. let me say that I have a profound conviction that nothing will be done by Congress to repudiate in any way our obligations or to weaken our 5-20s.[2] Meanwhile the great remedy will begin.

It is a great calamity that A. J. was not impeached a year ago. Every day of delay has postponed specie payment, & opened the door for repudiation. This was always so obvious to me that I was pained when I saw accomplished financiers throw themselves in the way of the great remedy.

Specie payts will come from the general health of the body politic,— from successful reconstruction—& from harmony between the two branches of the govt. now at feud. Without this it is an impossibility. With this it will come promptly & easily. So it seems to me, & so I have constantly insisted.[3]

Ever Yours, Charles Sumner

ALS MHi (81/472, PCS)

1. Speaking in favor of the Finance Committee's proposal for payment of the national debt, Sherman stated that no 5-20 bond sold after the Legal Tender Act of 25 February 1862 was necessarily redeemable in gold. The Finance Committee also recommended that the U.S. Treasury, in order to pay its debt, issue coupon bonds payable at 5 percent in forty years and redeemable in coin in ten years (*Globe*, 40th Cong., 2nd sess., 1463–64; appendix, 180–89).

2. The House of Representatives had voted to impeach President Johnson on 24 February 1868. Concerned about Johnson's possible conviction, Atkinson wrote CS 25 February asking for reassurance that Johnson's potential successor, Benjamin Wade, would not "commit the country to disguised repudiation." Although he was critical of Johnson on other grounds, Atkinson wrote that in fiscal matters Johnson's removal would be "a great misfortune in its ultimate effect, while admitting that it appears to be a necessity" (Boston, 41/182, PCS).

3. Atkinson thanked CS for his letter and agreed that Sherman's speech was unsettling. "We businessmen seek stability by avoiding the changes which the statesman sees to be necessary in order that stability may be a reality" (29 February, 41/204).

To John Bright
private

Washington 24th March '67 [*1868*]

Dear Mr Bright,

I have yours of 7th March. It finds me under the pressure & anxiety of important events.

One of the great blunders of our history was that the Presdt. was not impeached two years ago.[1] This time has been lost to restoration, political & financial. Had this been done specie payments would have taken place already, & the cry of repudiation would not have been heard. Of course, so long as he remains in office, there can be no reconstruction & no specie payts. Of both of these propositions I have never doubted.

I say nothing of probabilities now; for the cable will give you results before my speculations can arrive.

I do not believe there will be any repudiation in any form.

I am happy to see the good tone about the Alabama;[2] but I am at a loss to know of what value the principle of Arbitration will be in the future, if England, its originator, declines its application to a matter in which as you admit, your govt was "unfriendly & injurious."[3] As a lover of peace & anxious for its foundations, I am infinitely pained by this result. To my mind, it is a terrible blow at Peace. If you can refuse in a case, where you think yourselves clearly right, another Power can do the same, & thus, under yr lead, Arbitration as a principle of International Law is sacrificed.

I do not write now to revive in any way the former offer. It has been rejected,[4] & there are so many here, who rejoice in it, that I presume we must look to some other solution.

The question of the *legality* of the Queen's Proclamation is delicate & novel; & yet, if it was "unfriendly & injurious" can it be consistent with the Law of Nations in an enlightened age? On this there is much to be presented, which thus far has been held back. The whole argt. founded on our blockade must be exploded, if the discussion proceeds.

Ever Yours,   Charles Sumner

P.S. I know no instance in history where one Power while at peace, did so much injury to another, as England did to the U. States during our rebellion, beginning with her concession to our rebels.

ALS   GBL   (81/505, PCS)

1. Bright wrote from Rochdale, "I lament Mr. Johnson's obstinacy & folly. . . . The world will probably think he cannot have a fair trial before the Senate. How is his power to be checked or suspended during the trial, or even after it, if convicted?" (41/272, PCS).

2. On 6 March 1868 Parliament once again debated the *Alabama* claims issue, when G. Shaw Lefevre stated that Lord Stanley should not regard the negotiations as closed and called for publication of the correspondence. Stanley replied to Lefevre that although Great Britain would still defend its concession of belligerent rights to the Confederacy, the principle of arbitration seemed acceptable to both sides. Both Gladstone and John Stuart Mill expressed hope (in varying degrees of optimism) that arbitration could proceed (*Hansard's Parliamentary Debates*, 3rd series, 190:1150–98).

3. Bright stated that "no Govt. could for a moment listen to" such a proposal as Seward's, that the "*legal right* of this Govt. to admit the belligerent rights of the South" was an issue eligible for arbitration. Bright believed in "*legal right*," he wrote, "tho' I wholly condemn the act itself & I think you have great reason to complain of it as unfriendly & injurious." If, however, continued Bright, Seward used the belligerent rights issue to argue that it "enabled English sailors, without the risk of being hanged as pirates, to engage in war against you under the Confederate flag," then his argument was "not unreasonable, & . . . it ought to be granted—& this I think is the general feeling here."

4. Seward had written Adams 13 January that the *Alabama* claims arbitration should be considered definitely closed. Bright wrote, "I learn what you doubtless know, that Mr. Seward has not wholly withdrawn from the question—altho' he professes to have given up 'Arbitration.' *I am sorry he is not more direct & explicit*" (41/272). Indeed, Seward wrote Adams 23 March that when the naturalization differences were resolved, the question of "adjusting the Alabama and other claims in a matter practically unexceptionable in either country" could be pursued (*Foreign Relations* [1868], part 1, 141, 183).

To Francis Lieber

Senate Chamber 27th March '68

My dear Lieber,

You will pardon my seeming remissness. I always read what you kindly write, even if I am unable to write in return.[1]

I ought at once to have reported on Mrs L's letter.[2] At once I saw Mr

Stanton; but I had no encouragement except his good-will. He had no vacancies & did not expect any. Carnot[3] stays & sleeps at the War Office, so that he may not be dislodged by any *ad interim* pretender.

I think you will like the German Treaty.[4] To my mind it is essentially just. It embodies the claim originally made by Cass & for a long time denied by Prussia. His claim represented "high-water mark" on this question in our country, & now Germany reaches this point. The Treaty was carried after debate by 39 to 8.

Monday the trial begins, &, if I can prevail, it shall proceed *de die in diem*,[5] without intermission, to the end. Some think it will last three weeks. If the managers press, I think it may be ended in 10 days.

Can I tempt you here?—[6]

Ever yours,   Charles Sumner

ALS MH-H (64/550, PCS)

1. Lieber had pasted on page 3 of his letter to CS of 19 March 1868 his one-page essay, "The National Polity is the Normal Type of Modern Government," asking CS to read it if and when "Impeachment and other things" allowed him the time (New York, 81/498, PCS).

2. Apparently Matilde Lieber had written CS about securing a West Point appointment for a relative, Edward Oppenheimer (Lieber to CS, 27 February, 81/476).

3. The press had also compared Stanton to the French statesman and military strategist Lazare Nicolas Carnot (1753–1823).

4. The treaty between the U.S. and the North German Confederation provided for mutual granting of citizenship to each country's emigrants. The Senate approved it on 26 March (*Executive Proceedings*, 16:208).

5. "From day to day."

6. Lieber responded he was not certain he could attend the impeachment trial and added, "I take it as a matter of course that all conversation about impeachment with Senators would be taboo'd" (28 March, 81/517).

To Thomas Wentworth Higginson

Senate Chamber
April 11th [1868]

Dear Mr Higginson

I have your note of the 7th and am much obliged to you for it.[1]

The newspapers are full of rumors about Mr. Chase,[2] but I cannot think there is the least foundation for them. I have had too much experience in these matters not to know how almost universally false such stories are, and I have known Mr. Chase too long and well to imagine that he has been governed by any unworthy motives, in the course he has taken.

I am pained to be obliged to differ from him so widely & to find that he is, as it seems to me, so much mistaken, but that he is going to prove false to the principles he has supported through life, I do not for an instant believe.

Faithfully yours   Charles Sumner

Col. T. W. Higginson
Newport R.I.

LS   NjMo   (81/538, PCS)

1. On 31 March 1868, after Chase expressed his right as presiding judge to rule on questions of evidence in the impeachment trial, CS proposed two motions protesting such right. Both motions were defeated (*Globe*, 40th Cong., 2nd sess., supplement, 59, 63). Higginson wrote (Newport, Rhode Island, 41/476, PCS) to thank CS for his recent opinion "The Chief Justice, Presiding in the Senate, Cannot Rule or Vote" (see Wks, 16:98–133).

2. Higginson asked CS if he had heard the story that Chase had earlier consulted certain Democrats about the presidential nomination, and advised checking out the story. Both the *New York Tribune* (1 April 1868:4) and the New York *Evening Post* (23 March 1868:2) printed reports about Chase's possible candidacy in 1868 .

To John Wolcott Phelps

Senate Chamber
April 18th. [?] 1868

Dear Sir

Your letter of the 18th. has been received, and while I agree with you that there are many things in the present situation to be regretted, I am not by any means equally confident that they could have been avoided.[1] Every man must have certain theories, principles by which governments should be conducted, but where we undertake to apply them to practical problems, there are many difficulties to be overcome, many concessions which must be made in order to accomplish the desired result. The old proverb has it "the shortest way across is often the longest way round," and nowhere is this truer than in legislation. It is not every Gordian knot that can be cut: some must be patiently untied.

Take the reconstruction question for example. We had to contend against ignorance, prejudice, disaffection at the South, against division in our own councils, dissatisfaction in the North, the result of financial distress, and against the power and influence of the President, which has all been thrown into the scale against us. Under these circumstances it seems to me more wonderful that we have succeeded so soon, than that we did not long ago. It is easy to point out mistakes after they have been made, but not always so easy not to make them. "The *ex post facto* obviousness of things" is a difficult thing to meet.

I agree with you that the Presidential chair has not always been filled by the most suitable men, but what can be done?[2] We could nominate Pres. Woolsey, but it would be impossible to elect him, and we must take the best man we can get to represent our principles, and trust to the influence of time and education to cure the evils of the present.

Yours truly   Charles Sumner

Gen. J. W. Phelps
Brattleboro Vt.

———————

LS OFH (81/552, PCS)

1. In his long letter to CS, Phelps bemoaned the lack of freedom in the executive branch of the U.S. government. Congress, wrote Phelps, had "bound the executive, neck and heels, that no man of character would wish to attempt the administration of it." He went on to characterize CS's behavior as typical of "the ochlocratic tendencies of the times," because, on the one hand, CS endorsed universal male suffrage while, on the other, he would deny the chief justice a vote in the impeachment trial (41/557, PCS).
2. Phelps stated that potential Republican nominee U. S. Grant was a weak candidate because he had vacillated in his support of the executive branch. He asked CS, "Would it not be better to take a man free from all compromises, all galled roses, all bad issues, like President Wolsey of Yale College, for instance, and thus infuse into our institutions some of their pristine spirit and purity?"

To Francis Lieber

Senate Chamber Saturday
[2 May 1868]

My dear Lieber,

I take it that the whole story in the *Sun* is a quiz.[1] Wade assures me that he has not spoken with a human being about appointments & that every story to the contrary was an invention. He has spoken with me on some possibilities of the future, telling me that I was the only person he had spoken with on the matter. I advised him at the proper moment & before taking any decisive step to see Genl. Grant. The latter is earnest for the condemnation of the Presdt.[2]

The trial lags. Our only remaining trouble is from the disposition of senators to talk after the arguments are finished. My proposition is to vote on the day after the argts.[3]—

There are senators, calling themselves republicans, who are Johnsonite in sentiments.[4] At the head of these is Fessenden, who has opposed every measure by which this country has been saved. Had he openly joined the enemy several years ago, it would have been better for us. He has sown trouble in our camp & been a constant ally to the enemy.

Ever yours,   Charles Sumner

ALS   MH-H   (64/527, PCS)

1. With his letter of 30 April 1868 Lieber enclosed a clipping from the New York *Sun* (30 April 1868) speculating that if Wade became president, Horace Greeley, as "head man of Mr. Wade's administration" would be named secretary of state, or "any place he is willing to accept" (New York, 81/572, PCS).

2. According to William McFeeley, Grant did not speak publicly on the issue, but privately supported impeachment (*Grant* [1981], 275–76).

3. Lieber replied that he agreed with CS that "the Senators have no business to argue the case among themselves" before voting, but he feared that, given the American "craving for oratorical display," CS's proposal would fail (4 May, 81/585). CS's motion that the Senate proceed immediately to a vote was tabled 7 May (*Globe*, 40th Cong., 2nd sess., supplement, 408–9).

4. Expressing some doubt that Johnson could be convicted, Lieber wrote, "A two thirds vote is a very difficult number in a novel case like this." The *New York Times* of 29 April 1868:1 predicted that at least one or two Republican senators would vote to acquit Johnson but that Fessenden would vote for conviction on some of the charges.

To Charles W. Slack

Senate Chamber 8th May '68

My dear Mr Slack,

I enclose a letter for the Collector, written at yr suggestion.[1] I hope Mr Warren may be appointed.

Soon after you receive this the conviction of the Presdt. will be recorded.[2] It has been beyond doubt from the beginning.

How can the country pardon these senators, who have interposed delay to this necessary judgment? Of course, I write this for yr private eye.

Ever sincerely Yours,   Charles Sumner

ALS OKtu (81/592, PCS)

1. The identity of the collector and the circumstances are unknown. Charles W. Slack (1825–85; editor of the Boston *Commonwealth*) had written CS 26 March 1868 that he wished to be considered for the collectorship of internal revenue in the Third District of Massachusetts in case of a vacancy (Boston, 41/410, PCS).

2. Slack wrote CS 8 May, "We are all anxious to know the result of the great trial. Many are *nervous*, but feel they can anchor to you" (42/011). On 6 May the impeachment case was given to the Senate; the *New York Times* expected a verdict by 11 May (7 May 1868:1).

To Henry I. Bowditch

Senate Chamber 21st May '68

My dear Dr,

I am in my seat always, not having been out of it five minutes during this weary session; but I have never heard any proposition to admit new senators in order to influence the conviction of a wicked Presdt; nor do I know any thing of any attempt to *dragoon* senators, who have voted for the criminal after deceiving their associates as is the case with some, if not all.[1]

Some strange stories have reached Boston. There are also painful reports that come from there. We are told that what is called "the legal mind" of Mass. is for acquittal. Give me a lawyer to betray a great cause. It was so on the Fugitive Slave Bill. All the lawyers sustained it, including even the Supreme Ct of Mass. Shameful record! There is a record of equal shame preparing for those who in the same spirit, on technicalities & quibbles, sustain the Presdt.

I have written to you more fully than to any one else on this subject. You were in the old warfare with Slavery, & I have only to say now, that impeacht was one of our great battles with the Slave Power. If it has been lost, it has been through the same men, who in times past have cost Liberty so much.

Bribery,[2] & personal vindictiveness towards Mr Wade have been the decisive influences—with very little of sound law or sound reason.

Ever Yours,   Charles Sumner

ALS MB (81/609, PCS)

1. On 16 May 1868 the Senate acquitted Johnson 35–19 (with seven Republicans voting for acquittal) of charges advanced in Article 11 that he had commited high crimes and misdemeanors (*Globe*, 40th Cong., 2nd sess., supplement, 412). The Senate then adjourned in order that Republicans could attend their convention in

Chicago 20–21 May; two more major articles would be voted on when the Senate reconvened on 26 May. Henry I. Bowditch (1808–92; a former abolitionist and professor at Harvard Medical School) wrote CS 18 May from Boston asking, "Do the leaders of the Republican Party mean to annihilate it? If so they cannot do a better thing than to attempt to *dragoon* Senators into voting for the conviction of the President." He informed CS that most Bostonians favored conviction but not by any "underhand dealing, as adjournment to admit Southern Senators—or by browbeating & calling actual Senators bad names" (42/090, PCS).

2. The House of Representatives approved on 16 May a motion to investigate charges of corruption in the Senate's vote on impeachment (*Globe*, 40th Cong., 2nd sess., 2503–5).

To Francis W. Bird

Senate Chamber—
28th May '68

My dear Bird,

The platform is good *minus* the second article, which is foolish & contemptible. The Democrats will have a great opportunity in exposing its Janus-faced character.[1]

I have to-day filed my Opinion on Impeachment.[2] Having opposed this system of filing, invented for our betrayal, as an apology for delay & an opportunity of self-vindication for the traitors, I came reluctantly & tardily into the idea. When I saw some of the enemy Opinions, I felt that I too must write.

My Opinion occupies 17 *columns* of the Globe. I intend it as a supplement to my speech on the Barbarism of Slavery. This I told Chase on the day of the vote. I have made it thorough.

Major Poor says that the interest in impeachment is gone, so that even the Journal will not print my Opinion.[3] In other days any thing of mine was printed. I doubt if I have ever done any thing so important. From beginning to end I vindicate impeachment & declare my vote to be "Guilty of All & infinitely more." I send slips to Journal to-day. Can you induce the printing?[4]

Ever Yours,   Charles Sumner

ALS   MH-H   (81/612a, PCS)

1. In his letter of 25 May 1868 Bird asked CS his opinion of the Republican Party platform, stating, "Under the circumstances we could not do better." Describing negotiations in the platform committee on the suffrage issue (the "second article," to which CS objected), Bird wrote that the article had been weak and apologetic regarding suffrage when it came from the subcommittee. Yet the final version, unsatisfactory as it was, "does not *deny* the power of Congress, & I yielded. I modified the first

part of the resolution & it stands in my words" (New York, 42/132, PCS). The second resolution's final version stated that Congress's guarantee of equal suffrage to "all loyal men at the South . . . must be maintained, while the question of suffrage in all loyal States properly belongs to the people of those States" (*New York Times*, 22 May 1868:1).

2. *Globe*, 40th Cong., 2nd. sess., supplement, 463–78.

3. Agreeing with newspaperman Ben:Perley Poore, Bird wrote CS that impeachment was "dead & the sooner Congress addresses itself to its regular business, the better. I think the attempt to detect corruption will fail."

4. Bird replied on 9 June, "The Boston papers will publish nothing without enormous pay." He recommended that CS have the opinion privately printed in Washington for distribution in Massachusetts (42/270).

To George William Curtis

Senate Chamber 30th May '68

My dear Curtis,

I fear that you must have judged me harshly, for my too long delay. Yr letter found me much occupied with other things, & this must be my apology.

I should value much the opportunity of seeing my excellent friend, Genl. Raeslaeff, so that I am tempted to those counsels which would bring him among us again, if it were only for a visit.[1] But I cannot answer yr inquiry on this ground.

We are now on the eve of a Presidential election, & already "economy" has become a battle-cry. With this is mingled an opposition towards Mr Seward's shemes of foreign acquisition. I am simply stating facts without expressing opinions. I doubt if any diplomatic unction can prevail at this time, so as to give a reasonable hope for the ratification of the Danish Treaty. It is now pending before the Senate Comttee. of Foreign Relations.[2] Had I submitted it to a vote there at any time since its communication to the Senate, it would have been rejected. Foreseeing this result, I have kept it back, thinking that it were better to have it fail through oblivion rather than by an adverse vote.

Since the Danish Treaty, there have been propositions from Dominica for the sale of Samana,[3] & these also are pending before the Comttee. There is therefore, an alternative. Which of the two to choose?—St Thomas or Samana? I think Mr Seward, if he could have his way, would say "Both." Most persons at this time say "Neither." Looking at this subject, under all the responsibilities of my position, & strongly impressed with the importance of carrying out the engagements made with Foreign Powers I confess that I cannot now see any ground to expect a ratification of the Danish Treaty.

Ever sincerely Yours,   Charles Sumner

P.S. Do we really want a Naval Station in the West Indies?[4] Sooner or later we shall have one, in the course of political events & without purchase.

ALS MH-H (81/613, PCS)

1. Curtis wrote CS 20 May 1868 informing CS that Waldemar Raasloff (1815–83; Danish minister to the U.S., 1859–66) was "anxious" about the status of the pending treaty providing for the sale of the West Indian islands St. Thomas and St. John to the U.S. Raasloff, wrote Curtis, was even considering returning to the U.S. to ensure the treaty's ratification (New York, 42/103, PCS).
2. The treaty had been referred to the Senate Foreign Relations Committee on 4 December 1867, and President Johnson's announcement of the Danish ratification followed on 24 February 1868 (*Executive Proceedings*, 16:4, 178). See Seward to CS, 18 January, 81/375.
3. The Foreign Relations Committee received a report from the secretary of state on 10 February requesting Senate action on the "transfer" of the Samana Peninsula and Samana Bay to the U.S. as proposed in a draft of a treaty with the Dominican Republic (ibid., 163).
4. CS also wrote Seward on 30 May requesting information about Germany's move to establish a naval station in the West Indies (81/616).

To Edward Atkinson

Senate Chamber 3d June '68

My dear Sir,

I think there is some misunderstanding with regard to doings here. The story of the caucus was a mistake.[1]

The story of "the Seven" is sad enough. There is very little doubt that at least two were corrupted by money, & I hear it said that the evidence also affects a third.[2] Two others of most influence were guilty of a duplicity, next in baseness to positive corruption, besides resorting to quibbles against their country. Grimes was always open, although he found in the end nothing but quibbles on which to stand.

The lawyers make a discreditable exhibition in this case. They have belittled their profession, as never before. As an old lawyer, jealous of the profession, I feel this keenly.[3]

Sincerely Yours,   Charles Sumner

ALS MHi (82/006, PCS)

1. Atkinson wrote CS 1 June 1868 (Boston, 42/183, PCS) that he was concerned about Republican "ostracism" of the seven Republican senators (Fessenden, Fowler,

Grimes, Henderson, Edmund G. Ross, Trumbull, and Peter F. Van Winkle) who had voted for Johnson's acquittal. Although dismayed at these senators' decision, Atkinson wrote CS that he was "proud of their independence" and voiced his respect for Fessenden, Grimes, and Henderson especially.

2. According to Donald, CS believed that Ross, at least, had been bribed (DD, 2:337). In Senate remarks 25 and 27 July, Henderson, Fowler, and Ross defended their votes and criticized the House committee's investigation of corruption (*Globe*, 40th Cong., 2nd sess., 4463–65, 4507–17).

3. Atkinson thanked CS for his reassurance that the report of exiling the seven Republicans was a "mis-statement" (5 June, 42/216).

To Edward Atkinson

Senate Chamber 18th June '68

My dear Sir,

I have never made any comment on the invitation to which you call my attention.[1] I leave this to others.

I first knew of it through my colleague Mr Wilson, who, turning round in his seat, handed me a paper containing this item, & he added—"this means mischief; it is aimed at you."

Then came Mr Wilkes of N.Y.[2] who repeated that Mr Stanton had spoken of it as "aimed at Mr S," & Mr Wilkes did not doubt this.

Then came a senator, one of the quibblers to whom F.[essenden] had shewn the letter, who very uproariously declared in the horse-car, that "it was a movement which must end in the ejection of Sumner from his seat."

Meanwhile I recd. two letters, one from a leading politician of Eastern Mass, & the other from a leading politician of Western Mass,[3] both saying that the enemy were beginning to shew their hands, & that this movement was aimed at me.

On all this I say nothing; & I write it now only in reply to yr communication. Of course men are supposed to mean the natural consequences of what they do. It will be for others & not for me to apply this rule to the present case.

When Chief Justice Shaw, by a wretched quibble, committed the judiciary of Mass to the constitutionality of the atrocious Fug. Slave Bill, I do not remember that there was any tender of a public dinner to him; nor did Chief Justice Taney receive such a complt. when he braved all good sentiments to sustain Slavery judicially. Each was brave & conscientious—in sustaining a bad cause.

When in 1776 the Admiralty Judge, Sir James Marriott, predecessor of Sir Jon. Scott, put forth his great quibble against our fathers, declaring solemnly, that as they hold their lands in common socage as of the borough of Greenwich in Kent, &, as this borough was represented in Parlt. therefore the colonists were represented.[4] Basil Montague in his beautiful Essay on the Perfect Lawyer (see his beautiful little volume) mentions this quibble as a perpetual example to be avoided by the good lawyer. I never heard that the Admiralty Judge was dined by our fathers or their reptives in England, out of Complt. to his wonderful invention & his courage in putting it forth.

The news from the South is painful. The triumph of the quibblers is marked with blood. This is fearful. Of course, all sympathy with the quibblers gives encouragement to the bad cause. Yr dinner will quicken bloodshed, & make rebellion joyous. Its influence is already felt by the re-action here in Washington. But this is not the first quibble in history which was a fountain of blood.

Until you wrote me, I did not know that your name was on the list.[5]

Sincerely yours,   Charles Sumner

ALS   MHi   (82/034, PCS)

1. Boston Republicans including Atkinson, Governor Bullock, John Murray Forbes, and Richard Henry Dana, Jr., signed a letter on 10 June 1868 inviting Fessenden to a public dinner at a date of his convenience. Fessenden declined on 25 June because of Senate business (*New York Times*, 1 July 1868:1). On 16 June Atkinson protested to CS about a recent notice in the Boston *Commonwealth* stating that the Fessenden dinner was "a demonstration" against CS. He deplored the fact that editor Slack had been "so stupid" as to print such a "mischievous and absurd allegation." Atkinson informed CS that although he had "gladly" signed the invitation to Fessenden, he and many of the others intended no "adverse expression to yourself" (42/334, PCS).

2. Probably George Wilkes (1817–85), editor of *Wilkes' Spirit of the Times* and a correspondent of CS's.

3. CS probably referred to letters from Bird, who wrote from Boston, "Conservatism is lifting its mischievous front again here, as usual," and from William Stowe of Springfield, who told CS the invitation "had an evil & a personal bearing" aimed at the impending Senate race (9 June, 10 June, 42/270, 280).

4. The statement on the colonists' representation by Sir James Marriott (1730?–1803) was actually made in 1782.

5. Atkinson replied that he saw no connection between the Marriott example and the "present case." He defended the Fessenden dinner, stating that it was organized to "protest against the intolerant spirit which has overwhelmed Messrs. Fessenden and Trumbull and Grimes" (22 June, 42/388).

To Edward W. Kinsley

Senate Chamber 24th June '68

Dear Mr Kinsley,

I have always liked Atkinson much.[1] Once I did something in securing him access to persons here & in commending him as "the pearl of

Boston merchants." On financial questions, he is instructive; but away from these he seems to have lost his wits, or rather to follow some superfine ideas, which are outside the sphere of the practical.

There are men in Boston who have always been willing to wound or at least to coldshoulder the senators chosen by Mass. Letters from A. seem to shew that he drifts into this [congregation?].[2] I am sorry, & wish it were otherwise. If he had as much experience of public affairs as of finances, his judgment would be more unerring.

I was glad to read of the great evng at East Walpole, when our *Bird* of Freedom had such a pleasant roost. I wish I had been there.[3]

Sincerely Yours,   Charles Sumner

ALS MH-H (82/050, PCS)

1. From Boston Kinsley wrote CS gossiping about the Fessenden dinner invitation: "Only think of Edward Atkinson being taken in" (20 June 1868, 42/382, PCS).

2. Besides letters printed here, CS and Atkinson had recently exchanged several others on the impeachment acquittal, the Fessenden dinner, and CS's place in the Republican party. CS had been especially perturbed by Atkinson's letter of 22 June, in which Atkinson stated that he was one "of a very large and as I believe the most judicious section of the Republican party who think it should have been the duty of Congress to make the best of Mr Johnson" (Atkinson to CS, 22 June, CS to Atkinson, 24 June, 42/388, 82/042).

3. In his 20 June letter Kinsley described the tribute to F. W. Bird attended by eight hundred people. CS contributed ten dollars to the celebration (Kinsley to CS, 6 May, 42/029).

To Edward L. Pierce

Senate Chamber 25th June '68

My dear Pierce,

If yr doubts are well-founded, where are we?[1] All the bills for the re-admission of rebel states proceed on the idea of fundamental conditions imposed by Congress. I have not a particle of doubt that they are valid as the Constitution itself.

Pardon me if I suggest that you yield too much to the old pretension of State Rights & do not open yr mind enough to that new power, now awakened into life, from the guarantee clause.[2] Critics of all kinds & even the Sup. Ct. admit that it is for Congress to enforce this clause, when in its judgment the exigency has arrived, & so doing to affix a meaning to republican govt. Next after the Dcltn. of Indep. & the Preamble of the Constitution, this is the most important clause of the Constitution. Let it be enforced, & you have Human Rights every where under the safeguard of the nation & an indestructible unity.

Pray think of these things.—I am glad that you agree with me about lawyers.[3] There I cannot be wrong.

I am astonished at [A]tkinson, who seems to rejoice in writing unpleasant things. But he is so giddy on politics that he hardly knows what he writes.

Ever Yours,   Charles Sumner

ALS   MH-H   (64/556, PCS)

1. On 10 June 1868, in connection with a bill to readmit North Carolina, South Carolina, Louisiana, Georgia, and Alabama, CS delivered an address, "Validity and Necessity of Fundamental Conditions of States." In it CS argued that in giving states the power to "determine the 'qualifications' of electors" and the "power to regulate suffrage," Congress could disfranchise the black race. He proposed that states should promise to grant equal rights and universal male suffrage before readmission (*Globe.*, 40th Cong., 2nd sess., 3024–27). Pierce disagreed with some of CS's arguments in his speech, writing that, while it was appropriate to impose conditions before admitting the states, "each state when fairly in the Union has as much power over its internal affairs as any other" (Milton, Massachusetts, 23 June, 42/411, PCS).

2. See CS to Richard Henry Dana, Jr., 8 February 1866.

3. In his letter Pierce complimented CS for his "Opinion in the Case of the Impeachment of Andrew Johnson," stating, "no mere lawyer ever could look at a large question in a large way."

To the Duchess of Argyll

Washington 30th June '68

My dear Duchess,

It is long since we have written to each other.[1] Perhaps the fault is mine. Meanwhile I have been much absorbed by our affairs.

The cable makes one hesitate to write of events, for before a letter can arrive, it is anticipated. For a long time but one result of impeachment was possible. Delay gave the Presdt. his opportunities, which were used so as to secure the one needed vote. I regard this as a great calamity. As soon as it was known at the South, that the Presdt. was acquitted, unionists, white & black, were insulted. I receive letters daily, shewing the malignant influence there, all quickened anew, which make me sad enough.[2] For my country this acquittal is terrible, but it has relieved me personally of great responsibilities. Mr Wade would have relied upon me, & wished me to leave the Senate.

Mr Johnson, just nominated to London, is very Anglican & desirous of settling every thing with you. This is the best part of him. A veteran lawyer, 72 years of age, accustomed to the conflicts of the bar, & a border-state man, he has experience & the point of honor. On my comttee. he has always supported me in my efforts to keep the peace & I am sincerely sorry to lose him. I moved his unanimous comfirmation by the Senate, which pleased him much.[3] He will not leave till 1st August.—I do not doubt that Grant will be our next Presdt so that, in all probability, the new Minister will have little more than an official visit in England; but he will have powers to treat especially on the naturalization question, & he is very sanguine that he can bring it to a close. Good! Our Fenians are as bad as yours.

I hope you have seen Longfellow with his little flock of children.[4] I am sure you must like him.

You too in England have had your preoccupations.[5] Yr Prime Minister & our Presdt are in similar situations. But your questions are not so fiery as ours; for ours are the unquenched flames of civil war. Remember me always to the Duke & believe me

Ever Sincerely Yours, Charles Sumner

How is yr Mother. Remember me kindly to her. I noted Lorne's entry into Parlt. A stage of life.

ALS CSmH (82/067, PCS)

1. The duchess's last recovered letter, from London on 5 February 1868, alluded to the Sumners' separation: "It grieves me *very* deeply to hear of private as well as public cares" (40/723, PCS).

2. For example, in the week the impeachment trial ended, CS received angry letters from David Root of Camden, New Jersey; William E. Webster of Boston; H. Snapp of Joliet, Illinois; Benjamin P. Chute of Arago, Nebraska; and Frederick Allen of Savannah, Georgia (42/117, 119, 128, 153, 181). The last wrote that "when we heard of the acquittal of andrew Johnson one of the great tyrannical usurpers that is now a living upon this continent I tel you it made many a truly loyal hearts Beat sad."

3. The Senate confirmed Reverdy Johnson on 12 June (*Executive Proceedings,* 16:257).

4. Longfellow had sailed for Europe with his family on 27 May and was then touring England (HWL, 5:238–46).

5. Disraeli had become prime minister in February 1868 and recently had called for a general election in November.

To Charles W. Slack

Senate Chamber 17th July '68

My dear Slack,

I have yr kind note.[1]

Better than any list supplied by me would be a reprint from the Index from any recent *Globe*—say the last—of the entries under my name. This will shew something of the variety of labor.

Six years ago this was done by the State Comttee. & it stifled that criticism. All the entries, with the references, were copied, shewing not only the number of subjects, but the frequency of speech & action with regard to them. If you will transfer this testimony to yr columns, you will present a broad-side. Merely look at my name & follow down the page.

Ever Yours,   Charles Sumner

ALS   OKtu   (82/111, PCS)

1. Slack wrote 15 July 1868, "Everybody is praising your Finance Speech. Still the Hunkers say you are not 'Practical.'" He asked, could CS send him a "list of the subjects you have discussed, or *reported*, not relating to the negro or anti-slavery?" Slack wanted to publish the list, because he thought CS would have a "*stronger* opposition" in the fall than in any former campaign, with Charles Francis Adams as a possible rival. Still, Slack assured CS, "God reigns, and you can beat the whole crowd if you go into the fight with a will!" (Boston, 42/696, PCS).

To J. A. Cowing

Senate Chamber
July 26th. [25] 1868

Dear Sir

I have your letter of the 25th and I need not say I have read it with attention.[1]

The Funding Bill as it passed the Senate seemed to me a wise and salutary measure but the House amendments have destroyed all that was valuable in it.[2] As it passed that body, it was worth nothing, and the action of the House seemed to indicate a prevailing indisposition to pass any measure of that nature now. What the Committee of Conference may have been able to agree on remains to be seen, but at this time of the session, it is very doubtful when the bill in any practical shape passes.

That will leave the question open for another six months, and by that time I hope the election of Grant will have given a death blow to all schemes of repudiation.[3] If the Public credit is once firmly established, our foundation is sure and we can approach the subject with greater hope of a satisfactory conclusion—I feel as if the Financial question will have virtually settled itself before we meet again, and we shall only have to arrange the practical details.

Accept my thanks for your letter, and believe me

Faithfully yours   Charles Sumner

J. A. Cowing Esq.
New York

P.S. Since writing this the Conference Committee have made their report.[4] You will see what it amounts to.

LS VtGEW (82/135, PCS)

1. No letter of 25 July 1868 from J. A. Cowing has been recovered. CS's clerk may have mistaken both dates, since the Senate did not meet on 26 July, a Sunday. In an earlier letter from New York Cowing asked for a copy of CS's 11 July speech, "Financial Reconstruction through Public Faith and Specie Payments." In that speech, CS supported the Senate's proposed funding bill and argued for resumption of specie payments and the gradual disappearance of greenbacks. Cowing wrote that he hoped the House would pass the Senate's bill declaring that only coin, i.e., gold, would be considered legal tender (13 July 42/667, PCS).

2. The bill passed the Senate 14 July and the House (after amendments) on 21 July. The House deleted the provision in the funding bill that legalized gold contracts and changed interest and maturity rates for U.S. bonds (*Globe*, 40th Cong., 2nd sess., 4050, 4310–12).

3. In his speech CS had declared, "so long as Andrew Johnson is President, the return to specie payments is impossible. . . . When General Grant said, 'Let us have peace,' he said also, 'Let us have specie payments'" (ibid., 3965).

4. The conference report removed certain amendments regarding the maturity of U.S. bonds, and the Senate agreed to the bill on 25 July, abandoning its provision for legalized gold contracts. The bill provided for issuing long-term bonds to pay the national debt with interest and principal payable in gold (*Globe*, 40th Cong., 2nd sess., 4466).

To Henry W. Longfellow

Washington 4th Aug. '68

My dear Longfellow,

This morning I was gladdened by yours from Shanklin,[1] a place of which I knew nothing until I learned from the Gazetter that it was a "maritime parish of the isle of Wight." Enough! I wish I were there, escaped from these heats.

Here I am;—Congress over & every body gone;—still detained by incessant work, & not knowing where to go, if I leave. I shall return to Boston, houseless, homeless.

The Duchess of Argyll writes of you in the most charming way & of "the trio of daughters at breakfast."[2] I hope they are enjoying their travels; but hope is unnecessary. They must be very happy.

I am curious about yr experiences, of which you say nothing. Is travel a bore? Are you better off at home? And yet there is much to enjoy. I covet a day at the National Gallery in London, & then at the Louvre. To see such art would fill my soul. It would be much also to feel relieved from all care & responsibility. By the way, the enemy are busy to do this for me, & talk of C. F. Adams as the candidate. Very well. If the people of Mass turn from me, I shall not complain. I have done my duty. My friends have no anxiety, & I have letters from unexpected quarters. You would be astonished at a very generous letter from Wm. Amory expressing "admiration & gratitude" on account of a recent speech on the Finances.[3] I mention this because he has for a long time been bitterly against me. But why should I trouble you with these things?

I often wish you had seen my house. Indeed, you should have come to me. I am trying to make it pretty inside. Do not laugh if I tell you I am buying pictures—originals! like George Brown in the Dame Blanche, who bought a chateau with his economies as sous-lieutenant. But I have some good pictures. Come & see them.

Every thing is auspicious politically. Grant will surely be elected. I was over-ruled in the Senate, when the Presdt. nominated a good Republican to Austria. I had kept the place open thus far & wished to do so until Motley was re-nominated. He is now in Boston & writes me uneasily about the action of the Senate.[4] Good bye! God bless you & all with you!

Ever affectnly Yours,   Charles Sumner

ALS   MH-H   (82/146, PCS)

1. 21 July 1868, 82/124, PCS.
2. Tunbridge Wells, 17 July, 42/704. Longfellow was traveling with his daughters, Alice, Edith, and Anne Allegra.
3. William Amory (1804–88) praised CS's speech but also remarked that the portions on Reconstruction illustrated CS's "usual dangerous ability," which had influenced both Congress and the U.S. "over to what, in my opinion, . . . is a political heresy" (Boston, 24 July, 43/058).
4. CS voted against Johnson's nominees for the post, Samuel S. Cox and Henry A. Smythe. On 25 July the Senate unanimously confirmed Henry M. Watt as minister to Austria (*Executive Proceedings*, 16:271, 323, 342). Motley wrote thanking CS for "constant & friendly efforts in regard to the very painful affair of the Austrian mission" (30 July, 43/110).

To William H. Claflin

Washington 9th Aug. '68

My dear Governor,

I hope you will not decide against being govr. until I have an opportunity of seeing you, which, I trust, will be very soon. You are the man for the party & the cause. If there are reasons, why you should not accept now, I should like to consider them with you. I know of but one, & that I will speak of when we meet.

It must be a source of no common satisfaction to find how the good people of our cwlth look to you. Massachusetts must be kept at the head of the column. Her ideas, sustained by an unwavering Constituency, have led thus far. I do not believe she will take any back-ward steps or adopt a policy which is no better than marking time. Forward is the word. Such at least is my motto.[1]

Ever sincerely Yours,   Charles Sumner

ALS   OFH   (82/154, PCS)

1. Claflin became the Radicals' candidate and was elected governor in November 1868.

To John Bright

Washington
13th Aug. '68

Dear Mr Bright,

I have been detained here by the death of Mr Stevens. Age & decay had reduced him so low that he could not resist a diarrhea. He was a hero; but no financier.[1] On Slavery & the suppression of the Rebellion he was always austere & fixed. His death will make no essential change, unless on the financial question where his activity & authority will no longer perplex. Here he erred; but in all else he was a great leader—to whom all gratitude & honor.

It is hard that the U. States should be so misrepresented by the London press. The *Times* has a correspondent who sees through rebel spectacles & writes with a rebel pen. I doubt if my name is ever mentioned without a misrepresentation.[2] But it is harder to bear the pretentious liberalism of the *News* correspondent, who is more mischievous than the other from his pretenses. It is strange that the *News* will tolerate such hostile perversion.[3]

I wish you well through yr great election.[4]

Ever Sincerely Yours,   Charles Sumner

ALS   GBL   (82/159, PCS)
Enc: Newspaper clipping

1. On 11 August 1868. CS's eulogy was delivered on 18 December (*Globe*, 40th Cong., 3rd sess., 149–51). Stevens had differed from CS in supporting greenback currency and a protective tariff (Eric Foner, *Reconstruction* [1988], 233).

2. The only recent criticism of CS was that in the London *Times*, 7 July 1868:12. The American correspondent, probably Joel Cook, called an exchange between CS and John Conness a "sharp discussion" and alluded to CS's considerable ability to postpone legislation when he wished.

3. E. L. Godkin served as American correspondent for the London *Daily News* (*The Gilded Age: Letters of E. L. Godkin*, ed. William M. Armstrong [1974], 12). In the *Daily News* Godkin praised the Republican senators voting for Johnson's acquittal (1 June 1868:1), satirized Wendell Phillips as making "a profession of extravagance" (22 May 1868:5), and complimented Democrats for their civilized behavior at their recent convention (18 July 1868:5). CS had enclosed an unidentified news clipping criticizing the *News*'s American correspondent because he appeared to be sympathetic to Radical Republicans but instead distorted their views.

4. Bright had written from Rochdale on 1 August, "We shall have a great contest; & from all I hear & see, I think we shall have a substantial & probably a large majority" (43/128, PCS).

To Anna Cabot Lodge

Coolidge House Friday evng
[21? *August* 1868][1]

Dear Mrs Lodge,

I am for a moment happy in the vision that you present of that bride who deserves all happiness. May she have it truly!

I do not know if Motley is a speaker. This is of small account, as the address,[2] when reprinted, will reach thousands, & such will be his audience.

I am at a loss to understand what lesson I need with regard to the *core* of my trouble.[3] The core is very simple. A wife was very wicked & false; turned away from all her vows; turned her house into a hell;—contracted a *liaison* with a foreigner; went off with him two miles on way to a cemetery; staid out at night & was let into the house after midnight; insulted her husband in every possible way; brought public shame upon the house; shewed herself an abandoned woman;—confessing all the time that she had no complaint to make. This is the core of the matter. Read the life of Lady [Halkett?] & of Lady Ellenboro,[4] if you wish to know her character—two bad women rolled into one. This is the core, & nothing else.

I should not write except to ban & protest against any semblance or spark of excuse or apology for this utterly indefensible wickedness. To suggest any such thing is to shew an insensibility to all moral principle

& to truth. It is worse; it is an attempt to throw blame upon an innocent person, who was full of generosity & long-continued silence. Against this I rebel; I protest with all the energy of my soul, as an infamy kindred to the infamy of her character.

Next to the original wickedness of her life is the wickedness taken up by her friends of making another responsible.

I had vowed myself to silence, for her sake, & for the sake of her child. But I am released from my vow. I shall not hesitate to speak of her as she deserves.

I hope you will not complain of me for my frankness. But I wish my friends to understand that on a case like this, where there is no question, I shall not hesitate. Bad woman! to be remembered only with hissing & scorn,—unworthy of her sex, on which she has brought shame.

Dear Mrs Lodge,[5] You must bear this kindly. As a deeply wronged person—wronged even by the suggestions of yr kind note—(as if any *man* or woman could say any thing to extenuate this wickedness) I cannot forbear letting you know my feelings.

Ever Yours, Charles Sumner

P.S.—On looking over yr note I find words about marriage— "what it demands from *both* as a *mutual* contract." If this is intended to apply to my case, you misunderstand the facts. Nobody ever recognized this more completely than I did, or more completely performed all. I was encountered by misconduct, persistent, atrocious, devilish, all of which I bore with patience & silence—when at last she conceived the idea of throwing the blame upon me. The whole story is too painful & without a tittle of excuse or apology, or any thing but baseness, falsehood & wickedness, revealing the worst things of a degraded woman.

Pardon me for annoying you; but I am unwilling for a moment that I should seem in yr mind to have justified the lesson which you propose to teach. On marriage I have been an idealist. I have seen it through visions, & I gave myself to it with a complete surrender; when I was rewarded by the most unpardonable misconduct. But enough. Do not misunderstand me. It is hard to have suffered from this misconduct; & now all is aggravated by this misrepresentation.

C. S.

ALS   MHi   (82/171, PCS)

1. This letter is tentatively dated as a response to Anna Lodge's incomplete letter of 16 August 1868 (Nahant, 43/205, PCS) to CS. No clues to the wedding to which CS referred have been uncovered.

2. Anna Lodge may have referred to Motley's campaigning activities for Grant.

3. Anna Lodge wrote CS that she knew CS was "doing what seems to *you* right under the circumstances," but she was "tempted to risk telling you wherein I think you wrong." She urged CS to be silent regarding Alice Sumner's behavior; "never breathe your convictions, for you would then lose the sympathy & sincere interest, which, believe me, you *now* inspire in your *opponents* as well as your true friends in Boston." She considered Alice Sumner "Heartless, self-willed, undisciplined & *wholly unjustifiable* in her conduct to you, but [*not*] *guilty* in the way you think her."

4. CS may mean Anne Halkett (1622–99), who had been the lover of Joseph Bampfield, a royalist colonel, and later reluctantly married Sir James Halkett; Jane Digby Ellenborough was divorced in 1830 by Edward Law, earl of Ellenborough, on grounds of adultery.

5. This paragraph, with its separate salutation, is on the reverse of page 7 of the holograph letter.

To Anson Burlingame

Boston 6th Sept. '68

My dear Burlingame,

I was sorry not to see you before you left, partly for pleasant chat, but more for some interchange of thought on the Treaty & the vista opened.[1]

I am not suprized at the *Times*. You are doubtless prepared for it. The Standard's article shews that there is a difference in the press.[2] This is a good sign.

I do not know that you have information with regard to the probable course of the British govt. I have some reason to believe that it has conferred with the French Govt, & that the two will act together. I understand that Ld Stanley, while entertaining a natural English regret that the mission did not begin with England, is not hostile to it; but that he desires concessions from China, partly to sustain govt. in ratifying the treaty. The concession mentioned was the navigation of the Yellow River. France will expect the adjustment of the outstanding question about her nationals. Such is what I hear from a good source.

I wish to see you go through with yr splendid mission, visiting all the great Powers, &, having brought them all into kindly relations with China, then return to the ancient empire & there exert the just influence of yr position in opening its gates to mankind. This yr work.

Ever sincerely Yours,   Charles Sumner

ALS   DLC   (82/186, PCS)

1. Burlingame had arrived in the U.S. in May 1868 with a delegation of Chinese diplomats in order to negotiate a new treaty between the U.S. and China opening up

commercial relations between the two countries. That treaty was signed 4 July and ratified by the Senate 24 July. In June CS had been part of a Senate welcoming committee for Burlingame and his delegation and in August had spoken at a Boston dinner honoring Burlingame and the Chinese visitors. The group sailed for Europe on 9 September (Burlingame to CS, 23 May 1868, 42/121, PCS; *Executive Proceedings*, 16:355–56; *Globe*, 40th Cong., 2nd sess., 3215; Wks, 16:318–25; *New York Times*, 10 September 1868:2).

2. The London *Times* criticized the U.S. treaty with China as a threat to British interests (2 September 1868:9). The London *Standard*, however, believed that the treaty was evidence of "the Chinese preparing for an advance by opening windows in the great wall" separating China from the West (3 September 1868, reprinted in the *New York Tribune*, 4 September 1868:1).

To Henry W. Longfellow

Coolidge-House—Boston
17th [*and* 20] Sept. '68

My dear Longfellow,

Here am I in the third story looking from the back of this house over a stable & a machine shop, where I hear constantly the tread of horses & the hiss of steam. To this I have come at last in Boston. For the time this is my home—all that I have here. I miss you always. The consciousness that you were within reach was companionship, &, then, I could take the omnibus & find myself soon under a friendly roof. Nothing of this now.

Of course, I am solitary. I have seen the Motleys several times, who are well installed in the Warren house, Park St, but hardly any body else, except on business or politics. He is much enraged with Seward & looks anxiously for restoration to his post at Vienna, which he considers the only reparation that can be made to him. I do not think he has commenced work. Some have talked of him for Congress in Mr Twitchell's District;[1] but he prefers Vienna to Washington.

Speaking of politics, you will let me confess the satisfaction I have in the unanimity & enthusiasm with which I have been nominated by the State Convention for a fourth term as senator.[2] R. H. Dana called to tell me that there was no opposition to my re-nomination. So at last I have conquered;—after a life of struggle. Meanwhile I am losing my voice, so that it is still uncertain if I can speak during the present canvass. I am in the hands of Dr [*Henry I.*] Bowditch, who finds the bronchial muscles weakened, as if from over work. This is hard for me at this time. He is applying electricity.

But I have said too much of myself. Pardon; 1000 pardons.—Poor Owen[3] is in terrible difficulty. Scraps which I enclose will tell you all.

He says that he fired into the top of the tree, not knowing that any body was there, & meaning to frighten the trespassers. This incident adds to his complications. Was there ever a house that seemed more tumble-down? Dorè[4] could get ideas in his grounds for another sketch of the Enchanted Princess. As I drove to his door, the driver was obliged to part the branches, & all about was over-grown & wild. And now comes human blood to disfigure the scene. He has been reading proofs for me & talks always of you with sincere & beautiful affection, touching me to the heart.

Fields has shown me yr note from Lugano, with Italy in the background.[5] I think I could enjoy that; but I am not sure that I can enjoy any thing more. I remember well that pass of St Gothard, & the vallies descending to Bellinzona. I turned to Maggiore.

We are in the midst of a Presidential election, & the excitement promises to be intense. I do not doubt the result. The defeat of Grant now would be as bad as his defeat at Richmond. All our friends are confident.

Washington—20th Sept. Tomorrow will be a session for a day mainly to provide for another session in October.[6] All this is caused by the failure to remove Johnson. With him out of the way there would have been no occasion for this most troublesome precaution.——Tell me yr plans, & how the children enjoy travel. All for them is happiness, with no echoes from other days. You must be happy in watching their happiness. Give them my love. Fields is jubilant about the tragedies, which he will launch according to the Lugano decree. Good bye! God bless you!

Ever affectionately Yours,   Charles Sumner

P.S. It is pleasant to be in my own house;—so far as any thing is pleasant. A great contrast to the close quarters of a hotel.

I drove by yr house on my way to Mt Auburn. The semi-circular window was open, also one window in the nursery. I wished to stop & go in.

ALS   MH-H   (82/194, PCS)

1. Ginery Twichell (1811–83), U.S. congressman (Rep., Mass.), 1867–73.
2. Republicans meeting at Worcester 9 September 1868 adopted a resolution calling for CS's reelection (*New York Tribune*, 10 September 1868:1).
3. John Owen (1805–82), Cambridge publisher.
4. Gustav Doré (1832?–83), French illustrator.

5. Letter of 23 August, HWL, 5:259. In it Longfellow asked Fields to publish his *New England Tragedies* on 10 October.

6. The assembled Congress simply agreed to convene again on 16 October and 10 November (*Globe*, 40th Cong., 2nd sess., 4518–20). Republicans had called these sessions in case, in their judgment, Johnson failed to carry out Reconstruction measures. Writing Edwin D. Morgan on 4 November that the November session was unnecessary, CS stated, "I do not doubt that the power to come together has been effective, as a *police* against the Administration" (Boston, 82/214, PCS).

To John Russell Young[1]

Boston 24th Sept. '68

Dear Mr Young,

Occupied by the pleasant things you said I forgot two minor points on which I wished to say a word.

(1) Why does G. W. S.—who is so splendidly true & liberal, advocate court dress for our ministers? Did he ever read Sartor Resartus?[2] The taylor is not to be disregarded. Our republic must be emancipated from the *Clothes-Philosophy* of courts; not of society; but of courts. Until this is done we are not on an equality with other powers. The rule is fixed, that any foreigner may appear before the sovereign in the dress which he would wear before his own sovereign. Accordingly in London a Hungarian wears the double jacket which is his national costume, a Turk wears his fez, &, I insist that our American Minister should wear the simple dress of a gentleman in the evng.

This rule of ours is a part of the system by which the Republic will make itself manifest in Europe. It will be follow[ed]. Cobden told me that he never had been to court, & never would go, on account of the dress required, which he would not wear. He would rejoice in our new rule. I am sure that Bright likes it.[3]

(2) The other point was one, briefly prescribed in my little speech at the flag-raising of Ward 6. Why not insist upon calling the democrats "the Rebel Party."?[4] Fasten [*MS incomplete*]

AL   DLC   (82/198, PCS)

1. John Russell Young (1840–99), managing editor, *New York Tribune*.

2. A notice by the *Tribune*'s London correspondent George W. Smalley (1833–1916) had apparently appeared recently in the *Tribune*. CS refers to Thomas Carlyle's satirical work (1833–34) emphasizing that all institutions were simply "clothes" and therefore ephemeral.

3. Young replied on 26 September that he had sent CS's letter to Smalley (New York, 43/323, PCS). Writing from London on 2 December, Smalley acknowledged

CS's criticism of Smalley's "poor little paragraph on Court Dress," and stated that he had no "obstinate opinion" on it. In fact, declared Smalley, noting that many Americans in Britain wanted Reverdy Johnson recalled, "I am more concerned that you should get a decent representative than that he should wear decent clothes" (43/659).

4. In his speech for the Grant-Colfax ticket, "The Rebel Party" (14 September 1868), CS stated that Southerners had taken over the Democratic party: "But, whatever name they adopt, they are the same Rebels who, after defeat on many bloody fields, at last surrendered to General Grant, and, by the blessing of God and the exertions of the good people, will surrender to him again" (Wks, 16:327). Young replied he liked CS's suggestion: "We shall use it effectively in the canvass."

To [Elihu B. Washburne?]

Boston
11th Dec. [October] '68[1]

My dear Sir,

Mr Motley will deliver an address on the Presidential Election on the 20th. It is carefully prepared & treats the question admirably, with just allusions to Grant.

Of course, the *Tribune* will be glad to print this the morning after its delivery; but can not it appear in all the morning papers of New York?—I can send in advance the sheets. What say you?

Ever yours,   Charles Sumner

Skies bright!

ALS   MHi   (82/236, PCS)

1. CS must surely have misdated this letter, because he was not in Boston in December. Evidence points to October, because Motley gave his address "Four Questions for the People," endorsing Grant, on the 20th of that month. In pencil on the document, not in CS's hand, is written "To Hon E. B. Washburne." Washburne (1816–87; U.S. congressman [Whig, Rep., Ill.], 1853–69) was a chief organizer of Grant's presidential campaign.

To Francis Lieber
private

Boston 4th Nov. '68
—day after election.

My dear Lieber,

I have just read yr good letter, & am sorry that my vague language was so vague.[1] But how can one who has suffered as I be happy? Life is very heavy.

A minor trouble has been in my throat which has prevented me from speaking. The vocal organs have been strained, & I was losing my voice. For some weeks I have been under medical treatment, & forbidden to speak in public. Once I did speak. This forbearance was a disappointment; for I longed to do my part.[2]

But this is small, when there is a serious sorrow, from the misconduct of one who should have been true.

The headship of the first commttee. of the Senate is equal in position to any thing in our govt. under the Presdt., & it leaves to the Senator great opportunities.[3] Had Mr Lincoln lived I think I should have been obliged to determine then, if I would supersede Mr Seward. The thought troubled me at the time; for how could I leave reconstruction & Equal Rights unsettled in the Senate? Nobody has ever heard me say that I would accept any place out of the Senate, if it were offered to me. I admit, however, that my country has a right to determine where I can work best.

Ever Yours,   Charles Sumner

ALS MH-H (64/591, PCS)

1. No letter from Lieber has been recovered. CS apparently referred to his letter of 1 November 1868 to Lieber, in which he described his poor health and unhappiness (64/589, PCS).

2. Republicans won solidly in the Massachusetts legislature, assuring CS of reelection.

3. Lieber probably expressed the hope, as had other correspondents, that CS would become secretary of state in Grant's administration. See Samuel Gridley Howe to CS, Boston, 10 September, 82/188; John Russell Young to CS, New York, 26 September, 43/323; and George Smalley to CS, London, 2 December, 43/658.

To Samuel Gridley Howe
private

Senate Chamber 7th Decbr. '68

My dear Howe,

I write now from my desk on the first day of the session by way of P.S. to my letter of yesterday.[1]

Latterly I have been led to think more than ever of the uncertainty of life. Perhaps the little interest I have in it has made me notice symptoms that in a gayer mood I might have neglected. Suffice it to say, that I have now but one solicitude; it is to print a revised edition of my speeches before I die. If this were done, I should be ready to go.

These speeches are my life. As a connected series, they will illustrate the progress of the great battle with Slavery, & what I have done in it.

I hope it is not unpardonable in me to desire to see them together especially as I have nothing else.

Sometimes I think of giving up my house or cutting off expenditures in order to devote my means to this object; but I am so comfortable in my surroundings, &, at my time of life & in my public position, feel their necessity so much, that I hesitate.

Therefore, I left the question of publication to Fields.[2] All I desire is the edition, although it will impose an onerous labor upon me; but I can do it better than any body else.

I am thus communicative, because I wish you to understand my feelings on this matter.

Ever yours,   Charles Sumner

ALS   MH-H   (64/597, PCS)

1. CS wrote Howe 5 December 1868 seeking advice about an edition of his speeches. CS wanted to have editorial control; because of his concern about the cost of such a publication, he wondered if a subscription drive beforehand would be appropriate (Washington, 64/593, PCS).

2. Fields replied 14 January 1869, recommending that CS accept the offer of Lee & Shepard, the Boston publisher. Although Fields wrote that he would like the contract, he thought Lee & Shepard better equipped to secure prepublication subscriptions (Boston, 44/389).

VII

CONFLICTS WITH GRANT

January 1869 – March 1874

T HE ELECTION OF
Grant marked for Sumner not only a change from the much-despised
Johnson administration but also a shift in his interests. Recovered let-
ters in 1869 indicate that he focused almost entirely on foreign policy.
To be sure, Sumner had been commenting since 1862 on Britain's
"adverse sympathies" with the Confederacy (to John Bright, 5 August
1862) and, since the war, the stalled *Alabama* claims negotiations.
Sumner continued to advocate settlement by arbitration and to blame
Britain for the delay.

Sumner's change of focus from domestic politics may have resulted
from frustration over the Senate's failure to convict Andrew Johnson in
May 1868. More importantly, Sumner probably hoped to be named
secretary of state (see to Francis Lieber, 4 November 1868). When he
was not, Sumner nevertheless saw an opportunity to control foreign
policy with a supposedly ignorant president in the White House and
his old friend Hamilton Fish heading the State Department.

Sumner was correct in asserting that his main points in "Claims on
England" were not new (to the duchess of Argyll, 18 May 1869) but
consistent with what he had written and spoken earlier. Publicly as well
as privately Sumner had faulted Britain for conceding belligerent status
to the Confederates and for permitting construction of their cruisers.
From the beginning of the Civil War (see to Richard Henry Dana, Jr.,
30 June 1861) Sumner had feared that a Northern blockade would
imply that the Union regarded the Confederacy as a separate nation.
But once the Union had established the blockade, he maintained that
it meant no such thing, that the Confederacy was still no more than an
insurrectionary body and thus not entitled to the belligerent status
Britain granted it in May 1861. Although he later hedged on terminology to make himself appear in complete agreement with the Grant
administration on British policy, Sumner still stated that the British
concession was the "first link in the chain by which the liability was
fixed" (to John Sherman, 1 May 1871). In this stance Sumner and

Seward agreed (see to John Bright, 10, 16 December 1867), and Sumner praised Seward's "persistency" (to Adam Badeau, 26 July 1869).

Sumner dominated foreign policy for most of 1869, as these letters show. When in 1870 the Santo Domingo annexation issue eclipsed the *Alabama* claims negotiations in both his and Grant's minds, the break between the two became public, and the result had to be Sumner's deposition as chair of the Foreign Relations Committee. Sumner's initial opposition to the Santo Domingo treaty was not simply antagonism to Grant. In the early 1850s Sumner had shown concern for the independence of Haiti and later for keeping the West Indies free from U. S. involvement (see Sumner to Wharncliffe, 19 December 1852, to John Bigelow, 17 June 1854, and to George W. Curtis, 30 May 1868). That Sumner refused to drop these issues even after Grant's expansionist designs had been effectively stopped in the Senate is just one more example of Sumner's single-mindedness and lack of perspective.

Surprisingly, Sumner did drop his opposition to Grant and Fish's foreign policy on the Senate's final consideration of the Treaty of Washington in May 1872. David Donald has pointed out how the treaty in many respects met Sumner's demands for national claims. Thus the senator had no choice but to agree to ratification in May 1871. To his critics like Reverdy Johnson and Francis Lieber, Sumner asserted that the treaty reflected his policy. Yet to others like George Bemis, Lord de Grey, and George Smalley, Sumner regretted that it did not go far enough. He wrote de Grey, Smalley, and Sir Stafford Northcote about the treaty's failure to establish permanent principles for international maritime law: "we ought to have got more, and mankind should also" (to George Smalley, 18 June 1871). Ironically, the U. S. case prepared by Bancroft Davis and submitted to the Geneva arbitration tribunal in December 1871 contained a much stronger set of demands than Sumner's (see to Whitelaw Reid, 25 April 1872), despite Sumner's suggestion publicly and privately that Britain cede Canada to the U. S. as compensation for damages from the *Alabama* and other cruisers. When in May of 1872 the Senate considered a supplemental article to the treaty in which the U.S. agreed to withdraw all national claims, Sumner's silence is puzzling. He voted against the article, but apparently said little. Only brief statements as to his thinking survive (see to Reid, 25 April 1872, and to George Bemis, 20 May 1872). Some interpreters (Adrian Cooke, for example) say that Sumner was too ill to protest vigorously. Yet he had sufficient energy for a four-hour anti-Grant speech later that month.

It can be argued that Sumner did genuinely want peace, not war, between the United States and Britain, even if to some observers he sought it in strange ways. In other instances, such as advocating a cautious policy toward France during the Civil War, and in defending Lord Lyons's conduct (see to Francis Lieber, 3 May 1863), Sumner showed himself a diplomat and peace advocate. Perhaps, as on some Reconstruction issues, Sumner recognized that the Treaty of Washington and its subsequent article, promising peace, would have to suffice. He was no doubt sincere when he wrote Bright (8 August 1865), "our true objective should be to bring the two countries into relations of harmony & good will." Sumner had always declared that no monetary value could be put on the cruisers' damages and the prolongation of the war. Hence he did not gloat over the $15.5 million in damages the Geneva tribunal awarded to the U.S. To Bright he wrote that the settlement was "the beginning of an organized substitute for war. This is worth all its cost in debate & in money" (21 September 1872).

After his removal from the chair of the Foreign Relations Committee Sumner's declining health preoccupied him, and he returned to his mission to enact federal legislation ending all discrimination against blacks. He took refuge in the past, in editing his speeches. "I have always insisted that my life was in my speeches," he wrote Edward L. Pierce, 7 January 1870. In his final years, after officially repudiating Grant and endorsing Greeley for president in July 1872, Sumner broke with many men who had sided with him in his struggles: George William Curtis, Frederick Douglass, William Lloyd Garrison, Francis Lieber, Gerrit Smith, and Henry Wilson. "Why have I always been in the breach?" Sumner had earlier asked Longfellow (22 June 1870). Almost any friend or correspondent could have answered that question—but not Sumner. Publicly a man with sweeping visions, privately Sumner lacked insight. He continually failed to understand why or how his relationships were broken; he simply mused to Longfellow, "And yet it seems to be the same as at the beginning."

To John Bright

[*Washington, 17, 19 January 1869*]

Of course I read carefully all that you say, whether to the public, or better still, to myself. Your last letter was full of interest. All the treaties have been sent to the Senate in copy.[1] They would have been ratified at any time last year almost unanimously. I fear that time will be needed to smooth the way now. Our minister has advertised the questions by his numerous speeches, so that he has provoked the public attention if not opposition.[2] The Senate is not removed from popular influence; and I doubt if it will act until it begins to hear the public voice. Thus far nothing has been said on the question in the Senate or in my committee, but I have heard loose talk from senators to the effect that our minister has made it impossible to adopt anything he has done. I mention this, not to vindicate it, but only to give you a glimpse of floating impressions. All this troubles me. I think that never at any time have I felt so powerless over the question. This may change; but I think time will be needed. You are aware, of course, that the feeling towards Mr. Seward will not help the treaties. At this moment I do not know well enough the views of General Grant, which will necessarily exercise great influence.[3] It is some time since I spoke with him on the subject. He was then very exacting.

Tuesday, January 19. I finish this letter at my seat in the Senate. Last evening I met General Grant at dinner, and conversed with him briefly on the new treaties. I would not commit him, and do not think that he has any very precise policy. He did not seem to object to the naturalization and San Juan negotiations, but I think he had a different feeling with regard to the Claims convention. He asked why this could not be allowed to go over to the next Administration? This morning I called up the subject in my committee. There was nothing but general conversation, in the course of which it was remarked that Great Britain had never appreciated the wrong, the terrible wrong, done to us, not only in the cases of ships destroyed, but also in driving our commerce from the ocean. You know that I have never disguised the opinion that the concession of belligerent rights was wrongful; that there can be no ocean belligerency in a power without the capacity of administering justice on the ocean,—in other words, without prize-courts and ports. Of course, therefore, such a concession to pretenders without this capacity must be at the cost of the power which makes it. As a principle of law and justice I cannot see how this can be doubted. Denied or questioned, it must ultimately be adopted as essential to the safeguard of the seas. To what extent it will enter into our settlement I cannot now say. I wish I could write more fully and carefully, and see the future more clearly; but I write as well as I can under pressure and with business going on about me. There are topics in your letter of great interest.[4]

PL[5]   Prc, 4:368–69   (82/307, PCS)

1. Two treaties with Great Britain were signed 14 January 1869. The Johnson-Clarendon Convention, signed by Clarendon, the new foreign minister in the Gladstone government, established a commission of four representatives (two from the U.S. and two from Britain) to meet in Washington and rule on all claims from both countries. Any claims not settled by the commission would be referred to a mutually agreed-upon arbitrator, if possible; if not, the commission would cast lots to determine which arbitrator would decide a claim. The Treaty on San Juan Islands would settle a U.S.–Canadian boundary dispute. The naturalization treaty, signed 9 October 1868, would provide mutual citizenship privileges to immigrants. All three were referred to the Senate Foreign Relations Committee 19 January (Reverdy Johnson to Seward, 15 January 1869, *Foreign Relations* [1868–69], part 1, 400–405; *Executive Proceedings*, 16:443).

2. Reverdy Johnson had already come under serious U.S. criticism for acquiescing too readily and too publicly to British demands. Regarding Johnson, Bright wrote 25 December 1868 from Rochdale, "Your Minister here seems to have caused much disappointment with you—& he has caused me some of the same feeling. The general impression here is that he has spoken more than was necessary" (44/164, PCS).

3. Bright wrote, "I suspect neither your Minister nor ours understands what is really the position & the intention of Mr. Seward. . . . The impression here is that he does not want the matter settled, or that he feels his position in the Senate so feeble that he dare not bring any arrangement which is possible for him, before that Body with any chance of success." If Seward suspected that the "popular outcry" against Reverdy Johnson would cause the Senate to defeat the treaty, wrote Bright, it had better wait until the Grant administration was in place. CS wrote Dana 26 January 1869, "The claims question with England will go over to the next Admtion, & will probably become one of the greatest international litigations in history" (82/313).

4. Bright stated he thought that Lord Stanley (foreign minister in the now defunct Disraeli government) had "yielded everything that could reasonably be asked." He asked CS to inform him if he could about "the cause of the present obstacles to further progress in the negotiation." He concluded, "Our views are much alike, & our objects are precisely the same."

5. No holograph letter has been recovered.

To Benjamin Hall Wright

Senate Chamber March 12th [*1869*]

Dear Sir

I have your letter of the 10th and have read it with pleasure.[1] The feeling against the action suggested by General Grant both in Congress and in the country seems to have been very strong and I am glad the difficulty has disappeared. I hope General Grant will make no more mistakes.

Yours truly   Charles Sumner

B. H. Wright Esq
Rome N.Y.

LS   DLC   (82/354, PCS)

1. Benjamin Hall Wright (1801–81), an engineer in Rome, New York, wrote CS (10 March 1869, 45/449, PCS) applauding CS's action in objecting to the appointment of New York merchant Alexander T. Stewart as secretary of the Treasury. The Senate had confirmed Grant's nominee on 5 March, but when a statute forbidding any persons involved in trade or commerce from holding U.S. Treasury Department appointments was brought to light, Grant requested an exemption in Stewart's case. CS called for full Senate consideration before any vote, and on 9 March Grant withdrew his request (*Executive Proceedings*, 17:3–4; *Globe*, 41st Cong., 1st sess., 22, 34; *New York Times*, 10 March 1869:1).

To the Duchess of Argyll

Senate Chamber 6th April '69

My dear Duchess,

I was glad to have yr last letter; but I am mystified by what you say about something attributed to me. I have said nothing; not a word thus far.

It became my duty as chairman of the Comttee. to make a unanimous report against the Claims Convention;[1] but I have not spoken or even conversed on the subject, except with Motley, who has been here for several weeks.

The treaty has not been considered in the Senate; but will be, probably, early next week. Other business has been in the way. It is probable that on its consideration, I shall be obliged to state the case as it is understood by the Committee.

I have never ceased to regret that this terrible question was not considered by England at an earlier day; for it was easy to see that the more it was understood by our people, the more exacting they would be. Mr Johnson's course has aroused the country. Genl. Grant has very strong convictions on the question.

You will be glad to see Motley, whose business & aspiration will be to settle this question.[2] He is much in earnest, & has given attention to the case.

You speak of two children married. One is Edith. Which is the other?[3]

Ever yours & the Duke's,   Charles Sumner

ALS   CSmH   (82/378, PCS)

1. The Senate Foreign Relations Committee had recommended on 18 February 1869 that the Johnson-Clarendon Convention be rejected (*Executive Proceedings*, 16:483).

2. Motley was unanimously confirmed as minister to Great Britain on 13 April (ibid., 17:162).

3. The duchess replied on 1 May that her second son, Archibald, was a recent bridegroom (Kensington, 46/546, PCS). Edith Campbell (d. 1913) married Henry George Percy, seventh duke of Northumberland, in 1868.

To Hamilton Fish

Wednesday morng.
[*Washington 14 April 1869*]

My dear Fish,

I did not hear the list of consuls when read at the desk yesterday, but have just read it in the *Chronicle*.

I am astonished to find "J. C. Fletcher Consul at Palermo." [1] Eight years ago Mr. Lincoln, without saying a word to Seward, gave that place to me for the benefit of Louigi Monti, an Italian teacher at Cambridge, who had married a Boston lady, & was an intimate friend of Longfellow, I asked for it to oblige Longfellow & the family of the lady. [2] The salary is $1500. Only an Italian could live there on this pay.

I observe that hardly any of the numerous & very competent candidates from Mass are taken; but it seems to me hard that my only nominee on the consular list should be sacrificed. At this moment Longfellow is on a visit to Monti at Palermo, where he may hear by telegraph that a republican administration has displaced his host, leaving him poor & without support. Should this be so? [3]

Ever yours,   Charles Sumner

ALS   DLC   (82/396, PCS)

1. James Cooley Fletcher (1823–1901) was then a U.S. agent in Brazil.

2. See CS to Longfellow 16 March 1861. Monti's wife, Frances Parsons Monti (d. 1906).

3. From the State Department Secretary of State Fish replied at noon, 14 April 1869, expressing his regrets but explaining that Monti was a "total stranger" to him. Had CS spoken sooner, he would not have been dismissed (46/538, PCS). On 25 May CS wrote Longfellow, "Monti is safe" (82/485).

To John H. Clifford

Washington 5th May '69

My dear Govr,

I have already told Mr Grennell that I shall sustain any nomination for collector at New Bedford made by Mr Buffington. [1] It only remains that the latter should make the nomination.

I must thank you much for yr good sympathetic note on my last speech, which seems to be so well recd.[2] Many things I have done better, but here I have become the voice of my country, &, therefore, find praises to which I am unaccustomed.[3] But nobody has written me more kindly or authoritatively than yourself.

Sincerely Yours, Charles Sumner

P.S. Hooper & Motley are gone & I am here alone, expecting to stay till June. If you can come to Washington in this interval, I wish you would make my house yr home. Come!

ALS MHi (82/439, PCS)

1. Clifford wrote CS 2 May 1869 (New Bedford, 46/569, PCS) that he wished his relative, a Colonel Allen, to be collector of customs in New Bedford and looked to James Buffington (1817–75; U.S. congressman [Rep., Mass.], 1869–75) to nominate him. The incumbent, Grinnell, was a nephew of the collector of the port of New York, Moses H. Grinnell (1803–77).

2. CS delivered his speech opposing the Johnson-Clarendon Convention, "Claims on England," in executive session 13 April; the Senate voted 54–1 to reject the treaty (*Executive Proceedings*, 17:163). In his letter of 15 April Clifford wrote that CS had "developed in an unanswerable manner, the vital importance" of distinguishing between ocean and land belligerency (Boston, 46/221). CS had declared, "There is a dominion of the land and a dominion of the ocean. But, whatever power the rebels possessed on the land, they were always without power on the ocean. Admitting that they were belligerents on the land, they were never belligerents on the ocean" ("Claims on England" [1869], 5).

3. For example, J. G. Dudley, a stranger, wrote from New York that CS had "touched the key note of the sentiment of the American People"; from Rochester, Frederick Douglass declared, "Voices that once reached you hoarse with wrath and disparagement are now clear and melodious with praise"; William Amory wrote that CS's speech "deals courteously & in statesmanlike tone & phraseology very hard blows . . . to John Bull" (15 April, 26 April, 6 May, 46/224, 459, 628).

To Hamilton Fish

Washington, Monday morng
[17 May 1869]

My dear Fish,

On careful reflection it seems to me better that I should withdraw that sketch in pencil, which was an attempt on my part to harmonize the ideas of the Administration with a just statement of our case against England.[1] The sketch is inadequate & does injustice to the strength of our case, which I am unwilling in any way to weaken.

It will be for Congress to determine hereafter how much shall be claimed & on what grounds. The publication of the Alabama correspondence, which is now proceeding on the order of the Senate,[2] will be the signal for debate, & I do not doubt that this question will occupy much of the attention of the next session. Seward has always anticipated the time when Congress would take jurisdiction of it.

Under these circumstances I am more than ever satisfied, that, as chairman of the Senate Committee, I ought not in any way to be a party to a statement which abandons or enfeebles any of the just grounds of my country, as already expounded by Seward Adams & myself. As you were kind enough to give me an opportunity of expressing an opinion, I owe it to frankness to declare my dissent from the course proposed. I do this in all kindness and only under a sense of duty.

The only person I have spoken with on this question is Mr Cushing,[3] who, after perusing my speech again & consulting his books, affirms its absolute conformity with the Law of Nations & its moderation of tone. I am sure that good lawyers, who look into the question, must come to the same conclusion. I do not doubt what will be the judgment of Congress. It will not take any steps backwards.

I regret that Mr Motley's own programme[4] has not been adopted, believing as I do, that, it is in harmony with the public convictions, & with the law. It is rare that the cause of the country has so eloquent a defender. I wish he were allowed to speak according to his own enlightened discretion. The cause cannot suffer through him.

I write now with much diffidence, & only because I fear, that without this explanation my position may be misunderstood. We are beginning the greatest international debate of our history. I hope that nothing may be said at the outset for us to regret hereafter.[5]

Believe me, my dear Fish, with true regard,

Sincerely Yours,   Charles Sumner

ALS   DLC   (82/466, PCS)

1. Fish and CS had disagreed on how strongly the U.S. case should be based on the Queen's Proclamation of 13 May 1861, which conceded belligerent rights to the Confederacy. CS argued in his speech that the *Alabama* damages stemmed directly from Britain's concession. According to notes in the Fish Papers, CS asked to amend the original instructions to Motley, approved by the Cabinet on 15 May 1869. These instructions read: "The President wishes it to be understood that he does not complain of the fact of the accordance by Great Britain or any other nation of belligerent rights to the insurgent population during the late rebellion within the U.S. . . . He does not rest the claims of this nation against G. Britain upon the time of the issuing the proclamation of neutrality by the latter Gov.—." Fish objected to CS's first amendment, which read: "The Prest . . . does not mean to found upon this act any

special claim of damages. He regards it as the beginning of the unjustifiable conduct of England, & as constituting a part of the prolonged system which resulted so disastrously to the U. States. It necessarily enters into the discussion as part of the case." CS then modified his language to state: "The President wishes it understood, that the claims of the U. States are founded on actual losses, suffered by individual citizens or by the Nation. Questionable as was the original concession of belligerency under the circumstances when it was made, he regards it as a part of the case only so far as it shows the beginning of that course of conduct, which resulted so disastrously to the U. States. It is less important in itself than from what followed" (copies of Fish's draft and CS's version, Fish Papers; J. C. Bancroft Davis, *Mr. Fish and the Alabama Claims* [1893], 31–33; draft of second revision in CS's hand, 6, Fish Papers, Library of Congress).

2. U.S. Senate, *Alabama Claims*, Senate Ex. Doc. no. 11, serial sets 1394–98.

3. Cushing, now a Republican, practiced law in Washington and headed a commission to revise U.S. statutes. He and CS began to see each other socially in 1868. Claude Fuess states that in December 1868 CS had brought about Cushing's appointment as special envoy to Colombia to negotiate a canal treaty (*The Life of Caleb Cushing* [1923], 2:301).

4. Motley had prepared his own instructions and submitted them to Fish on 26 April 1869. In his "Memoir" Motley argued that the U.S. blockade of the Southern coast "was an act of sovereignty rather than of war" (14) and that the "virtual recognition by Great Britain of the so-called confederacy . . . was the fountain and origin of the evils by which we are now oppressed" (4). Motley termed the Queen's Proclamation "the first and almost fatal step" in the war because it "breathed into the so-called confederacy the breath of such life as it was ever destined to attain" (8) (typed copy in Fish Papers, Library of Congress; a note by "A. N." stated that the "original was given to Sumner").

5. Fish replied that he regretted receiving CS's note that morning. He wrote, "We have but one object & differ only as to some incidents—they may be of more importance than I suppose, or of less than you think" but scarcely enough to "break down an Administration." He hoped CS would reconsider his withdrawal (Washington, 17 May, 47/033, PCS).

To John Lothrop Motley

[*Washington 17 May 1869*]

At last the document is finished. Caleb Cushing dined here last evening, and we discussed the points thoroughly, there being no difference between us.[1] He had reperused my speech and examined the books, and was prepared to stand by my text as in complete conformity with the law of nations. He thought the paragraph I drew as a mode of settlement toned down the true doctrine and inadequately stated our case. I knew it was so, but I did it in order to harmonize the ideas of the Adminstration with our case. On reflection this morning, I wrote a note to Fish withdrawing my draft, and at the same time expressing my dissent from the draft he proposed. My purpose was to leave him to make his own statement, for which I should be in no respect responsible. Shortly after breakfast Cushing called, and went from me to the state department. After four hours he has just returned, saying that it is all settled to his satisfaction; that the clause abandoning our position on belligerency is given up, and that the rest of the paragraph is very much as I wrote it.[2]

Fish is going to give you a consular convention to negotiate, which has long been desired, but which England has always hesitated about, owing to the difficulty of reconciling some of the ordinary consular prerogatives with the common law.

The President is desirous to have it known that he recognizes as a right of sovereignty the concession of belligerency, as he may wish to use it with regard to Cuba.[3] It was the effort to state this principle that caused the embarrassment. Of course there is no doubt that a nation may do this thing precisely as it may make war; but if it does it without good reason it is an unfriendly act. Fish was also very desirous to separate England from France, and I drew a clause to meet this point. Obviously the two cases are different. Both did wrong in the concession of belligerency, but it was only in England that the concession was followed by blockade-runners and pirate ships. In France there was *damnum absque injuria*; in England, *damnun cum injuria*. And yet the English are busy over this alleged inconsistency of my speech in arraigning England and not arraigning France. But (1) There was no French treaty under discussion; and (2) There were no damages from France. All this is plain enough. I feel very grateful to Cushing, who has brought his authority to bear on Fish. I say to you for your encouragement that he agrees with me on all the points. To my mind, his opinion is the best we can have.

PL[4] Prc, 4:406 (82/471, PCS)

1. After receiving Fish's reply of 17 May 1869, CS sent it to someone, probably Cushing, with the note "Please read & return." CS informed his recipient that he had written Fish "withdrawing my pencil sketch as inadequate & doing injustice to the national cause" (47/033, PCS).

2. The final instructions read: "The necessity and propriety of the original concession of belligerency by Great Britain at the time it was made have been contested and are not admitted. They certainly are questionable, but the President regards that concession as part of the case only so far as it shows the beginning and the animus of that course of conduct which resulted so disastrously to the United States." The instructions closed with this paragraph: "You will, therefore, be pleased, in your social and private intercourse and conversation, as well as when it becomes necessary in your official conversation and intercourse, to adopt this view of the declaration of neutrality by Great Britain, and the other Powers, and to place the cause of grievance against Great Britain, not so much upon the issuance of her recognition of the insur-

gents' state of war, but upon her conduct under, and subsequent to, such recognition" (15 May 1869 [the original date remained in the revised version], "Recall of Minister Motley," 5).

3. Since October 1868 insurgents in Cuba had been waging a war against their ruler, Spain. A provisional Cuban government had been formed in 1868, and various agents, based mainly in New York, were pressuring the U.S. to recognize Cuban belligerency (Allan Nevins, *Hamilton Fish* [1937], 177–80; Joseph V. Fuller, "Hamilton Fish," *The American Secretaries of State and Their Diplomacy*, 7 [1928], 138–41).

4. No holograph letters from CS to Motley have been recovered.

To the Duchess of Argyll

Washington 18th May '69

My dear Duchess,

Friendship should always be frank; but it must not be unjust. You forget my duties to my own country & to truth; & you forget also that during the war I never failed to condemn that terrible & fatal Proclamation.[1] My words are of record in my speech of Sept. 1863 on which Ld Russell commented at Blairgowrie. What I have said lately, is only a mild repetition of what I said then.

I have never disguised that, in my opinion, the worst blunder in all English history was that Proclamation. I had always hoped that, in some way or other, it might pass out of sight, so at least that I might not be obliged to pronounce judgment upon it. For years I have been silent, almost to the neglect of the duties of my position. At last a treaty was signed on which I was constrained to act.

There seemed to be madness in such a negotiation begun after the people had chosen another Presdt. It was as if discarded servants had undertaken to sell their master's property. I never saw the treaty until it was sent to the Senate. At once it became known & was condemned by the Senate & the people; even in advance of its consideration by the committee. When I looked at it, I saw how utterly inappropriate & inadequate it was. A year or six months before, in the national mood at that time, it might have been accepted, not that our case was not the same then that it is now, but the Nation was less exacting. I was satisfied, that the treaty could not be ratified, & *that it ought not to be ratified*. Its ratification would have been an evil day for all who love peace, for it would have left an inappeasable sense of wrong in the national heart. I felt that the time had come for England to know our case. It became my duty to state it. My statement is adopted by the Senate & by the country.

Mr Motley was unanimously confirmed, on my motion, immediately after the rejection of the Treaty, as he had been originally nominated by the Presdt on my recommendation, &, as the Secy of State informs me "as a compliment" to me. Nobody could have been nominated or confirmed, whose position on our relations with England was doubtful. Of course Mr Motley agrees with me. His competitor Mr Jay is the author of the articles in the New York Tribune, which go so much beyond the speech you condemn.[2]

You know well that England by her course to us, has deeply offended & shocked all her best friends in the U. States. Talk with Motley or Longfellow, & they will tell you the truth. I do not think her case improved by recent manifestations—may I say it?—in the tone of yr letter.

The people here are in no hurry. They had rather wait. They are not disturbed by the sayings, that England will not entertain our claims. I fear that the majority here hope she will not. I do not agree with them. I wish settlement & concord; but this can be only by candor & fairness. Harshness & abuse will not do it.

The Presdt. does not desire Motley to press our claims. He willingly leaves to yr govt. to say when you are willing to consider them. But he is instructed specially to exhibit the difference, which yr letter fails to appreciate, between England & France.[3] Both erred in that fatal Proclamation; but no pirate-ships or blockade-runners, causing infinite detriment to the American people were allowed to leave France. We distinguish clearly between the two countries. England stands alone.

Nothing can better illustrate the weakness of the English defense, that the constant inquiry, "why not complain of France also"? The inquiry shows the blindness of English eyes to the wrong done us—in my judgment the greatest wrong ever done by a friendly Power to another friendly Power. So it has always seemed to me & so it seems now.

To yr inquiry about the Sibyl I answer, the justice of our claims has always been the same.[4]

And now, my dear Duchess, I ask—why write these things? Perhaps I err. I would not say any thing unkind or harsh; but I must leave yr letter unanswered or answer it frankly. I have said nothing except in plain reply.

The Motleys go by the Steamer that takes this letter—wife & three daughters.[5] His position will be difficult; but you know that he is no enemy of England. I hope there will be no unkindness; but with yr press, so embittered & so unjust, it is hard to see how any body can be decent. But I trust to returning reason & to that good sense which is English.

I am glad you added what you did about yr children, for there I sympathize with you completely. I follow the path of justice towards

Ireland which your cabinet is treading[6] & hope for that day of reconciliation which will be so precious. I hope for it also between England & the U. States.

I note that the Duke is again an author.[7] I do not wonder, when already so successful.

Good bye!

Ever sincerely Yours,   Charles Sumner

P.S. On a point of yr letter I add that the French Minister [*Jules Berthémy*], who has just reached Paris *en Congé* called on me before he went to know what he should say to the Emperor, on the question, whether France was embraced in our demands. Of course, I replied, that thus far no damages or actual losses had been traced to France or to any country but England.

The Senate has ordered the publication in some 10 8vo vols. of all the correspondance & papers, English & American, on the question of claims, so that the subject will be presented to Congress at the next session, & I doubt not will be the chief question, unless before then some solution is reached.

ALS   CSmH   (82/472, PCS)

1. Elizabeth Argyll wrote CS from Kensington 1 May 1869 (46/546, PCS) that CS's speech had been "a grievous disappointment." She found his chastisement of Britain for conceding belligerency to the Confederates "entirely unreasonable"; even America's own President Lincoln had made such a concession.

2. "The Alabama Wrong" by John Jay (recently confirmed as minister to Austria) appeared in the *New York Tribune*, 20 February 1869:6 and 22 February 1869:4.

3. France was not specifically named in Motley's instructions, which alluded to "other powers" conceding belligerent rights. However, "it was in England only that the concession was supplemented by acts causing direct damage to the United States" ("Recall of Minister Motley," 5). The duchess reminded CS that Britain had not acted alone regarding the Confederacy. "You must know well that the Fr. govt. thought this acknowledgement of Belligerency unavoidable."

4. The elapsed time since the damages only intensified the U.S. demand, CS had asserted in his speech: "If our demands are larger now than at our first call it is not the only time in history when such a rise has occurred ("Our Claims on England" [1869], 14). CS alluded there to the myth of Sibyl, who first offered to sell her collection of nine books to Tarquinius Superbus of Rome. When he refused, she burned three and offered the remaining six at the same price, which he accepted. The duchess chided CS that he should not have referred to that "very unreasonable old Sibyl as your authority."

5. Motley, his wife, Mary Benjamin Motley (d. 1874), and daughters, Elizabeth Ives, Mary, and Susan, sailed from New York 19 May.

6. The Gladstone government had on 1 March proposed the disestablishment of the Irish church, which Parliament was then debating.

7. *Primeval Man: An Examination of Some Recent Speculations* (1869).

To Anna Cabot Lodge

Washington—20th May '69

Dear Mrs Lodge,

I hear nothing of yr banquet, which surely must have been elegant & joyous.

At last they have sailed—content I hope; but with austere duties.[1] When we meet I can tell you things you will be interested to know. The Secy of State called on me to tell me that the Presdt made the nomination to England "out of compliment to Mr Sumner."

Of course this absorbs so much patronage, which Mass. might claim in other quarters, & it makes me peculiarly responsible for the success of the mission.

It is a great ⟨duty⟩ task which Motley now enters upon & memorable in history.

As you do not see the English papers, you hardly know how excited they have become against me—very much like the old slave-masters in other days. There is a daily broad-side against your innocent friend.[2]

Good bye!

Ever sincerely Yours   Charles Sumner

———————————

ALS   MHi   (TTR 82/478, PCS)

1. The *New York Times*'s Washington correspondent noted that details of Motley's instructions were "a matter of much speculation here" and believed that they "coincide" with CS's speech (18 May 1869:1).

2. The British press expressed concern as to the effect CS's speech would have on the stalled negotiations on the *Alabama* claims and how closely CS's speech, with its extraordinary demands, reflected the Grant administration's views. The London *Times* of 5 May called CS's argument one "of that intuitive sort which has been common in all the tribunals of despotism." CS, said the *Times*, was more responsible than any other man for the Civil War as well as for "the differences which keep the breach still open." Another *Times* editorial called him a "demagogue" (London *Morning Star* and London *Standard*, 30 April 1869, summarized in the *New York Times*, 1 May 1869:1; London *Times*, 3 May 1869:8, 5 May 1869:9, 7 May 1869:9).

To Francis Lieber

Washington 30th May '69

My dear Lieber,

I like much to commune with you on the Law of Nations, &, I wish you to begin by reading my speech

I have made no demand,—not a word of apology,—not a dollar; nor have I menaced, suggested or thought of "war." Your idea is derived from the recent English articles.[1]

On the contrary the Peace Society is about to publish my speech as a "peace tract."

My object was simply to expose our wrongs as plainly but as gently as possible; "with illustrations of how reparation has been made in other cases,—when England (1) expressed regret & (2) paid money.

I have been strengthened by a communication of the opinion of Mr Binney on the question of damages, who remarks that "the damages to our commerce may be measured by the contemporary gains to the British."

To my mind, our first duty is to make England see what she has done to us. How the case shall be settled—whether by money, more or less—by territorial compensation—by apologies—or by an amendment of the Law of Nations, is still an open question. Perhaps, all may be combined.

If I saw you, I could tell you what I will not write.

Private. Motley has prepared a masterly paper, sharp as a blade, & a model of composition, covering absolutely the grounds of my speech, in gross & in detail. He read the speech six times before it was delivered, & he was the only *person* who knew its contents. He accepted it *verbatim* & was willing to meet Lord Clarendon & all English Society on that basis. *This is absolutely for you alone.*

Ever Yours,   Charles Sumner

ALS   MH-H   (64/627, PCS

1. According to Frank Freidel, Lieber feared CS's speech could lead to war with England and was asked by Fish to write a letter urging a moderate course for both countries (*Francis Lieber* [1947], 398). Lieber's letter, "The Alabama or Laird Principle," did not specifically criticize CS but urged that the claims question be "honorably settled" and warned of the damages from privateering that the present conflict threatened (New York *Evening Post*, 29 May 1869:4).

To Charles W. Slack
private

Washington Sunday
[30 May 1869]

Dear Mr Slack,

I am at a loss to understand the publication of a malignant & bitter attack on me in the Cwlth by a foreigner *who has for some years felt it his duty to malign me.*[1] Do I deserve it? Am I the man he paints?

As for the editorial, it is equally incomprehensible.[2] Every body familiar with the history of the war should know two things, (1) that Mr S's wretched blunders in the shape of instructions were not known till 10 months after the fatal concession of belligerency to slave-driving rebels, &, therefore, could have no influence on that concession, & (2), even if they were known, they could not justly modify the duty of Anti-Slavery England not to acknowledge in any way a *new Power*, whose only declared reason of separate existence was Slavery as its corner-stone—all of which I have explained at great length, & put forth in formal resolutions, adopted by both Houses of Congress, & communicated to Foreign Powers. In short, I have done every thing except attack Mr Seward, as a foreigner has attacked me.[3]

Ever sincerely Yours,   Charles Sumner

ALS   OKtu (82/496, PCS)

1. Goldwin Smith's address to Cornell University students, 19 May 1869, refuted CS's charge that Great Britain had substantially aided the Confederacy (Boston *Commonwealth*, 29 May 1869:1–2).

2. Although the accompanying editorial defended CS, the *Commonwealth* agreed with Smith that Seward's policy was poorly formulated at the Civil War's beginning and declared that Seward's instructions to Charles Francis Adams and William L. Dayton were "the source of mortification to loyal men" (ibid.).

3. Slack replied that he had printed Smith's article at Francis W. Bird's request because Bird believed France was more at fault for encouraging the Confederacy than was Great Britain. Slack reassured CS that his "reputation and invaluable public service are . . . held dear by the *Comlth* and all its friends" (Boston, 1 June, 47/193, PCS). In his response of 3 June (82/511), CS refused to be mollified. He wrote that the "case is entirely different" with France because the U.S. could "trace *no damages* to France *as we can to England*." He wrote that if he were the person Smith had characterized in his speech, "you & others should call for my instant resignation."

To Benjamin F. Butler
private

Washington 3d June '69

My dear General,

I do not write for controversy. From the beginning of my public life, I have never stepped aside to criticise any person, who is aiming substantially in the same direction that I am. Of course, I shall not begin with you.

My object is simply to call yr attention to the opinion of the "law lords" on the *effect* of the Concession of Belligerency.[1] I do not speak of its *legality* but of its *effect*. Now according to these English authorities, without the concession, the building of a ship in England for the rebels would have been "piracy." It is not I who say this but the "law lords" of England.

From this it follows that the concession opened to the rebels the ship-yards & store-houses of England, lifting from the assistance they might supply the criminal character which it would have had otherwise, & placing under the smaller penalties of violated neutrality.

Therefore, in fact, the concession was the first stage in the building of the ships. I dwell upon it, not so much on account of the Alabama, as to embrace the consort ships with regard to which the evidence is not as positive as with regard to the Alabama.

With this brief explanation I venture to ask you to glance again at the part marked in the pamphlet I send.[2]

Pardon this trouble amidst these heats & believe me, dear Genl,[3]

Yours sincerely,   Charles Sumner

ALS   DLC   (82/506, PCS)

1. In an interview with a *Boston Post* correspondent on 28 May 1869 (*New York Times*, 31 May 1869:5), Congressman Butler stated that CS's speech had no legal basis, for Lincoln's proclamation of a blockade in effect recognized the Confederacy as belligerents. In addition, declared Butler, a recent Supreme Court decision had ruled against CS's argument that the Confederates were legally pirates, not belligerents.

2. CS probably marked the passage in his speech in which he argued that "Law Lords" in England such as Frederick Thesiger, first Baron Chelmsford, and Sir George Cornewall Lewis had declared that without a proclamation of belligerency, "the fitting out of a ship in England to cruise against the United States would have been an act of piracy." CS declared that the proclamation was "the first stage in the depredations on our commerce" ("Our Claims on England" [1869], 5).

3. Butler replied that he saw no "substantial" difference with CS on the *Alabama* claims issue as a whole, only some "as to the ground upon which we should put the action of the country." Butler argued, as he had in his interview, that Britain's chief purpose in according belligerent rights to the Confederacy was to "destroy our commerce" and would end up "destroying us as a nation." He believed that the U.S.'s suit in the claims case should be based on these British designs, not on Britain's proclamation of belligerency, which he saw only as part of a larger "scheme" (Lowell, 7 June, 47/234, PCS).

To Timothy O. Howe

Washington
3d June '69

My dear Judge,

I answer you as well as I can.

Imprimis, I cannot explain the Tribune. Can you? I never could. Its

London correspondent is admirable for character, knowledge & certitude.[1]

Grimes's letter was characteristic.[2] Its special object was to please our enemies in England by belittling my speech, which, according to him, was published at my "request," as was customary in the Senate. In the first place I made no such "request," nor did I make a suggestion on the subject, &, in the second place, I have never known the injunction of secrecy removed from any speech by a vote of the Senate. Certainly it is not usual.[3]

The *Chicago Tribune* is supposed to be under Grimes's influence. The President, in conversation lately, suggested that Trumbull had probably influenced its course latterly.[4]

The speech which I made the other day was a mild abstract of the earlier speech—on a much lower key—defecated, if I may so say, of everything to give offense, except so far as the statement of our wrongs might give offense.[5] These were stated frankly, & this is the cause of English rage. The English papers have bullied & think they have succeeded in driving us back. Have they?[6]

Ever sincerely Yours,   Charles Sumner

ALS   WHi   (82/509, PCS)

1. The *New York Tribune* and Smalley, its London correspondent, generally supported CS's speech. CS may have been annoyed at a recent *Tribune* editorial that stated that CS had spoken as a "moralist . . . rather than as a statesman" (24 May 1869:4).

2. In his letter of 31 May 1869 (Green Bay, Wisconsin, 47/164, PCS) Howe asked CS if it were true, as Smalley stated, that Senator Grimes was the author of a letter of 10 May to the London *Times* signed "An American Citizen" (reprinted in the *New York Tribune*, 29 May 1869:4). In that letter, which the *Tribune* attributed to Grimes, Grimes stated that the Senate supported CS in rejecting the Johnson-Clarendon Convention, but not his grounds for doing so.

3. In his letter Grimes stated that CS himself asked for the removal of secrecy. Zachariah Chandler, however, moved that the injunction of secrecy be lifted (13 April, *Executive Proceedings*, 17:163).

4. Howe asked CS about a recent article in the *Chicago Tribune* that stated that CS's speech did not reflect American opinion on the *Alabama* case. He asked CS to tell him "'what ails' the Chicago Tribune & the British Press."

5. In his letter Howe remarked on similarities between "Claims on England" and "Our Foreign Relations," delivered in 1863. He wondered why, since the tone of the earlier speech was "much more impassioned and denunciatory," the current British reaction was so much stronger.

6. Howe replied that everyone in Wisconsin was "quite self possessed" and unwilling to drop the *Alabama* claims case (Green Bay, 6 June, 47/231).

PUNCH, OR THE LONDON CHARIVARI.—May 15, 1869.

HUMBLE PIE (?)

JONATHAN (as Interpreted by Mr. Sumner). "WAAL, REVERDY! GUESS THIS LOT 'LL ABOUT DU FOR YOUR FRIEND JOHN BULL THAR."

REVERDY JOHNSON. "HA! I'VE DINED WITH HIM A GOOD DEAL LATELY, AND HE WON'T EAT *THAT*, I PROMISE YOU."

From **Punch**, *15 May 1869. "The English papers have bullied & think they have succeeded in driving us back. Have they?" (to Timothy O. Howe, 3 June 1869). Courtesy of the Massachusetts Historical Society.*

To *William E. Forster*
Private.

Washington, June 8th, 1869.

Dear Mr. Forster,

I had already read your speech before I received the copy which you kindly sent me.[1] *Si sic omnia!* If other English utterances were in the same tone, the differences between the two countries would be much nearer a settlement than I fear they are.

The last few weeks have witnessed a consentaneous effort in England to widen the breach, (1) by suppressing the statement of our grievances, (2) by daily misrepresentations of that statement, and (3) by abuse and vilification. Of course all this postpones the day of settlement, for there can be no settlement until a plain statement of our case is read and understood in England. This is now refused. I am sorry, because I desire a settlement, wherein I differ from many who would keep the question open.

Your speech is printed in our newspapers, and the articles denouncing America, the Senate, and myself. This is right. Many ask why the same fairness does not show itself in England. Not a press in England which has not attributed to me sentiments and allegations which could not have been attributed had the speech been candidly laid before their readers.

Even you, in your speech, complain of me for addressing these "fashionable men, who after all, did not guide the destinies of England."[2] Oh no! There is nothing of this in my speech. *I spoke only of the Government and its tastes*, which found an echo in Parliamentary cheers. It would have been entirely unworthy of the occasion, as it seems to me, had I stepped aside to accuse the "fashionable," or to praise the "working men." To the latter I have offered my homage at other times.

Pardon me if I call attention to another statement. You say, "if there be danger at all, it is from America."[3] How so? Not a word of it in the speech which English newspapers misrepresented without printing. At the time of its delivery the speech was hailed as "pacific," and I challenge any person to read it through and find a single note of war.

The secretary of our Peace Society[4] writes that he proposes to print it as a "peace tract," Certainly, in this spirit I tried to speak.

I have always had a deep sense of our wrongs from England—to my mind the most terrible ever offered by one friendly Power to another. These I expressed fully in my speech of September 10th, 1863, on which Lord Russell commented at Blairgowrie. Such was my love of peace—especially with England—that when our troubles were over I said nothing, hoping for a settlement. Never in the Senate or elsewhere did I utter a word. At last the late treaty was negotiated. As I think of it now, there was madness in that negotiation. It was made (1) after a new President had been elected, known to feel intensely on the *Alabama* question; and (2) after the country had been aroused by Mr. R. Johnson's maudlin career to a frame of mind which demanded its full dues. It was no sooner signed than the people condemned it, before the committee or Senate had acted. Had it been signed earlier by six months I think it might have been adopted. When it was determined to reject the treaty it became my duty to assign the reasons.

I hope you will talk freely with Motley, who was in Washington at the time, and who will tell you to what extent my speech represented the views of all here, from the President down to the doorkeeper, and he will tell you also my own desires and hopes.

Of course, it will be for England to open the negotiations again. If those who control her affairs prefer that the question should remain unsettled, there are many here, besides the numerous Irish, who will be pleased; but I am not in this number.

I should be glad to know if England now shares the opinions of the law lords; to the effect that, by the concession of belligerency, the builders of war vessels were relieved from the crime of piracy. If this be the law, as I cannot doubt, then did that false concession open the dockyards and arsenals of England to a pro-slavery rebellion? So it seems. I cannot see it otherwise, and therefore I regard the concession as the first stage of the great offence.

I hope you will see General Schenck,[5] who is the leader of our House of Representatives. He will talk frankly and wisely. Pardon my frankness,[6] and believe me, dear Forster,

Sincerely yours,   Charles Sumner

PL T. Wemyss Reid, *Life of Right Honourable W. E. Forster* (1888), 2:15–18 (82/515, PCS)

1. Addressing his Bradford constituents 20 May 1869, Forster stated his disappointment with CS's speech, but nevertheless praised his patriotism and expressed hopes for a peaceful resolution of the differences between the two nations over the *Alabama* claims (London *Times*, 22 May 1869:6).

2. Forster stated that Americans complained that they could not visit a British club or drawing room "without hearing some reproach against their country" and asked, were Republicans "to judge England by her fashionable clubs and her drawing rooms?" CS had forgotten the middle and working classes, who had supported the North in the Civil War.

3. Forster declared that he almost wished he were addressing Americans because perhaps he could persuade them of Britain's desire for peace. The "danger in America" he wished to dispel was caused, he stated, by the speech of his friend Mr. Sumner.

4. William C. Brown (d. 1870), secretary of the American Peace Society, 1847–70.

5. Robert C. Schenck (1809–90), then U.S. congressman (Rep., Ohio), 1863–70.

6. Forster replied briefly on 20 June from London that neither of them would benefit "by dwelling on our disagreements as to past facts" and that he was gratified that CS was not personally offended (Reid, 2:19; 82/530).

To John Lothrop Motley

[*Washington 11 June 1869*]

The President left for West Point day before yesterday. I was with him for an hour before he left, during which we discussed belligerency, and England and Cuba. He asked how it would do to issue a proclamation with regard to Cuba identical with that issued by Spain with regard to us.[1] I advised against it. He is very confident that the Cubans will succeed. On the same day I had a call from two Cubans,—one of whom was Aldama,[2] the richest man of the island and an old friend of mine,—who had come to solicit the concession of belligerency, saying that with it success was certain, and that without it the island would become a desert. I gave them no encouragement.

In the evening I had a prolonged talk with Fish, whom [*Edward*] Thornton had visited that day. Fish said to him that our claims were too large to be settled pecuniarily, and sounded him about Canada,[3] to which he replied that England did not wish to keep Canada, but could not part with it without the consent of the population. Fish desired to know of me how to state the amount of claims to England, to which I replied that I should make no "claim" or "demand."

PL   Prc, 4:409–10   (82/523, PCS)

1. CS probably refers to Spain's proclamation of neutrality in the Civil War, issued 17 June 1861 (*New York Times*, 28 May 1869:7).

2. Miguel Aldama supported the provisional government and became president later in 1869 (Allan Nevins, *Hamilton Fish* [1937], 338).

3. CS did not ask in his speech that Britain cede Canada to the U.S. as part of the *Alabama* settlement, but others, including Zachariah Chandler, had advanced this possibility (19 April, *Globe*, 41st Cong., special session, 727–28).

To Caleb Cushing

Washington Wednesday morg
[*16 June 1869*]

My dear General,

I saw Fish last evng & found him as always with me most friendly. We spoke of the attempt to make it appear that there were differences between us,[1] & I ventured to remark, that, whatever might be the effect of such efforts on my position, I feared more the influence on our case in England, & the position of our Legation. There should be union at home. He agreed, &, I think, would be glad to make a statement on the point.

I write this, for yr information, as I am about to leave for Boston

Sincerely Yours,   Charles Sumner

ALS   DLC   (82/518 [misdated 9 June 1869], PCS)

1. "Cymon," the *New York Times* Washington correspondent, wrote on 13 June 1869 that CS was "much displeased" with Motley's instructions for two reasons: (1) Motley was not instructed to reopen negotiations now and (2) he could not use the recognition of belligerency as an issue when negotiations began. CS "knows what MR. MOTLEY's instructions are as thoroughly as does that man who wrote them, and his pride probably prevents him from making a frank admission of the completeness of his defeat" (14 June 1869:1).

To Hamilton Fish

Boston 18th June '69

My dear Fish,

Here is a letter which has come back to me. You or Mrs Fish will do me the kindness to direct it.

If I were in Washington I should shew the letters I enclosed to Genl Cushing.[1] If you have no objection & happen to meet him, you can hand them to him & ask him to return them to me.

I am satisfied that the time has not come for Mr Motley to say any thing about demands, whether more or less. The first step is to make England see our grievance. She must understand our case. This will be the diagnosis which precedes the remedy.

Ever Yours,   Charles Sumner

ALS   DLC   (82/525, PCS)

1. By this date CS may have received Motley's letter of 7 June 1869 from London (47/241, PCS). In it Motley reported on the British outrage over CS's speech; the press claimed, wrote Motley, that CS sought Britain's *"national humiliation."* Motley assured CS he would continue to defend his speech but that Motley was reluctant to take up the "whole matter" of claims with Foreign Secretary Lord Clarendon at this early stage. The Motley letter may possibly be one of the letters CS said he would like to show to Cushing.

To John Lothrop Motley

[*Boston 20 June 1869*]

The late statements from Washington that there was no difference between Fish and myself have had a tranquillizing effect.[1] With more experience at Washington, our front would have been more perfect.

P.S. Paul Forbes arrived here three days ago directly from Madrid, with overtures from Prim about Cuba.[2] The language of the latter was "When a family is in distress, it sells its jewels." The idea seemed to be that the United States should mediate between Spain and the insurgents, the latter paying for their independence. The President is disposed to undertake the mediation if any representative of the insurgents can give assurances that the idea can be carried through. The President told me that he was entirely satisfied that England made the concession of belligerency "to injure us."

PL   Prc, 4:410   (82/531, PCS)

1. The New York *Evening Post* (19 June 1869:3) published a statement that "rumors of disagreement" between CS and the administration on the *Alabama* claims were "entirely unfounded." CS had assisted in and agreed with the instructions to Motley and had "signified" that the policy proposed "was as firm and vigorous as our foreign relations would now justify."

2. Paul Forbes, a cousin of John Murray Forbes, had proposed to Grant that Forbes serve as a private intermediary between the U.S. and Spain regarding Cuba. Juan Prim (d. 1870), a Spanish military leader, had actually taken over control of the Spanish government from Isabel II (Allan Nevins, *Hamilton Fish* [1937], 102, 121, 191–93).

To the Duchess of Argyll

Boston 22nd June '69

My dear Duchess,

I begin by answering yr inquiry. The blacks at the South have had a hard time through the treachery of the late Presdt.[1] Taking all things into account their success is considerable. They shew a disposition to learn, & some of them have been very successful. If the Presdt. had a more genuine sympathy with them, it would benefit them; but he wishes to do right.

I hope you have talked with Motley. You can say to him what you would say to me on our present troubles & misunderstanding. But I confess my present disappointment, especially when so good & calm a person as Mr Forster makes such a speech.[2] In tone it was all that could be desired; but, in other respects, it was painful. He attributes to me a position for which there is not one word of justification in my speech. Of course, he could not misrepresent. Therefore, like the newspapers, he commented & criticised without reading. Thus a sincere effort, made to explain an existing difficulty, *that you might really understand it*, is trifled with.

But it is more painful to find the levity with which Mr Forster talks of a question under the Law of Nations,[3] involving multitudinous graves, & enormous expenditures. He runs out of the House of Commons to the Library, takes down Wheaton, & finds the whole question settled! Here is one of the greatest questions of International Law, *absolutely without any authoritative precedent*, settled in this sciolistic style. To my mind this is cruel.

You in England must choose yr own course. It is easy, however, to see that you are again making the same terrible mistake, which was made at the beginning of the war. *You would not understand our case then*; & you will not understand it now. You believed false reports; & now your press,—especially the *Times*—has false witnesses to testify with regard to opinion here.[4] Do not believe them. Opinion here is united. There is no substantial difference among any who exercise influence over the question.

You will make a fearful mistake if you proceed on any idea that I am alone—or that there is a difference between me & Mr M. or the Presdt or the Secy of State. Mr M's instructions were submitted to me & altered by me in order to make an important point clearer.[5] Of course, the insult & misrepresentation directed upon me falls upon my country.

I enclose an article, which you should read carefully. It is written by Senator Anthony, one of the most peace-loving English senators, actually Presdt. of the Senate, & in the chair when I spoke.[6] If any body can speak for the Senate or for public-opinion, it is himself an old journalist & President of the Senate. But England has determined not to hear our case. Ld Russell & Ld Clarendon both refused point blank & now, when a statement is made expressly to enable her to understand the grievance, of which we complain, there is no end to the indignities which she thinks proper to heap upon the author. Of course, all this makes the final settlement more difficult. Already the Irish here clamor for war, & one of the chief anxieties of good men here is lest the counter-movement stimulated by the conduct of England shall take this direction.

Have I not said too much? One thing more. *Do not believe the Times witness*. Believe Mr Motley. The *Times* articles are written in the office of a semi-rebel & copper-head, whose plausible talents are devoted to misrepresentation. The *News* writer [*E. L. Godkin*] is an Englishman, who has never understood the country he has adopted.

Silence will now be the rule. Our administration has no desire to press the discussion. The Irish & Anglophobists all desire to keep the question open, & this is the desire of England. Alas! it must be opened before it can be settled. But, England insists that it shall be postponed until American retaliation can open it. Here I protest with all the energy of my soul. God bless you!

Ever Sincerely Yours,   Charles Sumner

ALS   CSmH   (82/532, PCS)

1. The duchess on 4 June 1869 wrote CS from Kensington asking about the condition of southern blacks: "Is it true that there is much death among them?" (47/ 212, PCS).

2. The duchess declared she did not want to discuss CS's speech further but was still "in the dark" as to CS's laying all the blame on Britain.

3. In his speech Forster admitted that at first he was inclined to regard Confederate ships as pirates but that after consulting the works of the international law scholar Henry Wheaton, he realized that in case of an insurrection, "any neutral country was bound to consider that to be a state of war, and could not look upon either party as pirates" (London *Times*, 22 May 1869:6).

4. The American correspondent of the London *Times*, probably Joel Cook, wrote 21 May that the views reflected in CS's speech "are repudiated by the sober second thoughts of the American people, while Secretary Fish, with his moderate views and his desire to soothe the bad feeling engendered from the Alabama controversy, is sustained." The correspondent maintained that CS's speech did not represent the U.S. government's stand and that a "social breach" existed between CS and the president (London *Times*, 3 June 1869:10).

5. See CS to Fish, 17 May 1869.

6. Anthony had sent CS a copy of his article, which had been published in the Providence *Journal* (21 June, 47/357). In the article Anthony wrote that CS's speech was "essentially a pacific one" and had full U.S. support (clipping, 82/553).

To Caleb Cushing
private

Boston 28th June '69

My dear General,

I am obliged by yr note just received.[1]

The statement to which you refer has, perhaps, tranquillized the press; but I question, if it does not contain expressions, which weaken our case at home & abroad.[2] I would never have said that the policy "was firm & vigorous as our foreign relations *could now justify.*" Our policy should always be firm & vigorous. These qualities are sometimes silent, as we are disposed to be now.

Nor do I understand why there should be any question about amount.[3] If we would succeed with England, we must shew confidence in our case. *Crede ut possis et potes*.[4]

But I submit. You will note the exaltation in England, at my expense. No such thing should have been permitted. Our front should have been perfect. It would have been easier for Motley, had this been the case.

I enclose an article by Senator Anthony, Presdt. of Senate & in the chair when I spoke.

Motley sends his kind regards to you.[5]

Believe me, dear General,

Sincerely Yours,   Charles Sumner

P.S. Is any thing doing about reciprocity?[6]

ALS   DLC   (82/540, PCS)

1. Cushing wrote CS from Washington that President Grant's reluctance to build the U.S. *Alabama* claims case on the belligerency issue was based on the pending Cuban question in which the U.S. might grant belligerent rights to Cuban insurgents (26 June 1869, 47/387, PCS; Prc, 4:407).

2. Cushing wrote that he had been "attentive to your wishes," as expressed in CS's letter of 16 June, and seen that Fish issued the statement of harmony between CS and the administration for the New York *Evening Post* (19 June 1869:3).

3. The *Evening Post*'s notice stated that CS differed with the administration only on the amount of damages.

4. "Believe that you can and you can."

5. On 16 June Motley wrote CS a lengthy letter describing conversations with various British leaders, including John Bright. Motley believed that he was correctly pursuing his instructions and would be "cautious & guarded" in public expression but "very plain in confidential talk with leading men" (London, 47/324).

6. Canadians were interested in a new reciprocity treaty with the U.S.

To George Bemis
private

Boston. 7th July '69
Coolidge House.

My dear Bemis,

Yours of 19th June has just come.[1] Do not judge me for not writing. All that I can do with the pen must go into work.

I wish I could converse with you on our case. Fish has more than once asked when you would return. I would not interfere with the requirements of health; but if these allow, pray come home & give us the advantage of yr knowledge & ability. They are needed. Nobody here is sufficiently informed.

You are mistaken in yr anxieties. B. F. B.[*utler*] can not obtain control of this question, so long as we do our duty. If we abandon it, be assured the politicians will take it up.

Our case must be stated in its points so that at length England will feel it. The convulsion under the recent attempt is the beginning.

The Alabama papers, ordered to be printed, will make 8 or 9 vols. I find that Mr Hunter did not think the Bunch papers of much importance.[2] It is not too late to have them included, as the work is proceeding according to a resolution of mine, "under the superintendance of the Secy of State."

The English are making the same blunder now which they made at the beginning of the war. There is no lie too big for them to swallow. *See* the *Times* correspondant *passim*, especially when he introduces my name. Don't believe him. *The Presdt, Secy of State, Minister to London & Chairman of Senate Comttee are all of one mind*, & you will see that R. J. in his despatch, vindicating his treaty has taken our ground on Belligerency.[3] Come home from that Paris where you are so happy; *ducite ab urbe domum.*[4]

I followed our friend Judge Fletcher to Mt Auburn.[5] He was worn & changed, so as hardly to be known. The day before his death he asked after you. Good bye! Let me hear from you.

Ever yours, Charles Sumner

P.S. I enclose this to Motley.[6] When in London don't fail to see Smalley, the *Tribune* correspondant. He is excellent.

ALS MHi (82/551, PCS)
Enc: two unidentified newspaper clippings.

1. Bemis wrote from Paris that both the U.S. and Great Britain seemed unyielding on the claims issue, and a rupture in diplomatic relations might ensue (copy, Fish Papers, Library of Congress).

2. William Hunter (1805–86), chief clerk in the State Department. In his reply from Paris (26 August 1869 [mislabeled "No Addressee"], 83/050, PCS), Bemis voiced his regret that correspondence between Robert Bunch, British consul at Charleston, and James M. Mason would not be published. Bemis and Motley both believed these letters contained more important evidence of Great Britain's recognition of the Confederates than the Queen's Proclamation of Neutrality.

3. Although the Johnson-Clarendon Convention contained no statement about

belligerent rights, in his dispatch to Seward 17 February from London, Reverdy Johnson stated that the grounds for the U.S. *Alabama* claims rested on the precipitous recognition Great Britain conferred on the Confederacy when it issued the Queen's Proclamation of Neutrality (*Foreign Relations* [1868], part 1, 371–74, 411–19). CS enclosed a clipping containing passages from Johnson's dispatch and underlined certain statements: (1) that even if Lincoln's blockade proclamation had been known to the British government, *"it furnished no justification for the action of this government"*; (2) the proclamation of neutrality meant that the *Alabama* and other ships could *"not have been in the estimation of English law as well as in the law of nations, piratical vessels"* (82/553). The *New York Times* printed these paragraphs (16 June 1869:5) with the comment that, despite Johnson's professions of difference with CS on belligerent rights, the extract showed that "Mr. Johnson then occupied the identical position now maintained by Mr. Sumner."

4. "Come back to your origins from the city."

5. Richard Fletcher died 21 June.

6. Besides the clipping mentioned above, CS enclosed for Motley a newspaper summary of Anthony's article supporting CS.

To Henry W. Longfellow

Coolidge House—8th July '69

My dear Longfellow,

Where are you? Climbing Alps? Traversing Germany? Enjoying the Rhine? Busy in Paris? I imagine the children more content than you.[1]

A few days ago rambling in Cambridge, I went to yr house, rang & knocked—was admitted, looked about that I might report to you. All was as you left it; & the books did not seem injured. I feared dampness. You are expected in the latter part of August. Shall you be here then?

Poor Thies[2] looks thin & pale. He talks of dying in two years. He has finished his catalogue, which belongs to the bibliography of engravings. It is done with care & knowledge.

Boston is dull enough. I see few people, & dine generally at the club in Park St. If you return my circle will be enlarged.

I have commenced the revision of my speeches for an edition like that of Edmund Burke.[3] Do not smile at my audacity. I am to fill 8 or 10 vols, & the booksellers propose to call them "Works." I do not like the term, but what else is there? "Speeches & Orations" would be better, if there were not some other things, like political letters & reports.

The revision tempts me to great work, beyond my anticipation. I have filed & amended those two early vols., so that it would have been as easy to re-write. If I could throw them into the fire, I would, & have an end of them; but since this is impossible, next to their destruction is a good edition revised & amended before I die.

If you care to know about our question with England, you should begin by disbelieving all the lies of the *Times*, especially where my name occurs. The Presdt,—the Secy of State, the Minister to England & the Chairman of the Senate Comttee. of Foreign Relations are *all agreed*. The report to the contrary is an invention. Good bye! Love to the children. Who is with you now!

Ever affectnly Yrs,   C. S.

I enclose an article which states what the Senate intended when it accepted my speech.

ALS MH-H (82/557, PCS)

1. Longfellow was then in Paris and planned to sail from Liverpool 21 August 1869 (Longfellow to John Nichol, 10 July, HWL, 5:285).

2. Louis Thies (d. 1871), curator of rare books at Harvard College Library, wrote 17 July about his plans to return to Europe (Cambridge, 47/519, PCS).

3. CS had already begun sending edited versions of his early speeches to John Owen for examination (see CS to Owen, 16 May, 82/464), and CS's publishers, Lee & Shepard, wrote him 13 July that its printers, Welch, Bigelow & Company, were ready for his copy (Boston, 47/499).

To Benjamin F. Butler

Boston 10th July '69

Dear General,

I am obliged by yr kindness in allowing me to peruse this interesting communication.[1]

The despatch of R. J. [*17 February 1869*] to which allusion is made, reached Mr Seward on the morning of 4th March. He took it at once to A. J. & it was sent with an Executive message to the Senate. As there was no Ex. session before 12 o'clk that day, the message & doct. were swept from the table into the office of the Secy of Senate, whence it was recovered *on my motion* & ordered to be printed.[2] I enclose a copy. Every senator had his regular copy. You will notice, that R. J. puts himself substantially upon the ground of my speech.

I do not doubt that this will be debated much at the next session.

Sincerely Yours,   Charles Sumner

ALS DLC (82/562, PCS)

1. With a brief accompanying note asking CS to observe the judicial maxim "*audi alterum partem*" ("listen to the other side"), Butler sent CS a confidential statement about Reverdy Johnson's recent visit to Washington ([3? July 1869], 82/596, PCS).

The document of 3 July in another hand, marked "copy," stated that Johnson claimed CS's speech "has alienated or neutralized all our friends in England," and that Britain would not pay any damages "based, as Mr. Sumner proposes, upon the recognition of the Confederate government." Motley, said Johnson, would have "nothing to do" in London except negotiate a claims treaty based on the Johnson-Clarendon Convention.

2. Although the Senate met 4 March, no record exists of CS's motion (*Globe*, 40th Cong., 3rd sess., 1864–67).

To Caleb Cushing

Boston 10th July '69

My dear General,

I am obliged by yr note of 8th. July.[1]

My desire is to act so that our example may give new force to International Law & help future Peace. For a Republic to give this example is much.

It is plain that there is nothing to justify this great concession to insurgent Cubans, unless you discard all rule & follow simply yr own passions or desires. They have not reached that point of reasonable certainty for the present & future, which alone can justify such a step on our part, unless we accept the hazards of war with Spain.

Two things I wish for Cuba—(1) Independence & (2) Emancipation, & both are certain to come very soon. But why should we assume needless responsibilities of money or arms?

Sincerely Yours,   Charles Sumner

ALS   DLC   (82/564, PCS)

1. Cushing wrote from Washington enclosing two unidentified newspaper clippings that, he said, indicated "how the cross-currents of Cuba act on the question of England." One clipping stated that the administration would like to drop the belligerency issue in the *Alabama* claims case and that some congressmen were pressuring Grant to that end. Wrote Cushing, "We are prone to assume that rebellion any & every where (except in the US) and under whatever circumstances, is necessarily right, and the national authority necessarily wrong." CS sent Cushing's letter on to another correspondent, possibly Fish, with the note "to be returned" (47/466, PCS).

To Hamilton Fish

Boston 10th. July '69

My dear Fish,

I am obliged by the opportunity of reading Motley No. 8. As soon as I have perused it again I shall return it to Mr Hunter.[1]—Nobody will know from me any thing about it.

I see that Mr Gladstone fortifies himself by an alleged excitement in our country.[2] Nobody here is excited. It is in England that the excitement prevails. The more I reflect upon our case & confer with our best people here the more I am satisfied that I did not go too far in the statement of our grievance. When the debate comes on, I think you will find that graves & epitaphs will count.

I enclose an article in the Advertiser, written by P. W. Chandler, one of our ablest lawyers.[3]

I send also a letter from Motley, showing some sensibility at the criticism on his speaking at Liverpool, & also a long conversation with Mr Bright. To the latter I have replied.[4] I beg you not to be anxious on this account. Mr B. has no just ground of complaint. His rage is a part of the prevailing anger.

I also send a letter from Bemis, & another from Michel Chevalier,[5] who, as you know, is high in the confidence of the Emperor.

The letters you can return.—I hope you are well & not too much oppressed by work.

Ever sincerely Yours,   Charles Sumner

ALS DLC (82/566, PCS)

1. After checking with Fish, Hunter had sent CS, at his request, a copy of Motley's "No. 8," his dispatch of 12 June 1869 to Fish. Hunter emphasized that CS must keep the document confidential, since its transmission to CS was highly unusual (Washington, 8 July 1869, 47/468, PCS).

2. In Parliament 8 July Gladstone stated that he "had no reason to believe" that U.S. rejection of the Johnson-Clarendon Convention precluded further negotiations. The U.S.'s suggestion for a delay came, said Gladstone, in "reference to the state of opinion and feeling in that country" (Hansard's Parliamentary Debates, 3rd series, 197:1425).

3. In an unsigned article Chandler wrote that the British had misunderstood and overreacted to CS's speech; because Motley presented no specific claim for damages, many Britons wrongly concluded that CS's speech did not reflect the administration's view (Boston Daily Advertiser, 10 July 1869:2).

4. Motley's letter of 16 June (47/324) expressed surprise that what he called his "meagre & vague although friendly" statement when welcomed by the American-British Chamber of Commerce at Liverpool on 31 May was so "strongly censured." At the welcome, Motley had declared his hope that the two nations would work closely together (London Times, 1 June 1869:12). Motley also described to CS his meeting with John Bright, who felt, said Motley, "suppressed wrath" over CS's speech, because CS had offered no basis for future negotiation. No letter from CS to Bright has been recovered; in fact there is no record of any correspondence between July 1869 and August 1871.

5. In his letter of 29 June (Paris, 47/401), Chevalier congratulated CS on his speech, which he said enjoyed a grand success in Europe. A copy is in the Fish Papers, Library of Congress.

To Hamilton Fish
private

Nahant (where I am on a visit
of a few days) 11th July '69

My dear Fish,

I have sent Motley's No 8 to Mr Hunter,—nobody having seen it or knowing any thing about it.[1]

The only point which troubles me is the intimation that the postponement was *on our account*.[2] I supposed it was to be on account of the known excitement in England; that, for the present we were not disposed to press the negotiation, as there was reason to believe that England was not in a mood to entertain it, but that we are ready for it at any time.

This brings me again to a view which I mentioned in my note of yesterday;—that we should confine ourselves at first to a statement of our case, *so that England may see its extent*. I despair of any practical result till this is done. When England sees the grievance, as we see it—when she learns that our generals from the Presdt down all believe that the war, with its deaths & its expenditures, with present taxation, was prolonged, through her conduct, & that this is the conviction of our people,—let her grasp this idea, & she will be ready for the *remedy*. But the remedy cannot be proposed until the case is understood, & the sooner that is stated the better. Should it not be before the meeting of Congress?—

Ever sincerely Yours,   Charles Sumner

ALS   DLC   (82/568, PCS)

1. In his dispatch of 12 June 1869 (No. 8) Motley described his meeting on 10 June with Lord Clarendon and the message Motley had presented then in pursuance of his instructions. Regarding the matter of Britain's concession of belligerent rights, Motley wrote that he had told Clarendon, "The famous proclamation of neutrality of May 13, 1861, was not considered justifiable by the United States Government, but the President wished it to be used, when our case should once more be presented, only as showing animus, and as being the fountainhead of the disasters which had been caused to the American people, both individually and collectively, by the hands of Englishmen. Other nations had issued proclamations contemporaneously, or nearly so, with that of Great Britain; but from Great Britain alone had there come a long series of deeds, injurious to the United States, as the fruits of the proclamation, while from other nations there had come no injury save the declaration itself" ("Recall of Mr. Motley," 9).

2. Motley had written that, as instructed, he advised Clarendon "to pause for a brief period—a limited interval—not longer than might be necessary for the subsi-

dence of violent emotions and public manifestations of excited feeling created by the rejection of the treaty." Clarendon agreed but commented that he doubted that Britain had manifested "any such intensity of feeling" as Motley had described as prevailing in the U.S. (ibid., 7–8).

To Hamilton Fish

Boston 21st July '69

My dear Fish,

More than being at yr beautiful & most tempting home I congratulate you on the success of that business with Spain.[1] If accomplished completely it will be one of the best things in our diplomacy.

How clear it is, that our true *policy*—saying nothing of international duty—has been from the beginning to keep on good terms with Spain. In this way we can do more for Cuba & at less cost than by any system of filibusterism or unjustifiable concession, with the hazard of war & infinite expense.

The Cubans can buy their independence cheaper than they can obtain it even with our help. A war for a few months would cost the purchase-money.

You ask what I had written to Motley, which put him on the defensive?—Nothing except that his speeches at Liverpool were criticised. I thought he ought to know this. It seems to me that he dealt very well with John Bright, whose conduct is not creditable.[2] Is it not a part of that prevailing madness which has made their press & every body else so unjust? I assure you, *he has no ground of complaint against me.*

I do not fear that politicians can control the Alabama question, if we do our duty. We must keep the case in our hands; but this can be only by showing that we are in earnest. *We must make England know & feel our grievance* before we make any proposition.

Ever sincerely Yours,   Charles Sumner

P.S. I imagine you with yr family about, for whom kind regards.

ALS   DLC   (82/577, PCS)

1. CS may have referred to Fish's confidential agreement calling for Spain to recognize Cuba in exchange for payment from the provisional government, a plan that the U.S. would guarantee. Slavery would also be abolished in Cuba. Paul Forbes cabled Fish on 20 July 1869 that Spain provisionally agreed to the terms (Allan Nevins, *Hamilton Fish* [1937], 193–94, 231). There is no evidence one way or another about CS's knowledge of these negotiations, although the *New York Times* re-

ported (16 July 1869:1) that the American minister to Spain, Daniel E. Sickles, had been entrusted with a delicate mission to persuade Spain to grant quasi-independence to Cuba.

2. Motley wrote that in his meeting with Bright, Motley had defended CS's speech as that of an "independent Senator," not as a diplomatic document; he stressed how strongly the U.S. supported CS's speech. Motley said that Bright felt Britain was "embarrassed" at the U.S. rejection of the Johnson-Clarendon Convention since, according to Bright, the treaty met U.S. demands satisfactorily (16 June, 47/324, PCS).

To Adam Badeau

Boston 26th July '69

My dear General,

I am obliged by yr good letter, but I have for sometime doubted, if it were advisable at least for me to try any longer against the spawn of misrepresentations in England.[1] My own system is so essentially pacific, I am so near a quaker in my convictions, & I have such ties with England even now, that I cannot allow personal indignities to sway me in an important public duty. Whatever may be said there, I shall hope to keep the peace.

But I confess that this recent outburst of dishonest attack, where nobody has read the speech, followed by falsehood & abuse of every hue, with the bad temper, haughty tone & brutal insolence which seemed almost universal, have disheartened me.[2] How, then, can the question be settled 'peacefully'? I am the most pacific advocate on our side. Others who take it up, will touch a different cord.

Already many look to war. B. F. B.[utler] told me recently that it must come, as the people never would give back, & every body is profoundly convinced that England is equitably liable for several years of our war, with its deaths & taxation; George Bemis, writes me from Europe, that he is disheartened, for he does not see a solution except through war. *I do*; & I am not afraid of war, if our Administration will make England see & understand our case. This is no time to disown an authoritative statement, made under peculiar circumstances, & adopted, as speech never was before as the voice of the Senate & of the country. If we give back, *there are others who will take our places*, that will not give back.[3] It is our duty to conduct this debate closely, & make England know the wrong we have received & the convictions of our people. When this is done, we can take up the question of *remedy*, more or less; but first the grievance must be stated in length & breadth.

If I reply to yr inquiries, it is because I would not seem indifferent to yr desires.

You can report, whether I represented the Senate & the country—& the Presdt. too.[4] I think you can say, that never was any doubt about it. This point is stated well in Senator Anthony's article, & also in Mr P. W. Chandler's in the Advertiser, both of whom, belonging to the most moderate school, insist that the country agrees with me.

Of course, you know that the phrase "abject apology" & nothing like it can be found in the speech.[5] I never had the idea. But my *speech makes no demand, whether apology or money*, not a word of apology, not a cent of money. It shows, that we have suffered incalculable damages for which we have never received compensation or acknowledgment, & refers to other cases where money was paid with an apology. But [*one four-page section of the letter is missing*]

the world & for International Law. Talk with Mr Bemis on the "friendly" character of that concession. He knows its history. I never saw Mr Seward more like a caged tiger, or more profuse of oaths in every form that the English language supplies, than when prancing about the room denouncing the Proclamation of Belligerency, which he swore he would send to hell. To my mind the best point in his whole prolonged service at the State Depart. was his persistency in holding England responsible for the ⟨damages⟩ Proclamation. I never thought him sufficiently clear on the question, whether the Proclamation alone was ground of damages, or the proclamation with the detriment, from the ships & blockade-runners. The latter has always been my ground. We cannot give up the liability on this account, without weakening our case immeasurably.

It is easy to see that the English desire to limit the case to the Alabama. I embrace all the ships. But negligence, perhaps, can be shown only in the case of the Alabama. In the other ships we rely primarily upon the Proclamation, *without which they could not have been built*, so that the Proclamation becomes the first link in our case.

But I write on—too much, & now stop. I hope you enjoy London.— Society there is the best in the world.

If I can serve you in any way command me, & let me know from time to time how the drama appears. Be frank always where it is possible with Englishmen & let them know our case, so that when it is presented again they will not treat our honest well-meant effort with indignity.

Bon jour!

Ever sincerely Yours, Charles Sumner

I hope Mr Moran[6] is well. I know not what I have written; but I commit it to yr discretion.

ALS   NNHi   (82/585, PCS)

1. Adam Badeau (1831–95), aide to U. S. Grant, was then serving as an assistant to Motley at the American legation. He wrote CS from London 8 July 1869 (47/460, PCS) desiring to enlighten CS on some aspects of the British reaction to the *Alabama* issue that Motley might have overlooked. Badeau offered to pass on to his British contacts any elaboration or correction CS might have.

2. "Very few even prominent Englishmen," wrote Badeau, "have until now really read your speech."

3. From his talk with leading Liberals, Badeau concluded that they were disappointed that CS had not mentioned their support of the North during the war. He suggested, "If you should deem it proper in any way to let them or the world know that they are exonerated from the criticism which they maintain should be passed only on Tories or Whigs—I think their feeling towards you would be greatly mollified."

4. Badeau reported that many British were more angry with CS than the U.S. government, believing his speech "did not represent the sentiment of America."

5. In his Bradford address, William Forster had characterized CS's speech as appearing to demand "an apology,—almost, I might say, an abject apology" (London *Times*, 22 May 1869:6).

6. Benjamin Moran (1820–86), U.S. secretary of legation, London, 1864–74.

To John Bigelow

Boston, 30th July '69

My dear Editor,

—For so it is or is to be![1] The law-writers tell us that "time" is of the essence of a contract. I suppose they are right. If you were 10 years younger I should have no doubt on yr present temptation. I should say—yield.

I was hoping for you something different. I wished yr practised pen engaged in some solid book, which you could compose at yr own hours, & in yr own house, without the perpetual Charivari of a daily press. Perhaps, I am too Capuan & wish too easy a life.

Yr idea that the Times shall not edit you is excellent—with salt enough to save independence & to savor the paper.[2] Whichever way you go, my good wishes will be with you.

Ever sincerely Yours,   Charles Sumner

ALS   NSchU   (82/594, PCS)

1. Henry J. Raymond, *New York Times* editor and publisher, had died 18 June 1869 and CS wrote Bigelow congratulating him on taking Raymond's post (26 July, 82/589, PCS). Bigelow replied that he had indeed been invited to "take the direction" of the *Times*, but was not certain he would accept (Newport, 28 July, 47/561).

2. Bigelow inferred that CS had expressed "some misgivings scarcely disguised in yr note" and assured CS he had changed neither his "political philosophy nor editorial ethics"; he wrote, "it is proposed that I should edit the Times not that the Times should edit me." Bigelow ultimately refused the position.

To John Lothrop Motley

[Boston 17 August 1869]

I talked over our question with Fish,[1] and advised him strongly to present our case before the meeting of Congress, in length and breadth, with all its aggravations, so as to show our grievance; and at the same time to say that this was done to enable the British government to understand the feelings of our people; that we should rest without any demand of any kind, but that the British government should be invited to take it into candid consideration, to prepare the way for some equitable adjustment with a view to peace and reconciliation. I insisted that something of this nature must be done before the meeting of Congress, or there would be dissatisfaction. I think that I made an impression upon him, for he invited me to prepare such a paper. This I declined, saying that I was too much occupied otherwise, and besides I had made my statement. . . . There was a room kept for me at Fish's while the President was there, but I did not think it best to be there.[2] I arrived immediately afterwards. Fish was kind and confidential. I think he is weary of official life. He did not intend to remain after the meeting of Congress, but his purpose now is to stay for a year. I am pained at the attacks which I fear he must encounter. A vigorous presentment of our case will take from critics one of their weapons. . . . Fish thought that any negotiation on the claims should be at Washington, where the Senate can be consulted, as nothing can be done without the consent of that body. He had talked with John Rose of Canada,[3] who had sounded him about sending out the Duke of Argyll. The duke must not come unless to be successful. The case must not be embittered by another rejection.

PL   Prc, 4:412–13   (82/613, PCS)

1. Motley wrote CS 22 July 1869 (London, 47/537, PCS) that many "friends" in Britain did not understand the U.S. case "thoroughly," specifically the "intrigues" of April and May 1861, which had resulted in the Queen's Proclamation of Neutrality. His experience thus far, said Motley, had caused his views to be "entirely unmodified." CS had visited Fish at his Hudson River home 6–7 August.

2. Upon learning that Grant was to be a guest at Fish's house, CS postponed his own visit, for he did not wish to "be in the way" (Boston, 1 August, 3 August, 82/602, 604).

3. Sir John Rose (1820–88), then minister of finance for Canada, was in the U.S. to confer about a new reciprocity treaty between the U.S. and Great Britain.

To John H. Clifford

Coolidge House Thursday noon
[23 September 1869]

My dear Govr,

Your very kind note is the first voice that has reached me. I am glad you liked what I said.[1]

I intended to make repudiation impossible,—to warn Spain that she must prepare to go, but to keep my country out of the trouble,——& to let England see how & in what tone I judged her still,—also to prepare the way for Canada.[2] A good deal to attempt in one speech— prepared & begun since Sat. evng last. Not till Saturday last did I definitely accept the invitation to preside.[3]

Yr criticism is excellent.[4] Mat. Prior wrote as you said. Shall I confess that in the words about the Ocean, I was not sure if I quoted Bryant or Pope's translation of the account of the shield of Achilles? All was done in such haste, that there was no time for verification.

As to that pamphlet edition—I am tired of printing pamphlets,— & have done enough at my own expense.

Towards Cuba our course is very plain. Be kind with Spain; make her feel yr good-will, & then shew her the way history points. But do not expose our country to her Letters of Marque. People do not know Spain. Touch her pride, & it will cost you commerce. *I know it*. I wish you could talk with Fish about England. He needs it.

Every sincerely Yours,   Charles Sumner

ALS   MHi   (83/031, PCS)

1. Clifford wrote CS 22 September 1869 (New Bedford, 48/210, PCS) praising the "noble and timely thoughts" of CS's speech to the Republican State Convention 22 September.

2. Speaking on domestic affairs first, CS denounced both repudiation of the national debt and the continued use of greenbacks. On foreign affairs, CS called on Spain to grant independence to Cuba. The U.S. should not intervene, he said; any concession of belligerent rights to Cuban insurgents was unwise, especially since the insurgents had not consistently embraced emancipating Cuban slaves. As for Britain,

CS refused to "fix the measure of this great accountability." While it was up to Canadians to decide who would govern them, Americans believed that a union with Canada "with the good will of the mother country and the accord of both parties, must be the harbinger of infinite good" ("National Affairs at Home and Abroad" [1869], 12, 14, 16).

3. CS had written Fish 12 September that rumors that CS would speak soon on Cuba and the *Alabama* question were untrue (83/020).

4. Clifford made some corrections "for the great pamphlet edition which is to be known and read of all men." He referred to the epigrammist Matthew Prior (1664–1721), who "never *wrote* as the newspaper people made him read." The pamphlet edition of CS's speech contains at the close a brief adaptation from Pope's translation of the *Iliad*, book 18 (1750), "'poured round all old Ocean's' constant tides."

To Julia Kean Fish

Boston 29th Sept. '69

Dear Mrs Fish,

I have just recd. the enclosed letter concerning poor Mrs Lincoln. I do not recall the writer, but the account she gives accords with what I have heard from other quarters.[1]

I think that I know the failings of that lady, but I cannot forget that she is the widow of our President.[2]

This world is full of sorrow, & every where there is opportunity of charity. All true. But is not this a case for the nation?

The papers say that yr husband is at home. I congratulate him & the family.

I wish the Cuban question looked clearer, & nearer a solution. Spain must go, & the sooner she sees it the better for all.[3]

Ever sincerely Yours,   Charles Sumner

ALS   DLC   (83/039, PCS)

1. CS probably enclosed a letter from Sally B. Orme, wife of Philadelphia businessman James Orme, about the sorry state of Mary Todd Lincoln. Writing from Baden Baden, Germany, Mrs. Orme described her recent visit to Mary Lincoln's Frankfurt hotel, where she lived in a "small cheerless desolate looking room." Mrs. Orme asked, "is this not dreadful—that the wife of Abraham Lincoln should be so situated—." She asked that CS make public Mary Lincoln's condition (12 September 1869, 48/147, PCS).

2. CS had already tried to get Congress to provide a pension for Mary Lincoln during its recent session. She wrote CS 27 March from Frankfurt thanking him for "his kind perseverance in my behalf" (45/684). On 14 July 1870, Congress finally (and somewhat reluctantly) passed a bill allowing Mary Lincoln a pension of $3,000 a year (*Globe*, 41st Cong., 2nd sess., 1249–50, 5560).

3. Spain still showed every intention of putting down the Cuban insurrection (*New York Times*, 23 September 1869:1, 25 September 1869:8).

To Hamilton Fish

Boston 7th Oct '69

My dear Fish,

At last you are again at work—deserting the river-bank, which must be very glorious in its autumn dress. I wish I were there.

My last letter from Motley was red. at yr house. I send now the first since then which is more minute.[1]

I wish Spain were reasonable.[2] She must come to her senses, sooner or later. So must England.

The more I think of our relations with the latter, it seems to me that our first step is to make a clear & full statement of our grievance, without any claim of damages, so that England shall appreciate the feelings of our people. This will be the beginning of any future negotiation. If this could be sent out before Congress, & laid on the table with the message, it would be a basis for action.

Many years ago, when Mr Webster was Secy of State, I remember taking the great liberty of writing a letter to him, suggesting that our case against England at that time should be stated in the Presdt's message, with sufficient fullness to make it known to the world,—as the message went every where at home & abroad. I forget to what extent this suggestion was acted upon at that time; but you will remember that Mr Polk used the message as his vehicle against Mexico.

I do not doubt that England will propose terms which we can accept just so soon as she sees that we are in earnest, which she will see, if our govt. states the grievance in an elaborate paper, & the Presdt. sums it up in his message. Such a course will anticipate debate & action in Congress, &, it seems to me will keep the question in the hands of the Administration. Seward often threatened that he would refer the question to Congress, & then, said he, "England will learn that I am the gentlest of all."

You will observe that Motley in his letter speaks of a statement from us, which he thinks expedient.[3]

Believe me, dear Fish,

Ever sincerely Yours,   Charles Sumner

P.S. As I think of our pending questions I wish Fessenden were with us.[4] He was clear & honest,—& I am sure that we should have worked together. I am glad to know how kindly he felt to me before his death.

ALS   DLC   (83/055, PCS)

1. CS sent Fish Motley's letter of 12 September 1869 (Penmaenmawr, Wales, 48/137, PCS) with the note "to be read confidentially & returned. C. S."

2. The Spanish government had refused the U.S. plan for Spain to sell Cuba (*New York Times*, 13 October 1869:1).

3. Motley wrote in his 12 September letter that he agreed with CS that a "thorough, searching, outspoken statement of our case" should be presented to the British government, without calling for specific reparations. "In truth the damages are beyond estimate."

4. Fessenden died 8 September. A. L. Hobson of Portland, Maine, wrote CS shortly before Fessenden's death to tell him of a recent conversation with the senator in which Fessenden had said of his relations with CS, "I am happy to say that our differences are all settled & we are now good friends" (3 September, 48/098). CS delivered a eulogy on Fessenden 14 December (*Globe*, 41st Cong., 2nd sess., 112–13).

To Hamilton Fish

Boston 11th Oct. '69

My dear Fish,

I make haste to reply to yr inquiry about the liability of the Hornet.[1]

Is it enough to be satisfied that we have no statute agnst the Hornet? Under Washington, before any statute, ships were held under the Law of Nations, which is the law of the land. There is a famous case on this point in 1794. I have no books at hand, &, therefore, cannot give you the reference.

Now, by the Law of Nations, it seems to me that the owners of the Hornet were guilty the moment they began to do any thing for the preparation of the ship *knowing her ultimate purpose*. Showing this *scienter* & any the smallest act would be enough.

Of course this guilt continues in the ship, & makes it liable. Proceedings against her on this point would at least hold her.

I am sorry for yr criticism of Motley,[2] which I do not presume to judge, as I have not the *data*, nor have I ever seen the Bunch papers.[3] Assuming, however, that these illustrate the conduct of England, I do not see how they can be kept back—*valeat quantum*.[4] I am entirely satisfied—at least so it seems to me—that our case must be presented first to England fully, so that she must feel its extent & pressure. This will justify the Senate & will satisfy the public. Afterwards we can get some recognition of principle. I have no fear of war or any serious cry, *if the Administration covers the whole ground in its statement*. If this is done unsatisfactorily, then the cry will begin, & Congress will deal with it, as Seward always anticipated. My earnest desire now is to see it presented in such a way that no member of Congress will wish to add any thing. From yr letter I do not infer the character of the paper you have sent out.[5] If it is a statement of our case, so much the better.

Edge's pamphlet[6] must be judged by itself & its own internal merits.

Ever Yours, Charles Sumner

ALS DLC (83/061, PCS)

1. The *Hornet*, a privateer flying Cuban colors, was commanded by an ex-Confederate with a Southern crew. The ship had put into the port of Wilmington, North Carolina, ostensibly to load coal, but sources believed the movement was really to test U.S. reaction (*New York Times*, 1 October 1869:1, 5 October 1869:1, 9 October 1869:3). In his letter of 9 October 1869 Fish asked CS's advice. If the U.S. extended hospitality to the *Hornet*, then the U.S. recognized Cuba as a belligerent; on the other hand, "if we allow her to depart, we permit a hostile expedition from our shores" (Washington, 48/352, PCS).

2. Fish also discussed Motley's behavior in England: "his rhetoric is strong & wants a vent not consistent with the restraints required by his position. He did not follow his instructions in the interview with Ld Clarendon narrated in his No. 8." Fish explained that because of his "personal regard" for Motley, he had sent him only a "gentle" rebuke. However, in any other government, "such violations of instructions" would have resulted in "the most severe censure, probably by an immediate recall." Fish confessed that Motley's course might have been wiser but "the Administration thought otherwise" and Motley was obliged to obey his instructions. He asked CS, "Can we preserve peace if the accredited representative of our Government should endeavor to 'make such a detestable record against Gt Britain'? . . . Do we mean War? I know you do not & I do not—does he?"

3. Both Motley and George Bemis continued to urge the publication of correspondence of Robert Bunch and Confederate officials such as William Henry Trescot, a South Carolinian who served as an emissary from Jefferson Davis (Motley to CS, 12 September, Bemis to CS, 18 March, 48/137, 45/567). Fish claimed, however, that Motley was mistaken as to the correspondence's implications and it should not be published.

4. *Valeat quantum, valere potest*: "Let it pass for what it is worth."

5. Fish wrote that he had sent Motley a paper (No. 70, 25 September 1869) to be read to Lord Clarendon affirming the United States' "willingness to reopen negotiations *here*," whenever Britain deemed such a move appropriate. He hoped CS approved.

6. Frederick Milnes Edge, a British journalist who had been in the U.S. during the Civil War, had approached both CS and Motley with a plan to expose the British support of the Confederacy during the war (Edge to CS, London, 3 July, 9 August 1869, 47/431, 451, 655; Motley to CS, 12 September). In "Our Claims on England" CS had cited an earlier Edge pamphlet that calculated British damage to American ships. Fish wrote CS 9 October that he hoped Motley had not given Edge much encouragement in his proposed pamphlet, which seemed without solid evidence.

To Hamilton Fish

Springfield 9th Novbr. '69

My dear Fish,

I have yours of the 6th, which has been forwarded to me here where I have come to lecture. I do not expect to reach Washington till the Saturday before Congress, which is the day when I arrive generally. But I give you my views on the important points of yr letter at once.[1]

I do not think that at this moment any body here can *formularize* any proposal to England.[2] Time must intervene, in order to ascertain what the people will require. This will be seen in the probable debates of Congress. Should Congress show indifference, then the way will be open for you to make a proposal. Should Congress express itself decisively then again you would have a guide.

Here I remark on an obvious difference between the question now & at any previous time. Down to the mission of Reverdy Johnson, the country was indifferent, leaving Mr Seward free to make such proposal as he saw fit, &, I do not doubt, that with reasonable discretion in our Minister there, the country would have continued indifferent, leaving to the Secy of State the substantial control of the question. You know I have always said that the rejected Treaty would have been accepted six months earlier; not because our rights now are different from what they were then, but because the people are more exacting.

Reverdy Johnson made an appeal to the people stirring them up & making them feel their responsibility. The people acting on this appeal rejected his Treaty. The Senate did nothing but record their decision. It is a mistake to suppose that this was done by Mr S. or the Comtee on Foreign Relations or by the Senate itself.[3] They did little more than register the foregone conclusion; & this accounts for the singular unanimity with which it was received by the country.

All this shews that we must consult the public. Having jurisdiction of the question once, they will claim it again, & no Administration can venture on any proposal which shall oust this jurisdiction.

With this view, it seems to me our present course is to wait, unless England chooses to take the initiative. If England will cultivate a little decency it might do much to smooth the way. But I despair of any justice in that quarter. The last sentence of my much-abused speech contains an important practical suggestion, which England ought to profit by.[4]

Did I ever tell you of Fessenden's speech in committee? Just before the vote was taken, he said—"England has done us mischief enough,

God knows! but I don't care for her money. If she had ever said one good simple word of regret & good will, I could forget all the rest." Here is the beginning for England.

I should not be disposed to relax at all in the exigency of our claim, until England shews some good-will, or Congress becomes indifferent. She must feel its gravity, & that our Govt. is the simple agent of a people which still smarts under a sense of injury.

From the beginning I have had but one opinion on the wrong England has done us; but such has been my desire for peace, & so Philo-Anglican have I been, that I held my peace until I was obliged to speak. I often told Sir Fred. Bruce, that, notwithstanding my sense of the wrong my country had received, I would stand aside, provided the two countries could agree upon a treaty which the American people would accept. I said this also to Mr Thornton, but I distrust his candor or intelligence. He has not behaved well, & my present purpose is to say so in the Senate. He has been a mischief-maker, particularly with regard to me. My course has been simple & direct. Mr [Moorfield] Storey mentioned to me that he was present at a visit of Mr Thornton to me, at the time of R. J's appointment when I said to him, that "in my judgment England had done us greater wrong than was ever done by one civilized Power to another not afterwards washed out by the bloodiest of wars." He, therefore, knew my judgment on the question, & there was no need of the unworthy despatches he wrote.[5]

While I do not see the way to make any specific demand at present, I do not think we ought to relax in effort to make England feel our sense of wrong. To this end, I counsel still a careful, [explicative?] & firm statement in the Presdt's message.[6] This will have several influences (1) It will make the English people see the case in its gravity. (2) It will satisfy our people (3) It will supersede the efforts of others whose voice is for war.

I want peace,—& to this end settlement. But I see no chance of this until England changes her tune. As Danton[7] once said—"let us have a little prose & decency."

I shall be in Boston next Sunday & the Sunday after at the Brevort House, N.Y.

Ever Yours,   Charles Sumner

ALS   DLC   (83/087, PCS)

1. CS was then on a lecture tour presenting "A Question of Caste" in eastern cities. Fish wrote CS from Washington seeking his advice on a recent informal request from

Lord Clarendon via Sir Edward Thornton about the U.S. position on the *Alabama* claims. Fish said he was unwilling, until he could meet with CS, to respond to Thornton. Fish wished to know when CS would return to Washington (48/465, PCS).

2. Fish wrote that Thornton had asked "with much earnestness to give him an indication of what would be accepted by our Government," in a fairly "definite" statement. Fish asked CS if he would "note what you think will be sufficient to meet the [views?] of the Senate & of the Country, or will you formulate such proposition."

3. Thornton had said, wrote Fish, that because the Johnson-Clarendon Convention had been "'somewhat contumaciously rejected'" by the U.S., the British government saw "difficulties" in resuming negotiations.

4. CS's speech closed saying that a "generous expression" from Britain acknowledging its responsibility "would be the beginning of a just settlement" ("Our Claims on England" [1869], 14).

5. On 19 April 1869 Thornton sent Lord Clarendon six copies of CS's Senate speech on the *Alabama* claims and, in summarizing the speech, used words like "preposterous" to describe CS's argument that British support of the Confederacy prolonged the war. Thornton continued, "I know of no arguments more calculated than those contained in his speech to excite the passions of his impulsive countrymen, and to inflame that animosity which, unhappily, it is but too apparent they still feel against England" (*British Documents*, part 1, series C, 7:197–200).

6. In his annual message to Congress Grant approved the rejection of the Johnson-Clarendon Convention: "Not a word was found in the treaty, and not an inference could be drawn from it, to remove the sense of the unfriendliness of the course of Great Britain in our struggle for existence which had so deeply and universally impressed itself upon the people of this country." Grant looked forward to a "solution of this momentous question with an appreciation of what is due to the rights, dignity and honor" of both the U.S. and Britain (6 December, *Globe*, 41st Cong., 2nd sess., 6).

7. Georges-Jacques Danton (1759–94), French revolutionary leader.

To Francis Lieber

Senate Chamber 24th Decbr. '69

My dear Lieber,

I have read Laboulaye's Preface & also the introduction to Bluntshli with the constant praise of yr works, & the translation of yr code.[1] I like much what Laboulaye writes. He is a thinker & does not forget the demands of civilization.

One passage of Laboulaye, & the repetition of the same idea in the Introduction suggests a practical question of much importance. Both say that a nation maintaining Slavery should be put under the ban of the civilized world. This is very general. What is meant? How far should the ban extend? This brings me to the practical question.

How would it do to suspend diplomatic relations with Powers maintaining Slavery? This would bear on two countries only—Spain & Brazil. Such an act on our part could not fail to have important consequences. I do not think these two countries could stand against the pressure. Is not the probable result worth the effort?

With this idea, I have thought of introducing into the Senate, after the holidays, a resolution calling for the suspension of diplomatic relations with Slave-Powers. What say you?[2]

Even if the resolution were not adopted, would not its introduction by me have the desired effect, especially in Spain? The Cortez will meet in three weeks, & would hear of this movement by telegraph. Would it not make haste to decree Emancipation? *Qu'en dites vous?*[3]

Would not such a step on our part be in the line of our action [*letter is incomplete*]

AL   MH-H   (64/644, PCS)

1. Lieber wrote CS (New York, 11 December 1869, 83/138, PCS) that the president had been sent an advance copy of *Le Droit International Codifié . . . et Précédé d'une Préface par Édouard Laboulaye* (1870) by the German law scholar Johann Kaspar Bluntschli (1808–81). The work had been based on Lieber's code of military behavior, which he prepared for the Union army in 1863.

2. Lieber advised against introducing such a resolution. Other countries, such as China and Turkey, would also be targets. Moreover, the resolution would flout international law, which forbade the interference by other countries in domestic affairs (28 December, 83/175).

3. "What do you say?"

To Edward L. Pierce

private

Washington 7th Jan. '70

My dear Pierce,

I enclose the only subscription paper that I know any thing about. Any other has been adopted without my knowledge.[1]

The works are, of course, separate. The Life is separate, if there is to be a life.[2]

I have always insisted that my life was in my speeches & I have never desired any thing but a complete corrected edition of these. Next to destroying them, so that none should survive, I wish to see them revised & edited. In this object, which is near my heart, no body has taken such interest as Dr Phelps.[3] Through him others have been interested, who have assumed a certain portion of the preliminary expense, standing behind the publisher. Other expenses beyond anticipation will fall on me.

The work I have undertaken will be no sinecure, nor will it be free from pecuniary outlay. But I am an absolute stranger to the business arrangements. I do not know who is standing behind the Publishers, nor to what amount they are bound; nor do I know the contract or arrangement with Dr Phelps. I am doing my part of the work & assuming the pecuniary obligations incident to it. This is all.

I advised against any other Life than the Works. I am still of this opinion. But it seems hard that friends of mine should be so bitter towards one who, of his own accord,—after I had failed to obtain a publisher—obtained one for me with the capital needed in such an enterprize.

Why do you not speak to the Publishers on the blending the *two together*?[4] This is contrary to my understanding, & inconsistent with my purpose.

Sincerely Yours,   Charles Sumner

ALS   MH-H   (64/651, PCS)

1. Pierce wrote CS 4 January 1870 from Boston, objecting to the advertisement from the Boston publishers Lee & Shepard for CS's forthcoming works. A flyer advertising CS's works announced that Lee & Shepard would also publish "A Life of Charles Sumner, by Hon. Chas. A. Phelps [*1820–1902*], author of 'Life of U. S. Grant.'" One of CS's oldest friends, wrote Pierce, had refused to subscribe because of Phelps's involvement: "he is odious in this community" (49/248, PCS). CS had received similar protestations about Phelps from Charles Slack (Phelps was not intellectually able) and Francis W. Bird (Phelps was "distrusted" in Boston circles) (12 March, 21 June 1869, 45/478, 47/359).

2. Pierce wrote CS that he believed no biography should be written during the subject's lifetime. If one was undertaken, it should be a completely separate venture. Since CS was known to "revise and edit the works," readers would assume he had played a major part in the writing of the biography.

3. Phelps's letters to CS at this time contain details of the forthcoming publication and Phelps's desire for a political appointment (9 September 1869, [February? 1870], 12 March 1870, 48/126, 50/063, 167).

4. Although Lee & Shepard wrote CS 14 January approving Phelps's one-volume biography (49/349), shortly thereafter Phelps must have been dropped from the project. Pierce wrote CS 6 February expressing his and others' satisfaction that a "change has been made in the mode of publication" (Milton, 49/573).

To Samuel Gridley Howe

Senate Chamber 16th March '70

My dear Howe,

I am always glad to see yr writing, & only regret how little able I am now to be any thing more than an unresponding correspondant. My life is very crowded & fatigued

As to Cuba, I am obliged to say, that I have never seen any evidence that brings her insurgents within any rule of law, reason or humanity,[1] justifying our concession to them of *a flag on the ocean*. No nation can concede to insurgents a flag on the ocean, which is the present question, unless it bounds on the ocean, has ports & *the means of administering justice on the ocean*. Such is the requirement of civilization, in the interest of peace & to prevent the burning of ships on the ocean. Every captured ship must be carried into port & condemned as prize, & unless this can be done the captors are no better than pirates.

Can the U.S. take a step which will stultify the nation? Can we disregard the rule we have constantly invoked,— which to my mind is a safeguard of peace & security? Too much do I love peace—too strongly am I impressed by its importance to our country at this moment—too transcendant is our example—for me to be willing to adopt a course which will put all these in peril. I have no doubt that the concession of a flag on the ocean to Cuban insurgents would be a wrong to Spain. Such is my judgment. To my mind it is clear beyond question. Therefore, I cannot consent to it. But beyond my judgment of its wrongful character, is the positive peril of war, which it must create. I call it a peril only. But I have little doubt that it would be followed by Letters of Marque from Spain against our commerce, sweeping it from the ocean & drawing us into war, which would cost 500 millions at least. Boutwell[2] thinks 1000 millions. I do not think this ought to be encountered lightly.

If we must have war I prefer that the U.S. should declare at once openly that it sides with the insurgents, & accepts war with Spain; but let it not begin by *telling a lie*, in other words by declaring what is notoriously untrue.— Is the country ready for war? The Cuban junta wish it, for they are reckless, & they say that we should conquer Spain. Very well; but at what cost? I do not doubt that [*Juan*] Prim would accept a war with the U.S. (1) as confirming his power & (2) as affording what is called an "honorable" way of losing Cuba. Spain with her 18 millions might yield to our 40 millions, after doing us incalculable damage, & Cuba would be independent—& what then? Do we desire her annexation?

For myself, I desire her independence, & I see what seems to me the best way of obtaining it. Among these ways I discard (1) bribery of U. States officials, who are implicated on a large scale[3] & (2) war by the U.S. Both these agencies I repell.

I have reason to believe that the people will be indignant at the dishonest efforts made to compromise our country. At any rate when I am dead, there is nothing which I would have remembered about me more than the tenacity with which I have clung to the duty & policy of peace, when pressed as I have been for months. I believe in peace & I am against any act or declaration that will thwart or imperil civilization. If we can keep the peace, the world will be ours. Our only danger is from war.

I look to annexation at the North. I wish to have that whole zone from Newfoundland to Vancouver. But a war with Spain would postpone this triumph indefinitely.—Do not think unkindly of me because I cannot see these things otherwise

God bless you!

Ever & ever Yours,   Charles Sumner

P.S. Did you not write an article in favor of *one cent postage?* I remember yr effort, but I am not sure of the form it took. Please send me any thing on the subject.

Are you sure that the franking privilege is not valuable as an educator especially at the South & West? Can we afford to lose this agency in circulating speeches, & pamphlets?[4]

ALS   MH-H   (64/653, PCS)

1. Although the Cuban rebellion against Spain appeared to be failing, the New York–based organization of insurgents continued to press for U.S. support (*New York Times*, 3 January 1870:5, 13 January 1870:5). In February and March 1870 several resolutions had been introduced in the Senate to recognize a state of war between Cuba and Spain, and to protest Spanish cruelties, but consideration was either postponed or referred to the Senate Foreign Relations Committee. CS had spoken 15 December 1869 against recognition of the Cuban insurgents as belligerents (*Globe*, 41st Cong., 2nd sess., 1206, 1776–77, 144–45).

2. George S. Boutwell was then secretary of the Treasury.

3. In his dispatch to Daniel Sickles of 26 January 1870 Fish deplored the violation of U.S. laws by agents for the Cuban junta; they had employed armed bands to launch attacks from within the U.S. against Spain (*New York Times*, 22 February 1870:1).

4. On 10 June 1870 CS gave a Senate speech favoring one-cent postage for all, which he stated would substitute for the current franking privileges congressmen enjoyed (*Globe*, 41st Cong., 2nd sess., 4291–98).

To Hamilton Fish

Thursday mrng
[*Washington 17 March 1870*]

My dear Fish,

It is now more than *nine* years that I have been chairman of the Comtee of Foreign Relations in the Senate, during which long period all the diplomatic nominations & treaties have passed through my hands. Seward boasts that he negotiated ½ of all the treaties in our statute book;—then have I carried ½ through the Comttee & Senate,—giving to them my best attention.

In this responsible service I have sought the public interest to the best of my ability, with no other object in view. Often I have been obliged to differ from the Secy of State, & from the Presdt & often also from colleagues of the Comttee & from the Senate. Since the presidency of Grant I have differed less than ever before. I believe there are only two instances, &, now I find these the occasion of misunderstanding.[1] Must I accept every thing without any exercise of my own judgment? Then why have a committee? Certainly I cannot serve on any such terms.

I had supposed that experience was of some account, &, then behind all, I had supposed that every honest public servant in the exercise of his discretion, was entitled to a candid & considerate judgment. Clocks do not go alike. Men do not think alike. We must be just to each other, & recognize the rights of each in his place.

There are few in the govt who have a greater personal interest in these questions, or a longer responsibility for them before the country than myself. How then can I renounce the conclusions which, on my conscience, seem just?—It would be as if Grant had deserted his military duties.

But I am very weary, & unhappy & should be glad to give it all up. I want nothing but peace.—I forget—I did want one small place for a life-long friend[2]—a place which I created,—which I always intended for him—which he would honor—, & where the public interests would harmonize with his appointment—I waited through the Administration of A. J. for [this?] opportunity & now I wait through another Administration. This is the only personal desire that I have had, the only personal request that I have ever made. It could not be granted & I submit. But I do not think you should judge me unkindly because in the duties cast upon me I act according to the light of my experience, seeking always the good of my country—I cannot do otherwise. You must bear with me at least.[3]

Ever sincerely Yours,   Charles Sumner

ALS   DLC   (83/325, PCS)

1. On 10 January 1870 the Grant administration presented two treaties to the Senate regarding Santo Domingo: one provided for the lease of the bay and the Sa-

mana peninsula on that island; the second, for U.S. annexation of Santo Domingo. Both were referred immediately to the Senate Foreign Relations Committee. On 15 March the committee recommended 5–2 that the annexation treaty be rejected. The committee did not report on the lease agreement (*Executive Proceedings*, 17:334, 392; *New York Times*, 16 March 1870:1).

2. When Fish first became secretary of state, CS had unsuccessfully urged the appointment of Samuel Gridley Howe as minister to Greece (CS to Howe, 28 March 1869, 64/611, PCS).

3. Fish replied the same day, writing that CS's note had come just as he was leaving for the State Department. "I find that I was so very unfortunate last Evng. & that I have such an unhappy faculty of being misunderstood, that I fear to venture on any thing more than an acknowledgment of your letter & the assurance that however much misunderstood I am, very truly your friend[,] Hamilton Fish" (Washington, 50/202). The precise nature of their disagreement the previous evening is not known. While Fish did not personally support the annexation of Santo Domingo, he was obliged, as a member of the Grant administration, to serve the president's wishes (Allan Nevins, *Hamilton Fish* [1937], 270–73, 316).

To George Washington Greene

Senate Chamber
17th March '70

My dear Greene,

As you are a member of the Legislature, you can tell me of Anthony's chances.[1] I hope they are *good, better, best*. His experience ought not to be lost to the Senate, &, now, as one of the fathers, I feel anxious to preserve my companions about me. My life is often hard, & there are some here who are unkind. You know that Anthony is always sympathetic with me. Therefore, it is natural that I should like him.

I have been on the point of writing to Govr. Padelford,[2] whose pleasant countenance lighted the platform the evng I spoke in Providence, & also my old friend Mr [*Amos*] Barstow. When you see these excellent gentlemen give them my regards & ask how the case stands. Then, perhaps, you will write me; but on the latter point I despair.[3]

I have more pictures. If they were Raffaeles or Domenochinos,[4] I doubt not you could see them.

Ever sincerely Yours,   Charles Sumner

ALS   ICUJR   (83/329, PCS)

1. Henry B. Anthony was up for reelection.
2. Seth Padelford (1807–78), governor of Rhode Island, 1869–73.
3. Greene replied 26 March 1870 after conversing with various Rhode Island

authorities. He assured CS that although Anthony had a strong opponent, Anthony's friends were hopeful (East Greenwich, Rhode Island, 50/266, PCS).

4. Domenico Zampieri (1581–1641), like his predecessor Raphael, an Italian painter. According to Donald, CS's taste in paintings was questionable and he frequently paid more than the work was worth (DD, 2:325–26; see, e.g., invoices from H. N. Barlow, Washington art dealer, June 1868, 42/213, 368, 391).

To Hamilton Fish

20th March '70

My dear Fish,

I send a formal note asking for any papers not now in possession of the Comttee. on the St Domingo Treaty.

I am tempted to say a word for Schurtz in reply to yr criticism.[1] I have observed him closely from the moment this treaty was recd. He has been positive, but always with reasons, in which I do not doubt he is as sincere & patriotic as the President. Why should this be doubted?

I am anxious that this interesting question should be considered on its merits. Of course, I begin by admitting all that I understand the Presdt says in its favor,[2] but this leaves open great questions financial, political, & moral,—the latter to my mind of surpassing interest.

Ever sincerely Yours,   Charles Sumner

ALS   DLC   (83/339, PCS)

1. Carl Schurz, recently elected U.S. senator from Missouri, had voted in the Senate Foreign Relations Committee along with CS and three others to reject the treaty to annex Santo Domingo. Fish wrote the evening of 20 March 1870 that he meant no criticism of Schurz; Schurz had "other & higher grounds of objection, all of which I sincerely respect" (50/230, PCS).

2. Grant had been actively lobbying for his treaty. He had sent a letter to the Senate on 14 March asking for prompt consideration and, he hoped, ratification before the treaty was due to expire 29 March (*Executive Proceedings*, 17:389–90). On 17 March Grant visited the Senate to try to persuade various senators to support the treaty. Grant wrote Fish 22 March instructing him not to deal with CS over delaying consideration of the treaty; he feared Fish might agree to CS's plan. CS was "an enemy of the treaty; will kill it to-morrow if he can, and only favors delay probably to better secure its defeat" (letter in Fish Papers, Library of Congress).

To Henry W. Longfellow

Senate Chamber 21st March '70

Dear Longfellow,

Yr hand-writing has a gleam of the sun for me always—as I sit in my darkness. This morng I saw you reading Michelet.[1] Why can I not read Michelet or somebody else? For me there is nothing but perpetual fatigue.

Did I tell you that J. B. Smith made me a visit of 2 or 3 days? He seemed content.[2]

I hear nothing from J. O. on my debt to G. N.[3] He will write me in about 2 years; but he is an excellent critic, with an ear for language, which I know in few. His verbal emendations are often very felicitous, showing a sense or instinct for the proper adjective or noun. So much for J. O.

While I write the debate is going on.—All at once I have another responsibility. The Presdt. without any notice has negotiated a treaty for the annexation of St. Domingo. I have reported against it. (1) Nobody can tell the amount of the debt.[4] (2) We buy a civil war & a bloody *lis pendens*. (3) We commence a policy of annexation in the West Indies, incorporating tropical islands with our republic, when I incline to believe we should offer them a beneficent protectorate without incorporation. These are great questions, on which it is my misfortune to differ from the Presdt.

Good bye!

Ever Thine,   C. S.

ALS   MH-H   (83/342, PCS)
Enc: Newspaper clipping[5]

1. Longfellow wrote 17 March 1870 that a recent visitor to Washington reported that CS was "the leader of the Senate." In his letter of 19 March, Longfellow wrote he was reading *Précis de l'Histoire de France jusqu'à la Révolution Française* (1855) by the French historian Jules Michelet (1798–1874) (Cambridge, 83/330, 337, PCS).

2. Joshua B. Smith wrote CS a letter of thanks from Boston 17 March (50/210).

3. CS wrote both John Owen and George Nichols about payment for Nichols's editing of CS's collected works (to Nichols, 18 February; to Owen, 19 February, 83/281, 286).

4. The present Dominican government, under the rule of Buenaventura Báez, owed money, with a high rate of interest, to the British firm Hartmont. Article 3 of the treaty stipulated that all Dominican property "not specifically ceded" to the U.S. would be "pledged" toward payment of the republic's public debt; article 6 specified that the U.S. was "in no event to be liable" for any part of either the interest or the debt (DD, 2:440; *New York Times*, 13 January 1870:5). CS delivered an extensive speech in executive session on 24–25 March against the treaty (no text survives) (ibid., 25 March 1870:1).

5. CS had pasted onto his letter an unidentified clipping that reported that a Washington woman correspondent, "Shirley Dare," noted how CS "sits in the Senate like a great faithful hound, *casting watchful glances up the gallery*" [underlined by CS]. The paragraph continued, "To me the look seems searching for a face that never appears." Beside the clipping CS had written "!! never!—."

To Henry W. Longfellow

[*Washington, 29? April 1870*]

"A specimen!" [1]

AN MH-H (83/396, PCS)
Enc: Newspaper clipping from Easton, Pa., *Weekly Argus*

1. The clipping from the 28 April 1870 issue of the *Argus* stated, "SUMNER has been detected in an intrigue with Dinah Revels, wife of his brother Senator from Mississippi." CS's message appears above the clipping. No doubt the *Argus* was piqued by CS's promoting Hiram Revels. When other senators contested Revels's claim to his seat, CS spoke for Revels, declaring that with his confirmation "the primal truths declared by our fathers are practically recognized" (25 February, *Globe*, 41st Cong., 2nd sess., 1566–67).

To Mary Bucklin Claflin

Senate Chamber 10th May '70

My dear Mrs Claflin,

I needed no assurance from you to know that yr husband had done for Mr Revels all that hospitality or sympathy could suggest. [1]

I am glad to hear of Mr Revels's sucess & of all the kindness he received. [2] In this welcome I catch the triumph of a new civilization.

Believe me, dear Mrs Claflin,

Very faithfully Yours,   Charles Sumner

ALS MWA (83/422, PCS)

1. Mary Claflin (1825–96), wife of the Massachusetts governor William Claflin, had written CS twice regarding Hiram Revels's visit to Boston. On 4 May 1870 she explained that the fact that her husband could not receive Revels earlier at a reception should not be construed as a slur against the senator (Boston, 50/452, PCS).

2. In her letter of 9 May Mary Claflin assured CS of the Claflins' warm welcome. Revels's "general reception, and his own deportment have been *all* that you could desire" (50/473). When Revels spoke at Tremont Temple 4 May, Claflin introduced him (*Boston Daily Journal*, 5 May 1870:2).

To Henry W. Longfellow

[*Washington*] 22nd June [187]0

Dear Longfellow,

I like the new poem much. [1] It is sweet & beautiful—in itself the very bell told of. I have read it several times & always with delight.

The papers seem to like it.

It is 10 o'clk in the evng & I am in my seat, listening, talking, writing, reading—very busy & tired.[2] When do you move to Nahant? Hot weeks are before me here until the last of July if not later. I am cross & see things darkly. *Inter nos* there is much disappointment about the Presdt, who has no experience & little wisdom.[3] Alas!

I long for repose & every day vow that I will resign & disappear from the scene. I am too old for controversy & battle. Why have I been always in the breach? And yet it seems to be the same now as at the beginning.

Good bye! Good night!

Ever Yours,   C. S.

———————

ALS   MH-H   (83/477, PCS)

1. "The Alarm-Bell of Atri," *Atlantic Monthly* 26 (July 1870):1–3.

2. The Senate debated until midnight a bill to extend the Southern Pacific line from Texas to California (*Globe*, 41st Cong., 2nd sess., 4719–34).

3. Although the Santo Domingo treaty had lapsed, Grant on 31 May 1870 asked the Senate to reconsider it. Throughout June that body examined information it had requested from the president about foreign powers' financial interests in the Dominican Republic; about conditions under which U.S. agents had negotiated the annexation treaty, and the extent of the Republic's public debt; and about the Navy Department's instructions to officers on ships off the coast of the Dominican Republic (*Executive Proceedings*, 17:465–67, 474, 476, 480). In open session CS castigated Orville E. Babcock, a Grant aide who had helped negotiate the treaty, and stated that the negotiation had "for a long time been under suspicion" (8 June, *Globe*, 41st Cong., 2nd sess., 4194, 4199).

To Joseph L. Stackpole
private

[Washington] 26th June [1870]

Dear Mr Stackpole,

I fear that there is ground for the rumor to which you refer, but I shall not believe the thing possible until it is done.[1] I say to you *confidentially* that I have reason to believe that Mr. Grennell collector of N.Y., has been thought of as the successor.[2] This would settle N.Y. difficulties;—but the whole thing is beyond the line of ordinary credence.

The Presdt. has become much excited in his attempt to introduce St Domingo into the Union, & uses all his influence & his appointing power to advance his plan. This is supposed to have a bearing on the appointment at London.

I beg you to believe that all this is to me most painful & intolerable.

Faithfully yours,   Charles Sumner

26th June '70

private

P.S. Since writing you this morng, I learn that the Presdt. tendered the place of Mr Bancroft to Mr Grennell,[3] who refused it. It is said that he will accept the Naval Agency. But the Presdt. avows his determination to remove Mr Motley. My colleague conversed with him on the subject this morng. The Presdt wished somebody "more American," but my colleague thought St Domingo was at the bottom.

"More American"! Where is he? Show him. Of course, this is an excuse.

ALS   MH-H   (64/661, PCS)

1. Joseph L. Stackpole (1838–1904), a Boston lawyer and nephew of John L. Motley, wrote 25 June 1870 that newspapers of 24 June carried rumors that his uncle was to be recalled as minister to Great Britain. He wished to know if they were true (Boston, 51/156, PCS).

2. Stackpole wondered if Fish might be Motley's successor. Moses H. Grinnell had recently chaired a pro-annexation rally in New York (Prc, 4:442).

3. Bancroft remained in his post as minister to Germany. Grinnell became naval officer of customs.

To Hamilton Fish

[*Washington 28? June* 1870]

News to me!

C. S.

ANS   DLC   (83/484, PCS)
Enc: Newspaper clipping, "Washington Topics," New York *Evening Post*, 27 June 1870:4.[1]

1. The first two paragraphs of the article state that CS was prepared to deliver "an elaborate arraignment of the foreign policy of the administration" when the Senate met in executive session to consider the Santo Domingo treaty. The article continued, "Mr. Sumner is satisfied that his friend, Mr. Motley will be recalled from England." The Senate rejected the annexation treaty on 30 June, 28–28 (⅔ necessary to ratify) (*Executive Proceedings*, 17:503).

To Hamilton Fish

Sat. morng.
[*Washington 9 July 1870*]

My dear Fish,

Late last evng. the Senate ratified the two English treaties. As the Naturalization Treaty was read, one signature reminded us of death, the other of an injustice worse than death.[1] The blows of Providence are easier to bear than those of man.

Ever sincerely yours,   Charles Sumner

ALS   DLC   (83/493, PCS)

1. On 8 July the Senate ratified the convention dated 13 May 1870 between the U.S. and Great Britain on naturalization (*Executive Proceedings*, 17:514). The signers were Lord Clarendon, who died 27 June, and Motley. On 1 July Fish informed Motley that the president wished "to make a change in the mission" and therefore offered him "the opportunity of resigning, in case you feel inclined to do so" ("Recall of Minister Motley," 15).

To Hamilton Fish

Monday mrng
[*Washington 18 July 1870*]

My dear Fish,

The absurd assault made on Motley, first in the Senate[1] & then in the press,[2] makes it proper for his friends to correct at least the misrepresentations.

I enclose a statement by Mr Hooper & myself on one of the two points.[3] The other point will be treated separately.

This statement is made in justice to an absent friend. It will at least be furnished to him, if not printed at once.

I think you will agree that this correction ought to be made. If Mr Motley is to be removed, an affair 15 months old should not be brought forward against him by people who know nothing of it.[4]

Sincerely Yours,   Charles Sumner

ALS   DLC   (83/500, PCS)

1. On 14–15 July 1870 the Senate considered Grant's nominee to replace Motley, Frederick T. Frelinghuysen (1817–85; U.S. senator [Rep., N.J.], 1866–69, 1871–

77); on 15 July the nomination was confirmed, with CS abstaining (*Executive Proceedings*, 17:544–45, 547). During the closed session CS protested Frelinghuysen's confirmation in a two-hour speech, mainly on the grounds that Motley should not be removed. New York Senator Roscoe Conkling rebutted CS's charges, stating that, as minister to Great Britain, Motley stressed that the U.S. claim for damages proceeded from Britain's concession of belligerent rights. When in Britain, Motley had pursued his "own position," declared Conkling, instead of following the instructions Fish had given him in his letter of 15 May 1869 (Notes on speech, Conkling Papers, Library of Congress; *Boston Daily Advertiser*, 18 July 1870:4; *New York Times*, 16 July 1870:1).

2. The *New York Times* stated that reports that Motley was removed in revenge for CS's opposing the Santo Domingo treaty were "absurd"; Motley's own views on U.S. policy in the *Alabama* claims negotiations did not conform to those of the administration, declared the *Times*, and when Motley first spoke officially with Lord Clarendon on 10 June 1869, he "submitted" his own views instead of those of his government. Since then "the question of his recall has simply been a question of time" (ibid.).

3. In his dispatch to the *Boston Daily Journal* dated 21 July (22 July 1870:2) Ben: Perley Poore reproduced a conversation in April 1869 between CS and Fish. According to Poore, CS had said, "'Why not levy on Motley? Let him write a memoir, to be used in whole or part, or not at all, as you see fit.' Mr. Fish at once came into the idea, and authorized Mr. Sumner to invite Mr. Motley to do this. Mr. Sumner replied: 'Of course in your name.' To which Mr. Fish, according to the recollection of Mr. Sumner, assented with much good will. Accordingly, Mr. Sumner, in the name of Mr. Fish, asked Mr. Motley to write, who undertook the service in the discharge of his new duties, feeling that he could not excuse himself. He was at the time the guest of Hon. Samuel Hooper, who remembers well that Mr. Motley was engaged on a paper which, at the time, he understood was at the request of Mr. Fish. Mr. Hooper is sure that Mr. Motley was in [no?] respect a volunteer, and that the paper in question was spoken of at his table, while Mr. Fish was dining there, as a task imposed on Mr. Motley."

4. Fish replied, "My recollection is not in precise accord with yours as to the suggestion to him to write a paper being authorized in my name. The proposition was made by you to me that he should write or furnish a paper, to which I certainly & readily assented, without however understanding that I was placing any duties upon him, or doing else than assent to his doing what, from the source & manner of the suggestion, I supposed he was desirous of undertaking" (18 July, 51/313, PCS). Meanwhile Motley had on 14 July cabled and written Fish that he felt "compelled to decline" Grant's offer to resign because "no reasons are given me why I should resign the post" ("Recall of Minister Motley," 15–16).

To Hamilton Fish

Tuesday Mrng
[*Washington 19 July 1870*]

My dear Fish,

There was an "assault" on Motley in the Senate, which made honorable men hang their heads. The removal was bad, but the assault made it worse; & one ground was that he had *"volunteered* to write his instructions." Of course, I denied this point-blank. It was trivial enough,—but as an excuse for removal it was difficult to characterize, —&, I assure you, this was one of the two excuses!!!

The circumstances about writing that paper are very clear in my memory. *It never entered Motley's head*, until I told him from you that it would be agreeable to you.

By the way,—I asked Bancroft Davis[1] sometime ago to allow me to peruse Motley's paper. He told me that it was not on the files of the Depart. but in your possession. So much the better. Will you allow me to peruse it now? The way it was characterized in the Senate was so entirely different from my recollection, that I wish to see it again.[2]

I will return it promptly.

Sincerely yours,   Charles Sumner

ALS   DLC   (83/506, PCS)

1. J. C. Bancroft Davis (1822–1907), assistant secretary of state.
2. Fish sent with his note of 19 July 1870 a copy of Motley's "Memoir," which he said had "until Sunday last" not been out of his drawer since May or June of 1869. "The fact of the paper being written was known, so far as I was aware or had agency in making it known, to *very* few—none outside the Cabinet, & probably not all of them. I heard of it soon after from sources which surprised me." Fish asked CS to recall Fish's "comment upon it, at the time, in which you partially if not wholly concurred" (Washington, 51/317, PCS). Fish's diary indicates that on Sunday, 17 July, he showed Motley's "Memoir" to Senator Timothy Howe (vol. 1, Fish Papers, Library of Congress).

To George Bemis

Washington 22nd July '70

My dear Bemis,

Do not judge me because I have not written for an age.[1] I have no time for writing. More than ever I am absorbed by daily duty. I envy you the leisure that enables you to see Europe so well, & to write simply as it pleases you.

I hope that it will please you not only to write one of yr good letters so full of instruction, but to take up that famous pen which you keep & write again on the Alabama question.[2] You know well the topic best to discuss. I wish that you would round & complete the discussion, & then collect yr articles in a book hence forward to stand on shelves in libraries great & small to be taken down with honor & respect & to be quoted always.

Fish sent me yr minute epistle, which I read with wonder.[3] You should have been at home within reach to guide the editor. When shall we see you again? I long for a friendly symposium of talk. There is much for you to tell me, & I have something for you.

The removal of Motley is simply *brutal*. This is the only word to describe it. Add also heartless & cruel. I hope you will see him & strengthen him. The tragical death of Prévost-Paradol adds to the gloom.[4] He was with me half an hour three days before his suicide, speaking of the war, & his surprize at it, but saying that it was necessary,—also of literature & especially of Guizot, Thiers & St Beuve.[5] He evidently was a great admirer of Thiers.

Thus far sympathy here is with Germany & I shall be surprized if it does not increase. More than ever I detest war & those who wage it. It is terrible. Just so soon as the govts. of Europe are settled on the basis of popular rights, war will be impossible. Disarmament will then take place.

I hope that you will write at once. Give us another of yr papers. Good bye!

Ever Yours,   Charles Sumner

This a poor good-for-nothing little letter. You cannot do as badly if you should try.

ALS   MHi   (83/515, PCS)

1. Bemis wrote from Florence 3 May 1870 that he had not heard from CS since June 1869 (83/405, PCS).

2. In 1869 Bemis had published "Mr. Reverdy Johnson: The Alabama Negotiations, and Their Just Repudiation by the Senate of the United States."

3. Bemis informed CS of a 26-page "Bill of Particulars" he had sent Fish criticizing the publication of the *Alabama* claims diplomatic correspondence. The U.S. claims were weakened, wrote Bemis, because of the "insufficient & bungling" manner in which the papers had been presented.

4. Lucien Anatole Prévost-Paradol, the French ambassador to the U.S. (b. 1829), had committed suicide on 20 July. Reports were that he was despondent over France's declaration of war against the North German Confederation on 19 July. Napoleon III had been provoked by Chancellor Bismarck's publishing an edited statement from William I (the Ems telegram) that refused to assure France that no member of the Hohenzollern royal family would ever lay claim to the Spanish throne.

5. Charles A. Sainte-Beuve (1804–69), French literary critic.

To Timothy O. Howe

Washington
27th June [*July*] '70[1]

My dear Judge,

All packed & ready to start amidst these heats I acknowledge yr letter. When at home by the sounding sea I will consider yr suggestion about our ante-room.[2]

I make no issue with any body. I am a living witness on certain matters. Two days ago Mr Cushing dined here & I astonished him by saying that there was an attempt to shew a difference between the Motley memoir & the Fish despatch of 23d Sept.[3] He said it was "folly"—that the only difference between the two was in the "co-relation of the parts." I called his attention especially to the part of the memoir about belligence as a "fact" to which you refer.[4] He read it over deliberately & said it was in every sentence a "truism"—all reproduced in the Fish despatch. You will pardon me if I say that the memoir does not "argue" as you suppose.—Of the many "pretexts" for an unjustifiable act this is as bad as the rest—utterly absurd & adding to the brutal wrong. On this question I have no hesitation. I know it all, & I pronounce this removal unequalled in brutality & wrong by any governmental act bearing on office in our history. So it will be recorded, & as it is directed against an historic character, it will be avenged in an especial chapter.

Pardon me if I express astonishment at yr coldness when such an act is perpetrated.[5] Motley thought you his friend. I always thought you the friend of justice.

In this matter I have been no beginner; but I am so constituted that I cannot witness an act of wrong without being aroused in my inmost nature, & never outside of Slavery & its impulsions I have known any comparable to this where you, my dear Howe, are willing to be compurgator.

No—No! It is all a fearful blunder & offense,—& every "pretext" makes it worse.[6] Good bye!

Ever Yours,   Charles Sumner

ALS   WHi   (83/480, PCS)

1. Misdated by CS, as Howe's letter to CS and his endorsement on CS's letter indicate.

2. Howe wrote about the "embellishment" of the Senate reception room (Washington, 21 July 1870, 51/321, PCS).

3. CS must mean Fish's dispatch of 25 September 1869 (No. 70) to Motley (see CS to Fish 11 October 1869). In that dispatch, which Fish intended Motley to read to Lord Clarendon, Fish laid out the U.S. case against Great Britain on the *Alabama* claims issue, and stated that the British government should decide when negotiations should resume. Fish devoted twelve paragraphs of the long dispatch to the question of the Queen's Proclamation granting belligerent rights to the Confederacy and stated the U.S. objection to the "unseasonable precipitancy" of that act. He wrote that even though the president fully recognized the right of any nation to accord belligerent rights as it deemed appropriate, the U.S. regarded the Queen's Proclamation a "sign of a purpose of unfriendliness" to the U.S. and "friendliness" to the Confederacy (*British Documents*, part 1, series C, 7:235–40).

4. Howe wrote that it was a "fact" that Motley's "Memoir" differed from Fish's instructions of 15 May 1869 in that the latter conceded Britain's right to accord belligerent rights while the "Memoir" stated, as Howe wrote, that "recognition was itself the great offence against this country."

5. Howe had also supported Motley as minister to Great Britain, he wrote, and therefore shared the "mortification" of Republicans that the minister had displeased Grant.

6. CS was "mistaken," stated Howe, in thinking Motley was removed "to spite you." Howe was "anxious" for the "success" of Grant's administration, and viewed CS as a key figure in accomplishing this goal. Howe sent a copy of his 21 July letter to CS to Fish with a note stating that he hoped to clear up any "misapprehension" as to the alleged "accord" between himself and CS (21 July, Fish Papers, Library of Congress). Replying to Howe on 6 August, Fish described a recent interview with CS in which Fish argued that Grant had recalled Motley not because of differences with CS. "But I fear that nothing can change him—he is determined to believe himself the cause of whatever is done, & that he is the object against which all assaults, real or imagined, are aimed. . . . I have endeavored & shall endeavor to satisfy & reconcile him." Fish hoped that Howe could make CS understand that he had overestimated his support around the U.S.: "If he could be disabused, I think there is a possibility of preventing what otherwise seems to me his determination—an effort to divide the Republican Party and lead off whatever he can into opposition to the President" (Howe Papers, Wisconsin Historical Society).

To John Bigelow

Boston 7th Aug. —'70

My dear Bigelow,

The inquiries of yr letter with regard to Prévost-Paradol have been mostly answered by the papers.[1] He called on me the Saturday before his death, when he handed me yr letter. Our conversation was on the war, which took him by surprize—its necessity—probable duration—our neutrality—the Germans here—then on Guizot, Thiers & Sainte-Beuve. When he left Havre Hohenzollern had not been invited, & when he reached his hotel in New York, then, with the thermometer in the nineties, he learned that the conflict was at hand with unexpected responsibilities for him. Then came the thought of friends alienated. It was too much. He did as Charles York.[2]

The French Foreign Office, generous beyond precedent, telegraphed to send home his remains in the steamer that brought him out with his children, domestics & the 39 *caisses* which constituted his baggage, all at the expense of the govt. From the conversation with him I was led to anticipate much social & intellectual enjoyment.

The recall of Motley is simply brutal, & the pretexts are only aggravations. Genl. Butler says that Hoar was the first victim to St Domingo; Motley is another.[3] The President has had but one idea latterly;—it was to annex St Domingo. Punishment & reward were equally employed.

Remember me to the Bancrofts. I used to hear from them. Perhaps, it is my fault, that I do not now.[4] The Presdt. offered his place to Grennell, who had the good sense to refuse, & then to ask for the Naval Office. Then came a pressure for both, with ominous givings out from the Presdt. Meanwhile Baron Gerolt was most anxious that Bancroft should be retained, & I think spoke to Fish on the point, as he did to me.

Ever Sincerely Yours,   Charles Sumner

I shall always be glad of an inner glimpse of Europe—by a letter from you.

ALS NSchU (83/539, PCS)

1. Bigelow wrote he was "dreadfully shocked" to learn of Prévost-Paradol's suicide and asked CS what aside from the excessive heat in Washington "disposed him to destroy himself" (London, 23 July 1870, 51/324, PCS).

2. Prince Leopold of Hohenzollern-Sigmaringen (1835–1905). The death of Charles Yorke (1722–70) was rumored to be suicide. Under extreme party pressure not to accept the office of lord chancellor, Yorke died a few days after accepting the post.

3. E. Rockwood Hoar's resignation as attorney general on 23 June came at the request of Grant. Bigelow wrote CS that he thought Motley had been handled "very shabbily"; it was diplomatic custom to give "even a footman 30 days notice." He observed that such treatment of public officials would soon lead to "a rapid degeneration in their quality."

4. Bigelow replied from Berlin 2 October with a message from Bancroft. The minister had written CS several times but, receiving no reply, had "almost feared" that his letters "were of no interest" to CS (51/543).

To Timothy O. Howe
private

Boston 28th Aug. '70—

My dear Compurgator,

—for so you are in yr last epistle unless all definition is at fault. Do you not come from the vicinage of an offender & say that he is innocent? I know you change the issue;—but that is of no consequence.[1]

My allegation is that the removal of Mr Motley was an act of sheer brutality & utterly indefensible. You reply that it was not done out of spite to a senator, & then play compurgator. Don't be frightened by the word.

"What harm" said Dr Johnson to Goldsmith "does it do a man to call him Holofernes?"[2]

There is no sufficient reason for the removal—nothing—every thing assigned makes it worse by introducing pretexts & getting away from obvious truth. I have heard Fish's *decantatum* & told him that the case became more indefensible with every word he said. This is my judgment still.

Latterly I have been the guest of Longfellow at Nahant & then of Bryant on the Berkshire Hills,[3]—& both talked much & with generous indignation of the indignity to an illustrious citizen,—but they are only poets & of no account with a military Administration.

Yesterday Mr T. Hughes, M.P. our famous English friend[4] dined with our club. He expressed himself with happiest language of Mr Motley, whom he represented as doing so much for our country. His removal, he said, was incomprehensible beyond any thing of the kind that had ever occurred.

To-day Mr Bemis has been with me—our greatest master in the Alabama debate—just from London, where he saw Mr Motley intimately, only a fortnight ago. He says that Mr Motley is at a loss to understand the blow he has received—that he feels it bitterly—that the whole occurrence is incomprehensible to him—that he always regarded the Presdt & Secy. of State as his friends.

Thus from every quarter are we led to the same conclusion with regard to this ill-omened act by which a citizen who deserves well has been cruelly insulted—by which the two senators of a Republican State have been trifled with—& by which the State itself has been hurt in its regard for a cherished son;—& of the author of this act you are compurgator. This is all; not Holofernes, but compurgator.[5]

The whole country suffers also & the national cause. I do not doubt that M. can do more for us now in London than any other Minister, or commttee. of ministers we could send. Our object—at least my object—*is the withdrawal of the British flag from this hemisphere.* This should be my diplomacy. Who can aid this like M.?—

I envy you the quiet of the river's bank & the sight of yr rolling prairies;—but I must work at home.[6] Good bye!

Ever sincerely Yours,   Charles Sumner

Pardon these blots. A blot is my escutcheon—

———————————————

ALS WHi (83/555, PCS)

1. Howe's letter from Green Bay contained a list of five "wrongs," including the Brooks assault on CS, which Howe said were greater than Grant's recall of Motley; Howe denied that he was a "compurgator" in the recent recall. He stated that Grant may have "thought he had cause of complaint," which was sufficient reason for Motley's dismissal. At the top of the letter CS wrote, "To amuse you. C. S." (23 August 1870, 51/411, PCS). CS may have sent the letter to Samuel Hooper.

2. In *Anecdotes of the Late Samuel Johnson, LL.D.*, Hester Lynch Piozzi described newspapers' depiction of Goldsmith and Johnson as "the pedant and his flatterer" from *Love's Labour's Lost*. After Goldsmith expressed his annoyance, Dr. Johnson replied, "how is a man the worse I wonder in his health, purse, or character, for being called *Holofernes?*" (*Johnsonian Miscellanies*, ed. G. B. Hill [1897], 1:270).

3. CS visited Bryant at Cummington, Massachusetts, in mid-August (Bryant to CS, CS to Bryant, 1, 8 August, 51/368, 83/541).

4. Thomas Hughes (1822–96), author of *Tom Brown's School Days*.

5. Howe replied that he was not bothered with the label of either compurgator or Holofernes. Should not CS come right out and call him Holofernes? Howe hoped that CS's "singular selection of terms" did not mean he was losing his "fondness for the classics" (4 September, 51/447).

6. The two should drop their quarrel, suggested Howe in his 23 August letter, and find "more agreeable ways" of spending their time. He invited CS to Wisconsin.

To Hamilton Fish

Boston 6th Sept. '70

My dear Fish,

I have written no letter, nor have I printed or prompted a word of the numerous articles on Motley's removal—some of them sent to me marked,—as, for instance the *Springfield Republican* this moment recd.[1]

I think the *Advertiser* had in mind Wilson's much-admired letter,[2] so generally telegraphed & which has produced such an effect abroad. I have written nothing.

As Secy of State & one whom Motley once regarded as "friend," you cannot be indifferent to the painful feelings this event has caused. It is felt by the State as an indignity &, of course, an open expression of indifference if not hostility to her two senators, &, then, an unmitigated brutality to an illustrious citizen who supposed that "that the Presdt & Secy of State were his friends."

Since my return I have seen many persons from W. C. Bryant on the Berkshire hills to Longfellow at Nahant,—including politicians & business-men,—& there is but one sentiment of pain & indignation. The excuses assigned, of course, make it worse. Every body asks where was the cabinet? Why did not somebody resign rather than sanction an act of unjustifiable harshness by which the public service is such a loser.

Wilson was with me two days ago. He feels *stronger* about it now than before, & thinks its true character is more & more apparent.

Frelinghuysen was wise in not taking the office. How could he?—

At a dinner the other day, Boutwell undertook to interpose a word of apology (God save the mark!) &, the cry was—"this makes it worse"! He should have resigned rather than seen it go on.

I do not know that you care to hear these things. I send them in all kindness for you. Would to God the administration could be saved from this [load?]!

Sincerely Yours,   Charles Sumner

ALS   DLC   (83/565, PCS)

1. Fish wrote CS 3 September 1870, thanking him for, but puzzled by, the statement in the *Boston Daily Advertiser* (31 August 1870:2) that Motley had arrived in New York. Fish believed Motley to be still in London; yet, as he stated to CS, "I believe everything I read in Boston Journals or Periodicals." In a later letter, 5 September, Fish asked if CS had written any public letters on Motley's recall and if so would CS please furnish him with a copy (Garrison, New York, 51/442, 452, PCS). The notice in the *Springfield* (Mass.) *Daily Republican* (3 September 1870:2) stated that Motley had returned to the U.S. but Grant had not yet appointed his successor.

2. The *Advertiser* article referred to a letter by CS as "conclusive" proof that "the story of a difference of opinion between the Administration and the Minister concerning the Alabama claims is absolutely groundless." The *Advertiser* continued, "Why should Mr. Sumner have volunteered to write thus to the nation, unless he felt called upon to sustain a friend stricken solely by reason of friendship?" (31 August 1870:2). Henry Wilson, a supporter of the Santo Domingo treaty, had written President Grant 5 July asking him to reconsider Motley's removal. He reminded Grant of Massachusetts' support of him and stated that Republicans would regard Motley's removal not only "as a blow at him, but at Mr. Sumner." CS had read Wilson's letter in his Senate speech on Motley's removal 14 July (*Boston Daily Advertiser*, 18 July 1870:4).

To Caleb Cushing

Cotuit-port—8th Sept. '70
at Mr Hooper's

My dear General,

Let me refer you to pp. 163 *note* & 257 note in Mulford's work "The Nation," [1] for a statement on the belligerent question with England, applicable also to Cuba. The statement on p. 257 is masterly for simplicity & completeness.

The concession of belligerence, so he says, "was a deliberate act, *within her control* & the injuries to this nation which were resultant from it are therefore within her responsibility & may be submitted to arbitration." [2]

Who is Mr Mulford? I know nothing of him. He has written a very thoughtful masterfull book, showing scholarship, taste & good principles.

Bemis has returned satisfied—that the recent change in the English neutrality law[3] will be set up as a bar to us in our debate; & that they are determined to confine the question between us to the Alabama alone &, even on this ship, to the point of due diligence in preventing the escape. Will our excellent Secy. of State play into their hands? The best part of our case is on the belligerent question. This is applicable to *all the escaped ships*, & its pressure upon England will make her, more than any thing else see the policy of withdrawal from our hemisphere. I take our great object now should be the retreat of the English flag.

I think Bemis will write again.

Very faithfully Yours,　　　Charles Sumner

ALS　DLC　(83/572, PCS)

1. Elisha Mulford (1833–85), an Episcopal clergyman living in Pennsylvania, wrote *The Nation: The Foundations of Civil Order and Political Life in the U. States* (1870). On page 163 Mulford had written that Britain's alleged policy "was no neutrality," because concession of belligerent rights gave the Confederacy status as a nation and also certain protections "which were formed in international law only for nations."

2. CS added his own emphasis to the quotation from page 257 of Mulford's work.

3. The new law forbade any forces to organize in Great Britain against a "friendly power" or to willingly supply any materials to that power (Adrian Cook, *The Alabama Claims* [1975], 134).

To Hamilton Fish

Cotuit-port—14th Sept. [1870]
at Mr Hooper's

My dear Fish,

I enclose a memdum. calling attention to a new authority, better than Clarendon's Presdt. Wolsey,[1] &, if you can tell me any thing about him I shall be interested to know it.

I shall never read any thing of yours except with kindness, but you will pardon me if I confess the pain caused by some things in your last letter, showing misapprehension on several points.

(1) You speak of the Advertiser as "*falsely* representing Motley to have arrived in the U.S to make the *falsehood* the peg for an assault upon the Administration."[2] Of course you were not aware that the cable had announced the sailing of M. in the Java, & then again, on the arrival of

this steamer at New York, the telegraph to the evening papers in Boston announced his arrival. Nothing could be more natural than that a leading Boston paper should give him welcome. How could it be otherwise? He was returning after an unprecedented indignity & the paper gave expression simply to the general sentiment of the people. Of course, there was no "assault on the Administration," as you allege. The paper is strong for the Administration.

(2) You quote my words that I have never "printed or prompted a word of the numerous articles on M.'s removal," & then proceed to say that "several" have been attributed to me—especially one telegraphed from Washington by "Perley." Is this candid, my dear Fish? Did I not send you the statement telegraphed by "Perley," in advance of the telegraph?[3] Of course you know my responsibility for that—never concealed. At any time I am ready to change it to an affadavit. My denial was of the *articles editorial*, which have abounded, not one of which has come from me in any way. In their multitude & strength they are but the expression of a prevailing sentiment among many of the best friends of the Administration.

(3) You seem to me to have a mistaken idea of the statement telegraphed by "Perley." It was said in debate,[4] & the allegation was current elsewhere that M. had been guilty of the heinous offense of *volunteering* to write his instructions. This was eighteen months before his removal, & it was brought forward as a reason why now he should be sacrificed,—although constantly ministers have written their own instructions, as Caleb Cushing wrote his twice, &, as Mr Beach Lawrence tells me, Albert Gallatin[5] wrote his. But Motley *volunteered?* Such is the allegation. To which I reply: *Motley did not volunteer*, for I invited him in the name of the Secretary of State &, I did it after conversation with the latter, & with his full authority, as I distinctly remember, & Mr Hooper, at whose house Motley was staying remembers that it was so understood at the time. Now, you may question my recollection of the authority from you, but you cannot question my positive statement that M. was in no respect a *volunteer*. So this reason falls.

(4) You then proceed to use language very strong, saying that "the publisher [*Poore*] seems unappreciative of the *infamy*[6] to which he exposes that gentman [[Mr Hooper]] while attributing to him a statement, which (being inaccurate) I think he cannot have made." The statement did proceed from him. He made it, & has no doubt of its absolute accuracy. Where, my dear Fish, is the *infamy?* Even if there is inaccuracy, where the *infamy?* I am at a loss to understand. Of course the allegation of *infamy* attaches not only to the publisher, but to Mr H. & myself. Is it that Mr H & myself cannot make a simple statement

to explain an obvious misunderstanding? The *confidences* of the Depart. of State are opened to sustain an allegation, inconsistent with the truth, & to that we reply M. was no *volunteer*.

(5) You say Mr H. is represented "as betraying the confidence of his hospitality." How so? This is an allegation as difficult to sustain as that other, that M. was a *volunteer*. Surely, he could not have believed that you had taken sides so bitterly against M., that you would not welcome kindly his testimony tending to remove an obvious misapprehension & correct a statement with which to his knowledge your name had never been associated.

(6) You next say that you are led "to believe rumors" that you fall under Motley's "bitter vituperation."—Do not, I entreat you, "believe rumors," especially when inconsistent with every scrap of testimony. (1) Not a letter from M. has been recd by any body, since his removal— not by me, not by Hooper, not by any of his old friends, not even by his family.[7] Therefore no "bitter vituperation" has been written. (2) And I believe as little has been said. Ex-Govr. Washburne[8] & Mr Bemis, who have just returned, saw him for days in London after his removal, & conversed with him constantly & freely. He did not disguise from them his surprise. He could not understand the blow he had received; but he spoke always with "perfect gentleness," without one word of harshness or unkindness. John Bigelow wrote me from London under date of July 23d, & while condemning the removal in terms stronger than the *Boston Advertiser*, reported from Motley nothing but surprise. Mr Gordon Dexter wrote Mr Hooper, that, on reading the despatch announcing his approaching removal, which was communicated at 11 o'clk at night to the N.Y. Herald by Z.[achariah] Chandler M simply said it was impossible, "as the President & Secy. of State were *his friends*." This is all that has come to me showing his mood & I think you will agree there is nothing to sustain the new allegation, supplementary to the others, of "bitter vituperation."

(7) You then say—"If Mr M. be, as I suppose him to be a just man & a grateful one, *if he knows the truth*,[9] he would blister his tongue & tear out his heart before he would turn upon me." Now, in the first place, there is not one tittle of proof or a single reason of belief, that he has "turned upon" you or upon any body. He takes this blow gently. But what can he "know," leading him to believe, that he is under such peculiar obligations at this moment to the Secy of State? *This officer has become a party to his removal*. The Secy of State wrote & then telegraphed;—at least so it is understood. It was also understood in the Senate that the reasons urged against him were supplied by the Secy. of State[10]—that he allowed a Senator to assign as a reason for removal that

M. 15 months before had *volunteered* to write his instructions, & that he supplied to a senator his own injurious opinion of M's Memoir, calling it a "magazine article,"—this being another reason for removal 15 months after it was written. I know not if Motley knows these latter things; of course the first he knows officially.—I have written to M. only once,[11] &, while I did not hesitate to characterize his removal as it must be characterized in history, I did not introduce a single name. He will know nothing from me which can occasion any irritation towards persons.

Allow me to ask you, in all candor, if during these latter weeks you have spoken to me of M. with any friendliness? Did you not give support to the Presdt's first allegation that he was not enough American? Do you not still adhere to the theory that he volunteered to write his instructions? Do you not disparage his magnificent Memoir, which while precisely co-incident with the [25] Sept. [1869] despatch states the American case with at least equal force? Did you not even menace a McCracken exposure,[12] being a letter or communication last Decbr as to private conversation, without, as in the other McCracken case, giving him an opportunity of reply? These things do not seem to me very consistent with that "generosity," which lays him under such perpetual obligation.

But why go into these details? The removal was a mistake & a wrong. So it will be considered historically—the most grievous personal wrong ever done in the Depart. of State, & from the character of the victim not to be forgotten. This is at least my judgment. Sincerely & un-feignedly, & with the friendship of years stirring in me, I regret your participation in it. But you may ask "what could I do?" Let me give the remark which I hear constantly, "Mr Fish is a gentleman; why did he not resign?" Had you done this, there would have been no question as to yr position—no question as to yr sense of justice or friendship for Motley. Instead of this you vindicate the act.

All this I write in freedom—thinking, that, *after your letter to me*, I ought to write it,—that the misconceptions into which you have evidently fallen may be removed.—I hope this may be soon forgotten. It will not be kept alive by me. If I say any thing, it will be, as in the present letter, only in response to others, who assail our absent friend.

Believe me, my dear Fish,

Ever sincerely Yours, Charles Sumner

P.S. On re-perusal of yr note I am impressed by the energy with which you protest, that you are a "friend" of M.[13] Good. But having this friendship, why so sore at the simple sincere effort of his friends, who have nothing but kindness for you, stating their recollections of a matter which has been formally alleged to justify his removal?—This is as incomprehensible as the removal.—

An elaborate article in the *Independt* of Sept. 8th in many respects excellent & just to M. & regretful for the Administration, has another curious allegation, that M. had given offense by correspondance with Mr. Sumner![14] Now, I have not recd. a line from M. which you have not seen, & for months before his recall I had not written him one word on any political question—nor any thing but a note of introduction. The newspaper allegation seems sustained by a letter just recd. from a distinguished senator, giving what the Presdt said to the senator—that he wished the minister to represent him.[15] This is a new stone to hurl.

In speaking of M's removal as the most grievous *personal wrong* in the history of the Depart. of State, & destined to be chronicled hereafter, I did not remark on its absolute eccentricity. {It?} is unique,—a paragon—a "nonesuch." Never before has the Dep. of State played the part of King Pyrrhus's elephants[16] & trampled down its own friends—trampled down an illustrious citizen abroad—also the senators & reptives. of a Republican State & still more the people of this faithful state, & the sentiments of scholars & gentlemen throughout the country;—but is not all this fully [disclosed?] in the admirable letter of Senator Wilson addressed directly to the Presdt. protesting against this act?

C. S.

ALS DLC (83/579, PCS)

1. The "new authority" CS refers to is Elisha Mulford, author of the *The Nation.* Theodore Woolsey had both privately and publicly expressed his disagreement with CS's emphasis on Britain's concession of belligerent rights (Woolsey to CS, New Haven, 29 May 1869, 47/149, PCS; *New York Times*, 25 May 1869:5).

2. Fish had begun his letter of 10 September 1870 (Garrison, New York, 51/477) by thanking CS for an article on Prévost-Paradol. He went on to say that the writer of that article was "almost on a par with that of the writer in the Boston Advertiser who falsely represents Motley to have arrived in the U.S." CS underlined "falsely" and "falsehood," but his quotes from Fish's letter are accurate.

3. See CS to Fish, 18 July 1870.

4. The Senate's closed debate on the Frelinghuysen nomination. See CS to Fish 18 July 1870.

5. William Beach Lawrence (1800–81), acting governor of Rhode Island, 1851–52, and an international law scholar. Albert Gallatin (1761–1849), one of the Treaty of Ghent negotiators and U.S. minister to France, 1816–23; U.S. minister to Great Britain, 1826–27.

6. CS's emphasis.

7. After he had officially given up his post, Motley wrote 7 December that he had

not previously written CS about his removal because he wished to communicate "officially" with only the secretary of state (London, 51/697).

8. Emory Washburn sent CS a draft of a letter he had prepared for senators Sumner and Wilson to sign. The draft asked Motley to state his side of the controversy, along with any causes for "complaint or dissatisfaction" with the administration (Cambridge, 6 September, 51/463).

9. CS's emphasis.

10. Fish gave no reasons in his two telegrams of 1 and 12 July for dismissing Motley ("Recall of Minister Motley," 15).

11. None of CS's holograph letters has been recovered, and Pierce did not print this one. Motley undoubtedly wrote no letters to CS as part of his policy of silence, noted above.

12. See CS to Anna Cabot Lodge, 31 August 1867.

13. Fish closed his letter stating, "I have from more than one source been repaid ungenerously for friendship & have had kindness ignored. I should be sorry to have to add Mr M. to the list of those at whose hands generosity has met with ingratitude but I shall try to live through it."

14. The New York *Independent* (8 September 1870:4) examined and dismissed possible reasons, other than Grant's revenge against CS, for Motley's removal. One charge the *Independent* advanced and then discounted was that Motley's dispatches "displeased" Grant and Fish in their "curtness and formality" as contrasted with Motley's "voluminous correspondence" with CS, a contrast that implied (stated the *Independent*) that CS, not the administration, was Motley's superior.

15. Hoping to mend the breach between CS and the president, Justin Morrill (1810–98; U.S. senator [Rep., Vt.], 1867–98) wrote CS 5 September (Stafford, Vermont, 51/455) describing a visit he had with Grant before he left Washington. He had "protested" to Grant, Morrill wrote CS, against "any blow at you in consequence of your action" (an action Morrill called "conscientious") in defeating the Santo Domingo treaty. Morrill reported that Grant had replied he was not vengeful against CS but that Grant wished "to have his own views represented" in London.

16. In King Pyrrhus's invasion of Sparta (275 B.C.), the king's elephants went mad and trampled his own troops (*Plutarch's Lives*).

To Anna Cabot Lodge

Coolidge House Wednesday evng
[*21 September 1870*]

Dear Mrs Lodge,

I am obliged by the glimpse you gave me into the London home of our friends. I am glad that they are tranquil.[1] I cannot be. My sense of justice, & those great principles on which depends the universe, is disturbed.

I understand that A. A. Lawrence[2] returns very indignant;—so also does Ex-Govr Washburne. Meanwhile the Presdt finds it difficult to fill the place. That great & most tempting post has become a street beggar.[3] Alas! for our Administration. Such are the disappointments, which add to the burdens of life.

I enclose for perusal a letter which gives another glimpse.[4]

I am sorry at the minor key of yr note; but I do not doubt that your good genius will find enough to do, when you have done all that you can do for yr children.[5]

Good bye!

Ever sincerely yours Charles Sumner

Mr H. has returned from Cotuit. Nat. H.[6] is already 8 days at sea on his way from Liverpool

---

ALS MHi (TTR, 83/590, PCS)

1. Anna Lodge copied several paragraphs from a recent letter from Motley's daughter Mary and enclosed them in her letter of 16 September 1870 to CS. Remarking on CS's description of the Motleys' London life in her reply of 22 September, she wrote that her excerpts must have given CS an erroneous impression: the Motleys were "*far* from 'tranquil'" and quite distressed (Nahant, 51/495, 523, PCS).

2. Amos A. Lawrence, Boston merchant.

3. Besides Frelinghuysen, a number of senators, including Timothy O. Howe and Oliver P. Morton (1823–77; U.S. senator [Union Rep., Ind.], 1867–77), had declined the offer by this date (Howe to Fish, 3 September, Fish notes, [10 September 1870], Fish Papers, Library of Congress).

4. CS enclosed a letter of thanks to him from Mary Lincoln (York, England, 7 September, 51/468).

5. As her children married and moved away, Anna Lodge lamented that with "the vocation of daughter—wife & Mother over what farther mission Life has for me, *I* do not see" (51/495).

6. Nathaniel Hooper, brother of Samuel Hooper.

To the Duchess of Argyll

Boston 25th Sept. '70

My dear Duchess,

It is long since I have heard from you. Meanwhile this world shakes with contending armies. More than ever I detest war & all its work.

I never honored Mr Gladstone more than when he hesitated to compromise England & would not let her get into this bloody carnival.[1] I was glad that his declaration was so reserved & cautious—glad that he left to another the stronger word which his govt. required. This will be to his honor always.

I trust that this terrible war will be the death of war. To this end there must be disarmament. If I were near M. Jules Favre,[2] I would say—"offer Prussia a new civilization,—give a higher guaranty than any she asks, by the side of which the surrender of a fortress or province is vulgar,—*disarm*; send back to honest productive industry 400,000 men." In this work England might do much. I understand that Russia is ready. So at least her Minister assures me.[3]

Poor France! What will become of this nation! I see no chance for her except in disarmament. With these prodigious economies she would be able soon to repair her losses.

I like very much the Orleans princes, conferring something of the personal attachment which they so easily inspire, but I fear that their return will simply prepare the way for another revolution.[4]

I have written nothing about the removal of Mr Motley, which will always be considered a painful & indefensible incident in our diplomacy. There is no reason for it which can be named without causing a smile of derision or a burst of indignation.[5]—I hope that you are all well. God bless you!

Ever sincerely Yours,   Charles Sumner

ALS CSmH (83/591, PCS)

1. The Queen's Proclamation of Neutrality in the Franco-Prussian War was issued 19 July 1870. On that day the foreign minister, George Leveson-Gower, Lord Granville, instructed the lords commissioners of the Admiralty to forbid ships from either country to use any British port "for any warlike purpose" (London *Times*, 20 July 1870:10).

2. After the French were defeated at Sedan on 2 September, Napoleon III surrendered, and he was deposed 4 September. Jules Favre (1809–80) was foreign minister in the new government.

3. Konstantin Katacazy (1830–90), a correspondent of CS's, had been named Russia's minister to the U.S. in 1869 (Allan Nevins, *Hamilton Fish* [1937], 503).

4. CS knew and corresponded with Louis-Philippe Orléans, comte de Paris (1838–94), grandson of Louis Philippe and, with Henri Eugène Philippe Orléans, duc d'Aumale. With the collapse of Napoleon III's reign and the German siege of Paris, begun 19 September, the future of the Third Republic was uncertain.

5. The duchess replied 15 October, "Mr. Motley's recall is too sad a proceeding for me to speak of" (Inverary, 51/582, PCS).

To Hamilton Fish

Boston 29th Sept. '70

My dear Fish,

If there is much in your letter that pains me, there is something which pleases me. To all that you say of our friendship I respond with my whole heart, & I accept also your idea that there should be "no reserves."[1] Both good!

But I am disturbed by the animosity which you reveal to Motley &

the elaboration of yr effort to justify his disgrace. But "no reserves." You must bear with me kindly, while I speak of yr letter briefly point by point.

(1). As to the Advertiser,[2]—yr impassioned allegation was that it *"falsely represented* Mr M. to have arrived in U.S *to make the falsehood* the peg for assault on the administration." Here is distinct reduplicated charge of *falsehood*. *Answer.* The Advertiser, like every body else in Boston believed M had arrived as the cable telegraph had announced his coming in the Java, & the New York telegraph had announced his actual arrival. Clearly no "falsehood" in the Advertiser.

(2) Then comes the "Perley" despatch. I am at a loss to understand the gravity of the difference between us. The substance of my allegation is that M. was in no respect a *volunteer* in writing that memoir—that he wrote it *at my instance & request*, communicating also the desire of the Secy of State.[3] Now you may disown my authority to speak for you, though on that point my memory is explicit & positive; but you cannot in any way question my *personal testimony that I asked M. to write the Memoir*; & this at once exonerates him from the grievous burden of this accusation, which is made a chief reason for his disgrace.

(3) But you present a new point, & ask if the writing of the "Memoir" had not been entertained & begun before his confirmation. To this I answer, no, *no, no.* Hooper to whom I showed yr letter, containing this new count in the indictment, remembers well that M. came home from my house, saying—"I can't get off as soon as I expected; I have a job on my hands. I am to write a "Memoir" on our English claims."

(4) Both Hooper & myself are at a loss to understand your feeling. He has to-day read over the Perley report & finds it correct, according to his best recollection. Now, my dear Fish, you do not think Hooper "infamous"; I am sure you do not, although you say so.

(5). You still criticize the "Memoir."[4] But if there was objection to him on this account, why was he allowed to sail? why not recalled before he went? That "Memoir" *is absolutely co-incident with the* [25] *September despatch*, & I am not the only person who on consideration says so. Whenever it sees the light it will vindicate itself. If "essayish," so were Ld Clarendon's long "Notes";[5] but how superior Motley!

(6). As to yr misinformation about Motley's conversation,[6] Who can have talked with him as intimately as Bemis, Govr. Washburne, A. A. Lawrence? And now two days ago returned Mr. N. Hooper (brother of S. H) who breakfasted with M. 10th Sept., & reports that he was pained but gentle, saying nothing against any body

(7) You seem to complain because he has not answered yr *private* note *covering the letter of recall signed by you*. Are you aware that he has an-

swered no private letter,—not Hooper's, not mine? I am not aware that there is a private letter from him on this side of the Atlantic since his disgrace. Could he be expected to begin with the person who had helped deal the blow? The poet speaks of the lamb that "licks the hand just raised to take its blood."[7] This is beautiful, but human nature is not celestial or lamb-like enough to follow the example.

(8) You withdraw yr expressions of friendship for M.[8] Of course this is yr affair. It is for you to adopt towards him the course which yr feelings dictate. But I confess that I cannot understand how a "friend" could become a party to his disgrace, or, if unwilling to resign rather do the evil deed—how he can vindicate it & supply excuses as I understand you to do. What is yr last letter but an elaborate excuse?

(9) As to the menaced *McCracken* exposure! I understood you to say at my house in July last, standing at the door of my study, up stairs, that you held information or a letter showing *that M's conversation* (I think in Decbr) was inconsistent with his instructions. You may remember my indignant exclamation, & inquiry, if it was "Badeau." Your reply I remember; "I shall not tell you if it was or was not." In what does this differ from McCracken?[9] But Seward said that no report would be acted on in the State Depart. without giving the accused an opportunity of reply.

Again, as to McCracken! Wilson my colleague was with me last evng & gave me in brief a conversation of yours a fortnight ago, where you revived a story that M. had spoken against his country before the war, when, as Wilson said, he had evidently spoken against the disgraceful condition of his country from Slavery, & that then you said that as to M's character as Minister there were "two sides"—that you *had received letters* showing him unAmerican (this you said to me also)[.] Wilson was not sure whether you adopted [*Zachariah*] Chandler's accusation & called him outright "an English snob,"—b[ut] that was the idea.

This is my simple answer to yr inquiry about McCracken! Of course, under ordinary circumstances, you would repell such a mode of attack on a distinguished citizen, whom you h[ad] called "friend," & I am sure now that you will regret it. I am sure that you will be sorry for every impeachment of him, that you have allowed yourself to make. It is all contrary to your nature, or I have mistaken your character;—& I have not mistaken it. I know you too well to believe that you can look upon such things with sympathy,—& such is the estimate of you which I shall continue to cherish, as dear to my heart.

Allow me, my dear Fish, to make a suggestion. Try to write a des-patch, embodying the different reasons that have been assigned for M's disgrace—put them plainly as they should be put—& then read it over in a cool moment & I am sure there will not be a reason which you will not read with a smile of derision or with a blush of shame.

And then please to proceed & consider that in doing such a thing you hurt the feelings of a distinguished citizen—of two senators, one of whom is an old friend—of a whole delegation in Congress—& of the people of a Republican State, disposed especially to honor you. I might add also,—consider if you do not hurt an Administration in which we have a common interest, & also the good name of our country.

I have written, my dear Fish, as you invited "without reserves," in all simplicity, & with friendship welling in my heart. I am sorry for M. whose feelings are sorely tried, but you are to suffer in reputation from this far more than he can suffer. Every body says now—"How could he do it?" And this will be the question of history.

But in the face of this great mistake, by which so many have been pained, I cannot think of you except with constant friendship & longing for yr welfare, & especially for yr success as Secy of State. [10]

Ever sincerely Yours,   Charles Sumner

ALS   DLC   (83/601, PCS)

1. Replying to CS's letter of 14 September 1870, Fish wrote from Washington that friends "must understand each other, & must have no reserves—certainly none, when circumstances *seem* to bring them into some difference" (25 September, 53/530, PCS).

2. After characterizing the *Boston Daily Advertiser* article of 31 August as a "bitter, invidious side-thrust at the Administration," Fish wrote, "I really do not see that I should withdraw my opinion of that article, which contained nothing of 'welcome' to Mr Motley, but all of censure of the Administration." Aside from the passage quoted in CS's letter to Fish, 6 September, and its expression of sympathy for Motley, the *Advertiser* stated, "Such sudden changes, especially when arising so mysteriously, are extremely demoralizing, both at home and abroad (31 August 1870:2).

3. Fish stated that CS should not have had published any statement on the disputed details of how Motley came to write his "Memoir," "without adding to the statement of your recollection of the initiation of the Motley Mission, the fact of which you were apprised, that my recollection differed from yours."

4. Fish wrote, "I told you at the time, that I thought his 'Memoir' would be an excellent article for one of the English Reviews, if it could be published without being traced to any person in official position in this Country—After I had sent it to you (as Mr M had requested me to do) when late one Evening I found you in your Study, reading it, on my inquiry as to your opinion of it, I well remember your reply 'it is, as you say, rather *essayish* —but it is a well-written paper' to which I cordially assented."

5. Motley had written CS in May about the problem in responding to Clarendon's long "Note" appended to his dispatch of 6 November 1869 to Thornton and thus not truly official (London, 24 May 1870, 50/583). See *British Documents*, part 1, series C, 7:240–49, 251.

6. Fish stated he hoped he had been "misinformed as to Mr Motleys censure of

me" but cited as evidence to the contrary unidentified letters from "several Americans in Europe."

7. Fish wrote CS that along with the official request for Motley's resignation of 1 July he had included "a private personal, & unofficial note, expressing the pain which the discharge of that duty caused me & my deep regret that a change was to be made." "And licks the hand just rais'd to shed his blood," Alexander Pope, "Essay on Man," I:84.

8. "I take back all that I may have said having any appearance of a right to any friendship or consideration at his hands—"

9. Fish wrote he felt compelled to answer at least "one count" of CS's "arraignment" and denied that he would make such a threat "to any person for whom I professed regard." Fish objected to CS's "ex-cathedra-autocratic style" in the allusion to the McCracken letter. "You must excuse me for saying that this is offensive, but I say so, very deliberately & very earnestly and will not doubt that when the excitement in connection with this Motley business under which you seem to be laboring, has passed, you will see its injustice & cruelty." Fish had "not the most remote idea of what you allude to."

10. Fish had closed his 25 September letter with professions of friendship. However, the secretary apparently did not reply to CS's latest letter, or any others in 1870, except for a brief note, 26 October, acknowledging and returning to CS a letter he had sent from Michel Chevalier (Washington, 51/605).

To the Duchess of Argyll

Chicago—22nd Novbr. '70

My dear Duchess,

I take advantage of a resting-place in a journey[1] to acknowledge yr interesting letter, which contained so much. The engagement of yr son, though historic, is most important to you as the promise of happiness which I hope may be enjoyed to the end.[2] Assure him of my best wishes. I think of him often & shall now follow him with special aspiration & benediction.

You have probably heard from Mr Palfrey.—Longfellow to whom I communicated yr message, writes;

"These are happy days at Argyll Lodge & at Inverary & well they may be; for the Princess is a lovely woman in her own right & quite apart from her royal birth."[3]

I am glad that England keeps out of war. Do not let her be involved again. The Russian note[4] seemed to disturb yr equanimity, but I hope that there will be nothing more than notes.

This terrible war tasks patience. How dreary & ghastly. Louis Napoleon was the original offender & my sympathies were with Germany until the surrender of the Emperor,—when I think Germany erred in not offering peace on terms not wounding to France.[5] She had conquered by arms;—why not conquer by magnanimity also?

Why will not England push Disarmament? This was a favorite idea of Ld Aberdeen, expressed in Parlt., &, as I remember well, the subject of conversation.[6] It *is the idea now of the Russian Govt.* Has not the time come for this immense & practical measure for permanent peace?

The Senate meets 5th Decbr, when I shall be in Washington. Good Bye!

Ever yours & the Duke's,   Charles Sumner

ALS   CSmH   (83/654, PCS)

1. CS had embarked on a lecture tour 17 October 1870, delivering an old lecture, "Lafayette," and, on the Franco-Prussian War, "The Duel between France and Germany, with Its Lesson to Civilization" (Wks, 18:177–253).

2. The Argylls' son, the marquess of Lorne, had become engaged to Princess Louise (1848–1939), daughter of Queen Victoria.

3. Cambridge, 14 November, 83/645, PCS.

4. The duchess had expressed regrets over "this terrible war" (Inverary, 15 October, 51/582). On 13 November the Russian chancellor Alexander Gorchakov issued a statement that Russia no longer considered herself bound by the 1856 Treaty of Paris, which prohibited military activities in the Black Sea (*New York Times*, 14 November 1870:1).

5. CS argued these points, as well as pleading for disarmament, in his lecture on the war.

6. CS had visited the British statesman Lord Aberdeen 16–19 October 1857 (Journal, Prc, 3:552).

To Gerrit Smith
Private

Senate Chamber 7th Decbr. '70

My dear friend,

I think often of the pleasant Sunday I passed under yr roof.[1]

What you told me of yr son interested me much.[2] I wish that he could be encouraged to persevere & apply his rare gifts to that branch of science for which he has shown such attachment. In this way he can do much & acquire a good renown.

Can you not help the colored people in Haiti? The Minister of the Black Republic [*Stephen Preston*] is much disturbed by the attempt of our govt. to establish itself on their island. The persistance of the

Presdt. must be encountered.[3] Will you not write one of yr letters or make an appeal for the Colored race? Let us hear from you.

Ever sincerely Yours,   Charles Sumner

ALS NSyU (84/005, PCS)

1. Smith had invited CS to stay with him when CS lectured in nearby Canastota 5 November 1870 (Peterboro, New York, 9 October, 51/578, PCS).
2. Probably Green Smith (b. 1842).
3. In his annual message to Congress, 5 December, President Grant gave numerous reasons in favor of the annexation of the Dominican Republic, including the argument that the republic could give "remunerative wages to tens of thousands of laborers not now upon the island." He urged "early action" upon Congress to acquire the country, and specifically recommended that Congress authorize him to appoint a commission to negotiate a new annexation treaty. On 9 December CS offered a resolution in the Senate calling for the president to furnish the Senate with complete correspondence regarding annexation, especially with regard to Haiti, which bordered the Dominican Republic (*Globe*, 41st Cong., 3rd sess., 6–7; 51).

To Edward L. Pierce
private—

Senate Chamber. 15th. Decbr. '70

My dear Pierce,

I have had a hard battle, & my last! I shall never go into another conference with the Mass. delegation.[1]

One of the delegation gave as a reason for voting against you, that, if you were recommended, B. F. B.[*utler*] would transfer the contest & then the question would be between the nominee of a St Domingo-reptive, & that of an anti-St Domingo senator, when B. F. B. would prevail.[2]

Courage! You will have a grand career

Ever Yours,   Charles Sumner

ALS MH-H (64/670, PCS)

1. CS had kept Pierce informed in letters of 10 and 12 December 1870 (64/666, 668, PCS) as to Pierce's chances for appointment as U.S. district attorney for Massachusetts. Both Henry Wilson and CS had voted for Pierce, wrote CS, and he had spoken strongly in favor of Pierce's nomination.
2. Butler's choice, David H. Mason, was nominated by Grant on 15 December and confirmed by the Senate 22 December (*Executive Proceedings*, 17:586, 593).

To Mary Clemmer Ames[1]

Thursday morng
[*Washington 22 December 1870*]

My dear Mrs Ames,

Yr card was mislaid, & I spent half an hour Sunday in trying to find you,—ringing at several doors of 14th St.

I trust that you will not find me as bad as I have been painted.[2] I am in earnest, & since Slavery my moral nature has not been so much aroused as by the course of our govt. in this St D. business. I cannot help it. So I see it on the evidence supplied by our own govt.

I long to help the people on that island by helping the establisht. of peace & reconciliation; but this can not be done by a war dance of great guns. Our good offices should be tendered at once to bring about tranquility. The Haytian Minister assures me of the desire of his govt. for a firm treaty of peace which shall adjust all questions of boundary & debt.[3] Blessed are the peace-makers! Among these let me be enrolled.

The strange effort yesterday to cut off debate shews that the friends of the St D. scheme dare not face the question, although they have the commission on their side.[4] It reminded me of 1852, when both political parties insisted that Slavery should not be discussed & denied me a hearing in the Senate. I obtained it by an amendment to an Appropriation Bill.

Sincerely Yours,   Charles Sumner

ALS   OFH   (84/019, PCS)

1. Mary Clemmer Ames (1839–84), Washington journalist and correspondent for the New York *Independent*.

2. On 21 December 1870 the Senate debated Morton's resolution authorizing Grant to appoint a commission to obtain information on Santo Domingo. In his speech (later called "Naboth's Vineyard") CS argued that Grant desired to take over the Republic of Haiti as well as the Dominican Republic and that a vote for Morton's resolution was a vote for annexation, "a new step in a measure of violence." CS called Grant's request for a commission unnecessary, "an act of supererogation." He compared Grant to former president Buchanan, who had tried to influence policy by changing a Senate committee, an indication, said CS, of "the extent to which the President has fallen into the line of bad examples." In the evening session Senators Morton, James W. Nye, Howe, Chandler, and Conkling criticized CS's speech. Morton called the speech an attack on Grant "most unprovoked and indefensible"; Chandler termed the speech a "brutal assault" and said, "President Grant will live in the memory of his countrymen and his laurels will be fresh and green when the Senator from Massachusetts will be forgotten." In his remarks, Conkling called for the reorganization of the Senate Foreign Relations Committee. The committee should be "no longer led by a Senator who has launched against the Administration an assault more

bitter than has proceeded from any Democratic member of this body" (*Globe*, 41st Cong., 3rd sess., 226–31, 236–38, 242–46).

3. Stephen Preston wrote 9 December that he had written Fish seeking what implications the president's message on Santo Domingo had for the independence of Haiti. Preston added that Haiti considered CS its good friend (Washington, 51/715, PCS).

4. Senators Conkling and Morton stated that Morton's resolution could be quickly passed that day. At 6:37 A.M. 22 December the Senate approved the resolution 32–9. CS, Schurz, and Justin Morrill were among those opposing it (*Globe*, 41st Cong., 3rd sess., 222, 271).

To William Lloyd Garrison

Washington 29th Dec. '70

Dear Mr Garrison,

Yr letter is cheering, & reminded me of other days.[1] I find now that same old heartlessness & violence, which prevailed against Kansas—showing how when people embark in such a policy they act & speak accordingly.

When you read my speech, you will see that it was strictly to the point, discussing the subject-matter & avoiding all allusion to the Presdt, except where the case positively required.

The Haitian Minister had been to me full of emotion at the message of the President as "trampling his country under foot." I could not refer to despatches or docts.[2] Therefore, I was driven to take up the message & draw from that as much as I could.

I was in earnest, & determined if possible to arrest this sacrifice. The only answer was a flood of personalities. Nothing has been baser than the *Advertiser*.[3] Its allegation was absolutely false. At the [west?] I am generally sustained. In Boston——you know.

There is a menace to displace me from the Comttee. on F. Relations, of which I have been chairman 10 years. This is a sop to Cerberus.[4] It is founded on my difference with the Administration on this question, & the character of my speech. You will receive the speech soon, & I commend it to yr perusal. Consider, if you please, that docty. evidence known to me could not be used.

Gerritt Smith writes as you do. What will W.[*endell*] P.[*hillips*] say?

Ever sincerely Yours,   Charles Sumner

ALS MB (84/033, PCS)

1. Garrison wrote 26 December 1870 affirming that he supported CS "with all my understanding, heart and soul" on the Santo Domingo issue. He knew CS would stand firm against "any vial of rhetorical abuse, or by any menace of personal malice, or by any Presidential overbearing" (Roxbury, 52/109, PCS).

2. In his speech "Naboth's Vineyard" CS accused the U.S. Navy of threatening the Haitian government, adding, "I wish I could give you the official evidence on this assumption; but I am assured, on evidence which I regard as beyond question, that this incident has occurred" (Globe, 41st Cong., 3rd sess., 229). As Donald explains, CS could not cite confidential documents unless his motion to have the complete correspondence published was approved (DD, 2:469).

3. The *Boston Daily Advertiser* (23 December 1870:2) criticized CS's "bitter denunciation of the President for causes not germane to the issue" and stated that by abandoning his previous "strong position" against annexation, CS had embarked on a course "which must result in impairing his own public influence or in the humiliation of the President; for these are the only alternatives." In another editorial (28 December 1870:2) the *Advertiser* chided CS for introducing into the debate on Morton's resolution rumors that the president sought to change the Senate Foreign Relations Committee. The *Advertiser* also praised CS's leadership of that committee, however, and stated that any removal of CS would be "less injurious to Mr. Sumner than to the administration."

4. The watchdog guarding Hades, i.e., Fish.

To Gerrit Smith

Washington 30th Decbr. '70

My dear friend,

I have already asked you to send yr excellent letter to every member of the two Houses of Congress.[1] I wish that you would send me also some extra copies.

Never before was executive pressure brought to bear with the same force. If the Senate were a regiment, it could not be more under drill. This is one of the painful aspects of this Presidential effort.[2]

Ever Yours,   Charles Sumner

ALS NSyU (84/042, PCS)

1. In his 25 December 1870 letter, Smith enclosed copies of his public letter of 22 December to U.S. representative John C. Churchill (Peterboro, New York, 52/097, PCS). In that letter Smith argued against the annexation of Santo Domingo, concluding, "Oh, how much better than this scheme of the President would be our nation's proclamation, if sacredly observed by herself, that to these races belong the tropics—given to them by God, and not to be taken from them by man!"

2. Smith responded on 1 January 1871, stating it would be "preposterous" for CS to be removed as chairman of the Senate Foreign Relations Committee: "The country would not stand the high-handed measure" (52/209).

To George Bemis

Washington 31st Dec. '70

My dear Bemis,

Don't believe what you read of me in the papers, unless it harmonizes with yr ideas. I know nothing of the "interview" to which you refer, & what you quote is unfounded.[1] I have approved R. J's statement of the legal substitution of the underwriter for the assured, where there has been a loss & payment. This is all.

I always read you with pleasure on the Claims question,—& what is more with substantial accord. Yr last letter states the question on the concession of belligerent rights grandly.[2] I wish I could inspire you with what I feel to be yr duty in this case. You must write. On this subject you are "the only One." Begin on belligerence; then in other articles, take up statute amendt, & the amendt. of the Decltn. of Paris. *Note.* Do you see that the Longmans have just published an Essay on Blockade?—You must go forward. I know that you can be useful to yr country, while you make a name for yourself.

Never was I more right than in this St Domingo business. It a case of oppression & hardship, which I am trying to arrest.

W. W. Story's Castle of St Angelo[3] is very learned

Ever Yours,   Charles Sumner

How unjust to me is the Advertiser—as in the olden time! The spirit seems wicked, while I am trying to stop a wrong.

ALS   MHi   (84/044, PCS)

1. Bemis wrote CS 28 December 1870 asking if a recent Chicago *Republican* interview with CS as he met with former Republican congressman Isaac Arnold were true, in that CS said he approved Reverdy Johnson's promoting the Johnson-Clarendon Convention abroad (Boston, 84/029, PCS). The *Boston Morning Journal* (5 December 1870:2) discounted the *Republican* article, calling it a third party's "unauthorized report from the memory of what transpired at a private meeting between friends."

2. Bemis wrote that he wanted to urge Robert C. Schenck, the new minister to Great Britain, not to settle the *Alabama* claims case for "a few paltry millions" without acknowledgment from Great Britain of her error in conceding belligerent rights to the Confederacy.

3. Part 1 of Story's essay appeared in *Blackwood's* magazine 108 (December 1870):754–73.

To Whitelaw Reid[1]
private, & confidential

Senate Chamber 12th. Jan. '71

Dear Mr Reid,

I have not read the Motley correspondance, except the first & last paragraphs of the reply,[2] which were to me simply disgusting—knowing, as I do this whole case; but I have read yr notice,[3] & I write to correct an idea at least so far as it may refer to me.

You say that "Mr M's appointment must have been pressed upon Genl. Grant with an urgency which, though he deferred to it, he did not the less keenly feel to have been excessive & annoying."—I never spoke to the Presdt. on the subject but twice, &, the first time casually on the stairs of the White House, & never in any way asked or urged the appointment. This is not my habit. I stated to Genl. Grant, that, with his admission, I desired to make suggestions with regard to our diplomatic service in Europe. After insisting upon experience & culture I proceeded to recommend strongly the retention of Mr Marsh at Florence, Mr Morris at Constantinople,[4] Mr. Bancroft at Berlin, & I then added, that this list would be properly completed by appointing Dr Howe at Athens & Mr Motley at London, where he had already a position of influence, & I assigned reasons why I thought he could do much there. This was my only conversation with the Presdt. on the subject.

When what is called the "brief" for the appointment was made out in the State Department, it stood thus:

John Lothrop Motley,	Mass. —
John Jay	New York
Horace Greeley	New York.

This was shown me by the Secy of State before presentation to the Presdt.

I doubt not that other persons spoke to the Presdt, but I contented myself with the opinion & recommendation I have mentioned, which, it seems was sustained by the State Depart. After the appointment was made & Mr Motley had left, the President spoke to me of him as "the right man for the place." The first intimation of dissatisfaction was after the St Domingo difference, when the Presdt said he wished somebody in London "more American." The idea about Ld C's death which I am told plays a part is simply ridiculous. A fortnight before that Mr Fish tendered the mission to me[5]—after intreating me to abandon my opposition to the St Dom. scheme.[6]

Yours very truly,   Charles Sumner

ALS DLC (84/096, PCS)

1. Whitelaw Reid (1837–1912), then assistant editor, *New York Tribune*.
2. By order of the Senate, "Recall of Minister Motley" was furnished to that body on 9 January 1871. CS refers to Fish's reply of 30 December 1870 to Benjamin Moran, defending the administration's decision to recall Motley (27–37). In his last paragraph Fish stated that Motley's protest against his recall (7 December 1870, 17–26) illogically connected two unrelated events: the defeat of the Santo Domingo annexation treaty and the administration's request for Motley's resignation. Instead, wrote Fish, Grant had long planned to recall Motley, and the death of Lord Clarendon on 27 June 1870 made the recall timely (37).
3. The *New York Tribune* editorial (11 January 1871:4) praised Fish's account of the removal but regretted the occasion for it.
4. Edward Joy Morris (1815–81), U.S. minister to Turkey, 1861–70.
5. According to Fish's diary, Benjamin F. Butler and Simon Cameron urged Grant to appoint CS as minister in order to remove him from the Senate (vol. 1, 27 June 1870, Fish Papers, Library of Congress). See DD, 2:455–56, on the disagreement between Fish and CS as to when Fish suggested that CS become the minister to England. Allan Nevins says the suggestion occurred on 27 June and was an impulsive one (*Hamilton Fish* [1937], 369–70).
6. In his response of 15 January (New York, 52/342, PCS) Reid agreed that Fish's ending paragraphs exhibited "fatal defects of taste." He informed CS that Greeley, not he, had written the editorial and if a subsequent version were published, CS's "facts" would be taken into account.

To Hamilton Fish

Jan 17/71

Memorandum for Mr. Fish in reply to his inquiries.

(1) The idea of Sir John Rose[1] is that all questions and sources of irritation between England & the United States should be removed absolutely & forever, that we may be at peace really & good neighbors;[2]—and to this end all points of difference should be considered together.—Nothing could be better than this initial idea. It should be the starting-point.

(2) The greatest trouble, if not peril,—being a constant source of anxiety & disturbance—is from Fenianism which is excited by the proximity of the British flag in Canada.[3] Therefore, the withdrawal of the British flag cannot be abandoned as a condition or preliminary of such a settlement as is now proposed.[4] To make the settlement complete the withdrawal should be from this hemisphere, including Provinces & islands.[5]

(3) No proposition for a joint Commission can be accepted unless the terms of submission are such as to leave no reasonable doubt of a favorable result. There must not be another failure.

(4) A discrimination in favor of claims arising from the depredations of any particular ship will dishonor the claims arising from the depredations of other ships, which the American Government cannot afford to do;—nor should the English Government expect it, if they would sincerely remove all occasions of difference.[6]

(signed) C. S.

C   Fish Diary, vol. 2, Fish Papers, DLC

1. On 10 January 1871 the Senate approved referral to the Senate Foreign Relations Committee of a resolution authorizing the president to appoint a commission "to determine the claims for damages committed upon our commerce by British cruisers" (*Globe*, 41st Cong., 3rd sess., 392). CS wrote Bemis 18 January (Washington, 84/110, PCS) that Rose was now in Washington "with proposals, or rather to sound our govt. The English pray for settlement, as never before." Rose described two meetings with CS in dispatches to Lord Granville of 16 and 19 January (*British Documents*, part 1, series C, 7:308–11). On 16 January Rose wrote, "I confess to some feeling of discouragement if the Government, as seems to be the case, make the acquiescence or co-operation of Mr. Sumner and the Committee on Foreign Relations a condition to taking any step. Whether it be that Mr. Sumner does not see the prospect of his own handiwork being sufficiently prominent, or whether he truly entertains the large views about territorial cessions, &c., I cannot say; but, on reflecting over our conversation, I fail to find in it any other motive than a vindication of himself, and the purpose of keeping the solution of the question in his own hands."

2. Preceding this phrase on the copy in Fish's diary is the letter "(a)." In the margin Fish wrote, "(a) if as Mr S. proposes the British are to withdraw from this Hemisphere . . . we shall no longer be 'neighbors.'"

3. Fish here added a "(b)" and in the margin wrote, "(b) *Fenianism* is not excited by this proximity. It exists elsewhere."

4. Adding "(c)" here, Fish noted marginally, "(c) the alleged cause of difference must be abandoned before a settlement is attempted!"

5. In a memorandum that Rose prepared for Granville's consideration, c. 27 January, Rose quoted, without comment, this statement from CS's memorandum (ibid., 327–28).

6. CS copied this last paragraph in his 18 January letter to Bemis, stating, "Mr Fish has asked my judgt." CS wrote Bemis that Cushing agreed with CS against "allowing any discrimination in favor of a particular ship. Nothing would please the English more."

To Gerrit Smith

Senate Chamber 17th Jan. '71

My dear friend,

Mr White informed me that he had written to you, proposing that you should come here as peace-maker between the Presdt & myself.[1] Others have seen the Presdt. in this behalf, & his reply was that if he

were not Presdt he "should demand personal satisfaction of Mr Sumner."
I know not for what. I have done nothing but my duty;—nor have I
ever made any personal impeachment of him. I have criticised his public course & this was all,—& only in the exigency of debate in order to
arrest a bad measure.

The debate[2] has had great effect, which may be seen in these things;

(1) Delay—so that there can be no snap judgment by joint-resolution
before the 4th March, as was the original plot.

(2) A good commission.[3] The Presdt. was obliged to appoint well-
known men.

(3) The attention of the country which has been aroused!

(4) Congress has been kept from committing itself to the plot.
All these things have been obtained by this debate.

I have examined the Spanish docts in 1861–63, relating to the occupation of Dominica, & find that Spain boasted that, at the period of
the invitation & vote, there was "not a single Spanish bottom in the
waters of the island, not a Spanish soldier on the land or an emigrant or
agent in the territory." —What a contrast between our Republic & the
old monarchy! Surely we ought not to be outdone in justice or forbearance! When our Commissioners arrive with their war-vessel, there will
be four war vessels of the U. States, including the Dictator our most
powerful monitor. Why this display of force?

The Haytian Minister here acted as interpreter when our Commodore
menaced his govt,[4] & he has related to me the incident.

The Minister has printed 1000 copies of my speech with yr "beautiful
letter,"[5] as he calls it, at the end. He is full of gratitude to you. The
point you present is made, & must be considered.

Ever sincerely Yours,   Charles Sumner

ALS   NSyU   (84/108, PCS)

1. Andrew Dickson White (1832–1918; president of Cornell University, 1868–
85) had recently been named a member of the commission to obtain information on
Santo Domingo. Smith wrote CS 20 January 1871 that he agreed with White that
the breach between the president and CS was a "national calamity." Grant was "patriotic & honest—but he is not reasonable & well-tempered" if he were acting to
have CS removed from the Senate Foreign Relations Committee, wrote Smith, and
he did not believe that CS had "assailed" Grant's "integrity" (Peterboro, 52/381,
PCS).
2. When the Morton resolution authorizing a commission passed the House and
was referred back to the Senate, CS unsuccessfully proposed several amendments and

motions for delay (10–12 January, *Globe*, 41st Cong., 3rd sess., 403–5, 426, 430–31). Both Houses approved the resolution on 12 January (ibid., 457).

3. Other members were Samuel Gridley Howe and Benjamin F. Wade, with Frederick Douglass serving as secretary.

4. Charles H. Poor (1808–82), then commander of the North Atlantic fleet, sent a notice 10 February 1870 to Haitian president Nisage Saget that the U.S. Navy would permit no interference by Haitians with the Dominican government. Poor reported to the secretary of the navy on 12 February that Haitian officials were "displeased with what they considered a menace on the part of the United States accompanied with force" (U.S. Senate, *Correspondence with and Orders Issued to Commander of our Naval Squadron in Waters of Island of San Domingo*, Senate Ex. Doc. no. 34, 1871, 14, serial set 1440).

5. To John C. Churchill; see CS to Smith, 30 December 1870.

To Hamilton Fish

Senate Chamber Jan. 19. 1871

Sir:

Since my memorandum of Jan. 17 1871 in reply to the inquiries with which you honored me in relation to the terms of settlement with Great Britain, I have been induced to consider more particularly the idea to which you called my attention of making a discrimination in favor of the claims arising from the depredations of a particular ship to the dishonor of claims arising from other ships.

I fear that in my memorandum I did not express sufficiently my sense of the wrong done to good citizens by this proposition, if such it may be called. If I express my repugnance to it now, it is because you invited my judgment upon it while you seemed disposed to adopt it in pending negotiations with Great Britain.

I take the liberty of mentioning that meeting General Banks this evening at Mr. Hooper's, I found he shared my repugnance to this proposition, which he called repudiation.[1]

I have the honor to be, sir,

Your obedient servant   Charles Sumner

The Secretary of State [*in CS's hand*]
Honorable Hamilton Fish
Secretary of State

LS   DLC   (84/115, PCS)

1. CS added these last four words in his own hand.

To Hamilton Fish

Washington Jan. 22. 1871

Sir,

In reply to your communication of 21st Jan.[1] I have the honor to say that I understood you to ask my opinion on the proposition to require from England the payment of losses by the Alabama, leaving the losses by other ships unmentioned and at the same time you led me to believe that this proposition was yours. This impression was confirmed by the circumstance that Mr. Patterson when he first broached the subject to me in advance of our interview[2] told me that this was your idea.

I am glad to be assured by your letter that I am mistaken in supposing that you have any such idea.

In reply to the other part of your letter,[3] I have to say that you are mistaken in supposing that I have spoken of any "proposed negotiation" with any body not a member of the Committee of Foreign Relations or even of the Senate. You are probably not aware that the House Committee of Foreign Affairs has before it a bill providing for the audit and payment of American claims on England for the depredations of her ships. Nothing more natural than that meeting the chairman of the Committee [Nathaniel P. Banks] I should inquire if he were disposed to sanction any discrimination in favor of the claims arising from a particular ship. His energetic reply that such a discrimination would be repudiation lead me to ask him to use his just influence with the Administration to prevent such a step. Accordingly when making the protest which I felt it my duty to do, I added words which I now repeat;

"I take the liberty of mentioning that meeting General Banks this evening at Mr. Hooper's, I found he shared my repugnance to this proposition which he called repudiation."

I hope I did not err in using his authority against a proposition which from your remarks to me and also to Mr. Patterson I was induced to believe had your favor, while I regretted to find it too much in harmony with recent things from the Department.

I have the honor to be, Sir,

your faithful servant,   Charles Sumner

Honorable Hamilton Fish
Secretary of State

LS   DLC   (84/120, PCS)

1. Fish wrote that he thought CS was "mistaken in attributing to me, any expression of disposition to adopt the idea of 'making a discrimination in favor of the claims arising from the depredations of a particular ship'" (Letterbook copy, Fish Papers, Library of Congress).

2. James W. Patterson (1823–93), U.S. senator (Rep., N.H.), 1867–73, and a member of the Senate Foreign Relations Committee. Patterson wrote Fish 12 January 1871 that after a long conversation with CS that morning, CS had agreed to receive Fish "kindly" despite what, according to Patterson, CS "deems the President's bloody lawsuit with San Domingo" (Fish Papers, Library of Congress).

3. In his 21 January letter Fish also stated that he considered his conversation with CS regarding the proposed negotiations with Britain as confidential, as was appropriate for communication between the two bodies they represented. "I remark therefore with surprise and regret that you have communicated a part at least of the questions which had been presented to you in confidence, to a Gentleman not a member of the Committee, or even of the Senate."

To Hamilton Fish

Senate Chamber—
Committee Room of Foreign Relations
Jan. 28. 1871

Sir

I hope you will pardon me if I call your attention to my communication two weeks ago inviting you to furnish the draft of a bill to carry out the recommendation of the President in his annual message with regard to the claims on England.

In considering this important question it is desirable that the Committee should have the advantage of a bill embodying precisely the views of the Department of State.

I have the honor to be, Sir,

Your obedient servant,   Charles Sumner

Honorable Hamilton Fish
Secretary of State

———————————

LS   DNA   (84/131, PCS)

To George Bemis

Senate Chamber 2nd Feb. '71

My dear Bemis,

I have yr letter, being 3 days work & am very grateful. The two others I recd.[1]—

I wish I could have the advantage of intercourse with you;—& still more, do I wish that you would take the pen & state our case.

I have just recd. from the Secy of State the draft of a bill. It provides for a Commission to examine "certain claims agnst the Govt of GB & Ireland"—in respect to *any vessel* which during the late rebellion committed maritime torts—(without naming any vessel) considering (1) whether the facts about equipment & shelter of such ship created a liability for her acts & (2) the "actual damages sustained" by claimants. The Commissioners to report "their conclusions to the Presdt for such further action as shall be necessary.["] The Presdt. is to notify the British Govt of the Commission & invite it to take part in its proceedings.

You will see how moderate is this proposition,[2] & it submits to a Commission appointed by the Presdt to determine the ships liable. Let me hear from you.[3]

Ever yours,   Charles Sumner

ALS MHi (84/147, PCS)

1. In his letters Bemis supplied CS with examples and citations on the 1861 British concession of belligerency issue. On 26 January 1871 he advised CS not to speak on the *Alabama* claims negotiations; Bemis thought a speech unnecessary, and he lacked the time to assist CS in preparation (26, 31 January, 1 February, 52/409, 432, 84/143, PCS).

2. As correspondence in *British Documents on Foreign Affairs* indicates, Sir John Rose, Sir Edward Thornton, Lord Granville, and Fish were planning a joint agreement to establish arbitration of the *Alabama* claims, with an eye toward prompt Senate approval (Rose to Granville, 12 January and 31 January, part 1, series C, 7:305–6, 325–26). Rose apprised Granville on 21 January of a plan to remove CS from the Senate Foreign Relations Committee after the next Congress convened (315). On 9 February Grant announced the appointment of a Joint High Commission to negotiate differences between the U.S. and Britain on "acts committed by the vessels which have given rise to the claims known as the 'Alabama claims.'" The Senate confirmed the commissioners on 10 February, with CS supporting the resolution (*Executive Proceedings*, 17:644, 651).

3. Bemis's next letter contained little comment on the *Alabama* claims except for his fear the U.S. was rushing too quickly toward a settlement (Boston, 10 February, 52/498).

To Whitelaw Reid

Washington 25th Feb. '71

Dear Mr Reid,

I have been much touched by the revelation of yr note, which was entirely unexpected.[1] But I beg you to believe that I do not consider myself a candidate for any thing,—unless it be the good will of good men.

Mr Greeley & myself are of the same age, both born in 1811; but he is an older as well as better soldier than I. My controversy has been constant for more than a quarter of a century, & during some of this time he has thought kindly of me. If he is disposed to be sharp on me it is because he follows a rule different from mine. My rule has always been never to assail or criticize those who agree with me sincerely in object & aim, although I could not accept their methods.

But I have had enough of combat & am very weary. And yet combat is before me. I cannot look without moral repugnance on this whole St D. business & especially the treatment of the Black Republic.

I hope to be in my seat tomorrow for an hour.[2] Believe me, dear Mr Reid,

Sincerely Yours,   Charles Sumner

ALS DLC (84/179, PCS)

1. Writing CS on 22 February 1871, Reid quoted a paragraph from John Bigelow of Boston wondering why CS had never become a candidate for president: perhaps, thought Bigelow, CS had "'more capacity for making friends for his principles than for himself'" (New York, 52/612, PCS).

2. CS had been ill since 18 February with an attack of angina pectoris (Prc, 4:462).

To Edward L. Pierce

Washington 5th March '71

My dear Pierce,

I am not anxious; nor should I have written to you even as briefly as I did of the vilipending article, except that you had alluded to it.[1] Let it pass.

It was easy for me to see who did it—a person[2] never in my house & who knows nothing of my life or friends. But when did any solid journal of Boston fail in flings at me?

Slack's long political article in the *Cwlth* is more disheartening.[3] How little he knows of the real movement & how little what he invites for the country!

Had the portrait been without the article I should like to send it to friends; but I am not disposed to circulate an elaborate insult. But I am not anxious.

Ever Yours,   Charles Sumner

ALS   MH-H   (64/688, PCS)

1. Urging CS for both political and health reasons not to speak on the Santo Domingo issue, Pierce had also referred, in his letter from Boston of 27 February 1871, to a sketch in *Every Saturday* (4 March 1871, Sumner scrapbook, vol. 2, Houghton Library) that, wrote Pierce, was "unworthy of the paper" (52/648, PCS). The article praised CS for his goals and his scholarly predilections, but criticized him for his "gaslight theories and philosophical abstractions." The senator, stated the article, frequently "seems to have no conception whatever of the force of words he utters in condemnation." After CS had replied that if the article were true he deserved another angina attack, Pierce assured CS not to exaggerate the sketch's importance; CS was too significant to be wounded by such criticism (1, 3 March, 64/687, 52/698).

2. Pierce wrote that Sidney Andrews, a Washington journalist, was reputed to have written the article.

3. The Boston *Commonwealth* editorial called the Grant administration's policy one "of justice, of economy, and of peace" and looked to Grant's "triumphant re-election." It called the question of the Santo Domingo annexation an "open one" and advised the country to await the report of the "unbiased and competent commission" (4 March 1871:2).

To Edward Eggleston[1]
confidential

Senate Chamber 10th March 71

My dear Sir,

The Presdt. has such relations with me as he chooses. I have never declined to see him or confer with him. If there is a quarrel it is all on his side.[2]

The Secy of State sent to me through Senator Patterson, to know how I would receive him if he came to my house on business. I replied; "that I had a deep sense of wrong from him; but that I should receive him at any time, or confer with him, on public business." Accordingly he came to my house and I received him kindly. Afterwards, when meeting him socially, I gave him the cold shoulder.[3]

This matter is now discussing in the Senate & Schurz is speaking admirably.[4]

Faithfully yours,   Charles Sumner

Mr Fish insulted me personally in his despatch to Mr Motley.[5]

ALS (photostat)   DLC   (84/198, PCS)

1. Edward Eggleston (1837–1902), then editor of the New York *Independent*, in 1877 sent a copy of this letter to the New York *Evening Post*.

2. Eggleston had sent CS (New York, 7 March 1871, 52/714, PCS) an advance copy of an editorial that appeared in the *Independent* on 9 March 1871:4. In that editorial Eggleston defended CS's right to differ publicly with Grant; such diversity strengthened the Republican party. "If General Grant should come before the people for re-election, the voice of Charles Sumner would be all the more powerful in his favor from the fact that it had not spared to criticize what he deemed the mistakes of the President."

3. CS wrote Theodore Tilton 25 March (84/215) that after Fish's dispatch to Motley, noted below, was made public, CS decided that Fish "could not expect social relations with me, & that, if he expected, self-respect on my part forbade them. . . . Accordingly I recd. the Secy at my house, when he came for my counsels on the English negotiation—talked with him fully & kindly, but without one word except on official business." Sir John Rose described CS's attitude toward Fish as one of "marked coldness" when they all dined at Robert Schenck's on 20 January (*British Documents*, part 1, series C, 7:315).

4. The Senate debated for over four hours a resolution on committees for the 42nd Congress. At issue was the proposal from the Republican caucus, which had met 9–10 March and voted 26–21, 23–21 to remove CS from the Foreign Relations Committee. Schurz argued that the differences between the president and CS did not warrant CS's removal and that CS had "discharged" his duties "with great credit" to the committee as well as the country. The Senate approved the resolution on committees, 33–9 with 25 abstaining, including CS, Schurz, and Wilson (*Globe*, 42nd Cong., 1st sess., 35, 53).

5. Fish had written in his 30 December 1870 dispatch to Moran that Motley must be aware that "many Senators opposed the San Domingo treaty openly, generously, and with as much efficiency as did the distinguished Senator to whom he refers, and have nevertheless continued to enjoy the undiminished confidence and the friendship of the President—than whom no man living is more tolerant of honest and manly differences of opinion, is more single or sincere in his desire for the public welfare, is more disinterested or regardless of what concerns himself, is more frank and confiding in his own dealings, is more sensitive to a betrayal of confidence, or would look with more scorn and contempt upon one who uses the words and the assurances of friendship to cover a secret and determined purpose of hostility," a passage quoted by Schurz in his speech defending CS (ibid., 36; "Recall of Minister Motley," 36–37).

To Ira Harris

Washington 11th March '71

My dear Judge,

I met the editor of the Evng Journal at yr house[1] & he conversed with me in a friendly way.

I observe that he says of me "had he been content with a fair & candid opposition to measures which did not command his approval" &c[2] Of course, here is an allegation that I have not been fair & candid &. Now I write for no purpose of controversy, but if you are at liberty I wish you would be good enough to ask the editor to be good enough where I have not been fair & candid. Let him point out the place, & I will apologize at once before the country.[3] This is all a superlative transpicu-

ous humbug! I know the case & how I have conducted it, —& I know—
—Grant!

Ever Yours   Charles Sumner

ALS PHi (84/202, PCS)

1. Charles E. Smith (1842–1908), associate editor of the *Albany Evening Journal*.

2. In an editorial published 10 March 1871:2, the *Evening Journal* argued that, because CS was likely to oppose the *Alabama* claims treaty and because he had allowed "his feelings to betray him into an attitude of rancorous hostility," the Republican caucus's decision to remove him was sound.

3. Both Harris and Smith responded to CS, Harris in a brief letter lamenting CS's removal and explaining that he had shown CS's letter to Smith (Albany, 15 March, 53/298, PCS). Smith wrote that there had been no "abatement of the 'friendly' feeling evinced towards you when we met." Republicans could not afford to quarrel, however; they must "bear and forbear" (53/383). To assure CS of his esteem, Smith sent CS a later editorial from the *Evening Journal* (13 March 1871:2), one that called upon CS to pursue a "course of honorable and high-minded elevation above the mere impulse of resentment," a course that befitted CS's "dignified character" (16 March, 53/383).

To Moses Coit Tyler

<u>private</u>

Senate Chamber 31st March '71

My dear Professor,

I cannot thank you enough for the good words you write me.[1]

Amidst the gush of sympathy & the torrent of approbation[2] pouring upon me, I am deeply afflicted, when I think of differences with friends & the shism in our party, for whose unity I have labored always.

Nothing could have led me to this Controversy except the hope to do something for our Constitutional safeguards & to elevate our country to a higher plane of International Ethics.

Meanwhile uncertainty & discord prevail on the whole island of St. Domingo. Had our Presdt gone there, in the Xtian. spirit, not to buy or annex, but to make peace & establish harmony, civilization would have been promoted, & we should have been nearer the just end. For years I have been in favor of doing all possible good to the people there & I shall not depart from this rule. But the first step is to put ourselves right, &, if the strong arm of force is to be employed it must be by the authority of Congress & not by Caesarian will.

Thanks again for yr good words, & believe me, dear Prof—

Sincerely Yours,   Charles Sumner

ALS NIC (84/224, PCS)

1. Moses Coit Tyler (1835–1900), then professor of English at the University of Michigan, wrote CS 17 March 1871 about his ouster from the Senate Foreign Relations Committee; those who had organized the removal were "given over by the gods to madness." Tyler assured CS that "no other public man, since Washington, has had in his life time such a concurrence of loyalty & affection, as that which now sweeps over the dividing stakes of party, & bears all hearts to your service" (Ann Arbor, 53/414, PCS).

2. The Sumner correspondence contains as much mail over this political assault as that over the 1856 physical assault. Among the letters of sympathy were ones from Agassiz, who wrote simply, "I am and ever shall remain truly & faithfully your friend," and George T. Downing, a black caterer, who deplored "the outrage upon you, our dearest friend" (Cambridge, 9 March, 52/739; Richmond, 17 March, 53/396). On the other side, a writer signing himself "Rad" wrote from Richmond 15 March that CS deserved his demotion, "after all your persecution of the South so-called, and your adhesion to the Rads" (53/354).

To Francis W. Bird
private—

Washington 16th April '71

My dear Bird,

My relations with Presdt. Lincoln were of unbroken intimacy always & constantly. I arrived at City Point as one of his party the day after his visit to Richmond, but went with Mrs Lincoln. For 4 days we were together Thursday, Friday, Saturday & Sunday when he deposited me at my own door. The next Friday he was assassinated.

On the Sunday on board the steamer, he read Macbeth aloud, &, in private conversation with me, said—"they say I have been under Seward's influence; I have counselled with you twice as much as I ever did with him"; & this same remark has been reported to me as said by him to others. I have been more than once told that, had he lived, he would have offered me to the Depart of State, &, his course toward me made me sometimes think that I should be called to decide the question, whether to quit the Senate.

My relations with all his cabinet were friendly & confidential,—including Blair, who has often said that Mr Lincoln intended to offer me Seward's place.

I send you these facts to be used discreetly.[1]

Ever Yours,   Charles Sumner

P.S. Alas! the disturbing influence of office! If there were no offices in Mass!—

ALS   MH-H   (84/240, PCS)

1. CS followed up this letter with another one 17 April 1871, stating that his opposition to Lincoln's Reconstruction plan for Louisiana did not sever their friendship (Washington, 84/247, PCS). In his article "President Lincoln and Senator Sumner" (Boston *Commonwealth*, 29 April 1871:2) Bird refuted allegations that CS's "arrogance" had also caused a break with another president. Calling such charges "grossly and notoriously false," Bird used the details from CS's two letters to state that differences "in grave matters of public policy" did not affect "the friendly relations between those two magnanimous and great men."

To Benjamin F. Butler

Senate Chamber Tuesday
[*18 April 1871*]

My dear Genl,

I am obliged by the kindness of yr letter & the trouble you have taken. Evidently I was very infelicitous in conveying to you an idea of the paper in question; for you have misconceived the greater part of it & its character.[1]

In considering whether to launch it, I find a determining consideration in justice to Mr Motley, who is vindicated completely, & then on the other side a hesitation to expose Mr Fish, which is done completely.

Faithfully Yours,   Charles Sumner

There are no comttee. letters in question, nor is there any third person except Mr Motley, whose case is exhibited in its true light, & most damning to the Secy.[2]

———

ALS   DLC   (84/249, PCS)

1. CS had prepared a paper, "Personal Relations with the President and Secretary of State," at the end of March 1871 (Wks, 19:99–124). Butler wrote CS 16 April (copy, Washington, 84/242, PCS) that he had "reflected much" on their conversation about CS's break with Fish. He assured CS that he "could hardly take sides" in the rift because he believed his friendship with CS "has been without *disturbance* for many years." Still, he advised CS to "examine very carefully whether there is now in the public mind such evidence of assault by Mr Fish upon you as will justify the publication of private notes and private conversations between you." Butler feared that CS's attempt to defend himself might seem more like "an attack" and could "recoil upon yourself."

2. Fish noted in his diary on 21 April (vol. 3, Fish Papers, Library of Congress) that Butler read to him a copy of his letter of 16 April to CS. Fish told Butler that any publication of correspondence or conversations would not "in any way enable S. to sustain any complaint against me."

To Francis W. Bird
private

Washington 20th April '71

My dear Bird,

What is the meaning of the report & resolutions on St Domingo in the Mass. Legislature?[1] Of course, if passed, my efforts on this question will be weakened & my enemies will rejoice. Do I deserve this blow? Never have I acted more simply & sincerely for the good of my country, & for the elevation of the African race.

Is that report worthy of Mass?—

It is said here that the Collecter of the Port managed it,[2]—& that he was prompted by Butler.

[*William*] Sprague told me that it was impossible to contend with power. Never before did patronage exert such sway. If there were no offices Mass. would be a noble, generous, beautiful unit![3]—

God Bless you!

Ever yours,   Charles Sumner

ALS   MH-H   (84/253, PCS)

1. On 13 April 1871 Representative Ensign H. Kellog of Pittsfield submitted a report and a resolution that the Massachusetts House of Representatives approve the U.S. government's plan to annex Santo Domingo (*Boston Morning Journal*, 14 April 1871:1).

2. Thomas Russell (1825–87), collector of customs at Boston and Charlestown. Bird agreed in his reply of 29 April (Boston, 54/398, PCS) that Russell was probably behind the resolution, which would advance Benjamin F. Butler's interests. Bird doubted the resolution could pass either house of the Massachusetts legislature, and the resolution was ultimately tabled (Willard P. Phillips to CS, Boston, 2 May, 54/438).

3. Replying to a similar query from CS, Edward L. Pierce explained that in Massachusetts the "mass of men are indifferent to what becomes of a *negro* country" and the annexation issue was not worth splitting the Republican party (Boston, 22 April, 54/333).

To William Lloyd Garrison

Washington 26th. April—'71

Dear Mr Garrison,

I am by no means certain that the Dominicans desire annexion.[1] Evidently they desire peace, security & a stable govt.; but it is very questionable whether they would consent without a pang to the loss of national life.

Baez is an immense intriguer & he made it his business to blind the commission. Cabral, who is a better than Baez, writes that it is impossible to know the real sentiments of the people in the way adopted by the Commr.[2] Then it is known that there is a large number of exiles, some of the best men in the country, sent out by Baez, who, if at home, would exert a just influence.

Behind is the terrible question, being a bloody lawsuit, with Hayti & its population of 800,000. This people & govt are sorely tried. We are to them as a hawk to chickens.

To my mind our duty is plain;—make peace between the two govts on the island, & then help each govt.—so that the African race may be encouraged by an example of self-govt.

This whole measure was conceived in heartless indifference to the colored race. It was born of Cazneau & Fabens,[3] the same who in 1854 proposed annexion in the interest of Slavery; & now it is in a kindred interest.

Never has our country been so much demoralized by Presidential influence as now. The Senate & the people are subjugated. Genl. Banks says "one man does the thinking for all, & he has no cabinet." This is hard. Even our excellent Dr Howe catches the fever of submission. I complained to him that the support of the ships about St Domingo had cost the country two millions of dollars supposing that this would disturb his sense of economy if not of justice, when he replied, like an Administration politician,—"but they must be employed somewhere."—"No"! said I, "cut down the Navy, & save this money." But a very small portion of this sum if spent on a peaceful mission or the healing of difficulties & the elevation of the people of the island would have brought tranquility, good will & all other blessings. Howe seems to have a partizan spite against the Haytians;—so has Douglass.[4] Their friendship is exclusively for the Dominicans. I am for both, & think it our duty to obtain peace between them,—instead of organizing dominion, if not war.

Ever sincerely Yours,   Charles Sumner

ALS MB (84/256, PCS)

1. Garrison wrote CS 24 April 1871 thanking him for his 27 March speech on Santo Domingo, "Violations of International Law and Usurpations of War Powers." Garrison regretted that the commissioners' report (submitted to the cabinet on 31 March) strengthened the president's case in stating that most Dominicans wished annexation (Roxbury, 54/342, PCS).

2. In his speech of 27 March CS characterized Báez as a "conspirator, and trickster . . . without patriotism, without truth," allying with the U.S. solely for his own gain (*Globe*, 42nd Cong., 1st sess., 296). The *Report of the Commission of Inquiry to Santo Domingo* stated, however, that the Báez government exercised "full and peaceable possession" over all parts of the republic except on the Haitian border, that the Dominicans enjoyed full political rights, and that no secret promises of land or gifts had been made between U.S. and Dominican authorities (U.S. Senate, *Report of the Commission of Inquiry to Santo Domingo*, Senate Ex. Doc. no. 9, 1871, 6, 176, serial set 1466). José Maria Cabral was president of the country from 1866, after Báez's ouster, to 1868, when Cabral in turn was deposed by Báez's forces. The Cabral letter CS cites is unrecovered; in a letter of 23 February to CS Cabral had, however, stated that any reports that he favored annexation were untrue (Dominican Republic, 52/440).

3. Both Joseph W. Fabens (1821–75) and William L. Cazneau had engaged in land speculation in Santo Domingo in the 1850s and 1860s; in 1870 they promoted annexation, with Grant's approval, chiefly for their own pecuniary advantage (Charles Tansill, *The United States and Santo Domingo, 1798–1873* [1938], 411–13).

4. Douglass wrote from New York that he regretted not seeing CS when in Washington and hoped to arrange a meeting soon: "Your qualifications to advise in all matters of philanthropy and patriotism find recognition no where more readily than with me though to you the fact may seem quite otherwise" (27 April, 54/379).

To Lord de Grey [1]

Thursday [27 April 1871]
[Washington]

Dear Lord de Grey,

I forward a telegram just recd. from Chicago.[2] I am earnest that you should see a prairie, which next after Niagara is nature in grandeur & beauty. Chicago stands on the edge of a prairie.—And you must not fail in giving an hour to Trenton, which is beautiful & most picturesque.[3]

Sincerely Yours,   Charles Sumner

ALS   GBL   (84/270, PCS)

1. George Frederick Robinson, third earl de Grey and later marquess of Ripon (1827–1909), headed the Joint High Commission to negotiate a settlement for the *Alabama* claims, and had been in Washington since 23 February 1871 with other commission members Sir Stafford Northcote, later Lord Iddesleigh (1818–87), law professor Montague Bernard, and Sir John A. MacDonald, prime minister of Canada.

2. James H. Bowen, president of the Calumet and Chicago Canal and Dock Company, wrote and telegraphed CS 27 April, inviting the commission to visit Chicago with all expenses paid (84/265, 54/372, PCS).

3. De Grey replied that such a trip was doubtful, but they could discuss Bowen's invitation "when we have the pleasure of dining with you on Saturday" (Washington, 3 May, 54/447). CS had already entertained the British members of the commission twice, once with their wives. He wrote Longfellow, "they are pleasant, refined, cultured—& I like them, as is my wont with such people" (Washington, 27 April, 84/268).

To Isabella Beecher Hooker

Washington 27th April '71

My dear Mrs Hooker,

Yr letter of April 12th has been "on the table" too long.[1]

I beg you to believe that I am not insensible to yr kind appreciation of what I have done.[2] I hope in the future to be none the less worthy of yr good will.

The frank can be used only at the P.O. where its author resides.[3] It cannot be sent off to be used in other places.

If I can be of service in circulating yr docts. it will give me pleasure.

The Senate will resume its session May 10th, & I expect to remain here till the middle of June.

Sincerely Yours,   Charles Sumner

ALS   CtHS   (84/266, PCS)

1. Isabella Beecher Hooker (1822–1907), half sister of Harriet Beecher Stowe, wrote CS asking him to speak before the forthcoming National Woman Suffrage Convention in New York 11–12 May 1871. If CS could not speak, she asked him at least to write a letter for the group, stating that women should have equal rights with blacks (Hartford, Connecticut, 12 April, 54/245, PCS). Hooker enclosed a copy of "An Appeal to Women of the United States by the National Woman Suffrage and Educational Committee." In it the committee, headed by Hooker, argued that the civil rights enacted in the Fourteenth and Fifteenth Amendments should be consistently extended to women (Elizabeth Cady Stanton, Susan B. Anthony, Matilda Joslyn Gage, *History of Woman Suffrage* [1881], 2:485–88).

2. Hooker also enclosed a copy of an article that she had written, "Who Shall Be the Next President" (New York *Independent*, 6 April 1871:9). She urged Republicans to nominate CS as one who would "assure the women of these United States that their rights under the Constitution shall be respected."

3. Hooker asked if CS would send out letters connected to her work in women's suffrage under his frank: "since men have had the franking privilege for near a hundred years in order to maintain their hold on government, it seems but fair that women should be permitted to argue the question of their rights of citizenship under the same privilege."

To George Bemis

Washington Saturday
[*29 April 1871*]

My dear Bemis,[1]

I hear nothing from you. What say you to the settlement?

(1) England in the treaty expresses regret for the escape of the ships.[2]

(2) Principles are recognized, which, it is supposed, will cover liability for the escaped ships.[3]

Write.[4] Do.

Ever Yrs   C. S.

ALS   MHi   (84/272, PCS)

1. Fish had suggested Bemis as an assistant to J. C. Bancroft Davis, the secretary for the Joint High Commission, but Boutwell remonstrated because Bemis was considered too close to CS (Fish Diary, vol. 2, 19 February 1871, Fish Papers, Library of Congress).

2. The Joint High Commissioners had argued over the proper expression of regret from Britain, which would be part of the preamble to the Treaty of Washington (see Her Majesty's High Commissioners to Lord Granville, Granville to the same, 8 April, 10 April, 15 April, 18–20 April 1871, *British Documents*, part 1, series C, 7:377, 380–82, 8:1, 6). The final version stated as Article 1: "Her Britannic Majesty has authorized Her High Commissioners and Plenipotentiaries to express, in a friendly spirit, the regret felt by Her Majesty's Government for the escape, under whatever circumstances, of the Alabama and other vessels from British ports, and for the depredations committed by those vessels" ("Treaty of Washington," *Foreign Relations* [1872], part 2, 12).

3. Article 6 of the treaty laid down three conditions in which a neutral government should prevent the arming and departure of a ship intended to war against a nation "with which it is at peace"; article 7 stated that a tribunal would establish first whether Great Britain had violated any of these rules and, if it had, award "a sum in gross to be paid by Great Britain to the United States for all the claims referred to it" (ibid., 14–15).

4. CS telegraphed Bemis on 8 May for his advice on the treaty (Washington, 84/298, PCS), and on 9 May Bemis sent an "Elaboration" to be passed on to American commissioner E. Rockwood Hoar (54/472). Bemis wrote CS two days after the Senate began its consideration of the treaty (15 May) that the treaty would not do justice to U.S. claimants. He called the treaty "a *miserable abortion*; *a wholesale 'sell'*; & an *ignominious surrender of every thing valuable*" (Boston, 17 May, 531, 603).

To John Sherman

Washington 1st May '71

Dear Mr Sherman,

I have just read yr letter with a certain surprize which I cannot disguise.[1] Yr indictment against me contains a new count, which makes its appearance for the first time. Certainly it was not mentioned in the Senate, nor did I ever hear of it elsewhere. It could not be mentioned by any one familiar with the case.

(1) You say that "Mr S. *insisted* that the hasty proclamation by G.B. &c was the foundation, the *gravamen* of the Alabama claims." I hope that I

do not take too great a liberty in asking you to point out where I have taken any such ground. Never did I take it in any speech, or any where. On the contrary I have always insisted that the "foundation & *gravamen*" of our claims were the *damages received*, & that the Proclamation was the first link in the chain by which the liability was fixed. This was the ground in the Senate speech which had yr approbation, & also in my speech of Sept. 22nd. 1869 which I send marked.[2] You will see that I there make a distinction between England & France, both of which conceded belligerent rights; but only from England did damages come.

(2) You say that on this question "the Presdt. & Mr S. differed widely." If so there is no official evidence of it. On the contrary the official evidence is the other way.

(a) I drew the instructions to Mr Motley of May 16 1869, relating to belligerent rights & have now before me the original draft in my own hand-writing.[3]

(b) The despatch of Sept. 25th. 1869, which states our case completely & is the only authentic statement by this Administration was proposed & planned by me. *I was invited to write it*, but declined. I suggested who should write it, & it was written accordingly.

(c) I have before me Mr Fish's letter to me of Oct. 1869 describing this last despatch & saying that it was according to my "views."[4]

(d) In Novbr. 1869 the British govt made overtures for negotiation, when Mr Fish wrote me, asking me "to formulate the proposition."[5]

(e) Jan 16th 1871 Mr Fish came to my house to ask me what we should require of England.

And now in the face of this history, I understand you are making a public allegation of a difference between the Administration & myself, *where I had actually held the pen for the Administration* [or?] *been invited to do so*, & you assign this as a reason for displacing me from a position I had occupied 10 years.

(3) You say that on the English question the Senate was against me. I am not aware of any expression of the Senate on this question since my speech which you at least approved. Nor am I aware that the Senate has ever condemned the despatches written by me or at my suggestion.

(4) You introduce falsehoods of "interviewers," which have been point-blank denied by me, & which I deny again.[6] Never have I any way alluded to the "motives" of the Presdt.

(5) You say that the Presdt. "sought the advice & counsel of Mr S." A mistake. He may have sought my vote, which I did not promise; but he never sought "advice & counsel."[7]

I hope you will pardon this brief & hurried correction of some of the errors into which you have fallen.—I have a careful statement of these matters prepared, which your letter will compel me to disclose, where the personal relations with the Secy are precisely set forth, with his appeals to me on the very questions, where you represent me as against him.

The episode of Mr Motley is explained by the record.

Faithfully Yours,   Charles Sumner

P.S. The claims of our people if the treaty is adopted, are to go before a commission.[8] Is it expedient to discredit in advance any position, by which the liability of England may be fixed? I have alw[ays] insisted that her liabil[ity] was for *actual damages*, & that this liability is fixed—

(1) By the proclamat[ion] without which the ships could not have been built, no[r] could a blockade-runn[er] have been equipped.

(2) Negligence in all[ow]ing the escape.

(3) Welcome, hospital[ity] & supplies in the colonial ports.

ALS   DLC   (84/289, PCS)

1. In casting his vote on 10 March 1871 for the removal of CS from the Senate Foreign Relations Committee, Sherman explained that he felt bound by the Republican caucus's decision (*Globe*, 42nd Cong., 1st sess., 50–51). Sherman's letter to the Springfield, Ohio, *Republic* of 24 April (reprinted in the *New York Times*, 30 April 1871:1) stated that he had tried to prevent CS's removal and attributed CS's demotion to his foreign policy differences with the Grant administration. Furthermore, wrote Sherman, CS "did not, and could not, and would not represent the views of his Republican colleagues" on the forthcoming *Alabama* negotiations.

2. CS made two statements on belligerence in this speech: belligerency "may be illustrated in the three different cases of war, independence, and belligerence. In each case the declaration is an exercise of high prerogative, inherent in every nation, and kindred to that of eminent domain . . . and so a nation recognizing belligerence where it does not exist in fact becomes a wrong-doer also." CS declared, "There can be no doubt, that, through English complicity, our carrying trade was transferred to English bottoms; our foreign commerce sacrificed, while our loss was England's gain; our blockade rendered more expensive; and generally that our war, with all its fearful cost of blood and treasure, was prolonged indefinitely. This terrible complicity began with the wrongful recognition of rebel belligerence, under whose shelter pirate ships were built and supplies sent forth" ("National Affairs at Home and Abroad" [1869], 13, 14).

3. See CS to Fish, 17 May 1869, and to Motley, same date.

4. See CS to Timothy Howe, 27 July 1870, note 3. Fish wrote that he had instructed Motley to read this dispatch to Lord Clarendon, a document "which I ⟨think⟩ hope you will be satisfied with" (Washington, 9 October 1869, 48/352, PCS).

5. See CS to Fish, 9 November 1869.

6. Sherman had written that CS's "most extreme and active opposition" to the

Santo Domingo treaty had been then "aggravated by alleged public conversations with Mr. SUMNER by 'interviewers,' in which the motives of the President and others were impugned."

7. Sources disagree as to exactly what CS promised when Grant called on him in early January 1870 seeking support for the treaty annexing Santo Domingo. John W. Forney, who was present at the meeting, declared he could not recall CS's precise statement, but "understood" that CS stated that he "would cheerfully support the treaty." CS denied such support, stating "the language is fixed absolutely in my memory: 'Mr. President,' I said, 'I am an Administration man, and whatever you do will always find in me the most careful and candid consideration'" (Forney to Orville Babcock, 6 June 1870; CS remarks, 21 December, *Globe*, 41st Cong., 3rd sess., 242–43). According to Donald, despite whatever was actually said, Grant left CS's home with the impression CS would support the treaty (DD, 2:434–38).

8. The Treaty of Washington called for arbitration at Geneva by representatives from Great Britain, the U.S., Brazil, Italy, and Switzerland. Work was completed on the treaty 8 May.

To Edward L. Pierce

Senate Chamber 12th May '71

My dear good friend,

You seem to like what I do when it is done, but are anxious always in advance lest I should do something amiss. It never entered my head to make the speech you imagine.[1]

I have an account of my "personal relations" with him, which has been drawn up for two months to be put forth, if thought best, in precise answer to the allegation against me. At present I am occupied with the treaty.[2]

What means my much-valued friend of many years, Mrs Howe? I have seen words of bitterness about me from her. I do not deserve them. In other days she has praised me when I did not deserve as well as now.

As for Grant—*wait*. Never did I utter truer words or more needful than when I said that half the thought & expense, bestowed upon the pacification of the South which he has given to St Domingo, & there would have been no Ku Klux.

Good bye!

Ever Yours,   Charles Sumner

ALS   MH-H   (64/692, PCS)

1. Pierce wrote 8 May 1871 (Boston, 54/468, PCS) that he heard CS might make a speech "reviewing Fish's foreign policy," and advised him not to do so. Fish was

"not your peer—and he has no hold on the country," declared Pierce, and such a speech would only give CS's enemies another opportunity to show his differences with other Republicans. He admired CS's speech supporting the anti-Ku Klux Klan bill, 13 April, which Pierce thought had recouped some of CS's old Republican support.

2. Pierce wrote that he hoped CS could approve the Treaty of Washington "conscientiously with all your heart. I rejoice at every opportunity afforded for you to show yourself *en rapport* with your old associates save in one measure only."

To John Sherman

Washington 12th May '71

Mr Sumner ventures to call Mr Sherman's attention to the despatch signed "Hamilton Fish," & dated Sept 25th 1869—being pp. 107–115 among the papers accompanying the treaty. This is the last *official* statement of the Administration on the question of belligerence. It was written at Mr Sumner's suggestion by a gentleman indicated for this purpose by him, & was intended to be in precise harmony with his "views."[1] This Mr Fish declared in a private autograph note [9 *October 1869*] which Mr Sumner has.

Mr Sherman will next be good enough to glance at Mr Sumner's Worcester speech made 23d Oct. [*September*] 1869, two days before the date of the despatch, & which was printed in Washington the day before such date. He will find the most precise agreement between the despatch & speech, especially on the question of belligerence.

As the despatch is the last official declaration of the Administration on this question, according to the papers communicated to the Senate, so is the speech Mr Sumner's last public word. He has said nothing since.

And yet, in the face of this open unimpeachable testimony Mr Sherm[an] charges Mr Sumner;

(1) With a position on the belligerent question which he never adopted.

(2) With difference on this question from the Administration; And then Mr Sherman

(3) Announces to the world that this alleged "differe[nce"] invented by himself, was the reason & in his judgt. sufficient reason for insulting an old Senator.[2]

C. S.

ALS   DLC   (84/307, PCS)

1. See CS to Motley 17 August 1869. Caleb Cushing was the "gentleman" to whom CS refers.

2. Sherman apparently replied (draft, Washington, 15 May, 84/310, PCS). He wrote that he was "surprise[d]" at the "tone and temper" of CS's latest letter. Sherman insisted that his letter to the Springfield, Ohio, *Republic* "contained nothing but what I supposed were conceded facts," borne out by CS's speeches and other "public documents." As for CS's points, Sherman stated that the authorship of the 25 September 1869 dispatch was immaterial: "It is the act of Mr Fish." He agreed that CS's Worcester speech (which he termed "very general") "is not inconsistent" with the Fish dispatch, but he maintained that the dispatch did differ from CS's earlier "Our Claims on England" speech in which CS had emphasized the British concession of belligerency more strongly. Sherman had meant CS no "injustice," he wrote, but "you [push?] the matter entirely too far when you take my statement . . . as an evidence of an intention to insult you."

To Lord de Grey

[*Washington*] 23d May 1871

Dear Lord de Grey,[1]

I enclose copies of amendts. which I have drawn up in the hope of doing something for the improvement of Intern. Law. I shall not press them to a division.[2]

I see that the invention of the newspapers has found new advertisement in your House.[3] Again *bon voyage*![4]

Sincerely Yours,   Charles Sumner

ALS   GBL   (84/315, PCS)

1. Lord de Grey wrote on 15 May 1871 that he had just learned that Lord John Russell was to speak in Parliament 22 May objecting to parts of the Treaty of Washington. He assumed that CS would not be "surprized" at Russell's response, but, Lord de Grey wrote, "it shows the difficulties that we shall have to encounter" (Washington, 54/520, PCS). To Granville, de Grey telegraphed on 9 May that CS was "doubtful and hesitating" about the treaty. On 16 May de Grey telegraphed Granville, "Every reason to believe Mr. Sumner will support" (*British Documents*, part 1, series C, 8:30, 33).

2. CS enclosed a copy of two printed amendments (rules four and five) to article 6 of the treaty, which would bind a neutral government to deny protection to armed vessels. On 24 May CS did, indeed, propose these amendments as well as a new article, which would protect private property on a neutral vessel from capture on the high seas; all were defeated (*Executive Proceedings*, 18:106–7).

3. In Parliament 22 May, Thomas Maitland, eleventh earl of Lauderdale, took note of a telegram printed in the British papers about an alleged CS speech against the treaty, in which CS argued that the British statement of regret was "inadequate" (*Hansard's Parliamentary Debates*, 3rd series, 206:1101–2). Although the *New York Herald* reported CS as delivering a lengthy speech on the treaty (20 May 1871:3), CS dismissed the report as "pure invention" when the Senate discussed leaks of the treaty

on 22 May (*Globe*, 42nd Cong., special sess., 890). On 24 May he voted for the treaty, which was ratified 50–12 (*Executive Proceedings*, 18:108).

4. The British commissioners left Washington 24 May. From London, de Grey thanked CS for his letter and the amendments; perhaps in the future CS's "views" on private property "will prevail; but at present they would meet with much opposition on both sides of the Atlantic." He concluded, "It has been a great satisfaction to me & to my colleagues to find that you were able to give your vote in favour of our work" (17 June, 54/677).

To Whitelaw Reid

Washington 30 May '71

Dear Mr Reid,

I call yr attention to a passage of my speech in the *Globe* where I set forth yr submission to illegal process.[1]

Do you think the Sec of State competent to represent us in the Arbitration of our claims at Geneva?[2] Is there a single point in our case which he understands? Would not his appointment sacrifice the claimants?

Very truly Yours,   Charles Sumner

ALS   DLC   (84/318, PCS)

1. Two *New York Tribune* correspondents, Z. L. White and H. J. Ramsdell, had been taken into custody for refusing to identify how they had obtained a copy of the Treaty of Washington, which the Senate, under usual executive session rules, had intended to be kept private, but which had been printed in the *Tribune*. On 27 May 1871 CS had supported a motion to discharge the two men and praised Reid for appearing before the investigating committee when he was not legally required to do so (*Globe*, 42nd Cong., special session, 920–23). The Washington correspondent for the *New York Tribune* praised CS's speech against detaining recusant witnesses (29 May 1871:1).

2. A short editorial in the *Tribune* (29 May 1871:4) endorsed the rumored choice of Hamilton Fish as chief negotiator in the *Alabama* claims negotiation. Fish, said the *Tribune*, "will command the approval of those best informed and the entire satisfaction of the Country." Reid replied that his compliment to Fish had been in deference to Greeley, who "esteems Mr Fish much more highly than either you or I" (New York, 31 May, 54/597, PCS).

To Henry Wilson

Washington June 2nd '71

My dear Wilson,

Here are two letters, which I cannot forbear writing.[1] Other friends are aged or dead.

I fear that I did not impress you by my perfect willingness to encounter any denials of Mr Fish. He can only make the case worse, & the reports of his sayings let him down enormously. He came to my house at 9 o'clk in the evng & stayed till midnight, pressing me all the time to abandon my opposition to the St Dom. scheme.[2] When I remained firm, he said—"There is the English mission. Take it. It is yours." I know nothing of his authority. But the absence of authority cannot change the character of the act on his part.

(1) The offer was to get me out of the way or to compromise me.

(2) The offer was made anterior to the death of Lord Clarendon, thus showing that this event did not determine the recall of Motley as was alleged.

Major Poor thinks these counter-sayings of Mr Fish justify me in making my statement. Until this is done, the country & the Senate cannot appreciate the conduct of the Secy or my forbearance.

If I can be any service to you at home or abroad, during yr absence pray let me know.

Good bye! May you have a pleasant voyage, a happy tour & return strengthened for our common duties.[3]

Sincerely Yours, Charles Sumner

ALS DLC (84/322, PCS)

1. Wilson was sailing for England in a few days.
2. See CS to Whitelaw Reid, 12 January 1871, note 5.
3. Wilson replied 6 June 1871 (New York, 54/635, PCS) thanking CS for the letters of introduction. Wilson added, "the more I reflect upon it the more I feel that you had better not print your paper concerning Fish." Sometime in June CS sent Claflin, Pierce, and Gerrit Smith, among others, a printed copy of his "Personal Relations with the President" (Wks, 19:99–124) marked "unpublished—private & confidential—not to go out of Mr ——'s hands" (84/334, 338, 64/694). The article was not published until after CS's death.

To George W. Smalley[1]

[Washington 18 June 1871]

I am sorry that so conspicuous a negotiation did not end in more for international law.[2] We ought to have got more, and mankind should also. There should have been a consecration of the great principle of immunity of private property on the ocean; also the denunciation as a pirate of any ship plundering and burning prizes at sea without taking them into port for adjudication; also the recognition of the duty of a neutral Power to exclude from its ports in time of war any armed vessel engaged in hostilities which does not hold a commission delivered in some port of military or naval equipment in the actual occupation of the commissioning Government. These provisions deal with evils which became manifest during our war, and I always hoped that the final Treaty would not neglect them. With such safeguards for civilization, I would have been content with less for my own country. Such a Treaty I could not have opposed even if it gave us nothing.[3]

PL   London *Times*, 15 February 1872:10

1. Smalley and CS had discussed the Treaty of Washington when Smalley was in Washington the week of 12 June 1871 (Smalley to CS, Boston, 6 June; New York, 9 June; Chicago, 21 June; 54/631, 647, 685, PCS). Smalley later wrote CS that he hoped he had not "interpreted too liberally the permission you gave to quote you" when he included this extract from CS's letter to him (unrecovered) in a letter Smalley wrote to the London *Times* (London, 15 February 1872, 56/485).

2. To Bemis CS had written, 5 June, "We have lost where we should not" (Washington, 84/324).

3. In acknowledging CS's letter Smalley wrote on 21 June that "what you say as to the omission in the treaty" should be expressed publicly. He asked, and received (New York, 30 June, 55/027), permission to show CS's letter, especially CS's last remark, to John Bright: "there ought to be a cordial understanding between you and him" (54/685).

To Sir Stafford Northcote

Washington 18th July '71

My dear Sir Stafford,

I congratulate you upon being once more at home with family and friends—to say nothing of the green-cushioned bench.

Your work has found the welcome it deserved—at least in England. The opposition was little more than Pharnaces to Caesar.[1]

Here the Treaty is still on trial & will be until after the award.

It is hard to think that so good an opportunity was lost for doing so much to improve the Law of Nations & especially to limit the sphere & peril of war. Believing most profoundly that this is the present duty—shall I say mission?—of England, I cannot comprehend the lukewarmness in important quarters.[2] I write freely, because I saw how you inclined in this direction.

Had our Treaty secured the immunity of private ppty, I could have seen our claims reduced to a minimum. And this seems to me the obvious policy of England, who has more to gain by such a rule than any other Power.[3]

Since you left the photographer has made another experiment & I send you the result, according to promise.

Ever sincerely yours,   Charles Sumner

I leave here for Boston this week.

ALS   GBL   (84/369, PCS)

   1. On 12 June 1871 the House of Lords defeated Lord Russell's motion that the government withdraw the Treaty of Washington (*Hansard's Parliamentary Debates*, 3rd series, 206:1901). Caesar defeated Pharnaces (63–47 B.C.) in 47 B.C.

   2. In the House of Commons on 12 June, Sir Roundell Palmer (1812–95; solicitor-general, 1863–66; later first earl of Selborne) asked a question about the second rule of article 6, which forbade a neutral government from allowing a belligerent the use of its ports or territorial waters. Palmer asked if the rule would be interpreted by the U.S. "in the same limited sense" as it was in Great Britain and if any communication could be issued to "guard against its being accepted or understood in any larger sense." Gladstone replied that Fish had declared that he hoped the two governments could issue a "joint declaration which should place the meaning of this Rule beyond all chance of misconstruction" (ibid., 1903–5).

   3. Replying 9 August (London, 55/168, PCS), Northcote wrote that Britain had achieved "a much better settlement than would have been afforded by the Johnson-Clarendon convention; and, though I should have individually preferred a still broader measure, I am not dissatisfied with what we have got."

To Carl Schurz

Washington 1st Aug. '71

My dear Schurtz,

   I am still here,—& nobody is more surprised than myself. I am like that Genoese Doge taken to Versailles, who, when asked what he thought the most remarkable thing, said—"finding himself here."

   I shall be on my way to Boston when this reaches you.

   Of course, the Presdt's message pretending to abandon the St Dom. folly, besides its most uncandid allegations & suggestions, was not sincere. I did not so regard it at the time.[1]

   The flag still flies at Samana with two steamers,—all this under pretence of that lease which lapsed four months from its date.[2] Parties in New York, probably Spofford & Tileston have advanced $150 000 on account of the 2nd year's rent, in the hope of making Congress pay it. The Presdt. may be silent for the present, but with a re-election, he would push his scheme desperately. I know of two different persons with whom he has been corresponding on the subject. Of this I am sure.

Genl. Boynton[3] promised to send you an Inquirer of Phila, containing a letter from Samana, on which he relied, to the effect that our Navy is to support Baez—the same old story!

I shall watch for yr speech, which I know will be able & eloquent; & I doubt not firm & searching. There is a *dementia* in the Republican party. We must save it.[4]

Good bye!

Ever yours, Charles Sumner

ALS DLC (84/384, PCS)

1. Schurz wrote from St. Louis that he had seen recent news reports of U.S. naval orders to a squadron near Santo Domingo, and wondered if CS had any more information (27 July 1871, 55/121, PCS). When Grant sent the Santo Domingo commissioners' report to the Senate 5 April he recommended that no further action be taken; the people should be allowed to reach their own opinions on the annexation issue (*Globe*, 42nd Cong., 1st sess., 469–70).

2. The U.S. lease of Samana Bay in Santo Domingo had expired 1 July 1870. The mercantile firm Spofford, Tileston and Company, which had invested with Joseph Fabens in land on Samana Bay, were running a steamship line to New York (Charles Tansill, *The United States and Santo Domingo* [1938], 463, 346, 350).

3. H. V. N. Boynton, Associated Press news correspondent, who accompanied the Commission of Inquiry to Santo Domingo.

4. In a speech to a German audience in Chicago 12 August Schurz reiterated his opposition to the annexation of Santo Domingo and said he and CS had a right to differ with the president if they chose (*New York Times*, 13 August 1871:1). Replying to CS's letter on 14 August Schurz declared that the Republican party could succeed only "by making it the party of reforms and by suppressing the bad influences governing it" (Chicago, 55/197).

To Samuel Gridley Howe

Washington 3d Aug. '71

My dear Howe,

I have not replied to yr last letter, because I hesitate to write to you of any thing where you & I, usually in such accord, are so far asunder. I cannot see any thing in this business as you see it—nothing![1]

To me the whole business is a crime, beginning in simple greed of beautiful land, instigated primarily by a pro-slavery rebel Cazneau & his accomplice Fabens. It is the case of Ahab & Naboth's vinyard,[2]— according to all the Presdt's speeches & conversations, to the return of

the Commrs. So it is to me; but I do not wish to say more on that to
you.

If the Presdt. writes & talks humanity to you, it is for a purpose. It
is not in him.[3]

I deplore the attempt to put on its legs the sham lease, which is dead
as Julius Caesar & cannot stand five minutes' debate! Sending out
money under such a pretense is a mockery. You know that the Presdt's
friends did not dare to present the case at the last meeting of Congress!

You must pardon my sympathy with the Haytians which dates to my
childhood. My father was in Hayti shortly after leaving college, & his
stories of the people there are among my earliest memories. He did not
describe the people as you do. Then came the embittered discussion
about the recognition of their Independence,—ending in a Bill drawn
by me & carried through the Senate, by which that Independence was
recognized.[4] Since then they have been almost my wards. I feel a wrong
to them keenly, & when I heard yr harsh words about them—when I
heard your indifference to their claims, & Wade's oaths against even
hearing their side,[5] I felt that there was not only a shocking violation
of the first principles of justice [ante?] alteram [partem?][6] but downright
inhumanity.

Sending arms to the island is only to feed civil war! You send a sword
when I would send peace, which is the longing of my life to which
in every fibre of my being I am devoted. I would give peace to both
parties—to Baez & Saget—to the whole island; & there is a way, cheap,
economical, simple, constitutional, legal, humane; it is by peaceful
efforts to make peace under the guarantee of the U. States & put each
party on its legs.

But in this there is nothing to gratify the *imperatorial* nature of the
Presdt. He began as Ahab, & he cannot change conduct.

How much has this war-dance about the island cost? At least three
millions! Imagine this vast sum devoted to the improvement of the
island & the establishment of education. It agonizes me to think of
these means thus diverted from a good purpose, &, worse still, employed to keep one million of people in distress!

I have read the admirable addresses of the Haytian towns on our war-
dance, & ask myself, if the towns of Mass. could put forth 40 addresses
comparable to these from the people that you objurgate & despise.

But the Haytians may be as bad as you represent them, they are
entitled to justice & the true duty of our country is peace & not war.

I hope you will pardon this freedom. So do I feel this difference, that,
when this question began, could I have foreseen that you were to rush
into it, so intensely, I should have been tempted to resign my seat in

the Senate. I shrink from controversy especially with a much-valued friend. But why did you not see the invitation to you as Agassiz to whom it came first saw it?[7]—

God bless you!

Ever affectionately Yrs,   Charles Sumner

ALS   MH-H   (64/705, PCS)

1. Since his return from Santo Domingo, Howe had enthusiastically embraced its annexation. At some point in 1871 Howe became a director of the Samana Bay Company, a corporation formed by Joseph Fabens and Spofford, Tileston and Company to develop the Samana peninsula (Harold Schwartz, *Samuel Gridley Howe* [1956], 310–13).

2. Ahab, king of Israel, had Naboth stoned to death in order to obtain his vineyard (1 Kings 21).

3. Howe had written President Grant 4 June urging the renewal of the U.S. lease of Samana Bay (Howe Papers, New-York Historical Society).

4. 24 April 1862. See CS to John Andrew, 27 April 1862. The Haitians offered a medal to CS 13 July 1871 in token of his efforts to defend "the dignity of a black people seeking to place itself, by its own efforts, at the banquet of the civilized world" (Wks, 19:154; Stephen Preston to CS, 8 June, 54/642, PCS). Preston wrote CS 11 July that the steamer *Tybee* under orders from the U.S. government was bringing arms and money to the Báez government. He wrote that Báez and influential people in Washington ("personnes influentes") believed that the fall of the Haitian government would help annexation (New York, 55/080).

5. A section of the report that Howe reputedly wrote described the "aggressive policy" of the Haitian government, "at whose head is a president elevated by a bloody insurrection, involving the murder of his predecessor." On 9 March, when the commission visited Haiti briefly, Wade objected to "any further communication" with representatives of José Maria Cabral, the exiled leader of Santo Domingo (U.S. Senate, *Report of the Commission of Inquiry to Santo Domingo*, Senate Ex. Doc. no. 9, 1871, 8, 54, serial set 1466).

6. "Before another part."

7. Asked to serve as a commisioner, Agassiz had refused, out of deference to CS (CS to Francis W. Bird, 25 April 1871, 84/263). In a letter to the *New York Tribune*, 23 August, Howe used a passage from CS's "Prophetic Voices Concerning America" as grounds for annexing Santo Domingo. Howe regretted the criticism of the U.S. naval force in Santo Domingo waters and stated that even if Grant had been "technically wrong" sending the fleet there, his annexation policy was "morally right" (*Letters on the Proposed Annexation of Santo Domingo* [1871], 5–6).

To James Jackson Jarves

Nahant 19th Aug. '71

My dear Jarvis,

On reaching here from Washington I was happy to find yr note, from which I learn that you are among us,—& I am glad of it,—for you are needed.

I hope our people will secure yr pictures.[1] I understand well that they will not please the multitude at once, but I am sure that they are of great value as illustrating the origin & history of Italian art, besides having several specimens of special interest & beauty; & this is substantially the opinion of Mr T.[homas] G.[old] Appleton with whom I have conversed on the subject.

I have corresponded & conferred with the Trustees of the Corcoran Gallery on acquiring them; but they have not yet organized their museum, &, I think, are not strong enough in money.[2] I urged the pictures strongly. If Boston cannot have them, then I desired them at Washington.

I hope to see you soon, when we will talk on these things,—& you will tell me the news of Italian Art. I read yr book with great interest.[3]

Sincerely Yours,   Charles Sumner

ALS CtYB (84/397, PCS)

1. James Jackson Jarves (1818–88), an art collector and critic, had written upon his return from Europe about a possible sale of his collection of 119 early Italian masters, which had been on deposit at Yale University. Needing to sell them as soon as possible, Jarves hoped to get $60,000 for them. He wondered if trustees for the prospective Boston Museum of Fine Arts would be interested. If not, he asked CS to look into other possibilities in Washington (Boston, 8 August 1871, 55/160, PCS; *New York Tribune*, 10 November 1871:5).

2. The Corcoran Gallery of Art in Washington, D.C., was opened on 22 February 1872.

3. Jarves's *Art Thoughts, The Experiences and Observations of an American Amateur in Europe* was first published in 1869. Later Jarves wrote that he would sell his pictures for $28,000, "which is less than half of their appraised valuation" (New York, 7 December, 55/618). The collection was sold at auction to Yale University.

To Francis Lieber

Nahant Sunday
[20 August 1871]

My dear Lieber,

I was glad to see so much of you & wished for more.[1]

I find here yr letter of 24th July, & note yr comment on Motley; saying he was willing to go to England on my speech,—which you condemn.[2]—Do you not forget Fish's despatch of 25th Sept—written by Caleb Cushing—which covered my speech absolutely, so that Clarendon said it was "Sumner's speech in a diplomatic note."[3]

I know not if I told you that Lord de Grey told me that, without my speech the Treaty could not have been made & that he had worked by it as by a chart. Every point I made against the R. Johnson Treaty is met in the Treaty.—Of course, the amount of damages belongs to the evidence, & will be considered at Geneva.

Ever Yours,   Charles Sumner

ALS MH-H (64/699, PCS)

1. CS had dined with Lieber while in New York (Lieber to CS, New York, 11 August 1871, 84/392, PCS).
2. On 24 July Lieber answered CS's request for Lieber's opinion on "Personal Relations with the President," which CS had sent him earlier. Lieber wrote that the "threatening ruin" from the Democrats meant that intraparty conflicts should be suppressed. He thought CS's speech would either damage the Republican party "very seriously" or isolate CS entirely. Lieber recalled his letter of May 1869 in which he doubted CS's claim that Motley, as minister to Great Britain, would follow only CS's views. Lieber thought at the time such procedure "not foreboding a happy or speedy settlement of our difficulties" (New York, 84/373).
3. Notes made on 23 October 1869 by Charles S. A. Abbott, third Lord Tenterden (later secretary to the Joint High Commission), for Lord Clarendon stated that the Fish dispatch was, "in fact, a reproduction of the speech made by Mr. Sumner." Clarendon on 6 November 1869 sent an edited version of these notes to Thornton (*British Documents*, part 1, series C, 7:241, 251).

To Gerrit Smith
private

Nahant—Mass. 20th Aug. '71

My dear friend,

Yr note & its enclosure reached me at this retreat where I am with my friend Longfellow. I regret much that I cannot see the Presidential question as you see it.[1]

I know few politicians who think that Grant can be re-elected. Greeley told me last week that he looked upon his defeat as inevitable. Forney, who is friendly to him & has just accepted the collectorship of Phila., told me that he did not see how he could be re-elected, although he thought he would obtain the nomination;—to which I replied that he could not be nominated if it appeared that he could not be re-elected.

Therefore when you ask me to withdraw opposition to Grant, you ask me to aid in the defeat of the Republican Party. I have too much interest in this party to do any such thing.

But waiving the question of his success—he does not deserve the nomination. "One term" is enough for any body—especially for one who, being tried, is found so incapable,—so personal—so selfish—so vindictive, & so entirely pre-occupied by himself. All who have known him best testify to his incapacity. Don't forget Stanton's judgment.[2]

It is hard to see the Ku Klux raging & good people dying through his lukewarmness & indifference. It is my solemn judgt, which at the proper time I shall declare, that the much-criticized Ku Klux legislation of the last Congress would have been *entirely unnecessary*,[3] if this Republican President had shown a decent energy in enforcing existing law & in manifesting sympathy with the oppressed there. *On him is that innocent blood*,—which flowed while he circulated at entertainments, excursions, horse-races. Instead of being at Long-Branch[4] a good Presdt. would have been at Savannah & Mobile or at least he would have made himself felt in those places.

Consider, then, the insincerity of his message about St Dom. One million of blacks are now kept in anxiety & terror by the Republican Presdt, whom you hail as representing "moral ideas"! Instead of abandoning his ill-omened Scheme,—he is now pressing it—working at home, like Hamlet's ghost, under ground & at the island with a most expensive fleet. His war-dance about the island has cost several millions. Instead of making peace between the two contending parties, & setting each on its legs, in the spirit of disinterested benevolence, he sends money to Baez under pretense of a sham treaty to keep alive civil war. Nothing has aroused me more since the Fug. Sl. Bill & the outrages in Kansas. The same old spirit is revived in the treatment of the Haytian Republic.

And I am asked to help the re-nomination of such a man. Impossible! I love the Republican—love my country too well to have a hand in such a thing.

In these conclusions I am governed by no personal feelings—more than I had to Franklin Pierce or James Buchanan! How can I, an old public servant, devoted to a cause, turn aside on any personal feelings?—No,—my dear friend, I write in sadness & sincerity, hoping yet to do something by which the cause of our country shall be saved. Think of five years under his vindictive imperialism! Surely *you* must hesitate.

Grant is full of personal enmities. He has quarelled with two members of his cabinet—a Minister to England—a chairman of a Senate Comttee.—one or two of the diplomatic corps——the governor of a territory[5]—& numerous others, *all good & faithful Republicans* or friendly to him. I was always his true friend—never breathing a word except in kindness & respect—anxious for the welfare of his Administration—& yet, when I felt it my duty to oppose his St Dom. scheme, *always without one word of allusion to him*, he was moved to vindictiveness. Ask any member of the Comttee. or any Senator, if in the debates of the Comttee. or Ex. session, I made any allusion to him, except to express a regret that he had entered upon this mistaken policy. And yet the vengance came.

Afterwards when he still persevered I felt it my duty to arraign him openly. Had I been a reptive. I should have felt it my duty to move his impeachment. —I shall be astonished if at the next session his impeachment is not moved. His chance of impeachment is better than that of re-election.

Why, then, press him for candidate? Unquestionably the hardest possible to elect—& unquestionably the poorest calling himself Republican!—There are 40 good Republicans in the Union, any one of whom can be nominated without hazard to the party &, when elected will be a better Presdt. So I believe on my conscience, & on this belief I must act. At proper time I shall communicate Mr Stanton's dying judgment.[6]

Ever Sincerely Yours,   Charles Sumner

ALS NySU (84/399, PCS)

1. Smith wrote on 8 August 1871 that he knew CS did not think highly of Grant but he believed Grant was the only candidate to stop the Democrats. First the Republican party must be united, wrote Smith, and CS should have "the wisdom & magnanimity to say that it must be" (Peterboro, 55/162, PCS).

2. In a subsequent letter, 28 August, CS quoted Stanton's dying words regarding Grant; according to CS, Stanton had referred to his "'duty to study him, & he did study him night & day . . . & he then declared his utter incapacity'" (84/409).

3. The act to enforce the provisions of the Fourteenth Amendment (known as the Ku Klux Klan Act), which Congress passed 18 April 1871, gave federal authorities the power to prosecute crimes involving the infringement of civil rights (Globe, 42nd Cong., 1st sess., 779).

4. Grant's vacation home in New Jersey.

5. Both Hoar and Jacob D. Cox had been dismissed from the cabinet in 1870, the latter from his post as secretary of the Interior. James Mitchell Ashley had been removed as governor of the Montana Territory in 1870.

6. Smith replied that although he was a little less disposed to Grant after CS's "long, frank & friendly letter" he did not think any other Republican could defeat a Democratic candidate (23 August, 55/233).

To Caleb Cushing

Coolidge House Thursday
[21? September 1871]

My dear Genl,

I called at Young's hoping to find you but you were gone. I still hope for that pleasure.

I am sincerely glad you are to take part for us at Geneva; but I am in despair, & so are others at the thought of Bancroft Davis stating our case.[1] He wants ability & character.

I have conversed with many here about him. He is a "rotten egg," & is so regarded by all the most important persons in our state. The legislative report is correct,[2]—so I am informed by Govr Claflin & Mr Bird.

I protest against his agency & shall deem it my duty at the proper time to assign reasons.

Such a man to state our case! The idea is absurd.

The more I study this Treaty & go behind the scenes, the more I am impressed by the worse than mediocrity in the negotiation on our part. The instructions of the British Commrs. shew that they were authorized to concede more than is in the Treaty.[3] But how expect any thing from the Secy of State! I do not agree with Bemis in speaking of the "lost cause"; but I feel that all yr great resources will be needed to repair the blunders already made, & the dead weight of Davis in the case.

Ever Sincerely Yours,   Charles Sumner

Staempti is an intense republican,—not very popular in Switzerland, & taken in preference to Bluntschli, who was of Zurich, but is now "serviteur de Bismarch"—& on our case too superficial. De la Rive would have been taken,[4] but it was feared that his English associations would "give umbrage at Washington."

ALS   DLC   (84/441, PCS)

1. Cushing had been named one of the counselors for the Geneva arbitration, scheduled for December 1871. J. C. Bancroft Davis had been appointed American agent, or secretary, for the U.S. delegation to the Geneva arbitration.

2. At CS's request, Edward L. Pierce was looking into Davis's connections with the Boston, Hartford and Erie Railroad; Pierce reported on a $60,000 sum that Davis received from a Mr. Eldridge seeking "advantages and contracts beneficial" to the railroad (CS to Pierce, New York, 27 November, 64/720; Pierce to CS, Milton, Massachusetts, 55/621).

3. Lord Granville's instructions to the British commissioners, 9 February, stated that Britain upheld the principle of arbitration as set forth in the Johnson-Clarendon Convention, but continued, "you are at liberty to transmit for their consideration any other proposal which may be suggested for determining and closing the question of these claims. For the escape of the 'Alabama' and consequent injury to the commerce of the United States, Her Majesty's Government authorize you to express their regret in such terms as would be agreeable to the Government of the United States and not inconsistent with the position hitherto maintained by Her Majesty's Government as to the international obligations of neutral nations" (*British Documents*, part 1, series C, 7:319).

4. Jacob Staempfti (1820–79), former president of the Swiss Republic, was one of the five arbitrators. CS possibly referred to historian William de la Rive (1827–1900).

To Edward L. Pierce

Coolidge House Sunday
[*24 September 1871*]

My dear Pierce,
Can I see you here before 12 o'clk Monday?—I think I can explain
B. F. B's ways & means, & the *coup d'état* which I forsee.[1]

Ever Yours,   Charles Sumner

ALS   MH-H   (64/716, PCS)

1. The Republican State Convention, to be held 26 September 1871 at Worcester, promised to be a showdown between pro- and anti-Butler forces over the gubernatorial nomination. Butler was opposed by William B. Washburn (1820–87; U.S. congressman [Rep., Mass.], 1863–71). Some correspondents urged CS to speak out strongly against Butler (Clement Hugh Hill, 8 September; Alexander H. Rice, 18, 19 September, 55/305, 327, 332, PCS), while others, such as Ben: Perley Poore, advised CS not to desert Butler in favor of a "namby-pamby conservative, who never stood squarely behind you" (Newburyport, 19 September, 55/329). Ultimately, CS decided not to attend the convention, which nominated Washburn. Butler on 2 October sent CS a quotation from the *Springfield Daily Republican* "in memory of a former friendship . . . in order that you may see what you have so well earned." The *Republican* stated that, although CS and Wilson had expressed opposition to Butler, they "'timidly staid away from the Convention, and can claim very little of the credit of securing his defeat'" (Boston, 55/375).

To Carl Schurz
private

Boston 25th Sept. '71

My dear Genl,
I have not seen yr Nashville speech complete,—but admire the extracts much.
I doubt if Jeff. Davis & his *confrères* ought to have the license of office-holding again.[1] I have always said that when the time had come, nobody should outdo me in generosity to the South. You insist that the time has come.
Yr statement against Grant is most powerful.[2] The more I think of

him & his doings, the more I feel his incompetency & wrong-headedness. I tremble for my country when I contemplate the possibility of this man being fastened upon us for another four years. What can be done to make this impossible? I also tremble when I think of reconstruction, with Liberty & Equality, committed for four years to the tender mercies of the Democrats. Which way is daylight?

Hooper has a letter from Washington, which says, that the State Dep. has distributed the balance on hand among the Venezuela claimants, according to their certificates!—But this is only an incident to the flagrant demoralization which prevails. What next?

I wish a Presdt with a little common sense, common justice & common liberality who is not always brutal or vindictive. Think of the Presidential quarrels—ending in indignity to two members of the cabinet—the chairman of a Senate Comttee—distinguished senators—a Minister to London—the dean of the diplomatic corps, an excellent friend who has returned home embittered to our country & now the Russian Minister, whose govt. I am assured, has approved his course entirely;[3]—to say nothing of numerous other cases. Verily we have "a man of quarrels" for Presdt.

I hope Mrs Schurz & yr children are well not forgetting the infant Astyanax.

Let me hear from you & give me yr vista of the Future.[4] The New York & Mass. Conventions this week may have an important influence.[5]

Ever Yours,   Charles Sumner

ALS DLC (84/429, PCS)

1. In his Nashville speech, 20 September 1871, Schurz declared that a general amnesty to ex-Confederates "should no longer be delayed" (*Speeches, Correspondence and Political Papers of Carl Schurz*, ed. Frederic Bancroft [1913], 2:258).

2. In pursuing his policy of annexing Santo Domingo after the Senate had rejected the treaty, Grant "violates the Constitution," stated Schurz. He told his southern audience that he would not work to reelect one "whose reelection . . . will be a justification and encouragement to all future Presidents in committing acts of usurpation reaching still further" (ibid., 272).

3. CS's "excellent friend" was probably Henry S. Sanford, a correspondent of long-standing. Sanford had originally been appointed as minister to Spain in 1869, but the Senate delayed confirmation and Grant then appointed Daniel E. Sickles. Sanford subsequently resigned as minister to Belgium (see Sanford to CS, Brussels, 3 May 1869, 46/595, PCS). Konstantin Katacazy had for some time been embroiled in a series of quarrels with Secretary Fish, most recently for trying to obstruct the Treaty of Washington and for writing articles hostile to the president. Katacazy wrote CS 21 August that Fish wished to have Katacazy recalled, but that his only charge was that "ma personnalité lui est désagréable" (my personality is disagreeable to him) (Staten Island, 55/223). Fish informed the Russian government in the fall of 1871

that Katacazy should be recalled, and on 16 December he was (Allan Nevins, *Hamilton Fish* [1937], 503–11).

4. Schurz wrote from St. Louis 30 September (55/366) summing up informally the points he had made in his Nashville speech. He refused to support Grant or a Democrat for president and looked toward a third party. Young men in the South, he wrote, were ready "to uphold the new order of things *in every direction*, if they are generously treated." Schurz believed the South would provide "a power fit to absorb the best elements of both parties" and CS should lead that party.

5. The New York Republicans, meeting at Syracuse 27–28 September, threatened to split over rival delegations seeking to represent the Tammany Hall district (*New York Times*, 26 September 1871:4, 5).

To Reverdy Johnson
private

Cotuit—Mass. 27th Sept '71
—at Mr Hooper's for 3 days—

Dear Mr Johnson,

I am glad you felt it yr duty to call Sir Roundell Palmer to account for his speech & especially for that part in which he reduces the sphere of Arbitration to a *minimum*, if not "to the little end of nothing." [1] This great boon can be of little value, if a nation is privileged at any time to set up a point of honor, feigned or real, against its application.

Arbitration, according to the Congress of Paris, & according to common sense, is a substitute for War, precisely as a judicial tribunal became the substitute for the Ordeal by Battle. As well insist on the old Ordeal in certain cases instead of a court, as adopt the argument of Sir Roundell. If Arbitration is what it ought to be, it is for just such cases as Sir Roundell discusses. Its sphere should be co-extensive with War.

I had read this part of Sir Roundell's speech with something of feeling, & enjoyed relief by yr generous treatment of the question.

You content yourself by showing the liability of England from failure of due diligence with regard to the ships,—without considering the other grounds or saying any thing on the Rule of Damages. The latter question seems to me important under the existing Treaty. Shall it be merely the value of individual ships & cargoes, or the larger damages foreshadowed by Mr Cobden in his speech in Parlt[2] & his letter to Mr Edge? I do not doubt that it ought to be the latter, &, I understand this is the opinion of Mr Horace Binney.

I do not understand yr limitation of our grounds on pp. 19 & 20. It seems to me that we may take any ground at Geneva that could have been taken under your Treaty, & especially the first of yr grounds mentioned on p. 12.[3]

I hope you will pardon me if I suggest that on p. 11 you seem to have confounded my position with that of Mr Seward. I never insisted "as a *sine qua non* to any settlement by arbitration that the question of belligerency should be embraced."[4] Mr Seward always did. Therefore, I have abandoned no view on this point. Nor did I ever insist that England by its Proclamation of Neutrality, without subsequent damages, become liable to us. This was Mr Seward's position; never mine.

My position was identical with yr own as admirably stated in yr despatch of Feb. '69 & reproduced in yr pamphlet on p. 12. The Proclamation I presented as one link in the chain by which the liability of England was fixed. The two other links were—(1) the escape of the ships & (2) the hospitality to the ships in English ports.

Showing the liability the next question is the Rule of Damages. But all these questions seem to me open under the existing Treaty &, I understand, will be presented at Geneva.[5]

But I have little confidence of any satisfactory result. I fail to see in the present Administration any thing pointing that way. Imagine this great lawsuit intrusted to Mr Bancroft Davis!

Believe me, my dear Sir,

very truly Yours,   Charles Sumner

P.S. Your statement of my position on p. 11 is that which has been constantly made by the English journals, not one of whom printed my speech.—My position appears in the Senate speech April—1869 also in the speech at Worcester Sept 23d 1869 & is co-incident in all respects with that of the despatch of Sept 26th 1869, signed by Mr Fish, &, on the question of liability co-incident with yr despatch of Feb. '69.[6] The English did not choose to understand me & their misapprehension has been substituted for the truth. I am not surprized that the frequent repetition of this substitution has made an impression on you.[7]

ALS MdHi (84/434, PCS)

1. In his pamphlet "A Reply to a Recent Speech of Sir Roundell Palmer on the Washington Treaty and the Alabama Claims" (1871), Johnson rebutted Palmer's assertions in his Parliament speech of 4 August 1871. Palmer criticized the Johnson-Clarendon Convention because he feared the arbitrators would have debated the validity of the Queen's Proclamation of May 1861. In his pamphlet Johnson wrote, "the honor of England actually demanded that every question in controversy between the Kingdom and the United States which could not be settled by negotiation between themselves, should be submitted to arbitration" (4–5).

2. CS had cited this speech extensively in his "Our Claims on England." Cobden's speech of 13 May 1864 protested the specific and national damages that Great Britain

had inflicted upon the U.S. (*Hansard's Parliamentary Debates*, 3rd series, 175:496–505).

3. Johnson here named three grounds upon which the U.S. could base its claims: (1) Great Britain had violated international neutrality laws; (2) if not, the laws it passed "were intentionally left so defective"; (3) Britain failed to enforce any laws passed. On page 12 Johnson stated that the U.S. based its case on two grounds: (1) "the Proclamation of Neutrality was contrary to Public Law"; (2) Britain did not "exert proper care and dilligence."

4. Johnson wrote that CS's "support of the recent Treaty, I think, does him honor." He went on to state that CS's speech against the Johnson-Clarendon Convention was, however, "extravagant and unjust towards England." Now, by voting for the Treaty of Washington, CS had "abandoned" his stand on the belligerency question as well as "his pretension" that Great Britain "owed an indemnity to the United States themselves which could only be adjusted by millions of treasure and an apology."

5. Johnson responded (Baltimore, 4 October, 55/389) that he understood the treaty not to allow for any general or national damages, only those to individuals, and these were "to be limited to the value of the property destroyed."

6. See CS to George Bemis, 7 July 1869.

7. In his reply Johnson wrote that he had intended no "injustice" to CS in commenting on CS's April 1869 speech. Johnson had recalled in that speech, he wrote, that CS based the U.S. claims case on the British Proclamation of Neutrality, "but in this I am, of course, mistaken, as you have a more perfect recollection of the speech than I can have."

To Edward L. Pierce

Washington 27th Dec. '71

My dear Pierce,

Will you not help my Bill for Equal Rights?[1] Call it cap-stone, or key-stone, it is the final measure for the safeguard of our colored fellow-citizens. It will make them comfortable & happy.

Republican Senators must see its importance. My excellent colleague thinks more of Amnesty.[2]

God forbid that if my colleague were assaulted as I have been I should leave him in the lurch![3]

Ever Yours,   Charles Sumner

ALS   MH-H   (64/722, PCS)

1. On 7 December 1871 CS revived his Supplementary Civil Rights Bill, a measure he had been pressing since 13 May 1870. The bill stipulated that all citizens of the U.S. be "entitled to the equal and impartial enjoyment of any accommodation, advantage, facility or privilege" in all modes of transportation; in all schools; in restaurants, inns, and theaters. In addition, no citizen could be dismissed as a juror "by reason of race, color, or previous condition of servitude." Any laws that discriminated against persons of color were to be repealed or annulled. When the Senate

received a bill granting amnesty to ex-Confederate officials from the House on 20
December, CS moved his bill as an amendment (*Globe*, 42nd Cong., 2nd sess., 36,
241–45).

2. In support of his amendment, CS had declared that, since a bill was proposed
"that we should be generous to those who were engaged in the rebellion, I insist upon
justice to the colored race every where throughout this land." Henry Wilson responded that, although he disliked parts of the bill granting amnesty to ex-
Confederates, he would vote for it "not as a measure of justice to the South or equality
among citizens" but "as a thing of charity and mercy, of unmerited grace." He hoped
CS's bill could be considered separately at a future time (*Globe*, 42nd Cong., 2nd
sess., 20 December 1871, 240, 248–49).

3. Devoting his response to CS's letter chiefly to other topics, Pierce replied 14
January 1872, "I will do what I can, though I have been and still am a good deal
preoccupied" (Milton, Massachusetts, 56/139, PCS).

To Charles N. Hunter

Washington 29th Dec. '71

Dear Sir,

It is not in my power to be with you at yr celebration of Emancipation.[1]

Allow me to say that on that anniversary you should pledge yourselves to insist upon Equal Rights & not to stop until they are secured.

There is a Bill now pending in the Senate, having this object. Will
not our colored-fellow-citizens help its passage? They should make
themselves felt.

How a Republican can hesitate, it is difficult to understand—especially a Republican owing his seat to colored votes. There are some who
urge Amnesty first. I am for Justice first. I begin with Justice to the
colored race. When this is assured, it will be easy to grant the other.

Accept my thanks for the invitation with which you honor me &
believe me, dear Sir,

Faithfully Yours,   Charles Sumner

Chas N. Hunter Secretary &c[2]

ALS   NcD   (84/479, PCS)

1. Charles N. Hunter (c. 1852–1931), then assistant cashier at the Freedmen's
Savings and Trust Company, Raleigh, and later a newspaperman and school principal,
sent CS an invitation on behalf of the colored people of Wake County and North
Carolina to attend their Grand Emancipation Celebration, 1 January 1872. Hunter
wrote that he and his fellow freedmen wished to "behold one who has ever stood as a
wall of brass in defense of the liberties of our people" (Raleigh, 22 December 1871,
55/716, PCS).

2. Written in another hand.

To George William Curtis

[Washington] 30th Dec. '71

My dear Curtis,

The room at Hooper's shall be ready, but do not forget, that, on arrival you are to dine at 6 o'clk with me. I expect you at my pot-luck.[1]

I envy you holidays at such a home & with the Shaw family near.

I wish you would help my Bill for Equal Rights. The colored people are stirring, &, I think, will show force at the opening of Congress. It is first in order as an amendt. to the Amnesty Bill.

My Bill is an application on the national theatre of an argt. made by me in Boston as long ago as 1849 where I first employed the term Equality before the Law. Its theory is that in all institutions, functions or privileges created or regulated by law, there shall be no discrimination on account of color. Now is the time to secure this immense boon, which is the final fulfillment of the promises of the Declaration of Indep. Pass this,—& let me drop, & oblige yr colleagues in support of Grant. Willingly will I go. Give me up; but save the Bill.[2]

Good bye!

Ever Sincerely Yours,   Charles Sumner

AL   MH-H   (84/482, PCS)

1. Curtis wrote CS 26 December 1871 (Staten Island, New York, 56/009, PCS) about his forthcoming trip to Washington. He added, "In all the battling meanwhile, I mean that you & I shan't fight if *I* can help it!!"

2. *Harper's Weekly* (30 December 1871:2) devoted a column of praise to CS's Supplemental Civil Rights Bill.

To Henry W. Longfellow

Washington 25th Feb. '72

Yr handwriting,[1] dear Longfellow, is like sunshine from my large pile of letters,—& is next to seeing you.

Today is charming but I am at home working always. There is no end to it. I am weary, & often say, how much longer must this last?

I have been gratified by the success of the Civil Rights Bill.[2] I begin to believe it will become a law. Then will there be joy. Very few measures of equal importance have ever been presented. It will be the cap-stone of my work. Then, perhaps, I had better withdraw & leave to others this laborious life.

My proofs linger painfully.[3] Years & labor & money must yet be spent before the work is completed. And who will care for the ponderous collection? J.[ohn] O.[wen] will be faithful always, but he is good & original.

Here is a letter from R. W. E., which you will read with interest. Curtis thought it worth more than any diploma or office.[4] I am much touched by it, & shall keep it among my treasures. Good bye! God bless you!

Always Yours,   Charles Sumner

ALS   MH-H   (84/536, PCS)

1. Either Longfellow's letter of 15 February or [25? February 1872] from Cambridge, 56/481, 532, PCS.

2. On 15, 17, 31 January and 5 February CS spoke for his amendment to the amnesty bill. The amendment passed the Senate 9 February, with Vice President Schuyler Colfax breaking the 28–28 tie. However, the amnesty bill as amended failed (33–19) to receive the necessary two-thirds vote (*Globe*, 42nd Cong., 2nd sess., 381–91, 429–35, 726–30, 821–25, 828, 919, 929).

3. CS was working at this time on volume 5 of his works, covering speeches through July 1861.

4. Emerson stayed with CS 5–7 January, a visit he described as "throughout interesting & agreeable" in a letter to Lidian Emerson on 9 January: CS "works incessantly at his desk with a selfpossession that no company can disturb, & yet fails not to supply every want, convenience, & furtherance to his guests" (*Letters of Ralph Waldo Emerson*, ed. Ralph L. Rusk [1939], 6:195). Although Longfellow returned Emerson's letter, c. 28 January, to CS (56/537), it is unrecovered. According to Emerson's daughter, the letter contained both praise and political advice for CS (Ellen Tucker Emerson to Edward Emerson, 4 March 1872, *The Letters of Ellen Tucker Emerson* [1982], 1:646–47).

To Wendell Phillips

[Washington] 10 March '72

My dear Phillips,

Yr words cheer always.[1]

There was a menace of my old pangs on the heart,—but bromide of potassium & rest are bringing relief. Nothing would have been known of it, except that I was constrained to excuse myself from duties in the Senate & thus tell my case.[2]

The political future causes much anxiety. I have a profound sense of Grant's unfitness for the Presidential office. He is the man of rings, &

the great quareller. He has a military ring at the White House, & a senatorial ring here. He has quarelled more than all other Presdts. together.

How do you cast the horoscope? Which way do you incline?[3]

Ever Yours,   Charles Sumner

ALS   MHi   (84/553, PCS)

1. In his letter to CS of 3 March (56/571, PCS) Phillips expressed concern for CS's health and urged him to take care of himself "for our sakes who want to lean on you & so need a strong man."

2. CS had been intermittently absent, because of an angina attack, from 4 to 16 March (Prc, 4:510).

3. Phillips had recently supported Benjamin F. Butler for governor and on 15 January 1872 had included a tribute to him in a speech to ex-soldiers in Dayton, Ohio (Irving Bartlett, *Wendell Phillips* [1961], 357–61; *New York Times*, 16 January 1872:1). Phillips wrote CS 11 April ([Boston?], 57/126) that if the burgeoning Liberal Republican movement hoped to get "support from the *Labor* movement—it will get *none* for *C. F. Adams* or *Trumbull* or *G.[ratz] Brown*. I should myself & I judge most others of that ilk, would support Grant in preference to either of those three."

To Samuel Bowles

[*Washington*] 14th March '72

Dear Mr Bowles,

I have read yr note carefully,[1] & shall do what after consideration seems best. Meanwhile I shall be glad to hear from you.[2]

Ever Yours,   Charles Sumner

ALS   CtY   (84/555, PCS)

1. In his letter of 9 March 1872 Samuel Bowles (1826–78), editor of the *Springfield Daily Republican*, urged CS to endorse the nominating convention of Liberal Republicans scheduled to meet in Cincinnati 1 May. Before the convention, wrote Bowles, CS should "present your arraignment of Gen. Grant,—both of course within the line of fealty to the republican party, and, indeed, especially as duties owed to the republican party. We can save the party now, only by changing its candidate." He informed CS that Massachusetts "waits for you in this matter." He thought anti-Grant Republicans must work to prevent either a division in the party or "the necessity of any of us leaving it" (Springfield, Massachusetts, 56/605, PCS).

2. Bowles responded on 18 March, congratulating CS on the announcement, 15 March, that CS would preside at the Cincinnati convention (*Boston Daily Advertiser*, 16 March 1872:1). Bowles expressed hope that "a bold, vigorous movement" would dislodge Grant's grip on the Republican party and that congressmen would speak out against the president (56/649).

To Henry Wilson

Senate Chamber 18th March '72

My dear Sir,

Major Poore astonished me yesterday by showing me a telegram in the Boston *Advertiser*, setting forth sundry things about me & attributing to me certain sayings.[1]

From beginning to end in every allegation & every sentence this telegram is a strange & unaccountable mistake. Not one thing set forth about me or attributed to me is true, except that I had an interview with you—very brief, casual & confidential.

As every body refers this telegram to you, I think you will see the propriety of pronouncing it at least so far as you are concerned a wretched humbug.

If this is founded on any conversation between us, ⟨you have surely made⟩ there is a strange mistake. I never said to you nor have I said to any body, what is attributed to me about my future course; nor did I say what is attributed to me about yourself.

If you think proper to hand over to the public in turn all conversations ⟨of a private intimate character you hold⟩ with ⟨your⟩ a colleague, [*inserted from margin*] who has been your friend, & always treated with trust & kindness [*insert ends*] I think I may justly expect that they shall be stated with reasonable accuracy & I suppose you will not object to my stating yr conversation at my house this winter concerning Genl Grant when you said "Well, he is a *cuss*" with a good accent on *cuss*.

Truly Yrs   C. S.

P.S. Since writing this letter I have recd one from you[2] which shows that this strange jumble is traced to you. I hear also of yr conversation with others about me.

Dft   MH-H   (64/728, PCS)

1. Along with its announcement that CS would preside over the Liberal Republican convention, the *Boston Daily Advertiser* telegram (16 March 1872:1) went on to state that CS had told Wilson that CS's break with Grant was irreconcilable; CS planned to "attack the President and his administration with all the vigor and effect at his command." CS had also allegedly informed Wilson that "their political paths must soon openly diverge."

2. In his letter, 17 March 1872 (Washington, 56/645, PCS), Wilson wrote "in haste" that he had not wished to have their political differences made public. Of their break over Grant, Wilson stated, "I have feared it for months—have worked for a

long time to prevent it. . . . I have not seen a moment for more than twenty [*years*] that I would not do anything in my power for you." Wilson "clung" to the hope that the two could remain "personal friends." CS wrote Edward L. Pierce, "Wilson after a cock & bull story about me has run off to Conn. He is stranger than fiction" (22 March, 64/730). Massachusetts Republicans on 10 April endorsed Wilson for vice president (*New York Times*, 11 April 1872:1).

To Edward W. Kinsley
private

Washington 24th March '72

Dear Mr Kinsley,

Why will Mr Slack make misstatements about me?[1]—I have no quarrel with the Presdt. *He* has attacked me while I was in the discharge of public duties, treating him with all honor, & he has persisted in the attack. Mr Slack insults me by charging me with being controlled by a sense of personal injury. Humbug! I should despise myself, if even such conduct as the Presdt towards me could affect my public conduct. I am a public servant, & am governed by duty as such.

I have a profound sense of Genl. Grant's unfittness for the high office he holds & I tremble for my country at the thought of his re-election. The youth of this great Republic & mankind need a better example. Mr Slack does not think so; but I hope he will not misrepresent me.[2]

Ever sincerely Yours,   Charles Sumner

ALS   MBU   (84/561, PCS)

1. In an editorial, the Boston *Commonwealth* (23 March 1872:2) discounted recent rumors that CS would attend the Cincinnati convention, and welcomed CS's recent statement to a visitor that he would wait for the Republican convention before taking a stand in the forthcoming presidential election. "Unquestionably," wrote the *Commonwealth*, CS "feels deeply grieved at the indignity of his displacement from the foreign-relations committee and the recall of his friend Motley." The *Commonwealth* predicted that CS would "oppose the renomination of President Grant with vigor" but would then "doubtless remain passive" after Grant's certain renomination.

2. Replying belatedly on 8 April, Kinsley apologized for Slack's "unfortunate . . . wording of some paragraph in his paper," and assured CS that Slack remained his good friend. Kinsley informed CS that there was no organized opposition to Grant in Massachusetts. CS's friends would probably leave the Republican party if CS believed it necessary, "but your friends do not feel that that time has come." Kinsley would, he wrote, "as lief have Grant, as most any Republican" except CS (Boston, 57/100, PCS).

To Edward W. Kinsley

private

Senate Chamber 10th April '72

My dear Kinsley,

I did not write to promote any personal interest. I have none. I am a candidate for nothing. I desire no office. But I am not insensible to misrepresentation & injustice.

Never was the Boston press so hardened & hermetically sealed against even Fair Play where I am concerned. Even Slack cannot do justice to me. This madness for Grant upsets every thing. All this is laying up mortification & regret for the future.

Grant is *unfit*, & this will be confessed in history. I have no personal griefs—to influence me by a hair's breadth. I know my sincerity, & the sense of duty which governs me. His treatment of the Black Republic deserves impeacht. & it shews an insensibility to law & Constitution; so also the violation of our neutral duties & an act of Congress in the sale of Arms to belligerent France. Then comes his indifference to duty, making his office a plaything & a perquisite—all of which must be met, if the Republicans are guilty of the suicidal folly of renominating him.

The French Arms inquiry has already sustained me *in every essential point*, & before it is finished, will probably sustain me on the question of discrepancy between the accounts of the War & Treasury. But the Boston press, will never let this be known. [1]

I claim very little; but I have done the State some service, & I am trying to do more now. [2]

Ever Yours,   Charles Sumner

ALS ViWWL (84/572, PCS)

1. On 28 February 1872 CS spoke for his resolution that a select committee investigate the sale of arms from the U.S. War Department to France during its recent war against Prussia. In his speech CS declared that Americans had a right to know "if there is any . . . bog anywhere about our Ordnance Office, where millions whole have sunk." When the Senate committee subsequently called CS before it on 26–27 March, CS protested, saying that such a summons was "of doubtful propriety" and that the committee was not an unbiased body (*Globe*, 42nd Cong., 2nd sess., 1258–63; U.S. Senate, Select Committee on Sales of Arms to France, *Sale of Ordnance Stores*, Senate Report no. 183, 1872, 321–23, 335, 835–42, serial set 1497). Both the *Boston Daily Advertiser* (29 March 1872:2) and the *Boston Daily Journal* (27 March 1872:2) criticized CS for refusing to tell what he knew.

2. Kinsley replied that only one man could defeat Grant: CS (Boston, 24 April, 57/225, PCS).

To Hiram Barney
private

Senate Chamber 12th April '72

Dear Mr Barney,

That scrap is an invention, absolutely without authority.[1] Never have I said to any body what I shall do, if the Republican Convention commits the suicidal folly of pushing Grant for another term—least of all have I said that I withdrew opposition to Grant.

If I am silent it is because I can do nothing by which the cause of the colored people is in any way weakened or compromised. I stand by them always; but I do not regard Grant as a competent reptive. of their cause. How will it be with the other side?

I hope for the passage of the Civil Rights Bill in the House next Monday.[2] When this is a law, reconstruction is crowned.

Therefore, your first letter was most welcome.[3]

Ever yours,   Charles Sumner

ALS CSmH (84/575, PCS)

1. Hiram Barney (1811–95), a New York lawyer, enclosed an unidentified newspaper clipping with his letter of 10 April 1872 to CS (New York, 57/114, PCS). The clipping referred to a Washington *National Republican* statement that CS had declared he would "make no further opposition" to Grant's nomination and would support him if he were nominated in Philadelphia in June.

2. Barney wrote that if the Civil Rights Bill were adopted, "the mission of the republican party is ended." The House adjourned on 15 April after briefly discussing its Civil Rights Bill (similar to CS's) and on 20 May declined to consider it (*Globe*, 42nd Cong., 2nd sess., 2440–41, 3649). For the failure of a civil rights bill in this congressional session see DD, 2:545–47.

3. In his earlier letter to CS, 6 April (57/089), Barney had asked CS to speak out publicly for the Liberal Republican movement and its upcoming convention. In his second letter, Barney wrote that when he had seen the *National Republican* item about CS, he feared his first letter had been offensive.

To Henry W. Longfellow

Senate Chamber 25th April '72

Dear Longfellow,

You will be glad to hear of N. A. who dined with me yesterday, hale & hopeful.[1] He is Midas in capacity. Last year he bought a piece of land here for $8000, & now finds it more than doubled. He seems to have great expectations in South Carolina, not merely pecuniary, but politi-

WILL ROBINSON CRUSOE (SUMNER) FORSAKE HIS MAN FRIDAY?

From Harper's Weekly, *20 April 1872. "If I am silent it is because I can do nothing by which the cause of the colored people is in any way weakened or compromised" (to Hiram Barney, 12 April 1872). Cartoon by Thomas Nast. Courtesy of the U.S. Senate Collection.*

cal;—but I found that he had not taken steps to establish a domicile there which would be necessary to his Congressional aspirations.

I do not know if you note the disturbance of the political sky with the uncertainity as to the future. The Boston press has more than its habitual meanness, if not falsehood. It is promised to Grant, & its agents here, who do not incline that way, are warned that all their despatches must be for Grant, & no friendship for any Senator must interfere with this rescript. The papers there are hermetically sealed against all which does not make for Grant.

Meanwhile I say nothing, though under great pressure, being determined when the whole field is clear to take that position in which I can best serve the country & especially continue to maintain the rights of the African race.[2] As the discussion proceeds I think Grant's chances become less. But I do not prophecy. Schurtz thinks Grant, if he continues a candidate, will not have more than 6 States in the Electoral College. My hope is that he may have the patriotism to withdraw & give us peace. His name divides instead of uniting—the party.[3] — Good bye!

Ever Yours,   C. S.

ALS   MH-H   (84/577, PCS)

    1. Longfellow's brother-in-law, Nathan Appleton (1843–1906).

    2. Francis W. Bird repeatedly implored CS to speak out against Grant and asked CS's permission to place his name in nomination for president at the Cincinnati convention (Boston and Pittsburgh, 11, 15, 18, 23 April, 57/122, 159, 193, 217, PCS). After the New Orleans Convention of Colored People met 11 April, the black clergyman Henry McNeal Turner wrote CS that their resolution denouncing the Cincinnati convention had passed only because Liberal Republicans such as Schurz and Trumbull had voted against the Civil Rights Bill in the Senate. Turner wrote that he had, however, prevented the group from passing a resolution endorsing Grant's re-nomination and he would follow CS's advice exactly in the forthcoming campaign (New York Times, 12 April 1872:1; George Downing to CS, New Orleans, 17 April; Turner to CS, Savannah, 20 April; 57/188, 205). David A. Wells, economist and Liberal Republican, who had visited CS in Washington in order to get his endorsement of the Cincinnati convention, wrote CS 14 April that it seemed "pretty evident" from the New Orleans convention that the Grant organizers were "using the colored people to prevent your endorsement of the Cincinnati Convention." In his letter he begged CS not to "abandon a movement which more than any other man you have helped to commence" (Norwich, Connecticut, 57/155; DD, 2:542–43).

    3. Longfellow wrote CS 14 May (Cambridge, 57/340), "I was glad you had nothing to do with the Cincinnati Convention." He stated that "American politics puzzle me and annoy me, . . . and I turn away in rather a cowardly manner to more congenial things."

To Whitelaw Reid
private

Senate Chamber 25th April '72

Dear Mr Reid,

I enclose an extract from the Presdt's Message Dec 6—1869, where he states briefly the case *re* England. It is important in 2 aspects;

(1) As the highest notice to the world, including England, on the point what were "generically" the Alabama claims.[1]

(2) That the Presdt adopted before the world the claims for consequential damages, or as they should be called "national" damages. Such I called them in my speech.

This correction leaves open the question which will be uppermost next week as to the taste, or propriety of the Bancroft-Davis statement & claim. I do not doubt that every thing necessary could have been set forth ⟨without raising⟩ in a way to make us irresistible & blameless. But what could you expect from the hands to which this business was entrusted? Does H.[*amilton*] F.[*ish*] know any thing about it?

Of course England does not appear any better than our Administration.[2]

Ever Yours,   Charles Sumner

ALS   RPB   (84/579, PCS)

1. Since January 1872 the British and American governments had been arguing unofficially as to whether U.S. indirect claims had been, in fact, included in the Treaty of Washington (Adrian Cook, *The Alabama Claims* [1975], 217–25; see CS to Reverdy Johnson, 27 September 1871). Bancroft Davis's lengthy American case, prepared November 1871 and submitted to the Geneva tribunal on 15 December, included a section on indirect claims (*Foreign Relations* [1872], part 2, 1:1–204). Stating that it was not possible to calculate "the vast injury which these [*British-built*] cruisers caused in prolonging the war," Davis asked the tribunal to determine whether the U.S. should be reimbursed for all cruisers' damages to the U.S. after the Battle of Gettysburg (when, argued Davis, the Confederacy operated offensively only at sea) (188–90). When the Senate briefly discussed Britain's intentions regarding indirect claims 6 and 9 February 1872, CS remained silent (*Globe*, 42nd Cong., 2nd sess., 840–42, 907–9). Most recently Britain had presented its case, denying the U.S. right to submit a claim for indirect damages. In an editorial 24 April 1872:4 the *New York Tribune* stated that the U.S. had a right to submit any claims to arbitration, but how best to present and define those claims "is another matter entirely." The *Tribune* noted that none of "our leading publicists," or legislators, British or American, had presented thus far "any indication of a satisfactory and honorable solution" to these differences which had "causelessly arisen."

2. In an editorial 29 April 1872:4 the *Tribune* adopted similar language to that in CS's points (1) and (2). The *Tribune* lamented the fact that the "American case is virtually surrendered." It quoted a paragraph from Grant's December 1869 presidential message that pointed out that the Johnson-Clarendon Convention had treated widespread and long-range "'injuries resulting to the United States'" as mere "'ordi-

nary claims.'" Such injuries, Grant had declared, were "'in the increased rates of insurance; in the diminution of exports and imports, and other obstructions to domestic industry and production; in its effects upon the foreign commerce of the country; in the decrease and transfer to Great Britain of our commercial marine; in the prolongation of the war, and the increased cost, both in treasure and in lives, of its suppression.'"

To [George S. Boutwell?]
private & *confidential*

Washington [*c. 30 April 1872*]

My dear Govr,

Anxious to save the Republican party, now imperilled by selfish men, I turn to you. The cause of trouble is a man whose name divides instead of uniting the party. Let him withdraw. How after receiving honor from the party he insists upon dividing it & plunging the country into an internecine feud can be understood only when we consider the selfishness & vindictiveness of his nature.

You have a right to be heard. Appeal to him. Ask him to withdraw positively & unreservedly, & give us peace.

I write to you for yr private eye, according to our long intimacy, & with a sincere desire that we may all be saved the trial impending should he persevere.

Ever sincerely Yours,   Charles Sumner

P.S. An old M.C. now here tells me that he is astonished to find beyond the few Presdtial [strikers?] *nobody for him.*[1]

ALS   MLNHS   (84/603, PCS)

1. As a Radical friend of CS's and Grant's secretary of the Treasury, Boutwell is tentatively identified as CS's addressee. Boutwell wrote CS 19 June 1872, after Grant's nomination for the presidency, acknowledging an unrecovered CS letter of 15 June and expressing the "kindest feelings" for CS, but declaring that after eight years of close relationship with Grant, "I look upon him as a patriotic and honest man, capable in the place he occupies" (Groton, Massachusetts, 58/192, PCS). The date of CS's letter is based on similarities in language to CS's to Longfellow 25 April, above.

To Edward L. Pierce
private

[*Washington c. 8 May 1872*]

How you can call this article[1] "well-toned," I do not understand.

Have I ever failed in Republicanism? Has my voice been "drowned by intimidation or tuned to expediency"?[2] Have I not alone this winter pressed the principles of the Republ. Party to their consummation, while the Presdt was holding back? I am against Grant & Grantism,— & because I do not surrender[,] the Journal which has deserted to this unrepublican cause, insults me with the charge of desertion. My vows are not to Grantism.

Then the *Journal* talks of the Presdt's gross attack on me when I had never named him except in kindness & honor involving the degradation of an illustrious Mass. citizen in foreign service as having "a mixture of right & wrong."[3] The Presdt was the assailant & wrong-doer—all of which will yet appear.

C. S.

Who is responsible for the present rending of the Republican party? I insist that it is those Republicans who urged Grant & Grantism against the public conscience, & the known conviction of men who were in a situation to understand the case. Set this down as true; nobody here is for Grant & Grantism unless an office-holder or a ring-man. The *Journal* should have opposed the sacrifice of the party. *It should now*, although I fear it is too late.[4]

ALS   MH-H   (64/733, PCS)

1. Enclosed with this letter was a *Boston Evening Journal* editorial (6 May 1872:2; 64/735, PCS) entitled "Where is Charles Sumner?" The *Journal* found it hard to conceive of CS's "going over to the Democratic party, either formally or practically." The paper begged CS to review the whole political scene and endorse the Republican party's nominee. If the Democrats took the White House, the *Journal* contended, "Republican benefactions to the country in securing which Mr. Sumner has spent his whole public life, would be imperiled."

2. The *Journal* regretted that Republicans had not recently heard "the rallying call of one whose voice was never drowned."

3. The *Journal* called on CS to put behind him Grant's "undeserved and gross injury" to him, and termed their feud "a mixture of right and wrong on both sides."

4. Pierce replied 20 May 1872 that the Cincinnati convention's nomination of Horace Greeley on 3 May was not popular in Massachusetts, even among those who attended the convention. Although many Republicans might dislike Grant, they would stay with the party (Boston, 57/392).

To Charles W. Slack
private

Sunday
[*Washington 12 May 1872*]

My dear Slack,

I must thank you for the simple & direct denial of a falsehood about me carried by Baez who knows not truth, & which Mrs Howe should not have put in circulation.[1]

My course in this business has been simple & sincere. I have always thought that the West India Islands belonged to the blacks, but whenever there was any talk of annexion which was very slight I listened kindly saying nothing except that I should consider what had been said. This was my course to the Presdt.

In this whole business I know the absolute purity of my motives & my simple desire for what was best.

Persons are strangely changed when they begin to advocate the St Dom. scheme,—& so, pardon me, when they begin to advocate Grant. I can never think of my old friend Dr Howe without affection & admiration; but I condemn that influence which practised on his noble nature.

Boutwell was here for 2 hours today. He is the only person I see who does not regard Grant's election as already lost. If Grant is imposed on the country there will be no party issue—no question between the two parties, Republican & Democratic—but simply a personal issue between Greeley & Grant—between the two G's—the *great* G & the little g. On such an issue can a good Republican hesitate? Is not the pen mightier than the sword? The two are about to meet. The pen cannot be defeated. Let us save our party from being a personal party.[2]

Sincerely Yours,   Charles Sumner

ALS   OKtu   (84/680, misdated [? July 1872], PCS)

1. The Boston *Commonwealth* was printing a series of letters from Julia Ward Howe about her recent trip to Santo Domingo in February 1872. The Howes traveled to the island in order that Samuel Gridley Howe, as director of the Samana Bay Company, could negotiate an agreement to lease the bay (Harold Schwartz, *Samuel Gridley Howe* [1956], 313–14). In letter no. 4 (11 May 1872:2) Julia Howe reported that in a meeting with President Báez, Báez commented on CS's sudden change of opinion (from "entire approbation" to opposition) on Santo Domingo annexation. In a note appended to the Howe letter, the editor wrote that Mrs. Howe "must be wholly mistaken," for CS had never promised to support annexation. The editor concluded that CS would not "tie himself up by promises without conditions, as none more than Dr. Howe and his family have reason to know."

2. Slack replied 15 May that he was gratified to receive CS's "kindly note of Sunday" after so many differences over news items that had been "misinterpreted and misrepresented." He informed CS that CS's "dislike" of Grant was not popular in Massachusetts. Grant was after all the Republican party's leader and "old soldiers of the Republican cause should pardon many imperfections" (Boston, 57/347, PCS).

To Whitelaw Reid
private

Senate Chamber—15th May '72

Dear Mr Reid,

Perhaps I have no right to make any suggestion as to the conduct of the *Tribune*, but I cannot forbear expressing the hope that the withdrawal of H. G.[1] will be followed by an open exposure & treatment of the pretensions of Genl. Grant as a civilian.

It looks now as if the Presdtial. election would be a *personal* issue. Such the friends of H. G. should make it. The party argt. would be, then, of less avail. But the people must be prepared for this issue. Any thing that shews the unfitness of our military chief or illustrates his character will be in order.[2]

Sincerely Yours,   Charles Sumner

ALS   DLC   (84/587, PCS)

1. Greeley issued a statement that he would, "until further notice, exercise no control or supervision" over the *New York Tribune* (*New York Tribune*, 15 May 1872:4), and Reid became editor.

2. Reid replied 16 May 1872 that CS's note "strikes the exact chord we want." He asked if CS would write a series of anti-Grant editorials for the *Tribune* and promised to keep CS's authorship a secret if he wished (New York, 57/356, PCS).

To George Bemis

[*Washington*] May 20th [187]2

My dear Bemis,

I send you a House doct which contains longer & argumentative notes.[1] The Senate collection is larger, with sundry later notes; but ours is printed confidentially. The *Herald* boasts that it has printed all.[2]

I wish you would give me yr views on this strange proposition.[3]

(1) Should the claims be withdrawn?

(2) If withdrawn, should it not be by diplomatic or Executive act,— as by note or instructions to our agent & counsel.

(3) Is there any occasion or propriety for doing it by the treaty-making power?

(4) Is the proposed rule advisable?

Fish has sacrificed our case by the way in which he has treated it. I never called our damages "indirect" or "consequential," but always "national."

Was there ever such a muddle?

Ever yours,   Charles Sumner

Don't play the cynic & cold shoulder, but let me hear from you fully.[4]

ALS   MHi   (84/592, PCS)

1. Possibly House Ex. Doc. no. 282 or 324 (serial set 1517–19, 1521) containing the British case submitted to the Geneva arbitration and appendices of past correspondence. These papers were submitted to the House, per its request, on 24 and 26 April 1872.

2. On 15 May the *New York Herald* printed some 38,500 words, it claimed, of the entire U.S.–British correspondence on the U.S. case submitted to Geneva (16 May 1872:7).

3. After numerous cables across the Atlantic, on 10 May the British finally submitted a "Supplementary Article" for the Senate's consideration. Reviewing first both the British and American interpretations of the Treaty of Washington's statement on indirect claims, the article then stipulated, "Whereas the President of the United States, while adhering to his contention that the said claims were included in the Treaty, adopts for the future the principle contained in the second of the said contentions, so far as to declare that it will hereafter guide the conduct of the Government of the United States, and the two countries are therefore agreed in this respect: In consideration thereof the President of the United States, by and with the advice and consent of the Senate thereof, consents that he will make no claim on the part of the United States, in respect of indirect losses as aforesaid, before the Tribunal of Arbitration, at Geneva" (*Foreign Relations* [1872], part 2, 2:500).

4. The Senate began consideration of the supplementary article 13 May. On 25 May CS offered an amendment that "the determination of this question belongs properly to the discretion of the President in the conduct of the case before the tribunal of arbitration"; it was defeated 4–46. Subsequently the Senate ratified the supplementary article (43–8) after some change in wording. CS voted against its ratification (*Executive Proceedings*, 18:248–49, 262–65).

To William Lloyd Garrison
private

Washington 3d June '72

Dear Mr Garrison,

You will not doubt that I have recd yr frank note with pain,—for, I value yr sympathy & good opinion much. But I should have been untrue to my own sense of duty had I not spoken.[1]

I have a deep conviction of the Presdt's utter unfitness, & his evil & demoralizing example. I think I let you know this in our conversation last autumn.

Both of us have been charged in other days with saying too much & with bitterness in treating those who stood in the way of truth. I am sustained now as then.

As you do not see the Presdt. as I do, you are in the situation of those who did not see Slavery as we did.[2]

Sincerely Yours,   Charles Sumner

ALS NjMo (84/607, PCS)

1. On 31 May 1872 CS delivered a strong attack on Grant, "Republicanism vs. Grantism," in the Senate. Besides criticizing Grant for nepotism, cronyism, gift-taking, and violation of the Constitution in trying to annex Santo Domingo, CS stated that his party's "creed ceases to be Republicanism and becomes Grantism; its members cease to be Republicans and become Grant-men. It is no longer a *political* party, but a *personal* party. For myself, I say openly, I am no man's man, nor do I belong to any personal party" (*Globe*, 42nd Cong., 2nd sess., 4110–22). On 1 June Garrison wrote that CS's speech was "ill-judged, ill-timed, and so extravagant in its charges and bitter in its personalities as to neutralize whatever of just criticism can be found in it." He told CS, "You cannot separate General Grant from the party which put him in the Presidential chair, and which means to keep him in it, if possible, another term, being satisfied with his patriotism, integrity, and general administration; and, therefore, in stigmatizing him as an unscrupulous usurper and a venal self-seeker, you virtually pronounce it to be equally corrupt and untrustworthy" (Roxbury, 57/482, PCS). Garrison sent a slightly changed copy of his letter to the *Boston Journal* and it appeared in other newspapers as well (*Letters of William Lloyd Garrison*, vol. 6, ed. Walter M. Merrill and Louis Ruchames [1981], 231).

2. CS's mail reflects overwhelming support for his speech; blacks such as John H. Cook and W. U. Saunders wrote to congratulate him (Washington, 11 June, Baltimore, 13 June, 58/093, 128). Other critics beside Garrison included George William Curtis and John Greenleaf Whittier (Staten Island, 5 June, Amesbury, 12 June, 57/645, 58/111). Republicans convening in Philadelphia 5 June nominated Grant and Henry Wilson for president and vice president.

To Francis W. Bird
private

Washington Tuesday evng
[11 June 1872]

My dear Bird,

I lose no time in acknowledging yr letter & paper which came this evng. I see little of the Boston press, & I am at a loss to understand yr allusions to my correspondance with enemies,—& the disclosing my purposes.[1] Since my speech I have written—

(1) 1 letter to Longfellow

(2) 1 to Garrison acknowledging his letter immediately on its receipt, supposing it to be private

(3) 1 to Clarke acknowledging his defense.

(4) 1 to John Owen my proof-reader.

This is all—no "enemy" here.[2]

Nor have I even given a hint to a human being as to my future course. My right hand has never spoken it to the left. Of this I shall not speak until I can see the whole field, & especially the bearing on the colored race. I mean to fail in nothing by which they may be helped.

Therefore, all stories as to what I shall do or shall not, are inventions. Nobody will know my purpose sooner than yourself,—for I honor you constantly. But I seek two things (1) the protection of the colored race & (2) the defeat of Grant.

Ever Sincerely Yours,   Charles Sumner

I am at work here & shall probably remain till August. I have no other home.

I hope Howe is well.

ALS   MH-H   (84/601, PCS)

1. Bird's initial reaction to CS's speech was positive: "It is terrific, and if done six weeks ago, would have done terrible execution" (East Walpole, 3 June 1872, 57/525, PCS). No information as to Bird's allusion has been recovered. The Boston *Commonwealth* criticized CS's speech as not accounting for "difference of temperament" between Grant and himself. "Mr. Sumner has been ungenerously and contumeliously treated. . . . [B]ut, so far as we have gathered their sentiments since this speech, there is scarcely one that approves it as wholly just, or as likely to add to his fame" (8 June 1872:2).

2. Of the letters CS lists, those recovered are (besides the one to Garrison, above) one to James Freeman Clarke [7 June], 84/610, and two to Longfellow, 7 and 10 June, 84/613, 618. Between 1 and 11 June CS also wrote to Elihu Burritt on the peace movement, to Samuel Gridley Howe on a political appointment, to Francis Lieber answering a scholarly question, and to Anna Cabot Lodge justifying his speech (84/605, 609, 612, 617).

To Hiram Barney
<u>private</u>

Washington
4th July '72

Dear Mr Barney,

What is the outlook?[1] The Democrats will nominate G? What then?

(1) Will the whole party sustain him?

(2) To what extent will there be defection from the Republicans? I hear of sporadic cases, & note the manifestation in Ill. The Boston *Journal* puts New York among states sure for Grant. I had supposed otherwise. How is this?

I write to you, because I know yr sympathies & that you are calm.

Ever Yours   Charles Sumner

How do you forecast Penn? Grant's friends admit defeat in Oct. but insist that they *shall* recover the State in Novbr.[2]

ALS   CSmH   (84/621, PCS)

1. Barney kept CS informed of New York politics and on 15 June 1872 (New York, 58/144, PCS) Barney wrote CS that the New York *Evening Post* would probably support Grant. A slim chance for a change would be the withdrawal of Greeley, but probably, he wrote CS, "we shall have to defeat Grant with Greeley."

2. Barney gave CS an updated report on 6 July (58/304). Barney expected the Democrats to nominate Greeley in Baltimore on 9 July and the Republicans in the countryside, but not the city, to vote for Greeley. He calculated that New York, Illinois, and twelve other states would definitely elect Greeley, and perhaps another four states as well. Although not a strong supporter of Greeley, Barney wrote, "he is the only hope of salvation from Grantism."

To Francis W. Bird
<u>private</u>

Washington 9th July '72

My dear Bird,[1]

W. B. S. means Mr Spooner. He has been unjust to me for sometime.

I hear from Robinson who is against Greeley.[2] So are the colored people.[3] My anxiety is there, & my purpose is to take the course which will be best for them.

Ever Yours,   Charles Sumner

I hope Howe is well; but I do not hear from him. I suppose he too is another W. B. S.

ALS   MH-H   (84/624, PCS)

1. CS's most recent recovered letter from Bird was that of c. 1 July 1872 in which Bird enclosed a request from the New York National Liberal Republican Headquarters for CS to speak or write on behalf of the new party. Bird wrote that Massachusetts was ready; "we only need you for a leader" (Boston, 58/275, PCS).

2. William Stevens Robinson, then clerk of the Massachusetts House of Representatives, had written CS 16 May that Greeley was a "most unfit man for President." He did not provide an appealing alternative to Grant, said Robinson, and could not reform U.S. politics. "His nerveless grasp could not even suppress the local Ku Klux, much less another Southern rebellion" (Boston, 57/358). Unless CS misdated his letter to Bird, he could not have received Robinson's of 11 July, which again expressed dissatisfaction with both Greeley and Grant.

3. As indicated above, CS to Garrison 3 June 1872, most of CS's mail from blacks supported his anti-Grant stand (see also William N. Taylor to CS, New York, 24 June, 58/242). Frederick Douglass, however, wrote CS 5 July from New York that, while he admired CS's recent speech, he disagreed with him about Grant. He asked CS to "take part with neither [*candidate*] in the present canvass—and leave the rest to time and events" (58/300).

To Gerrit Smith
private

Washington 9th July '72

Dear Mr Smith,

You supposed that I should call yr remarks unjust? Did you not feel that they were unjust?[1]

I write for no controversy. You make a personal assault on me & charge me with personal motives,—forgetting the elaborate conversations at your house & afterwards at my own where I disclosed to you my deep sense of Genl. Grant's unfitness—& the extent to which my conscience had been shocked by his conduct.[2] You forget how I unfolded to you my interest in Hayti & her struggling people, which I was taught in childhood to cherish,—how happy I was in carrying through the act acknowledging the independence of the Black Republic,—how from that time I watched its fortunes & tried to serve it—how, when I became aware of the utterly heartless & insensate conduct of Grant to that people, I was indignant, as when Kansas was assailed, the case being as bad as that of Kansas,—you forget how sympathetically you listened *then*; & now, when acting simply according to these convictions, hoping to do something for my country, you assail me by substituting personal motives for that honest judgment which on my conscience I was obliged to give. I never deserved your sympathy & support more than now, &, never, in the course of a life which has had your praise was I more sincere & simple in the discharge of my duty.

In sustaining yr allegation of personal "dislike," you are pleased to invent with regard to my early life.[3] If you will kindly ask any body familiar with it, you will see how imaginative you have been. But I am at a loss to understand what my early life has to do with this.

I never disliked Grant. When you allege that, you again invent. On the contrary I was his sincere friend & supporter until I became aware of his course in Hayti, & the more I think of that, the more utterly indefensible it appears. It is *revolting.*—so I see it, & for this reason I began to judge him.

Is it just, when these things were known to you, that you should hunt for personal motives? I deny the whole imputation, in gross & detail.

Would it not have been more candid, more in accordance with the friendship which I had supposed safe against decay so long as life lasted, for you to have recognized the strength of my convictions, & not questioned their honesty or sought to weaken them by invention about my early life?

I believe Grant essentially unjust, & I am sorry to see that his defenders seem inspired by his character. This is natural.

I send you a speech marked, & ask if you are just to me with regard to the Douglass incident.[4] It was because Douglass had recd indignity on board the boat, that the neglect of the Presdt became conspicuous. You say, "certainly it is that Mr Douglass is *insensible of it.*" Believe me I did not refer to this incident until Mr Douglass in my own house, a fortnight before the speech, had complained of it.

You are mistaken about Mr Stanton.[5] I have abundance of concurring testimony. His most intimate friend during the latter months of his life, Mr Hooper, confirms it fully, & so do many others. And why should it not be known? I am in earnest. I wished to save the Republican party from the infliction of a second term, & what I said was true.

In defending his gift-taking,[6] you forget that it is "gift-taking compensated by office," which is the unprecedented offense.

I have before me yr letters of last autumn, very different from the assault you now make, where you say in reply to frank statements that you "*know* that they all proceed from deep convictions & an honest heart." You then add; "The idea of Grant's nomination would be as painful to me as it is to you, if I had your exceedingly unfavorable opinions of him"—Then again you say; "It was not necessary for you to vindicate yourself to me. You have lived for yr country & for all mankind."—I will not quote the praise that follows. Besides all this you say "I cannot ask you to vote for Grant, nor even to forbear voting against him."[7]

Then you were not disposed to assail me & to find excuses in imagined contrasts of early life.

It is very painful for me to write this. But it seems to me that your own sense of justice will recognize its truth

Once you stood by the Slave; stand by Hayti now, which represents the Slave.

Sincerely Yours,   Charles Sumner

ALS NSyU (84/628, PCS)
Enc: "Speech of Gerrit Smith to his Neighbors in Peterboro, N.Y., June 22 1872"[8]

1. On 22 June 1872 Smith delivered a speech emphatically endorsing the Republican party and its nominees. The Republicans offered the only guarantee for the black man's future, argued Smith. In the latter part of the speech Smith criticized "Republicanism vs. Grantism." He sent a copy of "Speech of Gerrit Smith," remarking that CS would consider Smith's treatment of CS "unjust but not unkind" (Peterboro, New York, 5 July, 58/301, PCS).
2. See CS to Smith, 20 August 1871.
3. In his speech Smith offered as a motive for CS's "intense dislike" of Grant the different backgrounds of the two: "Mr. Sumner was born in affluence and bred in elegance" and had had "intercourse with some of the most cultured minds" in the U.S. and Europe. "President Grant, on the contrary, was a poor boy and a laboring man." Although, declared Smith, CS would not "undervalue" Grant, CS "would be one of the last men to see in him fitness for statesmanship or for the Presidency."
4. In "Republicanism vs. Grantism," CS had attacked Grant for slighting Frederick Douglass; Douglass had been "repelled from the common table of the mail-steamer on the Potomac" and later had not been invited with the Santo Domingo commissioners to the White House (*Globe*, 42nd Cong., 2nd sess., 4120). Where Smith maintained in his speech that the "incident exists but in Mr. Sumner's imagination," CS wrote "false."
5. Smith called CS's use of Stanton's dying words on Grant's unfitness for the presidency "but one other unjustifiable attempt . . . to depreciate the President." CS had emphasized too strongly the "strange thoughts" of a dying man, claimed Smith, for Stanton had habitually spoken of Grant "in terms of exalted praise."
6. Smith declared that "to single him out for blame in the case proves that General Grant is a basely persecuted man."
7. Letters of 23, 31 August 1871, Peterboro, 55/233, 274.
8. On his copy of Smith's speech CS wrote, "I return this for yr *private* eye. I intend no public controversy. To you shall belong the exclusive honor of attacking an old friend without cause. C. S. Yr allusions to me are unfounded in truth, besides unjust & studiously insulting. C. S."

To Gerrit Smith
private

Washington 17th July '72

Dear Mr Smith,

I am disappointed & pained by yr letter.[1] You have here seen fit to print about me an unjust & unfriendly assault, &, when yr attention is called to it, you vindicate it.

I do not write for controversy; but I wish to specify;

(1) You charge me with being governed by a dislike to the Presdt. which you trace to my condition in early life, when I tell you, that down to his outrage upon the Haytian Republic, I had never uttered a word or harbored a thought of him except in kindness.

(2) To sustain yr allegation about the origin of my sentiments towards him, you are pleased to indulge in an invention with regard to my early life. Should we ever meet again I shall be willing to recount my early life; but I shall not write about it. Suffice it to say, that, knowing nothing about it, you invent in order to sustain an unfriendly theory

(3) You say that Frederick Douglass never complained of the Presdt's conduct as an indignity, when I tell you that, *"in my own house,* two weeks before I made the speech, he did complain to me; but here again you misrepresent the way in which I use the treatment of F. D.

(4) You are pleased to be astonished that I should be indignant at the outrage on the Black Republic, because you & Garrison are not indignant.[2] But are you & Garrison keepers of my conscience? I must act on the mandate within, as you did, when you condemned the surrender of fugitive slaves & the Crime against Kansas, although many persons did not share yr judgment. My conscience was shocked by the Presdt's course towards the Black Republic precisely as yours was on these other things. He was guilty of one of the greatest crimes in our political history, revealing a heartless, lawless & tyrannical nature. And, because, you, who from partizan considerations choose to sustain the criminal, will not see it so, therefore I am condemned. Not so would you have written in other days.

But all who support an unjust man forthwith become unjust, & I am sorry that you are no exception.

While attacking an old friend like myself I wonder that you spared another old friend Chase, who does not disguise his partiality for Greeley or his opinion that he will be elected & make an excellent Presdt.[3] Why not attack him & invent some discreditable reason for his conduct?

Sincerely yours,   Charles Sumner

I enclose a letter just recd. which refers to you.[4]

Another letter from a friend in Boston to whom you sent yr assault complains of its "injustice."

ALS   NSyU   (84/640, PCS)

1. Smith replied 14 July 1872 to CS's charges (Geneva, New York, 58/402, PCS). He had not intended, he wrote, "any dishonor" to CS and hoped CS had not yet decided to vote for Greeley. "May Heaven save you from doing so!"

2. Smith asked CS why Grant's policy toward Santo Domingo and Haiti "appears so much worse in yours than in any other person's eyes." Although CS was the good friend of the black, so was Garrison, wrote Smith. "Good men were in full sympathy with the President" in his annexation policy.

3. Writing CS 2 August, Salmon P. Chase stated that his opposition to Grant stemmed mainly from "delayed amnesty and interference with Supreme Court in the matter of legal tender" (Narragansett, Rhode Island, 59/055).

4. The P.S. is not included in PCS. Smith replied on 21 July that the letter from D. C. [Curtiss?] which CS sent him might express honest opinions, but they were nonetheless wrong (58/524). The correspondence between CS and Smith continued in this, mainly repetitious, vein until 12 August, with Smith still professing friendship and respect for CS.

To Heman Lincoln Chase
private

Washington 20th July '72

My dear Sir,

Are you not under a misapprehension with regard to my position? You speak of "reconciliation," as if there were something to be done or explained between the Presdt & myself.[1] There is nothing. I am a public servant, trained to duty & no personal grievance can sway me. I seek the good of my country, & especially the protection of the colored race.

In my judgment Genl. Grant is *absolutely & completely unfit* to be Presdt & unworthy of a re-election. On my conscience I so find, after personal knowledge & great opportunity of ascertaining his character. His course towards the 800,000 blacks of Hayti deserves execration. It is one of the crimes of our history, & has exercised a painful influence over that struggling people. But in this he showed his selfish, heartless & tyrannical nature. Will you kindly tell me how I can support such a man? I ask sincerely for help; but I appeal to yr conscience & not to any party prejudice.

Down to my acquaintance with his conduct there as revealed in docts & in the conversation of the Haytian Minister, I was his steadfast friend

& supporter, & when I tried to rectify this alarming abuse & usurpation, he became angry & vindictive. Personally I care not for this; but it is part of that character which had full swing against the unhappy Black Republic & which did not hesitate to connive at the imprismt. of an excellent fellow citizen, Mr Hatch of Conn.[2]

Then again I am a Republican, devoted to Republicanism, & anxious to advance the cause. How can I vote for Grantism? In the individuality of the Phila candidate, that Republicanism to which I am vowed is all lost in discreditable & impossible pretensions which no good Republican can defend. I do not accept Grantism—or this new Philadelphia gospel. My soul rejects it. What can I do?

Believe me—not without a pang can I part from those with whom I have been so long associated. But are not the best Republicans now sustaining Greeley?[3] I have never declared for him, &, therefore, I ask, are not the more eminent statesmen of the party against Grant? You have for him the senatorial ring, whose names are familiar but I suppose no Republican would hesitate to say that as Republicans—in weight & character—Greeley, Trumbull & Schurz surpass them all. To these add now the admirable Govr Blair[4] of Michigan, a model of purity & ability.

Is not the coming contest typified in the two candidates—each a platform—Greeley with large heart & head, embracing all that is good & Grant representing Grantism?—

Daily I receive letters from all parts of the country & especially from colored persons asking counsel.[5] Thus far I have been silent, & I should be glad to continue so. Be assured—I wish to be silent. But can I refuse to answer these inquiries? And must I not answer according to my conscience?

Accept my thanks & believe me, my dear Sir,

Faithfully Yours,   Charles Sumner

ALS   MH-H   (84/646, PCS)

1. Heman Lincoln Chase (1829–84) wrote CS that he was "pained" over the "unhappy differences" between CS and the president. He understood why CS would feel the president had injured him, but Chase hoped that a "reconciliation" could occur (Boston, 18 July 1872, 58/476, PCS).

2. Orville E. Babcock, William Cazneau, and Joseph Fabens had had Davis Hatch, a Connecticut businessman, imprisoned in Santo Domingo in early 1870 in order to keep him from testifying against the annexation treaty. A majority of a Senate committee investigating the Hatch imprisonment found Hatch's imprisonment justified (Charles Tansill, *The United States and Santo Domingo* [1938], 395).

3. Would not opposing the Republican party be "injurious to interests to which your whole life has been devoted?" Chase asked CS. Did Horace Greeley truly "inspire confidence"?

4. Austin Blair (1818–94), U.S. congressman (Rep., Mich.), 1867–73.

5. Robert A. Gray wrote from Harrisonburg, Virginia, asking CS if blacks could depend on Greeley, while from Alexandria, Virginia, G. W. Mitchell declared that "no colored or white man, devoted to human rights," could support Greeley (17, 18 July, 58/459, 482). On 19 July Frederick Douglass wrote CS that his present position was a "subject of deeper solicitude" than ever before. Douglass urged CS not to "give up the almost dumb millions to whom you have been mind and voice during a quarter of a century" (Washington, 58/492). A joint letter signed by twenty-four black citizens of Washington, D.C., asked CS, "as the purest and best friend of our race," to advise them how to vote. They believed that "thousands of the intelligent colored voters of the country will be guided in their action by your statement and advice" (A. T. Augusta et al. to CS, 11 July, 84/635; Wks, 20:174).

"*Will the senator from Massachusetts do this, to make his words good?*" From Harper's Weekly, 17 August 1872. "*I do not accept Grantism—or this new Philadelphia gospel. My soul rejects it. What can I do?*" (to Herman Lincoln Chase, 20 July 1872). Cartoon by Thomas Nast. Courtesy of the U.S. Senate Collection.

To Hugh J. Campbell

Washington 3d Aug. '72

Dear Sir,

I have been detained in Washington through all the heats of this summer & now my face must be turned North rather than South. But I beg you to believe me grateful for the invitation with which you have honored me[1]

You are right in opposing the usurpations of the Custom House in the affairs of Louisiana.[2] Such conduct, though supported by the Administration, is so hostile to Republican Institutions & utterly indefensible, that all good Republicans should co-operate against it.

Pardon me if I add, that, unhappily this usurpation is only a type of the injurious pretensions so manifest in Presdt. Grant since his entry into civil life. The soldier to whom the country was so grateful is lost in the President.

The opportunity is now presented of placing an original Abolitionist in the White House, who while guarding the rights of the colored people, will seek concord. Because Democrats have adopted him as their candidate, I shall not be deterred from voting for him.

Besides securing a good Presdt. you must see that no persons receive your votes as Representatives in Congress, who will not at all times stand by the Equal Rights of our colored fellow-citizens.

Believe me, dear Sir,

Faithfully Yours,   Charles Sumner

Honble Hugh J. Campbell

ALS C   MH-H   (64/738, PCS)

1. On 23 July 1872 Hugh J. Campbell, a militia commander and president of the Central Executive Committee of the Regular Republican party of Louisiana, telegraphed CS from New Orleans, inviting him to attend their meeting 6 August (58/547, PCS). In a subsequent letter, 31 July (58/684), Campbell asked CS for copies of his "Republicanism vs. Grantism" speech and of his "Letter to Colored Citizens," 29 July 1872 (Wks, 20:173–95), in which CS endorsed Greeley for president: "Unquestionably the surest trust of the colored people is in Horace Greeley." Campbell wrote CS that his recent letter had "produced a profound impression here in the minds of the colored people" and Campbell's committee wished to circulate as many copies of it as possible. Blacks such as T. R. Geda of Burlington, New Jersey, John M. Taphet et al. of New York City, J. G. Frisbie of New York, and Edwin Belcher of Augusta (1 August, 3 August, 5 August, 59/001, 100, 110, 135) protested or questioned CS's endorsement. Generally, however, CS's mail supported his decision (see letters from Robert Morris of Boston, Edward H. Ogden of Philadelphia, W. U.

Saunders, William Schouler, all 1 August, Colored Citizens of Arkansas, 5 August, 59/018, 019, 029, 30, 146). CS received a letter of appreciation from Greeley. CS's endorsement, wrote Greeley, "fixes the Democrats by holding them to new pledges to treat the colored men as equals and fellow citizens" (New York, 31 July, 58/675).

2. Republicans in Louisiana had split into two factions, one a loose coalition of Liberal Republicans and some Democrats and the other organized around the Custom House Republicans, so named because officials there owed their appointments to the Grant administration (Joe G. Taylor, *Louisiana Reconstructed* [1974], 227–29, 210; Eric Foner, *Reconstruction* [1988], 506).

To Jacob D. Cox

Washington 6th Aug. '72

My dear Sir,

I am obliged by yr interesting & instructive letter.[1]

A friend with whom I was conversing the day before I recd yr letter on yr change of relations with the Presdt, remarked that there was a mystification on the question which ought to be removed by a plain statement. This is supplied by yr letter.

I know not if you would be willing to have this printed; but if not I wish you would write another for publication, so that the country may understand the case. Will you kindly consider this?[2]

Meanwhile accept my best wishes & believe me, dear Sir,

Faithfully Yours,   Charles Sumner

ALS OO (85/019, PCS)

1. CS had written Cox on 1 August 1872 (85/001, PCS) enclosing a clipping regarding Cox's forced resignation as U.S. secretary of the Interior in 1870 and asking if the story were true. In his reply, 3 August (Cincinnati, 59/102), Cox gave CS more details of differences between Grant and himself over Cox's refusal to allow a fraudulent claim to mineral lands. Cox wrote that he had "no confidence in any real purpose of Civil Service Reform on the part of President Grant."

2. Cox replied that he did not wish to "renew a personal controversy" by publishing any letter about affairs of 1870 (9 August, 59/260).

To Sarah J. Luce

private

Washington 11th Aug. '72

Dear Miss Luce,

Yr letter was kindness from an unexpected quarter. Accept the sincere thanks of one whose life has known trial.[1]

Hardest to bear is the injustice of friends. Mr Slack does not seem capable of making a correct statement with regard to me. All his allegations are false.[2]

Never did any human being make any tender or proposal to me from the Presdt.[3] On the other hand, I always said that the Presdt could choose his relations with me. The alienation was begun & continued by him. Of this be sure.

I have faith in Horace Greely, & sustain him in that faith, believing that the country will prosper more under him, & be elevated in character beyond any thing to be expected under Grant, who is in my judgment without elevation, & positively unfit.

It is not pleasant to differ from friends. Nothing but an irresistible sense of duty could carry me to this alternative. I could not help it—especially when I saw, that, though Horace Greeley accepted by the Democrats, there was a well-founded hope of that reconciliation which, in all my speeches I have declared to be my most earnest desire.

If Mr Slack has pleasure in his present course, he will persevere. But I doubt not he will regret it.

For yr kindness again I thank you.

Sincerely Yours,   Charles Sumner

ALS   N   (85/035, PCS)

1. Sarah J. Luce, apparently a relative of Charles W. Slack's, wrote CS that Slack had showed "us, at the house" CS's letter to him (unrecovered) and invited her to respond. She had arisen during the night determined to write CS at "this hour of trial" hoping to comfort him "when such a torrent of abuse from your old associates is rolling up like pestilential vapors around you." She urged CS to "stand firm. The greater the cross the brighter the crown" (Boston, 7 August 1872, 59/213, PCS).

2. Slack thought his latest editorial in the Boston *Commonwealth* was "moderate and fair," wrote Luce, but she disagreed. In that editorial (3 August 1872:2) Slack described his "grief" that "the foremost statesman of our country" would endorse Greeley for president. Such a move represented CS's "fall from his high pinnacle of public and political effort." The *Commonwealth* attributed CS's desertion of the Republican party solely to his "fierce and disheartening quarrel" with Grant, and called the endorsement "the extreme of folly and infatuation!"

3. Grant had "again and again signified his willingness" for a reconciliation, stated the *Commonwealth*, but CS had not agreed to one.

To John Greenleaf Whittier

Washington—11th Aug. '72

My dear Whittier,

I have not read Mr Garrison's letter.[1] Some one said it was unkind & I made up my mind at once not to read it—of course never to answer it. I never allowed myself to have controversy with him in other days, when we differed on methods, because, I knew he was earnest against slavery. I shall join in no controversy now.

Never have I acted more absolutely under the mandate of duty not to be disobeyed than in my present course. Profoundly convinced of Grant's unfitness & feeling that a man like Greeley Presdt would mark an epoch for humanity I could not resist the opportunity, especially when Democrats took him as their candidate & pledged themselves to all that is contained in the Cincinnati Platform.[2] From the beginning while insisting upon all possible securities & safeguards I have pleaded for reconciliation. This is the word which recurs constantly in my speeches. The South insisted that I was revengeful. Never. And now the time has come for me to shew the mood in which I acted.[3]

This is a painful experience. But we are not choosers in this world. Certainly I did not choose this.

I wish we could meet. All this hot summer I have passed here—but expect to be in Boston Wednesday.

God bless you!

Ever sincerely Yours,   Charles Sumner

ALS   MiMp   (85/037, PCS)

1. On 5 August 1872 the *Boston Journal* printed a public letter, dated 3 August, from William Lloyd Garrison to CS responding to CS's "Letter to Colored Citizens" endorsing Greeley. In his letter Garrison accused CS of deliberately timing his endorsement to influence the first state elections of 1872, those in North Carolina on 1 August: "You have," wrote Garrison, "unfairly availed yourself of opportunities to work a fatal division in the Republican ranks." CS was no stronger an antislavery leader than vice presidential candidate Henry Wilson, asserted Garrison, and CS's claims for Greeley's being "a life-time abolitionalist" were wholly without support (Dft, 85/006, PCS; *Letters of William Lloyd Garrison*, vol. 6, ed. Walter M. Merrill and Louis Ruchames [1981], 238–50). Whittier wrote CS from Amesbury that he hoped CS would not answer Garrison's "extraordinary letter," which disturbed Whittier in its "unfairness, or misapprehension" (8 August, 59/256).

2. The first two principles of the Liberal Republican platform called for the U.S. government "so to mete out equal and exact justice to all," and affirmed support for the Thirteenth, Fourteenth, and Fifteenth Amendments (*New York Times*, 4 May 1872:1).

3. In his "Letter to Colored Citizens" CS urged black voters to "consider carefully whether they should not take advantage of the unexpected opening, and recognize the 'bail-bond' given at Baltimore as the assurance of peace, and unite with me in holding the parties to the full performance of its conditions. Provided always that their rights are fixed, I am sure it cannot be best for the colored people to band together in a hostile camp, provoking antagonism and keeping alive the separation of races" (Wks, 20:193).

To Samuel Gridley Howe

Coolidge House Monday
[2 September 1872]

My dear Howe,

I am pained to learn of yr accident. You will be as badly off as I am.

Bird was with me when yr note came. He will see you tomorrow. When I am gone, the wild beasts will doubtless prey upon me. It will be for my friends to say what truth & justice require.[1]

I know the integrity of my life in all things, & I am sure that there are persons who will hereafter regret what they say now.

God bless you!

Ever Yrs,   C. S.

Passengers are aboard at 9 o'clock. But I go from T wharf in a tug at 11 o'clk. If you are not too feeble I shall be glad to shake hand with you there.

ALS   MH-H   (85/052, PCS)

1. CS was to sail for England on 3 September 1872. A letter signed by both Howe and Francis W. Bird published in the *Boston Daily Advertiser* 4 September 1872 (enclosed in Longfellow to CS, Nahant, 3 September, 59/482, PCS) stated that CS's "sudden departure" should not be construed as an evasion of the political campaign but that "absolute rest for a considerable period was prescribed as necessary."

To Francis W. Bird

for yr *private eye*

Liverpool Sept. 15th '72

My dear Bird,

You have doubtless recd. my cable despatch of yesterday declining absolutely my nomination for Govr.[1] This is all that was needed for the public & I trust it has been acted on promptly. What I write now is for *you alone*.

I heard of this nomination shortly after landing yesterday evng but could not believe it until it was shewn me in the London Times.[2] I lost no time in sending my declination, which is positive & without any possibility of change. I could not & would not serve as Govr; therefore, it is not honest for me to be a candidate. But it is not necessary to give reasons. Few things in my political life have troubled me more. Nothing has ever placed me in a position which at the time & under the circumstances was so painful. If I add that it has cost me a night without sleep you will appreciate at least the sensibility of my condition. I landed, feeling that I had gained by the voyage, but this has thrown me back & I expect today a weary journey to London.

I came abroad for rest & repose, & you put me in a position, which makes these impossible. How you, who have so kindly appreciated my condition, could have consented to this, I do not understand.[3]

I hope, my dear Bird, there will be no hesitation in this matter. *My name must be withdrawn at once*; but I assume that it has been. I cannot be a candidate. This is impossible, & it is strange to me that you do not see it. I must be left to my independence, so far at least as to fight this battle according to my own sense of duty & the line I have marked for myself. In this line the governorship has no place.—I write this positively, fearing lest some persons may over-bear you, & insist upon the nomination. I *insist on withdrawal* & shall make this effective; but I rely upon you. The utter recklessness of this nomination, & the total disregard of my feelings & sentiments, & of my position, surprize me. The possibility never entered my head.

Sincerely yours,   Charles Sumner

ALS   MH-H   (85/062, PCS)

1. Bird telegraphed CS 14 September 1872 from Boston, "Wait for letters concerning nomination" (59/502, PCS). On 11 September the Worcester convention of Democrats and Liberal Republicans had nominated CS for governor (Edward Avery and Nathaniel P. Banks to CS, Boston, 14 September, 59/503). CS apparently sent several telegrams of withdrawal (CS to Bird, 18 September, 85/065).

2. London *Times* (13 September 1872:10).

3. Bird wrote 15 September that he had done all he could to prevent CS's nomination; he could have stopped the movement in favor of CS in the conference committee "had not Banks with infinite warmth, & with his great magnetizing power, entered the field." Once CS's name was brought before the whole convention, "nothing could resist it." He hoped that CS would at least "by silence acquiesce" and not formally decline. CS's nomination, he wrote, "furnishes the best possible proof that they [*Democrats*] are sincere in the New Departure" (East Walpole, Massachusetts, 59/504).

To John Bright

London Maurigny's Hotel
Sept. 21st '72

My dear Mr Bright,

I was glad to see once more yr friendly hand.[1]

I am about to start for Paris to return here in about 3 weeks & to sail from Liverpool in the packet of 14th Novbr;—but I hope that we may meet before I go.

Let us make as much as possible of the Geneva precedent,[2] which I cannot but think is the beginning of an organized substitute for war. This is worth all its cost in debate & in money.

I wish I were entirely well; but if I were, I should not be here. Physicians & friends insisted that I must seek rest,—& so I weary myself with sights, streets & pictures; but this is rest.

I hope when we meet that I may find you again restored, so that we may have the advantage of yr splendid powers. Good bye!

Ever sincerely Yours,   Charles Sumner

ALS   GBL   (85/072, PCS)

1. Bright wrote CS from Glasgow that, learning of CS's arrival in London, he hoped to see CS "for a talk on what is doing on your side of the water" (17 September 1872, 59/526, PCS).

2. Bright wrote, "You will be glad, as I am, that the long dispute is disposed of, so far as arbitration can dispose of it." On 13 September 1872 the Geneva arbitrators awarded a gross sum of £3,200,000 ($15.5 million) to the U.S. for damages from the *Alabama* and other British-built ships (London *Times*, 14 September 1872:5).

To Edward Avery and Nathaniel Banks

Paris. 6th Oct. '72

Gentlemen,

I have been honored by your communication of the 14th. September in which you mention that the Democratic State Convention & the Liberal Republican State Convention had united in nominating me as their candidate for Governor of Massachusetts.[1]

This nomination was made while I was on a voyage to Europe & without any previous hint or suggestion that it was contemplated by any body. It was an entire surprize to me. I heard of it first on landing at Liverpool & lost no time in sending two separate cable despatches to Mr Bird absolutely declining it & insisting on its withdrawal.

For me there was no other alternative. I had left home with reluctance to exchange the fatigues & excitements of a political contest for that repose which had become essential to the re-establishment of my health. Good friends who knew my condition urged this step—to which I was reconciled only by the consideration that my physician had forbidden for a time all public labor on my part. The prompt declination which I sent was rendered necessary by the system of [life?] I had commenced.

In acknowledging your communication I beg to repeat this declination & to insist on the withdrawal of my name—most sincerely desiring that no person should vote for me. Beyond this personal wish, which I trust will not be disregarded, is the consideration, that, if chosen, I could not serve. At the same time I express my grateful sense of the trust reposed in me by the two Conventions which united in this nomination. My acknowledgments are especially due to the Convention representing fellow citizens to whom I have been for a long time opposed on important public questions. I beg them to believe that I am not insensible to their good will, which is enhanced by the sign it affords that past differences are absorbed in a common desire to secure for our country the incomparable blessings of peace & reconciliation under the safeguard of good government & with the principles of the Declaration of Independence as our rule of conduct. Hoping earnestly for the triumph of this cause, I am, gentlemen,

very faithfully Yours,   Charles Sumner

Hon. Edward Avery Presdt of the Democratic State Convention
Hon. N. P. Banks Presdt of the Liberal Republican State Convent.

ALS   MH-H   (85/080, PCS)

1. Bird wrote CS 17 September 1872 that although CS's withdrawal was a "grievous disappointment to our people, particularly to our democratic friends," he could understand it. He asked CS that in his letter officially declining the nomination he "ring out a brave watchword for the campaign" (Boston, 59/524, PCS). Sending this letter to Avery and Banks in care of Bird, CS wrote that he had not seen the newspapers and hoped his name had been withdrawn (6 October, 85/079).

To Henry W. Longfellow

Fenton's Hotel London
26th Oct. '72

My dear Longfellow,

On reaching here yesterday I was gladdened by yr letter of Oct. 4th.[1] Rain & fog have obscured London since my arrival; but as I drove from the station in a Hansom it seemed mighty.

Leaving Paris I stopped at Brussells & Antwerp on my way to visit Motley at the Hague. At Brussells I met Solvyns, just appointed minister to London,[2] who spoke with pleasure of meeting you at Lucerne.

Motley occupied the house of Cornelius de Witt, one of the best in town, very spacious & filled with pictures; but he was packing to leave on account of his wife's health who needs a dryer winter than can be had at the Hague. His position is all that could be desired. The remarkable Queen[3] is the familiar friend of his family & he is honored on all sides. When I saw his reception every where here & the gratitude of the Dutch people I shared anew his indignation at the base treatment he recd. from our govt., absolutely without precedent in our history or in the history of diplomacy—showing an utter want of justice or decency. How can such things rule in our country?

I have not read an American paper since I sailed out of Boston harbor. But I read two clippings enclosed by a correspondent (E. L. P.) from G. W. T. [C.].[4] Why will not Curtis let me alone? He praises me & then stabs me. He has been intimate with me all the winter in almost daily intercourse, with every opportunity of knowing the truth, but the necessity of his position compels him, like the other courtiers, to take up inventions. I have been pained & made unhappy at his course, which recalls Osric in Hamlet.[5]

I hear nothing of my slow-paced vols; but hope that the horses are moving. That is another load lifted for the present.

I think the Republic is safe at last in France. It is the only possible govt. there & this is beginning to be recognized. I liked Thiers.[6]

Pictures were fascinating, but I found less time for them than I anticipated—amidst the whirl of sights & temptations. I left Paris without seeing the Bois de Boulogne.

Have I already told you that Lowell wishes himself at home? I am always glad to see Emerson; but fear in this wilderness we may not meet.[7] Good bye! Yr family are once more all about you, except Charles of whom the Count de Gabriac spoke with great warmth & kindness.[8] Love to all.

Ever Thine—   C. S.

ALS MH-H (85/085, PCS)

1. Cambridge, 59/617, PCS.
2. Henry Solvyns, former Belgian minister to Italy (London *Times*, 30 October 1872:10).
3. Sophie (1818–77), wife of William III of the Netherlands.
4. One of the unidentified clippings Pierce sent CS may be a *Harper's Weekly* article of 21 September 1872. In a column on CS, George William Curtis wrote that CS's "judgment seems to us to be wholly unsound, and the course which he advises full of peril to the very cause that he seeks to serve."
5. The servile courtier in act 5.
6. When in Paris CS dined with Adolph Thiers, then president of the Third Republic (Prc, 4:538).

7. Both James Russell Lowell and Ralph Waldo Emerson were touring Europe.

8. Alexis de Gabriac, a French nobleman, whom Charles Longfellow had met en route to India in 1868 (HWL, 5:272, 571).

To the Duchess of Argyll

Rochdale at Mr Bright's

Nov. 14th—'72

My dear Duchess,

It is now after midnight & at 3 o'clk P.M. I sail. I am sorry to leave England & have been tempted to stay longer. But I should not be happy away from my post. This terrible calamity which has befallen Boston adds to my anxieties.[1]

I have enjoyed England & English people. It is hard for me to return without seeing you; but I have felt the kindness of yr family.

I was glad to see George Howard & his bright wife in their artist home. Dinner at Ld. Granville's & two nights at Chatsworth were most interesting.[2] At dinner at the latter place I found myself between two ladies, whom I had never forgotten, one of whom I had seen at Castle Howard & the other at Althrop,—both charming. From there I came to Mr B. today, & we have been talking for 10 hours.[3]

Saturday I was at Frampton Court where were the Motleys & the Queen of Holland. In London I saw Mrs Grote & Lady Augusta Stanley, also the S's of Alderley,[4]—also pictures, books, streets & sights, enjoying myself constantly, & gaining strength. If not entirely well I return much improved.

England is beautiful & English people are captivating.

I am glad to hear from Mr Bright of yr health & strength.

I cannot pardon myself for not visiting Inverary, & once more seeing you & yr family, to whom I send kindest regards. Goodbye![5]

Ever, dear Duchess,

Sincerely Yours,   Charles Sumner

The fire in Boston is a warning to England. I know not why all London may not burn in the same way.

ALS   CSmH   (85/087, PCS)

1. A fire in Boston, beginning 9 November 1872, killed thirteen people and caused $75 million damage.

2. The duchess's cousin, George James Howard, later ninth earl of Carlisle (1843–1911), and his wife Rosalind Stanley. Invitations from Lord Granville and James

Lacuita, on behalf of William Cavendish, seventh duke of Devonshire (1808–91), came to CS in London (Walmar Castle, 7 November; Edinburgh, 6 November, 59/ 741, 737, PCS).

3. Reflecting later on their last conversation on American and British politics, Bright wrote that CS left him "with the impression that he felt himself seriously ill, and that his life of work was nearly ended" (Prc, 4:543).

4. Motley's granddaughter was christened at Frampton Court. The others CS mentions are the writer Harriet Lewin Grote (1792–1878), Lady Augusta Stanley (c. 1822–76), wife of the dean of Westminster, and Henry Edward Stanley, third baron Stanley of Alderley (1827–1903), and his wife Fabia (d. 1905).

5. The duchess had pressed CS to visit her but then realized the inconvenience for him (Inverary, c. 26, c. 30 October, 60/057, 059). On 15 November she thanked him for his farewell letter and hoped they would meet again: "God has brought your heart's desire for your Country to pass—and I think everything else must be small, & not worth anxiety by comparison" (60/012).

To Whitelaw Reid

Phila. 29th Novbr. —'72
at Mr Furness's on way to
Washington—

Dear Mr Reid,

From my Dr. yesterday[1] I heard in authentic words the condition of Mr Greeley & I left New York with a heavy heart.[2] I do not doubt that the killing blow has been the perfidy & ingratitude which he experienced & the base attacks on his life & character. There is ample room for remorse in certain quarters.[3]

Ever sincerely Yours,   Charles Sumner

ALS   DLC   (85/091, PCS)

1. After arriving in New York 26 November 1872 CS consulted with Dr. Charles E. Brown-Séquard there (Prc, 4:544).

2. In the presidential election Grant defeated Greeley 3,597,132 to 2,834,125 and carried all the Northern states. Since mid-November, Greeley's mental condition had been unstable and he had been placed in a private sanitorium.

3. Reid acknowledged CS's letter the same day, stating he had just come from Greeley's deathbed. He hoped CS would write a "tribute to his [Greeley's] memory" for the New York Tribune (New York, 60/050, PCS).

To Willard P. Phillips

Washington 21st Dec. '72

My dear Phillips—
"Faithful found among the faithless!"—
I cannot comprehend this tempest.[1] The resolution, which is treated

so severely, is an "old inhabitant." I have already brought it forward in substance twice before this last motion, & recd the warm commendation of General [*Winfield*] Scott & Genl. [*Robert*] Anderson.[2]

I should not have introduced it the other day, if Major Poore had not called my attention to it & reminded me that it was the only one of all

"*Let us have complete restoration, while you are about it.*" From Harper's Weekly, *28 December 1872.* "*I know that I deserved better of Mass. than now*" (*to Willard P. Phillips, 21 December 1872*). *Cartoon by Thomas Nast. Courtesy of the U.S. Senate Collection.*

my early propositions in the Senate which had not been adopted. He thought the present a good time for it, & he is now surprized at its reception.

I think when it is understood, some of the assailants will regret their course. It will be vindicated fully, not only by myself but by others.

Meanwhile I am submitting to medical treatment chiefly by poisons to act on the spinal cord.

Yours is the only letter which has revealed any thing of the temper of the House.[3]

I know that I deserved better of Mass. than now. It was our State, which led in requiring all safe-guards for Liberty & Equality. I covet for her that other honor of leading in reconciliation. First in civilization Mass. must insist that our flags shall be brought into conformity with the requirements of civilization.

For yr friendship I am most grateful, while I am astonished at others.

Ever Sincerely Yours,   Charles Sumner

I should like to see Dr T's[4] letter. He is always excellent & most friendly.

ALS   MH-H   (85/107, PCS)

1. CS had introduced a bill on 2 December 1872 to expunge from the U.S. Army register and battle flags all "names of battles with fellow-citizens" (*Globe*, 42nd Cong., 3rd sess., 2). On 18 December the Massachusetts House of Representatives passed a motion of censure against CS, stating that "such a bill would be an insult to the loyal soldiery of the nation" (copy of resolution, Sumner Papers, Houghton Library). Phillips, a member of the Massachusetts House, wrote CS that his supporters did "all they could" to prevent the resolution and believed if the resolution had come up a second time "the whole thing would have been indefinitely postponed" (Boston, 18 December, 60/188, PCS).

2. CS had introduced a similar resolution on 8 May 1862, and on 27 February 1865 offered a resolution that no picture in the Capitol depict a Civil War battle (*Globe*, 37th Cong., 2nd sess., 2010; 38th Cong., 2nd sess., 1126).

3. CS's mail was soon to reflect indignation over the resolution (e.g., J. R. Potter, Boston, 19 December; John N. Barbour, Boston, 20 December; Wendell Phillips, [Boston], 20 December; Herbert Radclyffe, Boston, 20 December; 60/200, 201, 206, 208).

4. In his reply Phillips enclosed the letter (Phillips Papers, Houghton Library) from James Thompson (1805–81), an early Free Soiler from Worcester. Phillips had read Thompson's letter protesting the censure in the Massachusetts House. Supplying further details of the close vote to censure CS, Phillips added that he suspected Ben: Perley Poore, Butler's friend, of "malice aforethought" in suggesting that CS reintroduce the resolution. Nearly all the "instigators and advocates" of the censure resolution, wrote Phillips, were Butler supporters (North Andover, 27 December, 60/271).

To Francis W. Bird
private

Washington 29th Jan. '73

My dear Bird,

A false alarm! I have not touched the book, except once a week to look over a single proof.[1]

It is true; I know something of the heartlessness & ingratitude of men. My rule of fidelity differs from that of many. I believe that I have been true to friends & to principles.

I think you must mistake about E. L. P.[2] But how explain Howe? His reckless abandonment of an old friend is painful, especially when it runs to false charges.

When shall you arrive?[3]

Ever Yours,   Charles Sumner

———————————

ALS MH-H (85/147, PCS)

1. Bird had written CS 27 January 1873 concerned about CS's health (CS had not been present in the Senate since 19 December 1872; Prc, 4:549). It would "injure you far less," wrote Bird, to attend Senate sessions, "where with, perhaps, more excitement, there would be change which of itself is relief, than to drudge constantly over one kind of work" (East Walpole, Massachusetts, 60/439, PCS).

2. Edward L. Pierce had been negligent, Bird declared, in not working harder to convince certain Massachusetts legislators not to support the resolution censuring CS: "Ten words from him would have changed the two votes from his district." (On this letter Pierce wrote, much later, that Bird had been "very unjust" to him; Pierce had tried to persuade a key legislator and had testified on CS's behalf before a legislative committee.)

3. Bird wrote he hoped soon to visit CS in Washington in order to discuss the "state of things" in Massachusetts "with more frankness than, I fear, attends the information you get from others."

To Willard P. Phillips
private

Washington 23d Feb. '73

My dear Phillips,

The movement is a surprize to me,—entirely unexpected. So much for friends!—& what good & great names are signed to the petitions![1]

My health seems to be returning, so that I hope soon to be in my seat.

Smith is always true, & so is [*James*] Wormley here. Such friendship as I have had from these two make me forget the injustice & desertion of others. I wish Smith to visit me at the Inauguration. Pray send him.[2]

Ever Yours,   Charles Sumner

ALS   MH-H   (85/156, PCS)

1. Phillips wrote to inform CS that John Greenleaf Whittier had organized preparation of a petition calling upon the Massachusetts House to rescind its censure of CS. Phillips was especially pleased that Vice President Henry Wilson had agreed to sign the petition; his letter and the petition would be printed in the *Boston Morning Journal* (Boston, 21 February 1873, 60/578, PCS). Other signers included Agassiz, Peleg W. Chandler, Claflin, Dana, James T. Fields, George S. Hillard, Oliver Wendell Holmes, Howe, Longfellow, and Slack (*Journal*, 21 February 1873:2; 22 February 1873:3). Wendell Phillips wrote CS that he had not been asked to sign the first petition and enclosed a copy of his own request to the General Court of Massachusetts for rescission ([Boston], 22 February, 60/582).

2. Phillips replied that representative Joshua B. Smith was very active in preparing the petition to present to the Committee on Federal Relations; he would like to visit CS, but was needed in Boston (27 February, 60/595).

To Willard P. Phillips
private

Washington 16th March '73

My dear Phillips,

Yr friendship touches me much; but I am at a loss how after all my work through the war, accompanied by my action on the flag May 8th 1862 & Feb. 27th 1865, any body can charge me with insulting the soldier.[1] The whole story is a preposterous invention.

How impressive & beautiful were Whittier & Wendell Phillips. Clarke was direct & forcible. I have seen nothing but a fragment of Pierce,—& a very elaborate attack which I cannot understand from Winslow.[2] He must think strangely of me.

I am sure the time will come soon when that proposition of mine will be recognized; & the insults to which it is now exposed will make it more honored. Mass. can not afford to stand alone among civilized nations.[3]

Ever Yours,   Charles Sumner

ALS   MH-H   (85/167, PCS)

1. In their frequent letters in February and March, CS supplied Phillips with information on how the practice of placing names of military victories on flags began,

and Phillips kept CS posted on the progress of the anticensure movement (CS to Phillips, 1, 2 March 1873, Phillips to CS, 28 February, 4, 14, 16 March, 85/159, 161, 60/602, 629, 690, 698, PCS). In his letter of 28 February Phillips wrote he was working to persuade an Abington legislator who had "always believed" in CS and even named his son for CS, but was "in great doubt what to do lest he should offend the soldiers."

2. On 5 and 6 March the Committee on Federal Relations held hearings on the censure of CS at which James Freeman Clarke and Edward L. Pierce testified on CS's behalf (*Boston Morning Journal*, 6 March 1873:4; 7 March 1873:4), but the committee turned down the petitioners' motion to rescind (House Document no. 141, Sumner Papers, Houghton Library). Whittier's letter of 8 March supporting CS appeared in the *Boston Daily Advertiser* 10 March 1873:2, and Wendell Phillips's on 11 March 1873:4. In the Senate Ezra D. Winslow questioned whether the Massachusetts legislature should "remain mute and meek, while her most honored son so speaks and acts as to give pain to thousands of her brave veterans, thousands of her best citizens" (*Boston Morning Journal*, 14 March 1873:4).

3. On 19 March the motion to rescind the previous legislature's censure of CS failed. Pierce had already warned CS that the motion would not pass because it had not been "managed with tact." The chief argument against the motion, wrote both Pierce and Willard Phillips, was that the present legislature believed it was not empowered to pass judgment on what was merely the previous legislature's expression of opinion. Phillips added that some voted against the recent motion because of CS's opposition to Grant. He noted that George S. Boutwell, CS's new colleague in the Senate, had not signed any petitions supporting CS (Milton, Massachusetts, 16 March; Boston, 21 March, 60/700, 733).

To Horace H. Furness

Washington 7th May [*1873*]

Dear Mr Furness,

The article you kindly send is entirely new to me, although a year old.[1] Do you intend that I shall keep it?

Who is Rudolph Doehn?[2] And what have been his sources of information?

I trust yr good father is entirely well

Sincerely Yours,   Charles Sumner

ALS   PU   (85/203, PCS)

1. Horace H. Furness (1833–1912), a Shakespearean scholar and son of William Henry Furness, sent CS an article from the German publication *Unsere Zeit*, 15 April 1872, on CS's "public life and labours." He wrote that he hoped the piece would give CS "some satisfaction to see with what clear vision the past twenty years of our history have been read by the Germans" (Philadelphia, 2 May 1873, 61/122, PCS).

2. Doehn was apparently the author of the article. Furness replied he had no information on him but would inquire of German friends ([May 1873], 61/247).

To Louis Agassiz

Washington 12th May '73

My dear Agassiz,

Yr letter is very interesting & the incident you mention is striking.

I have just read Dr Loring's speech, & envied him the opportunity & the way in which he improved it. His speech is able, & must exert an influence in elevating our educational standard in Mass. It will be hard now to disparage the appropriations you desire.[1]

As a review of what had been done elsewere & a tribute to you I enjoyed it much. But is he right when he says (p 14) —"perhaps no great discovery remains to be made"?[2]

Surely we have not yet reached the bounds of knowledge. More is unknown than is known. Greater discoveries than all before are to crown the future. So at least I like to think.

I hope you are well & strong. I am feeble still, getting about with difficulty.

Bon jour!

Ever yours,   Charles Sumner

Hooper has had a hard month, but he is now doing well.

ALS   MH-H   (85/209, PCS)

1. In his speech before the Massachusetts Senate, Loring argued that Harvard's Museum of Comparative Zoology, which Agassiz headed, had performed an important role in the development of science and should be funded by the legislature ("Speech of Hon. George B. Loring on the Museum of Comparative Zoology in Senate, March 26, 1873" [1873]).
2. In comparing the Harvard museum's accomplishments with those of similar European institutions, Loring reviewed scientific discoveries over the preceding hundred years and declared that "the age of discovery is past" (ibid., 14).

To Hiram Barney

Washington 24th May '73

Dear Mr Barney,

I do not wish a newspaper controversy & therefore say nothing in reply to Mr Parsons.[1]

The Ch Justice was saddened by the Administration.

Ever Yours,   Charles Sumner

ALS   CSmH   (85/218, PCS)

1. Salmon P. Chase had died 7 May 1873 of a paralytic stroke. In a *New York Tribune* interview (8 May 1873:5) CS stated that Chase had "grieved at the tendency of the present Administration." Richard C. Parsons (1826–99; U.S. congressman [Rep., Ohio], 1873–75) wrote a letter of rebuttal stating that CS was mistaken, for Chase believed Grant to be "an absolutely honest, incorruptible, and patriotic man" (*New York Tribune*, 21 May 1873:6). In his letter accompanying the Parsons clipping, Barney wrote that he agreed with CS's assertion and thought he had supporting evidence from Chase (New York, 22 May, 61/211, PCS).

To Carl Schurz

Washington 14th June '73

My dear Schurz,

You will be astonished that I am still here; but the weather thus far has been very agreeable & I could be no where so well as in my own house.

For the last six weeks I have been gaining constantly, &, though yet conscious of something that is not health, I feel that my enemy is disappearing. I am more hopeful than I have been at any time before.

I see nothing denoting change in the country. The Grant party has the offices & the machinery, & is sustained in what it does. The Presdt. is a-pleasuring always. But all this you must discern, even from yr distant travels.

I trust that yr family is well & that the newspapers are right in their report of what has befallen that "most estimable woman."[1] This reminds me of Agassiz's good fortune. One of his daughters in Boston with her husband, Quincy Shaw, has presented him $100,000 cash[2]— being the case of a *dot* by a daughter to her father!

While in Europe,[3] please ascertain the practice with regard to regimental flags, & the names of battles in civil war. Something can be obtained in Prussia, Austria, France. I know it must be; but I should be glad to have an authentic report from you.

Before this reaches you I shall be in Boston, perhaps at Nahant. Good bye!

Ever sincerely Yours,   Charles Sumner

Two lives of Chase are in hand—one by Judge Warden of Ohio & the other by Schukers, for a long time private Secy of Chase.[4]

ALS DLC (85/229, PCS)
Enc: unidentified newspaper clipping

1. The clipping CS enclosed stated that Margaretha M. Schurz, Schurz's wife, had inherited the equivalent of $170,000 in Prussian thalers.
2. Pauline Agassiz Shaw (1841–1917) and Quincy Adams Shaw (1825–1908) had given $100,000 to the Museum of Comparative Zoology at Harvard (Agassiz to CS, Cambridge, 26 June 1873, 61/330, PCS).
3. Schurz had written CS 25 April, giving his address in Hamburg (New York, 61/105).
4. Both biographers, Robert B. Warden (1824–88) and Jacob W. Schuckers (fl. 1874–94), had written to CS seeking assistance with their projects (Washington, 7 May, and New York, [26], 28 May, 20 June, 61/143, 234, 236, 314).

To the Duchess of Argyll

Washington 30th July '73

My dear Duchess,

I write hoping to hear from you.[1] I fear that you are not very well; but I shall believe to the contrary until I learn how you are. My own health seems returned—after a winter & spring of considerable trial under treatment by Dr Brown-Séquard.

I have been distressed by the telegraphic news of the death of the Bishop of Winchester,[2] who was a very engaging person with a fund of health to last long. So sudden a blow must have been much felt in England.

I cannot forbear rejoicing in the vote on Mr Richard's motion, although I observe that Mr Gladstone opposed it.[3] I do not like to see him on the wrong side, & I am sure that in ten years his mistake will be apparent. I know no reform promising so much good. As I reflect upon it, the imagination fails in the attempt to picture the incalculable advantage which must ensue from the diversion of such enormous means—so that they shall no longer be lost in unproductive service. With the millions of men & the millions of money now occupied in the War System, applied to purposes of peace the world would begin to smile. Pardon my enthusiasm, but this cause is very dear to me, & I rejoice that England has taken the lead in it although the Prime Minister hesitates.

I wait with anxiety for the condemnation of that wretch who calls himself Tichbourne,—an impostor beyond any in history from the false Nero & the faux Sebastiens of Portugal[4] down to our day. I trust that English justice will not let him slip.

I think often of my few days in England last autumn,—which I enjoyed much.

I like Mr Russell Gurney[5] & am sorry that he returns so soon to England. He seems a Tory of a mild type.

Our country is prosperous & growing in riches;—I hope also in what is much better.

I enclose two letters one from a former slave, son of a Va member of Congress & the other describing a former slave brother of a Ga. Senator. Remember kindly to the Duke

Ever sincerely yours,   Charles Sumner

Before you receive this I shall be on the seashore with Mr Longfellow near Boston.

ALS   CSmH   (85/260, PCS)

1. CS's letter crossed one from the duchess to him (Maidenhead, 28 July [1873], 61/399).

2. Samuel Wilberforce, bishop of Oxford, died suddenly 19 July.

3. Henry Richard spoke 8 July in favor of establishing a "general and permanent system of International Arbitration," which the House of Commons approved 98–88. Speaking against the motion, Gladstone argued that arbitration should be confined to specific differences between countries and that a permanent system might commit the government too broadly and unwisely (*Hansard's Parliamentary Debates*, 3rd series, 217:52–73, 74–82, 87–88). CS wrote Richard a letter of appreciation on 10 July (Wks, 20:273–74). On 2 December CS offered a similar resolution in the Senate, that the U.S. "recommend the adoption of arbitration as a just and practical method for the determination of international differences" (*Cong. Rec.*, 43rd Cong., 1st sess., 3).

4. Arthur Orton (1834–98) claimed to be Roger Tichborne, a long-lost heir of the Tichborne family. After having lost his suit for recognition as the legal heir, Orton was sued by the Tichborne family for perjury in April. Agrippina, mother of Nero (37–68), persuaded Roman emperor Claudius to favor her son over his own. Although Sebastian (1554–78), king of Portugal, was killed in battle, several imposters claimed to be the true king.

5. Russell Gurney (1804–78), London barrister, privy councillor.

To Samuel Gridley Howe

Cotuit 18th Sept. '73
at Mr Hooper's

My dear Howe,

Yr good letter[1] followed me to this much out-of-the-way sea-side, where I came from Nahant,—but return to Boston at the beginning of the week—very reluctantly, for I long for repose & the passive life of reading, which is with me an immense resource.

You are not the only friend who declares against my lecturing. Long-fellow & Bird are both strong against it.[2] But Dr B. Séquard did not seem unwilling that I should try. I have a double motive, first, as I have something to say, but more, I fear to better my finances. I lost by the fire my insurance stock, & I spent a good deal in Europe, for which I have a note in the bank payable Decbr 1st. The back-pay, which I handed back, would have covered this liability.[3]

Only in the lecture field can I make any thing. I know no senatorial way. This is my excuse.

I am sorry at yr report of yourself.[4] I had hoped you were to have many green years of life, & so I will hope still.

Meanwhile my book is a considerable draft upon me intellectually & financially. The labor of revision, examinations & annotation is beyond my original calculation. But it seems as if the vols may have on this account some value as a help to history. Why should I live, except to complete this work, which will probably reach 15 vols?

I suppose you will be in Boston Saturday, & so send this note there.

Bon jour! God bless you!

Ever Yours,   Charles Sumner

I have written too frankly about my affairs except for yr eye.

I was glad to see yr daughter Julia with her husband on the way to the Bird wedding,[5] where you were missed.

Why not obtain the Greek mission now? The Minister has returned home, & had a public reception at Troy?—Troy N. Y.—*bien entendu*![6]

ALS   MH-H   (85/280, PCS)

1. Howe wrote from Newport 7 September 1873 that his silence had not repre-sented "indifference" to CS. His and others' friendship had given "a value & charm to my life" (Howe Papers, Houghton Library).

2. Longfellow wrote George Washington Greene that CS's plan to lecture was "folly" (29 August, HWL, 5:681). Howe begged CS not to lecture or risk "any other peril to your health, except at the stern call of duty to your fellow men."

3. Pierce estimates CS spent $6,000 on rare books and engravings (Prc, 4:541). Invoices from booksellers and picture dealers are included on reels 59–60, Septem-ber–November 1872, PCS. U.S. senators had recently received an annual salary in-crease from $5,000 to $7,500, including two years' worth of back pay (Robert Byrd, Senate speech, 14 July 1989, *Cong. Rec.*, 101st Cong., 1st sess., 8013). CS protested his back pay and considered for a time giving it to a Massachusetts charity for wounded Civil War veterans or for black troops (to Edward L. Pierce, Washington, 25 March, 64/760).

4. Howe wrote, "I thought, a year ago; that I should survive you; but see now, that I shall not."

5. Bird's daughter was married in early September (Prc, 4:564). Howe's daughter Julia (1844–86) married Michael Anagnos (1837–1906), director of the Perkins Institute, in 1870. Howe wrote Bird on 1 September (South Portsmouth, New Hampshire, Howe Papers, Houghton Library) that an important meeting of the Samana Bay Company prevented him from attending the wedding.

6. John M. Francis (1823–97) was minister to Greece 1871–73; "of course!"

To George Harrington

Boston 15th Nov. '73

Dear Mr Harrington,

I hear nothing from you. Meanwhile the pressure for something practical increases.[1]

There must be no inflation. God forbid!

Can we succeed without contraction? My compound-interest bill would bring that gradually & surely.[2] Should not the return be prompt? Can we wait?

If the Secy[3] had power to go into the market for gold, paying with bonds at market price, would not that enable him to pay specie at once? Knowing that it could be had, the call for it would cease?

Sincerely Yours,   Charles Sumner

———————————

ALS   CSmH   (85/300, PCS)

1. Harrington, then a writer in New York, had written CS 16 October 1873 (61/589, PCS) that, in light of the economic distress known as the Panic of 1873, Congress was certain to discuss finance in the forthcoming session. Harrington was working on a brief that he hoped CS could use in senatorial debates.

2. CS introduced his bill on 11 December. It called for compound interest notes as a substitute for legal tender notes. CS denounced inflation and called contraction of the currency the "heroic method" to cure inflation while substitution was "the gentler method, as efficacious as contraction." The bill was referred to the Committee on Finance (*Cong. Rec.*, 43rd Cong., 1st sess., 142–44).

3. William A. Richardson (1821–96).

To Edward L. Pierce

Washington 26th Dec. '73

My dear Pierce,

You will be glad to know that the speech you prompted went off well—if noise, cheers & white napkins (mistaken for handkerchiefs) flourishing in the air are a sign.[1]

In a corner sat the saints of the Custom-House, Murphy, Arthur, Bliss, Frank Howe[2] & their followers, watching to see that I did not undermine the social fabric of which they are the pious guardians. I am told that they were disturbed by the enthusiasm when I entered, &, still more so by my speech, which they could not criticise.

The Presdt of the Society [*Elliot C. Cowdin*] reports some one as saying, "Sumner did give a terrific knock at the Presdt, when, speaking of Miles Standish paying 50 per interest on a loan, he said so much for a soldier on a financial expedition!"[3] But the whole company roared so loud that the saints had no chance. Perhaps at the time they did not think that Capt. Miles Standish was the predecessor of our Presdt. But all this is for you. I was very prudent & never once named Grant during my visit to N.Y.

Ever Yours,   Charles Sumner

And so Baez the usurper has fallen. I [gave?] a speech in which I described him.[4]

ALS   MH-H   (64/774, PCS)

1. On 22 December 1873 CS delivered "Our Pilgrim Forefathers" at a dinner of the New England Society at Delmonico's in New York (Wks, 20:291–300).

2. Thomas Murphy, collector of customs in New York. Chester A. Arthur, collector of the port of New York, 1871–78. Probably George Bliss (1830–97), then U.S. district attorney for New York. Frank Howe, also a custom house official. The New York Custom House, run by Murphy, a Grant appointee, had in 1872 been investigated on charges of corruption and favoritism to certain importers (Allan Nevins, *Hamilton Fish* [1937], 593–95).

3. CS had described Standish borrowing £150 in England to maintain the Massachusetts colony (Wks, 20:294–95).

4. On 26 November a sizable portion of the Dominican Republic had revolted against the Báez government, and a new president was elected 22 December (*New York Times*, 11 December 1873:1). For CS's description of Báez see CS to Garrison, 26 April 1871, note 2.

To Joshua B. Smith

Washington 1st Jan. '74

Dear Mr Smith,

I wish you a happy New Year, & trust that this note will find you improved in health.

I regret much to see how little pluck there is among the colored representatives. They are considering how to surrender on the Civil Rights Bill, through fear of the Presdt!![1]

I enclose a letter from Mr Potter of Arlington.[2] My answer was that I had nothing to do or say in the premises. I think you will agree with me.

Sincerely Yours,   Charles Sumner

ALS   NcD   (85/333, PCS)

1. On 2 December 1873, at the opening of the 43rd Congress, CS once again introduced his Supplementary Civil Rights Bill (see CS to Pierce, 27 December 1871) and argued, unsuccessfully, that it need not be referred to a Senate committee (*Cong. Rec.*, 43rd Cong., 1st sess., 2). Of the seven black representatives in the 43rd Congress, two had by this date publicly supported a civil rights bill: Richard H. Cain, who introduced a bill in the House 4 December, and Joseph S. Rainey, who spoke for it on 19 December. Later in the session, on 6, 10 January, and 7 February 1874, Robert B. Elliott, Cain, and Alonzo J. Ransier spoke supporting either the House bill or CS's bill. After CS's death, both James T. Rapier and Ransier spoke in favor of CS's bill, on 9 June (*Cong. Rec.*, 43rd Cong., 1st sess., 64, 343–44, 407–10, 565–67, 1311–14, 4782–86; Eric Foner, *Reconstruction* [1988], 533–34, 538).

2. Possibly a letter from Joseph S. Potter, a Massachusetts legislator.

To Caleb Cushing

Senate Chamber Friday
2'oclk [*9 January 1874*]

You are nominated Chief Justice.[1] May you be happy & successful!

C. S.

ALS   DLC   (85/337, PCS)

1. Grant sent Cushing's nomination to the Senate on this date (*Executive Proceedings*, 19:212).

To Francis W. Bird

[*Washington*] 15th Jan [187]4

My dear Bird,

I should never have nominated or recommended C. C. as C.J.[1] But I was called to consider his name being before the Senate, if I could vote for his rejection. Now I know him well,—having seen him for the last ten years constantly & I know his position on questions in which I am deeply interested. I trust him absolutely &, believe, if the occasion had occurred,[2] he would have vindicated our ideas judicially far better than any probable nominee of Grant.

I do not write in the dark, for I have talked with him on these questions, & have seen his sympathy with me.

You know that I do not cherish old differences & animosities. How many have I seen advanced to the front who were once bitterly the other way!

Knowing C. C. as I did, would it not have been mean & craven for me to turn against him, or to skulk in silence? This is not my way with friends. Such is not my idea of friendship. But no earthly friendship could make me put in jeopardy our cause.

I confess that I am glad of the sensibility shown for the safeguard of reconstruction. Thank Robinson;[3] but what shall we do with other possible nominees? Who will vouch for B. R. C.?[4] And who will vouch for some accepted Republicans with whom *technicality* is a peril to *principle?*

Shew this privately to W. S. R. Tell him that I am better than he seems to fear.

Ever Yours,   Charles Sumner

ALS   MH-H   (85/340, PCS)

1. Bird wrote CS on 13 January 1874 (East Walpole, 61/778, PCS) that all CS's friends in Massachusetts with whom Bird had talked were against Cushing's nomination: "His conservatism is bred in the bone & he will never change." In addition, Bird wrote CS, "He cheated me once flagrantly & I believe it is characteristic of him."

2. Grant withdrew Cushing's nomination on 13 January, citing information that "induces me to withdraw him from nomination." In March 1861 Cushing had recommended a friend as a clerk in the Confederate government (*Executive Proceedings*, 19:218; Prc, 4:585).

3. William Stevens Robinson was presumably the author of a letter to the editors of the *Boston Evening Journal* that supported Cushing and stated that CS's support of Cushing's nomination was sufficient evidence of Cushing's "loyalty to the Union and to the policy of reconstruction" (12 January 1874:2).

4. Benjamin R. Curtis, former U.S. Supreme Court justice.

To Samuel Bowles
private

[*Washington*]
[*c. 24 January* 1874]

Dear Mr Bolles,

I wonder if I deserve this.[1] The remarks I made were unprepared & were aimed absolutely at the case of Mr Waite, whom I regard as *the poorest of the three*. I hoped by showing what Chief Justices were[,] to warn against an appointment of which the warmest praise was that he would be "a respectable judge," & whose opinions on vital questions were unknown. I could not take the responsibility of voting for such a person & I tried to warn others. But there was a fear of something worse & a longing to get rid of the question & all were helped by Thurman[2] who had a personal friendship for the candidate & an Ohio sentiment. I lament the conclusion & regret that I was able to do so little against it.[3]

Truly Yours,   Charles Sumner

ALS CtY (85/346, PCS)
Enc: Newspaper clipping, *Springfield Daily Republican*, 23 January 1874:4.

1. The clipping attached to CS's letter stated that CS had delayed the confirmation process of Morrison R. Waite (1816–88), an Ohio judge who had served as counsel at the Geneva arbitration, in order to adjust "one of his fine speeches" to a different nominee than CS had expected. Declared the *Republican*, CS "must have himself felt it rather a lame conclusion to come down to merely negative praise of the new candidate, of whom he could speak only by report."
2. Allen G. Thurman (1813–95), U.S. senator (Dem., Ohio), 1869–81.
3. The Senate considered Waite's nomination on 20 and 21 January 1874 and approved it, 63–0, 21 January. CS was not recorded as voting (*Executive Proceedings*, 19:226–27). Pierce says that, although no notes of CS's speech survive, "the outline of the senator's thought is likely to have been in his mind for a speech in support of Cushing's nomination" (4:588).

To Apphia Horner Howard[1]

Senate Chamber 11th Feb. '74

Dear Mrs Howard,

Yr handwriting was an olive-branch & then its words seemed the voice of the dove.

How you could hesitate to adopt that resolution, which has been approved by the foremost generals of the Nat. Army—has always seemed one of those incomprehensible divergencies & ideosyncracies to which a free citizen, even without a vote, is entitled,—although at the expense of good sense, history, patriotism—to say nothing of Xtianity even without Quakerism. The case has always been too clear for argt., & evidently some persons are candidates for penitential sheets. But you are no longer on the list. I am glad on yr account.[2]

Ever sincerely yours,   Charles Sumner

ALS MHa (85/361, PCS)

1. Apphia Horner Howard (1832–1903), a journalist from Georgetown, Massachusetts, had earlier opposed CS's battle flags resolution (CS to Howard, 14 June 1873, 85/227, PCS).

2. Willard Phillips sent CS a telegram 11 February 1874 from Boston notifying him that the Massachusetts Senate had voted 26–7 to rescind the earlier motion of censure against CS (61/802, PCS). Phillips's two other telegrams, 13 and 25 February, informed CS that the Massachusetts House had also voted, 118–46, for rescission and that copies of the new resolution were being sent to CS's congressional colleagues (61/811, 835). On 10 March, on the motion of George S. Boutwell, the announcement of the Massachusetts legislature's rescission was read in the Senate (*Cong. Rec.*, 43rd Cong., 1st sess., 2085).

To Samuel Bowles
private

Senate Chamber
3d March '74

Dear Mr Bowles,

I am at a loss to understand the mystification about my course on a recent event,—which was at once frank, unreserved & open.[1]

I had no hint or suspicion of Simmons's nomination until it was on the table of the Senate; nor had I ever heard his name mentioned for the collectorship—never a suggestion of it.

I never met any such company as reported at Mr Hooper's;[2] nor have I met Genl. B. any where except in the Senate for more than three years (I except H. L. P's dinner to the City Comttee. & the delegation).[3]

From the moment I heard of the nomination I expressed myself without reserve & from that time daily I conferred with Mr Boutwell, Mr Pierce & others freely always declaring my opposition & pleading with my colleague to oppose it. In Exec. Session I made my opposition known in repeated speeches, explicit & positive.

How the counter-statements could have originated—I leave to others to determine. Two different theories may explain it.

Sincerely Yours,   Charles Sumner

ALS CtY (85/374, PCS)

1. The *Springfield Daily Republican* (2 March 1874:4) criticized CS for initially remaining neutral and then, along with Boutwell, issuing only a "feeble protest" over the nomination of William A. Simmons (1840–1916) as collector of the port of Boston. After Grant, at the behest of Butler, had sent Simmons's name to the Senate on 16 February 1874, many anti-Butler men urged CS to prevent the confirmation if

he could, for Simmons had managed Butler's unsuccessful gubernatorial campaign in 1873. Governor William B. Washburn wrote CS that Simmons's appointment would mean the end of the Republican party in Massachusetts. Despite the adverse report from the Committee on Commerce, chaired by George S. Boutwell, the Senate confirmed Simmons on 27 February, with both CS and Boutwell dissenting (*Executive Proceedings*, 19:251, 259, 260; Washburn to CS, Boston, 18 February, 61/289, PCS; Dale Baum, *The Civil War Party System* [1984], 187–89).

2. The *Republican* stated that Simmons's nomination was first initiated at a dinner party at Samuel Hooper's, attended by Boutwell, Butler, and CS. CS, stated the *Republican*, "played the part of disinterested spectator" and agreed to remain silent in exchange for Butler's support in CS's forthcoming reelection bid.

3. Henry L. Pierce, recently elected U.S. congressman, gave a dinner at Wormley's in early February for the Massachusetts congressional delegation (Prc, 4:590).

To William Washburn

Senate Chamber
9th March '74

My dear Govr,

I am against capital punishmt; but if any man ever deserved a halter it is Baez, who proposes to visit Boston.[1]

I know his history intimately. He is a usurper, whose hands have been red with innocent blood, & who had the terrible audacity of conceiving the idea of keeping an American citizen in a dungeon to prevent his return to New York where it was feared he would write against the Treaty, & this crime he actually perpetrated.

If he comes to Boston he ought to be driven out by an indignant public sentiment.

Sincerely Yours,   Charles Sumner

ALS   MLNHS   (85/377, PCS)

1. Báez had been visiting in the U.S., and on 28 February 1874, just as he was about to depart for Boston, he was arrested in New York. Davis Hatch (the "American citizen" CS refers to) had brought a suit of $65,000 in damages against Báez for Hatch's false arrest in the Dominican Republic. On 4 March Báez's lawyers protested his arrest, claiming that Báez's acts were legitimately carried out in his capacity as president of the Dominican Republic and that some of Hatch's allegations were untrue (*New York Times*, 1 March 1874:1, 4 March 1874:2).

INDEX

Sumner's opinions on various subjects are indexed under that topic (e.g., Disarmament, Fugitive slave laws). A (??) after a name indicates tentative identification. Normally, the first or second page reference for a person contains identifying information.

Jackson, James, and Harper's Ferry investigation, II: 15–16
Jackson, Patrick Tracy, I: 257, 260
Jackson, Robert M. S., I: 464–65, 469
Jackson, Thomas "Stonewall," II: 117
Jackson, William, I: 286
James II of England, II: 377
James, J. W., I: 146–47
Jarves, James Jackson
  letter to, II: 567–68
  Art Thoughts, II: 568
  sale of art collection, CS on, II: 568
Jarvis, Edward, II: 7
  on Calhoun's justification of slavery, I: 138–39
  memorial for the American Statistical Society, I: 138–39
  "Remarks on the Census," I: 237
Jay, Eleanor Field (Mrs. John), I: 130–31, 294
Jay, John (1745–1829), I: 294–95
  charge at Richmond on neutrality, II: 242
Jay, John (1817–94), I: 329, 460; II: 537
  letters to, I: 129–31, 294–95, 375–76, 399–400, 401–2, 402–3, 403–4, 432–33, 450–51, 470–71, 473–74, 536–37; II: 42–43, 61–62, 76, 79–80, 144–45, 179, 242, 285
  on conscription, II: 179
  on CS as secretary of state, II: 285
  and diplomatic appointment, II: 61–62, 266, 403
  and emancipation, II: 76
  on foreign intervention, II: 144–45
  and Kansas admission, I: 451
  and Lemmon case, I: 375
  and presidential election, I: 471
  and secession crisis, II: 43
  speeches and writings
    "The Alabama Wrong," II: 463–64
    "America Free, or America Slave," CS on, I: 471
    "Caste and Slavery," CS on, I: 129–31
    "First Abolitionist Society of New York," I: 399–400
Jay, William, I: 130–31, 224, 432, 451; II: 43
  "Address to Inhabitants of New Mexico," I: 284–85, 294–95
  The Kossuth Excitement, I: 349

Jefferson, Thomas, I: 95; II: 205
  CS on, I: 265–66
  letter on neutrality, I: 118, 120
Jeffrey, Lord Francis, I: 48, 51, 58
Jenkins, Fred (Shadrack), I: 323
Jenks, Richard Pulling, I: 8–9
Jewett, Charles Coffin, I: 419–20
Jewett, John Punchard
  publishes *The Key to Uncle Tom's Cabin*, I: 375
  publishes *Uncle Tom's Cabin*, I: 373
Jewett, William Cornell, on French mediation in Civil War, II: 141–42
Johnson, Mr., I: 445
Johnson, Andrew, II: 347, 362, 392, 401, 404, 409, 414, 430, 444, 502
  letters to, II: 252, 312, 344–45
  and amnesty, II: 291, 294
  and black suffrage, CS on, II: 290, 298–300
  and Colorado admission, II: 364–65
  and conciliation to South, CS on, II: 307–8, 310–22, 324, 325, 329–30, 332–36, 339–42, 344–47, 349–51, 354
  CS evaluates, II: 358–59, 365, 374–76, 380, 416
  CS meets with, II: 346
  and elections of 1866, II: 380–81
  and Fenianism, CS on, II: 383–84
  impeachment of, II: 386, 423, 427–28, 430–31, 434, 451
  impeachment of, CS on, II: 420, 421, 425–26
  at inauguration, CS on, II: 272
  and Lincoln assassination, II: 295
  and Mississippi proclamation, II: 307
  and national debt, CS on, II: 437
  and New Orleans massacre, II: 380–81
  North Carolina proclamation, CS on, II: 303, 305
  and Pierpont government, II: 302
  political ambitions, CS on, II: 341–42
  and presidential election, 1864, CS on, II: 252
  and readmission, CS on, II: 352
  and Reconstruction Act of 1867, II: 399
  removes Stanton, CS on, II: 401–2
  and retaliation, II: 297